EMPIRICAL LABOR ECONOMICS

Empirical
Labor Economics

The Search Approach

THERESA J. DEVINE

NICHOLAS M. KIEFER

New York   Oxford
OXFORD UNIVERSITY PRESS
1991

Oxford University Press

Oxford   New York   Toronto
Delhi   Bombay   Calcutta   Madras   Karachi
Petaling Jaya   Singapore   Hong Kong   Tokyo
Nairobi   Dar es Salaam   Cape Town
Melbourne   Auckland

and associated companies in
Berlin   Ibadan

Library of Congress Cataloging-in-Publication Data
Devine, Theresa J.
Empirical labor economics : the search approach /
Theresa J. Devine and Nicholas M. Kiefer.
p.   cm.   Includes bibliographical references.
ISBN 0-19-505936-0
1. Labor economics.   I. Kiefer, Nicholas M., 1951–   .   II. Title.
HD4901.D49 1991
331—dc20   90-6852   CIP

1 4 6 8 9 7 5 3 1

Printed in the United States of America
on acid-free paper

Preface

Workers differ in capabilities and training; jobs differ in requirements, compensation, and working conditions. Matching workers and jobs takes time and information. Labor markets do not operate like the market for winter wheat. The search approach to labor economics extends the neoclassical theory by incorporating issues of uncertainty and information explicitly. As a result a close link between econometric and theoretical modeling can be maintained.

Information asymmetries, information lags, and strategies for coping with uncertainty are now important features of economic models in a variety of fields. At the macro level, these issues are important components of models of the business cycle and models of rational expectations equilibrium, including search equilibrium. At the micro level it is difficult to find an area that does not exploit models involving information issues. Despite active theoretical development, the "new economics of information" has had little empirical impact in applied areas. Labor economics is the happy exception.

Our objective is to survey the empirical literature in labor economics from a search point of view. We interpret "the search approach" broadly, to include most stochastic models of the labor market. As it turned out, many studies that do not explicitly take a search approach can be interpreted within the search framework. The studies we review range from simple presentation of descriptive statistics to sophisticated nonlinear models requiring development of novel econometric techniques. We expect that many of these developments will find applications in other areas of economics. The labor applications to date have been primarily microeconomic studies and this is reflected in our coverage.

We are grateful to the many scholars who have discussed their work with us, often at length and in detail, and who have helped the project by sending us reprints and working papers. We are especially grateful for discussions and support from Ken Burdett, George Jakubson, Larry Kahn, Shelly Lundberg, Dale Mortensen, Lars Muus, George Neumann, Geert Ridder, Sunil Sharma, and Insan Tunali. We are grateful for the financial support of the National Science Foundation and, during the early and slow phase of the writing, the Guggenheim Foundation. Our interest in the search approach to labor economics continues, so we would appreciate continuing to receive working papers and reprints: Professor Theresa J. Devine, Department of Economics, The Pennsylvania State University, 417 Kern Building, University Park, PA 16802; and Professor Nicholas M. Kiefer, Department of Economics, Cornell University, 476 Uris Hall, Ithaca, NY 14853.

University Park, Penn.   T.J.D.
Ithaca, N.Y.   N.M.K.
September 1990

Contents

List of Tables

EMPIRICAL LABOR ECONOMICS

1

Introduction

Understanding the labor market is central to understanding the modern economy. It is the largest "single" market in most economies, with compensation to labor accounting for more than half of Gross Domestic Product (GDP) in the United States, the United Kingdom, and the European Economic Community.[1] The operation of this market is a fascinating and complicated process. Workers differ in their abilities, attitudes, and tastes. Productivity depends not only on a worker's abilities, but on how well a worker is matched to a job. An exceptionally talented carpenter might be a mediocre waiter. Complicating matters, workers in a labor market typically do not know the full range of opportunities available— what firms have openings in what fields, and at what wages. They must devote time and energy to finding out. Similarly, firms do not know the talents of a particular applicant. An employer must forecast a prospective employee's performance on the basis of his or her experience, training, and other observable characteristics. Even after a match is made—that is, a worker locates and accepts employment—information is accumulated about the quality of the match. If the job or the worker turns out to be a disappointment, the employee and firm will look for more attractive opportunities. Finally, as the characteristics of the economy, the individual, and the firm change over time, matches that were once good can become bad. The result is turnover and search for new possibilities. Thus, the labor market is noisy; uncertainty and incomplete information are prevalent. It is also dynamic; acquiring and processing information take time. These characteristics make the labor market quite different from the spot markets analyzed in static neoclassical microeconomic theory.

Given this contrast, how useful is the simple, static neoclassical labor market model? In that model, workers choose their labor supply by maximizing utility, a function of income and leisure, subject to a budget constraint in which prices (including the wage) are given. The term *leisure* here refers to nonmarket time—of course, this need not be time devoted to rest or recreation as in the conventional usage. Workers who are employed adjust hours of work on the margin, so that the marginal utility gain resulting from an increase in consumption earned by an additional hour of work is exactly equal to the marginal disutility associated with sacrificing an additional hour of leisure. The alternative to employment in this model is nonparticipation. An agent will not enter the labor force if the wage he or she could obtain is less than the value of nonmarket time. This case can arise for an individual who has substantial nonlabor income (e.g., from investments or from the earnings of a family member) and who therefore has a low marginal utility of consumption. It can also arise for an individual with substantial domestic responsibility, and therefore a high marginal value of time. Leisure is thus treated like any other commodity. On the demand side of this labor market, firms are assumed to maximize profits, taking wages and the price of output as given. A firm knows it can hire as many worker-hours as it wishes at the going wage; the problem is to settle on a level of employment. Aggregate demand and aggregate supply in a labor market are derived by summation of the individual demand and supply functions. The market wage is given by the intersection of demand and supply.

This static theory has been extraordinarily useful for organizing economists' thoughts about the operation of the labor market at the microeconomic level. In particular, it has been useful in analyzing the effects of policies such as the minimum wage, the negative income tax, and other income maintenance programs. These analyses are now a standard part of every economics undergraduate's training. The model has also been useful in organizing and interpreting data at the level of the individual worker, although the success here has been less dramatic. In particular, the profession has become accustomed to notoriously poor fits in wage determination and labor–supply equations.[2]

On the other hand, the simple, static model is hopelessly deficient in explaining macroeconomic events. Unemployment, for example, does not appear as an equilibrium phenomenon. Available discussions of unemployment appeal to an exogenous wage rate set above the equilibrium level—perhaps with a mention of "downward rigidity" or nominal wage contracts. Inflation plays no role. This unsatisfactory situation led theorists to attempt to model the labor market closely—taking account of the information flows involved—in hopes that a more realistic model of the labor market would lead to a greater understanding of inflation, unemployment, and the business cycle.

The new "economics of imperfect information" was invented to deal with problems of uncertainty and matching. Many of the now classic works on the economics of incomplete information and the new theory of search as applied to macroeconomic problems appeared in the celebrated "Phelps volume," published in 1970.[3] The principal application from the outset was to the labor market. This research has led to a growing literature often placed under the heading "job search" theory.

The theory of job search treats uncertainty in the labor market explicitly. The central idea is that unemployment can have investment aspects. This idea is older than the modern mathematical models.[4] A remarkable early discussion is given by W. H. Hutt (1939), who considers unemployed workers evaluating employment prospects—prospecting for jobs. Hutt raises the possibility that the less conspicuous form of waste involved in suboptimal employment (i.e., workers in the wrong jobs) may be more important than the obvious idle capacity associated with unemployment. This real possibility remains unexplored. Woytinsky (1942) also considered investment aspects of unemployment in a discussion of quits. Hicks (1964) noted that imperfect knowledge about job opportunities leads to investment of time in seeking information, and hence to unemployment. Despite this insight, Hicks did not pursue the idea that unemployment can have a productive side. Stigler's (1961, 1962) papers gave the first formal (mathematical) analysis of the optimal search strategy of an unemployed worker.

Together these papers alerted the profession that unemployment could be studied using the standard microeconomic approach: assume unemployed workers are rational and optimize subject to information constraints and other constraints, and then work out the behavioral implications.

Search models maintain the austere intellectual rigor of Walrasian economics (agents maximize utility subject to constraints, and no agent will knowingly forgo an opportunity for improvement) while dropping the assumption of simultaneous transactions under complete information. The assumption of complete information is replaced by an assumption about expectations—typically the assumption of rational expectations. With this assumption, no agent is biased (i.e., systematically surprised). The picture is one in which firms look for workers, unemployed workers (and perhaps dissatisfied employed workers) look for jobs, and matches are made at random, with probabilities that depend on the activities of the workers and the firms.

The basic features of the simplest job search model are easily described. An unemployed worker looks for a job offer each period. A job offer consists of an offer of employment at a stated wage rate; the worker knows the distribution of wage rates, and each offer is an independent draw from this distribution. The notion is that the worker knows the general features of the wage distribution in an area, but does not know specifically which plants or firms offer which wage. Of course, the relevant distribution may be specific to an occupation or an industry, as well as a geographic region. The probability that a worker receives an offer in a given period can be fixed or can depend on the worker's search effort. The early sequential search models simply assume this probability is one, so an unemployed worker obtains an offer each period and either accepts employment at the offered wage, or waits and looks again the next period. The "period" is an abstract notion that presents no problem for the theory, but requires some care in empirical work. The most frequent approaches are to define the period as a week or to recast the model in continuous time. Simple models also assume that offers are received only by unemployed workers, so that accepting an offer forecloses the possibility of receiving another. Of course, workers do receive and accept alternative offers while employed; search models basically require that an unemployed worker is more likely to get an offer than an employed worker. Suppose the worker's objective is maximization of the present discounted value of lifetime income. When the offer distribution is fixed over time, the worker's income and search costs are constant over time, and the worker expects to hold the job accepted a long time (formally, forever), the optimal policy is simple to describe. It is a *reservation wage* policy; the worker determines a reservation wage and then accepts the first offer that exceeds the reservation wage. The reservation wage is the wage that equates the marginal costs and expected marginal benefits of continued search. Details of the argument establishing the optimality of the reservation wage policy are given in Chapter 2.

Even this simple structure has appealing implications from a modeling point of view. First, unemployed workers can expect to remain unemployed for a while before finding a suitable job. Thus, the model is consistent with unemployment. Second, unemployment is productive—it is basically an investment in information (or, perhaps, an investment in luck). This means that welfare statements about unemployment have to be made carefully. Third, employed workers may or may not be "on their labor supply curve," depending on what assumptions are made about the marginal adjustment of hours of work. Thus, the link between the wage rate and the marginal value of leisure can be broken, a necessary condition for Keynesian unemployment. Finally, a researcher is typically not lucky enough to have good data on reservation wages or rejected offers, but unemployment spell lengths are often observed—and the stochastic specification of our theoretical model is tight enough to deliver a likelihood function for these data. To illustrate this point, note that the probability that an unemployed worker will find employment is a constant over the course of a spell. Thus, the model implies a specific probability distribution for unemployment durations—geometric in discrete time, exponential in continuous time.

Without much additional structure, the simple search model also delivers insight on macroeconomic policy issues. Indeed the model is now standard fare in macroeconomics courses (e.g., see Sargent's text, 1987).

Consider an economy in which unemployed workers search for employment and become employed with some probability, new entrants enter the labor market in each period, and workers retire at some constant rate. Retirement is not a feature of our simple model, but suppose (correctly) that it introduces no major complications to the policy calculation relevant to new entrants. Suppose that the economy is in equilibrium, so that the flow of workers into employment is offset by retirements, holding employment constant, and the flow of workers out of unemployment is exactly compensated by new entrants, holding unemployment constant. Now suppose an exogenous demand shock occurs, increasing the demand for all goods. The response of firms, in addition to raising prices, is to raise wages in an attempt to hire additional workers. Thus, the distribution of wage offers shifts toward higher wages. Suppose unemployed workers are not aware of the demand shock; they assume that they are searching from the fixed distribution prior to the demand shock. Searchers will obtain higher offers because of the shift and will accept "too high" a proportion of offers because they have not adjusted their reservation wages. This story suggests a possible foundation for the Phillips curve, the well-known negative correlation between the unemployment rate and the rate of the change in prices. This argument was pursued by Mortensen (1970a,b). Of course, workers will catch on to the general increase in demand and adjust their reservation wages eventually; when that occurs, the unemployment rate will rise toward its former level. Thus, the story provides, at best, a potential argument underlying a short-run Phillips curve. Since workers cannot be presumed to be fooled repeatedly and systematically in a well-specified model, the argument here is not complete, but it is suggestive.

The equilibrium rate of unemployment is certainly an object of interest. Can it be affected by policy? What sort of policies? The search approach emphasizes flows into and out of unemployment, rather than stocks, such as the level of unemployment at a particular time (which are the focus of the neoclassical model). Indeed, in a wide class of models, the equilibrium rate of unemployment depends only on the flows into and out of unemployment (and possibly into and out of the labor force), not on the initial distribution of workers across labor market states or on the distribution in any period. Thus, a policy that temporarily increases employment, such as a subsidized jobs program, will not affect the equilibrium unemployment rate unless it changes, permanently, the rates at which workers find or lose jobs. On the other hand, policies that affect the flows have the potential to be successful. A major policy issue here is the effect of Unemployment Insurance benefits. Do benefits cause workers to be more choosy by reducing the cost of search and therefore increasing the reservation wage? If so, is this bad? Alternative policies improve the available information about jobs by providing centralized listings of vacancies, for example, as in job banks. In the search framework these policies increase the arrival probability of offers and decrease the per-offer costs of search.

Although explaining unemployment in a coherent framework was the initial focus of search theory, it has become clear that the approach has applications in other areas of labor economics. Search ideas are useful in human capital economics, program evaluation, the analysis of occupational choice, the economics of migration, and the economics of marriage and divorce. In assessing the return to schooling, for example, the search model provides a framework in which the effect of schooling on wages (a classic topic) can be combined with an effect on unemployment experience over the worker's lifetime to produce an estimate of the effect of schooling on total lifetime earnings. The same holds for analysis of occupational choice. In assessing the effect of a job training program, the search model provides a theoretical framework for studying effects on wages and employment separately and for combining these to find an overall effect on earnings. Models of discrete choice over time and models of matching often fit into a search framework (broadly interpreted). Thus, the development of search models has affected microeconomic theory and practice, as well as macroeconomics. Indeed, although search notions have had a profound impact on macroeconomic theory, the impact on empirical practice has been primarily seen in microeconomic studies of the labor market.

Before turning to a discussion of empirical matters, let us sketch some elaborations of our simple model to give an idea of the range of theoretical models that have been examined. First, we have concentrated on the constant reservation wage case. This is obtained when the offer distribution and arrival probability are constant and the worker's horizon is infinite. The general result is, essentially, that a reservation wage policy is optimal when the offer distribution is known. In general, the reservation wage could be different in each period. Thus, the policy is characterized by a sequence of reservation wages, not just a single number. If the reservation wage varies over time or over duration of an unemployment spell, the distribution of durations is different from that implied by a constant reservation wage model. The question of a recall option becomes important when the offer distribution changes over time. Can an offer, once declined, be accepted in a later period? In the stationary model with a constant reservation wage the recall option is irrelevant since it would never be exercised. In other models it is important to be specific about the recall possibilities. When the offer distribution is unknown the optimal policy may not be a reservation wage policy. We have also considered a fixed offer arrival probability and concentrated on the acceptance decision. It is possible to model time allocated to search in a model in which the arrival probability depends on search intensity. Most of the literature concentrates on the acceptance decision; the generation of offers deserves more attention. Finally, it is feasible to introduce equilibrium considerations. Firms can be modeled as choosing the wage to offer to workers, knowing that the choice of a wage will affect turnover. Burdett and Mortensen (1989) obtain an explicit functional form for the equilibrium wage distribution and consequently the reservation wage in a dynamic equilibrium model of the labor market.

Most of this book presents a survey of empirical work in the search framework based on microeconomic data, that is, information on individual workers, households, or firms. In any empirical analysis, the nature of the available data—what is observed and for whom—affects both the specification of an empirical model and the estimation procedure. Empirical work within the search framework is no exception. As the available information varies widely across studies, it is worth spending a moment considering what information might be available and how it compares with what one would like to see.

From our brief sketch of the job search model, it is clear that having data on wage offers, reservation wages, and completed unemployment spell durations for a random sample of workers would pose a very attractive situation for a researcher. Something is typically missing. Only one study appears to have access to data on rejected offers and relatively few have access to observations on something that can reasonably be interpreted as a reservation wage (or the "asking," "minimum acceptance," or "critical" wage in the older terminology). These data are typically generated by survey questions pertaining to lowest acceptable wages and interpretation as a reservation wage is less than straightforward in some cases. Similarly, the use of alternative search methods (newspapers, employment agencies, direct employer contact, etc.) is reported rarely, and observations on numbers of offers are even more scarce. Data on unemployment spell durations and accepted wages are widely available, but these are not problem free.

Data limitations place a constraint on a researcher in terms of potential approaches, but the force of the constraint depends on the objective of the study. The objective will determine not only the questions to which answers are sought, but also the willingness on the part of the researcher to adhere to a tight theoretical structure when specifying an empirical model. Objectives in the empirical search literature range from measurement of a particular parameter or effect (e.g., the effect of Unemployment Insurance Benefits payments on unemployment duration) through determination of whether the data at hand behave in rough conformity with the predictions of the theory, to tests of particular tight parametrizations of search models against specific alternatives. Note that search theory itself is never tested. The models we can write down precisely enough to be subject to test are patently false. The question is whether one can write down models that are simple enough to be useful, yet not disastrously at odds with labor market data. As will be seen, the evidence is mixed. Empirical search models have provided insights into the workings of the labor market at the individual level. They have raised new questions. However, they have not yet led to significant advances in understanding macroeconomic phenomena.

With these factors in mind, our discussion of the literature is organized according to the major variables that are observed and analyzed. Chapter 2 introduces a formal specification of a search model. This specification is not as general as possible by any means, but it provides a useful framework for interpreting empirical work. Extensions of the basic model that are actually or potentially useful in empirical work are also treated. Chapter 3 considers some issues of estimation and inference. Chapters 4 and 5 focus on studies that address the experience of unemployed workers. Studies that make use of "direct" evidence on individual reservation wages are reviewed in Chapter 4, starting with regression studies. Search theoretic arguments guide the choice of regressors in these studies and also provide rough specification diagnostics by suggesting signs for regression coefficients. In that no theoretical restrictions are exploited or imposed for the purpose of identifying the parameters of the theoretical structure, these are considered "reduced-form" studies. We turn then to studies that exploit the underlying theory in a variety of ways to identify structural parameters within particular formulations of the job search model.[5]

Data on unemployment spell durations are widely available for the United States and elsewhere. Accepted wage data are often available as well. Some of the studies discussed in Chapter 4 analyze unemployment spell duration data and wage data along with reservation wage data. In Chapter 5, attention turns to studies that analyze unemployment duration and wage data in the absence of observations on reservation wages. Studies that use search theory to interpret regressions of unemployment duration or its natural logarithm are the first subject. In some cases, regressions of realized wage gains are also included. Analyses of duration data based on the hazard function approach (see Chapter 3) are next and "structural studies" follow. These use a variety of techniques that require data on spell durations and wages, alone, to identify the structural parameters of particular specifications of job search models.

In Chapters 4 and 5, we pay particular attention to reported (or implied) effects of unemployment benefits on unemployment spell durations. The magnitude and duration of benefit payments to unemployed workers are widely thought to affect the flow of insured workers from unemployment to employment, and hence to affect the natural rate of unemployment. Understanding and measuring these effects are important for designing an efficient benefit system—one that promotes employment without reducing the utility of workers. Since the "benefit effect" has been the focus of many studies, this provides a rough measure of sensitivity to alternative approaches and different data sets, while providing a measure of the degree of consensus on an important issue.

Analyses based on multistate search models are the topic of Chapter 6. The theoretical models that underlie the empirical analyses here address movements of workers out of employment as well as unemployment, and, in some cases, they also allow movement in and out of the labor force. Most of these studies use the hazard function approach and focus on incidence and durations of spells, not on wages. Studies that distinguish temporary layoffs and permanent separations are also covered in this chapter. Chapter 7 reviews analyses of data on the search strategies of unemployed workers and the arrival rates of offers. Discrete choice models are exploited here, as well as regression, hazard function, and a variety of structural approaches. Chapter 8 shifts attention to employed workers and considers data on job exits and job-to-job transitions without intervening spells of unemployment. These papers model the quit decision in an "on-the-job search" or "matching" framework. This chapter also reviews some recent studies of the wage–tenure relationship, in light of the implications of job search and matching models. In Chapter 9, experimental evidence on search is reviewed. Do subjects in laboratory settings designed to mimic search environments behave as search theory predicts? The few empirical investigations into search behavior on the demand side of the market are reviewed in Chapter 10. Chapter 11 draws conclusions and suggests directions for new research.

The average quality of the literature we review is very high (and the quantity is oppressive). Empirical labor economics is a sophisticated enterprise. We find that the search approach provides a useful organizing framework for a large body of results. On a policy issue, we see that unemployment benefits do affect unemployment durations, but a particular number, such as the benefit elasticity of duration, has been impossible to pin down. The overall effect is complicated and appears to depend critically on the potential duration of benefit receipt as well as amount. The effect of benefits on the reservation wage has been emphasized in modeling; there is empirical evidence that the effect works through search effort and choice of search techniques as well. The simplest search models assume that the probability that a worker will get an offer in a given period is fixed. We note direct and indirect evidence that offer arrivals vary across workers and that search intensity varies as well. Indeed, one recurring impression from studies on the supply and demand sides of the labor market is that variation in offers across individuals is more important in explaining variation in unemployment durations than is variation in reservation wages. Our notes for future research emphasize the need to understand the process by which offers are made (as a result of efforts of workers and firms alike), as a complement to the current focus on the process by which offers are accepted. Demand and equilibrium are essentially wide open topics.

Notes

1. Compensation to employees by domestic producers represented 60 percent of GDP in the United States, 56 percent of GDP in the United Kingdom, and 52 percent of GDP in the European Economic Community in 1985 (OECD, 1988).

2. The neoclassical model and variations are presented in detail in leading labor economics textbooks by Ehrenberg and Smith (1988) and Hamermesh and Rees (1988). These texts also review the empirical literature. Cain and Watts (1973) present an ambitious attempt to take the neoclassical model seriously in interpreting cross-sectional data on labor supply. Killingsworth (1983) provides a thorough and insightful survey of the empirical literature on deterministic models of labor supply, though he politely avoids detailed discussion of the fits of the empirical models.

3. Phelps (1970). Many of the papers in this volume are motivated by a concern with explaining inflation as well as unemployment. The first sequential job search models, McCall (1970) and Mortensen (1970a,b), appearing about the same time, focus on the unemployment generated by optimal search by workers. For applications of the economics of information outside the labor market, see Diamond and Rothschild (1978) and McCall (1980), for example.

4. A very determined reading can find search unemployment in Marshall, Beveridge, and Pigou (Feinberg, 1978).

5. It should be noted that the use of the terms *structural* and *reduced form* differs slightly here from that used elsewhere (e.g., Ridder and Gorter, 1986). What is and is not structural is a controversial and sometimes mystical discussion not taken up here. Here, the term refers to studies that make use of theoretical restrictions on parameters in econometric specifications.

2

The Search Framework: Theory

The search approach was developed as a model for the behavior of unemployed workers. Subsequent developments treat the decision to participate in the labor market and the decision to change jobs or leave a job. To fix ideas, let us focus on the original problem—the search behavior of an unemployed worker. This worker is assumed to be actively looking for employment. The worker is not sure where to look, however, and may uncover unappealing opportunities before finding a suitable job. Unappealing opportunities are those that are dominated by further search. That is, the worker prefers to continue looking. On our making an assumption about the distribution of job opportunities in the labor market, the worker's search policy leads to a distribution of time spent unemployed (searching), and to a distribution for the characteristics of the job on employment. Although these distributions are not observable for a particular worker, one can hope to learn them by observing a large sample of similar workers.

Some specific assumptions are necessary to firm up this discussion and to make it possible to find an optimal policy for the worker. Let us begin with a discrete time model, in which the worker, by dint of search efforts, obtains one job offer in each period. Now, jobs have many characteristics, including wages, hours, benefits, working conditions, and amiability of co-workers and supervisors. Assume that the wage is the most important—the item on which the worker bases the decision to accept or decline employment. Hours are assumed fixed, for the present, so "wages" and "earnings" are equivalent characterizations of a job. Setting hours equal to one allows the convenience of using the notation w to refer to earnings as well as wages. The worker does not know where which jobs—that is, values of w—are available, but does know the general characteristics of the local labor market. This situation is modeled by assuming that jobs are distributed according to some distribution $F(w)$, known to the worker. Job offers are assumed to be independent draws from the distribution F. Thus, the worker does not know which firms are "more likely" to offer good jobs than others. The worker is just as likely to obtain a high offer on the tenth draw as on the first, or the hundredth. This assumption, together with some others, leads, as we shall see, to tremendous simplification in the model—namely, the worker who is unemployed for 30 weeks faces exactly the same job prospects as the newly unemployed worker. Thus, the search strategy does not depend on time spent unemployed.

11

The assumption that job offers are independent draws from a common distribution is not innocuous and can be relaxed. An alternative assumption is that workers know which firms typically offer the best jobs. Suppose firms have different wage distributions so an offer to a worker is a draw from a firm-specific distribution. Under the assumption that each firm can be sampled only once, the worker will sample firms in a specific order depending on the associated offer distributions. This case is referred to as *systematic search*. The case of a common distribution, in which the worker samples offers from firms in an arbitrary order, is known as *random search*.

Another assumption we will need is that the worker's income while unemployed is fixed. The source of this income is, perhaps, unemployment insurance payments (in a system that does not vary benefits over the course of a spell of unemployment), annuity income, or income due to another family member. Suppose that the worker is risk neutral, so that income and utility can be taken to be the same, and that the worker wishes to maximize the expected present discounted value of income. The worker discounts future income at rate r. This rate is assumed for simplicity to be known and constant. Finally, the worker assumes that the next job will be held forever, so that the present discounted value of a job paying w is w/r. This drastic assumption (implying as it does that the worker expects to live forever) aids substantially in simplifying the analysis and turns out not to make much difference as long as the discount rate is greater than zero and retirement (or death) is not too close.

The important implication of all these assumptions is that the worker who is newly unemployed is in exactly the same situation as the worker who is unemployed 2 weeks, 4 months, or 10 months. Utility while unemployed is the same—there is no despair, or exhaustion of benefit payments, or ennui. Job prospects are the same—there is no useful signal to employers in the length of time the worker has been unemployed. Each offer is an independent draw from the distribution F and offers continue to arrive once each period. As a result, the worker's decision to accept or reject an offer does not depend on how long he has been unemployed. Although our setting is dynamic, and indeed time is crucial to the search argument as it provides the friction leading to the existence of unemployment, the decision problem we must analyze is simple and can be approached as a static optimization problem.

During each period of unemployment the worker receives one job offer consisting of a wage, w, and decides whether to accept the job or to decline the job and wait for the next period's offer. Since all periods are the same apart from the particular wage offered, we can study the acceptance decision for an arbitrary period. If the worker accepts the job, the value is the present discounted value of earning w in the current and each future period, namely w/r. What is the value of declining the offer and continuing to search? This value does not depend on any particular offered wage, although it does depend on the wage distribution F. Let V^* be the present discounted expected value of entering this labor market and following an optimal job search strategy. V^* thus depends on the distribution F, through the expectation, and on the optimal strategy, which we have not yet considered. With our assumptions, V^* does not depend on when the worker enters the market, or on whether the worker has been unemployed for some time. Recall that the worker faces the decision problem under identical conditions, apart from the particular wage offered, in each period. Thus, the present discounted value of following the optimal search strategy in the labor market is, for each worker, constant over the duration of a spell of unemployment. Now we can return to the question of the value of declining the outstanding offer w and continuing to search.

This value is given by the sum of this period's unemployment income, b, say, and the discounted value of following the optimal strategy in all future periods, $V^*/(1 + r)$.

At this point we have the value of employment at wage w, w/r, and the current expected value of continuing to search, $b + V^*/(1 + r)$. Clearly the worker should choose the option with the highest value. Now, the value of employment is an increasing function of the wage offered, while the value of continued search is a constant. These functions are given in Figure 2.1. There must be some values of the wage for which employment is the desirable alternative, otherwise it would not be worthwhile for the worker to enter this labor market. We assume there are some wages that are not acceptable, or the worker would always accept the first offer and the model would be useless for studying unemployment. The wage at which the value of employment is equal to the value of continuing to search is the *reservation wage*. The optimal action for a worker who is offered wage w is therefore to accept the offer if w is higher than the reservation wage, and to decline the offer and continue to search otherwise.

The argument so far has considered the decision problem for a worker in one period, facing the options of employment at wage w or following an optimal search strategy in the future. Recall that V^* involves an optimization. However, since V^* is constant over time, our analysis applies for any period, and furthermore the reservation wage is the same in each period. Consequently, the optimal strategy for a worker in this labor market is a reservation wage strategy: accept the first offer greater than the reservation wage; decline all others. Further interpretation of the reservation wage, and of V^*, is provided in the next section, which presents a mathematical development of a job search model.

A Model of Job Search

The model developed in this section will serve as a basic framework for studying the empirical papers reviewed in subsequent chapters. Essentially, the model is the same as

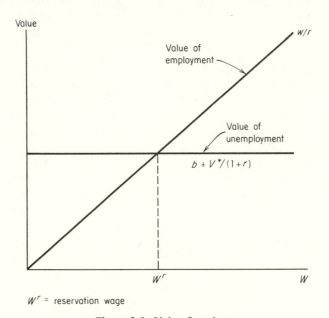

W^r = reservation wage

Figure 2.1. Value functions.

that described informally above; the major difference is that this section treats a continuous time version in which job offers are received at random intervals rather than once each period. Offers arrive to a searching worker according to a Poisson process. This implies that the probability of obtaining an offer in a given (short) interval of time is proportional to the length of that interval. The intuition is that Poisson time, in which discrete events occur at random intervals, is just a random distortion of real discrete time, in which events occur each period. The length of the period between events (offers) is random, instead of fixed.[1] For the rest of this section we restrict attention, as above, to the experience of unemployed workers seeking employment. A number of simplifying assumptions are useful:

1. A worker seeks to maximize the expected present value of income, discounted to the present over an infinite horizon at rate r.
2. The income flow while unemployed, net of any search costs, is b and it is constant over the duration of a given spell.
3. Offers are received while unemployed according to a Poisson process with parameter δ. The probability of receiving at least one offer within a short interval of length h is thus $\delta h + o(h)$, where $o(h)$ is the probability of receiving more than one offer in the interval and $o(h)/h \to 0$ as $h \to 0$. The parameter δ is the arrival rate of offers.
4. A job offer is summarized by a wage rate w. If accepted, this wage will be received continuously over the tenure of employment in the job.
5. Successive job offers received over the course of a spell of unemployment are independent realizations from a known wage offer distribution with finite mean and variance, cumulative distribution function $F(w)$, and density $f(w)$.
6. Once rejected, an offer cannot be recalled.
7. When accepted, a job will last forever.

Assumption 1, income maximization, is not crucial to the general implications of the model, although it leads to simpler and more readily interpreted derivations than the utility maximization case. Assumption 2, constant income flow while unemployed, is crucial for the constant reservation wage policy. The model can be analyzed without this assumption, but the calculations are substantially more complex. The assumption seems reasonable in samples in which most spells are of short duration—perhaps it is less plausible for spells of unemployment of a year or more. The Poisson arrival assumption 3 is convenient and tractable. In the discrete time case an analogous assumption is that offers arrive with constant probability each period. The crucial implications of the Poisson assumption are that offers arrive one at a time and that the probability of receiving an offer does not depend on the duration of a spell. In this respect, the model described here is quite different from the nonsequential search model examined in a pioneering paper by Stigler (1961). Stigler studied the "optimal sample size" problem—how many costly applications to make in a single period. Assumption 4, that a wage will be received continuously over the tenure of employment, is not crucial either. The important point is that the value of holding a job forever is an increasing function of the offered wage. Assumption 5, a known offer distribution, is important. There is no practical alternative to this assumption for generating tractable empirical models. Assumption 6, no recall, is not important. With the assumptions we have made, a recall option would never be exercised if available. With a constant reservation wage, if an offer is unacceptable today, it will be unacceptable tomorrow as well. Assumption 7, that the job will last forever, is not crucial. Incorporating Poisson layoffs changes the model trivially. Incorporating retirement at a fixed date in the future changes the calculation in principle, but in practice the change is trivial if the horizon is long and the discount rate is positive. To illustrate this, note that the difference in present value between $1/year over 25 years and $1/year forever with an annual discount rate of 10 percent is only $0.82.

Since the net income flow while unemployed is a constant, offers are independent and identically distributed, and the offer distribution and arrival rate are both known and time invariant, the value of unemployed search for the worker under these assumptions, V^u, will be a constant over the duration of a spell. It is defined implicitly by the equation

$$V^u = \frac{1}{1 + rh} bh + \frac{\delta h}{1 + rh} E_w \left[\max\{V^e(w), V^u\} \right]$$
$$+ (1 - \delta h) \frac{1}{1 + rh} V^u + o(h)K \tag{2.1}$$

where h is the length of a short period of time. The first term on the right side of this equation is the discounted present value of net unemployment income over the interval h. The second is the probability of receiving an offer in the interval h times the discounted expected value of following the optimal policy if an offer w is received, where $V^e(w)$ denotes the present value of accepting the offer. The third term is the probability of no offer in the interval h times the discounted value of optimal search thereafter. The last term accounts for the returns to search in the event of more than one offer; $o(h)$ is the probability of receiving more than one offer and K is the value of following an optimal policy if more than one offer is obtained. Under the Poisson arrival process, $\lim o(h)/h = 0$ as $h \to 0$.

The expected present value of accepting an offer w in this model, $V^e(w)$, is simply the present value of expected lifetime income at that wage:

$$V^e(w) = \frac{w}{r} \tag{2.2}$$

Since $V^e(w)$ is continuous and strictly increasing in w and V^u does not depend on the offer w, it follows that the optimal strategy for the worker is a time-invariant reservation wage policy: accept w if $w \geq w^r$, where the reservation wage w^r is a minimum acceptable wage offer defined by equating the expected present value of employment and the expected present value of continued optimal search, that is,

$$V^e(w^r) = \frac{w^r}{r} = V^u \tag{2.3}$$

The time invariance of the policy follows directly from the stationarity of the worker's environment. We are simply being a little more formal here about the situation in Figure 2.1.

Substitution of Equations 2.2 and 2.3 for $V^e(w)$ and V^u in Equation 2.1 yields

$$\frac{w^r}{r} = \frac{1}{1 + rh} bh + \frac{\delta h}{1 + rh} E_w \left[\max\left\{ \frac{w}{r}, \frac{w^r}{r} \right\} \right]$$
$$+ \frac{(1 - \delta h)}{1 + rh} \frac{w^r}{r} + u(h) \tag{2.4}$$

Rearranging terms and passing to the limit, this optimality condition may be written as

$$w^r = b + \frac{\delta}{r} \int_{w^r}^{\infty} (w - w^r) \, dF(w) \tag{2.5}$$

Finally, by evaluating the integral in Equation 2.5 and rearranging terms, the condition may be rewritten in a form that more readily affords an intuitive interpretation of w^r:

$$(w^r - b)r = (E_w[w \mid w \geq w^r] - w^r)[1 - F(w^r)]\delta \tag{2.6}$$

The left-hand side of Equation 2.6 gives the marginal cost of rejecting an offer equal to w^r and continuing to search. This is the imputed interest income flow on the difference between incomes in the two alternatives. The right-hand side gives the marginal expected gain in future earnings from continued search, given that an offer will be accepted only if it exceeds the reservation wage, times the instantaneous probability that an acceptable offer will be received. That is, the right-hand side gives the expected marginal return to continued optimal search. The reservation wage, which represents the optimal policy for the worker, is thus simply the wage rate that equates the marginal cost and marginal benefit of search activity.[2]

We have focused on the decision problem for a worker who is actively looking for employment. Of course, the worker can be assured of an income of b plus direct costs of search—simply by not bothering to search (recall that b is nonemployment income net of search costs). If direct costs of search are sufficiently high, or the expected returns sufficiently low, the worker will not enter the labor market. Some of the studies we discuss treat this labor force participation decision jointly with the employment decision.

Our primary interest is the empirical implications of this simple model. Focusing first on the reservation wage, it is important to distinguish between the concept defined here and the reservation wage that appears in deterministic models used to explain labor force participation decisions. There, an individual's tastes, fixed costs of working, and the shadow price of time determined by nonmarket productivity determine the reservation wage. The worker is assumed to face a given wage and the reservation wage does not depend on its level. In contrast, the optimal reservation wage defined by Equation 2.5 depends on market opportunities as summarized in the wage-offer distribution and offer-arrival rate, as well as supply-side factors.

Without adding any additional structure to the model, the following "derivative" restrictions for the reservation wage with respect to net income while unemployed, the discount rate, the arrival rate, and the mean of the offer distribution can be derived simply by differentiating the optimality condition (Equation 2.5):

$$dw^r/db = r/(r + \delta[1 - F(w^r)]) \in (0, 1) \tag{2.7a}$$

$$dw^r/dr = -\frac{1}{r} \frac{E_w[w \mid w \geq w^r] - w^r}{[1 + r/(\delta[1 - F(w^r)])]} < 0 \tag{2.7b}$$

$$dw^r/d\delta = \frac{E_w[w \mid w \geq w^r] - w^r}{\delta + (r/[1 - F(w^r)])} > 0 \tag{2.7c}$$

$$dw^r/d\mu = \frac{1}{1 + (r/\delta[1 - F(w^r)])} \in (0, 1) \tag{2.7d}$$

It can also be shown that the reservation wage will increase with increased uncertainty in the offer distribution in the sense of a mean preserving spread.[3]

These implications have obvious intuitive appeal. Without additional structure, the model also has specific implications for the distribution of unemployment spell lengths. Let τh denote the probability that the worker will become reemployed in a short interval of length h. This is simply the probability that an acceptable offer will be received over the interval h and it may be expressed as the product of two terms. The first is the probability that any offers will be received in the interval h. This is $\delta h + o(h)$ under the Poisson arrival process we have assumed. The second is the conditional probability that once an offer is received, it will be accepted under the worker's optimal policy. We will refer to this as the acceptance probability and denote it by $\pi(w^r)$:

$$\pi(w^r) = \int_{w^r}^{\infty} f(w)\, dw$$
$$= 1 - F(w^r) \tag{2.8}$$

Thus,

$$\tau h = (\delta h + o(h))\pi(w^r) \tag{2.9}$$

and by dividing through by h in Equation 2.9 and taking limits as $h \to 0$, we arrive at

$$\tau = \delta\pi(w^r) \tag{2.10}$$

the transition rate between the states of unemployment and employment, also referred to as the instantaneous reemployment probability or hazard rate. Note that τ does not depend on elapsed duration, nor does it depend on calendar time, because neither the acceptance strategy of the worker nor the environment he or she faces depends on these measures of time. This in turn has implications for the distribution of unemployment spell durations. The implied distribution is exponential.

If we let T denote the duration of a completed spell of unemployment with cumulative distribution function $G(t)$ and density $g(t)$, it follows from the definition of conditional probability that

$$\tau h = Pr(t < T \leq t + h \mid T > t) = \frac{g(t)h}{1 - G(t)} \tag{2.11}$$

Solving this equation for t and rearranging terms yields

$$S(t) = 1 - G(t) = \exp\{-\tau t\} \tag{2.12}$$

referred to as the *Survivor function*, which gives the probability of a spell lasting at least t and from which we find the density for T,

$$g(t) = \tau \exp\{-\tau t\} \tag{2.13}$$

The simple model specified here thus implies that completed durations have an exponential distribution with parameter τ so that the expected length of a completed spell is given by

$$E(T) = 1/\tau \tag{2.14}$$

Responses of τ (and thus of mean durations) to changes in net unemployment income, the discount rate, and the mean of the offer distribution may also be derived without additional structure. From the definition of τ given in Equation 2.10, these can be shown to be

$$d\tau/db = -r\delta f(w^r)/(r + \tau) < 0 \tag{2.15a}$$

$$d\tau/dr = \delta(f(w^r)/r)\frac{E_w[w \mid w \geq w^r] - w^r}{1 + (r/\tau)} > 0 \tag{2.15b}$$

$$d\tau/d\mu = \delta f(w^r)r/(r + \tau) > 0 \tag{2.15c}$$

The response of τ to changes in either the arrival rate δ or a mean preserving spread of the offer distribution, however, does depend on the shape of $f(w)$.

From the definition of τ, we can see that changes in δ will have a positive direct effect, but there will also be an indirect effect through w^r. From Equation 2.7 we know that this will be negative, but its magnitude is indeterminate without additional information on the offer distribution.[4]

More precisely, from Equation 2.10 we have

$$\partial\tau/\partial\delta = \pi(w^r)[1 - (\tau/(\tau + r))H'(w^r)] \tag{2.16}$$

where $H(w^r) = E_w[w \mid w \geq w^r]$, the mean of the accepted-wage distribution. Now, the model implies that the density for accepted wages is

$$f_a(w) = f(w)/\pi(w^r), \quad \text{for } w \geq w^r \tag{2.17}$$
$$= 0, \text{ otherwise}$$

so that

$$H(w^r) = E_w[w \mid w \geq w^r] = \int_{w^r}^{\infty} w\, \frac{f(w)}{\pi(w^r)}\, dw \tag{2.18}$$

It can easily be shown that the mean accepted wage is increasing in the truncation point of the distribution, that is,

$$H'(w^r) > 0 \tag{2.19}$$

but a restriction on the magnitude of this derivative requires restrictions on the shape of the accepted offer density $f_a(w)$ and therefore $f(w)$. Going back to the arrival rate derivative, a sufficient condition for Equation 2.16 to be nonpositive (negative) is $H'(w^r) \leq (<) 1$. Assuming that the density $f(w)$ is log concave is sufficient for the weak inequality to be satisfied and strict log concavity is sufficient for a strict inequality and thus for a negative effect for increases the arrival rate effect on mean durations. Exponential, uniform, and normal all represent specifications for the offer distribution that satisfy this condition. When $H'(w^r) > 1$, however, the level of the discount rate affects the results for Equation 2.15. In particular, for large enough values of r, an increase in the arrival rate may lead to a decline in the transition rate out of unemployment and thus to an increase in mean durations.[5]

The implications of the model for changes in the expected wage, $E[w \mid w \geq w^r]$, with changes in the variables b, r, μ, and δ, are also of interest. From Equations 2.17 and 2.19, it is straightforward to show that

$$dE_w[w \mid w \geq w^r]/db > 0 \tag{2.20a}$$

$$dE_w[w \mid w \geq w^r]/dr < 0 \tag{2.20b}$$

$$dE_w[w \mid w \geq w^r]/d\delta > 0 \tag{2.20c}$$

Additional derivative restrictions require additional information on the shape of $f(w)$, however, again because of opposite direct and indirect effects.[6]

Variations and Extensions

The assumptions maintained in our model are restrictive. Here, we consider some ways in which these assumptions might be relaxed. Our objective is not to survey all recent developments in search theory, but rather to consider potential ways that a few variations in assumptions might lead to different implications, or to more relevant empirical models. The surveys by Lippman and McCall (1976) and Mortensen (1986b) give details on the variety of models that have been studied. In following chapters we consider additional extensions that have been made in empirical applications.

Nonstationarity

For the most part, the assumptions of the basic model serve to ensure that the environment and therefore the optimal policy of the worker do not vary over the course of a spell. The assumption of an infinite horizon, for example, allows abstraction from any "aging" effects that might arise in the evaluation of the returns to search if working lives are finite. With a finite horizon, there will be a decline in the value of the returns on accepting a given offer the later in a given spell it is received.[7] An infinite horizon implies that the return on an offer is independent of when in a spell the offer is received.

The assumption of a constant income flow while unemployed also serves to maintain the invariance of the optimal policy over the course of a spell of unemployment. It might seem particularly objectionable. Fixed assets and the possibility of exhausting unemployment benefits render this assumption implausible for long spells of unemployment.[8] When benefit entitlement is of limited duration, for example, it can be shown that the reservation wage will decline (and the hazard will therefore rise) up to the date of exhaustion and then remain constant in a spell.[9]

Time invariance of the arrival rate and the offer distribution over the entire duration of a spell might also be restrictive. It might be argued that employers interpret a long spell of unemployment as a signal that a worker is a "lemon," for example, in which case the arrival rate might be expected to decline as a spell continues.[10] Human capital might actually be diminished by time spent out of work. Again, a decline in the arrival rate of offers might be expected and the offer distribution might shift down or change shape, as well. Alternatively, a worker (feeling either discouraged or desperate) may adjust his or her search effort and methods over the course of a given spell. A worker may look initially only into the best jobs available for a person with his or her skills, but look into less desirable opportunities later in a spell. This is known as *systematic search*. In either of these cases, the distribution of offers would effectively vary with duration and the arrival rate might rise or decline or do both as a result of such strategy changes. Alternatively, a worker may not know the actual distribution of offers he or she faces, but instead start out with a prior and update it on the receipt of each successive offer.[11]

All of these considerations suggest that incorporating nonstationarity into the model is appropriate. Consider the job search model when generalized to allow for variation over the duration of a spell in the reservation wage, the offer distribution, and the probability that an offer will be received for any of the reasons considered. Assume a reservation wage policy is optimal. This will be the case when the offer distribution is known and may apply while it is unknown (depending on the specification). Let $w^r(t)$ denote the reservation wage, $f_t(w)$ denote the offer distribution, and $\delta(t)$ denote the arrival rate at elapsed duration t. The conditional probability that an acceptable offer will be received in the interval $[t, t + h]$, given that a spell has lasted to t, will now be defined as

$$\tau(t)h = [\delta(t)h + o(h)]\pi_t(w^r(t)) \tag{2.21}$$

where

$$\pi_t(s) = \int_{w^r(s)}^{\infty} f_t(w)\ dw \tag{2.22}$$

Following the same procedure as before, we find the hazard rate for this model,

$$\tau(t) = \delta(t)\pi_t(w^r(t)) \tag{2.23}$$

the Survivor function,

$$S(t) = 1 - G(t) = \exp\left\{-\int_0^t \tau(u)\ du\right\} \tag{2.24}$$

and the density for completed durations T,

$$g(t) = \tau(t)\exp\left\{-\int_0^t \tau(u)\ du\right\} \tag{2.25}$$

Taken together, the considerations outlined do not imply a particular pattern for variation in the reservation wage and the hazard rate over the duration of a spell. Instead, they imply that the form of the hazard and thus the distribution for durations will depend heavily on the details of the specification of the theoretical structure.[12]

Just as the simple model abstracts from variation in the probability of leaving unemployment over the course of a spell, it abstracts from dependence on calendar time. Business cycles and seasonal variation in some areas of the labor market represent two obvious factors that might lead one to incorporate dependence on calendar time into the model. For example, the paths followed by the arrival rate or offer distribution might be modeled as depending on the calendar date of entry into the state of unemployment. Lippman and McCall (1976) allow the state of the economy, characterized by wage offer distributions, to evolve though discrete time according to a Markov chain. They find that the worker's optimal search strategy is a reservation wage policy with state-dependent reservation wages.

Systematic Search

The case of systematic search allows wage offer distributions to differ across firms. Of course, for this model to be different from the random search model there must be a restriction that each firm can be sampled only once, otherwise the firm with the "best" offer distribution would be sampled repeatedly. Salop (1973) considers a model with N

firms. Each firm is characterized by a wage offer distribution and an offer probability. The probability of "no offer" is modeled as part of the offer distribution by adding a mass point at zero wage. Workers know these offer distributions and offer probabilities, and apply to firms once each period. The worker must accept a job offer within N periods and the accepted job is held forever. The worker's decision problem is to choose the order in which firms are sampled and the reservation wage for each firm (naturally, the reservation wage for a firm depends on where in the order it is sampled).

Let f_j be the density (corresponding to the absolutely continuous part of the offer distribution) of wages at the jth firm sampled in the optimal ordering of firms, let w_j^r be the corresponding reservation wage, and let Π_j be the acceptance probability

$$\Pi_j = \int_{w_j^r}^{\infty} f_j(w) \, dw$$

The expected wage at firm j on acceptance is $h_j = (1/\Pi_j) \int_{w_j^r}^{\infty} f_j(w) \, dw$. Salop shows that the optimal search policy is given by an ordering of firms and a sequence of reservation wages satisfying

$$w_{j-1}^r = (1 + r)^{-1}(\Pi_j h_j + (1 - \Pi_j)w_j^r)$$

Firms are ordered according to $\Pi_j h_j/(r + \Pi_j)$ descending. It is possible that several orderings and sequences of reservation wages will satisfy these relations; the optimal ordering is the one leading to the largest expected value of income.

The model implies that the sequence of reservation wages is decreasing (note that $w_N^r = 0$). This is potentially relevant for many of the empirical studies we review. The ordering scheme implies that a worker choosing between two firms offering equal expected wages Πh (the probability the offer is acceptable multiplied by the expected value of the wage given the offer is acceptable) will first sample high wage–low probability firms. Note that the assumption of no recall is crucial in this model.[13]

Utility Maximization

Beyond the stationarity of the basic model, the behavioral assumption of income maximization might also seem too simplistic. It is equivalent to an assumption of risk neutrality and allows us to abstract from potential effects of risk aversion and nonlabor income on worker behavior. Maximization of a utility function defined as an increasing function of income, $u(w)$ where $u'(w) > 0$, could be specified instead without affecting the basic implications of the model. The intuitively appealing result that a more risk-averse individual will have a lower reservation wage can be established.[14]

With the assumption of income maximization, we are also ignoring the value of time spent not working. A multiplicative utility function defined over leisure and income might be specified instead. If we treat leisure when employed L_e and leisure when unemployed L_u as exogenous, the optimality condition for the reservation wage can be written as

$$u(w^r) = (u(L_u)/u(L_e))u(b) + (\delta/r) \int_{w^r}^{\infty} \{u(w) - u(w^r)\} \, dF(w) \qquad (2.26)$$

The optimal policy for the worker and basic implications of the model will be unaffected in this case if $u'(w) > 0$. If we drop the assumptions of separability across income and leisure or the exogeneity of leisure time in the two states, things become more complicated. For example, time devoted to search may be specified as a choice variable or offers may vary in terms of both hours of work and wages. In these cases, assumptions with respect to complementarity and substitutability of income and leisure will affect the basic implications of the model.[15]

Layoffs and Quits

To now, we have focused on the experience of a worker only when unemployed. The assumption that a worker will hold a job forever once an offer is accepted leaves no avenue for a worker to become unemployed, nor does it allow for job changes. In place of assumption 7, it might be assumed instead that

7′. When employed, a worker may be placed on permanent layoff, where the arrival of layoffs follows a Poisson process with parameter a.

A layoff, in this case, does not depend on current tenure. Job durations T_e follow an exponential distribution with parameter a. Expected tenure in any job taken is thus

$$E(T_e) = 1/a \qquad (2.27)$$

Layoffs such as these may be interpreted as being generated by some exogenous random factors. Alternatively, such separations may be motivated by a simple "matching" theoretical structure, although it is difficult to get a constant layoff rate in the matching structure.

Under either the matching or layoff interpretations, the present value of expected lifetime income at a wage rate w will be defined by

$$V^e(w) = \frac{1}{1 + rh} wh + \frac{1}{1 + rh} [(1 - ah)V^e(w) + ahV^u] + o(h)K \qquad (2.28)$$

The first term on the right is the present value of income, which will be received over a short interval of length h. The second is the present value of expected lifetime income at the end of this period, a weighted average of the worker's expected income if he or she remains employed at w and expected income if he or she is laid off and searches thereafter. The weights are simply the probabilities of each of these events occurring over the interval h. The third term is the probability of more than one offer multiplied by the associated value of following the optimal policy in that case. Under the Poisson assumption, $o(h)h \to 0$ as $h \to 0$.

Letting $h \to 0$ and solving for $V^e(w)$ yields

$$V^e(w) = \frac{w}{r + a} + \frac{aV^u}{r + a} \qquad (2.29)$$

which is continuous and strictly increasing in w. It follows that the wealth-maximizing and therefore optimal policy for the worker is a reservation wage policy: accept any wage w such that $w \geq w^r$, where the reservation wage w^r solves $V^e(w^r) = V^u$ or, equivalently,

$$\frac{w^r}{r} = V^u \qquad (2.30)$$

as before. The optimality condition for this model can be derived as in the simpler model and written as

$$w^r = b + \frac{\delta}{r + a} \int_{w^r}^{\infty} (w - w^r) \, dF(w) \qquad (2.31)$$

The effect of adding this assumption, alone, to the basic unemployed search model can thus be interpreted as equivalent to a change in the definition of the rate at which expected returns to search are discounted from r to $r^* = r + a$. The optimality and existence of a reservation wage policy, its time invariance, and the implications derived for the simple model are not affected, since the defining conditions for the values of employment and unemployed search are otherwise unchanged. The implications of Equations 2.7 and 2.15 carry over directly.

On-the-job search can be incorporated into the theoretical structure, in which case workers may move from job to job as well as between unemployment and employment. The value of an offer will be affected by the prospects of subsequent opportunities that might arise after taking the offer. A reservation policy will continue to be optimal for the worker, but there will be two reservation wages in this case, one for unemployment and another for employment. The relative values of these reservation wages will depend on the arrival rates and offer distributions in the two respective states. For example, if the arrival rates and offer distributions do not depend on the state occupied, then the reservation wage when unemployed can be shown to be equal to income while unemployed, holding all else constant.[16] On-the-job search models are reviewed in Chapter 8.

Variation in the optimal policy as an employment spell continues may be implied by more complicated models, which explicitly address experience when employed. In the case of either quits or layoffs, the relevant parameters might be modeled as depending on tenure in a job due to specific human capital accumulation or learning, for example.[17] As in the model focusing on unemployment alone, the pattern of variation with duration will depend on the precise theoretical structure here as well. Matching and alternative models of job-exit behavior are also reviewed in Chapter 8.

Steady States in a Two-State Model

The transition rate from unemployment to employment τ_{ue} in the model with layoffs is defined as in Equation 2.10 (with appropriate reinterpretation of the parameters under Equation 2.31). The transition rate from employment into unemployment τ_{eu} is simply the parameter a (workers have no choice in this transition). Since neither transition rate depends on the length of time spent in the state occupied in the current spell or on the worker's previous experience, they are said to possess the *Markov property*. The model implies that a worker's labor market history can be described by a continuous time Markov chain and steady-state probabilities that a worker will be in each of the two labor market states may be calculated. Letting the steady-state probabilities be denoted by $p^* = (p_e^*, p_u^*)$ and letting the probabilities that the states e and u are occupied at time $t = 0$ be denoted by $p^0 = (p_e^0, p_u^0)$, mild regularity conditions imply that $p^t \to p^*$ as $t \to \infty$. In a steady state, it must be the case that the flow into unemployment $\tau_{eu} p_e^*$ equals the flow out $\tau_{ue} p_u^*$. One interpretation of p_u^* is that it represents the proportion of an individual's life that will be spent unemployed. Alternatively, it can be interpreted as the proportion of a homogeneous population occupying state j. It follows that an expression for the "natural" unemployment rate is given by the solution:

$$u^* = p_u^* = \tau_{eu}/(\tau_{eu} + \tau_{ue}) \tag{2.32}$$

Three-State Models

Our discussion to now has abstracted from movements in and out of the labor force. In doing this, we have effectively restricted our attention to the experience of permanent members of the labor force.[18] If one is interested in studying labor market histories, a model of the labor market state space consisting of employment, unemployment, and nonparticipation may be appropriate. In such a framework, a worker chooses over time to occupy one of these three states. Movements among the states can be modeled as responses to random events, as before, and a labor market history thus may be represented as a stochastic process. Consider, for example, the following structure.[19]

Let u_j denote the utility flow when state j is currently occupied, with j = e (employment), u (unemployment), or n (nonparticipation). Since only relative utilities will matter to a worker, u_n may be set to zero and let $u_e = z + \epsilon$ and $u_u = b$. The term z is a human capital or mean wage and predictions of the effects of different z, due perhaps to different levels of education, ability, or labor market experience, provide a rough specification check in empirical work. Now these flows may change from time to time with the arrival of events in the form of random changes in ϵ or b. In particular, events may be described as independent random draws from a distribution $F(\epsilon, b)$, which workers know. Suppose, also, that workers know the processes governing the arrivals, but not the precise timing of such events when in any of the three states. In particular, suppose that the timings of information arrivals are Poisson with parameters δ_j. Restrictions on the relative values of δ_j may be appropriate. Nonparticipation is a situation in which workers are available for work but not actively seeking it. Arrivals when employed can plausibly be expected to arrive less frequently then when unemployed. Thus, it might thus be assumed that δ_u exceeds both δ_n and δ_e.

As in the simpler structures, the existence and uniqueness of state-dependent value functions can be established given mild restrictions. Given that state j is currently occupied, that the utility flows in employment, unemployment, and nonparticipation are $z + \epsilon$, b, and 0, respectively, and that all future decisions will be made optimally, these may be written as

$$V^j(z + \epsilon, b) = \frac{1}{1 + rh} [u_j h + \delta_j h E][\max_{k=e,u,n} V^k(z + \epsilon, b)]$$

$$+ (1 - \delta h)V^j(z + \epsilon, b)] + o(h) \tag{2.33}$$

$$= (u_j + \delta_j E[\max_{k=e,u,n} V^k(z + \epsilon, b)])/(\delta_j + r)$$

for j = e, u, n, where the second expression follows from rearranging terms, dividing through by h, and taking limits as $h \to 0$.

An analog to the reservation wage policy in the simpler models considered can be defined in terms of acceptance sets. Let $A_j(z)$ be defined over the space of doubletons (ϵ, b) as those values such that state j is preferred to the alternatives, given z, that is,

$$A_j(z) = \{(\epsilon, b) \mid V^j(z + \epsilon, b) = \max_{k=e,u,n} V^k(z + \epsilon, b)\} \tag{2.34}$$

These spaces are determined by critical values of e and u and characterize the optimal strategy for a worker on realization of an event. Precisely, the optimal strategy for a worker can be summarized in three numbers, $\epsilon(z)$, $b(z)$, and $\alpha(b; z)$ such that

$$V^e(z + \epsilon, b) \gtrless V^n(z + \epsilon, b) \text{ as } \epsilon \gtrless \epsilon(z) \tag{2.35a}$$
$$V^u(z + \epsilon, b) \gtrless V^n(z + \epsilon, b) \text{ as } b \gtrless b(z) \tag{2.35b}$$
$$V^e(z + \epsilon, b) \gtrless V^u(z + \epsilon, b) \text{ as } \epsilon \gtrless \alpha(b; \epsilon) \tag{2.35c}$$

where $\partial\alpha(b; z)/\partial\epsilon = (r + \delta_e)/(r + \delta_u)$. The acceptance regions A_j are graphed in (ϵ, b) space in Figure 2.2 for two values of z.[20]

As before, the empirical implications of the model are of primary interest. The transition rate from state i to j, $i, j = $ e, u, n, $i \neq j$, can be written

$$\tau_{ij}(z) = \delta_i\pi_j(z) \tag{2.36}$$

where

$$\pi_j(z) = \int_{A_j(z)} dF(\epsilon, b) \tag{2.37}$$

is the acceptance probability for state j. From any one of the three states that a worker may occupy there are two potential destinations so that the hazard rate for leaving a state for i, $i = $ e, u, n is defined as

$$\tau_i(z) = \sum_{\substack{j=e,u,n \\ j \neq i}} \tau_{ij}(z) \tag{2.38}$$

which does not depend on the length of time spent in state i. Thus, spell durations in any given state i have an exponential distribution with parameter $\tau_i(z)$. Let $G_i(t|z)$ be the corresponding cumulative distribution function. The conditional probability that state j will be entered on completion of a spell in state i is $\tau_{ij}(z)/\tau_i(z)$ for $j \neq i$. It follows

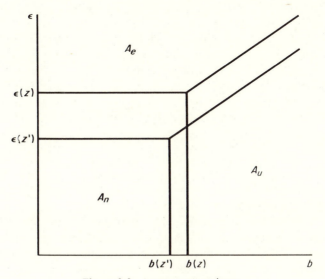

Figure 2.2. Acceptance regions.

that the density for a completed spell in i of length t that ends with a transition into j is given by

$$g_{ij}(t|z) = (\tau_{ij}(z)/\tau_i(z))g_i(t|z) \qquad (2.39)$$
$$= \tau_{ij}(z)[1 - G_i(t|z)]$$

for i, j = e, u, n, $i \neq j$.[21]

When the variable z is interpreted as the mean of the wage offer distribution faced by the worker, derivative restrictions can be derived for the reservation values $\epsilon(z)$, $b(z)$, and $\alpha(b; z)$ for the structure as it stands; namely, it can be shown that

$$\epsilon'(z) < 0 \qquad (2.40a)$$
$$b'(z) < 0 \qquad (2.40b)$$
$$\partial\alpha(b; z)/\partial z = 0 \qquad (2.40c)$$

These in turn imply that $\pi_e(z)$ (the likelihood of choosing employment after an event) will be positively related to z and $\pi_n(z)$ (the likelihood of choosing nonparticipation) will be negatively related to z. Without additional restrictions, the relation between z and $\pi_u(z)$ is ambiguous. From Equation 2.40, derivative restrictions for the transition rate $\tau_{ij}(z)$ with respect to z follow directly for $i \neq j$, i = e, u, n, and j = e, n. Note that because the δ_i are assumed independent of the mean offer z, all transition rate responses to changes in z are due to a change in the acceptance probability. These effects are illustrated in Figure 2.2. It is certainly plausible that variables affecting z could affect arrivals as well; this is an open area for modeling efforts.

As in the simpler models, the model specified here is Markov in the sense that a worker's labor market history provides no information about the rate at which movement from the state currently occupied into alternative states will occur. The model thus implies that a worker's labor market history follows a continuous-time Markov chain and steady-state probabilities that a worker will be in each of the three labor market states can be calculated straightforwardly.

Letting the steady-state probabilities be denoted by $p^* = (p_e^*, p_u^*, p_n^*)$ and letting the probabilities that the states e, u, and n are occupied at time $t = 0$ be denoted by $p^0 = (p_e^0, p_u^0, p_n^0)$, mild regularity conditions imply that $p^t \to p^*$ as $t \to \infty$; further, p^*, the limiting distribution, is independent of p^0. Thus, changes in the distribution of workers across states in any period do not affect the steady state. As above, p_j^* may be interpreted as the proportion of an individual's life spent in state j or, alternatively, as the proportion of a homogeneous population occupying state j in the long run. Using the properties that these proportions must sum to 1 and, in a steady state, the flow into a state must equal the flow out of a state, the steady-state distribution is given by

$$p_e^* = \delta_u\delta_n\pi_e(z)/(\delta_u\delta_n\pi_e(z) + \delta_e\delta_n\pi_u(z) + \delta_e\delta_u\pi_n(z))$$
$$p_u^* = \delta_e\delta_n\pi_u(z)/(\delta_u\delta_n\pi_e(z) + \delta_e\delta_n\pi_u(z) + \delta_e\delta_u\pi_n(z)) \qquad (2.41)$$
$$p_n^* = \delta_e\delta_u\pi_n(z)/(\delta_u\delta_n\pi_e(z) + \delta_e\delta_n\pi_u(z) + \delta_e\delta_u\pi_n(z))$$

Under the assumptions made above on the relative values of the arrival rates δ_j, it can be shown that the steady-state employment proportion will be an increasing function of the fixed wage component z, while the nonparticipation proportion will be a decreasing proportion. Variation in the unemployment proportion, however, will depend on the relative responsiveness of the two alternative proportions.[22]

Variation with spell durations can be incorporated into the model sketched here.

Alternative or more detailed specifications of the state space representing the labor market might also be considered. For example, part-time employment might be introduced as a distinct state. Our intent here has merely been to indicate the possibilities for multistate modeling. Many variations may be useful, depending on the question and the data available. As we review the empirical literature in Chapters 4 to 10, we sketch additional extensions of the basic model that have proved useful in applications.

Notes

1. For details on Poisson processes, see Karlin and Taylor (1985, Chapter 4); for a discussion in the search context, see Mortensen (1986b).

2. The optimality condition that defines the reservation wage for the worker follows directly from dynamic programming. It asserts that a worker's current optimal choice maximizes the sum of the flow of utility in the current period and the mathematical expectation of the worker's discounted flow of utility over the future, given that all future decisions will be made optimally.

3. The distribution F is a mean preserving spread of the distribution G if they have the same mean and $\int_0^y (F - G)\, dw \geq 0$ for all y.

4. Changes in the mean of the offer distribution also have direct and indirect effects, but we have bounds on the magnitude of the reservation wage response and this allows us to sign the effect on π and therefore τ.

5. Log concavity ensures that the slope of the truncated offer density does not exceed unity. See Burdett and Ondrich (1985) for the detailed derivation of the conditions discussed here and Vroman (1985) and Burdett and Muus (1989) for additional details on log concavity.

6. See Burdett and Ondrich (1985).

7. See Gronau (1971).

8. Beyond these potential changes in pecuniary income, adverse psychological effects of long-term unemployment have been documented (Hayes and Nutman, 1981). If we were explicitly allowing for a utility flow from time spent not working, we might want to incorporate this into the model.

9. The theoretical literature on supply-side search effects of unemployment benefit programs is extensive. For analysis of limited duration of benefits, see Mortensen (1977, 1986b, 1990). For treatment of other program characteristics, see Ben-Horim and Zuckerman (1987), Burdett (1979b), Burdett and Wright (1986), Hamermesh (1979), Hey and Mavromaras (1981), Lang (1985, 1986), Lippman and McCall (1980), Rosen (1977), Shavell (1979), Wright (1986a,b, 1987), Wright and Hotchkiss (1988), Wright and Loberg (1987), and Zuckerman (1985).

10. See Berkovitch (1990), Borjas and Heckman (1980), Phelps (1972), and Vishwanath (1989) for analysis of "scar" and "stigma" effects of time spent unemployed.

11. In this case, a solution for the reservation wage may not exist, as noted by Rothschild (1973). See Burdett and Vishwanath (1988b) for a theoretical analysis of worker behavior when the offer distribution is unknown.

12. See van den Berg (1990a) for a theoretical study of a search model with duration dependence. In fact, the class of nonstationary models consistent with search theory is somewhat smaller than might be expected. This is treated by Burdett and Sharma (1988).

13. See Burdett (1975), Kahn and Low (1987), and McCall and McCall (1981) for additional analysis of systematic search. Weitzman (1979), Roberts and Weitzman (1980), and Vishwanath (1988) also present related results.

14. Kohn and Shavell (1974) present an early treatment of utility-maximizing search. Danforth (1979) and Hall et al. (1979) present search models in which utility-maximizing workers face "imperfect" capital markets and draw down assets as they search while unemployed, and examine the role of risk averse behavior. Ionnides (1981) extends these models to examine search and savings behavior when layoffs are possible.

15. Mortensen (1977) examines endogenous search intensity, with a focus on the effects of variation in UI program characteristics and the effects of anticipated entitlement to benefits. Seater (1977) and Siven (1974) present early treatments of the separability of labor market time and consumption decisions. Kiefer (1987) and Blau (1988) treat the case of job offers that differ both in hours and in wages (on the empirical importance of tied wage-hour offers in a static context; Kapteyn et al., 1989), and Borjas and Goldberg (1978) and Wilde (1979) examine the effects of variation in alternative nonwage characteristics of offers on acceptance strategies. Lundberg (1981) considers joint decision making in a household utility-maximizing search model.

16. See Burdett (1978, 1979a,b), Mortensen (1977, 1986b, 1988), and Burdett and Mortensen (1978) for theoretical models that incorporate on-the-job search, alone and together with choice of search intensity.

17. An extensive amount of theoretical work has been done on learning about job matches. See Jovanovic (1979a,b) and Wilde (1979) for early examples.

18. Alternatively, this approach might be described as not making a distinction between unemployment and not being in the labor force (i.e., treating all nonemployment as unemployment).

19. The model to be sketched here is essentially that set out in Burdett et al. (1980, 1984a,b).

20. Note that $\partial V^j(z + \epsilon, b)/\partial \epsilon = 1/(r + \partial_j)$ for $j = e$ and zero, otherwise, and $\partial V^j(z + \epsilon, b)/\partial b = 1/(r + \delta_j)$ for $j = u$ and zero, otherwise. The proof of the optimal strategy given in Equation 2.35 follows directly from this. Note also that the dependence of the critical values of e and b on z is essentially the same at the dependence of w^r on the parameters of the offer distribution $f(w)$ in the model considered earlier. The existence and uniqueness of the value functions (Equation 2.33) follow from Blackwell's theorem (Blackwell, 1965), since the functional equations that implicitly define them satisfy the sufficient conditions for a contraction. See Sharma (1988) for details.

21. The density $g_{ij}(t|z)$ does not integrate to 1. Its integral from zero to infinity is τ_{ij}/τ_i, the probability, not conditional on duration, that a spell in state i will end with a transition to state j. For this reason $g_{ij}(t|z)$ is often referred to as a subdensity or an improper density.

22. Specifically, it will be an increasing function of z when $|\partial p_e/\partial z| > |\partial p_n/\partial z|$ and a decreasing function of z when the opposite inequality holds. See Burdett et al. (1984a,b) for details on this and a discussion of cases in which the Markov property of the model will fail to hold.

3

The Search Framework: Econometrics

Search models for the behavior of the unemployed have implications for reservation wages over time. These in turn have implications for the distribution of unemployment durations across individuals and for the distribution of accepted wages. The econometric problem is to use data to assess and refine the search approach. What features of the search model are consistent with patterns found in the data? What features are clearly at odds with the data? Are some of the variations and extensions listed in Chapter 2 better for understanding economies and economic behavior than the simple model—or should alternatives be developed? The inference problem is complicated by the fact that reservation wages are rarely observed (studies with observations on reservation wages are presented in Chapter 4). Without observations on reservation wages, researchers must rely on data on unemployment durations and wages.

The discussion in this chapter concentrates on unemployment duration and reemployment wages, though many of the issues treated arise as well in the study of employment duration data and job-to-job transition data. In the first section we treat some general considerations: the formulation of the joint wage and duration density, the likelihood function when regarded as a function of parameters, and the issue of censoring. Censoring is a ubiquitous problem in duration and wage data. We then turn to a discussion of specification alternatives in the context of data on wages and durations. These alternatives range from tightly specified structural models to illustrative regressions. This section also introduces the discussion of unmeasured heterogeneity. Next, we treat the case of wage data alone. This is followed by a treatment of duration data alone. As this is a somewhat newer topic for economists, it is treated in some detail. We first consider homogeneous worker data (no covariates) and deal with nonparametric and maximum likelihood approaches. Explanatory variables are then introduced. The setting is slightly more complicated (and less satisfactorily resolved) than introducing covariates into linear regressions. Finally we consider competing risks models, in which a spell can end for any of several reasons (e.g., a spell of unemployment can end with employment or upon withdrawal from the labor force). The next section introduces data

29

ket histories. In this kind of data, individuals are followed through sequential spells of employment (perhaps with changes of jobs), unemployment, and potentially nonparticipation.

General Estimation Issues

Estimation of search models is conceptually straightforward though often tricky in application. The model of Chapter 2 yields an exponential density for durations (Equation 2.13), $g(t) = \tau \exp\{-\tau t\}$, and a density for accepted wages (Equation 2.17), $f_a(w) = f(w)/\pi(w^r)$ for $w \geq w^r$. The parameter τ is equal to the product of the offer arrival rate and the acceptance probability, $\tau = \delta\pi(w^r)$, where $\pi(w^r)$ is the probability of receiving an offer greater than w^r, $\int_{w^r}^{\infty} f(w)\,dw$ with $f(w)$ the wage offer distribution. The densities of wages and durations are related in that they depend on common parameters—those determining w^r and $f(w)$—but the random variables wages and durations are independent in this model. Thus, the joint density of wages and durations is given by $p(w, t) = g(t)f_a(w)$. With the data density at hand, we are well on our way to doing estimation and inference based on the likelihood function.

The distribution of wages and durations can be expected to differ across individuals, perhaps due to variation in levels of human capital investment or differences in search costs. Introducing a vector of explanatory variables for the ith individual, x_i, and a parameter vector θ, the density of wages and durations for individual i is given by $p(w, t|x_i, \theta)$. The likelihood function for θ based on a sample of N independent observations is

$$L(\theta) = \prod_{i=1}^{N} p(w_i, t_i \mid x_i, \theta) \tag{3.1}$$

For the present we are not being specific about the way the explanatory variables and coefficients enter, but note that there are complicated relationships between parameters of the offer distribution and parameters of the reservation wage function due to the assumption of optimal search.

Structural models, which impose restrictions implied by the theory, are typically estimated by numerical maximization of the likelihood function. This maximization problem depends heavily on the specific distributional assumptions made, so producing estimates requires substantial programming and computing effort. As we will see, one of the standard regularity conditions can be violated in some specifications [the parameters of the reservation wage function can enter the limits of integration in $\pi(w^r)$], implying that some care must be taken in computing and interpreting coefficients and, particularly, asymptotic standard errors.

This estimation strategy is conceptually straightforward, once we accept the need to do numerical optimization, and forgo the use of a canned computer program. Using economic theory as far as possible, and then using judgment, we develop a joint density for the data conditional on parameters. With a sample of independent observations, the likelihood function is given by the product of these densities, and we study the likelihood to learn about parameters. In practice, the major additional difficulty of censoring must be addressed.

Censoring

Duration data are typically censored. That is, some of the observed spells are typically incomplete. For example, in a survey of workers with a follow-up survey at a later date, some of the workers will have experienced a spell of unemployment and then become reemployed. Others may have become unemployed and remain unemployed at the end of the study period. For these workers, the exact duration of unemployment is unobserved, as is the reemployment wage. Figure 3.1 illustrates the relationship between calendar time and duration and shows a censored spell.

Our data typically consist of a measured spell length together with the information on whether the spell was censored. Let T^*, a random variable, be a spell length for an individual in the absence of censoring, and let c be the censoring time measured from the time origin for the spell. Then the random variable that will be observed is the smaller of T^* and c, or $T = \min\{T^*, c\}$. We also know whether the observation is censored ($T = c$) or uncensored ($T = T^*$). Often the censoring times are known constants (given the time origin), for example, the end of a fixed-length panel survey. In another type of censoring, c is a predetermined constant common across observations, as when data measured in weeks from 1 to 26 are followed by a category "more than 26 weeks." Rather general forms of random censoring can be allowed, although it is crucial to assume that individuals whose spells are censored at time c are representative of all individuals who have spell lengths at least equal to c, perhaps after allowance for

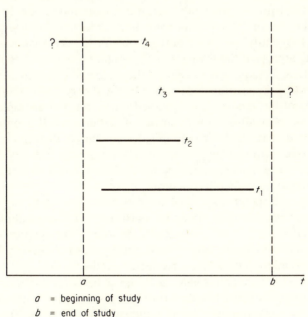

a = beginning of study
b = end of study
t_1, t_2 = complete spells
t_3 = right-censored spell
t_4 = left-censored spell

Figure 3.1. Classification of observed durations.

explanatory variables. Thus, if we regard the censoring time c as a random variable, it must be independent of T^*, after taking account of other factors. Censored spells contribute only a probability term $\int_c^\infty g(t)\,dt$, to the likelihood function.

The censoring we have considered so far is *right censoring*—the ending date of a spell is not observed. In some sampling methods, the measurement of duration begins when the individual enters the study, and thus the time origin is unknown (as is the true duration). This is known as *left censoring*. A spell of this type is illustrated in Figure 3.1 (t_4). This type of censoring is less common and difficult to deal with unless duration has an exponential distribution. In the exponential case, the distribution of duration after elapsed time t does not depend on t and so the distribution of remaining duration in left-censored spells is the same as the distribution for uncensored spells.

Note that wages are also censored in most cases—only offers above the reservation wage *(accepted wages)* are typically observed. This fact is taken into account in the construction of the density of accepted wages $f_a(w)$ from the density of the offers $f(w)$. Of course, inference about the shape of the offer distribution below the reservation wage depends crucially on a parametric assumption.

Specification Alternatives: Wage and Duration Data

Specifying the joint density of wages and durations allows (in principle) the imposition and potential testing of all the restrictions of job search theory. On the other hand, the tight specification requires some rather arbitrary assumptions on functional forms. Thus, if a model does not "fit" right, or some implications of the theory are rejected, it is often difficult to identify the source of the problem. An alterntive research strategy is to focus on some aspects of the search model, remaining agnostic about others. A natural approach along these lines is to analyze the wage and duration distributions separately—not imposing the relationship implied by the theory. Using this strategy, particular implications of the model can be studied bit by bit. For example, if reservation wage observations are available, they can be studied directly. If unemployment durations are more readily available or more reliably measured, they can be studied alone. These data sets offer information on the same question, since theory links the movement of reservation wages over duration to the distribution of durations. Accepted wage distributions can also be studied in isolation.

Regression models are often specified as a first approach, and the signs of coefficients are checked to see whether they satisfy the derivative conditions implied by a search model (e.g., Equations 2.7, 2.15, and 2.20). In the rest of this chapter, we review some methods of estimation that have been used in empirical search models. First, we set out a particular specification that leads to a regression model for the log of duration and the log of the accepted wage. This model provides a basis for interpreting regressions reported in a variety of studies. We then turn to a discussion of nonlinear models, typically estimated by maximum likelihood. Following this, we consider analysis of wage data alone, then analysis of duration data alone. Duration data are usually analyzed using hazard functions, which are reviewed. (Chapter 5 provides an extension of this hazard function discussion.) Finally, we briefly discuss analysis of labor market history data.

A Specification Leading to Linear Regressions

A convenient specification for the wage offer distribution faced by an individual is the Pareto, with density

$$f(w) = \alpha w_0^\alpha / w^{\alpha+1} \tag{3.2}$$

where w_0 and α are the lower bound and scale parameter of the distribution, respectively. This distribution has a long right tail. Provided $\alpha > 1$ the expected value of w is $\alpha w_0 / (\alpha - 1)$; if $\alpha > 2$ the variance is $\alpha w_0^2 / ((\alpha - 1)^2 (\alpha - 2))$. The Pareto distribution is widely used to describe the distribution of income, firm size, city size, etc. However, there is no compelling economic argument for using the Pareto as a wage offer distribution, and this is a potential source of lack of fit or of ambiguity in the interpretation of results. The probability an offer will be acceptable, given the reservation wage w^r, is

$$\pi(w^r) = (w_0/w^r)^\alpha \tag{3.3}$$

Now, to introduce heterogeneity into this model we specify the following functional forms:

$$(\delta w_0^\alpha)_i = \exp\{x_i\beta + u_{1i}\} \tag{3.4}$$

and

$$w_i^r = \exp\{x_i\Gamma + u_{2i}\} \tag{3.5}$$

where x_i is a vector of regressors that might include demographic and skill characteristics, nonemployment income information (unemployment benefits, in particular), determinants of the costs of search, and measures of local labor market conditions. Since it is extremely unlikely that the solution to the optimality condition (Equation 2.6) for the reservation wage will take the loglinear form assumed, Equation 3.5 must be regarded as an approximation to the reservation wage. Nevertheless, this approach represents a start because we have some notion from theoretical analysis about the signs of the effects of the regressors on the reservation wage. Furthermore, specification checks can be made on the basis of residuals once the model has been fit.

Note that all variables in Equation 3.4 must enter Equation 3.5. This follows because the reservation wage is a function of the parameters of the offer distribution and the arrival rate. Some variables can enter Equation 3.5 without entering Equation 3.4, however, since variables that influence search costs, in a general sense, need not affect productivity on the job.

To obtain a regression specification, consider the following result:

Proposition 1. Let duration T_i be distributed exponentially with hazard rate $\tau(x_i)$. Then,

$$\text{a. } E(T_i) = 1/\tau(x_i)$$

and

$$\text{b. } E(\ln T_i) = -\ln \tau(x_i) + \Phi(1)$$

where Φ is the digamma function.

Proof. a. Obvious—it is a property of the exponential distribution. b. A change of variables to $z = \ln T$, with Jacobian $\exp\{z\}$, results in the density $p(z) = \tau \exp\{z\} \exp\{-\tau$

exp$\{z\}\}$. The moment generating function for this distribution is

$$m(\theta) = E(\exp\{\theta z\}) = E(t^\theta) = \int_0^\infty \tau t^\theta \exp\{-t\tau\}\, dt$$

$$= \int_0^\infty u^\theta \exp\{-u\}\, du$$

$$= \tau^{-\phi}\, \Gamma(\theta + 1)$$

where Γ is the gamma function. Evaluating the first derivative of this last expression at the point $\theta = 0$ gives the stated result.

The hazard rate for the distribution specified above is

$$\tau(x_i) = \exp\{x_i(\beta - \alpha\Gamma) + u_{1i} - \alpha u_{2i}\} \tag{3.6}$$

so that application of Proposition 1 yields a regression specification of the form

$$\ln t_i = x_i(\alpha\Gamma - \beta) + \Phi(1) + \epsilon_{1i} \tag{3.7}$$

where the error term ϵ_{1i} incorporates u_1, u_2, and the deviation of $\ln t_i$ from its expected value.

This model is sufficiently parameterized to allow calculation of the expected value of the log of the accepted wage as well. A useful property of the Pareto distributions is that left truncations of the distribution are also Pareto. From the offer distribution (Equation 3.2) and the acceptance probability (Equation 3.3), it follows that the density of accepted wages is

$$f(w\,|\,w > w^r) = \alpha(w^r)^\alpha/w^{\alpha+1} \tag{3.8}$$

and by changing variables to $z = \ln w$ with Jacobian $\exp\{z\}$, we have

$$p(z) = \alpha(w^r)^\alpha \exp\{-\alpha z\}, \qquad \ln w^r < z \tag{3.9}$$

where z has expected value

$$E(z) = \alpha(w^r)^\alpha \int_{\ln w^r}^\infty z \exp\{(-\alpha z\}\, dz$$

$$= 1/\alpha + \ln w^r \tag{3.10}$$

The second expression is obtained on integration by parts. Using this result we have a regression specification for the accepted wage offer distribution.

$$\ln w_i = 1/\alpha + x_i\Gamma + \epsilon_{2i} \tag{3.11}$$

Lancaster (1985b) noted that it is sensible to think of Equations 3.7 and 3.11 as reduced form relationships since they give the endogenous variables as functions of the regressors alone. We may wish to isolate the structural parameters of the model. On writing the simultaneous equation system

$$\ln t_i = \alpha \ln w_i - x_i\beta + c + v_{1i} \tag{3.12a}$$

$$\ln w_i = 1/\alpha + x_i\Gamma + \epsilon_{2i} \tag{3.12b}$$

we can see that identification of reservation wage parameters requires variables in x_i that affect the reservation wage without directly affecting the arrival rate and offer distribution (i.e., zero restrictions on β are needed). Note that the variance of ln (w) is $1/\alpha^2$. This is useful in practice as it allows a quick check on the Pareto specification.

The appealing aspect of this regression model is that the estimated parameters can be related to the underlying theoretical structure. Obviously, the theoretical specification on which it is based is quite specific and thus restrictive, but alternatives could be considered.

On estimation, it is appropriate to ask whether the results are in accord with the theory. A quick check is whether the signs of the "effects" of regressors are consistent with theory. More can be done because the model is specific in its distributional implications. In particular, we may be interested in checking whether the reservation wage is constant. The specifications can be analyzed using residual plots.

If there is censoring in the duration data, then the specified model is inappropriate as it stands. It can be modified, however. If there is random right censoring, for example, a Tobit-like model for the conditional mean of log durations could be specified. Alternatively, we might wish to move away from linear regression models, which tend to emphasize mean durations or mean log durations, and consider maximum likelihood estimation.

Maximum Likelihood Estimation

Given a parameterization of the wage offer distribution $f(w)$, say $f(w \mid \theta, x_i)$, observations of the net income while unemployed b (there is some hope of having data on b), and values for the arrival rage of δ and the discount rate r (one of these can be estimated, sometimes), the reservation wage for individual i can be obtained from Equation 2.5, repeated here

$$w^r = b + (\delta/r) \int_{w^r}^{\infty} (w - w^r) \, dF(w)$$

This equation gives the essential restriction implied by search theory. The reservation wage is a function of market opportunities, not merely the value of nonmarket time as in the older literature. Thus, w_i^r is determined by x_i, θ, b, δ and r and the functional form is specified exactly once the form of the offer distribution is specified. This restriction implies that accepted wages, completed durations, and censored durations all convey information about the same set of parameters. For the offer distibutions that have been specified in the literature, the optimality condition is extraordinarily difficult to impose. Often there is no closed form expression for the reservation wage as a function of parameters and data—the implicit Equations 2.5 are the best one can do. Most authors have made some approximation, using either an expansion of the function w^r (although this function may be unknown, some of its derivatives are signed) or an expansion of the integrand in Equation 2.5. After making the approximation, maximum likelihood is then applied to estimating the parameters in the joint density of accepted wages, completed spells, and censored spells. Since there is no settled technique for estimating these structural models, the techniques used by individual researchers are described along with their studies below. In nonstationary job search models, the reservation wage changes with duration and a condition similar to Equation 2.5 holds in every period in a discrete time model; a differential equation determines the reservation wage in continuous time.

It is important to note that exact imposition of the optimality condition 2.5 typically leads to a nonregular estimation problem. Write the reservation wage function as a function of a scalar unknown parameter of the offer distribution, $w^r(\theta)$ (suppressing dependence on additional variables for the moment). Then the density of accepted wages is given by $f_a(w \mid \theta) = f(w \mid \theta) / \pi(w^r(\theta))$ for $w \geq w^r$. Suppose data were available on all wages offered so that we observed a sample from $f(w \mid \theta)$. Then we could use the fact that $\int_0^\infty f(w \mid \theta) \, dw = 1$ to infer that $\int_0^\infty f' \, dw = 0$ where f' denotes differentiation with respect to θ. Noting that this is the same as $\int_0^\infty (f'/f) f \, dw = Ed \ln f/d\theta = 0$, we have some confidence that solving the likelihood equation $d \ln L/d\theta = 0$ to obtain values of θ will give consistent estimates; the sample average will approximate the expectation taken using the true value of θ. (This argument harmlessly ignores a variety of other regularity conditions.)

When we consider the truncated distribution $f_a(w \mid \theta)$ we note that $\int_{w^r(\theta)}^\infty f_a(w \mid \theta) \, dw = 1$ and hence $\int_{w^r(\theta)}^\infty f'_a \, dw - (dw^r/d\theta) f(wr \mid \theta) = 0$. Thus $Ed \ln f_a/d\theta$, evaluated at the true value of θ, is not equal to zero, which means solving the likelihood equation does not lead to consistent estimation. In fact, the likelihood equation does not have a solution in many simple settings.

Let $w[1]$ be the minimum observed wage in the sample. Then a little more analysis shows that in the one-parameter setting we are considering, $\hat{\theta} = (w^r)^{-1}(w[1])$ (i.e., the inverse function of w^r) is the maximum likelihood estimator in large samples (see Christensen and Kiefer, 1990). This is interesting; the parameter of the wage distribution does not depend on the pattern of observed wages except through their minimum value. In the more relevant K-parameter setting with explanatory variables, the estimation problem is more complicated but the lessons are the same. Estimation involves solving a complicated nonlinear programming problem. Some studies have used gradient methods to estimate these models, using a penalty function that assigns very low likelihood values when a trial value of θ is such that $w < w^r(\theta)$ for some observed w. There are much more efficient computational methods for estimating θ. The maximum likelihood estimator in this nonstandard setting retains its property of consistency. (Of course, the constraints $w_i \geq w^r_i(\theta)$ for each observation must be imposed in calculating the maximum.) Computation of appropriate estimates of standard errors requires care. Methods of estimation and inference for these models are still being developed.

Note that the strategy of estimating w^r for a homogeneous sample by the minimum accepted wage and then estimating the "other" parameters by "maximum likelihood" conditional on the reservation wage does not give maximum likelihood estimates, as it ignores restriction 2.5. Theory requires that all parameters enter the reservation wage function. On the other hand, estimating w^r by the minimum, then using the distribution of accepted wages to estimate the parameters separately leads to a specification check. One can see whether the estimated w^r and the separately estimated θ satisfy Equation 2.5.

One easy and sensible, although ad hoc, method of avoiding the nonstandard estimation situation is to introduce an error term in the reservation wage equation, writing $w^r = w^r(\theta) + \epsilon$. With this modification (and a suitable distribution for ϵ), the range of acceptable wages does not depend on unknown parameters. Thus the limits of integration when calculating the expected value of the derivative of the density do not depend on the values of unknown parameters. Standard maximum likelihood methods can be used. This strategy is adopted by a number of authors.

Unmeasured heterogeneity arises when different individuals in a sample have different distributions of the dependent variable, even after controlling for explanatory variables. It can arise as a result of functional form misspecification (e.g., leaving out a regressor), failure to include a needed squared term in a variable, or the presence of important but unobservable variables. Unmeasured heterogeneity is a potential problem in nonlinear models generally; it is not peculiar to job-search or duration models.

Heterogeneity due to unobservable "individual effects" has been treated in nonlinear search models using a random effects specification. Write the density for the ith wage-duration pair conditional on the unobservable v_i

$$p(w, t \,|\, x_i, \theta, v_i) \qquad (3.13)$$

where v_i enters, for example, the mean of the wage offer distribution underlying the development of the density $p(\cdot)$. Under the assumption that v is distributed with the distribution $h(v \,|\, \sigma)$, the marginal distribution of the observables w and t is given by

$$p(w, t \,|\, x_i, \theta, \sigma) = \int_{-\infty}^{\infty} p(w, t \,|\, x_i, \theta, v)h(v \,|\, \sigma) \, dv \qquad (3.14)$$

The likelihood function based on $p(w, t \,|\, x_i, \theta, \sigma)$ can be used to estimate the parameters θ and σ. With appropriate choice of $h(v \,|\, \sigma)$, the parameter σ, perhaps a standard deviation, can be interpreted as measuring the extent of heterogeneity. It has proven useful in some applications to specify a discrete distribtuion for v—perhaps with only two or three support points. There is a growing impression that misspecification of the "mixing distribution" h is not as damaging to inference as misspecification of the distribution $p(w, t \,|\, x, \theta, v)$, but it is difficult to say anything precise about this issue without further specification of the model.

Models for Wage Data Alone

Suppose data are available on reemployment wages but not unemployment spell durations. Is it possible to say anything about a search model using these data? Yes, if we are willing to restrict attention to a model with a constant reservation wage. The density of accepted wages is given by Equation 2.17 as

$$f_a(w) = f(w)/\pi(w^r), \qquad w \geq w^r$$

where $\pi(w^r)$ is the acceptance probability $\int_{w^r}^{\infty} f(w) \, dw$. Adding a parameterization in θ and explanatory variables,

$$f_a(w \,|\, \theta, x_i) = f(w \,|\, \theta, x_i) \Big/ \int_{w^r}^{\infty} f(w) \,|\, \theta, x_i) \, dw \qquad (3.15)$$

Of course, w^r depends on θ, x_i, and f through the optimality condition (Equation 2.5). A natural approach is to form the likelihood function based on the densities of Equation 3.15 and obtain maximum likelihood estimates of the parameters using an assumption about the parametric form of f (possibly trying several different functional forms, in practice). Identification in this model is tricky. Since wage data are observed only above the reservation wage, and since the optimality condition (Equation 2.5) does not involve the density below the reservation wage, the lower tail of the wage offer density is not determined by the data and must be tied down by a parametric assumption. Not all parametric assumptions secure identification; the assumed density has to have the property that knowledge of the upper portion determines the complete density.[1] Note that exact imposition of the optimality condition (Equation 2.5) leads to a nonstandard estimation problem, as described above and treated in detail by Christensen and Kiefer (1990).

A modified regression approach for wage data can be taken. Suppose that the offer distribution has the form

$$\ln w_i = x_i'\beta + \epsilon_i^0 \tag{3.16}$$

with ϵ_i^0 normally distributed with mean zero and variance σ^2. Thus, the offer (actually, log offer) distribution differs across individuals only in its mean. Suppose also that the reservation wage of the *i*th individual is given by

$$\ln w_i^r = z_i'\gamma + \epsilon_i^r \tag{3.17}$$

with ϵ_i^r also normally distributed. Note that it is incredibly unlikely that the reservation wage satisfying the optimality condition (Equation 2.5) will take the form $\exp\{z'\gamma\}$. Hence the presence of the error term, which can also capture interindividual variation in w^r not captured by variation in characteristics z_i. An individual accepts a job only if $s_i = \ln w_i - \ln w^r > 0$. We can now write the model

$$\ln w_i = x_i'\beta + \epsilon_i^0, \quad \text{if } s_i > 0 \tag{3.18}$$
$$s_i = x_i'\beta - z_i'\gamma + \epsilon_i$$

where $\epsilon_i = \epsilon_i^0 - \epsilon_i^r$.

The model is in the same technical form as models for *selectivity bias*. Note that the expected value of the error term in the wage equation for the observed sample is nonzero, since we need the expectation conditional on $s_i > 0$, and, in fact, the expectation depends on the characteristics z_i, as well as on the x_i. The model can be estimated by maximum likelihood, or by a two-step method proposed by Heckman (1979). This class of models is discussed in detail by Tunali (1986). Our formulation requires that all variables included in x also be included in z, since the reservation wage function depends on the mean of the offer distribution. However, variables affecting cost of search can be included in z and not in x. Indeed, identification of the reservation wage function requires that some variables affecting the reservation wage not affect the mean-wage offer. On this point, and for a further development of the estimation method, see Kiefer and Neumann (1979a).

Models for Duration Data Alone

Econometric methods for analysis of duration data are rapidly being developed and imported from biometrics. These methods are based on specification of the hazard function, rather than the data density. Of course, it is straightforward to go back and forth between hazards and densities, so the only difference in approach is convenience in specification, estimation, and interpretation. Applications to labor market duration are natural (Silcock [1954] provided a remarkable early study of employment duration using hazard functions) and now numerous. Nevertheless, because the methods are still fairly new in economics, we review basic techniques here in detail and provide additional discussion in Chapter 5.[2]

The probability distribution of duration can be specified by the distribution function $F(t) = Pr(T \leq t)$, the corresponding density function $f(t) = dF(t)/dt$, the survivor function $S(t) = 1 - F(t) = Pr(T > t)$, or the *hazard function*

$$\lambda(t) = -d \ln S(t)/dt = f(t)/S(t)$$

The hazard function provides a convenient definition of duration dependence. Positive duration dependence exists at the point t^* if $d\lambda(t)/dt > 0$ at $t = t^*$. Positive duration dependence means that the probability that a spell will end shortly increases as the spell increases in length. Negative duration dependence exists at t^* if $d\lambda(t)/dt < 0$ at $t = t^*$. (The more straightforward statistical terminology *increasing hazard* and *decreasing hazard* does not seem to have caught on in economics.)

The *integrated hazard*

$$\Lambda(t) = \int_0^t \lambda(u) \, du \tag{3.19}$$

is also useful function in practice, though it does not have a convenient interpretation. It is the basic ingredient in a variety of specification checks. It is easy to see by a change of variables that $\Lambda(t)$, regarded as a random variable, has a standard exponential distribution.

Nonparametric (Graphic) Methods

Nonparametric methods are useful for displaying data on durations and for preliminary analyses of homogeneous observations, perhaps to suggest functional forms, with homogeneity perhaps being achieved by grouping according to observed variables. The sample survivor function for a sample of n observations with no censoring is $\hat{S}(t) = n^{-1}$ {number of sample points $\geq t$}. A modification is required to allow for censoring. Suppose the completed durations in our sample of size n are ordered from smallest to largest, $t_1 < t_2 < \cdots < t_K$. The number of completed durations K is less than n because some observations are censored and because of ties. Ties occur when two or more observations have the same duration. Let h_j be the number of completed spells of duration t_j, for $j = 1, \cdots, K$. Let m_j be the number of observations censored between t_j and t_{j+1}. Let M_k be the number of observations with durations greater than t_K, the longest complete duration. Then n_j, the number of spells neither completed nor censored before duration t_j, is

$$n_j = \sum_{i \geq j}^{K} (m_i + h_i) \tag{3.20}$$

The hazard $\lambda(t_j)$ is the probability of completing a spell at duration t_j, conditional on the spell's reaching duration t_j. A natural estimator for $\lambda(t_j)$ is $\hat{\lambda}(t_j) = h_j/n_j$, the number of "failures" at duration t_j divided by the number "at risk" at duration t_j. The corresponding estimator for the survivor function is $\hat{S}(t_j) = \Pi_{i=1}^{j} (n_i - h_i/n_i)$, which is the *Kaplan-Meier* estimator (Kaplan and Meier, 1958). Essentially, this estimator is obtained by setting the estimated probability of completion of a spell at t_j equal to the observed relative frequency of completion at t_j. It is possible to interpret this estimator as a maximum likelihood estimator (see Johansen, 1978).

Maximum Likelihood Estimation

Suppose that the family of duration distributions under consideration has been specified, so that the data distribution is known up to a vector of parameters θ. The family may have been chosen on the basis of a particular economic theory, convenience, and perhaps some preliminary nonparametric analysis.

Write the density of a duration of length t and $f(t, \theta)$. If a sample of n completed spells is available and each individual's spell is independent of the others, the likelihood function is

$$L^*(\theta) = \prod_{i=1}^{n} f(t_i, \theta) \tag{3.21}$$

as usual. In other words, the likelihood function is the joint probability distribution of the sample as a function of parameters θ. When a spell is censored at duration t_j, the only information available is that the duration was at least t_j. Consequently the contribution to likelihood from that observation is $S(t_j, \theta)$, the probability that the duration is longer than t_j. Let $d_k = 1$ if the kth spell is uncensored and $d_k = 0$ if censored. Then the log likelihood function $L(\theta)$ is

$$L(\theta) = \sum_{i=1}^{n} d_i \ln f(t_i, \theta) + \sum_{i=1}^{n} (1 - d_i) \ln S(t_i, \theta) \tag{3.22}$$

which has completed spells contributing a density term $f(t_i, \theta)$ and censored spells contributing a probability $S(t_i, \theta)$. Because the density is the product of the hazard and the survivor function, $f(t, \theta) = \lambda(t, \theta)S(t, \theta)$, and the log of the survivor function is minus the integrated hazard $\ln S(t, \theta) = -\Lambda(t, \theta)$, the log likelihood function can be written in terms of the hazard function

$$L(\theta) = \sum_{i=1}^{n} d_i \ln \lambda(t_i, \theta) - \sum_{i=1}^{n} \Lambda(t_i, \theta) \tag{3.23}$$

In practice it is usual to do an analysis based on asymptotic properties of maximum likelihood methods. Under a variety of well-known sets of sufficient conditions, the maximum likelihood estimator $\hat{\theta}$ is consistent for θ and $\sqrt{n}\,(\hat{\theta} - \theta)$ is normally distributed with mean zero and variance $-[n^{-1}\partial^2 L(\theta)/\partial\theta\partial\theta']^{-1}$.

Consider as an example the exponential model with $\lambda(t, \gamma) = \gamma$ and $\Lambda(t, \gamma) = \gamma t$. The log likelihood function is then

$$L(\gamma) = \sum_{i=1}^{n} d_i \ln \gamma - \gamma \sum_{i=1}^{n} t_i \tag{3.24}$$

with first derivative

$$\partial L(\gamma)/\partial\gamma = \gamma^{-1} \sum_{i=1}^{n} d_i - \sum_{i=1}^{n} t_i \tag{3.25}$$

When this is set to zero we derive the maximum likelihood estimator

$$\hat{\gamma} = \sum_{i=1}^{n} d_i \Big/ \sum_{i=1}^{n} t_i \tag{3.26}$$

with approximate variance

$$V(\hat{\gamma}) = -[\partial^2 L(\gamma)/\partial\gamma^2]^{-1} \qquad (3.27)$$

$$= \gamma^2 \bigg/ \sum_{i=1}^{n} d_i$$

Note the effect of censoring. If censored spells were treated as complete, the maximum likelihood estimator would be $\gamma_c = n/\Sigma t_i \geq \Sigma d_i/\Sigma t_i = \hat{\gamma}$.

Another popular specification is the Weibull model, with $\lambda(t, \sigma, \gamma) = \alpha\gamma t^{\alpha-1}$, α, $\gamma > 0$. This specification allows duration dependence. If $\alpha > 1$, the model has positive duration dependence—the conditional probability a spell will end increases with the length of the spell. If $\alpha < 1$ the hazard function is decreasing. If $\alpha = 0$, the hazard is constant—this is the exponential case. Thus, the Weibull is a simple, one-parameter (additional) extension of the exponential allowing for duration dependence.

Explanatory Variables

Explanatory variables can affect the distribution of durations in many ways. In ordinary regression models it is natural to assume, at least as a starting point, that explanatory variables affect the distribution of the dependent variable by moving its mean around. There is no analogous clear-cut starting point for including explanatory variables in duration models. The proportional hazard specification (discussed in the following) is popular and simple to interpret: the effect of regressors is to multiply the hazard function itself by a scale factor. The accelerated failure time model (also to be discussed) has seen less use in economics but is also easy to interpret: the effect of regressors is to rescale the time axis. More general models allow interaction between regressors and duration. As in most nonlinear models, the interpretation of the coefficients of the explanatory variables depends on the specification. In the general case, the coefficient does not have a clean interpretation as a partial derivative analogous to the interpretation of coefficients in the linear regression model. The sign of the coefficient indicates the direction of the effect of the explanatory variable on the conditional probability of completing a spell. The numerical value of this effect (i.e., the partial derivative) depends on duration and in general on other included variables.

In the proportional hazard model, the hazard function, depending on a vector of explanatory variables x with unknown coefficients (β, λ_0), is factored as $\lambda(t, x, \beta, \lambda_0) = \Phi(x, \beta)\lambda_0(t)$, where λ is a "baseline" hazard corresponding to $\Phi(\cdot) = 1$. It is a common (and sensible) practice to measure the regressors so that $\Phi(\cdot) = 1$ at the mean value of the regressors. Then λ_0 has an interpretation as the hazard function for the mean individual in the sample. Note that the coefficients designated θ previously have been separated into β and λ_0. In this specification the effect of the explanatory variables is to multiply the hazard λ_0 by a factor Φ that does not depend on duration.

With the proportional hazard specification we have $\partial \ln \lambda(t, x, \theta)/\partial x = \partial \ln \Phi(x, \beta)/\partial x$, so the proportional effect of x on the conditional probability of ending a spell does not depend on duration. In the imporant special case $\Phi(x, \beta) = \exp\{x'\beta\}$

$$\partial \ln \lambda(t,x,\theta)/\partial x = \beta \qquad (3.28)$$

so the coefficient can be interpreted as the constant proportional effect of x on the conditional probability of completing a spell. This specification admits a convenient interpretation as a linear model. Thus we have Proposition 2.

Proposition 2. The proportional hazard model $\lambda(t, x, \theta) = \lambda_0(t) \exp\{x'\beta\}$ can be written in the linear model form $-\ln \Lambda_0 t) = x'\beta + \epsilon$, where ϵ has the distribution function $F(\epsilon) = \exp\{-\exp\{\epsilon\}\}$.

Proof. With $\lambda(t, x, \theta) = \exp\{x'\beta\}\lambda_0(t)$ the survivor function for t is given by $S(t) = \exp\{-\Lambda_0(t)\exp\{x'\beta\}\}$, where $\Lambda_0(t) = \int\lambda_0(u)\, du$ is the integrated baseline hazard. Consider the random variable ϵ defined by $\epsilon = -\ln \Lambda_0(t) - x'\beta$. To calculate the distribution of ϵ, write

$$Pr(\epsilon < E) = Pr(-\ln \Lambda_0(t) < E + x'\beta) \qquad (3.29)$$
$$= Pr(t > \Lambda_0^{-1}(\exp\{-E - x'\beta\}))$$

This probability can be evaluated using the survivor function for t, giving

$$Pr(\epsilon < E) = \exp\{-\Lambda_0(\Lambda_0^{-1}(\exp\{-E - x'\beta\}))\exp\{x'\beta\}\} \qquad (3.30)$$
$$= \exp\{-\exp\{-E\}\}$$

which is the cumulative distribution function for the type-1 extreme value distribution. Thus, we can write the proportional hazard model in the form $-\ln \Lambda_0(t) = t^* = x'\beta + \epsilon$ a linear model for t^* in which the error term has a fully specified distribution.

To illustrate the linear model interpretation, we consider the exponential model with parameter $\gamma = \exp\{x'\beta\}$ and $\lambda_0(t) = 1$. Then, $-\ln t = t^* = x'\beta + u$. Regressions of this form appear in some of the studies we review.

The *partial likelihood approach* suggested by Cox (1972, 1975) is a semiparametric method for estimating β in the proportional hazard model without specifying the form of the baseline hazard function λ_0. Suppose the completed durations are ordered, $t_1 < t_2 < \cdots < t_n$. Suppose there is no censoring and there are no ties in the durations. The conditional probability that observation 1 concludes a spell at duration t_1, given that any of the n observations could have been concluded at duration t_1, is

$$\frac{\lambda(t_1, x_1, \beta)}{\displaystyle\sum_{i=1}^{n} \lambda(t_1, x_i, \beta)} \qquad (3.31)$$

With the proportional hazard assumption $\lambda(t,x,\beta) = \Phi(x,\beta)\lambda_0(t)$, this expression reduces to

$$\frac{\Phi(x_1, \beta)}{\displaystyle\sum_{i=1}^{n} \Phi(x_i, \beta)} \qquad (3.32)$$

and this quantity is the contribution of the shortest duration observed to the partial likelihood. Similarly, the contribution of the jth shortest duration is $\Phi(x_j, \beta/ \sum_{i=j}^{n} \Phi(x_i, \beta)$. The likelihood is formed as the product of the individual contributions and the resulting log likelihood function is

$$L(\beta) = \sum_{i=1}^{n} \left[\ln \Phi(x_i, \beta) - \ln \left(\sum_{j=i}^{n} \Phi(x_j, \beta) \right) \right] \tag{3.33}$$

The intuition here is that, in the absence of all information about the baseline hazard, only the order of the durations provides information about the unknown coefficients. Censoring is easily handled in the partial likelihood framework.

In the *accelerated lifetime* model, the effect of explanatory variables is to rescale time directly. If the baseline survivor function is $S_0(t)$, then the survivor function for an individual with characteristics x is $S(t, x, \beta) = S_0(t\Phi(x, \beta))\Phi(x, \beta)$. The density is $f(t, x, \beta) = f_0(t\Phi(x, \beta))\Phi(x, \beta)$.

In the special case $\Phi(x, \beta) = \exp\{x'\beta\}$, the accelerated lifetime model can be given a linear model interpretation. We have

Proposition 3. The acclerated lifetime model $S(t, x, \beta) = S_0(t\Phi(x, \beta))\Phi(x, \beta)$ can be written in the linear model form $-\ln t = x'\beta + v$, where v has the density $f_0(\exp\{-v\}) \exp\{-v\}$.

Proof. Change variables to $v = -\ln t - x'\beta$, and use an argument parallel to that in the proof of Proposition 2.

This representation of the model can lead to specification checks and suggestions for informative plots, as in the discussion following the linear model representation of the proportional hazard model. It also gives a convenient interpretation of the coefficients of explanatory variables: $\partial \ln t/\partial x = -\beta$.

Both the proportional hazard and the accelerated lifetime specifications restrict interdependence between the explanatory variables and duration in determining the hazard. In some cases, more flexible interaction between x and t must be allowed. Since the hazard function must be nonnegative, a convenient specification is $\lambda(t, x, \beta) = \exp\{g(t, x, \beta)\}$ where the function g is somewhat arbitrary but can be specified to include polynomials and step functions in t and x as necessary. The likelihood function based on this hazard can be used to obtain parameter estimates.[3]

Additional discussion of the hazard function approach is given in Chapter 5. Hazard function notions are easily extended to models in which a spell can end for different reasons—the setting of "competing risks."

Competing Risks

The competing risks framework considers models in which spells can end with a transition into any of several destination states. For example, a spell of employment could end with a transition to unemployment or an exit from the labor force. A three-state model of this type was presented in Chapter 1; the destination-specific hazard rates τ_{ij} are given in Equation 2.36 and the hazard rate for the distribution of a spell in state i is given in Equation 2.38 as $\tau_i = \sum_{j \neq i} \tau_{ij}$. Competing risks models, on parameterization of the hazard functions, can be fit by maximum likelihood or other methods as described above. When estimating the parameters of τ_{ij}, spells ending with a transition to state $k \neq j$ are regarded as censored. Thus, sensible specifications of competing risk models typically involve a lot of censoring and regression approaches are unsuitable.

Labor Market Histories

In longitudinal or panel data sets, a sample of individuals is followed over time and individuals in the sample may experience several transitions between labor market states. Job changes, short spells of unemployment, and occasional withdrawals from the labor force are not uncommon, particularly for seasonal workers or for new entrants to the labor force. Under suitable assumptions, the separate spell lengths (and associated wages when relevant) for a particular individual can be taken to be independent across spells. This means, for example, that the distribution of the length of the current spell of employment for a worker does not depend on the length of the preceding spell of unemployment. Furthermore, the distribution of the length of a spell of employment in a particular job does not depend on whether it was preceded by a spell of unemployment, employment in a different job, or nonparticipation. This independence property is strong, but without it (or some similar very strong assumption), empirical work is almost ruled out since an individual's history could depend on high-dimensional unobservables, expected to be correlated with practically everything.

An assumption of this sort is implicit in analysis of single spell data, since we typically assume that we are sampling from a homogeneous population, after controlling for explanatory variables. (Of course, some control for unobservable heterogeneity can be made, as previously described.) The assumption needed is that the process governing state to state transitions together with times spent in each state is a *semi-Markov process.* A semi-Markov process, or Markov renewal process, is a stochastic process in which transition from state to state (abstracting from durations in states) follow a Markov chain, while durations in states have origin and destination state-specific probability distributions. In the case in which these distributions are exponential, the process is a Markov process. With this assumption, sequences of spell lengths can be studied using hazard function methods, as described above. Different spells for the same individaul are independent and are typically treated as different observations. A conceptually simple generalization allows individual-specific effects (unobservables?) to be present. These effects induce correlation across spell lengths for a particular individual. Nevertheless, the process governing the labor market history for that individual is assumed to be semi-Markov, conditional on the value of the effect. The semi-Markov framework allows straightforward calculation of steady-state distributions of labor market time across states, generalizing calculations reported in Chapter 2.[4] More details on Markov and semi-Markov models are given in Chapter 6.

With the material in this chapter as background, we now turn to the econometric studies. Some of these use special and novel techniques, developed to fit the particular application. We treat these methods as they they appear.

Notes

1. For example, the Pareto distribution is not completely determined by its upper tail, since the lower support point w_0 is not identified. The normal is determined by its upper tail. Any density that is analytic can be determined from knowledge of the upper tail.

2. Discussions of duration analysis aimed at economists are provided by Kiefer (1988b) and Lancaster (1990). Additional references include Cox (1962), Cox and Oakes (1984), Kalbfleish and Prentice (1980), Lawless (1982), and Miller (1981).

3. Our discussion has focused on methods for working with individual unemployment spell observations, together with observations on covariates. Applications of actuarial and lifetable methods (and extensions thereof) to calculate average unemployment spell lengths and average unemployment exit probabilities using unemployment duration data by groups of individuals have been numerous (e.g., Cripps and Darling, 1974; McAuley, 1975; Kaitz, 1970; Salant, 1977; Frank, 1978; Bowers and Harkness, 1979; Akerlof and Main, 1980, 1981; Sider, 1985). For evidence on the relative merits of nonparameteric methods taken directly from the statistics literature and parametric extensions with the economics literature, see Pedersen and Smith (1983), Baker and Trivedi (1985), and Horrigan (1987). Alternative methods for the analysis of interval duration data—giving for each individual an interval for duration—are available; e.g., see Kiefer (1988) and Wurzel (1990).

4. For more on semi-Markov processes, see Heyman and Sobel (1982, Chap. 9).

4

Direct Evidence on
Reservation Wages

An individual's sequence of reservation wages takes center stage in theoretical search models, but practical data problems preclude this in empirical work—a reservation wage cannot be directly observed. The best an empirical researcher might hope for are responses to a question such as "What is the lowest wage you would be willing to accept?"—perhaps asked frequently over the course of a single unemployment spell. Unfortunately, such data are rare. We found just a few studies that have access to more than one reservation wage observation per worker. Melnik and Saks (1977) have two reservation wage observations for a sample of college seniors at Michigan State. Lynch (1983) has multiple responses to a reservation wage question for some workers in her sample of London youth—but only a small number who remain unemployed between interviews held 6 months apart.[1] Single interview responses have represented the primary source of direct evidence on reservation wages to date.

In this chapter, we discuss studies that have access to reservation wage data. We start with studies that take a regression approach. Several questions are addressed here, but the most frequent is whether the reservation wage declines over the course of an unemployment spell. Several studies also analyze the effects of unemployment benefits on reservation wages and unemployment spell lengths. We turn next to studies that exploit both reservation wage data and other unusual data to estimate the parameters of very specific search models. These are structural studies, using the terminology of Chapter 2.[2] With one exception, these studies use stationary frameworks; thus, movement in the reservation wage is not a focal point. However, benefit effects on the reservation wage and unemployment spell lengths receive a significant amount of attention. The structural studies also examine the response of reservation wages and unemployment spell lengths to variation in the offer arrival rate—without direct evidence on this variable.

Regression Studies

Kasper (1967) appears to have been the first to analyze reservation wage data—his objective being to investigate the pattern of movement in the reservation wage over the duration of a spell of unemployment. We discuss his work first and then turn to studies by Barnes (1975), Sant (1977), and Melnik and Saks (1977). These researchers first investigate the pattern of movement in the reservation wage using an approach similar to Kasper's. They then take different approaches to test particular hypotheses regarding the source of nonstationarity. The next study we discuss, by Miller and Volker (1987), investigates movement in the reservation wages of Australian youth.

We turn next to studies that use stationary job search models as a theoretical basis for their analyses. Warner et al. (1980) investigate potential sources of variation in unemployment spell lengths across workers—both direct and indirect (i.e., through variation in reservation wages). Feldstein and Poterba (1984) focus on variation in reservation wage–previous wage ratios. In both studies, the role of unemployment benefits is of primary concern. Holzer (1986b) focuses on differences in accepted wages and unemployment spell durations between young black workers and young white workers in the United States. He investigates the extent to which observed differences represent differences in reservation wages and alternative factors suggested by search theory. Sandell (1980a) studies unemployment duration and reservation wage data for married females in the United States.

The next papers we discuss address the issue of simultaneous determination of the reservation wage and unemployment spell length. Crosslin and Stevens (1977) appear to have been the first to recognize that coefficient estimates for reservation wage equations will be biased when single equation methods are used. They specify a two-equation model, based on a variety of search theoretic arguments and estimate the model using two stage least squares. Sandell (1980b) again focuses on the experience of females in the United States, but fits a two equation model for the reservation wage in this study. In each of these papers, the econometric models are tied loosely to theoretical structures and the identifying restrictions imposed are not easily interpreted. Jones (1988) takes a regression approach that is more closely tied to his theoretical model; his empirical model is essentially the exponential duration model set out in Chapter 3—modified to exploit available reservation wage data. Lancaster and Chesher (1984) specify a simultaneous equations model that generalizes the model used by Jones (1988) to allow for duration dependence in the reservation wage.

Kasper (1967)

Kasper addresses two questions: (1) "Are unemployed workers willing to accept a wage lower than that received in their previous job?" and (2) "Does the asking wage decline with the duration of a spell of unemployment?" These questions are motivated by an interest in the role of labor supply in producing sluggish labor market adjustment, as opposed to a formal search model. Nevertheless, his reasoning is clearly in the search framework.

Kasper argues that "an observer" would expect a worker to be unwilling to take a new job unless it offered a wage above the worker's previous wage, discounted by the probability of recall to the former job. The bases of this claim are an expected loss of nonwage benefits in the transition and a lower offer arrival rate if search is continued once on a new job. The hypothesis of a declining reservation wage is generated by two classical arguments. First, the marginal utility of leisure should decline as leisure accumulates. (Kasper thus provides an early application of the notion of a non-time-separable utility function.) Second, the drawing down of assets should lead to an increase in the marginal utility of income.

Kasper works with data for a sample of 3,000 unemployed workers who filed for extended benefits with the Minnesota Department of Employment Security between April and September 1961. The workers were asked "what wage are you seeking?" as well as the wage in their previous jobs. Kasper acknowledges the inherent difficulties in interpreting responses to the reservation wage question, but he also suggests some plausible incentives for workers to provide accurate answers in this particular survey. Workers who responded with an overly low wage might expect to be placed at that wage, whereas those with an unrealistically high asking wage might risk loss of their benefit eligibility. Duration is measured here as the number of months between the survey date and the date the previous job was lost, that is, all spells are right censored. Kasper also observes unemployment benefit status in the following February, but no additional information for the intervening period.

Kasper finds that asking wages are generally less than previous wages; on average, the difference is 2 percent in nominal terms and roughly 3.5 percent in real terms. To investigate the question of nonstationarity, Kasper fits a simple regression of the proportional difference between the previous wage w_p and the asking wage w_a on elapsed duration t. He reports the following results:

$$(w_p - w_a)/w_p = -0.808 + 0.375t \qquad R^2 = 0.068$$
$$(0.857) \quad (0.099)$$

where standard errors are in parentheses. This translates into a 0.3 percent decline in the asking wage per month. The basic result—that the asking wage declines with elapsed duration—holds up under a variety of respecifications.[3] However, on the basis of all regression results and some auxiliary analyses (e.g., scatter plots of grouped means), Kasper concludes that it takes between 2 and 6 months for the decline to begin and that the decline eventually tapers off.

Barnes (1975)

Barnes follows a strategy similar to Kasper's in his attempt to determine whether asking wages decline with duration. He then investigates whether movement in the asking wage reflects a decline in the expected returns to search, due to shortened periods over which returns to search may be collected (Gronau, 1971, or downward revisions in the perceived wage offer distribution (McCall, 1970).

Barnes works with data for a sample of 2,475 unemployed U.S. workers who were registered with Employment Service offices in 12 cities in 6 states in 1962. Responses to a question on the "lowest acceptable wage" serve as his reservation wage observations and self-reported months of unemployment in the current spell provide his duration data; all spells are therefore right censored. Workers were asked their wage rates and tenure in the job they had held the longest in the previous 5-year period. They were also asked if they had held another job since the one held longest, but nothing more about such jobs. Barnes treats the job held longest as the previous job. Responses to a (vague) question about whether a worker currently had good or bad expectations about job offers at an acceptable level of pay are also available.

To measure the impact of duration on asking wages, Barnes fits a regression of "asking wage flexibility," defined as the ratio of the asking wage w_a to the previous wage w_p, on a quadratic in duration t. The following results are reported:

$$(w_a/w_p)100 = -90.628 - 1.282t + 0.044t^2 \qquad R^2 = 0.009$$
$$ (7.511) \quad (0.289) \quad (0.013)$$

where standard errors are in parentheses. These results suggest that asking wage flexibility does decline, but it eventually tapers off. Barnes notes that when a linear model is fit to his data, his coefficient estimate is approximately the same as Kasper's 0.3 percentage point decline. He also notes that his findings are similar to the above when the same regression is fit separately for groups in an age partition and for groups in a partition based on whether or not the job held longest was the last job held.

To examine the source of the decline, Barnes fits a variety of regression equations. He first reports the following:

$$(w_a/w_p)100 = 81.261 - 0.007 \text{ age} - 0.025 \text{ tenure}$$
$$ (8.264) \quad (0.039) \qquad (0.037)$$
$$ - 0.121 \text{ job} - 11.411 \text{ perc} \qquad R^2 = 0.046$$
$$ (0.275) \qquad (1.100)$$

where tenure refers to tenure in the job held longest, job is a dummy variable that takes on a value of 1 if the last job was the job held longest, and perc is a dummy variable that indicates poor expectations about job offers at an acceptable level. Barnes interprets the results for the coefficients for age, tenure, the job as evidence against Gronau's explanation for a decline in the asking wage with duration and he interprets the magnitude and significance of the coefficient for perc as evidence in favor of McCall's explanation for a declining reservation wage. Given that duration is not controlled in the regression, this interpretation is not obvious. Barnes also reports the following results:

$$\text{perc} = 0.0993 + 0.0866t - 0.008t^2 \qquad R^2 = 0.1119$$

(Standard errors are not reported.) Noting that a regression is inappropriate given that perc is dichotomous, he nevertheless interprets the results as additional evidence in support of the learning explanation for the decline in the reservation wage.

Sant (1977)

Sant also considers the case of an unknown offer distribution and the effects of "learning" on movement in the reservation wage. For an individual who faces an offer distribution $F(x|\theta)$, he defines the reservation wage at elapsed duration t as

$$w^r(t) = f(F(x|\theta), G(\theta), t)$$

where θ denotes a vector of unknown parameters that characterizes the offer distribution and $G(\theta)$ denotes the worker's prior beliefs about the distribution of θ. To demonstrate that reservation wages might rise or decline with duration when workers sample from an unknown offer distribution, Sant cites known results for the case of inference about the mean of a normal distribution with known variance when sampling is done sequentially with a normal prior. In this case, movement in the reservation wage depends directly on the difference between the mean wage offer faced and the level of the reservation wage.[4]

Sant works with data for cross-sections of unemployed workers collected in the National Longitudinal Survey of Young Males (age 14 to 25 in 1966) for the years 1967–1969; the sample size is not reported. Responses to the question "What wage are you willing to accept?" provide his reservation wage data. Weeks unemployed during the year preceding an interview (which may be spread over more than one spell) are used as a measure of spell duration. Multiple observations for a worker may be present, but they are treated as independent (including matching observations censored at interview dates).

Sant works with a partition of his sample based on education level, IQ, race, geographic location, and year in which the unemployment spell took place. For each group with six or more observations, he first estimates an approximation to the reservation wage of the form

$$\ln w^r(t) = \alpha + \delta t + \epsilon_1$$

The intercept α is interpreted as the log of the worker's initial reservation wage μ_0, the coefficient δ for duration t is interpreted as the effect of learning on the worker's reservation wage, and ϵ_1 is a random disturbance. Standard errors are not reported, but sample sizes are very small and Sant warns that caution should be used in interpreting the results for δ because they are imprecise. Nevertheless, looking across the results for different groups, there is some evidence of variation in the reservation wage with duration—but not a monotonic decline. Both positive and negative signs for δ are reported. Given this finding, Sant fits log wage regressions of the form,

$$\ln (w) = \beta + \gamma \text{ experience} + \epsilon_2$$

where experience refers to years in the labor market and ϵ_2 is a random disturbance. Sant interprets the intercept β as the log of the mean of the true offer distribution μ. Then, letting μ_0^* and μ^* denote the estimates for μ_0 and μ obtained from these regressions, he calculates the difference

$$\mu_0^* - \mu^*$$

for each group and compares these to the δ estimates, δ^*. The simple correlation between this difference and δ^* is -0.74 across groups and a simple regression provides the following results.

$$\delta^* = 0.0003 - 0.058 \,(\mu_0^* - \mu^*)$$
$$(0.006)$$

where the standard error is in parentheses. Sant interprets these results as evidence that movement in the reservation wage depends systematically on the relationship between the initial reservation wage and the mean of the offer distribution—as predicted by his simple learning model.

Melnik and Saks (1977)

Melnik and Saks also investigate the behavior of the reservation wage when the offer distribution is assumed unknown. They do so, however, with the advantage of repeated observations on the reservation wage and other unusual wage and interview data.

Their sample consists of 132 graduating seniors in business and engineering at Michigan State University who were interviewed in February and May 1975.[5] The key questions in the first survey were "What do you think the most frequent gross starting salary would be for someone with your qualifications?" and "Assuming a satisfactory job were offered to you, at what gross salary would you accept it?" Responses to the first question provide Melnik and Saks with data on students' initial estimates of the modal wage. Responses to the second question provide initial observations on the reservation wage. Beyond their majors, grades, and other background questions, students were also asked about the number of on-campus interviews they had prior to the February survey, their use of job search methods other than the Placement Service, and the desirability of certain nonpecuniary job characteristics (e.g., company size, location, and potential for long-run advancement). In the May follow-up survey, all students were asked about their total number of on-campus interviews and "On the basis of your experience in the job market, what do you think the most frequent gross starting salary is for someone with your qualifications?". Students who had accepted offers (52 percent) were asked about starting salaries and nonpecuniary characteristics of their jobs. Students who had not yet secured employment were asked their current reservation wage. In addition to the survey data, Melnik and Saks also have data provided by the campus Placement Service to students on salaries received by previous graduates for each academic field.[6]

Melnik and Saks first report regression results for the first reported modal offer estimates. The explanatory variables are the preceding year's average salary within field, grade point average, number of interviews, and an interaction of the number of interviews with field. As expected, they find that students rely heavily on previous students' experience when predicting the mode of their own offer distributions and that deviations from this follow grade point averages closely. The results for the numbers of interviews provide evidence of a significant effect in just a few fields. Results are also reported for a regression of the initial reservation wage on the reported modal wage, number of interviews, grade point average, sex, marital status, parenthood, the proportion of education self-financed, and whether the student has applied to graduate school. Only the estimated coefficient for the perceived mode is significant at standard levels (0.956, standard error 0.053). This estimate is roughly consistent with the prediction of the search model that the slope of the reservation wage with respect to the mean offer is less than one (but nearly one).

Melnik and Saks are most interested in the relationships between the extent of interviewing and rates of change in the modal wage estimate and reservation wage. The authors first note that the two sets of responses for the modal wage indicate that the perceived distribution changes from being nearly symmetric to being sharply skewed to the right. They then report estimates for two alternative modal wage regression specifications. Both include the total number of interviews and the proportion of these interviews that took place between survey dates; the first specification also includes interactions between the number of interviews and fields, whereas the second includes dummy variables for fields alone.

Overall, the results provide little evidence that the interview process affects students' perceptions; neither interview variable is significant. Moreover, the error sum of squares is lower for the second of the two specifications, leading Melnik and Saks to conclude that "information is assimilated from a variety of sources and perceptions of modal wage can be regarded as relatively independent of interviewing" (p. 120).

For the rate of change of the reservation wage, Melnik and Saks again report results for two specifications. The first includes the number of interviews held between surveys, the rate of change of the perceived modal wage, and a job match variable related to nonpecuniary job characteristics. The job match variable is a variable that can take on a value between zero and one—zero if no job was taken and one if an accepted job had all desired characteristics, and the proportion of desired characteristics, otherwise. The number of interviews is treated as endogenous in the second specification and the system is estimated using two-stage least squares. In both cases, the accepted wage is used as the reservation wage for those who accepted a job by May, making interpretation of the results somewhat difficult. Still the results provide evidence that the rate of change in the reservation wage follows the rate of change in the perceived modal offer quite closely. Also, those who take jobs that best match their nonpecuniary desires appear to accept job offers that are quite close to their initial reservation wages. The results for the interview variables are quite interesting. When the number of interviews is treated as exogenous, the coefficient is insignificant. However, when interviewing is treated as endogenous, the results suggest that the reservation wage declines by about 1 percent with each additional interview. In both regressions, the constant is insignificant, that is, there is no evidence of pure duration dependence.

Melnik and Saks also report regression results for the number of interviews that include the rate of change of the reservation wage, first treated as exogenous and then treated as endogenous. Neither set of results provides evidence of causality in this direction. The results suggest that only the number of possible interviews in a student's major field and the number of search methods other than the Placement Service have significant effects on the flow of interviews. They also estimate a linear probability model for the probability of being employed by May, which includes the ratio of the reservation wage to the perceived modal wage, the number of interviews between February and May, the proportion of all interviews between February and May, the rates of change of reservation wages and modal wages, and a number of controls as regressors. Here, only the interview variables appear significant.

Miller and Volker (1987)

Miller and Volker report results from a detailed empirical analysis of the youth labor market in Australia—including analysis of its dynamics within the search framework. Their data are for a sample of workers, aged 19–25, who had completed secondary education (grade 10 in Australia) by the 1985 interviews of the Australian Longitudinal Survey (ALS). The ALS sample consists of 12,000 individuals, aged 15–24 in 1985, with 3,000 selected from a list of registered long-term unemployed and 9,000 selected from an area sample for all but sparsely settled areas. Miller and Volker work only with data for persons in the latter group for whom all relevant questions had valid responses, so their sample may be viewed as roughly representative for Australian youth. Answers to the question "What is the lowest weekly pay you would accept to work in any (full-time/part-time) job?" provide reservation wage data. In addition, they have detailed information on the use of job search methods and labor market histories. Their unemployment duration data are for weeks of active search for employment. In studying the behavior of reservation wages, Miller and Volker restrict their sample to workers, aged 19–24, who were seeking full-time work—to avoid effects of variations in intended hours of work. This gives them samples of 300 males and 164 females.

Miller and Volker use these data to estimate regressions of the form

$$\ln(w^r) = b_0 + b_1 x + b_3 d(t)$$

separately for males and females. The vector x includes log nonlabor income, demographic characteristics, education variables, and experience. The variable $d(t)$, defined as $1/(1 + \text{duration})$, is their measure of direct duration dependence. The results provide evidence of an intial decline in the reservation wage with duration, but it is roughly constant thereafter. In particular, for males, the results imply a 15 percent decline by the end of about 6 months, but little change thereafter. For females, the overall drop is much larger—roughly 35 percent—with most of the decline in the first few months; after 9 months, there is essentially no change. Some interesting results appear for the other regressors. Male workers with university degrees have much higher reservation wages (about 50 percent higher) than their counterparts. No similar education effect appears for females, however, and labor market experience has a negligible effect on the reservation wages of both groups. Miller and Volker interpret these variables as determinants of a worker's previous wage, but they might also affect the costs of search. In the latter case, the results might be interpreted as evidence of offsetting effects. Neither coefficient for nonlabor income differs significantly from zero, but Miller and Volker note that there is little sample variation in the amount of unemployment benefit received.[7]

Warner, Poindexter, and Fearn (1980)

The studies discussed thus far focus on testing the constant reservation wage hypothesis. In this study, Warner et al. maintain this assumption throughout their analysis. Their objective is to determine the relative influences of the unemployment benefits, the offer distribution, methods of search, and expected tenure in employment on the weekly probability of leaving unemployment—both directly and indirectly—that is, through the effects of these variables on the reservation wage.

Their data are for workers in four U.S. cities (Baltimore, Boston, Chicago, and Cleveland) collected in the 1970 Census of Employment. Responses to a question on the "lowest acceptable hourly pay" are available for 330 workers who experienced unemployment in the year preceding the survey. Completed unemployment spell durations, measured in weeks, and receipt of unemployment compensation are also observed for these workers, but not benefit amounts. Observations on wages and current tenure in employment are available for 11,059 workers who were employed at the time of the survey. Warner et al. use results from linear regressions of these variables on age, race, sex, education, occupation, and city to calculate instruments for mean wage offers and expected job tenures for the unemployed. An instrument for the standard deviaiton of the offer distribution is also constructed using the residuals from the wage regressions (averages are calculated for groups within an age, race, sex, occupation, and city partition). Warner et al. note that the instruments for the parameters of the offer distribution will differ systematically from those of the true distribution due to the use of accepted (as opposed to offered) wages in their wage regressions. They also note that the expected tenure instrument is likely to be biased downward due to the use of elapsed as opposed to completed tenure in employment.

Results for two log reservation wage regressions are reported—one that contains the expected job tenure instrument and a second reduced form specification that includes the determinants of tenure. The results for the elasticity of the reservation wage with respect to the mean of the offer distribution are 0.79 (standard error 0.101) and 0.87 (standard error 0.137), respectively. The coefficients for the offer variance are also positive, but small relative to reported standard errors. This result may simply reflect the use of accepted wage data, since the variance of the truncated distribution may be smaller than that of the true offer distribution under some specifications. The coefficients for receipt of unemployment benefits imply that the reservation wage is between 6.4 and 8.5 percent higher for recipients, but the effect is only marginally significant in the reduced form specification. Some interesting results for the use of different search methods also appear. The alternative methods of search are the standards that appear in Census surveys: newspaper, private employment agency, state employment agency, direct application to employer, friends or relatives, and union. The use of friends and relatives or a union has a signficant positive effect on the reservation wage. These results may reflect a pure union wage differential, as well as effects on the offer arrival rate.

Results are also reported for regressions of the log of the weekly probability of leaving unemployment, measured as the ratio of the number of times unemployed to total weeks of unemployment.[8] This method can be regarded as a semiparametric method of inferring the effects of regressors on the hazard (which is basically assumed to be a step function). Individuals with lower reservation wages and individuals who face higher mean wages are found to have higher probabilities of leaving unemployment, while recipients or unemployment compensation are found to have lower probabilities of leaving unemployment, given their reservation wages. For all search methods, however, there is no evidence of a significant effect on duration.

Feldstein and Poterba (1984)

Feldstein and Poterba study reservation wage data for a large sample of unemployed U.S. workers collected in a special supplement to the May 1976 Current Population Survey. Specifically, their sample consists of 2,228 workers, classified as unemployed, but neither new entrants nor reentrants, who completed supplemental questionnaires and provided responses to questions on both previous earnings and reservation wages. Their reservation wage data are generated by a two-part question: "What kind of work were you looking for (in the period 18 April through 15 May)?" and "What is the lowest wage or salary you would accept (before deductions) for this type of work?"

Feldstein and Poterba focus on the ratio of the reported reservation wage to the previous wage. They start by presenting mean ratios of the reservation wage to the highest wage in the preceding 27-year period, calculated for both the full sample and by reason for job separation—job losers on layoff, other job losers, and job leavers.[9] These numbers are interesting on their own. All group means are above 1 (1.01–1.09), except the mean for job losers (0.98); the median ratio for the sample is 1.0. As for variation with duration, mean reservation wage ratios by calculated spell lengths provide some evidence of a decline in the reservation wage. For job losers who were not on layoff and had durations of 50 or more weeks, the ratio is 0.91, a figure roughly consistent (though not strictly comparable) with the rate of decline reported by Barnes.

Feldstein and Poterba are primarily interested in the relationship between the unemployment insurance replacement ratio and the reservation wage ratio. Restricting their sample to those who report benefits, they fit regressions of the form

$$(w^r/w_p)100 = b_0 + b_1 F + b_2 N + bx$$

separately for the reasons for job separation groups, where w^r and w_p denote the reported reservation and previous wages, respectively, F denotes the unemployment insurance replacement ratio, N denotes the ratio of nonwage income (other than unemployment insurance) to the previous wage, and x includes age, race, sex, education, and dummy variables for receipt of welfare payments, receipt of supplemental unemployment benefits, other workers present, and marital status.[10]

The results for b_1 are all positive and significant, and exhibit expected variation across groups: 0.294 (standard error 0.184) for job leavers, 0.129 (standard error 0.057) for job losers on layoff, and 0.417 (0.070) for other job losers. The remaining results provide little evidence of demographic variation. One notable finding is that nonemployment income (from sources other than unemployment insurance), receipt of supplementary unemployment benefits, and receipt of welfare payments all have positive effects on the reservation wage ratios of workers who experienced permanent layoffs, but there is no strong evidence of these effects for other groups.

Holzer (1986b)

Holzer is also guided by the stationary job search model in his analysis of data for males in the United States, collected in the 1979 and 1980 Waves of the National Longitudinal Survey (NLS) of the New Youth Cohort. All workers in the sample were aged 16 to 21 in 1979 and not enrolled in school. The reservation wage data available here are generated by two questions in the 1979 survey: "What type of work have you been looking for?" and "What would the wage or salary have to be for you to be willing to take it?" Spell durations are measured as weeks of nonemployment between the 1979 and 1980 interviews. Thus, all spells are left censored and there may be multiple spells for some workers. Accepted wage data are taken from the 1980 interview.

Holzer's objective is to determine whether differences in unemployment rates and mean accepted wages observed for young black males versus young white males can be explained primarily by differences in reservation wages. Toward this end, Holzer first reports reservation wage differentials between black youths and white youths. He calculates these using results from regressions of the log reservation wage on either a predicted wage or predicted weeks worked in the previous year, fit by region and by employment status. The differentials are set equal to the difference between the predicted reservation wages for black youths using black sample mean characteristics and the coefficients from the two regressions. These indicate a differential of 10–16 percent between the reservation wages of black youths and white youths. This suggests that black youths set higher reservation wages—relative to the labor demand they face.

Holzer further investigates his question by fitting duration and postunemployment wage regressions on reported reservation wages, separately for black workers and white workers, first including and then excluding those who reported that they had not been actively seeking work in the month preceding the 1979 interview. He also reports results for weighted regressions, based on the sampling weights provided in the data set.[11] In each case, a variety of controls are included—occupation, industry, and union status for those who worked in the previous year, experience, schooling, "knowledge of the world of work" (an NLS variable), household income, region, urban residence, marital status, a dummy variable for workers with library cards, and a dummy variable for those who did not work in the previous year. When the samples are restricted to workers who reported that they were actively seeking work, the estimates for the elasticity of mean duration with respect to the reservation wage for blacks are positive and significant (ordinary least squares [OLS] 1.62 [standard error 0.528] weighted least squares [WLS]

1.456 [standard error 0.518], but the estimates are insignificant for whites (OLS −0.113 [standard error 0.476], WLS 0.286 [standard error 0.420]). When all nonemployed workers are included, the coefficient estimates are reduced substantially for both the black and white samples and even the elasticities for black youth appear to be just marginally significant. In contrast, the estimated reservation wage elasticities in the postunemployment wage regressions are significant and positive across the board for white workers, while the estimates for black workers are relatively small, generally insignificant at standard levels, and quite sensitive to the specification of other regressors. These elasticities are somewhat difficult to interpret (a 10 percent increase in the reservation wage leading to a 1 percent increase in the accepted wage?) and may reflect data or specification problems.

Incomplete spells are included in the duration regressions and only those who are reemployed are included in the wage regressions. There is no attempt to control for censoring in the duration regressions nor to control for potential selectivity bias in the wage regressions. The potential endogeneity of the reservation wage in the duration regression (perhaps due to measurement error) is not addressed. The ratio of the reservation wage to the accepted wage is above unity for almost half of the workers who become reemployed (44 percent of white workers and 46 percent of black workers), which might indicate that there are problems with the reservation wage data. All of these factors make interpretation of the regression results somewhat difficult. Holzer notes that the sample statistics are roughly consistent with the regression results, that is, that longer spells of joblessness experienced by black youths relative to white youths cannot be attributed solely to differences in reservation wages. The reservation wages reported by the two groups do not differ significantly, on average. (The mean reservation wage for black youths is slightly lower than the mean for white youths in this sample.) On the other hand, the mean accepted wage for white workers is substantially higher than the mean accepted wage for black workers. Note, however, that potential change in the reservation wage with duration is ignored in such comparisons.

Sandell (1980a)

Although much of the empirical search literature focuses on the experience of male workers, Sandell focuses on the unemployment experience of married women in the United States. Specifically, Sandell examines the effects of reservation wages on unemployment spell durations and postunemployment earnings using data for a sample of 85 workers collected in the 1968–72 interviews of the National Longitudinal Survey of Women (aged 25–49 in 1972). Reservation wage data are generated by responses to the question "How much would the job have to pay for you to be willing to take it?" The duration data are for left-censored spells, measured in weeks, that were completed prior to the respondends' next interviews; this measure is used because reservation wage data are available only for the unemployed, and accepted wages are observed only for the reemployed.

Sandell reports results for regression equations of the form:

$$\ln d = a_0 + a_1 \ln(w_o/w^r) + ax$$

where d denotes spell duration, w_o denotes an instrument for the mean of the offer distribution, and w^r denotes the reported reservation wage. The wage ratio is intended to serve as a proxy for the acceptance probability, and x includes regressors specified as determinants of the arrival rate of offers—the local or national unemployment rate, local population size, and dummy variables for race, involuntary unemployment (versus a quit), and year of observation. Predicted mean offers are calculated from wage regressions, fit separately for whites and nonwhites using postunemployment wage observations.

The results for a_1 provide some evidence of a positive relationship between durations and the level of the reservation wage; the estimates are positive, but appear sensitive to specification of the unemployment measure. This is not surprising, given the endogeneity of the reservation wage and the censoring in the duration data. In particular, the coefficient estimate is substantially smaller when the national unemployment rate is included, as opposed to the local. The results for remaining regressors are as expected—higher unemployment (local or national), involuntary separation, and living in a smaller market are all associated with longer spells.[12] The only surprising result is a negative coefficient for race being black. Though small relative to the reported standard error, a finding of shorter durations for black workers contrasts with the findings of others. It may be that the predicted wage captures the effect found elsewhere.

Mixed results are reported for a variety of postunemployment earnings regressions. When the accepted wage is regressed on the reservation wage and the predicted mean wage, the coefficient for the reservation wage is positive and significant (0.618, standard error 0.13), while the mean wage appears irrelevant. However, when the log ratio of the accepted wage to the mean wage is regressed on the log ratio of the reservation wage to the mean wage, the coefficient estimate is positive, but small relative to the reported standard errors.

Crosslin and Stevens (1977)

Crosslin and Stevens appear to have been the first to incorporate simultaneous determination of reservation wages and durations into their estimation procedure. They specify a two-equation model of the form

$$w^r(t)/w^r(0) = a_0 + a_1 t + a_2 w_p + \epsilon_1$$
$$t = b_0 + b_1(w^r(t)/w^r(0)) + \Sigma_j b_j x_j + \epsilon_2$$

where $w^r(s)$ denotes the reservation wage at duration s, w_p denotes the previous wage, and t denotes elapsed duration. The additional regressors include the proportion of household income normally derived from the individual's labor market earnings, the weekly unemployment insurance benefit, sex, and race. Search theory is used as a guide in specifying this model, but only loosely. In particular, the exclusion restrictions do not really have a clear search theoretic interpretation.

Crosslin and Stevens fit the model using data for participants in a job search experiment conducted by the Missouri Division of Employment Security in the St. Louis SMSA from September 1971 to March 1973. Initially, a random sample of 3,334 workers was selected from unemployment insurance recipients who claimed a third week's benefits, excluding those with known recall dates and those who normally secured employment through a union. These workers were then assigned randomly to treatment and control groups and initial interviews were conducted about 4 weeks later with 2,598 workers. A second interview was attempted with those who remained unemployed at the time of the first interviews—if and when unemployment insurance claims were terminated. Interviews with all participants were also attempted at the end of each worker's benefit year (i.e., 1 year after the date that the initial unemployment insurance claim was filed). Beyond the data from these interviews, administrative records are also available for each worker. Crosslin and Stevens restrict their sample to 690 workers for whom two reservation wage responses are available—one from the initial interview and a second from a later date.[13] Durations are measured as days of compensated unemployment; thus, some spells are censored. Throughout their analysis, Crosslin and Stevens work separately with two subsamples—those who receive the legislated maximum weekly benefit amount (57 percent of the sample) and those who receive less than the maximum.

Both two-stage least-squares and single-equation results for the reservation wage equation are reported. The coefficient estimates for duration differ substantially across procedures and across subsamples. For those receiving less than the benefit maximum, the two-stage least-squares estimate is negative and statistically significant, -0.00185 (standard error 0.00069), while the single equation estimate is positive and quite small, 0.00009 (standard error 0.000012). For the maximum benefit group, the sign pattern is the same, but both estimates are small; the two-stage least-squares estimate is -0.00031 (standard error 0.00014) and single-equation estimate is 0.00101 (standard error 0.00058). The average monthly decline in the reservation wage implied by the two-stage least-squares results are 3.03 percent for the maximum benefit group and 5.6 percent for those with benefits below the maximum.

Crosslin and Stevens also report reduced form estimates for the duration equation for each of the two groups. Overall, the coefficients are estimated imprecisely. In particular, benefits appear irrelevant for the below maximum benefit subsample (among whom benefit levels do vary).

Sandell (1980b)

In this study, Sandell estimates a two-equation linear model for the reservation wage, with the unemployment spell length treated as endogenous. His data are for a sample of 80 married women with spouses present, collected in the NLS (the source used in his 1980a study, previously discussed) who were unemployed at the time of either the 1967, 1969, 1971, or 1972 interviews and who had worked in the year preceding the relevant survey. The latter restriction is to avoid the issues associated with reentrants. Note, however, that this also eliminates left-censored spells present in the sample studied previously by Sandell.

The duration regression includes the local unemployment rate, local labor market size, a dummy variable for receipt of unemployment benefits, a dummy variable for involuntary unemployment, number of children, husband's income, race, dummy variables for the year of observation, and an instrument for the expected hourly wage—either the previous wage or a predicted wage.[14] Under both specifications, the coefficients for the unemployment rate are positive and significant and benefit recipients appear to have much longer spell durations. The estimates for the benefit shift are 16.267 (standard error 2.538) in the previous wage regression and 16.311 (standard error 2.585) in the predicted wage regression. An interesting result appears for the expected wage. When the previous wage is used, its coefficient is negative and significant (-0.034 [standard error 0.171). The coefficient for the predicted wage is about the same magnitude in the alternative regression, but insignificant (-0.035 [standard error 0.03]). None of the remaining coefficients differs significantly from zero in either model.

Sandell fits two-second-stage reservation wage regressions that include the predicted spell durations corresponding to the alternative expected wage measures. The additional regressors listed are all included, except for the year of observation. The basis of this identifying restriction is not clear. The estimated coefficients for duration are large and negative in both models: -4.533 (standard error 2.26) using the previous wage and -6.634 (standard error 3.00) using the predicted wage, where the scale is cents per hour. These translate into 2.65 and 3.93 percent declines per week. The large positive estimate for unemployment benefit receipt is accurately described by Sandell as "perhaps the most startling result" (p. 375) (73.935 [standard error 36.24] using the previous wage and 108.722 [standard error 40.873]). The coefficients for husband's income are positive and significant, as predicted by simple search models, but all other estimates are imprecise.

Jones (1988)

Search theory motivates the questions asked in the regression studies discussed thus far and it is used as a guide in the specification of regression equations. The links between theoretical and empirical models, however, are not very tight. In Chapter 3, we saw that a somewhat tighter link could be maintained between a theoretical structure and a regression specification. Jones takes a similar approach to the exponential duration model set out there to test the basic implication of the stationary job search model— that holding the arrival rate and offer distribution constant, workers who experience unemployment spells of longer duration have higher reservation wages. Specifically, he uses a variation of the regression specification in Chapter 3, which exploits his reservation data.

Under a Pareto specification for the offer distribution, the transition rate out of unemployment can be written as

$$\tau = \delta(w_0 w^r)^\alpha$$

Jones incorporates heterogeneity in the offer distribution and arrival rate. Indexing individuals by i, he adopts the specification,

$$(\delta w_0^\alpha)_i = \exp(x_i'\beta + u_i)$$

where β is a vector of unknown parameters and u_i is a random error. The transition rate for worker i is then

$$\tau_i = (w_i^r)^{-\alpha} \exp(x_i'\beta + u_i)$$

In Chapter 3, we assumed that reservation wage data were not available and therefore parameterized w_i^r. However, with access to (perfectly measured) reservation wage data, application of Proposition 1 implies that the parameters of the model can be estimated consistently by applying ordinary least squares to the regression equation

$$\log t_i = \alpha \log w_i^\tau - x_i'\beta - u_i$$

Maintaining the stationarity of the search model, Jones recognizes that the reported reservation wages are nevertheless likely to be correlated with omitted variables included in the disturbance term. To avoid potential simultaneity bias, he uses a predicted reservation wage in estimation, based on results from the regression

$$\log w^r = b_0 + x_i'b_1 + z_i'b_2 + \epsilon_i$$

where z_i includes variables that affect the transition rate only through their effects on the reservation wage. The parameters for the log duration regression are identified by these exclusion restrictions.

Jones fits this model using data for a sample of 854 unemployed British workers collected by the Economist Intelligence Unit in September 1982. The reservation wage data are based on answers to the question "What is the lowest amount in (weekly) take-home pay that you would be prepared to accept from a new job?" The responses to this question are available to Jones only in interval form less than £30, 30–40, . . . , 90–100, 100–125, . . . , 175–200, and more than 200. Jones uses the midpoints of the closed intervals, and £25 and £225 for the lower and upper open intervals, respectively. The available duration measure is months of registered unemployment, up to the interview date. The regressors x_i include a quadratic in age, sex, marital status, years of education, a dummy variable for technical qualification, and (to account for regional variation in labor market conditions) either 10 regional dummies or the regional registered unemployment rate. Weekly benefit amounts are not directly available from the survey data, but types of benefits received are reported. Jones uses this information, family composition data, and program rules to impute weekly benefit amounts for each worker. Jones then includes either the total benefit amount or the benefit components in z.

The results for the two-equation model provide evidence of a significant, direct relationship between spell lengths and reservation wages, but the magnitude of the estimated effect is fairly sensitive to model specification. When the imputed benefit amount is included in the first stage reservation wage regression, the α estimates are 5.62 (standard error 1.975) with the regional dummy variables and 7.159 (standard error 2.982) with the local unemployment rate. These can be interpreted as elasticities. Alternatively, under the Pareto specification for offers, these estimates imply log offer variances of 0.03 and 0.02. When the benefit components are included, the α estimates are positive and significant, but much smaller, 2.73 (standard error 0.749) with regional dummy variables and 2.665 (0.790); the implied log offer variances are 0.13 and 0.14, respectively. The estimated coefficients for other variables have sensible signs, but their magnitude and precision also vary substantially. When the imputed benefit is used in the first stage, males, younger workers, married workers, and workers with technical qualifications appear to have relatively shorter spells than their counterparts. Durations also appear quite responsive to local market conditions (using either measure). The quadratic in age appears to be supported by the data (with a minimum at about age 45). A negligible education effect appears, but Jones attributes this to lack of sample variation. On the other hand, the coefficient estimates in the models using the benefit components in the first stage are smaller in absolute magnitude and generally less precise. In particular, age and marital status appear to have negligible effects on durations in these regressions.

Jones checks these results in a variety of ways. Most important, he reports results for the duration regression fit using the reported reservation wages—as a check on the role of unobserved heterogeneity. When just the local labor market variables are included as regressors, the coefficients for the reservation wage are quite close to the two-stage results. However, when personal characteristics are added, the α estimates are negligible (0.005 [standard error 0.137] with regional dummy variables and −0.017 [standard error 0.135] with the local unemployment rate). This contrast in results suggests that heterogeneity in the offer distribution and arrival rate not captured by the regressors (x) is substantial and that it plays an important role in the determination of the reservation wage.

Jones also reports results for the two equation model fit separately for job losers (477 workers) and job leavers (265 workers), using the regional dummy variables as the measure of local labor market conditions. Overall, the coefficient estimates have signs similar to those reported for the full sample, but they are imprecise for both groups. In particular, although the α estimates are comparable to the full sample estimates in terms of magnitude, only the job leaver estimate is significantly different from zero at standard levels; the estimates are 5.458 (standard error 2.688) for job leavers and 7.374 (standard error 5.248) for job losers. These results suggest that the search process differs across these groups and, possibly, between new entrants (the omitted group) and previously employed workers. As a check on the maintained assumption of stationarity Jones also fits the two equation model separately for workers with reported durations of at least 3 months, at least 6 months, and at least 12 months. In all three cases, the sign pattern of the coefficient estimates is similar to the pattern reported for the full sample, but all estimates are imprecise. The α estimates are relatively small in all three cases—1.291 (standard error 0.758) for the 3 months or more sample, 1.636 (standard error 0.922) for the 6 months or more sample, and 0.883 (standard error 0.807) for the year or more sample. To some extent, these results may reflect the reduced sample sizes; alternatively, they might be viewed as evidence against the maintained assumption of stationarity.

Lancaster and Chesher (1984)

Lancaster and Chesher follow a regression approach in their analysis of durations and reservation wages. They specify a Pareto offer distribution, with density

$$f(w) = \alpha w_0^\alpha / w^{(\alpha+1)}, \qquad w \geq w_0$$

and a time-invariant offer arrival rate δ, and allow for linear-in-logs duration dependence in the reservation wage.

$$w^r(t) = w^r(0)t^\rho$$

where t refers to elapsed duration. This in turn leads to a fully simultaneous system for the reservation wage and log durations of the form

$$\log w_i^r(t) = \rho \log t_i + x_i'\beta + \beta_0 + \epsilon_{1i}$$
$$\log t_i = \alpha \log w_i^r(t) - x_i'\Gamma + \Gamma_0 + \epsilon_{2i}$$

Lancaster and Chesher fit their model separately for two samples of registered unemployed workers in the United Kingdom. The first consists of 627 males in three cities (Newcastle-upon-Tyne, Coventry, and London) who were surveyed by Oxford University in 1972. The second consists of 653 males, and the data were collected in a national survey for Political and Economic Planning (PEP) in 1974. All workers in these samples reported that they were looking for work at the time of the survey and durations are measured as weeks unemployed as of the survey date. Reservation wage data are generated by the questions: "What is the lowest wage you would accept in a new full-time job?" and "Would you tell me the lowest amount you would be prepared to accept after stoppages?"

The specification for x_i includes a quadratic in age, years of education, dummy variables for disability, marital status, and technical qualification, number of dependents, and city dummy variables (Oxford) or the local unemployment rate (PEP). A restriction on the parameters in the duration equation is required for identification of the reservation wage parameters.[15] Lancaster and Chesher assume that the number of dependent children influences spell duration only through its effect on the reservation wage; under this restriction, Γ is exactly identified. (Note, however, that ρ and β are not.)

Two-stage least-squares results are reported for the duration equation for each sample. The α estimates have the correct sign, but they are imprecise and differ substantially across samples: 2.755 (standard error 1.553) for Oxford and 0.891 (standard error 0.765) for PEP. These α estimates can be interpreted as elasticities of duration with respect to the reservation wage. Alternatively, under the Pareto distribution, they translate into log offer variances of 0.13 (Oxford) and 1.26 (PEP), which might be viewed as rather large. The coefficient estimates for the other regressors are generally precise and seem sensible. Durations appear responsive to local labor market conditions; the PEP results imply an elasticity of about 0.3 for durations with respect to the unemployment rate. Married workers and workers with more years of schooling have shorter durations. The quadratic in age also appears to be supported by the data; the results suggest that mean durations have a minimum at age 25 (Oxford) and a maximum at 51 (PEP).

Results for a model with unemployment benefit levels included are not reported. Lancaster and Chesher note that no sensible results were found for benefits and attribute this to endogeneity introduced by duration determined benefit levels during the sample period. Reduced form estimates for log duration are also reported; these are generally consistent with the findings described above.

Summary

The key results from the studies discussed in this section are summarized in Table 4.1. Given the variety of populations sampled and the diverse econometric approaches followed, it is not suprising that a wide range of estimates appear. Potential simultaneity bias and the various censoring schemes in the different studies provide ample reasons to be cautious when making inferences. Still, when taken together, the results reported here provide at least some evidence of a decline in the reservation wage with duration— at least over part of a spell of unemployment. The decline appears to occur in the initial part of spells for younger workers and in the latter part for older workers. As for benefit effects, reservation wages do appear responsive to benefit receipt and levels—but a summary estimate appears beyond reach. Durations of spells of unemployment depend positively on reported reservation wages and positively on benefits. These results are consistent with the search model. Finally, reservation wages appear to depend on mean offers in the predicted way (positively, with slopes less than but close to 1).

Structural Studies

In this section, we turn to studies that estimate structural parameters of very precisely specified job search models. We start with a study by Lancaster and Chesher (1983), who cleverly "deduce" average benefit elasticities and arrival rate elasticities for both mean durations and reservation wages, along with other parameters in a stationary, representative agent job search model. Their approach is based on treating their sample of workers from the United Kingdom as a random sample from a homogeneous population.

Lynch (1983) and Holzer (1986a) follow variations of the Lancaster and Chesher approach in their analyses of data for young workers in London and young black workers in the United States, respectively. Lynch focuses on the benefit elasticities and checks the sensitivity of her results to specification of the offer distribution. She also investigates heterogeneity among workers by using the deduction method for race and sex subsamples. Holzer also takes a deduction approach, but focuses on the discount rates implied by the optimality condition of a stationary job search model. He also takes a grouped data approach to examine heterogeneity; specifically, he considers variation according to sources and levels of nonemployment income. Ridder and Gorter (1986) use a variety of methods to analyze data for a sample of Dutch workers, including the Lancaster and Chesher deduction method. Most of the energy in the paper, however, is directed toward solving the optimality condition directly for the structural parameters of a stationary job search model, which incorporates heterogeneity among workers.[16] In the next and last study of this section, van den Berg (1990a) extends the approach of Ridder and Gorter to examine the effects of a one time change in benefit levels on the level of the reservation wage.

Lancaster and Chesher (1983)

Lancaster and Chesher carry out a highly structured and ingenious analysis of reservation wage data and responses to the question: "How much take-home pay would you expect to earn in a new job?" The authors interpret the answer to this question as the mean of the distribution of acceptable offers for an individual, $E(w \mid w \geq w^r)$, and then proceed to deduce additional parameters of the stationary job search model set out in Chapter 2. Their data are for 642 workers in the PEP sample analyzed in their 1984 study previously discussed; the sample here is restricted to those who provided answers to the expected wage question.

Lancaster and Chesher exploit the fact that the optimality condition given in Equation 2.5 may be useful for calculating elasticities of interest. Recall that this condition is

$$w^r = b + \frac{\delta}{r} \int_{w^r}^{\infty} (w - w^r) \, dF(w)$$

Interpreting b as unemployment benefits, Lancaster and Chesher note that benefit elasticities can be derived from the optimality condition simply by using the implicit function theorem. The elasticities of the reservation wage and the transition rate are

$$d\ln w^r / d\ln b = (b/w^r)(1 + \tau/r)^{-1}$$

and

$$d\ln \tau / d\ln b = - (f(w^r)/(1 - F(w^r))) \, b \, (1 + \tau/r)^{-1}$$

Since $E(T) = 1/\tau$ in the stationary model, the negative of the latter also gives the elasticity of expected duration with respect to b. Elasticities of the reservation wage and transition rate with respect to the arrival rate can also be derived; these are

$$d\ln w^r / d\ln \delta = ((w^r - b)/w^r)(1 + \tau/r)^{-1}$$

and

$$d\ln \tau / d\ln \delta = 1 - (f(w^r)/[1 - F(w^r)])(w^r - b)(1 + \tau/r)^{-1}$$

Here, again, the negative of the latter gives the elasticity of mean duration.

Table 4.1. Regression Studies: Single Equation Models

Study	Data	Dependent Variables	Findings for Reservation Wage
Kasper (1967) Movement in the reservation wage	United States, 1961 Extended benefit recipients, Minnesota	Proportional difference between reservation wage and previous wage	Declines 0.32 percent per month after delay of 2–6 months
Barnes (1975) Movement in the reservation wage	United States, 1962 Registered unemployed, six states	Ratio of reservation wage to previous wage	Decreases at decreasing rate: 0.27 percent per week in months 1–3; 0.17 percent after 12 months
Sant (1977) Movement in the reservation wage	United States, 1967–1969 NLS young males (14–25 in 1966)	Log reservation wage regression by education, IQ, race, location, and year	Increases and decreases with duration: -0.052–0.064 percent change per week; change depends directly on initial difference between mean offers and initial reservation wage
Melnik and Saks (1977) Reservation wages, perceived modal wages, and interviewing	United States, 1975 Michigan State University seniors	1. Perceived modal offer wage 2. Reservation wage 3. Change in perceived modal wage 4. Change in reservation wage	Approximately equal to perceived modal offer, and declines with number of interviews
Miller and Volker (1987) Movement in reservation wage	Australia, 1985 ALS youth (15–24)	Log reservation wage, by sex	Males: 15 percent decline by 6 months, then constant; females: 35 percent decline by 9 months, then constant
Warner, Poindexter, and Fearn (1980) Reservation wages and unemployment benefits, expected tenure, and the offer distribution	United States, 1970 Census of employment: Baltimore, Boston, Chicago, Cleveland	1. Log reservation wage 2. Log weekly probability of leaving unemployment defined as (number of spells/total weeks unemployment)	Increases with mean offer; higher for benefit recipients Employment probability increases with mean offer and decreases with reservation wage; higher for benefit recipients.
Feldstein and Poterba (1984) Reservation wages and benefit replacement rates	United States, 1976 May CPS special supplement	Ratio of reservation wage to previous wage, by reason for separation	Ratio increases with replacement ratio and declines slowly with duration

Study	Data	Model	Findings
Holzer (1986b) Reservation wages and differences in spell lengths and wages by race	United States, 1979–1980 NLS New youth cohort, males (16–21)	1. Log reservation wage, by race 2. Log duration by race 3. Log accepted wage, by race	Black–white reservation wage differential: 10–16 percent Elasticity of duration with respect to reservation wage: black sample, 0.59–1.46; white sample, −0.113–0.286 Elasticity of accepted wage with respect to reservation wage: black sample, 0.09–0.44; white sample, 0.4–0.67
Sandell (1980b) Unemployment spell durations and reservation wages	United States, 1968–1972 NLS married women (35–49 in 1972)	1. Log duration 2. Postunemployment wage regression	Increases with reservation wage Some evidence of positive relationship between accepted wage and reservation wage
Crosslin and Stevens (1977) Durations and reservation wages and spell	United States, 1971–1973 Job search experiment UI recipients, St. Louis, Missouri	Ratio of current to initial reservation wage, with endogenous days of compensated unemployment, by maximum benefit/below maximum benefit status	3.03 percent decline per month for maximum benefit group; 5.6 percent decline per month for below maximum benefit group
Sandell (1980a) Durations and reservation wages	Unites States, 1967–1972 NLS married women (35–49 in 1972)	Reservation wage with endogenous durations	Declines 2.65–3.93 percent per week
Jones (1988) Durations and reservation wages	United Kingdom, 1982 EUI registered unemployed	Log durations with endogenous log reservation wage	Positive elasticity of duration with respect to reservation wage; significant benefit effect (magnitude sensitive); evidence of unmeasured heterogeneity
Lancaster and Chesher (1984) Durations and reservation wages	United Kingdom, 1970s 1972 Oxford survey (3 cities); 1974 PEP survey nationwide registered unemployed males	Log duration with endogenous reservation wage	Elasticity of duration with respect to reservation wage 0.9–2.3 (imprecise)

As they stand, these formulas are defined in terms of the discount rate r and transition rate τ. However, from the integrated formulation of the optimality condition (Equation 2.7), we see that

$$\tau/r = (w^r - b)/(E[w \,|\, w > w^r] - w^r)$$

Thus, the elasticities for the reservation wage with respect to b and δ can be written simply in terms of w^r, b, and $E[w \,|\, w > w^r]$. (Note that these equations can be obtained from Equation 2.7 to bring the derivatives into elasticity form.)

By treating their sample as a random sample from a homogeneous population, Lancaster and Chesher are able to calculate estimates for the reservation wage elasticities by simply applying the formulas set out to sample means for the relevant variables. They report 0.135 as the average elasticity of the reservation wage with respect to benefits and 0.107 as the average elasticity of the reservation wage with respect to the arrival rate. Lancaster and Chesher also calculate these elasticities for groups within a partition of their sample by elapsed spell length—as a check on the fit of the model. There is some variation in the benefit elasticity; the estimates range from 0.11 and 0.17, with those in the 13- to 26-week range having the highest. The arrival rate elasticities are all close; the range is 0.09 to 0.12, with the 13- to 26-week group at the low end in this case.

Calculation of the elasticities for the transition rate τ with respect to benefits and the arrival rate requires specification of a parametric family for the offer distribution. Lancaster and Chesher choose the Pareto distribution, which has density

$$f(w) = \alpha w_0^\alpha / w^{(\alpha+1)}, \qquad w \geq w_0, = 0, \text{ otherwise}$$

In this case, the ratio of the density to the upper tail area that appears in the formulas for the elasticities is given by

$$f(w^r)/(1 - F(w^r)) = \alpha/w^r$$

and this may be calculated from the available data since

$$E(w \,|\, w \geq w^r) = w^r/(1 - \alpha^{-1})$$

Lancaster and Chesher report 7.63 as the average value for α, which corresponds to a variance in log wage offers of 0.017. The implied elasticities for expected duration are 1.03 for benefits and 0.19 for the arrival rate. As before, estimates are reported for spell length groups. The benefit elasticities are quite close here; the range is 1.0–1.2. The arrival rate elasticities exhibit somewhat greater variation; the range is -0.09 to -0.19, with the 13- to 26-week group at the high end and the 35- to 52-week group at the low end.

Lynch (1983)

Lynch uses the approach of Lancaster and Chesher to calculate elasticity estimates and then carries out some useful specification checks. In particular, she calculates the duration elasticities using both Pareto and exponential offer specifications. Her data were collected in a survey of young people living in the greater London area in March 1979 who planned to leave school that summer at the minimum legal age of sixteen; the initial sample consisted of 1,922 individuals. Approximately every 6 months after the departure from school, interviews were conducted with those who remained in the labor force and information on labor market activity was collected. The dropout rate from the sample was substantial; by November 1980, about 70 percent of the original sample remained in the labor force.

Lynch works separately with samples of workers who were actively looking for work at either the April 1980 or November 1980 interviews; the respective sample sizes are 70 and 53. She also carries out calculations by race and by sex using the November sample. These group samples are very small, but the results provide at least some information about demographic variation in young worker behavior. The three key questions that Lynch exploits are (1) "What is the lowest weekly wage you would accept before tax and other deductions?" (2) "How much do you expect to earn before tax and other deductions?" and (3) "How do you manage for money while you are out of work and how much does that amount to each week?"

The benefit elasticities for the reservation wage are all very close—0.080 for the April sample, 0.106 for the November sample, and 0.099 to 0.109 across race and sex subgroups in the November sample. The arrival rate elasticities for the reservation wage are also close across samples—0.148 for the April sample and 0.146 for the November sample, but there is nonnegligible variation across subgroups in the November sample. Males appear more responsive than females (0.161 vs. 0.128), and nonwhite workers appear more responsive than white workers (0.168 vs. 0.141).

The duration elasticity appears quite sensitive to the specification of the offer distribution as Pareto versus exponential. Focusing first on the results for the Pareto distribution, the estimates for the elasticity of duration with respect to benefits are 0.336 for the April sample, 0.483 for the November sample, and 0.439–0.493 across groups in the November sample. The arrival rate elasticities for duration are all very close—0.323 for the April sample, 0.298 for the November sample, and 0.281–0.303 across groups in the November sample. The estimate for α is 5.26 for the November sample, which implies a log offer variance of 0.036.[17] The results for the exponential offer specification differ substantially from the Pareto results. For the November sample, the benefit elasticities are all larger and exhibit greater variation across subsamples within partitions. The sample average is 0.559, and the range across groups is 0.489–0.619; in this case, females and white workers appear more responsive than their counterparts. On the other hand, the April average is 0.306, a slightly smaller number than found under the Pareto. The arrival rate elasticities are smaller for the November sample. The sample average is 0.252 and the range is 0.230–0.270 across race and sex groups, with males and nonwhites appearing more responsive. The April estimate is 0.357, which is slightly higher.

As a rough check on the maintained assumption of a constant reservation wage, Lynch fits a log reservation wage regression on log unemployment income, log duration, and a set of control variables. All estimates are imprecise. In particular, the coefficient for duration is −0.002 (standard error 0.002), so that a null of no duration dependence in the reservation wage cannot be rejected at standard levels. Similarly, the coefficient for log unemployment income is 0.013 (standard error 0.044). Lynch also notes that when the elasticities are calculated for groups in a sample partition by spell length, there is no evidence of variation with duration. Moreover, among workers who remained unemployed between April and November, only 20 percent reported lower reservation wages.

Holzer (1986a)

The integrated form of the optimality condition can be solved for the discount rate and written as

$$r = \tau(w^r - b)/(E[w \mid w \geq w^r] - w^r)$$

Holzer works with this equation and the formula for the benefit elasticity for the reservation wage derived by Lancaster and Chesher (1983) in his analysis of behavior of unemployed black youth. His data were collected in the National Bureau of Economic Research (NBER) Survey of Inner City Black Youth in 1979 and 1980. The sample with which he works consists of 447 black males, aged 16–24, from predominantly black and low income city blocks of Boston, Chicago, and Philadelphia, who were not enrolled in school in the year preceding their interviews. These data provide observations on some unusual items. Two forms of reservation wage data are available. First, each youth was asked what kind of job he was looking for and then "What is the lowest hourly pay . . . you'd be willing to take on that job?" The youths were also asked for the lowest acceptable pay on "any job" and, on average, these amounts are lower than those pertaining to particular jobs. Self-reported income sources (including illegal activities) and amounts are also available for each worker. Following Lancaster and Chesher, responses to a question about expected hourly earnings in the job "sought" are interpreted as the means of accepted offer distributions. The duration data pertain to total weeks without work over all spells in the year preceding the interview, including the ongoing spell, and all spells are measured in 2-week units.

Holzer's objective is to determine whether the observed behavior of black youths is consistent with income maximization. Toward this end, he calculates annual discount rate estimates using each reservation wage measure, first for his full sample and then for subsamples grouped according to sources and levels of nonwage income. The only required variable that Holzer does not observe directly is the transition rate, so he uses the inverse of the sample mean for durations. Since the durations include multiple spells and ongoing spells, these estimates are likely to be biased—and the bias may be positive or negative.

The estimates for the annual discount rate range between 0.213 and 0.297 for the full sample, depending on the measure of nonwage income used. The range across subsamples is much broader, 0.196–0.533, where the estimates at the upper end are for the reservation wages reported for "any job" and groups with reported nonwage income above $100 per week.

Holzer also calculates nonwage income elasticities for the reservation wage using the Lancaster and Chesher formula and a variety of nonwage income measures b. These range from 0.018 to 0.049, with the magnitude depending on the type of nonwage income included. In particular, the low estimate of 0.018 is obtained when only government transfer payments and unemployment insurance benefits are included. To check his results, Holzer fits separate log reservation wage regressions on the log expected wage and each of the nonwage income variables. Evaluated at the sample means, these elasticity estimates are even smaller than the deduced estimates. The range is 0.005–0.010; the largest in this case is for transfers and unemployment insurance benefits, but it is still extremely small.

Ridder and Gorter (1986)

Ridder and Gorter use a variety of methods to analyze reservation wage data collected by the Netherlands Institute for Public Opinion between October and December 1983. The sample design for the survey was a stratified random sample from the Amsterdam male population, aged 30–55 in September 1983, consisting of a random sample (RS), a stock sample of individuals who were registered as unemployed on September 1, 1983 (SS), and a flow sample of individuals who registered as unemployed between August 22 and September 7, 1983 (FS). Together, the usable portions provide a sample of 428 workers (201 in the RS, 124 in the SS, and 103 in the FS), with 205 workers unemployed at the interview date. These data are attractive because each worker was asked to reconstruct his labor market history from September 1973 through the interview date—a full 10-year period. Furthermore, each unemployed worker was asked the minimum, maximum, and average wage earned by persons with similar abilities, the wage he expected to receive, and his lowest acceptable wage. In this study, Ridder and Gorter restrict their sample to 99 unemployed workers for whom responses to all of these questions are available and exploit the very unusual wage distribution data to carry out a structural analysis of job search behavior.

Ridder and Gorter work with a model in which workers maximize utility functions defined over income and leisure, as in Equation 2.26. In particular, they assume that a worker's utility function can be represented by $u(L_j) \log(x)$, where L_j denotes leisure in state j and x denotes income. Ridder and Gorter also assume that workers know that they will remain employed in their jobs until some exogenously determined date, T. This is similar to the Poisson layoff process described in Chapter 2; in particular, the optimality of the constant reservation wage policy is not affected. Recall that the expected duration of employment in any given job in the random layoff model for worker i is $1/a_i$ and workers account for this in calculating the returns to an offer. The same holds here, that is, the discount rate in the present model is

$$r^* = \frac{1 - \exp(-rT)}{r}$$

Taking all of these assumptions together, the optimality condition for their model can be written as

$$\log(w^r) = (u(L_u)/u(L_e)) \log(b)$$
$$+ \frac{\delta}{r^*} \int_{w^r}^{\infty} \{\log(w) - \log(w^r)\} \, dF(w)$$

Ridder and Gorter interpret this stationary specification as an approximation to a nonstationary model, that is, a snapshot at a point in time when the worker expects everything to remain stable thereafter. In particular, benefits, the offer arrival rate, and the offer distribution are expected to remain constant from the moment of observation.

The objective of Ridder and Gorter is to estimate the parameters of this optimality condition—the reservation wage w^r, the utility of leisure ratio, the arrival rate δ, and the offer distribution, F. This is where the unusual wage data enter their approach. Ridder and Gorter assume that individuals face Pareto offer distributions, so that

$$f(w) = \alpha w_0^\alpha / w^{(\alpha+1)}, \qquad w \geq w_0$$

and

$$E(w) = (\alpha/(\alpha - 1))w_0$$

With the reported minimum wage equated with w_0 and the reported mean wage equated with $E(w)$, a solution for α follows directly. The wage data, alone, thus provide complete information on the offer distribution faced by each worker in their sample and the optimality condition can be written as

$$\log(w^r) = (u(L_u)/u(L_e)) \log(b) + (\delta/r)(1/\alpha)(w/w^r)^\alpha$$

From here, Ridder and Gorter specify functional forms for the utility of leisure ratio $u(L_u)/u(L_e)$, the arrival rate δ, and the discount rate r. On substitution, the optimality equation for a worker i is defined as

$$\log(w_i^r) = \exp\{X_i'\beta\} \log(b_i) + \exp\{Z_i'\Gamma + \Gamma_0\}(1/\alpha_i)(w_{0i}/w_i^r)^{\alpha_i}$$

where the vectors β and $\Gamma + \Gamma_0$ and the reservation wages w_i^r represent the unknown structural parameters of the model. The discount rate is specified as $\exp \Gamma_0$; it cannot be distinguished from the coefficient for the constant term in Z.

Ridder and Gorter estimate these parameters using an iterative two-step procedure. Their first step is to solve the optimality equation for w_i^r for each worker in their sample using numerical methods. These estimates, w_i^{r0}, represent nonlinear functions of the remaining parameters of the model. The second step is to use these estimates and the survey responses to the reservation wage question to obtain initial estimates of the parameters β and $\Gamma + \Gamma_0$. Specifically, nonlinear least squares is applied to the equation

$$w_i^r = w_i^{r0} + \epsilon_i$$

where w_i^r denotes the reported reservation wage of worker i and the ϵ_i are independently and identically distributed random "optimization" errors. This two-step procedure is iterated to convergence, yielding final estimates w_i^{r*}, β^*, and $(\Gamma + \Gamma_0)^*$.

Before reporting their results from this structural analysis, Ridder and Gorter report results for what they describe as an exploratory log reservation wage regression that includes both unemployment benefits and duration as regressors. The additional regressors include age, the unemployment benefit level, the number of previous spells of unemployment, and dummy variables for marital status, migrant status, secondary education, elementary education, and presence of another wage earner in the household. The estimate for the unemployment benefit coefficient is positive and significant at the 5 percent level and it implies an elasticity of 0.311 at the sample means. This is the only significant coefficient, however, and the overall fit of the model is not very good ($R^2 = 0.27$). In particular, the coefficient for elapsed duration is virtually zero (0.0016 [standard error 0.21]). Ridder and Gorter note that this duration result lends support to their stationary approximation to the search problem. However, they also recognize that the overall results most likely reflect simultaneity bias. As discussed in Chapter 3, if duration is simultaneously determined with the reservation wage, then no identifying restrictions are readily available to correct for the simultaneity in the linear model; all variables that affect elapsed duration must also affect the reservation wage. Ridder and Gorter do not pursue this issue, since their primary objective is not a test of the stationary model, but structural analysis based on the model instead.

The specification for the arrival rate regressors includes age, the length of the current unemployment spell, the number of unemployment spells in the preceding 10 years, and dummy variables for marital status, migrant status, elementary education, secondary education, and a living partner with income. The specification for the utility of leisure ratio regressors includes age, marital status, and duration of the current spell of unemployment. Note that duration is included in these specifications because of the interpretation of the model as an approximation to a nonstationary model at a point in time; that is, the arrival rate and utility ratio are treated as if they are constants following the observed date.

Overall, the results are mixed, the result for an R^2-like measure for the reservation wage estimates $(((\Sigma w_i^{r*2})/(\Sigma w_i^{r2}))\ = 0.95)$ compares favorably with the least-squares results; the nonlinearity of the optimality condition thus appears to be captured well by their specification. Also, the sample average of reservation wage residuals does not differ significantly from zero; that is, there appear to be no systematic optimization errors. However, setting these summary measures of fit aside, the results can be regarded as disappointing (particularly given the effort that goes into getting them). Although most signs are plausible, none of the coefficient estimates differs significantly from zero at standard levels. This may be interpreted as evidence against the stationary search model of their parameterization. Alternatively, it may simply be their data; the sample size is relatively small and results from consistency checks are not favorable to their interpretation of the wage data. In particular, the responses indicate that the workers were confused by the questions pertaining to reservation wage and expected wages. Twenty individuals reported reservation wages above the wages they expected to receive. Ridder and Gorter use their results to calculate a variety of parameters. The estimate for the Pareto parameter α is 7.4 (standard deviation 1.0), which implies a log offer variance of 0.018. The implied benefit elasticity for the reservation wage is 0.45 at the sample mean and the benefit elasticity for mean duration is 3.33, implying that a 5 percent reduction in benefits would produce a 2-month decrease in the average spell duration at the sample mean (about 14 months). Ridder and Gorter also use an estimate of the transition rate (based on completed spell durations in their sample) and an annual discount rate of 10 percent to calculate the sample mean acceptance probability and yearly offer arrival rate; these estimates are 0.59 and 1.46, respectively. Finally, the results for the utility of leisure ratio imply that, on average, there is no difference between the utility of lesiure when employed and the utility of leisure when unemployed.

As a check on their results, Ridder and Gorter use the Lancaster and Chesher approach to calculate the benefit elasticity for the reservation wage using the subsample of workers who report expected wages above reservation wages. The result is 0.37, a number close to their other elasticity estimates.

van den Berg (1990a)

van den Berg extends the analysis of Ridder and Gorter to consider the effects of variation in the level of benefits. In particular, he focuses on the effects of a one time change in the level of benefits on the reservation wage and mean unemployment spell durations.

As noted in our discussion of the Ridder and Gorter study, the stationary job search model may be interpreted as an approximation to a nonstationary model. More precisely, consider the simple multiplicative utility maximization formulation of the search model. Let $b(t)$ denote the value of benefits at time t, let $w^r(t)$ denote the reservation wage at time t, and let v denote the utility of leisure ratio (taken to be a constant over the duration of a spell). Focusing on variation in the benefit level alone (i.e., treating the offer distribution $F(w) = 1 - \pi(w)$ and the arrival rate δ as constants), the path followed by the reservation wage with duration is defined by the differential equation,

$$u'(w^r(t))w^{r'}(t) = ru(w^r(t)) - rvu(b(t))$$

$$- \delta \int_{w^r(t)}^{\infty} u'(w)\pi(w)\,dw$$

Now, suppose that the time axis along which duration is measured $[0, \infty)$ is divided into intervals such that, along each interval, the benefit level is a constant. For example, suppose that the benefit level is b_1 in the interval $[0, t^*)$ and b_2 in the interval $[t^*, \infty)$, where $b_1 > b_2$. After t^*, the reservation wage is a constant, which solves this equation with $w^{r'}(t) = 0$ and $b(t) = b_2$. This is the interpretation used by Ridder and Gorter. Before t^*, $w^r(t)$ follows this equation and the solution can be calculated using the boundary condition $w^r(t^*)$. As shown by Mortensen (1977), $w^{r'}(t) < 0$ for $t < t^*$ in the case of a one time drop in benefits, as described here.

van den Berg reviews these and more general results for nonstationary search models in the first part of his paper. He then focuses on a discrete one-time change in benefits in his empirical analysis because of its relevance in the Netherlands during the sample period. Prior to 1986 changes in the Dutch program, if an individual entered unemployment from employment, the benefit level equaled 80 percent of the previous wage for the first 6 months, 70 percent for about the next 18 months, and thereafter the individual became eligible for a needs-based public assistance benefit (i.e., a payment based on household size, dependents, and other household income). Exceptions to this pattern were new entrants and individuals with calculated unemployment benefit levels below the public assistance amount; these persons collected the public assistance benefit throughout their spells or for that part of the spell where this held (i.e., if the 80 percent to 70 percent drop put them under). For most unemployed workers in the Netherlands, the one-time drop in benefits at 24 months represented a good approximation.

van den Berg works with a sample of male workers selected from the Amsterdam sample studied by Ridder and Gorter. Thus, he has access to the unusual wage data. Complete benefit histories were not collected in the survey, but benefit levels at the survey date, previous wages, and elapsed durations are available. Together with the rules of the program, these data allow the benefit histories to be constructed. The sample with which van den Berg works consists of 136 male workers who were eligible for the standard benefit plan and who thus faced a significant drop in unemployment income at 24 months and 64 workers who faced no drop. van den Berg uses these data to estimate the solutions for reservation wages at the start of their spells and directly following the benefit drop at 24 months, the idea being to check to see whether behavior is in rough conformity with model. His approach to fitting the optimality conditions at each duration extends the approaches of Ridder and Gorter and Narendranathan and Nickell (1985, discussed in Chapter 5). van den Berg specifies the offer distribution to be of the form

$$f(w) = \frac{1}{w \log(\beta'/\alpha)} \qquad \alpha \le w \le \beta, 0 < \alpha < \beta < \infty$$

and he uses the special wage data to fit these for each worker in his sample. Specifically, observations on perceived minimum and maximum offers are not available for all workers in his sample, so van den Berg uses imputed values based on log linear regressions of each on a quadratic in log age, immigrant status, educational attainment, log experience (minimum only), and new entrant or reentrant status (minimum only). These first stage results are somewhat interesting on their own. They suggest that higher education and having a job prior to unemployment push up the minimum offer, that education and Dutch citizenship push up the maximum, and that remaining variables are irrelevant.

Reported reservation wages $w^r(t)$ are assumed to contain mean–zero measurement error, so that

$$w^r(t) = \tilde{w}^r(t) + \epsilon$$

where the tilde denotes the true value. The distribution of ϵ is specified as i.i.d. normal $N(0, \sigma^2)$ across individuals and independent of duration t. van den Berg uses this specification because reservation wages are not observed for all workers in this sample. As discussed in Chapter 3, incorporating measurement error in this way also avoids the issue of violation of the regularity conditions. van den Berg parameterizes both the arrival rate and the utility ratio as exponential functions of observable characteristics. Education levels and living partner's employment status are included as regressors in both; marital status and immigrant status are also included in the arrival rate specification.

van den Berg estimates the parameters of the model—the utility ratio and arrival rate parameters, the discount rate, and the variance of measurement error in the reservation wage—using the method of maximum likelihood. The basis for the likelihood is the joint distribution of spell durations and observed reservation wages, with censoring in the reservation wage and spell duration data incorporated appropriately. Using these estimates and values for initial benefits and benefits at 24 months, van den Berg is able to solve the optimality condition for values of the reservation wage and other parameters of interest.

Overall, the parameter estimates look sensible. Higher education appears to have a significant negative effect on the relative utility of unemployment and a significant positive effect on the offer arrival rate. Being married also pushes up the arrival rate, but other variables appear irrelevant. The annual discount rate estimate is 0.12 (standard error 0.035), which seems reasonable. Measurement error in the reported monthly reservation wage appears to be substnatial; the estimated standard deviation is 469 Dutch guilders (standard error 15.69).

van den Berg uses these estimates to calculate various search parameters for three different education groups. In all cases, the reservation wage decreases and the acceptance probability increases with duration. After 2 years, essentially all offers appear to be acceptable; the estimates for $\pi(w^r(t))$ start at 0.68–0.87 (the highest being for the highest education group) and reach 0.83–0.95. The monthly arrival rate estimates increase with education, but all are extremely low. The range is 0.04–0.06, implying that even workers in the highest education group wait over 16 months between offers.

Elasticity estimates are also reported by education group. Initially (i.e., at $t = 0$), the reservation wage elasticities with respect to current benefits are 0.15, 0.14, and 0.11 for the first, second, and third education level groups. The duration elasticities are similarly small—0.14, 0.16, and 0.07 for the three groups. However, after 2 years of unemployment (when benefit levels drop substantially), workers appear to be more responsive. The current benefit elasticities for the reservation wage are 0.23, 0.21, and 0.14.

The duration elasticity at 24 months is also much larger for the first and second education groups, 0.47 and 0.59, but it remains negligible at 0.06 for the highest education group.

Summary

Lancaster and Chesher (1983) do not report standard errors for the deduced elasticities, work only with averages of simple functions of the answers to survey questions, and do not control for heterogeneity, not even that due to regressors known to affect duration and wage offers. Nevertheless, the results obtained are sensible when interpreted in the context of a very simple model. This is extremely encouraging, but it should not be interpreted as strong evidence in favor of the simple stationary job search model. Lancaster and Chesher conclude their paper with some interesting theoretical sensitivity analysis. Specifically, they consider the implications of allowing risk aversion on the part of workers, entering leisure into the utility function, allowing choice of search intensity, and specifying a normal offer distribution in place of the Pareto. Each exercise casts doubt on the validity of their formulas—potential biases in both directions are implied. The contrast in the elasticities reported by Lynch (1983) using the Pareto versus exponential specifications for the offer distribution also presents reasons to exercise caution when interpreting these results.

The findings of Ridder and Gorter (1986) indicate the need for caution when using survey response data about characteristics of perceived wage distributions. Respondents' interpretations of the questions appear to vary substantially. Like Ridder and Gorter, Jones (1988, discussed in the previous section) finds that only 75 percent of the workers in his sample report expected wages above reported reservation wages. (Jones does not use the expected wage data.) The data analyzed by Lancaster and Chesher thus appear to be quite exceptional; this inconsistency appears for only 0.5 percent of their sample. Holzer's data suggest that simple rephrasing of a reservation wage question can produce very different results. Stephenson (1976) reports similar findings for a sample of Indianapolis youth. When asked "What is the minimum hourly wage rate or weekly take home pay you would accept at present?" white youth provided responses that averaged $2 and black youth provided responses that averaged $1.93. When asked "What hourly wage rate or weekly take home pay would you like to earn on this job you are looking for?" the averages were $2.78 for white youth and $2.75 for black youth.[18] Evidence in later chapters suggests that nonwage job characteristics are important. Reder (1978) reports that a nonnegligible proportion of M.B.A. candidates at the University of Chicago reject salary offers below those which they accept. The timing of offers may also come into play. Holzer's results also suggest that using alternative measures of nonemployment income can be expected to produce estimates of very different magnitude. On this note, Lynch reports that when weekly out-of-pocket costs of search are set equal to 5 pounds the (net) benefit elasticity for the reservation wage for her November sample is reduced to 0.057 (from 0.106), and the mean duration elasticity drops to 0.301 (from 0.483).

Table 4.2 summarizes the findings for key parameters in the studies in this section. Although there is substantial variation, some systematic evidence appears. First, the results reported by Holzer and Lynch suggest that longer spells experienced by young workers around 1980 in the United Kingdom and United States were not a direct consequence of high reservation wages induced by generous unemployment benefit levels.

Table 4.2. Structural Studies

Study	Data	Method	Findings for Reservation Wage
Lancaster and Chesher (1983)	United Kingdom, 1974 PEP registered unemployed	Deduction, using Pareto offer distribution	1. Elasticity with respect to benefits, 0.155; arrival rate, 0.107 2. Elasticity with respect to benefits, 1.03; arrival rate, 0.19 3. Log offer variance under Pareto: 0.017 (some variation by spell length)
Lynch (1983)	United Kingdom, 1980 London youth	Deduction, Pareto and exponential offer distributions, by interview date (April/November) and by race and sex for the November sample Log reservation wage regression	1. Elasticity with respect to benefits, 0.08–0.11; arrival rate, 0.13—0.17 2. Elasticity of duration with respect to benefits: Pareto, 0.34–0.49; exponential −0.23— −0.36 3. Log offer variance under Pareto: 0.036 Log benefit and log duration coefficients negligible
Holzer (1986a)	United States 1979–1980 NBER survey, Boston, Chicago, and Philadelphia; black males (16–24)	1. Deduction 2. Log reservation wage regression by type of nonwage income	Annual discount rates: 0.213–0.297; by income source and amount: 0.196–0.533 Elasticity with respect to nonwage income, by type: 0.018–0.049 Elasticity wage with respect to nonwage income: 0.005–0.010
Ridder and Gorter (1986)	Netherlands 1983 NIPO Amsterdam benefit recipients; males (30–55)	1. Solution to optimal condition for static model 2. Deduction 3. Log reservation wage regression	Elasticity with respect to benefits: 0.45 Elasticity of duration with respect to benefits: 3.33 Elasticity with respect to benefits: 0.37 Log offer variance: 0.018 δ (year) = 1.46 π = 0.59 Elasticity with respect to benefits: 0.311 No evidence of duration dependence
van den Berg (1988b)	Netherlands 1983 NIPO Amsterdam male benefit recipients (30–55)	Solution to optimality condition for nonstationary model, calculations at 0 and 24 months, by education group	Elasticity wage with respect to benefits at $t = 0$: 0.11–0.15; $t = 24$: 0.14–0.23 Elasticity with respect to future benefits at $t = 0$: 0.04–0.09 Elasticity of duration with respect to current benefits at $t = 0$: 0.07–0.16; $t = 24$: 0.06–0.59 δ (month): 0.04–0.06 π ($t = 0$): 0.68–0.87 π ($t = 24$): 0.83–0.95

Indeed, looking across studies, only Ridder and Gorter provide evidence of a large benefit effect on mean durations of male workers, young or old, and this result is overturned for these data by van den Berg. On the other hand, offer arrival rates appear to play an important role in determining spell lengths. Along this line, Lynch (1983) notes that only 15 percent of her April sample reported receipt of any offers when asked. Moreover, among these workers, the majority reported only one offer. Jones (1988, discussed in the previous section) reports similar evidence for his sample of British adults; for a period of 1 year, only 23 percent of his sample reported the rejection of an offer.

Studies based on direct measurement of reservation wages (via interviews or questionnaires) have demonstrated that some of the relationships predicted by the job search models are indeed present in the data. Reservation wages affect unemployment durations positively. Benefit payments appear to increase the reservation wage. There is evidence that variation in offer arrival rates affects reservation wages roughly as expected. Job prospects as measured by mean offers appear to affect reservation wages as predicted by the model (this is a prediction of magnitude as well as sign).

On the other hand, there is substantial evidence that reservation wages decline with duration. This finding suggests that attention to specification diagnostics is crucial when the constant reservation wage model is used.

Notes

1. Crosslin and Stevens (1977) use two observations that they interpret as reservation wages for each individual in their sample. However, it appears that the second observation may be an accepted wage offer.

2. There are two papers that exploit data on reservation wages for U.S. workers by Barron and Gilley (1981) and Barron and Mellow (1981a) that are not discussed in this chapter. Both are primarily concerned with choice of search intensity and based on a multistate framework. Discussion of these papers is reserved for Chapter 7.

3. Three alternative specifications are explored. The first is the same regression as in Equation 4.1, but fit using means for groups within a partition of the sample by spell length. The second is a regression using the same group means, but log duration is used in place of duration to detect nonlinearity in the relation. The third is estimation of the model separately for workers who had exhausted their benefits and workers who had not exhausted their benefits but no longer received them in the February following the survey.

4. DeGroot (1970) provides a derivation of these and other results for normal distributions. Also see Burdett and Vishwanath (1988a,b) for further discussion of learning about an unknown offer distribution.

5. The students surveyed in February were on line to sign-up for interviews with the campus Placement Service. The total number surveyed at that time was 222, but only 141 responded to the follow-up survey sent by mail in May and only 132 of these were complete. Because of the low response rate, Melnik and Saks did some follow-up work and found that the experience of those who had responded was fairly representative of that of the initial sample. The authors do not claim that this represents a representative sample of the U.S. labor force. Still, they note some desirable characteristics about the labor market studied—in terms of search theory: the market is highly structured, both the costs of search and available information in such a market are fairly uniform across student searchers, the students are price-takers, and grades provide a fairly objective ranking within fields.

6. In each survey, students were also asked: "What do you think the range of those starting salaries is? High _____ Low _____."

7. Miller and Volker also study unemployment and employment durations using a hazard function approach, but do not restrict their samples to those with reservation wages in these analyses. This part of their study is discussed in Chapter 6.

8. This approach follows Hall (1972). Within the sample of workers who experienced unemployment, 48 experienced more than one spell during the survey year. These observations are omitted from the sample used in the reservation wage analysis.

9. Feldstein and Poterba note that a small group of respondents is discarded because of extreme responses (a reservation wage-previous wage ratio of less than one-third or greater than three).

10. Although taxable at present, UI benefits were not taxable in 1976. Therefore, Feldstein and Poterba calculate F using a net income measure in the denominator. Specifically, they use .7 of reported income for all workers due to the absence of marginal tax rate information. They note that this will tend to overstate the replacement ratio and thus bias the estimate for b_1 toward zero. The sample sizes for job losers on layoff, other job losers, and job leavers are 246, 306, and 90, respectively.

11. In the NLS, there is an oversampling of low income whites and these weights are intended to allow one to generalize to the U.S. population.

12. Sandell reports essentially the same results for regressions of the form

$$\ln d = b_0 + b_1(w'_0 = w^{r1/2}) + bx$$

13. A detailed description of the data is not provided in this paper, but may be found in Crosslin and Stevens (1973). It is unclear from either source when the second reservation wage was solicited.

14. The predicted wages are calculated using the results from regressions of the log wage on education, experience, years spent outside the labor market after school, and tenure, fit separately for 416 black females and 1,061 white females using data collected in the 1967 NLS round of interviews. Note that both mean wage measures ignore truncation of the offer distribution at the reservation wage.

15. In principle, second moment restrictions may be used to identify the structural parameters of the model. In practice, this approach may be complicated by measurement error. See this paper and Lancaster (1985b) for an application and discussion.

16. The approach taken by Ridder and Gorter is a variation on the approach taken by Narendranathan and Nickell (1985), who do not have access to reservation wage data. We discuss the Narendranathan and Nickell study in Chapter 5.

17. Sample statistics are not reported for the April sample and therefore α cannot be calculated.

18. Stephenson (1976) fits a four equation model for reservation wages, search costs, unemployment durations, and expected job tenures (using responses to the first question as reservation wage observations). He states that two-stage least squares is used in estimation, but his empirical specification is not clear in the paper. Therefore we do not discuss it in detail. His recognition of the simultaneity is nevertheless noteworthy. Also, he reports that the reservation wage decreases by 0.06 percent per month, which is consistent with findings of little change in the reservation wage based on other samples of young workers.

5

Unemployment Duration and Wage Data

Whereas reservation wage data are infrequently available and often difficult to interpret, many microdata sets provide observations on unemployment spell durations, accepted wages, and previous earnings. A variety of approaches have been taken to analyze these data in the search framework—in the absence of reservation wage data. In this chapter, we review this work.[1]

We first look at studies that use search theory as a guide in model specification, but make no systematic attempt to identify parameters of the theoretical structure. These include regression and hazard function studies. The issue addressed most often in these studies is the effect of unemployment benefit levels on unemployment spell lengths. The hazard function studies also address the direction and extent of duration dependence in the hazard and the sensitivity of all parameter estimates to unmeasured heterogeneity. We turn next to structural studies. A variety of approaches are taken here, but all are similar in three respects: the empirical specification is closely linked to a very specific formulation of a job search model, the goal is to identify the parameters of the theoretical structure, and identification generally involves extensive use of restrictions implied by the theoretical formulation (as well as other, less satisfactory restrictions). Benefit effects on reservation wages and durations and duration dependence are examined in some of these structural studies. The relative importance of offer arrival rates versus acceptance probabilities in producing variation in unemployment spell lengths is also addressed. As in Chapter 4, this is done without direct evidence on the arrival process.

Regression Studies

We start this section with studies by Burgess and Kingston (1971, 1975, 1977), MacKay and Reid (1972), Ehrenberg and Oaxaca (1976), Classen (1977, 1979), and Holen (1977). These studies are all motivated by concern over the effect of unemployment benefits on the behavior of unemployed workers.[2] Search models developed by the mid-

1970s (essentially the model set out in Chapter 2) provided strong implications about the effect of benefit levels on unemployment spell durations and accepted wages. The theory also predicted the effects of potential duration of benefits (or benefit "entitlement") on unemployment spell lengths. The studies discussed here represent the first attempts to test these implications in the absence of "direct evidence" on reservation wages. Thus, they represent part of the foundation of the empirical search literature. Indeed the fact that a close tie could be maintained between theoretical and empirical specifications when working in the search framework was demonstrated by Ehrenberg and Oaxaca (1976, unpublished appendix).

Linear and log linear single equation regression models are typically used to analyze duration data. In Chapter 3, we saw that log duration regressions may be interpreted in the proportional hazards framework—they admit a constant hazard interpretation. However, recall that the disturbance terms in these models do not have normal distributions. Consequently, one must proceed cautiously when making inferences on the basis of reported standard errors. Complicating matters further, many of the studies work with data for unemployment insurance recipients. An obvious problem arises in terms of generalizing the results to the labor force as a whole. (Are unemployment recipients representative?) Moreover, the duration data in these studies generally pertain to weeks of compensated unemployment, so that very short spells are excluded and spells are generally censored at benefit exhaustion. Researchers typically recognized that censoring meant problems (though they may not have referred to censoring as such). In some studies, attempts are made to address the issue in regression specifications (e.g., a dummy variable is included for censored observations). Tobit models are also estimated, with benefit exhaustion (i.e., the censoring time) as a threshold. A third approach is restriction of the sample to uncensored observations. This approach is taken in studies that analyze data for samples of both benefit recipients and nonrecipients. The consequences of this sample restriction based on observed spell length are obvious; regressors specified as determinants of durations are systematically related to the disturbance terms and the coefficient estimates are likely to be biased. Taking all of these issues together, interpreting the results reported in the regression studies is less than straightforward, but it allows a comparison of findings across techniques and data.

Several studies also report results for linear and log linear postunemployment earnings regressions, which include benefit levels and benefit replacement rates as regressors. Interpreting the results as solid evidence regarding the effects of benefits on earnings is risky. First, earnings data are often taken from unemployment insurance administrative records and these data are generally truncated at insurable maximum earnings levels. In some studies, this truncation is addressed in the regression specification, but not always. Moreover, variation in the replacement ratio across individuals largely reflects state-to-state variation in a program parameter that may itself be tied quite closely to variation in earnings across states, that is, the states with high replacement ratios are likely to be high income states. (See Welch [1977] for additional discussion of this second issue.)

In the papers that follow, Feinberg (1978b), Kahn (1978), and Mellow (1978) focus on alternative hypotheses of simple search models. Feinberg studies the effects of risk aversion on search behavior. Kahn compares the empirical relevance of the finite horizon systematic search model (Salop, 1973) with the finite horizon random search model with recall (Lipmann and McCall, 1976). Mellow attempts to test the hypothesis of a negative relationship between search costs and the duration of unemployment. As in the benefit studies, problems with duration and wage data (and methods used to deal with these problems) generally make a tight interpretation of the reported results impossible. Nevertheless, the findings are suggestive.

We close the section with a study by Moffitt and Nicholson (1982). They analyze the effects of unemployment benefits on unemployment spell durations, but their approach is based on a static labor–leisure choice model, which generates hypotheses that are similar to those of the basic search model. We describe their model later.

Burgess and Kingston (1971)

Burgess and Kingston appear to have been the first to study the effects of unemployment benefits on spell lengths using microdata. Their data were collected in the Phoenix (Arizona) Service-to-Claimants Project, a job search assistance experiment conducted by the U.S. Department of Labor from September 1969 to April 1970. Participants in the experiment were selected randomly from all unemployment insurance claimants who were not "job-attached" (i.e., expecting recall within 30 days) and who were judged "job-ready" (i.e., intensive retraining or counseling was not required for reemployment). The sample analyzed here consists of 2,476 participants.

The primary concern of the study is measuring the effect of variation in the unemployment replacement ratio on unemployment spell durations. Their duration data pertain to weeks of compensated unemployment, which Burgess and Kingston recognize as potentially different from a worker's actual unemployment spell length. To check the effects of this distinction, they analyze data for the 1,029 workers who were known to have found employment when they discontinued their claims separately, in addition to working with the full sample. Specifically, they fit simple linear duration regressions and report the following results:

$$C = -10.75 + 0.09M - 0.54N - 0.55F + 1.73U, \quad R^2 = 0.32$$
$$\qquad\quad (0.038) \quad (0.386) \quad (0.145) \quad (0.05) \qquad N = 2476$$
$$D = -3.39 + 0.08M + 0.08N - 0.46F + 1.02U, \quad R^2 = 0.19$$
$$\qquad\quad (0.053) \quad (*) \qquad (0.170) \quad (0.066) \qquad N = 1029$$

where standard errors are given in parentheses, [3]C denotes claim length (discontinued or exhausted), D denotes discontinued claim lengths, M denotes potential duration of unemployment insurance benefits, N is a dummy variable for race ($N = 1$ for non-whites), F denotes the unemployment benefit replacement ratio (the weekly benefit divided by the average weekly wage in the worker's highest earnings quarter, i.e., the amount used to calculate benefit levels), and U is an unemployment measure (the ratio of the number of insured unemployed to the total civilian labor force, calculated by sex). The results exhibit some sensitivity to sample specification, but the coefficient for the replacement ratio is not affected substantially. In both cases, the estimated effect is large and negative—the opposite of what search theory predicts. Note, however, that this variable may be picking up effects of omitted variables that affect durations. The strongest result across both specifications is the estimated coefficient for the unemployment measure. The definition of this variable also makes the coefficient difficult to interpret; it may be measuring differences in spell length due to sex, coverage by unemployment insurance, or unemployment.

Burgess and Kingston (1975)

In this study, Burgess and Kingston work with data for the Phoenix reemployed discontinued claim sample from their previous study and data for analogous samples from Boston and the San Francisco–Oakland area collected in the same job search experiment. Thus, both very short and very long spells are excluded systematically. Overall, they have observations on 1,996 workers.

Their focus is the effect of the level of the benefit replacement ratio on unemployment spell lengths, as above. Here, however, they fit both duration and log duration regressions and use a much longer list of regressors. In addition to the benefit replacement ratio, potential duration of benefits, local unemployment rates (by city in this study), and race, they include categorical variables for age, education, sex, occupation, and reason for unemployment. They also report results for regressions fit separately by race and sex.

The coefficients for the benefit ratio are positive for the full sample, white males, white females, and nonwhite females. Relative to reported standard errors, however, the estimates are generally small. Only the white workers appear to be affected significantly by the replacement ratio, the elasticities being 0.15 for males and 0.31 for females. The replacement ratio coefficients for black males are actually negative, though small and statistically imprecise. As for the remaining variables, durations appear to increase with age and local unemployment, education seems irrelevant, and only the duration of white females appears to be affected significantly by the potential duration of benefits.

Burgess and Kingston (1977)

Burgess and Kingston report results for a postunemployment annual earnings regression, which they fit using data for the 1,719 workers in their Phoenix, Boston, San Francisco–Oakland sample for whom earnings data are available. The explanatory variables include weekly unemployment benefits, potential duration of benefits, spell duration, previous annual earnings, age, race, education, sex, length of residence, and city. Both benefit measures have estimated coefficients that are positive and significant (using t tests at standard levels), as implied by simple search models. The results suggest that a $1 increase in weekly benefits increases annual earnings by $25, while a 1 week increase in potential benefit duration increase annual earnings by about $70. The results also indicate that postunemployment earnings decline with the duration of a spell.

MacKay and Reid (1972)

MacKay and Reid analyze the effects of both lump sum and weekly unemployment benefits using data for male workers in the United Kingdom. Their sample consists of 613 workers who remained in the labor force (i.e., either searched or worked) following a layoff from one of 23 engineering plants in the West Midlands of England during the 1966–1968 period.[4] These data were collected for the express purpose of this study. Consequently, they have several attractive features. The plants were selected randomly and random samples, stratified by skill, were then selected from all workers who experienced layoffs at each plant.[5] Unemployment is measured as weeks of continuous unemployed search from the date of layoff up to the interview date (apparently more than a year later). Three percent of the sample remained unemployed continuously, while a third of the sample experienced either no spell or a spell of less than a week. MacKay and Reid include both in their sample, commenting that for the former, the true length of unemployment is understated (i.e., they recognized censoring). All workers were asked whether they had searched before being laid off, about the number of jobs held following the measured spell of unemployment, and whether separations from jobs in the period between the layoff and the interview were voluntary or involuntary. For all workers who experienced unemployment, data are also available on the number of employers contacted per week and the amounts of each type of unemployment benefit received. These include the statutory lump-sum "redundancy payment" (introduced in the United Kingdom in 1965), the flat-rate weekly benefit (based on marital status and numbers of dependents), and the earnings-related supplement (a weekly benefit based on family composition that became available in 1966 and provided a payment for the first 6 months of unemployment, equal to about one-third of the previous weekly earnings for a typical worker). For workers who experienced no unemployment, MacKay and Reid calculate each of these benefit amounts using data on individual and family characteristics, reasoning that expected benefits should influence on-the-job and unemployed search behavior.

MacKay and Reid weight their sample to represent layoffs at all engineering plants and fit linear duration regressions. The explanatory variables include the maximum weekly unemployment benefit amount received when unemployed (flat-rate plus earnings related), the lump-sum redundancy payment, the local vacancy rate, the number of employers contacted per week, and dummy variables for marital status, age group, skill level (skilled and semiskilled, relative to unskilled), and whether multiple jobs were left voluntarily following the layoff. Interpreting the results is somewhat difficult because of the zero duration and censored observations. Reservations aside, the estimated coefficient for the weekly benefit implies an elasticity of about 0.27 at the sample means. On the other hand, the estimated coefficient for the lump-sum benefit is positive, but small both in absolute terms and relative to its standard error. Job search prior to separation, search intensity, and voluntary mobility following the layoff all have large, negative coefficients, and durations all appear to be shorter for younger workers and married workers. Higher local vacancy rates also appear to have a large, negative effect on durations.

Ehrenberg and Oaxaca (1976)

Ehrenberg and Oaxaca also analyze the effects of unemployment insurance benefits on unemployment spell durations and subsequent wage gains. The stationary search model of Chapter 2, with the arrival rate δ set equal to 1 and offers specified as draws from a Pareto distribution, serves as the basis of their empirical analysis. The transition rate out of unemployment in this model is simply the acceptance probability

$$\begin{aligned} \tau &= \pi(w^r) \\ &= (w^r/w_0)^{-\alpha} \\ &= (w_0/w^r)^{\alpha} \end{aligned}$$

Heterogeneity is incorporated via the reservation wage using

$$\ln w_i^r = x_i' a$$

where the subscript refers to invidivual i. Using Proposition 1, this leads to a regression model of the form

$$\ln t_i = a_0 + a_1 F_i + \sum_{j=2}^{k} a_j x_{ji}$$

$$\ln(w_a/w_p)_i = b_0 + b_1 F_i + \sum_{j=2}^{k} b_j x_{ji}$$

where a_0 is interpreted as $\alpha \log w_0$, w_p and w_a denote pre- and postunemployment wages, respectively, and F denotes the benefit replacement ratio (the benefit level divided by preunemployment earnings). The additional regressors include the log previous wage w_p and a variety of controls for variation in the cost of search and the discount rate. Note that the parameters of the offer distribution (α and w_0) are assumed constant across individuals. It follows from the optimality condition that variation in transition rates across individuals must arise from differences in w_i^r due to differences in search costs, nonemployment income (i.e., benefits), and the discount rate.

Ehrenberg and Oaxaca fit the model separately for different age and sex cohorts using data collected in the National Longitudinal Surveys for the 1966–1971 period. Specifically, their samples consist of 464 young males (ages 14–24 in 1966), 613 young females (ages 14–24 in 1966), 274 older men (ages 44–59 in 1966), and 441 women (ages 30–44 in 1966). For each cohort, the observation period consists of 1 or more single year intervals between interviews, where the choice of years for each group is based on the availability of wage observations. To avoid the issue of censoring in their duration data, all cohort samples are also restricted to workers who were employed at (relevant) consecutive interview dates and experienced at least one spell of unemployment over the observation period. Consequently, unemployment spells of a year or more are systematically excluded. A second problem with the duration data is that only the total number of weeks unemployed between interview dates and the numbers of spells are observed, that is, exact spell lengths are not observed. Ehrenberg and Oaxaca therefore use the average spell duration between years. Additional sample restrictions are also used for each cohort. The young male and young female samples are restricted to workers who changed employers following their spells of unemployment. Separate results are also reported for nonstudents and for household heads (self or spouse for females) in these cohort samples. For women, the model is fit for the full sample and separately for 156 job changers. For older men, the sample period is restricted to 1967–1968 and results are reported only for 39 job changers who experienced one spell in this period, 51 job changers who experienced one or two spells, and 67 job changers who experienced one spell or more. Ehrenberg and Oaxaca note that the results for subsamples of older men who were voluntarily unemployed, on temporary layoff, or unemployed for unknown reasons provided no evidence of a benefit effect on durations or postunemployment wages.

Different sets of regressors are used for different groups, depending on the availability and relevance of different data. All include age, race, marital status, education, the local labor market size and unemployment rate, nonemployment income and asset variables, and measures of tenure or experience; the additional variables included in some but not other regressions include health status, number of dependents, and an NLS variable that measures "knowledge of the world of work."

Looking across all of the results for the log duration regressions, the explanatory power of the model is generally low ($R^2 = 0.05$–0.36, with the largest values for older men). The coefficient estimates have sensible signs, but they are generally small relative to their standard errors. This may simply reflect multicollinearity—between 13 and 19 regressors are included in the vector of controls for each of the groups in the specifications reported in the paper and there are references to alternative specifications including more. The coefficient estimates for the replacement ratio F are the one exception. For all groups, they are large and positive relative to the reported standard errors and imply that an increase in the replacement ratio increases the duration of an unemployment spell, as predicted. The replacement rate elasticities implied by these estimates vary between 0.04 and 0.21 across cohorts and samples when evaluated at sample means for F. These are also the benefit elasticities since

$$a_1 F = \frac{d \ln t}{d \ln F}\bigg|_{w_p} = \frac{d \ln t}{d \ln b - d \ln w_p} = \frac{d \ln t}{d \ln b}$$

where b denotes the level of benefits. Given the sample restriction to spells of a year or less, these elasticities are probably biased downward. Also, Ehrenberg and Oaxaca note that these estimates may understate the true elasticities because many workers in their samples receive no benefits and the sample means for F may thus be unreasonably low. (Group means range between 0.03 and 0.18.) When F is set to 0.5, for example, the elasticities are 0.19 for women (0.21 for job changers), 0.55 for older male job changers (0.825 if only one spell), 0.27 for young male job changers (0.46 for household heads), and 0.61 for young female job changers (0.75 for self or spouse household heads).

Most of the coefficient estimates in the earning gains regressions are also imprecise. In particular, there is some evidence that higher values for the replacement ratio have a positive effect on postunemployment earnings relative to previous earnings, but the effect is small in practical terms for both older men and women and it appears negligible for the younger cohorts.

Classen (1977)

Classen studies benefit effects on duration and earnings using data for samples of 3,235 unemployment insurance claimants in Pennsylvania and 5,129 unemployment insurance claimants in Arizona for the periods 1967–1968 and 1967–1969, respectively. The duration data are taken from the Continuous Wage and Benefit History (CWBH) files, a federally subsidized program in which several states maintain employment and unemployment insurance claim histories for random samples of workers selected quarterly from new claimants. Once in a sample, workers are followed until benefits are exhausted. An attractive feature of the data analyzed here is that maximum benefit levels were raised halfway through the observation periods for each state. Quarterly earnings data are also available for each worker from state unemployment insurance records, although only up to the insurable maximum. Durations pertain to weeks of compensated unemployment per successful claim, up to benefit exhaustion. Very short spells are thus excluded, very long spells are censored, and some durations are aggregated over multiple spells.

Classen uses these data to fit linear duration regressions for each state. No attempt is made to control for the censoring (although Classen does note that all coefficients are likely to be biased downward). The explanatory variables included in the Pennsylvania regression are the weekly benefit amount, sex, age, previous annual earnings, previous high quarter earnings, a measure of previous earnings stability (previous year earnings divided by high quarter earnings), industry dummy variables, and a dummy variable for observations in the year following the increase in maximum benefits. As in the other regression studies, the explanatory power of the model is low (adjusted $R^2 = 0.12$). The coefficient for benefits is large relative to its reported standard error and implies a 1.1 week increase with a $10 increase in the weekly benefit at the sample mean, which translates into an elasticity of about 0.6. The results also imply that older workers, low wage workers, and workers with less stable earnings in the previous year experience longer durations. A longer list of explanatory variables is used in the Arizona regression. In addition to the variables listed above, occupation, ethnic origin, reason for separation, the number of claims in the previous 5 years, previous employer type (private, government, military), and previous earnings in other states are included. The benefit coefficient for this sample is quite close to the Pennsylvania estimate; a 1.2 week increase in duration is implied for a $10 increase in weekly benefits, which translates into an elasticity of about 0.61. Results for other variables are qualitatively similar, except for sex; the coefficient estimate for the Arizona sample is large relative to the reported standard error and implies an average spell of 2 weeks longer for females. The lengthened list of regressors does not increase the explanatory power ($R^2 = 0.11$).

Both sets of results provide evidence of systematic variation across industries. This may reflect the large numbers of temporary layoffs in each sample (about two-thirds in the Pennsylvania sample). Classen notes that when the model is fit for workers who were recalled and workers who were not, the estimated coefficients for weekly benefits implied a 1.5 week increase in average claim duration for the Pennsylvania nonrecall group and a similar increase for the Arizona nonrecall group (result not reported). On the other hand, the benefit level has only a negligible effect on spell lengths of those on recall.

Results are also reported for postunemployment earnings regressions. These include the same explanatory variables as the duration regressions for each state. In both cases, the level of benefits appears irrelevant.

Classen (1979)

In this study, Classen again works with data taken from the CWBH files and administrative records for Pennsylvania and Arizona, but the samples analyzed here include workers who returned to work before collecting benefits, that is, very short spells (normally excluded when administrative records are used) are included. The sample sizes are 4,240 for Pennsylvania and 10,887 for Arizona.[6] As above, all analysis is done separately for each state.

Classen works with three regressions specifications for durations—a linear regression (as above), a log duration regression with all explanatory variables measured in logs, and a Tobit duration model with maximum duration of benefits defined as the threshold (to address the censoring in her data). The explanatory variables are those used in the Pennsylvania regressions of the previous study, with potential duration of benefits added in the linear and log linear models. During the observation period, the maximum number of weeks was 30 in Pennsylvania and 26 in Arizona, but potential duration for an individual might be less. The exact period of eligibility depends on annual and highest quarter earnings in the year preceding the filing of a claim for benefits, together with state-determined, maximum weekly benefit levels. Potential duration of benefits thus differs across workers within each state sample, as well as across states.

The linear regression results are essentially the same as those reported in the previous study for both states. The log linear results are similar, although benefit elasticities implied by the log linear results are somewhat larger—1.03 for Pennsylvania and 0.84 for Arizona. On the other hand, the benefit elasticities implied by the Tobit model are quite close to the linear regression results—0.65 for Pennsylvania and 0.71 for Arizona. The major difference between the Tobit results and the linear regression results appears for potential duration of benefits. All estimates for the potential duration coefficient are positive and large relative to their reported standard errors in the linear duration and log duration regressions, but these measure the effects of both an increase in potential duration and an extended period of observation. Not surprisingly, the Tobit coefficient estimate is about half the size of the linear regression estimate. The Tobit results imply that a 1 week increase in potential duration of benefits increases average claim duration by 0.7 weeks in Pennsylvania and 1.2 weeks in Arizona and the estimate for the Pennsylvania sample is small relative to the reported standard error.

Classen further explores the effects of benefits on durations, exploiting the presence of a legislated change in maximum benefit levels in both states. She fits piecewise linear regressions that incorporate the relationship between benefit levels, previous earnings, and the maximum benefit level. The results imply a larger benefit effect on durations than the simple linear regression results; at the sample means, the implied elasticities are 0.88 for Pennsylvania and 1.02 for Arizona. As in her previous study, Classen also examines differences in benefit effects between workers who were recalled and workers who changed employers. The estimated benefit coefficients for the nonrecall groups are large relative to the reported standard errors. A \$10 increase in weekly benefits is associated with a 2.3 week increase in average claim duration for nonrecalled workers in Pennsylvania and a 1.4 week increase in Arizona. On the other hand, the estimates for workers known to be on recall are small and less precise; the predicted effects of a \$10 increase in benefits are 0.8 and 0.7 week increase in duration in Pennsylvania and Arizona, respectively. Additional results for the recall and nonrecall regressions are not reported, but Classen notes that the coefficients for potential duration of benefits are nearly identical across groups in each state—providing additional evidence that the positive coefficients in the linear regressions largely reflect the truncation in the duration data.

Results for a variety of postunemployment earnings regressions are also reported. As in her previous study, the benefit level coefficients are positive, but negligible in size.

Newton and Rosen (1979)

Newton and Rosen also use a Tobit model to study the effects of unemployment benefit levels and potential duration of benefits on unemployment spell lengths. Their data are for a sample of 627 benefit recipients taken from unemployment files for Georgia for the period 1974–1976. Roughly half of these workers filed claims before July 1, 1975, when the maximum weekly benefit was increased, and the rest filed after the change. The duration data pertain to weeks of insured unemployment, up to the potential duration of benefits for each worker. Thus, short spells and long spells are excluded and some durations cover multiple spells. The maximum duration in the state is 26 weeks, but there is variation across workers that depends on earnings in the year preceding initial filing of a benefit claim. To avoid additional censoring, Newton and Rosen exclude workers who remained unemployed when the data were collected. As noted in the introduction, this practice potentially introduces a problem of sample selection bias. Precise data on weekly benefits are available, but earnings data are limited to gross quarterly earnings on the previous job and sex and race are the only personal characteristics observed.

The explanatory variables included in the Tobit model are a quadratic in the opportunity cost of unemployment (defined as net potential weekly earnings minus the weekly unemployment benefit), a quadratic in potential duration, an interaction of these two variables, sex, race, and the state unemployment rate at the time a claim was filed. The net potential earnings variable is set equal to one-twelfth of high quarter earnings minus an estimate for taxes; the latter is based on state and federal tax parameters and an assumption that each individual was married with two dependents and took a standard deduction.

Newton and Rosen fit the model for their full sample, by race, and by sex. The full sample results for the opportunity cost variables provide some evidence of a convex relationship for the full sample. The elasticity implied for duration with respect to the opportunity cost is -0.487 at the sample mean, which translates into a 1.8 week increase in spell duration with a 10 percentage point increase in benefits. Mean duration and the mean replacement ratio are not reported, but using rough estimates of 10 and 0.5, respectively, the implied benefit elasticity is 0.9. However, the results from estimation by race and by sex indicate that the effect may be negligible for nonwhite workers and for females. There is also some evidence of a positive relationship between actual duration and potential duration of benefits, but these estimates are generally imprecise.

Holen (1977)

Holen works with data from the same source as Burgess and Kingston, the Service-to-Claimants Project in 1969–1970. Her sample differs from theirs, however, in two important respects. First, Holen includes both participants and controls. Second, she works with data collected in five areas—San Francisco–Oakland, Phoenix, Boston, Seattle, and Minneapolis–St. Paul. Overall, the sample consists of 20,000 "job-ready" unemployment insurance recipients who did not expect to be recalled by their former employer. Beyond the large sample size and random receipt of job search assistance, an appealing aspect of these data is state-to-state variation in weeks of benefit eligibility and the rules used to calculate weekly benefits. Precise data on weekly benefits are also available. On the other hand, previous earnings are measured only up to the Social Security taxable maximum and the duration data pertain to weeks of compensated unemployment. Holen makes no attempt to control for the censoring in her duration data, but she does recognize potential biases. To correct for the truncation in the earnings data, she omits observations with earnings at or above the maximum level. Since this causes a systematic relationship between the disturbance term and regressors, coefficient estimates must be interpreted with more caution than usual.

Holen fits linear regressions of duration on sex, age, race, categorical education variables, occupation dummy variables, previous wages, potential duration of benefits, weekly benefit amounts, a measure of earnings stability (the number of quarters in which a worker had earnings in the previous year), receipt of special job search assistance, and city dummy variables or local unemployment rates. The estimated coefficients for the weekly benefit amount are positive and large relative to their standard errors and imply an increase in duration of 0.7–0.9 weeks with a $10 increase in the weekly benefit (the larger estimate being for the city dummy specification). Summary statistics are not reported for the sample, but rough estimates of the elasticities implied by the results can be calculated using an outside estimate for the ratio of average weekly benefits to mean durations. If we set this equal to 5 (in line with the data analyzed by Classen, for example), the elasticities are 0.35–0.45. The coefficient for the potential duration of benefits is large and positive, but this may simply reflect an extended period of observation as opposed to a policy effect. The estimated effects for receipt of special search assistance is large and negative; the participants in the experiment appear to have claims that are more than a week shorter than controls, on average. The results for remaining variables are consistent with those reported elsewhere. Older workers, females, nonwhite workers, workers with less than a high school diploma, and workers with less stable earnings patterns appear to have longer durations than their counterparts. Durations also appear quite responsive to the local unemployment rate.

Holen also fits postunemployment earnings regressions on the same sets of variables. The coefficient for the benefit level is positive and large relative to the reported standard error, but special search assistance appears irrelevant. The results for other variables seem sensible.

Kahn (1978)

Kahn analyzes the relationship between postunemployment earnings and duration. His objective is to test the empirical relevance of two alternative job search models: the finite horizon systematic search model with no recall presented by Salop (1973) and the finite horizon random search model with recall presented by Lipmann and McCall (1976). In both models, a risk-neutral worker samples one firm each period. Thereafter, the models part. In the systematic search model, the worker knows the offer wage distribution, which firms are offering what offers, and the probability of receiving an offer at any given firm. There is no recall and no resampling. In the random search model, the worker knows the distribution of offers but not their location and recall is permitted. The optimal policy is a declining reservation wage policy in both models, the decline being due to the finite horizon. The accepted wage is also predicted to decline with duration in the systematic search model, but not in the random search model with recall. In the latter, the accepted wage is a nondecreasing function of duration. This result relies heavily on the possibility of recall—with recall, the expected maximum offer will never decline with additional draws from the offer distribution. If the availability of recall is dropped from the random search model, the implications for accepted wages are the same in both models. Thus, Kahn's analysis might be interpreted as a test of the relevance of the recall assumption.

Kahn works with data for a sample of 759 workers collected in the 1967 Survey of Economic Opportunity. These data offer relatively large samples for age and sex groups (234 white males, 247 black males, 152 black females, and 126 white females), but they have several unattractive features. Most important, the duration measure available to Kahn is weeks unemployed in 1966. In addition to the possibility of right and left censoring, durations may be aggregated over multiple spells. The accepted wage data also have problems. The wage at the time of the 1967 interview is the only available measure and this may not be the wage accepted after a spell of unemployment in 1966; a worker may have experienced one or more job changes in 1967. Also, the survey design intentionally oversampled low income families.

To test the alternative hypotheses, Kahn starts by fitting accepted wage regressions separately by race and sex. In addition to duration, the explanatory variables include education, experience, the SMSA unemployment rate, the nonwhite percentage of the SMSA population, and dummy variables for marital status, recent migration, and region of the United States. The estimated coefficients for duration are negative for all groups except for white females, as implied by the systematic search model and the random search model without recall, but the estimates are small relative to reported standard errors.[7] The estimated coefficients for remaining regressors have familiar signs, but these are also imprecise.

Kahn recognizes the simultaneity of accepted wages and durations and reports two-stage least-squares estimates for a two-equation model with durations treated as endogenous. Specifically, duration regressions are fit using the variables previously specified, previous wages, and number of children. This last variable is included as a determinant of the reservation wage that should not affect accepted wages directly. However, because the accepted wage depends on the reservation wage directly, this is not an appropriate restriction and the results are difficult to interpret. Reservations aside, the reported estimates for the duration coefficient are all negative and, for all but white females, they differ significantly from zero at standard levels. The remaining results are essentially unaffected.

Feinberg (1976)

Feinberg sets out to determine the effects of risk and risk aversion on unemployment spell durations. Toward this end, he fits duration regressions using data for samples of male household heads collected in three waves of the Panel Study of Income Dynamics (PSID): 224 workers from the 1969 interviews, 246 workers for the 1970 interviews, and 358 workers from the 1971 interviews.[8] Feinberg works with each of the year samples separately because of the availability of different benefit data. Receipt of unemployment insurance benefits or workman's compensation during 1968 is reported for the 1969 sample, but not amounts. The combined total from these sources is reported for the 1970 and 1971 samples, and Feinberg uses this amount divided by the number of weeks unemployed as his measure of unemployment benefits. All durations are measured as weeks unemployed in the year preceding an interview. Thus, both right and left censoring may be present and durations may be aggregated over multiple spells. Data on assets and weekly travel-to-work costs are available for each worker in the sample and Feinberg uses these as measures of search costs. An index of "risk avoidance" is also available in the PSID and this is used as a measure of risk aversion.[9] Estimates for means and standard deviations of wage offer distributions are calculated using the frequency distributions reported for male earnings by occupation and SMSA in the 1970 Census of Population tables.[10] The standard deviation of offers is used as a measure of risk faced by a worker.

Results are reported for linear duration regressions for each year sample and also for groups in a partition of each year sample by race. The most general regressor specification includes all of the variables listed above, an interaction of the standard deviation of offers with the risk-aversion index, and dummy variables for occupation, race, and large city residence—but some of these variables are omitted for different samples.

The problems with the duration data, the use of some unusual variables, and this use of different regressor specifications make interpretation of the reported results somewhat difficult. Still, some interesting patterns appear.

The results for the full year samples suggest that both benefit receipt and higher benefit levels are associated with more time spent unemployed, on average. Spells of recipients appear to be about 2 weeks longer than spells of nonrecipients and a $10 increase in the benefit level is predicted to increase durations by 0.83 to 1.01 weeks. At the sample means for the 1970 and 1971 samples, the implied benefit elasticities are 0.95 and 1.44, respectively. However, looking at the results reported for the separate regressions by race, it appears that the full sample results understate the benefit effects for white workers slightly and overstate the benefit effects of these variables on nonwhite workers' unemployment by a large margin. Benefits appear irrelevant for nonwhite workers in the sample. The estimated coefficients for mean offers are generally negative, but small. They also appear quite sensitive to the benefit measure included, as one would expect. The estimated coefficient for the standard deviation of offers is generally positive, but this result also appears quite sensitive to specification of the remaining regressors. As for the risk-aversion index and its interaction with the offer standard deviation, the estimated coefficients are negative, but small relative to reported standard errors.

Mellow (1978)

Mellow works with data for a sample of 400 workers collected in the National Longitudinal Survey of Older Men (ages 45–59 in 1966) who were employed as wage or salary workers at both the 1966 and 1967 interviews and experienced a single job change in the year between. The job change restriction serves to eliminate multiple spells; unfortunately, the employment restriction excludes long spells systematically. Durations are measured as weeks unemployed and 173 of the workers report spells of 1 or more weeks.

Mellow's objective is to test the basic search hypothesis that higher search costs imply longer durations—without direct observations on the costs of search. Toward this end, he fits a simple regression of the form.

$$t = a_0 + a_1 (\ln w - \ln w^*) + \epsilon$$

where t demotes spell length, $\ln w$ is the log observed hourly wage in 1966 at his previous job, and w^* is the log of an estimate of the worker's mean wage. The latter is calculated using the worker's observed characteristics and the results from a basic log wage regression fit for all wage and salary workers interviewed in 1966.[11] Mellow interprets the residual as a measure of search costs faced by the worker. Although this interpretation is not clear-cut, the results are still interesting. For the full sample (i.e., including those with and without unemployment spells between jobs), he reports an estimate for a_1 of 3.47 (standard error 1.078, $R^2 = 0.026$). He also notes that when only those who experienced unemployment are included, the estimate for a_1 is 4.12 (standard error 1.856) and that when variables generally specified as determinants of search costs are included (e.g., assets and nonlabor income), the coefficients for these variables are small relative to their standard errors and the estimated coefficient for the log wage residual declines by only 10 percent.

Mellow also fits regressions for the proportional wage change between years. The explanatory variables include unemployment spell duration, a dummy variable for direct job changes, dummy variables for quits due to low wages on the previous job or the availability of a better opportunity and quits for other reasons (both versus a layoff), and a decomposition of the wage residual on the previous job into positive and negative parts. The results suggest that although workers who change jobs directly do significantly better, the wage changes of those who become unemployed increases with duration by about 1 percent per week. Both the negative and positive wage differentials for the previous job have negative coefficients, which might be interpreted as some evidence of an elimination of wage differentials with mobility, but both coefficients are small relative to reported standard errors. In Chapter 8, we discuss additional studies of wage changes with job mobility and, therewith, issues related to interpreting these results.

Moffitt and Nicholson (1982)

Moffitt and Nicholson analyze the effects of potential benefit durations and benefit levels on mean spell lengths, but take an approach that is different from those taken in the previously discussed studies. The approach here follows from a formulation of the problem in a standard labor–leisure framework. Individuals are modeled as choosing the optimal number of weeks of unemployment, given the net market wage they face and the potential duration of benefits. The budget constraint of the model is analogous to the kinked budget constraint of the standard labor supply model with a linear progressive tax structure. When eligible for benefits, the marginal wage is the net weekly gain over benefits and the replacement ratio is effectively like a proportional subsidy to time spent not working—available up to the exhaustion of benefits (i.e., the "kink"). Note, that there is no uncertainty in the model. A job at a known net wage just waits to be taken. Thus, there is no "search" interpretation for time spent unemployed. Nevertheless, the implications of the model are similar. The probability of longer unemployment spell increases with both the potential duration of benefits and the replacement ratio in this model.

To estimate the labor supply function implied by this model, Moffitt and Nicholson modify the maximum likelihood techniques used in earlier studies of segmented budget constraints.[12] Their data are for samples of 632 males and 439 females selected from a nationally representative sample of workers in the United States who experienced a layoff in 1974, collected regular extended benefits in 1975, and were eligible for an additional extension of benefits under the Federal Supplemental Benefits Program (FSB) that year.[13] Workers were interviewed in March 1976 and again in December 1977. Between the two interviews, retrospective labor market histories were collected for the entire period between the 1974 layoff and the second interview date. Moffitt and Nicholson restrict their samples to workers with all relevant data available who spent no more than 5 weeks outside the labor force over the sample period.

Interpreting the results is somewhat difficult. The dependent variable for the labor supply equation is the percentage of the observation period employed because the length of the observation period varies across workers in their sample. Nonemployment spells are also aggregated over two or more spells for some workers. Moffitt and Nicholson also note that people are rarely observed at the "kinks" of their budget constraint, that is the actual date of exhaustion. After experimentation with sample sizes around exhaustion dates, their preferred definition of the kink is the 6 percent of an individual's observation period surrounding the exhaustion date; the width of this band is 9.3 weeks for the mean observation period. Results are also reported for a 10 percent band and, overall, the results appear fairly sensitive to this specification. For example, the results imply that a 10 percent increase in the replacement ratio (net of taxes) produces an increase in average unemployment spell length of 1.46 weeks for males who do not exhaust benefits when the 6 percent band is used and an increase of 2.25 weeks when the 10 percent band is used. For female nonexhaustees, the corresponding estimates are 1.26 and 1.72 weeks. For male exhaustees, the estimates are 0.14 and 0.20 weeks. For female exhaustees the estimates are 0.08 and 0.10 weeks. The contrast in results for a 1 week increase in potential benefits for exhaustees is even greater. For males, the estimated increases in mean spell lengths are 0.01 and 0.41 weeks using the 6 and 10 percent bands, respectively. For female exhaustees, the effects are 0.01 and 0.20 weeks. Note that in this model, the nonexhaustees are not affected by the latter change in the budget constraint.

Summary

It is difficult to draw firm conclusions about the elasticity of mean durations with respect to benefit levels on the basis of the results reported in these studies. The estimates range from 0.03 to 1.44 (Table 5.1) and there are reasons to exercise caution in interpreting all of them. Nevertheless, these studies served well in a number of ways. They showed the existence of systematic relationships which are in accord with predictions of search theory. They indicated some of the major econometric issues that had to be addressed in the analysis of duration data within the search framework. Finally, they established the potential importance of some substantive issues. The findings of Ehrenberg and Oaxaca (1976) and others suggest that reasons for job exit are potentially important in explaining search behavior and benefit effects, particularly for some demographic groups. In particular, the findings of Classen (1977, 1979) and Ehrenberg and Oaxaca provide evidence of distinct differences between the experiences of workers on temporary versus permanent layoff. This is an area that continues to receive attention, as we will discuss in this and subsequent chapters. In general, the findings for benefits are similar—workers on recall are less responsive to program changes. Findings of a non-negligible effect for potential duration of benefits also appear in subsequent work, along with demographic differences in the sensivity to benefit levels.

Hazard Function Studies

We turn here to studies that model and estimate the hazard function for unemployment data directly. Relative to the regression approach, the hazard function approach represents an appealing route for two reasons: it allows more flexibility in specifying the duration distribution and censoring can be dealt with easily through appropriate specification of the sample likelihood. In Chapter 3, we reviewed basic aspects of the hazard function approach. Before proceeding with our review of the literature, we extend this discussion to consider some specifications that are commonly used and some major issues that have occupied a good deal of attention in the literature: time-varying explanatory variables, sampling issues, discrete-time models, and unmeasured heterogeneity.

Specifying the Hazard

The basic idea of the hazard function approach is to specify a functional form for the hazard rate out of unemployment in terms of explanatory variables that produce variation in the reservation wage (w^r), the offer distribution ($f(w)$), and the arrival rate (δ). The specification used most often in the search literature is the proportional hazards model (see the discussion in Chapter 3). Here, the hazard function at duration t is factored into a function of regressors x, which may or may not vary with duration of a spell, and a function of elapsed duration t,

$$\tau(x(t), t) = \lambda_0(t)\Phi(x(t)) \tag{5.1}$$

where λ_0 is referred to as the baseline hazard. Measures of human capital, unemployment benefits, local labor market conditions, and demographic characteristics may be included in the regressors $x(t)$. The defining characteristic of the proportional hazards specification is that all direct dependence of the hazard on duration is captured in the baseline hazard. That is, differences in $\tau(x(t), t)$ across individuals at a given duration t depend on t only through variation in regressors with time. For example, letting i and j index two different individuals, then

$$\tau_i(x_i(t^*), t^*) = a_{ij}(t^*)\tau_j(x_j(t^*), t^*) \tag{5.2a}$$

where

$$a_{ij}(t^*) = \Phi(x_i(t^*))/\Phi(x_j(t^*)) \tag{5.2b}$$

for all durations t^*. If the regressors do not vary with duration, then neither does the factor of proportionality. The direct dependence on t, captured by $\lambda_0(t)$, can be interpreted as a proxy for some economic process that is not captured in the regressor function (e.g., human capital depreciation or a signaling effect on the arrival rate that cannot be measured directly).

Given that the hazard is positive, a natural choice for the regressor function Φ is the exponential function, $\exp\{x(t)'\beta\}$, where β is a vector of unknown parameters. Specification of the baseline hazard is not entirely arbitrary, given this specification for Φ. It must be nonnegative and its integral over the positive axis must diverge to obtain a proper distribution function for durations. Intuitively, what this restriction means is that no individual can be expected to remain unemployed permanently. (If this condition is not satisfied, then the distribution is called improper or defective.) Most often, a particular parametric family for the duration distribution is specified. Along this line, consider a constant hazard specification, with $\lambda_0(t) = 1$. If the regressors are time invariant, then this specification corresponds to a time-invariant hazard

$$\tau(x) = \exp\{x'\beta\} \tag{5.3}$$

We have seen that this is equivalent to assuming that the random variable completed duration, T, has an exponential distribution with parameter τ and expected value

$$E[T] = \exp\{-x'\beta\} \tag{5.4}$$

Note that if the regressors are measured in logs, the coefficients β give the elasticities of the hazard and their negatives give the elasticities of expected duration. A generalization of the exponential model that is used frequently in the studies discussed below is the Weibull, where

$$\lambda_0(t) = \alpha t^{\alpha-1}, \qquad \alpha > 0 \tag{5.5}$$

With fixed regressors, the hazard in this case is

$$\tau(x, t) = \exp\{x'\beta\}\alpha t^{\alpha-1}, \qquad \alpha > 0 \tag{5.6}$$

Table 5.1. Regression Studies

Study	Data	Dependent Variable	Findings
Burgess and Kingston (1971) Benefit effects on duration	United States, 1969–1970 Job search experiment for UI recipients, Phoenix participants	1. Claim length (reemployed or censored) 2. Discontinued claim length	Duration decreases with replacement ratio
Burgess and Kingston (1975) Benefit effects on duration	United States, 1969–70 Job search experiment for UI recipients, Phoenix, Bay Area, Boston participants	1. Discontinued claim length 2. Log discontinued claim 3. Log discontinued claim, by sex and race	Elasticity of duration with respect to replacement ratio: white males, 0.15; white females, 0.3; black workers, negligible
Burgess and Kingston (1977) Benefit effects on postunemployment wage	United States 1969–1970 Job search experiments for UI claimants, Phoenix, Bay Area, Boston participants	Postunemployment wage	Earnings increase with benefit level and potential benefit duration; slight decrease with duration
MacKay and Reid (1972) Weekly vs. lump-sum benefit effects on duration	United Kingdom, 1968–1968 Workers at plants shut down in Westmidlands, males	Weeks of unemployed search	Elasticity of duration with respect to weekly benefit: 0.27; lump-sum benefit: negligible
Ehrenberg and Oaxaca (1976) Benefit effects on duration and postemployment wage	United States, 1966–1971 NLS young males: 1966–1967, 1967–1968, 1968–1969; young females: 1967–1968, 1968–1969, 1969–1970; older males: 1966–1967; older females: 1968–1969, 1969–1971	1. Log weeks of nonemployment, by age group and sex 2. Log postunemployment wage, by age group and sex	Elasticity of duration with respect to benefits: young males, 0.27–0.46; young females, 0.61–0.75; older men, 0.55–0.825; older women, 0.19–0.21 Earnings of older workers increase slightly with benefit levels; negligible effect for others
Classen (1977) Benefit effects on duration and postunemployment wage	United States, 1967–1969 CWBH UI recipients, Arizona: July 1967–July 1969; Pennsylvania: 1967–1968	1. Compensated weeks of unemployment per claim, by state 2. Postunemployment wage, by state	Elasticity of duration with respect to benefits: Pennsylvania: 0.6; Arizona: 0.61 No benefit effect Elasticity of duration with respect to benefits:

Study	Data	Dependent variable	Results
Classen (1979) Benefit effects on duration and postunemployment wage	United States, 1967–1969 UI claimants CWBH, Arizona: July 1967–July 1969; Pennsylvania: 1968–1969	1. Weeks of unemployment per claim 2. Log weeks of unemployment per claim 3. Tobit model (threshold = potential benefit duration) 4. Weeks of unemployment with piecewise linear benefit effect 5. Weeks per claim, by recall, no recall	Same as Classen (1977) Pennsylvania: 1.03; Arizona: 0.84 Pennsylvania: 0.65; Arizona: 0.71 Pennsylvania: 0.88; Arizona: 1.02 Benefit effect on durations of recalled about half the no recall response
Newton and Rosen (1979) Benefit effects on duration	United States, 1971–1976 UI claimants	Tobit model (threshold = potential benefit duration)	Elasticity of duration with respect to benefits: 0.9
Holen (1977) Benefit effects on duration and postunemployment wage	United States, 1969–1970 UI recipients, San Francisco, Phoenix, Boston, Seattle, Minneapolis; job search experiment participants and controls	Compensated weeks of unemployment per claim	Elasticity of duration with respect to benefits: 0.35–0.45
Kahn (1978) Postunemployment wages and duration	United States, 1966: SEO	Log postunemployment wage, by race and sex	Weak evidence of decline in earnings with duration
Feinberg (1976b) Effects of benefits, risk, and risk aversion on duration	United States, 1966–1970 PSID male household heads	Weeks unemployed within year, by year of observation, by race and year of observation	Elasticity of duration with respect to benefits: 0.95–1.44
Mellow (1978) Search costs and duration	United States, 1966–1967 NSL older men	Weeks unemployed	Duration increases with absolute deviation of previous wage from mean accepted wage
Moffitt and Nicholson (1982) Potential duration of benefit levels on duration (kinked budget constraint model)	United States, 1974–1977 benefit recipients eligible for extended Federal Supplemental Benefits	Percentage of observation period employed	Effect of 10 percent increase in replacement rate on weeks of unemployment: males, 1.5–2.3 week increase; females, 1.3–1.7 week increase

and durations have mean

$$E[T] = \exp\{-x'\beta/\alpha\}\Gamma[(\alpha + 1)/\alpha] \tag{5.7}$$

where Γ is the gamma function. Beyond convenient analytical properties (e.g., the integrated hazard has a closed form), the Weibull model is attractive because of the simple relation between the parameter α and duration dependence of the hazard. Since

$$\lambda_0'(t) \gtreqless 0 \quad \text{as} \quad \alpha \gtreqless 1 \tag{5.8}$$

the value of α gives the direction of movement in $\tau(x(t),t)$ with duration t, independent of that due to time-varying regressors.[14] Note, however, that although the Weibull baseline hazard allows variation in the hazard with duration, only monotonic variation is permitted. For some theoretical models, this may be suitable. More flexible distributions such as the log logistic or gamma might be used instead; an appealing aspect of the gamma distribution is that the exponential distribution (and thus the stationary job search model) represents a special case, as it does for the Weibull. Alternatively, one may stay in the proportional hazards framework, but choose not to specify a family for the duration distribution, that is, take a semiparametric or nonparametric approach to estimating the baseline hazard directly. A few of the studies that we review take this approach and we discuss their methods below. As discussed in Chapter 3, one might also depart from the proportional hazards model and consider an accelerated lifetime formulation, where the role of the regressors is to rescale time directly (as opposed to shifting the hazard). None of the studies reviewed in this chapter takes this last approach in studying unemployment durations, but the employment duration model fit by Farber (1980), for example, can be given this interpretation; we discuss this study in Chapter 6.

Sampling Specifications

As discussed in Chapter 3, once a functional form has been specified, the parameters of the model can often be estimated using the method of maximum likelihood. Censoring in the data is accounted for easily at this stage through appropriate specification of the likelihood function. Some sampling schemes are common across the studies we will discuss, so we review them for reference.

Suppose we have a sample of workers, all of whom became unemployed at the same time. If there is no censoring in the duration data, then the density implied by the hazard specification $g_i(t_i)$ is the appropriate contribution to the sample likelihood for an individual. If there is random right censoring, then the Survivor function $S_i(t_i) = [1 - G_i(t_i)]$ is entered. Left censoring is problematic if the duration distribution is not exponential—observed spells must be initialized and there is no standard way of doing this. Left-censored spells are typically omitted in the studies discussed below.[15]

It may be the case that starting calendar dates vary across individuals. Suppose that we have unemployment spell data for a cross section of workers. Unless the probability of entering unemployment at different calendar dates is a constant for each individual over time, this probability should be incorporated into the likelihood function. If we normalize time so that the survey calendar date is date 0, then the date of entry into unemployment for an individual i is $-t_i$. If we denote the density for the date of entry by $u_i(-t_i)$, then we can use Bayes' theorem to write the density of the entry date conditioned on being unemployed at time 0 (i.e., on a spell of length t_i) as

$$u_i(-t_i|0) = \frac{u_i(-t_i)[1 - G_i(t_i)]}{\int_0^\infty u_i(-e)[1 - G_i(e)] \, de} \qquad (5.9)$$

Here, t_i is referred to as the backward recurrence time and the conditional density, $u(-t_i|0)$ represents the appropriate contribution for individual i to the sample likelihood in place of the Survivor function. In practice, this is not straightforward; approximations are generally used when entry rate variation is incorporated. Often it is useful (less often, satisfactory) to assume that the rate of entry into a state is constant over time.

For example, suppose that two interviews are conducted h periods apart, that elapsed duration is observed at the first interview, which we will denote by s_i, and that the time of reemployment is observed if it falls between the first and the second interviews. Specification of the sample likelihood in terms of the backward recurrence time is appropriate, but evaluation of the integral in the denominator might be avoided here by conditioning the density on duration at the first interview and assuming entry rates are constant in the period preceding the first interview. Let a_i denote time spent unemployed following the first interview (the "forward recurrence time"), and let d_i be a dummy variable that indicates completion of a spell by the second interview. Then the contribution to the sample likelihood for individual i, is

$$L(s_i + a_i|s_i) = [g_i(s_i + a_i)/(1 - G_i(s_i))]^{d_i} \qquad (5.10)$$
$$\times [(G_i(s_i + h) - G_i(s_i))/(1 - G_i(s_i))]^{1-d_i}$$

Alternatively, it may be the case that only employment status is observed at the second interview. In this case, the contribution to the sample likelihood is

$$L(s_i + h|s_i) = [(1 - G_i(s_i + h))/(1 - G(s_i))]^{d_i} \qquad (5.11)$$
$$\times [G_i(s_i + h) - G_i(s_i))/(1 - G_i(s_i))]^{1-d_i}$$

where d_i again indicates an uncensored spell. Note that the likelihood is conditioned on s_i in both Equations 5.10 and 5.11, so that s_i is not regarded as a random variable, but a known quantity. (See Chesher and Lancaster [1981, 1983] and Ridder [1984] for additional discussion.)

Discrete-Time Models

We have focused on continuous time duration models. The duration distribution can also be formulated in discrete time. Letting $t = 0, 1, \ldots$ index periods of unemployment, the integrated hazard can be approximated by the sum $\Sigma_s \tau_s$, the summation from 1 to t, and the function $\exp\{-\tau_s\}$ can be approximated by $(1 - \tau_s)$. Together, these yield an approximation to the survivor function,

$$1 - G(t) \approx \prod_{s=1}^{t} (1 - \tau_s) \qquad (5.12)$$

This discrete time formulation has an intuitive appeal; Equation 5.12 states that the probability of a spell of length greater than t periods (approximately) equals the product of the conditional probabilities of failing to leave in each of the first t periods, $(1 - \tau_s)$, $s = 0, 1, \ldots t$. The conditional probability τ_t may again be modeled as a function of a vector of regressors $x(t)$ and (perhaps) elapsed duration t; as shown, this is equivalent to specifying the duration distribution directly. Some of the studies we review use the logistic formulation,

$$\tau(x(t), t) = (1 + \exp[-\{h(t) + \beta' x(t)\}])^{-1} \qquad (5.13)$$

where the pattern of duration dependence is given by the function $h(t)$. A kth-order polynomial is sometimes specified

$$h(t) = \sum_{i=1}^{k} \alpha_i t^i \qquad (5.14)$$

Setting $k \geq 2$ allows for nonmonotonic duration dependence. Maximum likelihood techniques can be used to estimate β and α. As in the continuous time case, the appropriate contributions to the sample likelihood function depend on the type of censoring present in the data. If uncensored, the contribution to the sample likelihood for individual i is

$$g_i(t_i) = \left[\prod_{s=0}^{t_i-1} (1 - \tau_i(s)) \right] \tau_i(t_i) \qquad (5.15)$$

For randomly right-censored observations, the contribution to the likelihood is the survivor function (Equation 5.12). Information about probabilities of entry at particular dates should also be incorporated when there is variation in the sample, using the discrete time analogue to Equation 5.9.

Unmeasured Heterogeneity and Misspecification

Implicit in the specifications discussed above is an assumption that the regressors $x(t)$ control for all heterogeneity across workers. In practice, this is not likely to be the case. Unmeasured and unobservable sources of heterogeneity are unavoidable. Functional form misspecification also translates into unmeasured heterogeneity. This is a common problem in the specification of econometric models, but the problem is potentially more critical here. Unmeasured heterogeneity leads to predictably biased inferences in duration models. If omitted variables are ignored, the estimated model may be biased toward negative duration dependence—even if the omitted variables are uncorrelated with included regressors. Intuitively, unobserved characteristics may lower the level of the hazards for some workers and therefore lengthen their unemployment spells. If these characteristics are not incorporated into the specification, the hazard at each duration t will be averaged over the unobservables for workers still unemployed at that time—but not recognized as such. There will be no explanation for the longer spells experienced by these workers relative to their observational equivalents other than a decline in the hazard with duration. Innate ability and self-motivation are obvious examples of such unobservables. Coefficient estimates for other regressors in the model may also be biased if unobserved heterogeneity is present, but unaccounted for in the hazard specification.

The most common method for dealing with unmeasured heterogeneity in the proportional hazards framework is to assume that it can be summarized by a multiplicative unit mean random disturbance term v that is distributed independently of both x and t with unknown variance σ^2. The hazard at duration t in this case is

$$\tau(x(t), t, v) = \lambda_0(t)\Phi(x(t))v \qquad (5.16)$$

So if there is no unmeasured heterogeneity (i.e., $\sigma^2 = 0$), the term v is absorbed into the constant term in the function Φ.

The duration distribution corresponding to this hazard specification is a mixture. Elbers and Ridder (1982) study nonparametric identification of this model. More often, however, parametric methods are used to estimate a specified mixing distribution. For example, many studies follow Lancaster (1979) and use a unit mean gamma distribution. The appeal of this specification is its convenient analytical properties. With a Weibull specification for the baseline hazard, durations in this case have mean

$$E[T] = \exp\{-x'\beta/\alpha\}[B(\alpha^{-1}, \sigma^{-2} - \alpha^{-1})/[\alpha^{-1}\sigma^{-2/\alpha}] \qquad (5.17)$$

where B denotes the beta function. (See Lancaster [1979, 1990] for additional discussion.)

Heckman and Singer (1984b) argue that inference with respect to duration dependence and the effects of regressors on the hazard may be extremely sensitive to the particular assumption invoked for the distribution of v. They advocate use of a nonparametric method due to Laird (1978) to estimate the mixing distribution. Nonparametric methods are used to estimate the mixing distribution in some of the studies to be discussed.

All of the studies we review assume that the multiplicative random component is distributed independently of included regressors. Chamberlain (1985) and others note the likelihood of this assumption being invalid and suggest estimation of fixed effects models when panel data are available. Alaouze (1987) explores this approach using U.S. data. Specifically, he fits a fixed effects model based on a gamma distribution for unemployment durations which allows general dependence between heterogeneity parameters and explanatory variables. He finds evidence of negative duration dependence.

For additional discussion of heterogeneity, misspecification, and alternative specification diagnostics for duration data models, see Butler et al. (1989), Chamberlain (1985), Chesher (1984), Chesher and Lancaster (1985), Chesher and Spady (1988), Heckman and Singer (1984a,b,c), Honoré (1990), Jensen (1987a), Kiefer (1984a,b, 1985a, 1988b), Lancaster (1979, 1985a,b, 1990), Lancaster and Nickell (1980), Nickell (1979a,b), Ridder (1986c), Ridder and Verbakel (1986), Sharma (1989), Trussell and Richards (1985), and Waldman (1985).

Our discussion has focused on reduced form techniques. The hazard function approach has been extended to estimate structural parameters of particular theoretical models. Chapter 3 outlined general aspects of the methods used in structural analyses and we discuss the specifics for each study in the next section of this chapter. Also, as noted in Chapter 3, the hazard function approach may be extended to the case of competing risks formulations for a duration distribution. This is done in the studies based on multistate models discussed in Chapter 6.

The Studies

We start our review of the literature with two papers that use the hazard function approach to study microdata on unemployment durations. Lancaster (1979) sets out the basics for a continuous time formulation of the duration distribution. He starts with nonstochastic constant and Weibull proportional hazard specifications with time-invariant regressors; he then uses a gamma mixing distribution to incorporate unmeasured heterogeneity. In fitting his models, Lancaster works with data for unemployed workers in the United Kingdom. Nickell (1979a,b) sets out the basics for a discrete formulation for the duration distribution. His basic hazard model is a logit specification with time-invariant regressors, a quadratic to capture duration dependence, and variation in the probability of entering unemployment across calendar time. He then extends the model to allow time variation in regressors and unobserved heterogeneity. His approach to modeling unobserved heterogeneity is nonparametric. Nickell also uses data for the United Kingdom when fitting his models.[16]

The thrust of these two papers and most of the papers that follow in this section is methodological. Nevertheless, all of the studies motivate their work by the need to obtain reliable estimates of the effects of unemployment benefits and other policy instruments on unemployment spell lengths. Atkinson et al. (1984) fit exponential and Weibull models for the duration distribution using data for male workers in the United Kingdom. Their concern is the basic issue of sensitivity to measurement of regressors. In particular, they focus on measurement of the benefit replacement ratio, labor demand, and taxes. Solon (1985) attempts to isolate the effect of taxing unemployment benefits on durations—a policy introduced in the United States in 1979. Toward this end, he modifies the Weibull model. Lynch (1985) uses a Weibull model to study the unemployment behavior of young workers in London. Podgursky and Swaim (1987) use a Weibull model to study durations of joblessness of U.S. workers following displacement. Narendranathan et al. (1985) address the sensitivity of estimated benefit effects to unmeasured heterogeneity and other issues of model specification. Ham and Rea (1987) extend the model presented by Nickell in their analysis of limits on the potential duration of benefits in Canada.

We close the section with studies that depart from parametric specification the baseline hazard. Dynarski and Sheffrin (1987) and Steinberg and Montforte (1987) use the partial likelihood method of Cox (discussed in Chapter 3), along with parametric methods. Dynarski and Sheffrin focus on the relationship between unemployment spell lengths and the unemployment rate in the United States, while Steinberg and Montforte study the effects of job training and search assistance programs on the unemployment spell lengths of displaced workers. Moffitt (1985) takes a nonparametric approach and Meyer (1988b) and Katz and Meyer (1988a) take a semiparametric approach to estimate the baseline hazard in their analyses of the effects of changes in the potential duration of unemployment benefits in the United States. We close with a second study by Meyer (1988a). His focus is the effect of reemployment bonuses on unemployment durations and his approach is again semiparametric.

Lancaster (1979)

Lancaster sets out the basics for application of the proportional hazards model in the search framework. He starts with the constant hazard model with fixed regressors (Equation 5.3),

$$\tau(x) = \exp\{x'\beta\}$$

and then goes on to consider the more general Weibull specification for the baseline hazard (Equation 5.14),

$$\tau(x,t) = \exp\{x'\beta\}\alpha t^{\alpha-1}, \qquad \alpha > 0$$

Lancaster works with data for a sample of 479 unskilled workers in the United Kingdom collected in a 1973 nationwide survey of the registered unemployed for Political and Economic Planning (PEP).[17] Two interviews were conducted, approximately 6 weeks apart, and elapsed duration at the time of the first interview and employment status at the second interview are available. Lancaster therefore uses a likelihood of the form of Equation 5.11. The explanatory variables are age, the local unemployment rate, and the benefit replacement rate (defined as total weekly unemployment benefits divided by net weekly pay on the previous job)—all measured in logs at their first interview values.

The results for the exponential model suggest that spell durations increase significantly with age, the unemployment rate, and the replacement ratio. Specifically, the replacement rate elasticity for the hazard is 0.43 (standard error 0.21) and the unemployment rate elasticity is 0.44 (0.17). On the other hand, the estimate of the Weibull parameter α is 0.77 (standard error 0.09) in Lancaster's second specification. Under the maintained hypotheses that both the Weibull proportional hazard model and the regressor specifications are correct, a null hypothesis of no duration dependence can be rejected in favor of negative duration dependence at the 5 percent level. The results for age and the unemployment rate for the Weibull model are almost identical to the constant hazard results, after rescaling by α. The estimate for replacement rate elasticity is somewhat larger, 0.53 after rescaling the coefficient estimate of 0.41 (standard error 0.21).

Lancaster proceeds to incorporate unobserved heterogeneity into his models using a unit mean gamma distribution with variance σ^2. For the Weibull model, the hazard is

$$\tau(x, t) = \alpha t^{\alpha-1} \exp \{x'\beta\}v, \qquad \alpha > 0$$

and the duration distribution is thus a gamma mixture of Weibulls; the exponential model simply restricts α to unity. For the constant hazard model, Lancaster's estimate for the error variance is 0.18 (standard error 0.08). The replacement ratio elasticity has approximately the same magnitude, but the standard errors for this and all other parameters are larger than before; none differs significantly from zero at standard levels. The error variance estimate in the Weibull model is much smaller, both in practical and statistical terms, 0.11 (standard error 0.17). The estimate for the Weibull parameter α is closer to one, 0.9 (standard error 0.22), but hypotheses of negative, positive, and no duration dependence cannot be rejected at standard significant levels. Similarly, the implied replacement rate elasticity estimate is about 0.6, which is larger than when unobserved heterogeneity is ignored. However, the standard error for the replacement rate coefficient is also larger and a null hypothesis of no benefit effect cannot be rejected.

Nickell (1979b)[18]

Nickell works with a discrete time formulation of the duration distribution. specifically, Nickell starts with a logit specification for the hazard (Equation 5.11),

$$\tau(x(t), t) = (1 + \exp [-(h(t) + \beta'x(t))])^{-1}$$

with a second-order polynomial for the duration dependence function $h(t)$ and linear splines to incorporate variation in the regressors with duration. Variation in the probability of entry at different dates is also incorporated into his empirical specification. Letting time be normalized so that the survey date is zero and letting $u_i(-t_i)$ denote the unconditional probability of entry for individual i at time $-t_i$, Nickell uses the approximation

$$u_i^*(-t_i) = u_i \cdot u(-t_i) \qquad (5.18)$$

in the discrete time analogue to Equation 5.9. the first term is an individual specific constant that is interpreted as the conditional probability that a person with i's characteristics would become unemployed, given that someone becomes unemployed. This is assumed constant over time. The second term is set equal to the aggregate flow into unemployment at the date $-t_i$. The justification offered for this approximation is that the composition of the inflow is not likely to have changed greatly over the time period relevant to this particular data set (about 2 years). The practical appeal of this approximation is that the first term cancels in calculating the conditional probability, simplifying matters greatly. There remains the issue of an infinite sum in the denominator of the conditional probability (corresponding to the integral in Equation 5.9); Nickell assumes that the inflow into unemployment is a constant at 100 or more weeks before the survey.

Nickell fits the model using data for a sample of 426 unemployed males in the United Kingdom drawn from the 1972 General Household Survey. The unemployment duration measure directly available from the survey is categorical (1–4, 4–13, 13–26, 26–52, and more than 52 weeks), but information on weeks worked allows calculation of a less coarse measure for spells of length less than a year. The regressors include occupation-specific local vacancy rates, age, marital status, a family needs variable (defined as $1 + 0.6 \times$ wife $+ 0.4 \times$ other dependents, approximately equal to the Supplementary Benefit scale), and a benefit replacement ratio calculated using program parameters and available income information. The results for this initial specification suggest that the replacement ratio has a large negative effect on the hazard; the implied elasticity for mean duration is 1.0. They also provide evidence of negative duration dependence.

Nickell goes beyond this basic specification in a couple of directions. He first allows the effect of the replacement ratio on the hazard to change with spell duration (i.e., duration dependence in the coefficient for the replacement ratio), with the date of the change determined by the data. On the basis of a likelihood ratio test, his results allow the constant effect of the replacement ratio to be rejected. Specifically, over the first 20 weeks of a spell, there is evidence of a large negative benefit effect on the hazard (elasticity 0.84), but virtually none for spells of greater length. Moreover, the coefficients in the duration dependence function no longer differ significantly from zero. Nickell examines the sensitivity of his findings to unmeasured heterogeneity using a two-point distribution for the intercept term, that is, he assumes that there are two types of individuals in the population. Both coefficient estimates and standard errors increase in absolute value, but the changes are small and there are no qualitative changes in their implications. In particular, time variation in the benefit effect is preserved; the implied replacement ratio elasticity for mean durations is about 0.95. Previous earnings are not included in the models for which results are reported, but Nickell notes that no income variables other than the replacement ratio had significant coefficients. The equivalence of the benefit and replacement ratio elasticities (as in Ehrenberg and Oaxaca, 1976) can thus be taken as holding (at least roughly) here. The results for other variables indicate that married workers and older workers have longer duration and that spell lengths are quite responsive to local labor market conditions.

Atkinson, Gomulka, Micklewright, and Rau (1984)

Atkinson et al. address the basic issue of sensitivity of results to specification and measurement of regressors—in response to what they perceive as the "prevailing wisdom concerning the relationship between the behavior of the unemployed and the unemployment insurance system—that higher benefits lead to longer durations" (p. 3). Their primary concern is the benefit replacement rate, but they also address measurement of labor market conditions and taxes.[19]

Atkinson et al. work with data for a sample of 1,231 men in the United Kingdom, aged 16 to 64, collected in the Family Expenditure Survey (FES) for the period 1972–1977. The FES provides unemployment spell data, measured in weeks, and a self-reported breakdown of unemployment income by benefit type. The detail of the income data and length of the sample period allow Atkinson et al. to experiment in a variety of directions (so many that keeping track of exactly what they are doing poses a difficult task).

Their basic model is the Weibull model used by Lancaster (Equation 5.6). Their duration observations are all censored and, therefore, they incorporate probabilities of entering unemployment into their likelihood specification using the same approximation as Nickell (Equation 5.9). Their basic regressor specification includes the replacement rate (or its log), the regional ratio of unemployment to vacancies, log age, and marital status. Their initial definition of the replacement rate is the ratio of unemployment income from all sources (based on application of standard rules to observed income and family characteristics and observed spell duration) to net employment income from all sources. The results for this model are not very different from those reported by others who use similar definitions (Nickell, 1979a,b, in particular). The Weibull parameter estimate is 0.49 (standard error 0.039), which implies negative duration dependence in the hazard. The coefficient for the log replacement rate is −0.577 (0.129), which translates into an estimate of 1.18 for the replacement rate elasticity for mean durations. The results also imply that married workers and younger workers have shorter durations than their counterparts and that durations increase significantly with increases in the unemployment to vacancy ratio.

Additional results are reported for models with alternative unemployment and employment income measures, partitions of the sample by spell length (less than 1 year, less than 2 years), and alternative specifications for the other regressors (e.g., entering a family needs variable). In all cases, there is evidence of negative duration dependence in the hazard, but the results for the replacement rate appear quite sensitive. The results for different sampling periods are particularly interesting. When they partition their sample according to observation before and after mid-1975—when the unemployment rate in the United Kingdom went above 5 percent—they find that the responsiveness of spell lengths to local labor market conditions was much greater in the high unemployment period, but there is no evidence that the replacement rate effect differed across periods when they fit the model for the full subsamples for each period. On the other hand, when they fit the model for samples with observed spell lengths of less than 1 year and less than 2 years, the response to the replacement rate appears to be much lower in the high unemployment period for both groups; a null hypothesis of no benefit effect cannot be rejected for the high unemployment period. Similar contrasts appear for the alternative sample and model respecifications. Overall, Atkinson et al. successfully demonstrate that a benefit effect of virtually any magnitude can be produced.

Solon (1985)

Solon uses a Weibull model to analyze the effects of taxing unemployment benefits, a policy introduced in the United States in 1979. His data consist of both survey responses and administrative records from the Continuous Wage and Benefit History (CWBH) file for the state of Georgia. Specifically, his sample consists of 6,610 workers who filed valid unemployment claims between January and June in either 1978 or 1979 (an application is considered "valid" if it is accepted and not preceded by an application that led to benefit receipt within the previous 52 weeks). Solon restricts his sample to workers who completed a survey at the time of filing for benefits, about one-third of all claimants. He notes that this low response rate could be due to employers filing claims when placing all or part of their work force on temporary layoff (which might actually be viewed as desirable). The survey data provide observations on personal characteristics and family earnings for the calendar year preceding the survey, but not whether an individual's benefits were taxed; Solon uses the available income data to determine taxation status. Weekly benefit amounts, potential duration of benefits, previous earnings, and weeks of compensated unemployment within a worker's benefit year (the 52 weeks following the date of a claim) are all available in the administrative data.[20] To account for the time between filing and receipt of benefits for workers who actually receive benefits and to account for the unemployment of those who become reemployed within the week following their filing (and thus never receive benefits), Solon adds 1 week to the number of compensated weeks and uses this as his measure of unemployment spell duration. The bias introduced by ignoring very short spells when using such administrative data is thus diminished. Duration is observed only up to maximum entitlement for 24 percent of the sample, but this is simply accounted for in the sample likelihood. A problem with the duration data that Solon cannot remedy is that total weeks compensated may be aggregated over two or more spells within a worker's benefit year.

Solon starts with the following Weibull specification for the hazard

$$\tau(x, t) = \alpha t^{\alpha-1} \exp\{-[\beta'x + \delta_1 b - \delta_2(d_t b)]\}, \qquad \alpha > 0$$

where b denotes the weekly benefit and d_t denotes a dummy variable that takes on the value of 1 for workers subject to taxation. Solon interprets the coefficient δ_1 as comparable to the benefit effect analyzed in other studies and δ_2 as a taxation effect. Since taxes were not deducted from benefit checks, he suspects that this might affect the estimate of δ_2. Specifically, he interprets δ_2 as equal to the product $\delta_1 \cdot p \cdot r$, where r denotes the rate at which benefits are taxed and $p \epsilon [0,1]$ is described as a coefficient of tax perception (i.e., if $p = 1$, then workers respond to the taxation of benefits as if their benefits were reduced by the same amount). This is essentially the same approach as that used by Rosen (1976) when estimating taxation effects on hours of labor supplied. Solon uses a flat rate approximation to the tax rate because family income is reported only in broad interval form and it is thus impossible to determine exact rates; specifically, he uses a tax rate of $r = 0.3$ taken from a study of effective tax rates in Georgia. The list of regressors is lengthy (30 regressors and a constant). It includes basic demographic characteristics (age, race, sex, marital status), occupation, high quarter and base period previous earnings, labor market status of spouse, the unemployment rate, the calendar month of the filing date, an indicator for expectations with respect to recall to one's former job, and a variety of interactions.

Solon reports an estimate for a α of 0.799 (standard error 0.01), which implies negative duration dependence. His estimate for δ_1 is 0.007 (standard error 0.001), which implies a proportionate change in expected duration of 0.0089 with a unit change in benefits. Summary statistics are not reported, but the implied elasticities at the minimum ($27) and the maximum benefit levels ($90) are 0.24 and 0.801. The estimate for the tax parameter δ_2 is 0.0016 (standard error 0.001). A null hypothesis of no taxation effect cannot be rejected at the 5 percent level on the basis of a t test, but Solon notes that a likelihood ratio test allows a null hypothesis of no effect to be rejected at the 5 percent level. This disagreement between asymptotically equivalent tests is annoying, but not uncommon. Solon also reports a summary of simulation results for the high income portion of his 1979 sample (i.e., those most likely taxed starting in 1979). The predicted effect of benefit taxation is a 1.2 week decrease in duration, on average.

Solon generalizes his model to allow for variation in benefit effects with remaining weeks of benefit entitlement. Letting E denote maximum entitlement plus 1 week (to account for the increment to observed durations), he specifies

$$\tau(x, t) = \alpha t^{\alpha-1} \exp \{-[\beta'x + \delta_1 b - \delta_2(d_t b)] + (\log E - \log t) \cdot (\phi_1 b + \phi_2(d_t b)\}$$

for $t < E$ and maintains his first specification for $t \geq E$. The estimates for δ_1, δ_2, and α are slightly smaller and have slightly larger standard errors, but their implications are unchanged. The α estimate is 0.719 (standard error 0.37), so that a constant baseline can be rejected at standard levels. The estimates for ϕ_1 and ϕ_2 are 0.001 (standard error 0.0004) and -0.0067 (standard error 0.00033), respectively. Thus, the magnitude of the benefit effect appears to decline as benefit exhaustion nears. The coefficients for remaining regressors have sensible signs. In particular, both sets of results suggest that durations increase with potential duration of benefits and they are longer among older workers and single workers. Recall expectations appear irrelevant, but this could reflect the sampling plan. Solon notes the potential effects of unmeasured heterogeneity, but he does not attempt to incorporate this into his model.

Lynch (1985)

Lynch analyzes duration data for a sample of London youth taken from the same source as the data in her earlier study—a longitudinal survey of young workers in the greater London area who left school at age 16 in summer 1979. (See Lynch [1983] in Chapter 4.) The sample analyzed here consists of 68 workers who were unemployed in April 1980, reinterviewed in November 1980, and provided responses to all relevant questions. For each worker, Lynch has information on both unemployment benefit receipt and self-reported unemployment income. Durations are measured as weeks of job search and the sampling scheme is such that elapsed duration at the first interview is observed and then either the completed spell length or employment status at the second interview. In specifying her sample likelihood, Lynch conditions on the first observed spell length, as in Equations 5.10 and 5.11. Accepted weekly wages are observed for workers employed at the November interview and Lynch uses the parameters of the tax system, worker characteristics, and the results from a log earnings regression fit for these data to calculate predicted mean weekly offer wages, net of taxes. Lynch notes potential problems of selection bias with these fitted wages because not all workers are reemployed. Another potential problem is that the observed wages are draws from the accepted wage distribution, as opposed to the full offer distribution.

Results for three Weibull proportional hazards models (Equation 5.6) are reported. The first includes a constant, race, educational qualifications (a dummy variable to indicate that exams were taken), sex, the log weekly benefit amount, and the predicted log wage. The signs of the coefficient estimates accord with expectations, but the standard errors are large, perhaps reflecting the small sample size; only the education qualification coefficient differs significantly from zero at the 5 percent level. The Weibull parameter estimate is 0.23 (standard error 0.25), which is significantly less than 1 and thus implies negative duration dependence. Qualitatively, these results are not affected when the replacement ratio is substituted for the log earnings and log benefit variables. The Weibull parameter estimate is slightly larger, 0.37 (standard error 0.21), but the finding of negative duration dependence remains intact. When the length of the previous spell is added to this second specification (to test for lagged duration dependence), the estimated coefficient is negative but small and insignificant and the remaining results are almost identical to the previous results, both quantitatively and qualitatively. In particular, the Weibull parameter is 0.38 (standard error 0.21), so that the finding of negative duration dependence again remains intact. Lynch also notes that estimates for a model with a gamma mixing distribution are also quite close to the above and that the variance estimate for the disturbance is close to zero.

None of the results provides evidence of a significant benefit effect on youth reemployment probabilities, but there are some potential problems in interpreting this finding. First, the unemployment income data are based on reported amounts. Thus, reporting money from parents and other sources is essentially random across individuals and it is quite possible that this reporting variation is what the unemployment income coefficient is picking up. No attempt is made to separate unemployment benefit income from other sources, but it is not clear that this would yield substantially different results because of the structure of the U.K. unemployment benefit program in the sample period. Lynch notes that only a minority of the 46 workers who were registered as unemployed were eligible for the regular weekly unemployment benefits; the rest received only a supplemental benefit, either because they failed to meet contribution requirements or because they quit their previous job. In addition to these measurement problems, the results for the replacement ratio in the second and third specifications might also reflect the use of the predicted wage in the denominator of the replacement ratio. The bottom line, however, is that Lynch finds no evidence of a significant benefit effect on the behavior of London youth.

Podgursky and Swaim (1987)

Podgursky and Swaim use a Weibull model to analyze the experience of U.S. workers following displacement. Their data are for a sample of 2,270 workers collected in the January 1984 Current Population Survey, which included a supplemental Displaced Worker Survey. Specifically, the supplement was administered to all individuals in the CPS sample aged 20 or more, who reportedly lost a job between 1979 and the interview date due to either a plant closing, an employer going out of business, a layoff from which the worker had not been recalled, or similar reasons. Podgursky and Swaim restrict their sample to workers aged 20–61 who were displaced prior to 1982, formerly employed as full-time wage and salary workers in nonagricultural jobs, and reported their reason for displacement was either a plant shutdown, employer relocation, a business failure, or job elimination (i.e., seasonal job separations, quits, separations for cause, and self-employed business failures are excluded).

The data are attractive because the CPS is a representative sample of the United States and extensive information on current and past labor force activity and earnings are available. The duration data, however, are problematic. Interviewers were told to determine the number of weeks a worker was without work but available for work between the time of displacement and the interview date. This would appear to differ from the normal definition of unemployment only in terms of the active job search requirement. However, differences between displacement and other separations were not clearly defined; in particular, the concept of a "temporary" job was not established prior to the survey. Interviewers and workers were left on their own to distinguish separations from temporary jobs and separations from jobs that could be categorized as a "displacement." The durations measured here are (roughly) net of such temporary employment spells. Thus, they may include multiple spells of joblessness, which in turn may include multiple spells of labor force withdrawal. Neither the number of spells nor the timing of spells is reported.[21] Podgursky and Swaim fit a Weibull hazard model (Equation 5.6) separately for subsamples of 1,044 blue-collar males, 372 blue-collar females, 430 white-collar males and 424 white-collar females. Not all of the workers in these samples experienced a spell of joblessness; in fitting the model, Podgursky and Swaim include those who did not and add 1 week to all observed spell lengths.[22] The explanatory variables are age, education, log previous usual weekly earnings (adjusted for trend growth), previous tenure, the percentage unionized in the industry of the previous job, the local unemployment rate at the time of displacement, and dummy variables for race, household headship, previous occupation, eligibility for unemployment insurance benefits, advance notice of displacement, displacement due to a plant shutdown, and year of displacement.

Given the problems with the duration data, the results are not easily interpreted, but some interesting patterns do appear. The Weibull parameter is significantly less than 1—and almost identical across groups (blue-collar males 0.754 [standard error 0.025], blue-collar females 0.753 [standard error 0.051], white-collar males 0.757 [standard error 0.038], and white-collar females 0.712 [standard error 0.041]). The results for the demographic variables are fairly consistent with expectations. White workers, male household heads, and workers with more education experience less joblessness. Male blue-collar workers in noncraft jobs and in heavily unionized industries experience significantly more joblessness. The coefficients for the previous wage and advance notice coefficients are insignificant for all groups except white-collar females; for the latter group, advance notice and higher wages are both associated with less joblessness. Age and unemployment insurance eligibility have a significant positive effect on the amount of joblessness experienced by blue-collar males, but no significant effect on other groups. The strongest results appear for the local unemployment rate and the plant shutdown variable. Higher unemployment rates are associated with significantly larger amounts of time without work for all workers, although the magnitude of the effect is much greater for females and blue-collar workers, relative to their counterparts. On the other hand, the amount of joblessness following a plant shutdown is significantly less than the amount following a layoff from a firm that remains in operation. This last finding is certainly interesting and might be kept in mind when we discuss the multistate studies of temporary versus permanent layoffs in Chapter 6.

Narendranathan, Nickell, and Stern (1985)

Narendranathan et al. work with alternative specifications of the Weibull model (Equation 5.6). Their objective is to address the issues raised by Atkinson et al. (1984) and Atkinson and Micklewright (1985), as well as other issues related to the sensitivity of estimated benefit effects to model specification.

Their data include both survey responses and administrative records for a sample of 1474 workers in the United Kingdom collected in the Department of Health and Social Security (DHSS) Cohort Study of the Unemployed, a panel survey that began in 1978. The administrative records provide detailed benefit and duration data. The available duration measure is the number of days in the first registered unemployment spell within a worker's benefit year. However, because benefit data for the first 4 weeks are missing for some proportion of the complete data set, Narendranathan et al. restrict their sample to those workers who experienced spells of at least 4 weeks. Age, marital status, ethnic group, housing tenure, education, training, health status, union membership, labor market history variables, the local unemployment rate, log weekly unemployment income, and an instrument for log weekly employment income from all sources comprise their basic list of regressors. Their instrument for employment income is based on results for a log earnings regression fit by skill group using data on previous earnings, age, and education.

The estimate for the Weibull parameter α in this model is 0.99 (standard error 0.254). The coefficient estimate for log unemployment income is -0.41 (standard error 0.032); together with the α estimate and the average share of benefits in unemployment income for their sample, the implied benefit elasticity for mean duration is 0.28. A small but statistically significant negative effect is reported for the unemployment rate and a large positive effect is reported for log income in employment. Remaining results are not reported but they are described as sensible.

Narendranathan et al. fit a wide array of variations of this basic model. Experimentation with alternative income measures for employment and unemployment yields some interesting results. The benefit elasticity is somewhat higher when only benefits are included, 0.33. The mean offer income elasticity, on the other hand, appears quite sensitive to the measure used; the range includes both positive and negative estimates. When they allow the benefit effect to vary with both age and duration, using an interaction term for the former and a linear spline for the latter, the results indicate that the benefit effect is smaller for older workers and that it declines with duration through the first 6 months. Thereafter, benefits appear irrelevant for all age groups but teens. The estimate for the Weibull parameter α in this model is 1.08 (standard error 0.043), which provides weak evidence of positive duration dependence. For workers with spells of 6 months or less, the implied benefit elasticities range from 0.65 for teens to 0.08 for older workers and the sample average is 0.28—precisely the same number reported for their basic specification. Qualitatively, the results for the coefficients for the local unemployment rate and log employed income are also unchanged. They also fit a model that allows for monotonic variation in the mean of the offer distribution, with the rate of change in the mean depending on a worker's skill group. The motivation for this is the notion that workers may search in "lower segments" of the labor market as their spells continue (i.e., a systematic search story). Letting w_0 denote the mean at the start of a spell and letting k index skill group, the mean offer wage at duration t is defined as

$$w(t) = w_1 t^{\delta_k - 1}$$

for a worker in skill group k so that the hazard can be written as

$$\tau(x_i, t) = \exp(x_i'\beta)\alpha t^{\alpha - 1 + \Sigma D_k \delta_k}$$

where D_k is a dummy variable that takes on a value of 1 if the worker is a member of skill group k and zero otherwise. Since the parameter α is not separately identified, $\alpha + \delta_k$ for the semiskilled and unskilled group is used as a baseline. Negative values for δ_k for the remaining groups are interpreted as evidence that the mean offers decline at a faster rate, for example, but note that this result might reflect a sharper decline in arrival rates or some other variable. They also allow the benefit effect to vary across skill groups. Overall, their results provide little evidence of variation in either δ_k or the benefit elasticity across skill groups; all elasticities are quite close to their previous estimates.

Simpler modifications of the basic model are also fit—incorporating tax rebates and allowing for variation in the effect of benefit levels across groups of workers having high versus low replacement rates. In the latter there is no significant evidence of a relationship between the benefit effect and the level of the replacement ratio. The results for the Weibull parameter, benefit elasticities, and other regressor coefficients in all of these alternative models differ only slightly from the results for the basic model. This also holds true when they incorporate unobserved heterogeneity into their model using a gamma mixing distribution. The benefit elasticity is 0.36, which is fairly close to their other estimates. However, corresponding to this estimate is an estimate of 2.09 for α (standard error 0.141), which the authors regard as "absurdly high." The estimate for the variance of the heterogeneity component v is 0.97 (standard error 0.104).

Moffitt (1985)

Moffitt takes a nonparametric approach to fitting the baseline hazard in his study of the effects of potential duration of unemployment insurance benefits and weekly benefit amounts on durations. His sample consists of 4,628 male benefit recipients in the United States selected from the Continuous Wage and Benefit History file (CWBH) for 13 states. The data in the CWBH are collected by state unemployment insurance offices under the supervision of the Department of Labor. Each month, a random sample of all new recipients is selected in each participating state and, each quarter, the administrative records for these new recipients and workers in previous samples are added to the existing file. Data collection for the file analyzed here (March 31, 1983) began at different times in different states between 1978 and 1980.

Durations are measured as weeks of compensated unemployment. Consequently, these data do not allow analysis of behavior before receipt or after exhaustion. More important, the spell durations available for some workers in the sample are aggregated over two or more spells. The sample is restricted to workers with gaps in recipiency that total 10 weeks or less, but it is not clear what proportion of all workers this represents or what the distribution of gaps looks like. Returns to former employers and entrance into new jobs are not distinguished; both permanent layoffs and temporary layoffs are thus included. The positive feature of these data is the availability of accurate information on benefit levels, potential duration of benefits (including changes in potential duration when extended benefits become available), the number of weeks of actual benefit receipt, and previous earnings. Basic demographic information is also available. Only a few observations last beyond 39 weeks and Moffitt treats these as censored at 39 weeks. Together with observations censored at the file date, about one-fourth of the sample is censored. Moffitt's total sample consists of two subsamples of roughly equal size. The first is a sample of workers who experienced a change in the potential duration of benefits beteen 26 and 39 weeks into their spells and he labels this the varying-duration sample. The second sample is drawn from the subsample of the CWBH that did not face extensions. He refers to this as the constant-duration sample. Throughout his analysis, Moffitt uses sampling weights.

Moffitt starts by calculating Kaplan–Meier estimates for the empirical hazard for the constant-duration sample and subgroups.[23] After a slight decline in the first 8 or so weeks, the hazard for the combined sample rises gradually through week 24. Thereafter, there are two significant spikes at 25 and 37 weeks.[24] When the sample is partitioned according to potential durations of less than and more than 26 weeks, there is little difference in the hazards over the first 20 weeks. Around 26 weeks, however, the hazard for those with longer benefit durations remains roughly constant (while those with 26 weeks of eligibility or less exit, or course). Hazards based on a partition by benefit level above and below the sample mean benefit level are also displayed. The hazard for the high benefit group lies below the low benefit hazard at 26 weeks, but this may simply reflect generosity across states, that is, a correlation between benefit levels and maximum duration of benefits, as opposed to a benefit level effect.

Moffitt's second round of preliminary analysis consists of regressions using the Kaplan–Meier Survivor estimates from the first round of analysis. He first fits a regression of $\ln(S_t)$ on t (without an intercept), which yields an estimate 0.7 (standard error 0.001) for the average hazard in the full sample. If the true distribution is exponential, the R^2 for this model should be 1.0 and his result is quite close (0.994). A regression of $\ln(-\ln(S_t))$ on $\ln(t)$ yields a coefficient estimate that represents the duration dependence parameter of a Weibull model and the result for the full sample is 0.986 (standard error 0.023) here—suggesting again that there is no duration dependence. Regression results for the benefit level and potential duration sample partitions are generally consistent with the hazards results. The first set of regressions produces expected differences in the average hazards and the results for the second set indicate positive duration dependence in the hazard for the low benefit group and negative duration dependence, otherwise.

Most of the energy in this study is devoted to estimation of a nonparametric proportional hazards model—the objective being to determine whether controlling for differences in potential duration produces an otherwise smooth hazard. The hazard function for individual i at week t is

$$\tau(t; x_i(t)) = \lambda_0(t) \exp(x_i(t)'\beta)$$

with the baseline hazard defined as a step function. Estimates of both the parameters β and the baseline hazard parameters (38, given the maximum observation period in the sample) are obtained using the method of maximum likelihood.

Results for a variety of specifications are reported. When the model is fit for the constant-duration sample with the benefit level and potential duration as the only regressors, both variables appear irrelevant. When age, race, education, the previous net wage, and the state unemployment rate (at the start of the spell) are added, the potential duration coefficient remains small and insignificant, while the benefit coefficient is negative and significant and the wage coefficient is positive and significant. Results for the remaining variables pose some contrasts to the findings of others. White workers are found to have significantly higher hazards, but although the age and unemployment rate coefficients are negative, as expected, they are not significantly different from zero at standard levels. The education coefficient is also negative (i.e., the opposite of what one expects), but insignificant at standard levels. Moffitt does not report the baseline parameter estimates for either specification, but notes that the bimodal distribution found in the preliminary analysis remains intact, that is, the regressors do not shift the entire distribution proportionately.

Moffitt next allows both the unemployment rate and potential duration to vary with duration and he fits the model using his combined sample. These results are somewhat different. The negative benefit level effect is maintained, but the potential duration variable has a significant, positive coefficient. The baseline results are not reported, but the bimodal distribution is again said to remain intact. Since the potential duration variable can pick up only a proportional shift, Moffitt reports that he attempted to pick up the spikes more directly by adding a time-until-exhaustion variable (i.e., potential duration at week t minus t). Simple search models with time-varying benefits predict a negative sign for this variable (e.g., Mortensen, 1977), but Moffitt reports that the coefficient in his model is positive and significant. The initial decline in the empirical hazard (perhaps due to recalls of workers on temporary layoff) appears to dominate the time-until-exhaustion effect. In view of these results, Moffit approximates the potential nonlinearity in the hazard using a time-until-exhaustion linear spline for 0–5, 6–10, and more than 10 weeks.[25] As expected, the data support this approximate quadratic specification; after the first 5 weeks of eligibility, the hazard declines with increases in the remaining weeks of benefits. The coefficient for potential duration is also negative and significant in this model; Moffitt suggests that this may reflect a wealth effect. Of course, the bottom line is the effect of these respecifications on the baseline results. Moffit reports that the spikes are diminished only slightly. In both sets of results for the combined sample, the results for the benefit level, the previous wage, and race are essentially the same as those described above for the constant-duration sample. The coefficients for education and the unemployment rate are also negative, as before, and significant in these models. It is not clear what produces the education result in this sample. For comparison, Moffit also fits an exponential model with the regressor specification of his third specification. All results (including the time-until-exhaustion spline) are nearly identical, that is, they are not sensitive to the baseline hazard specification.

The benefit elasticity implied by the nonparametric results is 0.36 at the sample mean, implying that a 10 percent increase in the weekly benefit level would increase mean spell duration by about one-half week. The elasticity for increases in the potential duration of benefits is 0.16 when measured at 26 weeks, implying that an increase in potential duration of 1 week would lengthen a spell by about a day. The unemployment rate elasticity is 0.12, which seems quite low; at the sample means, a one point percentage increase implies about a 1.4 day increase in mean duration. Given that extensions of benefits are tied closely to local unemployment rates, Moffit fits the exponential model with an interaction of the two included. The coefficient for the interaction is positive and significant, the coefficient for the unemployment rate more than quadruples, and the potential duration coefficient more than doubles. In sum, the disincentive effect of extending benefits is offset substantially by higher unemployment rates. For example, starting with unemployment at 6 percent and potential duration at 26 weeks, the net disincentive effect of a 3.2 week extension of potential benefit receipt would be zero if a one point increase in the unemployment rate occurred simultaneously.

Meyer (1988b)

Meyer also studies the effects of the level of unemployment insurance benefits and duration of eligibility on compensated unemployment, using a semiparametric econometric approach. His data are for a sample of 3,365 male benefit recipients in 12 states taken from the Continuous Wage and Benefit History sample studied by Moffitt (1985). Consequently, durations may be aggregated over multiple spells. The smaller sample size is due primarily to missing demographic data, although Meyer also notes that 36 observations were omitted due to negative values for time until exhaustion of benefits. Meyer notes that about 45 percent of his sample is taken from states and time periods that are not likely to have had changing benefit lengths (i.e., Moffit's constant-duration sample); for all but a check on his results, he uses the unweighted combined sample.

Meyer starts by fitting an empirical hazard using the Kaplan–Meier estimator. The pattern for his subsample is roughly similar to the pattern reported by Moffitt using the larger sample and the sampling weights. The hazard declines sharply in the first few weeks of a spell and then rises gradually through week 24. At 25 weeks, it rises sharply and remains high for about 4 weeks. It then declines and then jumps again sharply at 32, 35–36, and 38 weeks.[26] Meyer also calculates a remaining duration of benefits empirical hazard using an estimator similar to the Kaplan–Meier; it differs in that time is measured as time until benefit exhaustion (as opposed to time since a spell began). In the present application, benefit durations also vary across individuals at the start of their spells and then change for many individuals over the course of their spells; in calculating the hazard, some individuals are therefore counted more than once in some risk sets. Together with the aggregation of spells, this makes interpretation of the results somewhat difficult. Nevertheless, the results appear roughly consistent with the basic empirical hazard (i.e., as exhaustion nears, the hazard rises sharply) and they also provide some useful information. Specifically, spikes appear in this hazard around 13 weeks, at 24–25 weeks, and 37–38 weeks until exhaustion. Meyer suggests that these spikes may reflect employers' timing of recalls or workers' strategically planned starting dates for new jobs based on initial expectations about potential duration; when extended benefits become available, such plans may not be adjusted (Mortensen, 1990b). Alternatively, the spikes may simply represent a failure to claim extended benefits. Of course, a third explanation might be the aggregation of spells for individuals in measuring durations (e.g., spells of 13 weeks and 26 weeks may be merged). Meyer also presents the frequency distributions for both the initial length of benefit eligibility (i.e., the expected length when a spell starts) and the maximum eligibility period faced over the course of a spell. Each exhibits substantial variation, due to both variation in program parameters across states, extensions in some states during periods of high unemployment, and differences across individuals within states due to differences in work histories. There are also substantial differences across the distributions due to variation over time, both within and across states.

Meyer proceeds with a more formal analysis of his duration data. His approach to specifying the distribution of unemployment spell durations differs from the methods employed in the studies previously discussed. Specifically, Meyer works in a continuous time framework and uses a proportional hazards model, $\tau_i(t) = \lambda_0(t) \exp(x_i(t)'\beta)$, with the baseline hazard defined by

$$\alpha(t) = \ln \int_t^{t+1} \lambda_0(u) \, du \qquad (5.19)$$

where the $\alpha(t)$ are parameters that are estimated along with β using the method of maximum likelihood. Meyer refers to this method as *semiparametric.*[27] Following Moffitt, Meyer allows for variation over the first 39 weeks and treats longer spells as censored at this length (2.4 percent of his sample). Thus, there are 38 values estimated for α.

Meyer uses a variety of specifications for the explanatory variables. Following Moffitt (1985), he uses a spline in the time until actual benefit exhaustion to measure the effect of variation in the potential duration of benefits. Specifically, he allows different marginal effects when there are 1, 2–5, 6–10, 11–25, 26–40, and 41–54 weeks left.[28] Log weekly benefits and log previous weekly earnings net of taxes, the state unemployment rate at the start of a spell, categorical age group variables (17–24, 25–34, 35–44, 45–54), race, marital status, years of schooling, and number of dependents are also included in his basic specification. The estimated coefficient for the benefit level is large and negative and implies a benefit elasticity of 0.88 for the hazard at the sample mean. This translates into a 1.5 week increase in the length of a spell with a 10 percent increase in the replacement ratio. Meyer notes that this is on the high side of estimated replacement ratio effects and suggests the difference may be due to more accurate benefit and wage data. An alternative explanation may be aggregation over spells in measuring durations. The results also indicate that the hazard declines with increases in previous net earnings, age, and the state unemployment rate. The hazard rate is significantly higher for white workers and for married workers and it appears to be inversely related to years of schooling and the number of dependents.

Of particular interest are the results for the time-until-exhaustion spline. Overall, they provide some evidence of systematic variation in the hazard with remaining duration of benefits. After an initial decline, there is little change in the hazard over most of the period of eligibility. When there are 6 weeks left, however, the hazard increases, it continues to rise as exhaustion nears, and it jumps dramatically when there is 1 week left. Over the entire 6 weeks preceding exhaustion, the hazard roughly triples.[29] These findings are consistent with the spikes in the empirical hazard at the times of actual exhaustion of benefits, but the baseline hazard parameter estimates continue to indicate major spikes at 26, 28, 32, and 36 weeks. These correspond to the spikes in the time-until-exhaustion empirical hazard and may thus reflect unanticipated changes in benefit duration. Meyer investigates this possibility by adding a dummy variable that takes on a value of 1 in week t if benefits were scheduled to lapse that week, and zero otherwise. The point estimate for this scheduled lapse effect is large and positive; it implies a jump of over 400 percent in the hazard in scheduled lapse weeks. The spikes in the baseline parameter estimates at 26 and 36 weeks are also eliminated, although the spikes at 28 and 32 weeks are only slightly diminished. The results for benefit levels and remaining variables are essentially unchanged.

When dummy variables for state of residence are added to capture unmeasured heterogeneity that might influence wage and benefit levels, the time-until-exhaustion spline and scheduled lapse results are unaffected, but some other major changes appear. The benefit effect remains negative and significant, but it is reduced by about one-third. The coefficient for the number of dependents becomes insignificant. Most striking, the effect of an increase in the state unemployment rate changes from small and negative to positive and significant. Meyer suggests that the state fixed effects might be measuring variation in unemployment rates across states, while the state unemployment rates measure variation over time. The positive unemployment rate coeficient may thus indicate that spells tend to be shorter in periods of high unemployment (perhaps due to temporary layoffs), while workers in high unemployment states tend to have longer spells. (Note, however, that the longer durations appearing here may be the sum of multiple short spells.)

Meyer also reports results for two specifications with unobserved heterogeneity modeled as a multiplicative disturbance with a unit mean gamma distribution. With the scheduled lapse variables included, the heterogeneity variance estimate is 0.7901 (standard error 0.1953). Without these dummies, it is 0.756 (standard error 0.1943). All coefficient estimates tend to be slightly less negative when heterogeneity is incorporated, but only the benefit level effect changes appreciably. The estimate remains negative and significant, but its absolute value is reduced by about 25 percent. The baseline hazard estimates also change. Specifically, some evidence of positive duration dependence appears.

For comparison, Meyer reports results for Weibull models with and without the scheduled benefit lapse and state dummy variables. Overall, the coefficient estimates for the Weibull model are remarkably close to the corresponding semiparametric results. As for the fit of the Weibull model, the results from a likelihood ratio test allow rejection of the Weibull baseline hazard at standard levels when the time-until-exhaustion spline is omitted. However, in the more complete specification, the Weibull cannot be rejected at the 10 percent level. Estimates for the Weibull parameters are not reported, nor are their implications described.

Finally, Meyer reports results for his stochastic specification fit separately for the constant potential duration group, which he refers to as the nonrandom sample, and the remainder, which he refers to as his random sample. The results for the random sample are generally consistent with those reported for the full sample, except that the estimated benefit level effect is slightly smaller. The results for the sample in which potential benefit durations are not likely to have changed are similar, except for the time-until-exhaustion spline and the effect of the previous wage. These results imply that the hazard decreases significantly as time-until-exhaustion decreases from 40 to 12 weeks and that it remains roughly constant thereafter, that is, there is no significant increase just before exhaustion. (The 41–54 week part of the spline is omitted here.) The coefficient estimate for the log previous wage remains positive and significant, as before, but it is about half the size. For both subsamples, the estimated heterogeneity variance is negligible. Results for the baseline hazard are not reported.

Katz and Meyer (1988a)

Katz and Meyer estimate extensions of the models fit by Meyer (1988b) using the same CWBH data. They then use their results to simulate the effects of changes in both benefit levels and periods of benefit eligibility. Precisely, Katz and Meyer model the hazard as in Equation 5.19. Their basic specification for the explanatory variables is the same as Meyer's nonstochastic model with state dummy variables, except that the benefit and income variables are not measured in logs. Their second specification also includes potential duration of benefits (which they allow to change over the course of spell in the event that benefits are extended), interactions of the level of benefits with the age 17–24 dummy variable, and an interaction of the level of benefits with a dummy variable for 3 or fewer weeks until benefit exhaustion. The last component of the time-until-exhaustion spline for weeks 54–41 is omitted from this second model.

The results for the first specification are essentially the same as those reported by Meyer for his comparable specification, but the results for the model that controls for changes in potential duration present a slightly different picture. The jump in the hazard at 1 week before exhaustion is roughly the same across models, but the rise in the preceding 5 weeks disappears and a significant decrease appears as remaining benefit duration decreases from 26 to 12 weeks. The scheduled lapse effect is essentially unchanged (i.e., it is large and positive). The effect of the actual potential duration of benefits is negative, but not significantly different from zero at standard levels. The coefficient for the benefit level near exhaustion interaction is positive, but not significant at standard levels, that is, there is no evidence of a dramatic change in the benefit effect near the end of eligibility. The coefficient for the interaction of benefit levels and age 17–24 is large and negative—suggesting that the response of young workers to changes in benefit levels is relatively elastic. The results for the baseline hazard are not reported in this paper, nor are the results for the demographic control variables other than age. Presumably these are similar to those reported by Meyer.

Katz and Meyer note that it is difficult to translate predicted changes in the hazard into statements about mean spell lengths because of the nonlinearity of their model. They therefore use their results to simulate the effects of changes in benefit levels and potential durations on mean weeks of unemployment and mean weeks of compensated unemployment. Results are reported for simulations based on both sets of results described, with the maximum spell length weeks T set equal to 104 and the baseline hazard set equal to the sample average value for values of t beyond exhaustion. As Katz and Meyer note, all behavior after exhaustion is speculative. The base value for potential benefit duration D is 39 weeks. The key difference between the two sets of simulations is that responses to changes in D over the course of a spell are incorporated into the baseline hazard in the simulations based on the first specification results, but not in the second. In the latter, responses to changes in D are captured by the coefficient for D in the regressor function (i.e., the shift component).

Both sets of simulation results suggest that potential duration of unemployment insurance benefits has a strong impact on recipients' spell durations. Specifically, the results from their preferred second specification suggest that reducing potential duration from 39 to 26 weeks reduces mean compensated spell lengths by 16 percent, roughly the same reduction brought about by a 20 percent reduction in the level of benefits. The predicted changes in completed unemployment spell lengths are comparable, since average behavior is specified. On the other hand, the predicted changes in total benefit payments are quite different. The 13 week change in the period of eligibility reduces total receipts by 16 percent, while the reduced benefit level reduces total receipts by almost one-third (31.3 percent). The results for the first specification simulations are not very different. According to these results, the potential duration reduction produces a 20 percent reduction in weeks compensated and a 19 percent reduction in total benefit payments. The 20 percent benefit level reduction produces an 18 percent reduction in compensated spell lengths and a 31 percent decrease in total benefit payments.

Dynarski and Sheffrin (1987)

Dynarski and Sheffrin work with data for a sample of male and female household heads collected in the 1981 and 1982 interviews of the Panel Study of Income Dynamics (PSID).[30] Starting in 1981, the PSID asked household heads a supplemental set of retrospective questions about their labor market activity in the previous calendar year. Dynarski and Sheffrin are primarily interested in variation in unemployment spell lengths with variation in the unemployment rate. Consequently, a very attractive feature of these data is that they provide information not only on weeks unemployed (defined as time spent "unemployed or temporarily laid off"), but also on the calendar month and year in which each spell started. One shortcoming of the PSID is that only receipt of unemployment insurance benefits is observed; benefit levels are not. Overall, 1,278 household heads experienced at least one unemployment spell in the 1980–1981 period that they analyze. Treating spells as independent observations, their sample consists of 1,660 spells that began between January 1980 and December 1981 and either ended in 1981 or remained in progress at the April 1982 interview.

Since their primary interest is the effect of variation in the unemployment rate on reemployment and hypotheses concerning the baseline hazard are of secondary importance, Dynarski and Sheffrin use a partial-likelihood approach to estimate the hazard. Their specification includes both constant and time-varying regressors. The constant variables are age, race, sex, and dummy variables for the presence of a working spouse, coverage by unemployment insurance, industry, occupation, and the starting month of the spell. The unemployment rate is entered as time-varying by assigning the U.S. monthly unemployment rate to each month in a worker's spell.

White workers are found to have significantly higher hazards and unemployment benefit recipients have significantly lower hazards. Construction and manufacturing workers have significantly higher hazards than service workers, which might be expected given the seasonality of work in construction and generally higher incidence of temporary layoffs in manufacturing. In contrast to most results reported elsewhere, the hazard increases significantly with age, while sex, education, and occupation appear irrelevant. Employment status of the spouse also appears irrelevant, in contrast to the added-worker hypothesis. This result may simply reflect the time of measurement for this variable; changes in status may have occurred between the spell and the interview date when this variable appears to be measured. The unemployment rate is the variable of primary interest to Dynarski and Sheffrin. The coefficient is positive and significant, which they interpret as a temporary layoff effect, that is, the 1980–1981 period was one of rising unemployment and this result suggests an increased use of temporary layoffs of brief duration. For comparison, Dynarski and Sheffrin also present results with the unemployment rate fixed at its starting month level. The coefficient estimate here is positive, significant, and much larger. They note that part of the difference may be due to the positive time trend in the unemployment rate over the sample period. Substituting the index of industrial production for the unemployment rate produces essentially the same results. A plot of the coefficients for the starting month dummy variables is also provided. This suggests that the hazard is affected substantially by unmeasured cyclical factors proxied by the unemployment cohort variables.

Dynarski and Sheffrin do not report results for the baseline hazard recovered from these results, but note that the hazard exhibits slight positive duration dependence. For comparison, they also present results for exponential and Weibull models (Equation

5.6), with the unemployment rate fixed at its starting month level. The results for the explanatory variables are essentially the same as the partial-likelihood results for the fixed unemployment rate specification. The Weibull parameter is 1.079 (standard error 0.017), implying significant positive duration dependence, as in their nonparametric specification.

Steinberg and Montforte (1987)

Steinberg and Montforte use nonparametric, semiparametric, and fully parametric hazard function models to study the unemployment durations of displaced workers. Their data were generated by the first of a series of job search assistance and training experiments conducted by the U.S. Department of Labor—the Downriver Community Conference Economic Readjustment Activity (DCC) launched in July 1980 in Wayne County, Michigan. The DCC focused on the experience of workers at four auto industry-related plants that closed completely in June or July 1980 with two plants designated as controls and two as experimental. All workers on the layoff rosters at the latter were notified that they were eligible for program participation and approximately half participated. The program itself consisted of three parts: a 4-hour testing session, a 4-day jobseeking skills workshop, and training. Participation in the training component of the program was not mandatory for recipients of the job search assistance, so only about 56 percent of all participants received some form of training (high-technology in-class, other program-specific classroom, existing local programs, or on-the-job). The particular type depended on interests and test results. Retrospective interviews were held in the spring of 1982 with random samples of 509 workers laid off from the experimental plants and 493 workers from the control plants. Workers were asked about their labor market activity, income, assets, and demographic characteristics for the entire period following January 1, 1979. Unemployment durations are measured in weeks, but it is not clear whether or not spells following displacement are aggregated in the present analysis. Additional information from DCC administrative records is also available.

Steinberg and Montforte start their analyses by calculating the Kaplan—Meier estimates of the survivor functions separately for white and black workers at each plant. These results suggest that black workers fared worse than white workers following the plant shutdowns—and substantially worse at all but one plant (BASF, one of the experimentals). As for differences between experimental versus control plants, nonwhite workers laid off by the control plants appear to have left unemployment much more slowly. Among white workers, the survivor functions for all but the BASF plant are nearly identical. One explanation for the outlier behavior of BASF plant workers might be the lower average replacement ratio faced by the BASF workers—0.38 versus 0.94 for control workers and 0.55 for experimental workers (including BASF). In large part, the differences in replacement rates across plants reflected receipt of supplemental unemployment benefits (SUB); while 58.1 percent of all controls and 58.7 percent of all experimentals received SUB income, only 3.4 percent of the BASF experimentals received these benefits. Steinberg and Montforte also note that black workers faced higher replacement rates at all but one of the control plants.

More formal techniques are used next to examine this replacement rate explanation further and to evaluate program effects on durations. Steinberg and Montforte start by fitting Weibull, lognormal, and log logistic models. In all cases, the regressors are race, marital status, education, occupation dummy variables (operator, professional, and crafts versus other), log of years tenure at the layoff job, log general work experience, maximum potential weeks of benefits, the replacement ratio (total weekly benefits to layoff job-net weekly earnings), and the Detroit SMSA (monthly) unemployment rate at the time of layoff.

Two self-selection processes complicate the evaluation of program effects—the initial decision to participate in the program and the decision to receive training. Steinberg and Montforte choose not to model these decision processes explicitly. Instead, they include a set of dummy variables that yields estimates of interplant differences. Then, to obtain an estimate of the program effect, they simply divide the eligible plant dummy coefficients by the plant participation rate.[31]

The Weibull parameter estimate (baseline $\alpha t^{\alpha-1}$) is 0.912 (standard error 0.031), the log logistic parameter estimate is 0.705 (standard error 0.031), and the lognormal parameter estimate is 1.298 (standard error 0.050). These all suggest negative duration dependence—at least over a large part of a spell. The major difference in results across models is in the implied weights in the right tail of the baseline distribution. The differences in predicted mean durations are substantial: 101, 102, and 145 weeks for the lognormal, log logistic, and Weibull models.[32] The regressor coefficients have essentially the same implications across models. Perhaps most interesting are the results for replacement ratio. In all cases, it appears statistically irrelevant after controlling for the layoff plant. The same holds for the potential period of eligibility. The results for remaining variables are qualitatively similar to the findings reported by others. Black workers appear to have had spells that lasted roughly twice as long as the spells of white workers, while married workers had shorter spells than single workers. Workers that held positions in any skilled occupation and workers with more education also had shorter spells than their counterparts. Durations appear to have been significantly longer among workers with greater tenure. Given tenure, however, general labor market experience appears irrelevant at all standard levels of significance. The results for the unemployment rate imply a weak, negative relationship with spell lengths, but this may simply reflect measurement at the time of layoff.

The results for the interplant differences exhibit some variation across models, but overall they suggest that workers at the experimental plants experienced somewhat shorter spells than their counterparts at the control plants. However, the findings also suggest that experiences between control plants and between experimental plants were not similar. The outlier behavior of the BASF workers found in the Kaplan–Meier estimates remains in place after controlling for observed heterogeneity.

Steinberg and Montforte check their results in two ways. They first investigate the sensitivity of their regressors results to specification of the baseline by fitting a proportional hazards model with no prespecified baseline using the partial likelihood approach introduced by Cox (see Chapter 3). They also fit this model with time variation in the replacement ratio and the local unemployment rate. In the fixed regressor case, the results are almost identical to the previously described findings. On the other hand, some important differences appear when time variation in the regressors is incorporated. First, the hazard decreases significantly with increases in either the local unemployment rate or the replacement ratio. The implied elasticities of mean durations with respect to the replacement rate are about 0.80 for controls and 0.46 for experimentals. The unemployment rate elasticity is about 0.5. The results for the experimental (i.e., interplant) differences are also affected. Specifically, the results for the time-varying regressor model imply larger differences between workers at controls versus experimental plants and a closer alignment of results among experimentals and among controls.

Steinberg and Montforte do not report results for models with unobserved heterogeneity incorporated explicitly. They note, however, that their results from White's Information Matrix Test are not encouraging.

Meyer (1988a)

In this paper, Meyer analyzes data generated by the Reemployment Bonus Experiment conducted by the U.S. Department of Labor in Illinois. In this experiment, randomly selected unemployment insurance recipients were invited to participate in one of two programs. In the Claimant Experiment, a participant received $500 if he or she found a job within 11 weeks of his or her filing date and then kept the job for at least 4 months. In the Employer Experiment, employers received $500 if they hired a participant within 11 weeks of the filing date and the participant remained in the job for at least 4 months. Overall, about 4,000 claimants were selected for each experiment and another 4,000 were selected to serve as controls. Participation rates differed substantially across programs—84 percent in the Claimant Experiment versus 65 percent in the Employer Experiment. Success rates for participants in obtaining the bonuses also differed—16 percent for the Claimant Experiment versus about 4 percent for the Employer Experiment participants.[33]

Meyer starts his analysis by calculating the empirical hazards for first observed spells separately for participants in each experiment and also for controls. These suggest that hazards differed both across experiments and also between participants and controls—but only during the bonus eligibility period. Meyer also fits a semiparametric hazard model to the data for workers in the control and Claimant Experiment groups. (See the description of this model under Meyer [1988b]. In addition to controls for race, sex, and age, he includes log base period earnings, the log weekly benefit level, a dummy variable for workers in the Claimant Experiment group, and an interaction of this variable with dummy variables for spells lasting 11 weeks or less and spells lasting exactly 9 or 10 weeks (the second to pick up possible spikes). These results again suggest that the experimentals had significantly higher hazards during the bonus eligibility period, but not thereafter. Also, there is no evidence of a spike just before the end of the period. The results for remaining variables are consistent with those reported elsewhere. Black claimants, older claimants, and female claimants all have significantly lower hazards than their counterparts. The hazard also decreases with increases in the benefit level and with increases in base period earnings. Meyer experiments with a variety of interactions among the regressors. Basically, these results suggest that the effects of bonus eligibility in the first 11 weeks were greater for females and for claimants with high base period earnings. Unfortunately, the data do not indicate whether bonus recipients returned to former employers or found new jobs. (Both satisfied the program requirements for obtaining the bonus.) This would be an important factor to consider before making such bonus programs a permanent feature of the unemployment insurance system. Still, the mean spell duration for experimentals appears to have been significantly shorter than that of controls (more than a week shorter), suggesting that additional analysis of such bonuses would be worthwhile.

Summary

Table 5.2 summarizes the basic findings of the studies in this section for benefit effects and duration dependence, as well as evidence on the sensitivity of these results to incorporating unobserved heterogeneity into hazard specifications explicitly. Given the differences in populations sampled, definitions used for durations, and measures used for benefits and replacement ratios, and the wide variation in the specification of other regressors, the variation in results is not surprising. Still, some patterns emerge.

First, it appears that spell lengths are at least weakly sensitive to the level of benefits received, given the mean wage faced in the market, and that the degree of sensitivity varies with duration of the spell, labor market conditions, age, and other worker characteristics. Specifically, Nickell (1979a,b), Solon (1985), and others who allow for time variation in the benefit effect generally find that workers' responsiveness to the level of benefits declines as a spell continues. Nickell and Lynch (1985) present evidence of a nonlinear pattern in the benefit level effect with age. Atkinson et al. (1984) present evidence that sampling from different points in the business cycle can produce a wide range of estimates for the benefit effect—including no effect in unemployment periods. The hazards of nonwhite workers also appear to be less sensitive to benefit levels than do the hazards of white workers.

Not surprising, the findings for "duration dependence" in the hazard are quite sensitive to model specification. When additional sources of heterogeneity—both observed and unobserved—are incorporated into the hazard specification, variation in the hazard due to duration alone is diminished. This effect appears when time variation in regressors is allowed, as noted in the introduction to this section. Along this line, the findings of Moffitt (1985), Meyer (1988b), and Katz and Meyer (1988a) are generally consistent with the theoretical prediction of an increase in the hazard as exhaustion of benefits approaches. After controlling for the benefit receipt process, little duration dependence remains. Unfortunately, the results from these particular studies for time-until-exhaustion cannot be pushed too far because of the duration measure available in their data; their "spells" pertain to weeks of compensated unemployment within a benefit year and these may be spread over two or more actual spells of unemployment. (Similar aggregation issues pertain to the duration data analyzed by Solon [1985] and by Podgursky and Swaim [1987].)

As for findings not presented in the table, the results generally indicate that hazard rates are higher for white workers than for nonwhite workers (at least in the United States) and that hazard rates increase with years of education, decrease with tenure, and decrease with age. There is little evidence on differences between the hazard rates of males and females, since almost all of the studies focus on the experience of males. Almost across the board, there is evidence of a fairly strong, inverse relationship between local unemployment rates and the rate at which workers leave unemployment. Overall, these findings are consistent with those of the first section of this chapter and with the findings of Chapter 4.

Structural Studies

Only a few studies have used the optimality condition (Equation 2.5), or an approximation to it, in an attempt to estimate the parameters of a job search model in the

Table 5.2. Hazard Function Studies

Study	Data	Hazard Specification	Findings
Lancaster (1979) Continuous time hazard models	United Kingdom 1973 PEP registered unemployed	Proportional hazards 1. Constant baseline 2. Weibull ($\alpha t^{\alpha-1}$) 3. Constant, with gamma heterogeneity distribution 4. Weibull, with gamma heterogeneity distribution	Replacement rate elasticity 0.43 $\alpha = 0.77$ (S.E. 0.09) Replacement rate elasticity 0.53 Replacement rate elasticity 0.43 (S.E. large) Heterogeneity variance 0.18 (S.E. 0.08) $\alpha = 0.9$ (S.E. 0.22) Replacement rate elasticity 0.6 (S.E. large)
Nickell (1979a) Discrete time hazard models	United Kingdom, 1971–1972 GHS males	1. Logit, with quadratic in duration 2. Logit, with quadratic in duration and time variation in benefits 3. Logit, with quadratic in duration, and time variation in benefits, and 2 point heterogeneity distribution	Benefit/replacement rate elasticity 1.0; negative duration dependence Benefit/replacement rate elasticity 0.84 in weeks 1–20, negligible thereafter Negligible negative duration dependence Benefit/replacement rate elasticity 0.95 in weeks 1–20, negligible thereafter Negligible positive, then negative duration dependence
Atkinson, Gomulka, and Rau (1984) Sensitivity to regressor measurement and sample period	United Kingdom, 1972–1977 FES males	Proportional hazards 1. Weibull ($\alpha t^{\alpha-1}$) 2. Alternative regressors and samples specification	$\alpha = 0.49$ (S.E. 0.04) Replacement rate elasticity 1.18 Above results sensitive
Solon (1985) Taxation of benefits	United States, 1978–1979 UI claimants, Georgia	Proportional hazards 1. Weibull ($\alpha t^{\alpha-1}$) 2. Weibull, with time variation in benefit effect	$\alpha = 0.799$ (S.E. 0.01) Benefit elasticity 0.24–0.81 $\alpha = 0.719$ (S.E. 0.37) Benefit effect declines as exhaustion approaches
Lynch (1985)	United Kingdom, 1980 Youth (about 17)	Proportional hazards 1. Weibull ($\alpha t^{\alpha-1}$) 2. Weibull with gamma heterogeneity distribution	α estimates 0.23 (S.E. 0.25) to 0.38 (S.E. 0.21) No benefit effect Similar results; heterogeneity variance approximately zero
Podgursky and Swaim (1987) Effects of displacement	United States, 1979–1984 January 1984 CPS special supplemental survey of displaced workers	Proportional hazard Weibull ($\alpha t^{\alpha-1}$), by sex and occupation (blue/white collar)	α estimates 0.712 (S.E. 0.04) to 0.757 (S.E. 0.04)

Table 5.2. Hazard Function Studies (*continued*)

Study	Data	Hazard Specification	Findings
Narendranathan, Nickell, and Stern (1985) Sensitivity to model specification	United Kingdom, 1978 DHSS male benefit recipients	Proportional hazard 1. Weibull ($\alpha t^{\alpha-1}$) 2. Weibull with age and time variation in benefit effect	$\alpha = 0.99$ (S.E. 0.25); benefit elasticity 0.28 $\alpha = 1.08$ (S.E. 0.043); benefit effect declines with duration for first 6 months and with age; benefit elasticity 0.08–0.65, average 0.28
		3. Alternative regressors/samples 4. Weibull with gamma heterogeneity distribution	Similar results $\alpha = 2.09$ (S.E. 0.141) Benefit elasticity 0.36 Heterogeneity variance 0.97 (S.E. 0.104)
Moffitt (1985) Potential duration of benefits	United States 1983 CWBH male UI recipients, 13 states	Proportional hazard 1. Step function baseline, for workers with fixed benefit duration	Bimodal baseline Negative benefit level effect No potential benefit duration effect
		2. As in (1), with time variation in the unemployment rate and potential duration, for all workers	As in (1), except effect; positive benefit duration effect
		3. As in (2), with time-until-exhaustion added, for all workers	As in (2) and hazard decreases as time-until-exhaustion decreases
		4. Step function baseline, with time variation in the unemployment rate and potential and time-until-exhaustion spline for all workers	As in (3), except hazard decreases and then increases as time-until-exhaustion decreases and negative potential benefit duration effect Elasticity of duration with respect to benefits: 0.36 and with respect to potential benefit duration: 0.16
		5. Constant baseline	Similar results
Meyer (1988b) Potential duration of benefits	United States, 1983 CWBH male UI recipients, 12 states	Proportional hazard 1. Semiparametric continuous baseline, with time-until-exhaustion spline	Hazard roughly constant and then increases from 6 to 0 weeks before exhaustion; spikes at 26, 28, 32, and 36 weeks Benefit elasticity 0.88
		2. As in (1), with scheduled exhaustion dummy variable	Large positive scheduled exhaustion effect, only spikes at 28 and 32 weeks remain Benefit elasticity: 0.60
		3. As in (2), with state dummy variables	Similar results, except positive state unemployment rate effect Weak positive duration dependance

Katz and Meyer (1988a) Potential duration of benefits United States, 1983 CWBH male UI recipients, 12 states	4. As in (3), with gamma heterogeneity distribution 5. Weibull, $(\alpha t^{\alpha-1})$ 6. As in (4), fit separately for workers with and without changes in potential duration of benefits in benefit year 1. Semiparametric baseline, with time-until-exhaustion spline, scheduled exhaustion dummy variable, and state dummy variables 2. As in (1), with potential duration of benefits and variation in benefit effect with age and time-until-exhaustion	Heterogeneity variance: (2) 0.756 (S.E. 0.194), (3) 0.790 (S.E. 0.195) Similar results for regressors (α not reported) Heterogenity variances approximately zero Hazard decreases from 40 to 12 weeks before exhaustion and remains constant thereafter for constant benefit duration group Baselines not reported Large positive scheduled exhaustion effect Spikes at 28 and 32 weeks; positive state unemployment rate effect Hazard decreases as remaining benefit duration decreases from 26 to 12 weeks and jumps at 1 week before exhaustion; potential duration has a negative effect Benefit effect larger for ages 17–24; benefit level elasticity 0.8–0.9 Potential benefit duration elasticity 0.36–0.44 at 26 weeks, 0.48–0.5 at 35 weeks
Dynarski and Sheffrin (1987) Unemployment rates United States, 1980–1982 PSID household heads	Proportional hazard 1. Nonparametric baseline, time-varying unemployment rate 2. Weibull $(\alpha t^{\alpha-1})$	Hazard increases with increases in national unemployment rate Weak positive duration dependence Similar results; $\alpha = 1.079$ $\alpha = 1.079$ (S.E. 0.017)
Steinberg and Montefort (1987) Job search assistance and training programs United States, 1979–1982 Michigan experiment male displaced workers	Proportional hazards 1. Weibull $(\alpha t^{\alpha-1})$ 2. Log logistic 3. Lognormal 4. Nonparametric baseline 5. Nonparametric baseline (not recovered), with time variation in the replacement ratio and unemployment rate	$\alpha = 0.912$ (S.E. 0.031); no benefit level or benefit duration effects; programs shorten spells; predicted mean spell length 145 weeks As in (1), except negative duration dependence; predicted mean spell length 102 weeks As in (1) and (2), except for hazard; predicted mean spell length 101 weeks Baseline not recovered Replacement rate elasticity: 0.80 controls, 0.46 experimentals; programs shorten spells

S.E. = standard error.

absence of reservation wage data. In this section, we discuss studies that use wage and unemployment duration data toward this end.

We start with studies that incorporate heterogeneity among workers into theoretical and empirical specifications using extensions of the regression and hazard function approaches. For each of the basic elements in the theoretical structure, functional forms are defined over worker and labor market characteristics and vectors of unknown parameters. Theoretical and auxiliary restrictions are then used to identify the basic search theoretic elements. Three related works by Kiefer and Neumann (1979a, 1981) are discussed first. Their objective is to estimate an approximate solution to the optimality condition for the reservation wage in both stationary and nonstationary discrete-time versions of the basic model of Chapter 2. Their data are for workers in the United States. Narendranathan and Nickell (1985) take an alternative route to estimating individuals' reservation wages. They estimate the exact solution for the reservation wage defined by an approximation to the optimality condition for a continuous time, stationary job search model. Their data are for workers in the United Kingdom. The next papers we discuss by Devine (1988) and Wolpin (1987) extend the approach taken by Lancaster and Chesher (1983), based on the assumption of a random sample from a homogeneous population. Devine examines the extent to which variation in hazard rates across major demographic groups in the U.S. labor force can be attributed to systematic variation in arrival rates versus acceptance probabilites. Wolpin studies the transition from school to work for young males in the United States using a finite horizon search model.

Kiefer and Neumann (1979b)

Kiefer and Neumann work with a discrete time version of the stationary model of Chapter 2, with the assumption that exactly one offer is received per period, that is, the arrival rate is set equal to 1.[34] Thus, using our notation from that chapter, the optimality condition that defines the reservation wage for individual i is

$$w_i^r = b_i + \frac{1}{r_i} [E(w_i | w_i \geq w_i^r) - w_i^r] \pi_i(w_i^r)$$

To make the problem (more or less) empirically tractable, some additional assumptions are made. Specifically, log offers are taken to be independent draws from normal distributions that differ across workers only in terms of their means,

$$\ln(w_i) = x_i'\beta + u_{i1}, \qquad u_{i1} \sim N(0, \sigma_1^2) \tag{5.20}$$

so that

$$\ln(w_i^r) = z_i'\Gamma + u_{i2}, \qquad u_{i2} \sim N(0, \sigma_2^2) \tag{5.21}$$

can be interpreted as a log linear approximation to the solution for the reservation wage. To estimate the parameters β, Kiefer and Neumann exploit the theoretically implied restriction that accepted wages w_i^a must exceed the reservation wage, w_i^r, that is,

$$Y_i = \ln(w_i) - \ln(w_i^r)$$
$$= x_i'\beta - z_i'\Gamma + v_i \geq 0$$

where $v_i = u_{1i} - u_{2i} \sim N(0, \sigma^2 = \sigma_1^2 + \sigma_2^2 - 2\sigma_{12})$. This restriction is useful. It implies that

$$E[\ln(w_i^a)] = x_i'\beta + p\sigma\lambda_i$$

and

$$\text{Var}[\ln(w_i^a)] = \sigma_1^2(1 + p^2 y_i\lambda_i - p^2\lambda_i^2)$$

where

(a) $\lambda_i = \phi(-y_i)/[1 - \Phi(-y_i)]$
(b) $y_i = [x_i'\beta - z_i'\Gamma]/\sigma$
(c) $p = (\sigma_1^2 - \sigma_{12})/\sigma_1\sigma$

and ϕ and Φ denote the standard normal density and distribution function, respectively. Probit estimates of the normalized version of Y_i, $Y_i^* = Y_i/\sigma$ provide consistent estimates of λ_i, λ_i^*. Application of GLS to $\ln(w_i^a) = x_i'\beta + p\sigma\lambda_i^* + u_1 i$ then yields consistent and efficient estimates of β and estimates of σ_1^2 can then be obtained from the residuals.[35] This part of their analysis is fairly straightforward, but identifying the parameters of the reservation wage equation is not. Variation in the mean of the offer distribution produces variation in the reservation wage across individuals through expected gains from search. Thus, all elements of x_i must enter the vector z_i. The reservation wage may also vary with some of the regressors in x_i because of effects on costs of search, the discount rate, and income while unemployed. Omitting the subscript i for convenience, let z_0 denote regressors that affect w^r only through their effects on offers, let z_R denote regressors that affect w^r only through the discount rate and income net of search costs while unemployed (b), and let z_B denote regressors that may affect either. Then we have

$$\mu = E(\ln w) = z_0'\beta_0 + z_B'\beta_B$$

and

$$E(\ln w^r) = z_0'\Gamma_0 + z_B'\Gamma_B + z_R'\Gamma_R$$

where $\Gamma_0 = (\partial w^r/\partial\mu)\beta_0$ and $\Gamma_B = (\partial w^r/\partial\mu)\beta_B + \gamma$. Using these definitions, the normalized reemployment condition can be written as

$$Y^* = [(1 - (\partial w^r/\partial\mu)/\sigma]x'\beta - z_B'\gamma/\sigma - z_R'\Gamma_R/\sigma$$

This formulation implies that if z_R is nonempty, repeated estimation of the probit equation using an instrument for the mean on the first round estimates for β will yield estimates of $(1 - (\partial w^r/\partial\mu)/\sigma$, γ/σ, and Γ_R/σ. Identification of the basic reservation wage parameters can be otained directly, however, only if $\partial w^r/\partial\mu$ is known. Kiefer and Neumann show that

$$\partial w^r/\partial\mu = \tau(\tau + r) \in (0,1)$$

in their model, so that this case is excluded. However, this restriction is useful by itself. It allows identification of γ and Γ_R because $\partial w^r/\partial\mu$ can be estimated using data on durations and an outside estimate for information on the discount rate.

Kiefer and Neumann fit the model using data collected in October 1975 for the purpose of evaluating the Trade Adjustment Assistance Program (TAA). Their sample consists of 517 male workers in 14 states who experienced permanent layoffs in the

1969–1973 period. Kiefer and Neumann note that their sample is generally older, less educated, and more heavily unionized than the U.S. male population.[36] An appealing aspect is that workers on temporary layoff are excluded. Durations are measured in weeks and include both completed and right-censored spells. Accepted wages are observed for 327 workers.

Results are first reported for the first round probit for the employment condition and the accepted wage equation. Education, a quadratic in age, an interaction of age with education, the local unemployment rate, and tenure and log wages in the previous job are included in x_i. The specification for z_i includes the weekly unemployment insurance benefit, potential duration of benefits, number of dependents, and marital status, in addition to the regressors in x_i. In estimating the probit equation, the dependent variable is set equal to 1 for workers reemployed within 65 weeks, and zero otherwise. Kiefer and Neumann note that this choice is arbitrary, but that it makes no difference asymptotically given the stationarity of the reservation wage.

The results for the probit equation generally accord with predictions of search theory; exceptions to this are a positive coefficient estimate for potential duration of benefits and a negative education coefficient estimate, but neither is significantly different from zero at standard levels. The estimates of the offer wage equation parameters β are also sensible.

To identify the reservation wage equation parameters, tenure and wages in the previous job are both specified as affecting the reservation wage only through their effects on mean offers. Setting the annual discount rate equal to 0.1 and using the inverse of mean duration in their sample (34 weeks) as an estimate for τ, their estimate for $\partial w^r / \partial \mu$ is 0.94. The structural parameter estimates for the reservation wage equation based on this estimate appear consistent with predictions of the basic search model. In particular, reservation wages appear to increase with both unemployment benefits and mean wages; at the sample means, the benefit elasticity is about 0.02.

Kiefer and Neumann check their specification using both formal and informal methods. The coefficients for the regressors z_R specified as determinants of the reservation wage but not offers are essentially the same in the two sets of probit results, as they should be. The use of two variables in z_0 provides an overidentifying restriction; on the basis of a chi-square test, it cannot be rejected. On a less encouraging note, results from a Kolmorgorov–Smirnov test (which can be regarded as a test of the distributional assumptions and the overall model specification) are not favorable.[37]

Kiefer and Neumann (1979a)

In this study Kiefer and Neumann again work with a discrete time model, but they admit duration dependence in the reservation wage. Specifically, they replace Equations 5.19 and 5.20 with

$$\ln w_i(t) = x_i'\beta + u_{i1t}, \qquad u_{i1t} \sim N(0, \sigma_1^2) \tag{5.22}$$

and

$$\ln w_i^r(t) = z_i'\Gamma + gt + u_{2it}, \qquad u_{2it} \sim N(0, \sigma_2^2) \tag{5.23}$$

Thus, duration dependence in the reservation wage is approximated by exponential decay. The truncation point for the accepted wage distribution varies with duration in this model and depends on the actual realization of the job search process. Consequently, both spell duration and accepted wage information must be used to estimate the offer distribution parameters. Letting $Y_i(t)$ denote the employment condition redefined under Equations 5.22 and 5.23 and using the same notation otherwise, Kiefer and Neumann note that probit estimation could be applied to the normalized sequence $Y_i^*(t)$ for each individual to obtain estimates of the appropriate truncation corrections. They instead work with the joint distribution of accepted wages and durations and apply the method of maximum likelihood—since this exploits all information in their data simultaneously. The hazard function for their model is simply the acceptance probability, which under the normality assumption is

$$\tau_i(t) = \Phi(Y_i^*(t))$$

Thus, the joint probability of a spell ending in exactly t_i periods with acceptance of an offer w_i is

$$Pr(t_i, w_i) = \prod_{t=1}^{t_i-1} [1 - \tau_i(t)] \sigma_1^{-1} \phi((w_i - x_i\beta)/\sigma_1)$$
$$\times (1 - \Phi\{[-Y(t_i)/\sigma - p(w_i - x_i\beta\sigma_1)]/[1 - p^2]^{1/2}\}$$

This serves as the basis for their sample likelihood function for completed spells and the survivor function (Equation 5.10) is entered for observations on incomplete spells. To identify the parameters of the reservation wage equation, Kiefer and Neumann follow essentially the same procedure as in their analysis based on the stationary model. In particular, they rely on the derivative restriction for the reservation wage with respect to the mean to recover the basic parameters of the reservation wage equation from their estimates for β, σ_1, γ/σ, Γ_R/σ, $(1 - \partial w_i^r/\partial\mu)/\sigma$, and $p = (\sigma_1 - \sigma_{12})/\sigma\sigma_1$.

Kiefer and Neumann fit the model using the TAA data described. The specifications for the vectors x_i, z_i, and partition of z_i are also the same. Spells of more than 76 weeks are treated as censored here; Kiefer and Neumann note that this choice is based on the criteria that systematic changes in the reservation wage are likely to be captured by this point, but note that it is nevertheless somewhat arbitrary.

The estimates for the offer and reservation wage equations seem reasonable, except for the local unemployment rate. The coefficient in the normalized reservation wage equation is large, positive, and, in this case, statistically significant at the 5 percent level—raising an issue of causality of the specification. The elasticity of the reservation wage with respect to benefits implied by their results of 0.069 when evaluated at the sample mean. Their estimate for g/σ is -0.017 (standard error 0.001), which translates into an estimate of -0.0058 for g given their estimate for σ. Negative duration dependence is thus implied. Kiefer and Neumann also estimate a constant reservation wage model using the same procedure (i.e., Equations 5.22 and 5.23 with g set equal to zero). Overall, the coefficient estimates exhibit little sensitivity to this restriction (the benefit effect, in particular), but a decline in the reservation wage with duration cannot be rejected on the basis of a likelihood ratio test. Beyond this statistical support for the changing reservation wage model, Kolmogorov–Smirnov distributional tests are also performed to check the lognormality assumption used in both models. These results are not favorable for the constant reservation wage model (a finding consistent with that of their previous study [1979b]), but the lognormal offer distribution does appear to be supported using the results for the changing reservation wage specification.

With the changing reservation wage model, Kiefer and Neumann are able to account for about 30 percent of the variance in wage offers, leaving 70 percent to unobserved heterogeneity and pure chance. Since the relative magnitude of pure wage offer variation versus that due to measured and unmeasured population heterogeneity has implications for the relevance of search explanations, Kiefer and Neumann make an effort to analyze this formally. Specifically, they consider a decomposition of the residual in the wage offer equation of the form

$$u_{i1} = k u_{i2} + u_{i*}$$

where k is a scale factor relating individual specific disturbances in the reservation wage equation to market earnings, u_{i*} is considered purely random, and u_{i2} and u_{i*} are uncorrelated by construction. From this and the corresponding specifications

$$\sigma_{i1}^2 = k^2 \sigma_{i2}^2 + \sigma_{1*}^2$$

and

$$\sigma_{i12} = k^2 \sigma_{i2}^2$$

they derive an estimate for σ_{1*}^2 from their estimated covariance structure. For the constant and changing reservation wage specifications, respectively, their results imply that 4.3 and 8.5 percent of variation unexplained by the regressors x_i is due to pure randomness. This might be taken as casting some doubt on the relevance of search theory for explaining interindividual variation in wages.

Kiefer and Neumann (1981)

Kiefer and Neumann extend their previous work in a number of directions in this study. In particular, they go beyond the ex post approach to analyzing unobserved heterogeneity and directly incorporate it into their specification. First, they incorporate individual specific components into the mean of the offer distributions, replacing Equation 5.18 with

$$\ln w_i = x_i'\beta + f_i + u_{i1} \tag{5.24}$$

where $u_{i1} \sim N(0, \sigma_1^2)$ and $f_i \sim N(0, \sigma_f^2)$. They also allow the individual specific components to have direct effects on the reservation wage. Specifically, the solution to the optimality condition for the reservation wage is assumed to take the form

$$w_i^r = h(x_i'\beta + f_i, b_i)$$

Letting $h_{1i} = \partial w_i^r(t)/\partial(x_i'\beta + f_i)$ and $h_{2i} = \partial w_i^r(t)/\partial b_i$, they approximate $h_{2i}b_i$ by $z_i + f_i$. This leads to an empirical specification of the form

$$\ln w_i^r(t) = h_{1i}x_i'\beta + (h_{1i} + \theta)f_i + z_i'\Gamma \tag{5.25}$$

where the vector z_i includes all elements in x_i, as well as other regressors assumed to produce variation in w_i^r, as before. The employment condition in this case is

$$Y_i = (1 - h_{1i})x_i'\beta + (1 - h_{1i} - \theta)f_i - z_i'\Gamma + u_{1i} \tag{5.26}$$

Together with Equation 5.25, this forms the empirical model.

Kiefer and Neumann use the method of maximum likelihood to estimate the model. Conditional on f_i, the contribution to the sample likelihood of an incomplete spell of length t_i is the survivor function (Equation 5.12), with

$$\tau_i = \Phi \left[\frac{(1 - h_{1i})x_i'\beta + (1 - h_{1i} - \theta)f_i - z_i'\Gamma}{\sigma} \right] \quad (5.27)$$

Kiefer and Neumann also consider a specification that admits monotonic variation in the reservation wage with duration using the same specification as in their previous study. That is, the term gt_i is included in Equation 5.25 and it thus enters Equation 5.26 and the numerator of Equation 5.27 with a negative sign. In this case, the contribution for an incomplete spell is the survivor (Equation 5.10) evaluated at t_i. For a completed spell that ends in t_i with acceptance of a wage w_i, the contribution for the constant reservation wage model is the joint density

$$(1 - \tau_i(t))^{t_i - 1} \sigma^{-1} \phi \left[\frac{w_i - x_i'\beta - f_i}{\sigma} \right]$$

To move from the conditional likelihood to an unconditional likelihood, Kiefer and Neumann assume that the f_i follow a parametric distribution (i.e., a random effects specification for an error components model). In particular, they specify that the f_i follow a normal distribution with zero mean and unknown variance σ_f^2 and numerically integrate the f_i out of each term in the conditional likelihood. Note that the employment condition $w_i \geq w_i^r$ must be imposed in evaluating the density of accepted wages. The consequence is a set of complete estimating equations in place of Equations 5.25 and 5.26 with parameters β, Γ, θ, σ_f^2, and σ_1^2.

Kiefer and Neumann fit this model using the same data and specifications for x_i and z_i as in their previous studies. The derivative restriction $h_{1i} = \delta w_i^r / \delta \mu_i = \tau_i / (\tau_i + r_i)$ is also used for identification of the parameters of the reservation wage equation. However, as opposed to treating h_{1i} as a common parameter h_1 to be estimated (as done previously), they allow the derivative to vary across individuals in the same sample here and the cross-equation restriction it implies is imposed by solving the implicit equation numerically for each i. (Note that τ_i depends on h_{1i} and also on f_i.)

The estimates for both β and Γ are very similar to those found in their previous studies in both the constant and changing reservation wage models. In particular, the significantly negative tenure effect on mean offers reappears, as does the curiously positive unemployment rate effect on the reservation wage. The implied benefit elasticities for the reservation wage are 0.132 and 0.1 under the constant and changing reservation wage specifications, respectively; both are larger numbers than those implied by their earlier results. The estimate for g in this study is -0.023 (standard error 0.0011). Both the t statistic for the coefficient and a likelihood ratio across specifications (which are asymptotically equivalent tests) provide statistical support for a declining reservation wage. This estimated change is substantially smaller than their estimate with no control for individual specific components in the reservation wage—a finding consistent with the duration dependence and unobserved heterogeneity findings for hazard rates reported previously in the chapter. Note, however, that the estimated standard errors should be interpreted with more than the usual skepticism because imposition of the employment condition $w_i \geq w_i^r$ causes a violation of standard regularity conditions. (On this point, see Chapter 3.) The remaining coefficient estimates do not exhibit much sensitivity to this modification.

The variance results represent the major item of interest in the estimation results.

Under both specifications, the estimates of σ_1^2 and σ_f^2 are statistically significant at standard confidence levels and the estimate of the latter is approximately 10 times that of the former. This result can be interpreted as implying that omitted variables contribute almost 10 times as much to interindividual variation in wage offers as contributed by purely random factors (i.e., as the variation in offers faced by a searcher with given characteristics).

Narendranathan and Nickell (1985)

The approach taken by Kiefer and Neumann consists of estimation of an approximation to the solution of an exact formulation of the optimality condition. On the other hand, the approach taken by Narendranathan and Nickell might be described as estimation of the exact solution to an approximation to the optimality condition—for a somewhat more complicated theoretical model. Their theoretical model is essentially the stationary model set out in Chapter 4 in our discussion of the study by Ridder and Gorter (1986), with an additional assumption that the arrival rate varies with wage offers. Using our notation from the Ridder and Gorter discussion, the optimality condition that defines the reservation wage for worker i in their model can be written as

$$\log(w_i^r) = \frac{u(L_u)}{u(L_e)} \log(b_i) + \frac{1}{r_i} \int_{w_i^r}^{\infty} (\log(w_i) - \log(w_i^r))\delta_i(w_i)\, dF_i(w_i)$$

Narendranathan and Nickell specify functional forms for the arrival rate, the discount rate, and the leisure utility ratio defined over observable personal characteristics, local labor market conditions, income variables, and vectors of unknown parameters:

$$\frac{u(L_{ui})}{u(L_{ei})} = \exp(x_i'\beta), \qquad r_i = \exp(-\rho)$$

and

$$\delta_i(\gamma_i) = \exp(z_i'\Gamma + \phi\gamma_i)$$

where $\gamma_i = (\ln w_i - \mu_i)/\sigma$. On substitution, the optimality condition can thus be rewritten as

$$\log(w_i^r) = \exp(x_i'\beta) \log(b_i) + \exp(z_i'\Gamma + \rho) \qquad (5.28)$$
$$\times \int_{w_i^r}^{\infty} (\log(w_i) - \log(w_i^r)) \exp(\phi\gamma_i)\, dF_i(w_i)$$

Like Ridder and Gorter (1986), Narendranathan and Nickell set out to estimate the parameters of this optimality condition—but at a relative disadvantage. They do not have access to the special wage data that allows estimation of individual distributions under a Pareto specification. This complicates the estimation procedure substantially.

Narendranathan and Nickell assume that log offers are draws from normal distributions with means μ_i and variance σ^2 and estimate these parameters by fitting least-squares regressions to previous wage data. Previous wages are used for this purpose because accepted wages are observed for only a small proportion of their sample. They then use a series of approximations that allow them to write Equation 5.28 in terms of the standard normal distribution function and density. This in turn allows them to estimate an approximation to the solution for the reservation wage for each individual in their sample using numerical methods. Finally, using these reservation wage estimates, they apply the method of maximum likelihood to data on unemployment spell durations to estimate the remaining parameters of their model, (β, ρ, Γ), that is, they apply the hazard function approach under the constraint that the parameter estimates satisfy Equation 5.28. Our guess is that these reservation wages will come closer to satisfying the optimality condition than those generated by Kiefer and Neumann's log linear approximation, but this is only a guess.

Narendranathan and Nickell fit the model using data for the random subsample of 1,474 workers collected in the DHSS Cohort Study for the United Kingdom, the same source used by Narendranathan et al. (1985), as previously discussed. Age, marital status, race, education, skill qualifications, and work history over the previous year (all measured as categorical variables), and the local unemployment rate are included in the vector z. Marital status, age under 25, age over 54, and a dummy variable to indicate an unemployment spell in the year preceding the current spell are included in the vector x for the leisure utility ratio.

Overall, the arrival rate coefficients Γ are precisely estimated and the signs make sense. Individual offer arrival rates appear to vary significantly with race, skill level, and age—young, white, and highly skilled workers get more frequent offers than their counterparts. The coefficient for wage offers is both practically and statistically small; a null hypothesis of no effect for the level of a wage offer on the arrival rate cannot be rejected at standard levels. The results for the utility of leisure ratio also seem sensible; the constant estimate is -0.93 (standard error 0.344), which can be interpreted as a negative evaluation of leisure when unemployed relative to leisure when employed. Age appears irrelevant in this relative evaluation, while being married has a positive effect.

Narendranthan and Nickell report a variety of structural parameters implied these results, both for the full sample and for groups in a partition by age. For the reservation wage, the sample average benefit elasticity is 0.13, while the age group estimates range from 0.084 to 0.196 (the lowest being for the 45–54 groups). For duration, the sample average benefit elasticity is 0.26 and the range across age groups is 0.13 (over 55) to 0.30. Average daily arrival rates δ and acceptance probabilities $\pi(w^r)$ for the full sample and by age group are also calculated. For workers under 44, there is little variation in either parameter across age groups; the range is 0.017–0.024 for δ and 0.46–0.57 for $\pi(w^r)$. The results for workers over 45 are quite different. The average arrival rates are 0.008 for the 45–54 group and for the over 55 group and the average acceptance probabilities are 0.73 for the 45–54 group and 0.84 for workers over 55. For the full sample, the arrival rate δ is 0.018 and the acceptance probability $\pi(w^r)$ is 0.57.

As a basic consistency check on their reservation wage estimates, Narendranathan and Nickell check their levels against the accepted wages observed for approximately one-half of the full sample. They find that the accepted wages exceed the estimated reservation wages in about one-half of the observed cases. This finding may simply reflect the use of previous earnings data in estimating the parameters of the offer distributions; previous earnings are accepted wages and therefore the estimates for mean offers and reservation wages are likely to be biased upward. Of course, upward bias in the reservation wage is likely to lead to downward bias in the acceptance probabilities. On the other hand, the variance estimates for the offer distribution might be biased downward and this might bias the reservation wage estimates downward.

Given the method used to arrive at the reservation wage estimates, there is no simple way of testing hypotheses regarding the observed differences between accepted wages and the reservation wages estimates, but Narendranathan and Nickell experiment with alternative specifications. In particular, they try a right translation of the offer distribution, manipulation of the variance, and a regrouping of their sample for estimation of the offer distribution parameters. All fail to produce a major change in the proportion of accepted wages above reservation wage estimates. Restricting the wage coefficient in the arrival rate specification (ϕ) to a large and negative number and parameterizing the discount rate (r_i) both increase the proportion—but the latter modification produces the larger change and even this leaves the proportion at less than three quarters.

Results for the parameterized discount rate model provide some other interesting findings, however. The explanatory variables are age, race, marital status, skill level, and a dummy variable for less than 1 year tenure on the previous job (i.e., the local unemployment rate is used to distinguish the arrival rate and discount rate). The results indicate substantial variation in the discount rate with individual characteristics; white workers, workers over 55, married workers, and manual workers appear to have significantly higher discount rates than their counterparts. The results for the remaining parameters are qualitatively similar to those under the constant discount rate specification. The average benefit elasticities for the full sample are 0.162 for the reservation wage and 0.18 for mean durations, with ranges of 0.109–0.217 and 0.07–0.26, respectively, across age groups. The substantial drop in the duration elasticity reflects a decline for all groups and teens, in particular. The acceptance probability estimates differ substantially from those of the simpler model. For the full sample, the estimates are 0.162 for δ and 0.73 for $\pi(w^r)$, with ranges of 0.005–0.02 and 0.58–0.90, respectively, across age groups. In particular, workers under 35 have much higher acceptance probabilities according to this model. In this extended model, however, variation in transition rates across age groups appears to be driven primarily by variation in the arrival rate, as before.

Devine (1988)

As in the structural studies by Ridder and Gorter (1986) and Narendranathan and Nickell (1985), the general objective of this study is to distinguish the relative roles of acceptance probabilities and offer arrival rates in producing variation in transition rates out of unemployment. However, the focus here is variation across major demographic groups that comprise the labor force—as opposed to variation on the basis of all observable characteristics. The empirical approach differs accordingly. In particular, it aligns more closely with the approach of the Lancaster and Chesher (1983).

Workers within each labor force group are treated as a homogeneous population. On partitioning a representative sample of the labor force according to the characteristics of interest, the data for a particular group are then treated as a random sample from the relevant population. This allows estimation to be carried out separately for each group using methods that require replication. Interpreting the results for a group as representative measures for all group members, variation by worker characteristics is then analyzed by comparing the results across groups.

The transition rate equation of the stationary model of Chapter 2 serves as the empirical model for each group, that is, letting groups be indexed by c,

$$\tau_c = \delta_c \pi_c(w_c^r)$$

Given the stationarity of the model, the maximum likelihood estimate for the transition rate for each group can be calculated easily using the observations on unemployment duration for the group. The right-hand side is more involved. Assuming that observed wages are realizations of independently and identically distributed random variables with an arbitrary distribution function $F_c(w)$, a number of consistent estimators for w_c^r are available that require data on accepted wages for individuals in group c alone. An obvious candidate is the first-order statistic, which can be shown to be strongly consistent. A practical problem with using the observed minimum of accepted wages for workers of type c is its sensitivity to errors in measurement. Since any of the first m-order statistics (m fixed) and their averages can be shown to be consistent estimators for w^r, Devine works with the first two-order statistics separately and their average as a check on the sensitivity of her results.

With an estimate of the reservation wage and the transition rate for group c, if the distribution $F_c(w)$ were known, then a consistent estimate of the arrival rate would follow directly,

$$\delta_c^* = \tau_c^*/\pi_c\,(w_c^{r^*})$$

Obviously, $\pi_c(w) = 1 - F_c(w)$ is not known. If it is assumed that is F_c is a member of a parametric family $\{F(w|\theta_c)\}$; where the parameters θ_c are unknown, then the observations from the truncated distribution can sometimes be used to estimate θ_c (see Chapter 3). The normal and gamma families represent candidate families and both are attractive in that they are two-parameter families. Since the arrival rate estimate is likely to be sensitive to the choice of family, Devine carries out estimation of the full set of parameters for both specifications.

The method of moments is used to estimate θ_c. Since the theoretical moments of the truncated distribution are functions of the offer distribution parameters, equating the theoretical and sample moments for the truncated distribution provides a set of nonlinear simultaneous equations that may be solved for θ_c, the moments of the true offer distribution. Consistent estimates are obtained by solving the minimum distance problem

$$\min_{\theta_c} D(\theta_c) = [S_n - m(\theta_c)]'A[S_n - m(\theta_c)]$$

where S denotes the sample moments, m denotes the theoretical moments, and A is the inverse of the asymptotic covariance matrix for S_n, Ω^{-1}. In estimation, a consistent estimate Ω^* is calculated using sample moments. Asymptotically, the estimates are normally distributed and calculation of the covariance matrix is straightforward. Also, if the specification of the offer distribution is correct, $nD(\theta_c^*)$ has an asymptotic chi-square distribution with $k - p$ degrees of freedom, where k equals the number of moments used and p denotes the number of parameters in the vector θ_c for a given parametric specification. Devine works with two parameter families and three sample moments and she uses the test of the overidentifying restriction as a measure of goodness of fit.

Devine works with data collected in Waves 1–4 for the 1984 Panel of the Survey of Income and Program Participation, a longitudinal survey conducted by the U.S. Bureau of the Census. Waves 1–4 cover the period June 1983 to November 1984 and each worker is observed for up to 54 weeks during this period.[38] Durations are measured as weeks of joblessness (essentially defined as having no fixed employment arrangement). The sample consists of 5,214 workers who, over the course of the sample period, experienced an initialized spell of joblessness, did not report having a job in either an agricultural occupation or an agricultural industry, either worked full-time hours or reported part-time hours due to economic reasons, and remained age 64 or less at the end of the first completed spell of joblessness or the end of the survey (whichever came first). A restriction to the nonstudent population was desired, but enrollment data are not available for SIPP for the 1984 SIPP Panel. Using reported hourly wage rates where available and average hourly earnings otherwise, accepted wage observations are available for 3,396 persons in the sample.

The partition used in estimation is based on sex, race, and age (16–19, 20–24, 25–44, 45–64). Sample sizes differ substantially across the 16 groups and, even with the large total number of observations available, relatively small numbers of accepted wage observations are available for the oldest and youngest nonwhite groups (e.g., only 25 wages are observed for the oldest nonwhite males, versus 598 observations for prime-age white females). This must be kept in mind when interpreting the results.

Overall, the results for the parameter estimates under the gamma distribution are quite precise and appear insensitive to the choice of order statistic for the reservation wage estimator. Also, the chi-square statistics generally imply a good fit; the overidentifying restriction can be rejected at the 5 percent level for just a few groups. Both the mean and variance estimates vary substantially across groups but the estimates for the acceptance probability are close to 1 for all groups (0.91–1.0 for the average of the first two order statistics). Transition rates, on the other hand, differ substantially across groups (0.02–0.073) and a direct relationship thus appears between the variation in transition rates and variation in the arrival rate. The relatively longer spells of joblessness experienced by older workers, nonwhite workers, and females appear to be the result of relatively infrequent offers.

The results for the normal specification are similar in that there is limited variation in the acceptance probability across groups (except for a few outliers). Variation in the arrival rate thus appears to determine the transition rate. However, the average level of the acceptance probability using the full normal distribution is about 0.36. Devine notes that the normal distribution estimates for the mean center around zero (i.e., the distributions want to look like the gamma distributions). Since negative offers do not make sense, Devine notes that it is more appropriate to interpret her estimates as characterizing half-normal distributions. Doing a rough normalization for the mass below the mean, the truncated normal distribution estimates for the acceptance probabilities center at about three-fourths, which is not quite as different from the gamma results.

Wolpin (1987)

In his analysis of unemployment on graduation from high school, Wolpin takes a structural approach that differs substantially from those previously described. Wolpin modifies the discrete time version of the model set out in Chapter 2 so that workers face a finite search horizon and an offer probability that changes systematically with spell duration in a way that workers know. Fixed assets in a world of imperfect capital markets is offered as a possible rationale for the first of these assumptions. Together, these assumptions imply that a worker's reservation wage will vary systematically with duration.

Let T denote the end of the search horizon, let wage variables denote the discounted present value of offers (i.e., $V_e(w)$ in the notation previously used), and let β denote the subjective discount factor. Using previous notation otherwise, the reservation wage in his model is

$$w_t^r = b + \beta V_{ut+1} \tag{5.29}$$

for $t < T$, where the value of unemployed search is defined as

$$V_{ut} = \delta_t E[\max\{w_t, b + \beta V_{ut+1}\}] + (1 - \delta_t)E[b + \beta V_{ut+1}]$$
$$= \delta_t\{E(w_t \mid w_t \geq w_t^r)\pi(w_t^r) + w_t^r[1 - \pi(w_t^r)]\} + (1 - \delta_t)w_t^r \;^{39}$$

Substitution of Equation 5.30 into 5.27 yields a complex nonlinear difference equation. To solve for this sequence, Wolpin exploits the finite search horizon. Letting R denote time remaining until the end of life at T, the value of search at the search horizon T is

$$V_{uT} = [\delta_T E(w) + (1 - \delta_T)b] + \beta(1 - \delta_T)[\delta_{T+1}E(w) + (1 - \delta_{T+1})b] + \cdots$$
$$+ \beta^R(1 - \delta_T)(1 - \delta_{T+1}) \cdots (1 - \delta_{T+R-1})[\delta_{T+R}E(w) + (1 - \delta_{T+R})b]$$

since, for period T on, it follows directly from the assumption of a finite search horizon that a worker will accept the first offer received. Equivalently, the reservation wage is the minimum of the offer distribution faced,

$$w_t^r \leq w_{\min}$$

for $t \geq T$. If the offer probability is nonincreasing, it follows directly that the reservation wage will decline systematically with duration until the search horizon is reached.[40]

Wolpin's objective is to use data on durations and accepted wages to estimate the sequence of reservation wages and offer probabilities, income net of search costs while unemployed, and the offer distribution. Toward this end, he considers two alternative distributional assumptions for offers w_t: the normal, where

$$w_t = \overline{w} + u_t$$

and the log normal, where

$$\ln w_t = \ln \tilde{w} + u_t$$

where $u_t \sim N(0, \sigma_u^2)$. Using the definitions for the truncated means under these specifications, the value of unemployed search may be written as

$$V_{ut} = \delta_t\{\overline{w} + n_t\Phi(n_t/\sigma_u) + \sigma_u\phi(n_t/\sigma_u)\} + (1 - \delta_t)w_t^r$$

in the normal offer case and

$$V_{ut} = \delta_t\{\tilde{w}\exp((\tfrac{1}{2})\sigma_u^2)[1 - \Phi((n_t - \sigma_u^2)/\sigma_u)] + w_t^r\Phi(n_t/\sigma_u)\} + (1 - \delta_t)w_t^r$$

in the log normal case, where

$$w_t^r = \overline{w} + n_t \quad \text{and} \quad \ln w_t^r = \ln \tilde{w} + n_t$$

and Φ and ϕ denote the standard normal distribution function and density. For the offer probability sequence, Wolpin uses

$$\delta_t = \Phi(m_0 + m_1 t)$$

Given T, the sequence of reservation wages under either offer specification depends on only a few parameters ($\overline{w}$ or $\tilde{w}$, σ_u^2, b, d, m_0, and m_1). Given estimates for these parameters, the sequence of value functions may be solved recursively for the reservation wages, starting with V_{uT} and using numerical methods.

To estimate the parameters, Wolpin works with the joint distribution of unemployment spell durations and accepted wages. He assumes that the latter are measured with error. In particular, for observed wages, he defined

$$w_t^0 = \overline{w} + \theta_t \quad \text{and} \quad \ln w_t^0 = \ln \tilde{w} + \theta_t$$

for the normal and log normal cases, respectively, where

$$\theta_t = u_t + e_t, \qquad e_t \sim N(0, \sigma_e^2)$$

and the e_t and u_t are assumed stochastically independent. The sample likelihood is thus defined as

$$L = \prod_{i=1}^{K} \prod_{j=1}^{t_i-1} \left[\delta_j \Phi \left[\frac{n_j}{\sigma_u} \right] + (1 - \delta_j) \right] \times \left[\delta_{ti} \left(1 - \Phi \left[\frac{n_{ti} - p \left[\frac{\sigma_u}{\sigma_\theta} \right] \theta_t^i}{\sigma_u \sqrt{1 - p^2}} \right] \right) \frac{1}{\sigma_\theta} \phi \left[\frac{\theta_t^i}{\sigma_\theta} \right] \right]$$

$$\times \prod_{i=K+1}^{N} \prod_{j=1}^{t_i} \left[\delta_j \Phi \left[\frac{n_j}{\sigma_u} \right] + (1 - \delta_j) \right]$$

in the normal offer case, where $p = \sigma_u/\sigma_\theta$, $1 - p^2$ represents the fraction of the wage variance accounted for by measurement error, the first K spells are uncensored, and spells $K + 1$ through N are censored. The likelihood function for the log normal offer case is the same, but multiplied by the Jacobian of the transformation, $1/w_t$.

Wolpin fits this model using data for a sample of white males taken from the National Longitudinal Survey New Youth Cohort. His sample is restricted to workers who graduated from high school in 1979 and neither entered the military nor returned to school by the 1982 interview. Unemployment spells are measured as weeks without a "real" job, where the latter is defined as a job that is held for 3 or more months and involves working 30 or more hours per week. The sample size is 144, with 101 completed spells. Surprisingly, more than 30 percent of his sample had "real" jobs at the time of graduation. Wolpin assumes that the probability of getting a real job offer before graduation is a constant and solves for it using the observation that 61 weeks was the longest "real" job duration prior to graduation and the sample proportion for such jobs at the time of graduation. He uses 500 weeks for R and a discount rate of 5 percent to calculate the present value of lifetime income for an offer and the final search period value function, V_{uT}.

Wolpin reports that his results from estimation are extremely sensitive to the specification of the offer distribution. Specifically. results for the normal are described as so unreasonable that he presents only the log normal results. For the normal case, he notes that the estimates for mean offers and costs of search are negative, that the latter are unrealistically large, and that the discount factor is almost zero.

The log normal results are mixed. The reservation wage remains positive over the first 54 weeks of search, so 54 is used as an estimate for the search horizon following graduation. The mean weekly wage offer estimate is 188 dollars, about 17 dollars below the observed accepted mean. The arrival rate is 0.0128 in the first week of graduation and then declines to 0.0091 at T. Measurement error is found to account for only 1.2 percent of the total variation in offers.

Over the entire search period, the estimated reservation wage remains low; it starts at \$113 61 weeks prior to graduation (i.e., the first period of search), falls to \$79 in the first week following graduation, and then declines thereafter. One year after graduation, the results imply that the weekly reservation wage is just \$4. Corresponding to this is the unsettling result of $-\$104$ per week for net income while unemployed (b). As noted, Wolpin regards the negative of this as direct costs of search (i.e., he disregards income when not in a real job and searching, including that received from jobs that are not "real" by his definition). Incorporating this income would likely reduce this estimate of costs, but the absolute value nevertheless seems unreasonable.

Wolpin also reports results for a model that admits a limited amount of heterogeneity within his sample. Specifically, he specifies a functional form for the mean of the offer distribution:

$$\ln w = \ln \tilde{w} + \beta_1 AFQT + \beta_2 FS$$

where $AFQT$ is a dummy variable that takes a value of 1 if the individual's NLS ability test score is above average, and zero otherwise, and FS is a dummy variable for father's education that takes a value of 1 for high school graduation or more, and zero otherwise. The values for R, T, and the length of the search period prior to graduation are all set equal to the values estimated or used in the first specification and the costs of search and the path followed by the arrival rate are both assumed to be the same for all workers.[41]

The results for this model are qualitatively similar to those described for the representative agent model previously discussed. Mean offers vary as expected with $AFQT$ and FS, from a low of 173 for low ability youth with fathers without a high school diploma to a high of 250 for youth with the opposite characteristics. Measurement error accounts for 9.2 percent of the total variation in offers in this case; though small, this is a much higher proportion than in the simpler model. The reservation wage estimates also exhibit expected variation across groups—although all are very low, as before. Youth with above average ability scores and high school graduate fathers start out with a reservation wage of $163 and it declines to $140 by the week after graduation (roughly the minimum wage for a full-time job). For all other groups, the estimates are lower at all stages of the search process. The estimate for the weekly costs of search is $223, an even higher number than before.

The relative roles for the arrival rate of offers versus the acceptance probability in producing variation in the transition rates for individual workers over the course of the search period following graduation can be examined in Wolpin's model. Overall, the results provide evidence that the arrival rate is by far the dominant factor. The decline in the arrival rate more than offsets the decline in the reservation wage over the search horizon (acceptance probabilities remain above 0.88). The transition rate thus declines over the horizon.

As an informal check on his results, Wolpin compares the observed pattern for the transition rate out of unemployment to the pattern implied by his results for the model without regressors.[42] The patterns are very close for the first 26 weeks after graduation, but they diverge thereafter. Wolpin notes that this may reflect either the sample size or recall error in the reported durations. The mean duration implied by his results is 46.2 weeks, a number very close to the average spell length for his sample 45.6 weeks (complete and incomplete spells included).

Summary

Although the results of the structural analyses reviewed in this section are not identical across studies, some fairly clear patterns appear (Table 5.3).

First, although the male workers studied by Kiefer and Neumann and Narendranathan and Nickell appear to adjust their reservation wages in the theoretically predicted

Table 5.3. Structural Studies

Study	Data	Approach	Findings
Kiefer and Neumann (1979b) Stationary model	United States, 1969–1973 TAA males	Two-stage (probit and regression) procedure	Elasticity of reservation wage with respect to benefits 0.02
Kiefer and Neumann (1979a) Nonstationary model	United States, 1969–1973 TAA males	Maximum likelihood, test of stationarity	Change in reservation wage − 1.7 percent per week; Elasticity of reservation wage with respect to benefits 0.069; 4.3–8.5 percent of wage variation purely random
Kiefer and Neumann (1981) Fixed effects	United States 1969–1973 TAA males	Maximum likelihood, stationary and nonstationary models with individual-specific effects in mean wage offers and reservation wages	Change in reservation wage 0.2 percent per week; Elasticity of reservation wage with respect to benefits: stationary 0.132, nonstationary 0.1; 8.7 percent of unexplained wage variation purely random
Narendranathan and Nickell (1985) Stationary model with Poisson arrivals	United Kingdom, 1978 DHSS male benefit recipients	1. Solution for reservation wage in stationary search model, constant discount rate across workers	Elasticity of reservation wage with respect to benefits: sample 0.13, age groups 0.084–0.196; Elasticity of duration with respect to benefits: sample 0.26, age groups 0.13–0.3; δ (daily): sample 0.018, age groups 0.005–0.024; $\pi(w^r)$: sample 0.57, age groups 0.46–0.84
		2. As in (1), except parameterized discount rate	Elasticity of reservation wage with respect to benefits: sample 0.162, age groups 0.109–0.217; Elasticity of duration with respect to benefits: sample 0.18, age groups 0.07–0.26; δ (daily): sample 0.0162, age groups 0.005–0.02; $\pi(w^r)$: sample 0.73, age groups 0.58–0.9; Both models: longer spells due to lower arrival rates
Devine (1988) Arrival rates versus acceptance probabilities	United States, 1983–1984 SIPP 1984 panel	Representative agent stationary search model, by race, sex, and age group 1. Gamma offer distributions	$\pi(w^r)$: 0.91–1.0; δ (week): 0.02–0.073
		2. Truncated (at zero) normal offer distributions	$\pi(w^r)$: 0.6–1.0; δ (week): 0.05–0.23
Wolpin (1987) Finite horizon model	United States, 1979–1982 NLS New Youth Cohort, white male nonstudent high school graduates	Representative agent finite horizon search model 1. Lognormal offers	δ (week): first week after graduation 0.128; after 54 weeks 0.0091; $\pi(w^r)$: 0.88 in first week after graduation and rises thereafter
		2. Normal offers	Described as unreasonable
		3. Lognormal offers, by NLS ability score and father's education	Similar to (1)

direction when faced with higher benefit levels, the magnitude of the estimated response is small (elasticities: 0.02–0.217). Thus, mean durations are not predicted to change dramatically with large changes in benefit levels (elasticities 0.07–0.3). The latter estimates are noticeably smaller than those reported in the regression and hazard function studies reviewed earlier in this chapter. However, the magnitudes of both the reservation wage and mean duration elasticities reported here are not only consistent with the results of analyses of "direct evidence" discussed in Chapter 4—they are remarkably close.

A second pattern that emerges regards the relative influence of acceptance probabilities versus arrival rates in producing variation in transition rates across workers. According to the results reported here, workers almost always accept an offer—once an offer is received. The longer spells of joblessness experienced by some workers (older workers, nonwhite workers, skilled workers, and workers with less education, in particular) reflect infrequent offers. The results reported here suggest that the action is in the arrival rates. Under a tight interpretation of the job search model—with the arrival rate interpreted as exogenous—this infrequent offer finding shifts responsibility for longer spells of some workers to the demand side of the labor market. On the other hand, variation in arrival rates across workers may reflect variation in search effort. This is the route by which benefits could effect durations. The findings of the studies discussed here do not distinguish these potential sources of variation. We turn to analyses of this and related questions in Chapter 7.

The consistency of findings between the studies discussed here and those in Chapter 4 is encouraging (maybe empirical work is valuable). On a less encouraging note, the results from basic consistency checks reported here generally provide reason to hesitate before drawing any firm conclusions. In particular, the findings of Narendranathan and Nickell (1985), like those of Ridder and Gorter (1986) in their comparable study, suggest that caution must be exercised when attempting to fit structural models at the level of the individual worker. One explanation for the poor fit of their model may be the stationarity maintained in their analysis; the results of Kiefer and Neumann (1979a) discussed here, as well as those in previous sections, suggest that this may not be a good approximation. Their results may also reflect their parameterization of the offer distribution; formal and informal checks on the lognormal specification yield mixed results. Grouping the data to analyze variation across workers at levels somewhere between the micro- and macrolevel represents an alternative to focusing on variation across individual workers. Additional work using this approach seems potentially worthwhile.

This chapter has reviewed regression studies, hazard function studies, and structural studies—all based on unemployment duration and reemployment wage date.

The primary concern of the regression studies was the effect of UI benefits on unemployment spell lengths. Taken together, the results of these studies establish the existence of a positive effect for the size of UI payments on mean spell lengths (as predicted by theory), though not the magnitude of this effect. The results also suggest that potential duration of benefits may be important and that behavior may differ systematically between workers on temporary layoff and workers on permanent layoff. Demographic characteristics also appear important in determining spell lengths. Perhaps most important, these studies point to a clear need for application of econometric methods that conveniently allow for censoring.

The hazard function approach is the technology needed. Using this approach, it is straightforward to handle (at least right) censoring and to investigate questions of duration dependence. Overall, the results of the hazard function studies confirm the finding of a positive benefit level effect reported in the regression studies, but do not pin down its magnitude. Indeed the results of the hazard function studies suggest that attempting to estimate "a benefit effect" may be an inappropriate objective (or at least a less useful one than we once thought). There is evidence that the benefit level effect declines over the course of a spell, that it is sensitive to local and aggregate economic conditions, and that it varies with age and other demographic characteristics. When examined, potential duration of benefit receipt appears to be as important as the size of benefit payments. The type of layoff initiating a spell also appears to be quite important in determining benefit effects. That is, the contrast in benefit effects between workers on temporary layoff and workers on permanent layoff reported in regression studies is confirmed in results of the hazard function studies. Systematic differences beyond benefit effects also appear between spells initiated by involuntary and voluntary separations, and also among the various forms of the latter. A firm negative relation emerges between the hazard function and the local unemployment rate. As expected, increased control for heterogeneity—extra regressors, time-varying regressors, unobserved variables—reduces estimates of duration dependence. It seems clear that there is still room for improvement in specification.

The structural studies use a variety of specifications—each very tightly parameterized and each using somewhat arbitrary assumptions for the purpose at hand. It is fair to say that there is no clear winner (yet) in this specification contest. The most interesting result is the general finding of relatively high acceptance probabilities. This hints that variation in offer arrivals may be the major determinant of variation in unemployment durations. As for benefits, the results of structural studies show a positive but generally smaller effect than the regression and hazard function studies.

Notes

1. Several studies used aggregate time series and state level cross-sectional data to test the implications of search theory (e.g., Lininger, 1963; Holen and Horowitz, 1974; Jackman and Layard, 1988; Jackman et al., 1987; Layard and Nickell, 1986). The early microdata study by Burgess and Kingston (1971) actually represented a response to a study by Chapin (1971) who worked with state level cross-sectional unemployment duration data for the United States.

2. The papers by Ehrenberg and Oaxaca (1976), Holen (1977), Burgess and Kingston (1977), and Classen (1977) were presented together at a 1976 conference on the effects of unemployment insurance benefits on the experience of unemployed workers. Welch (1977) critiques each of these studies and provides his own perception of the strengths and weaknesses of search theory as a framework for analyzing the effects of unemployment insurance programs. Rosen (1977) and Katz and Hight (1977) offer additional comments. Munts and Garfinkel (1974) and others conducted additional empirical analyses of UI disincentive effects in the United States during this same period. See Fields (1977), Hamermesh (1977), and Danziger et al. (1981) for reviews of these early studies of U.S. data. Also, see Cousineau (1985) for a review of early analyses of Canadian data, including several unpublished studies.

3. These standard errors are calculated from reported t statistics. The asterisk indicates that a t statistic of zero is reported.

4. Engineering is defined here as "metal manufacturing, engineering and electrical goods, vehicles and aircraft, and other metal goods."

5. The response rate for the survey was 74.8 percent and yielded a sample of 876 usable interviews, including 218 females. MacKay and Reid exclude females from the sample analyzed here because only 13 percent received unemployment benefits. The additional reduction in sample size is due to exit from the labor force.

6. Given the differences in sample size, one suspects that there are additional differences in sample selection criteria.

7. The results for durations are −0.005 (standard error 0.0027) for black males, −0.007 (standard error 0.002) for black females, −0.008 (standard error 0.004) for white males, and 0.001 (standard error 0.012) for white females.

8. By design, about 40 percent of the initial 1968 sample of households interviewed in the Panel Study of Income Dynamics had incomes less than twice the federal poverty line; the remaining 60 percent represented a stratified random sample for the United States. The representative subsample can be identified using flags provided in the data set, but Feinberg notes that his sample is selected from the entire sample. This is typical in studies using the PSID, which we discuss.

9. The index can take values between 0 and 0.9 and its value is described as depending on the condition of cars, cigarette smoking, health and car insurance, use of seat belts, and savings available. It is not obvious how such a measure should be interpreted, particularly for low income workers. The variable assets is set equal to the sum of house value and car values and the variable liabilities is set equal to the sum of annual mortgage payments and rent payments.

10. The Census classification scheme consists of 125 SMSAs and eight occupational categories, giving a total of 800 classes. Feinberg uses the same standard deviation for each group for all 3 years and adjusts mean wages for inflation using consumer price indices for county of residence.

11. Mellow uses the coefficient estimates reported by Kalachek and Raines (1976), who fit a regression of the log wage on education, current job experience, training, race, age, health status, and additional personal characteristics for the 3,595 workers in the National Longitudinal Survey who were employed as wage and salary workers in 1966. The sample used by Mellow is a subsample of the Kalachek and Raines sample.

12. See Chapter 4 of Killingsworth (1983) for a discussion of these techniques.

13. The regular extension of benefits increased individuals' potential durations of benefits by 50 percent, up to a maximum total of 39 weeks. The FSB provided a 100 percent extension of the regular extended potential duration, up to a maximum total of 65 weeks. Combining state level variation in standard potential durations and individual level variation within states, there is a substantial amount of variation in potential duration in the overall sample.

14. The alternative parametrization for the Weibull, $\lambda_0(t) = t^\alpha$, is sometimes used. We note such cases in our discussion.

15. Ondrich (1985) discussed methods for dealing with left censoring when panel data are available.

16. Lancaster and Nickell (1980) present a joint discussion of their work in this area and this is followed by a discussion. We do not discuss this paper separately.

17. This sample is one of the two analyzed by Lancaster and Chesher (1983, 1984 discussed in Chapter 4).

18. Nickell (1979a) provides additional discussion of the findings reported here.

19. Atkinson and Micklewright (1985) provide an extended discussion of these same issues.

20. In Georgia, the potential period of entitlement depends on previous earnings and a range of possible benefits but may not exceed a statutory maximum of 26 weeks.

21. The multiple spell aspect of these durations is noted in the present paper. A modified version of the Displaced Worker Survey was administered in January 1986. In this version, workers were asked the number of employment spells in the period between displacement and the survey date, but not about the timing of these spells.

22. The proportions for the subsamples are not reported, but weighted tabulations indicate that 9.5 percent of all males and 6.7 percent of all females experienced no unemployment following displacement.

23. The varying-duration sample is excluded because of the nonstationarity introduced by the changes in potential duration.

24. There are also noticeable, though smaller spikes at 28 and 32 weeks in the plots.

25. This is done using the time-varying dummy variables: $Z_{1t} = P_t - t$, $Z_{2t} = \max(0, P_t - t - 5)$, and $Z_{3t} = \max(0, P_t - t - 10)$, where P_t refers to potential duration at t.

26. Meyer actually reports the estimates here and these are the times of the spikes. The reason for the 1 week systematic difference between the Moffitt hazard spikes and the Meyer hazard is not obvious.

27. The approach is described in detail in Han and Hausman (1990) and Meyer (1986). See also Prentice and Gloeckler (1978), Kiefer (1988b), and Horowitz and Neumann (1987).

28. The precise definition of the spline is: If t denotes the number of weeks until benefits are exhausted, then a set of variables for the intervals is defined as UI1 = 1 if $t = 1$, 0 otherwise; UI2–5 = $\min(6 - t, 4)$ if $t \le 5$, 0 otherwise, UI6–10 = $\min(11 - t, 5)$, 0 otherwise, etc.

29. Katz and Meyer (1988b) work with the same data. They note that part of the jump in the hazard in the last week may be spurious. Specifically, many states place a cap on the total amount of benefits an individual can receive in a benefit year. Thus, the payment in the final week of eligibility can be relatively small and some workers may simply choose not to pick it up. In the data analyzed here, this effect cannot be measured, but they note that results for different data indicate that this reduced payment effect on the hazard is not likely to be large.

30. As discussed earlier, the PSID sample includes an oversampling of low income households by design. Working with a random subsample is possible, but the sample used here is not restricted in this way.

31. Sex is not included as a regressor, not is it clear from the course of discussion whether or not females are included in the sample.

32. See Woodbury and Spiegelman (1987) for a complete description of the Illinois experiment. New Jersey, Pennsylvania, and Washington have also served as experimental sites. In the New Jersey and Pennsylvania experiments, participants also received job search assistance. Levine (1989) fits a representative agent search model to data from this experiment and a different bonus experiment in New Jersey. His objective is to "test" the basic search model, modified to include the potential reemployment bonus, by checking the fit of parameter estimates obtained using data for one state to experimental responses in the other. The model succeeds in predicting the pattern of program response, although the observed magnitude exceeds the predicted magnitude of the response. This seems about the best one might expect, given no control for heterogeneity, problems with the data, and the simple structure of the model.

33. The log-logistic hazard is $\alpha t^{\alpha-1}/(1 + t)^\alpha$. Thus, it is monotonically decreasing for $\alpha < 1$ and resembles the lognormal for $\alpha > 1$, with a maximum at $t + (\alpha - 1)^{1/\alpha}$.

34. This is the basic search model set out in the early papers by Mortensen (1970a,b) and McCall (1970).

35. OLS also yields consistent estimates, but not consistent standard errors. Kiefer and Neumann report results from application of both methods. This two-step estimation is discussed by Heckman (1979) and Lee (1978).

36. The mean age is 47.8 years, the mean years of schooling is 10.2 years, and the fraction unionized is 70.4 percent.

37. Fishe (1982) follows an approach quite similar to that of Kiefer and Neumann (1979b) in his analysis of different data. However, he adopts an exclusion restriction that is inconsistent with the rest of the model. Namely, he assumes that some regressors in the offer equation do not affect the reservation wage. His results are therefore difficult to interpret in terms of search theory.

38. The structure of the sampling plan and survey instruments for the SIPP are quite complicated. Devine provides a detailed discussion.

39. Wolpin does not explicitly consider receipt of nonemployment income, but refers only to direct costs of search. However, his "-c" is the same as net income when unemployed, i.e., b in the notation of Chapter 2.

40. The strategy of accepting a job early and quitting, in order to reinitialize the arrival probability process, must be ruled out by assumption. See Burdett and Sharma (1988). Note also that the assumptions that the search horizon is finite, i.e., that the period of search terminates at $t = T$, and that offers arrive in $t > T$ are somewhat at odds.

41. Wolpin notes that he estimated a model that allowed variation in the arrival rate path across workers, but a chi-square test did not allow rejection of the restriction to a uniform path across workers.

42. Wolpin restricts his attention to this case because of the small cell sizes when the sample is partitioned by *AFQT* and *FS*.

6

Labor Market Histories

We have restricted our attention so far to studies of the transition into employment. Here, we broaden the scope of our attention and examine analyses of labor market histories. We start with studies of worker movement in both directions between employment and unemployment (or nonemployment, more generally). Studies based on three-state models of the labor market, which distinguish unemployment and nonparticipation, follow. Studies in the third section focus on transitions out of unemployment, but distinguish unemployment spells following temporary and permanent layoffs. In the last section, we turn to studies based on alternative multistate models of the labor market that do not fit neatly into the categories listed above.

The data available here consist of observations on spell lengths in the relevant states and perhaps accepted or previous wages (reservation wages and offer arrival data are not available). We start each section with reduced-form studies. In all cases, the theoretical basis of analysis has a Markov or semi-Markov structure. The hazard function approach can thus be applied directly in the two-state studies. In the multistate studies, spells in any one state can end with a transition into more than one alternative state. The distribution of durations in each state thus has a "competing-risks" formulation and the hazard function approach can be used in these cases to model and estimate the destination specific (or "cause-specific") hazards. Structural studies follow the reduced form studies in each section. The approaches taken in these studies extend those used in structural studies of Chapters 4 and 5.[1]

Transitions in and out of Employment

We start this section with studies that use proportional hazards models to analyze transitions between employment and either unemployment or nonemployment. Burdett et al. (1985) analyze data for male family heads in the United States. Jensen (1987a) analyzes data for young workers in Denmark. Miller and Volker (1987) study data for young workers in Australia. We next turn to studies that use two-state models to address specific issues. Kiefer (1985a) analyzes data for male workers in the United States and focuses on returns-to-education measured in terms of effects on labor market transitions. Stephenson (1981) analyzes differences in labor market transitions between young white and nonwhite females in the United States. Tuma and Robins (1980) study the effects of a negative income tax on nonemployment and employment spell lengths using data from social experiments in the United States. Ridder (1988) analyzes the dynamic effects of training, employment, and recruitment programs using data for a sample of Dutch program participants. In the last study of this section, Flinn and Heckman (1982b) estimate the parameters of a representative agent model; their approach turns on treating their sample of young male workers in the United States as a random sample from a homogeneous population.

Burdett, Kiefer, and Sharma (1985)

In Chapter 2, we considered a two-state Markov model of labor market turnover in which employed workers face an exogenous probability of layoff. Burdett et al. (1985) generalize this model so that workers become unemployed in the event of a layoff or a quit—with each the result of a bad random draw from the distribution of offers faced. A worker's environment differs from the standard job search model in that (1) a worker's wage w may change from time to time when employed; (2) each new wage is a random draw from the same offer distribution faced when unemployed, $F(w)$; (3) the arrival of such changes follows a Poisson process with parameter δ_e, which the worker knows; (4) a worker may be laid off at any time; and (5) the probability of a layoff, $a(t_e)$, depends inversely on duration of the current employment spell, T_e. As in the simple search models, the optimal strategy for an income maximizing worker is a reservation wage policy. Specifically, an employed worker will remain employed if the new realization of the wage in the present job at tenure t_e, $w(t_e)$, exceeds the reservation wage at t_e, $w^r(t_e)$. The latter equates the present values of unemployed search and continued employment at t_e. It can be shown that $w^r(t_e)$ is (strictly) decreasing in t_e under the assumption that $a(t_e)$ is (strictly) decreasing in t_e. For an unemployed worker, the reservation wage is simply $w^r(0)$. Letting δ_u denote the arrival rate of offers when unemployed, and using our previous notation for the acceptance probabilities, the transition rates out of unemployment and out of employment for the model can be written as:

$$\tau_u = \delta_u \pi(w^r(0)), \qquad \text{and} \qquad \tau_e(t_e) = \delta_e \pi(w^r(t_e)) + a(t_e)$$

The transition rate out of unemployment τ_u is independent of previous experience in the labor market, including duration of the current spell t_u. Consequently, unemployment durations T_u have an exponential distribution with parameter τ_u, as in the simplest job search model. The transition rate out of employment $\tau_e(t_e)$ does not depend on the worker's labor market experience prior to the current spell, but it does depend on duration of the current spell. The density for employment durations T_e is thus

$$g_e(t_e) = \tau_e(t_e) \exp\left\{ -\int_0^{t_e} \tau_e(s) \, ds \right\}$$

The labor market history of a worker is thus a two-state semi-Markov process.[2]

Extending the hazard function approach to fit this model using labor market history data is straightforward. Each spell in a worker's labor market history is independent of those preceding and following it because of the semi-Markov property of the model; it thus enters separately into the sample likelihood function. For uncensored employment and unemployment spells, the contributions are the densities $g_e(t_e)$ and $g_u(t_u)$. For right- or left-censored unemployment spells, the contributions are the survivor function for unemployment evaluated at the observed lengths. The symmetry of the treatment of right- and left-censored spells is possible because of the memoryless property of the exponential unemployment duration distribution. The survivor function for employment $S_e(t_e)$ is entered for right-censored employment spells; left-censored employment spells are omitted to avoid the problem of initializing spells when the hazard depends on duration. Heterogeneity due to observable characteristics is incorporated into the structure using proportional hazards specifications. For unemployment, the hazard for individual i is defined as

$$\tau_{ui} = \exp\{x_i\beta_u\}$$

To allow for duration dependence in the employment hazard, a Weibull specification is used,

$$\tau_{ei}(t_e) = \alpha t_e^{\alpha-1} \exp\{x_i\beta_e\}$$

The model is fit using panel data for a sample of male family heads taken from the Public Use files from the Denver Income Maintenance Experiment (DIME). The DIME was an experiment conducted to investigate the effects of a negative income tax on labor supply. Low income and nonwhite populations were oversampled by design. Consequently, these data have the disadvantage of not being representative for the U.S. labor force. On the other hand, these data have appealing aspects for the present analysis. Families and individuals were interviewed quarterly between 1971 and 1974 and data were collected on demographic characteristics and labor market experience for the intervening periods. Information on the timing of changes in labor market status is sufficient to allow labor market histories to be constructed using standard CPS definitions.[3] Since assignment to treatment and control groups was random within combinations of stratification variables (pretransfer income and race), nonrandomness arising from experimental treatment effects can be avoided by working only with data for the controls and Burdett et al. do this.[4] Durations are measured in days and their sample consists of 1,707 employment spells (721 right censored) and 1,180 unemployment spells (374 right or left censored). (Nonparticipation spells are excluded.) Wages are also available for employed workers.

Results are reported for a specification for each transition rate that includes a quadratic in age, education, dummies for blacks and hispanics, and an instrument for the mean of the offer distribution. The mean offer instruments pertain to the quarter in which a spell occurred and they are calculated using results from log wage regressions on a quadratic in age, education, and race.[5] Results are also reported for regressor specifications that include a constant, alone, and then the quadratic in age, education, race, hispanic origin and the wage added successively.

Focusing first on the results for the employment to unemployment transition, the estimate for α is 0.69 (standard error 0.0182) using the full regressor specification, which implies negative duration dependence. This result is robust with respect to respecification of the regressors.[6] The coefficient estimates generally have expected signs and, for the most part, they differ significantly from zero at standard levels. The major exception is the coefficient for the wage variable; while negative, it is insignificant at standard levels. One explanation for this wage result might be wage changes associated with job-to-job transitions within single employment spells that are not distinguished in this analysis. Alternatively, it may reflect failure to distinguish voluntary and involuntary separations in measuring transitions into unemployment, and temporary versus permanent separations among the latter.

The findings for the unemployment to employment transition rate are similar to those discussed in Chapter 5. The results provide evidence of a large nonlinear age effect (positive and then negative) and a positive education effect. The coefficients for the non-white race dummy variables are large and negative, and the coefficient for black workers is larger in absolute value than the coefficient for hispanics. The estimated coefficient for the wage variable is positive and large, both in practical and statistical terms. Burdett et al. note that a Weibull specification for the unemployment duration distribution was also estimated. A complete set of results is not reported, but the estimate for α is reported as 0.84 (standard error 0.019), which might be interpreted as evidence against the constant unemployment hazard specification.

Burdett et al. do not estimate a model that incorporates unobserved heterogeneity, but they provide results from some formal specification analysis. Specifically, they consider the set of alternative specifications for the duration distribution with unobserved heterogeneity incorporated via a multiplicative disturbance in the hazard with unit mean and unknown variance (i.e., $\tau_e(v) = v\tau_e$, with τ_e defined as above and $v \backsim H(1, \sigma_v^2)$, for some continuous distribution H). The specification described above represents the degenerate case for v (i.e., $\sigma_v^2 = 0$), and they test this null against the alternatives using a Lagrange Multiplier test. This test is attractive because it requires no distributional assumption for v. (See Kiefer [1985b] and Sharma [1989]) for a detailed development of the test procedure.) The test results indicate the presence of unobserved heterogeneity in both the employment hazard and the unemployment hazard—even with the full list of regressors. Consequently, the findings for duration dependence described should be viewed with some caution.

Jensen (1987a)

Jensen takes an approach like that of Burdett et al. (1985) to study employment and unemployment duration data for young Danish workers. Specifically, Jensen fits Weibull proportional hazard models for the employment and unemployment hazard rates separately for males aged 17–21, females aged 17–21, males aged 22–24, and females aged 22–24. Each group sample consists of between 500 and 1,000 observations, selected randomly from a longitudinal data set constructed for about 5 percent of the Danish population using unemployment insurance and other administrative records.[7] Durations are measured in days and the period of observation is 1979–1980.

The explanatory variables of the model are labor market experience, the average hourly wage for the year of the spell, net taxable wealth, and dummy variables for non-metropolitan residence, children under age 17 (females only), completion of a vocational training program, industry, membership in particular unions, enrollment in the unemployment insurance program, and receipt of sickness benefits for 3 weeks or more in a given year.[8]

Results are given in Table 6.1 for Weibull parameters using

$$\tau_j(t_j) = t_j^\alpha \exp\{x_i\beta_j\}$$

Table 6.1. Weibull Parameter Estimates[a]

	Baseline: $\lambda_0(t) = t^\alpha$			
	F 17–21	M 17–21	F 22–24	M 22–24
τ_e	−0.44	−0.47	−0.48	−0.44
	(0.02)	(0.02)	(0.02)	(0.02)
τ_u	−0.19	−0.11	−0.15	−0.08
	(0.03)	(0.03)	(0.03)	(0.03)

[a]From Jensen (1987a). Standard errors are in parentheses.

for the hazard rate out of state j, j = employment, unemployment. Note that under this specification, duration dependence is indicated by the sign of the parameter α (as opposed to its value relative to unity under the alternative Weibull specification). All of these estimates are precise and they indicate substantial negative duration dependence in both hazard rates for all groups. The sickness variable has a positive effect on the transition rate out of employment, which makes sense, but the results for remaining variables are in some ways surprising. Metropolitan residence, for example, has a large negative effect on both transition rates. Labor market experience has large, positive coefficients in both transition rates for younger workers, but it appears irrelevant for workers in the 22–24 age groups. The estimated effects of both the wage and unemployment insurance receipt on the hazard rate out of unemployment are insignificant at standard levels for all groups. It may be that the wage results reflect combined (offsetting) effects of higher benefits due to higher wages and the direct effect of higher mean wages, although the benefit results are consistent with findings for young workers in the United States and United Kingdom. The estimated effects of unemployment insurance coverage on the hazard rate out of employment are positive and significant for all groups. The wage results for the hazard rate out of employment are most surprising. The wage coefficients are positive for all groups and they differ significantly from zero for all groups except males aged 22–24. To some extent, the complete set of findings for wages and insurance may reflect a relatively high incidence of temporary layoffs among high wage workers. Jensen and Westergaard-Nielsen (1990) explore this explanation and we discuss their study (along with other analyses of this question) later in this chapter.

Miller and Volker (1987)

Miller and Volker also fit Weibull proportional hazard models in their study of unemployment and employment duration data for Australian youth, aged 15–24, collected in the 1985 Australian Longitudinal Survey.[9] Relative to most studies, their sample sizes are quite large. For males, they have 2,443 single spell employment observations (2,067 right censored) and 819 single spell unemployment observations (443 right censored). For females, they have 2,123 single spell employment observations (1,816 right censored) and 622 single spell unemployment observations (318 right censored). Their hazard specification is $\tau_{ji}(t_j) = \alpha t^{\alpha-1} \exp\{x_i\beta_j\}$, for j = unemployment, employment.

Starting with employment durations, the regressors include categorical education variables (10, 11, or 12 years, trade qualifications, other postsecondary qualifications, university degree, and secondary school diploma), labor market experience, eight industry dummies, five dummy variables for foreign birthplaces, dummy variables for rural and small urban residence, five search method dummy variables, total number of children (males only), dummy variables for children under age 2 and children at least age 2 (females only), and dummy variables for marital status, partner's employment status, a poor command of English, and part-time jobs. For both males and females, the Weibull parameters for the employment hazard are significantly less than 1—0.5501 (standard error 0.035) for males and 0.6001 (standard error 0.038) for females—thus implying strong negative duration dependence. The results for remaining variables are generally consistent with expectations. Male workers who remain in school beyond grade 10 have longer employment durations that those who leave school earlier. This does not hold for females. Both males and females with diplomas or degrees appear to have significantly longer durations, but trade and other postsecondary qualifications do not significantly affect spell lengths. Labor market experience has a significant positive effect on employment spell lengths; this result is somewhat surprising—given the age range of 19–25. Married males have significantly longer durations, but no similar marriage effect appears for females. On the other hand, females with children under 2 have significantly shorter employment spells. Workers holding part-time jobs tend to exit more quickly. A rather interesting result appears for the search method variables; workers who use the public employment service have significantly shorter employment spells than workers who use direct application as their primary search method. Similarly, workers directed into public employment programs tend to have shorter spells. Industry seems to be a significant determinant of spell length; in particular, government workers and other nonpersonal service workers (e.g., finance or trade) appear to have relatively longer spells. Finally, employment status of partners appears to move together; workers with unemployed partners have significantly shorter employment spells. This may simply reflect local labor market conditions; no measure of local labor market tightness is included. Remaining variables appear irrelevant at standard levels of significance.

Turning to unemployment durations, the Weibull parameters are again close in size and both are significantly less than 1 (males 0.666 [standard error 0.038], females 0.676 [standard error 0.042]). The list of regressors is the same, except for the omission of the part-time and industry variables. Again, the results are generally precise and consistent with basic search theoretic hypotheses. Workers with higher education or postsecondary qualifications have significantly shorter unemployment spells, as do married workers and residents of large urban areas. The partner unemployment pattern found in the employment duration results also appears here, that is, workers with unemployed partners have significantly longer spells. Similarly, use of the public employment agency service is associated with longer unemployment spells for both males and females, relative to direct application to firms. Reliance on friends and relatives, on the other hand, is associated with significantly shorter unemployment spells.

Kiefer (1985a)

Kiefer presents some suggestive evidence on the rate-of-return to education—measured in terms of its effects on labor market transitions. Specifically, Kiefer fits a nonstochastic constant hazard specifiction for the two-state model using data for male workers in the United States taken from the Denver Income Maintenance Experiment (DIME). Treating a spell as an observation, his sample consists of 2,411 employment spells and 2,008 nonemployment spells (i.e., either unemployment or nonparticipation). Years of education, a quadratic in age, race, Hispanic origin, and a constant are included in each hazard specification.

Overall, the coefficient estimates are precise and consistent with findings reported elsewhere. Nonwhite and Hispanic workers appear to enter employment more slowly and leave employment more quickly than white workers. The transition rate out of nonemployment also decreases with age. The transition rate out of employment decreases with age initially, but eventually increases. As for the effect of education on spell lengths, the elasticities at the sample mean (11.0 years) are 0.76 for employment duration and -0.37 for nonemployment durations. For comparison, Kiefer reports results from OLS regressions, with and without dummy variables to indicate a censored spell. The implied employment and unemployment duration elasticities for education are 0.5 and -0.56 without the censoring dummy and 0.42 and -0.57 with the dummy variable added. Although close to each other, the magnitude of the employment elasticities differs substantially from those implied by the hazard function results—reinforcing the view that caution must be exercised in interpreting regression results.

Kiefer uses these results to calculate the effect of education on the steady-state nonemployment rate, p_n. Using the relation $p_n = \tau_e/(\tau_e + \tau_n)$, the proportionate effect of a change in education x on the nonemployment rate is

$$\frac{d \ln p_n}{dx} = \frac{d \ln \tau_e}{dx} - \frac{d \ln (\tau_e + \tau_u)}{dx}$$

The employment effect is calculated analogously. For these data, the estimates for p_n and p_e are 0.116 and 0.884 and the estimate for the proportionate education effect is -0.91. The education elasticity of the steady-state nonemployment rate is thus about -1.0 at the sample mean.

Stephenson (1981)

Stephenson studies the employment exit and entry behavior of young women using data collected in the National Longitudinal Survey of Young Women. His sample consists of 171 black and white women who left school in 1970, completed the 1970 to 1973 surveys, and had all relevant data available. Overall, Stephenson works with 201 nonemployment spells and 240 employment spells.

Stephenson's primary concern is the relationship between work during school and employment experience after leaving. Toward this end, he fits constant hazard models for the transition rates out of employment and unemployment using postschool duration observations. His explanatory variables are the local unemployment rate, an NLS ability index, and dummy variables for race, marital status, family low income status, high school graduate, region, presence of young children, residence in an SMSA, and vocational education. To measure job experience in school, Stephenson includes two dummy variables. The first indicates that a job was held during school and it ended 2 weeks after leaving school or before. The second indicates that a job was held during school and kept beyond 2 weeks after leaving school.

The coefficient estimates for both hazards have sensible signs but they are generally imprecise, probably as a result of the small sample size. The two exceptions are the dummy variables for high school graduate and holding a job during school (that does not continue beyond). The results imply that high school graduates have significantly longer employment spells, though their nonemployment spell lengths are not significantly shorter or longer. On the other hand, those who work while in school appear to have significantly shorter nonemployment spells, but neither shorter nor longer employment spells.

Stephenson also fits the models separately for white and black women. A likelihood ratio test allows rejection of the hypothesis that the coefficients are the same across groups. As for individual variables, the differences are in some ways striking. Focusing first on the transition out of nonemployment, these results suggest that the full sample result for in-school work experience largely reflects the experience of white women; the coefficient for black females is small and insignificant. On the other hand, nonemployment spells of young black women are longer in the South and they appear sensitive to the local unemployment rate—while spells of young white women appear unaffected by the values of these variables. The most interesting results for the hazards out of nonemployment are the low income family coefficients. They suggest that young white women in low income families have significantly longer nonemployment spells, while young black women in low income families have significantly shorter spells. The results for the hazard out of employment are closer to the full sample results. In particular, the high school graduate results hold for both groups. Nonwhite workers living outside the South and outside SMSAs also appear to have longer employment durations, but nothing else appears statistically relevent.

Tuma and Robins (1980)

Many of the studies we discuss in this chapter work with data generated by the Seattle and Denver Income Maintenance Experiments (SIME and DIME).[10] Typically, the samples are restricted to members of the control groups to avoid concern about treatment effects on behavior. Families in the treatment group (selected randomly from all participant families within each race and income group) experienced a change in disposable income at the time of enrollment. Specifically, the change y was determined by the negative income tax (NIT) formula:

$$y = G - Y_0(\beta_e - Y_0 d - \beta_0)$$

if the right-hand side was greater than zero, and zero otherwise, where G is a guaranteed income level based on family size, Y_0 is gross annual family income at enrollment, β_0 is the nonexperimental tax rate, β_e is an experimental tax rate, and d is a rate of decline. Different values for G and β_e (11 pairs in all) and two values of d were used in the experiments and the duration of the program was either 3 or 5 years.

In this study, Tuma and Robins work with data for both controls and treatment participants. Their objective is to determine the effects of the NIT on employment and nonemployment spell lengths. Toward this end, they fit constant hazard models for transitions out of employment and unemployment separately for husbands, wives, and female household heads. Using spells as the unit of observation, their samples consist of 2,991 husband employment spells, 1,692 wife employment spells, 1,523 female head employment spells, 1,837 husband nonemployment spells, 2,189 wife nonemployment spells, and 1,418 female head nonemployment spells. Roughly 60 percent of all families in the SIME and DIME were assigned to treatment groups, but a breakdown of the spells with respect to status is not reported. Hispanic workers are not included here; Tuma and Robins report that these data were not available when they were doing their research. Durations are measured in weeks and the sample period is the first 24 months of the experiment. The list of regressors is the same across both hazards and subsamples. The nonexperimental variables are a predicted value for normal income category, age, years of education, family size, number of children under 16, weeks worked in the year preceding the experiment, dummy variables for race and location, preexperimental disposable income, the preexperimental net hourly wage, and dummy variables for receipt of Manpower counseling and training subsidies. The categorical income and race variables are entered as controls for the stratified random assignment of treatment and control group status; Tuma and Robins note that separate analysis by stratification group was desired but precluded by limited sample sizes. The treatment variables are dummy variables to indicate participation in an NIT program and whether the program had a duration of either 3 or 5 years.

The results for the program effects are quite interesting. The estimated effect of the 5-year NIT treatment on the hazard out of employment is positive for all groups, but significant at standard levels only for husbands; for wives and female heads, the coefficients are small in both practical and statistical terms. Moreover, the results indicate that program duration is important insofar as employment exit behavioral effects are concerned. Even husbands' behavior appears unaffected when the program lasts only 3 years. The estimated effects of the 5-year NIT treatment on nonemployment exit rates are negative for all groups, as expected, and significant (at the 1 percent level). Restricting the program duration to 3 years appears to offset this, but only husbands appear essentially unaffected by treatment in the shorter program.

Results for additional variables are reported in an appendix. Blacks, older workers, and Seattle residents in each subsample appear to have longer employment spells. Seattle residents and older workers also have longer nonemployment spells, as do black men and female heads. Relative to white wives, however, black wives have shorter unemployment spells. More weeks worked in the previous year is associated with longer spells of employment after the start of the program and with faster movement into employment from nonemployment. Employment spell lengths increase with educational attainment among husbands, but not among wives or female heads. On the other hand, the duration of nonemployment spells of wives decreases with increases in educational attainment, but no similar effect appears for husbands and female heads. The results also suggest that employment spells are generally shorter and unemployment spells are generally longer among Manpower program participants, particularly when training is involved. The predicted effects are generally small, however, and not well determined statistically. Moreover, these measured effects may simply reflect time spent participating.

Ridder (1988)

Ridder attempts to determine the effects of training, recruitment, and employment programs on unemployment and employment spell lengths using data for a sample of 337 participants in such programs in 1979 and early 1980 in Rotterdam, the Netherlands. The participants were interviewed in May and June 1982, and for each worker, information was collected for the two spells preceding selection into a program and all subsequent spells up to the time of the interview. The major constraint faced by Ridder is the absence of data for a relevant control group. Selection into these programs was nonrandom, but precise rules are unknown.

Ridder models the labor market history of an individual as a nonstationary Markov process. Precisely, the density for a spell in state i, entered at time T_0, is defined as

$$f_i(t \mid t_0) = \tau_i(t_0 + t) \exp\left[-\int_0^t \tau_i(t_0 + s)\, ds\right]$$

where $\tau_i(t_0 + s)$ denotes the transition rate from state i into alternative states j, $\tau_i(s) = \sum_{j \neq i} \tau_{ij}(s)$, which may vary over time. In particular, a program effect on transition rates translates into a systematic difference before, during, and after participation. Now, if selection into the labor market programs was a random process, analysis of the labor market history data could proceed as in the studies discussed above. However, given that nonrandom selection procedures were used, Ridder uses the limited information he has about the selection process—that selection into any of the programs was more likely for unemployed individuals.

Precisely, Ridder treats the observed labor market history for an individual as con-sisting of two parts—a retrospective part for the period preceding selection for partici-pation and a prospective part for the period following selection. The prospective portion of the observed path consists of N completed spells and another spell in progress at the time of the interview. To account for the nonrandom selection of participants, Ridder conditions the prospective portion of the history on this transition. Beyond this, stan-dard procedures are followed in specifying the prospective contribution to the sample likelihood, that is, densities are entered for completed spells and the survivor function is entered for the spell in progress at the time of the interview.

Modeling the retrospective portion of the observed history—to determine program effects—is less straightforward. Ridder makes several simplifying assumptions to make the problem tractable. As noted, Ridder has observations on only two completed spells preceding the selection date. Accounting for the truncation of the second spell in prog-ress at the time of selection is straightforward; it is simply treated as a right-censored spell. The more complex problem is modeling the first spell. Ridder assumes that the transition rates in the period before selection are left continuous (i.e., that the environ-ment of the worker had no discrete changes, such as the program participation analyzed here), so that the entry rate into the state i is defined as

$$e_i(t) = \sum_{j \neq i} p_j(t)\tau_{ji}(t)$$

where $p_j(t)$ denotes the probability of being in state j at time t Normalizing time so that the selection date is time 0, then $-t_1 - t_2$ and $-t_2$ represent the starting times of the first and second retrospective spells, respectively, and the density for the observed ret-rospective history is

$$f(i_1, t_1, i_2, t_2) = e_{i1}(-t_1 - t_2)$$
$$\times \exp\left[-\int_0^{t_1} \tau_{i1}(-t_1 - t_2 + s)\, ds\right]$$
$$\times \tau_{i1 i2}(-t_2) \exp\left[-\int_0^{t_1} \tau_{i2}(-t_2 + s)\, ds\right]$$

where i_1 and i_2 denote the states occupied in the first and second retrospective spells. Assuming that the starting point of the history is sufficiently far in the past, the marginal probability of being in state i_2 at the time of selection is $p_{i2}(0)$. Thus, the density of the observed history conditioned on the state occupied at the time of selection is

$$f(i_1, t_1, t_2 | i_2) = \frac{f(i_1, t_1, i_2, t_2)}{p_{i2}(0)}$$

As it stands, the model is still quite complex. To simplify matters when turning to the data, Ridder restricts his attention to transitions between unemployment and employment. More important, he assumes that the economy was stable in the period preceding selection—so that transition rates between labor market states were constant over time. He also assumes that the entry rates are constant over time, that is, that the stochastic process representing a labor market history was in equilibrium at the time of selection. (He notes that the major deterioration in labor market conditions in the Netherlands started in the second half of 1980, that is, after the selection date.) It follows that

$$p_U(0) = e_E \frac{1}{\tau_E} \tau_{EU} \frac{1}{\tau_U}$$

where E and U refer to employment and unemployment, respectively. Upon substitution into the conditional density for the two state model, we have

$$f(E, t_E, t_U | U) = \tau_E \exp[-\tau_E t_E] \tau_U \exp[-\tau_U t_U]$$

which is simply the product of the densities for the spells preceding selection. This serves as the contribution to the likelihood for an individual who was unemployed at the selection date; the analogous density appears for those employed at the selection date.

Ridder uses the following specification for the transition rates:

$$\tau_{ij}(t, x; \beta) = \exp\{x'\beta_{1ij} + z(t)'\beta_{2ij}\}$$

for $i, j = $ U, E, $i \neq j$. The time-invariant regressors include age, sex, years of education, and dummy variables for minority workers, frequent spells of unemployment, and long spells of unemployment. Ridder describes these last two variables as controls for unmeasured heterogeneity. Several time-varying variables are included in $z(t)$. First, there are three time-varying dummy variables to measure program effects. The first takes a value of 1 after selection and zero before. To allow for variation in the program effects across demographic groups, interactions of this variable with age, sex, and minority dummy variables are also included. The second variable takes a value of 1 during program participation and zero otherwise. The third indicates program completion. Calendar time dummy variables are also included to control for changing labor market conditions.

Estimated effects of participation in the alternative programs on spell lengths are reported for workers in various sex, migrant, and age (less than 35, at least 35) groups. (A full set of coefficient estimates is not provided.) The estimates are generally imprecise, but some patterns nevertheless emerge. Focusing first on employment spells, younger females and migrant workers appear to benefit most from participation in any program, while males over 35 actually appear to have shorter employment spells following participation. Looking across programs, employment programs appear to be the most beneficial in terms of increasing employment spell lengths and training programs appear to be the least effective. The results for unemployment spell lengths are somewhat unsettling. They suggest that unemployment spells tend to be lengthened by participation in any of the programs and particularly by training program participation. Ridder notes that these pretreatment/posttreatment unemployment spell effects are likely to be biased. Specifically, the estimates are unbiased only if the transition rates out of unemployment are actually constant over time and selection of participants was random from the stock unemployed (e.g., duration of the spell in progress at the selection date did not matter).

Results are also reported for the dummy variables for the periods during program participation and after. During participation in employment programs, workers appear to have a higher probability of moving into unemployment and a higher probability of changing jobs. On the other hand, transition rates do not appear to be affected during participation in training and recruitment programs, but workers who complete these programs appear to have a significantly lower probability of becoming employed.

To bring all of his findings together, Ridder carries out a variety of simulations; specifically, the characteristics of a "typical" participant in each program are altered one at a time. These results suggest that labor market conditions significantly alter the observed outcomes of program participation. They also suggest that educational attainment plays an important role in producing variation in both the incidence and duration of unemployment spells across workers, as well as variation in employment spell lengths and the rate of job-to-job transitions—at least among the population of potential program participants. Finally, the labor market position of the employment program participants (male or female, migrant or nonmigrant) at the time of selection appears to have been weak relative to participants in the training and recruitment program participants. This translates into a warning to be cautious when examining the estimated multiplicative effects on spell lengths.[11]

Flinn and Heckman (1982b)[12]

The two-state Markov model of Chapter 2 serves as the theoretical basis for the analysis of Flinn and Heckman. Specifically, they work with a representative agent version under the matching interpretation for the random layoffs, with two alternative parametric assumptions for the match (i.e., offer) distribution—normal and exponential. Flinn and Heckman treat their data as a random sample from a homogeneous population and this simplifies the estimation problem immensely.

Precisely, Flinn and Heckman work with the joint distribution of accepted wages and nonemployment spell durations. Letting individuals be indexed by i, this is

$$h(t_i,w_i) = \tau \exp\{-\tau t_i\}f(w_i)/\pi(w^r), \qquad w_i \geq w^r$$
$$= \delta \exp\{-\tau t_i\}f(w_i), \qquad w_i \geq w^r$$

where the second expression follows from the definition of τ. The minimum accepted wage observed for their sample is used as an estimate for the reservation wage. This is the realization of the first-order statistic for accepted wages under the homogeneous population assumption and thus has the attractive property of consistency at a fast rate of convergence.[13] The sample likelihood is then conditioned on this estimate and maximized to obtain consistent estimates of the offer distribution parameters, the arrival rate δ, and the transition rate τ for the sample. For uncensored observations, the contribution to the sample likelihood is simply the joint density with the estimate for the reservation wage substituted for w^r. For censored spells, the contribution is the simply the survivor function, with the transition rate out of unemployment conditioned on the estimate for w^r. Note that the reservation wage estimate is not the maximum likelihood estimate. This procedure does not impose the optimality condition of Equation 2.5

relating the reservation wage to other parameters. (See Chapter 3 for additional discussion of this approach.)

To estimate the transition rate out of employment a, the method of maximum likelihood is applied separately to data on employment spell durations. With estimates for δ_u, w^r, a, the offer distribution, and an outside estimate for the discount rate, an estimate for net nonemployment income b is obtained by solving the optimality condition for the model,

$$b^* = w^{r*} - (r^* + a^*)^{-1}\delta^* \int_{w^{r*}}^{\infty} (w - w^{r*}) \, dF(w \mid w^{r*}, \theta^*)$$

where θ^* denotes the parameters of the offer distribution and the asterisks denote estimates. Finally, an estimate for the steady-state unemployment rate is obtained using the relation $u^* = p^* = a^*/(a^* + \tau_u^*)$

Flinn and Heckman work with data for a sample of white male high school graduates, ages 20 to 24, from the National Longitudinal Survey of Young Men who were not enrolled full-time in school when interviewed in 1971 and who were hourly workers if employed. Durations are measured in months. Overall, their sample consists of 231 nonemployment spells and 2,915 employment spells.

Two aspects of the results that are of particular interest are the level of the acceptance probability and the sensitivity of this result to the match specification. Under the exponential specification, the estimate for the acceptance probability is 0.60. Under the normal, the estimate is 0.92.[14] Thus, the results appear quite sensitive to the functional form specification of the offer distribution. The monthly arrival rate estimates are 0.20 in the exponential model and 0.132 in the normal model. In the normal case, the low transition rate of young workers appears to be due primarily to infrequent arrivals of any offers, but this hypothesis is not strongly supported by the exponential results.

The results for b^* under alternative estimates of 0.05 and 0.10 for the discount rate provide general specification checks. Under the normal, these estimates are -0.33 and -1.45, respectively, while under the exponential, they are -1.14 and -2.69. These can be interpreted as implying very high direct costs of search, very low income when out of work, or both. The estimate of the steady-state unemployment rate implied by the estimates for a and τ_u can be regarded as a rough check on the duration data. This is 0.225 and compares favorably with the actual nonemployment rate for this demographic group based on the CPS for this period, 0.245.[15]

Summary

The studies of this section provide a variety of interesting (and in some cases, curious) findings. These are summarized in Table 6.2. First, the results generally suggest a decreasing transition rate out of employment. There is also evidence of at least weak negative duration dependence in the transition rate into employment. In both cases, however, caution must be exercised in drawing conclusions because of potential biases due to unmeasured heterogeneity. On this note, the results from specification tests done by Burdett et al. (1985) are not encouraging. As for variation in the transition rates with the wage rate, neither Jensen nor Burdett et al. find evidence of a statistically significant negative relationship between the wage rate and the exit rate from employment. Jensen (1987a) actually finds evidence of the opposite, that is, a positive relationship between wage rates and transition rates out of employment. These findings are somewhat puz-

Table 6.2. Transitions in and out of Employment

Study	Data	Proportional Hazard Model Specification	Findings
		Hazard Function Studies	
Burdett, Kiefer and Sharma (1985)	United States, 1971–1974 DIME controls, male family heads	Constant and Weibull ($\alpha t^{\alpha-1}$) baselines	Employment: α = 0.69 (S.E. 0.02); Unemployment: α = 0.84 (S.E. 0.02) Lagrange multiplier test suggests unmeasured heterogeneity is important
Jensen (1987a)	Denmark, 1979–1980 Administrative records, youth	Weibull (t^{α}) baselines, by sex and age (17–21, 22–24)	Estimates of α Employment (S.E. small): females − 0.44 to −0.48; males −0.47 to −0.44 Unemployment (S.E. small): females −0.19 to −0.15; males −0.11 to −0.08
Miller and Volker (1987)	Australia, 1985 ALS youth	Weibull baseline ($\alpha t^{\alpha-1}$), by sex	Estimates of α Employment (S.E. small): males 0.55; females 0.6 Unemployment (S.E. small): males 0.67; females 0.68
Kiefer (1985a,b)	United States, 1971–1974 DIME controls, males	Constant baselines	Education elasticities for mean durations: nonemployment −0.37; employment 0.76
Stephenson (1981) Differences by race	United States, 1970–1973 NLS young women	1. Constant baseline hazards 2. Constant baselines, by race	High school graduates have longer employment spells Nonemployment spells are shorter for those who work while in school Hazards differ statistically by race
Tuma and Robins (1980) Dynamic effects of an NIT	United States, 1971–1972 SIME/DIME treatments and controls	Constant baselines, fit separately for husbands, wives, and female household heads	Husbands: 5-year NIT program increased hazard rates from employment and decreased hazard rates from nonemployment Wives and female heads: no NIT effect on hazard rates from employment; 3- and 5-year NIT programs decreased hazard rates from nonemployment
Ridder (1988) Dynamic effects of training, employment, and recruitment programs	Netherlands, 1979–1982 Program participants, Rotterdam	Constant baselines, with time-varying regressors for participation effects	Employment spell effects: females and minorities benefit, particularly from employment programs; males over 35 seem adversely affected Unemployment spell effects: spells lengthened by participation
		Structural Studies	
Flinn and Heckman (1982b)	United States, 1971 NLS young men, white high school graduates	Stationary representative agent model 1. Exponential offer distribution 2. Normal offer distribution	$\pi(w^r)$ = 0.60, δ (month) = 0.201 $\pi(w^r)$ = 0.92, δ (month) = 0.132

S.E. = standard error.

zling. A positive wage effect poses a direct contrast to the basic predictions of on-the-job search and matching models. One explanation might be a higher incidence of temporary layoffs among high wage workers; the reasons for separation are not distinguished in these studies. The findings for the wage effect on transition rates into employment are somewhat more clear. Burdett et al. (1985) find evidence of a positive relationship—as predicted by theory and as found in most studies in Chapters 4 and 5. Jensen (1987a) finds no evidence of a significant wage effect on the unemployment probability, but this may simply be due to correlation of wages and benefit levels; benefits are not included separately. Interpreting the (insignificant) earnings results reported by Tuma and Robins (1980) involves the same sorts of identification issues.

Education appears to play a major role in producing variation in transition rates both into and out of employment. Workers with higher levels of formal educational attainment appear to move out of employment more slowly and move into employment more quickly than workers with less education. Note, however, that the magnitude of the education effects does seem to differ across sexes and also by race. The results for training programs are somewhat mixed, as are the results for labor market experience. All told, these variables appear to have a positive effect on employment durations, but the magnitude is uncertain. Demographic differences in program effects also seem to be nonnegligible.

Among the most interesting policy findings in this section are those for the NIT experiments reported by Tuma and Robins (1980). Their results suggest that worker behavior was affected only slightly when the programs could be regarded as temporary, that is, when financial treatments lasted 3 as opposed to 5 years. However, when faced with a program of longer duration, workers—husbands, in particular—appear to have been affected significantly in ways consistent with predictions of simple search models.

Finally, the findings of Flinn and Heckman (1982b) can be regarded as a warning about sensitivity of structural results to parametric assumptions. Their results under an assumption of a normal distribution suggest that the young male workers accept any offer received, which represents a finding consistent with those of the structural studies of Chapters 4 and 5; their results of the case of an exponential offer distribution do not. The bottom line is that specification checks are essential.

Employment, Unemployment, and Nonparticipation

With the exception of the study by Burdett et al. (1985), the analyses of the previous section do not distinguish spells of unemployment and spells of nonparticipation. The same holds true for many of the studies discussed in earlier chapters. Generally, such merging of time spent out of work reflects data limitations, that is, insufficient information is available for the researcher to distinguish spells of the these two types. (Where relevant, we note this in our discussion of the individual studies.) In this section, we review studies that have access to (and make use of) data on spells in the alternative states of unemployment and nonparticipation. The key question is whether the two states are behaviorally distinct, that is, whether distinguishing the two spell types is important for the purpose of drawing inferences about transitions into employment. We start with a study by Burdett et al. (1984a) who estimate the three-state Markov model set out in Chapter 2. The theoretical model implies a competing-risks formulation for the distribution of durations in any one state and the destination (or "cause") specific hazards are modeled using a constant hazard specification. Weiner (1984) extends the empirical model of Burdett et al. to allow for duration dependence in all transition rates in a three-state model. His analysis focuses on the labor market flows underlying differences in the unemployment rates of black and white adult males in the United States. Lundberg (1985) investigates the dynamic aspects of the "added worker" hypothesis. Blau and Robins (1986b) study the effects of participation in public assistance programs on labor market transitions. Flinn and Heckman (1983) present results from a simple test of the hypothesis that employment and nonparticipation are behaviorally distinct states. In contrast to the other reduced form studies of this section, they use a Gompertz hazard model.

The study by Mortensen and Neumann (1984) that we discuss next appears to be the first attempt to distinguish information arrival rate and acceptance probability components of all transition rates in a three-state Markov model. In the last study of this section, van den Berg (1990b) extends the approaches of Ridder and Gorter (1986, discussed in Chapter 4) and Narendranathan and Nickell (1985, discussed in Chapter 5) to analyze labor market history data for a sample of male workers in the Netherlands. With this exception, all of the studies discussed in this section work with U.S. data.

Burdett, Kiefer, Mortensen, and Neumann (1984a)[16]

The basis for the empirical analysis carried out by Burdett et al. is the three-state Markov model set out in Chapter 2, generalized to allow for heterogeneity due to observed characteristics in both arrival rate and the offer distribution. Recall from Chapter 2 that the six transition rates τ_{ij} from state i to state j, i, j = e (employment), u (unemployment), n (nonparticipation), $i \neq j$, that together describe a worker's labor market history are defined as

$$\tau_{ij}(z) = \delta_i \pi_j(z)$$

where

$$\pi_j(z) = \int_{A_j(z)} dF(\epsilon, b)$$

$A_j(z)$ denotes the acceptance set for state j (with z interpreted as the mean of the offer distribution), and δ_i denotes the arrival rate of new information when in state i. In the empirical analysis, variation in δ_i across workers is also allowed, but wage effects on τ_{ij} are interpreted as entering through π_j alone.

The Markov property of the transition rates implies that the spell lengths in each of the three states are distributed independently for each worker in their sample, as well as across workers. Thus, each spell serves as a unit of observation. For a completed spell in state i that ends with a transition into state j, the contribution to the sample likelihood is the density

$$g_{ij}(t) = \tau_{ij} \exp[-\tau_i t]$$

where the transition rate between states i and j, τ_{ij}, is defined as a function of the characteristics for the individual who experienced this spell. Burdett et al. use the constant baseline hazard specification

$$\tau_{ij} = \exp(x\beta_{ij})$$

The transition rate out of state i, τ_i, is defined as the sum of the transition rates into the states other than i,

$$\tau_i = \sum_{j \neq i} \tau_{ij}$$

Transitions from i into states $k \neq j$ are thus treated as censored. For both right- and left-censored spells in each of the three states, the contribution to the likelihood is the survivor function evaluated at the observed length in state i,

$$S_i(t) = \exp[-\tau_i t]$$

Burdett et al. work with data collected in the Denver Income Maintenance Experiment (DIME).[17] The sample consists of both male and female workers in the control group and estimation is carried out separately for young workers (less than 21) and adults of each sex. Counting a spell in one of the three states as the unit of observation, there are 1,138 observations for young females, 2,524 for adult females, 1,119 for young males, and 1,571 for adult males. The regressor specification associated with each spell includes education, a quadratic in age, number of children, assets, race dummies for black and hispanic workers, an instrument for the log mean wage offer, and an interaction of race and the log wage instrument. The wage instruments are constructed using the results from log wage regressions fit by age and sex, using reported wages of employed workers for the job held longest in a given month; the regressors are age, education, and race. A wage instrument is available for each worker for each quarter in the sample period and the wage associated with a spell is from the quarter in which the transition out of the state occurred.[18]

The results provide evidence of substantial variation both across groups for each transition rate and across transition rates for each group. The number of coefficients (66 for each group) precludes a detailed discussion of all findings, but the results for the log wage coefficients (net of any race effects) are of particular interest, since the theoretical model has quite specific implications for the effects of mean offers.

The results for transition rates out of employment are consistent with the prediction that higher mean offers have a negative effect. The wage effect on transitions from employment into nonparticipation also appears to be about the same size or somewhat larger than the effect on transitions into unemployment.

The wage effects for transitions into employment by adults are positive, as predicted, and larger for transitions from nonparticipation. The wage results for youth transitions into employment are less clear-cut. For young black females, the wage effects on both transition rates are positive and significant, but only the transitions of nonparticipant young white females appear to be affected significantly by the mean wage faced. In contrast, the wage effect is positive for all unemployed young males, while young nonparticipant males appear unaffected.

The results for transitions between unemployment and nonparticipation are perhaps the most interesting. For adult males, the results are generally imprecise, that is, there is little evidence of systematic variation in transitions between the nonemployment two states with either the wage or demographic characteristics. The results for young males are also imprecise, except for a marginally significant negative wage effect on transitions from unemployment into nonparticipation. This wage finding is consistent with the predictions of the theoretical model, as well as the difference in the wage effects on young male transitions from employment into unemployment. For young females, there is some evidence that transition rates from nonparticipation into unemployment increase with the mean wage and decrease with education level and age. The nonemployment results for adult females are quite precise, though somewhat puzzling. Adult female transition rates between nonemployment states decrease significantly with education and increase with age (after an initial decline). These results also appear for transitions into employment, and they seem sensible. The surprising result is a large, positive wage effect on transitions in both directions between nonemployment states. The result for transition rates out of the labor force is not easily explained. Burdett et al. suggest that it might reflect an inverse relationship between wages and arrival rates for this group. Alternatively, it might reflect a correlation between wives' and husbands' wages, and a wealth effect on wives' labor supply.

Burdett et al. do not consider the effects of unemployment insurance benefits on the transition rates. Since these are proportional to earnings, the wage effects may in part reflect a benefit effect. In view of this, the results for the unemployment to nonparticipation transition rate might be viewed as even more perplexing since the benefit effect should be negative. Perhaps workers were simply more honest when responding to the DIME questions about actively seeking work.

Since estimation is carried out under the maintained hypothesis that labor market histories have a Markovian structure, Burdett et al. carry out some specification analysis. Specifically, they examine the exponential assumption for unemployment spell durations using plots of generalized residuals based on the results for each of the four age and sex groups. For young males, young females, and adult females, the specification appears adequate, but mean durations are noticeably underpredicted for adult males. Kolmogorov–Smirnov statistics are also calculated. At 5 percent significance levels, the null hypothesis that unemployment spell lengths have an exponential distribution can be rejected only for adult males; Burdett et al. note, however, that these statistics are conditional on the coefficient estimates and the nominal significance levels applied are thus inaccurate in the sense that they are not corrected for "degrees of freedom." They suggest that the statistic is best regarded as a summary measure of the visual diagnostic. They also note that chi-squared tests based on grouping the data into deciles produce qualitatively similar results for females and young males, relative to adult males. Kolmogorov–Smirnov results are also reported for models that include all regressors except the wage and then a constant alone—the objective being to determine (roughly) the role of heterogeneity versus true duration dependence. These test results suggest that findings of a declining hazard out of unemployment likely reflect unmeasured heterogeneity for groups other than adult males.

Finally Burdett et al. report results from steady-state analysis for a partition of each age and sex group by race and ethnic origin. The steady-state employment, unemployment, and nonparticipation rates implied by their results vary substantially across groups in ways reported elsewhere. Wage elasticities for labor force participation and unemployment rates are also reported. All unemployment rate elasticities are negative and the largest differences appear across age and race groups. This pattern comes across clearly in the wage–employment rate plots. For adult females and particularly adult males, the unemployment rates are nearly identical across groups at high wages, but diverge as the wage declines. For young workers, white unemployment levels are far below those of hispanic and black workers over the entire relevant wage scale. The pattern of variation in the labor force participation rate elasticities poses some contrast to these findings. All are positive, as expected, and there is some variation according to race—but the major differences appear between males and females.

Weiner (1984)

Weiner extends the empirical approach of Burdett et al. (1984a) to analyze differences in unemployment rates between black and white adult male workers. His objective is to determine whether differences in transition rates underlying differences in the unemployment rates between the two groups reflect differences in individual characteristics and economic opportunities or a difference in the groups' responses to the economic environment.

Weiner allows monotonic duration dependence in each of the transition rates in the three-state model. Specifically, he uses a Weibull model, $\tau_{ij}(t) = \exp(x\beta_{ij})t^{\alpha_{ij}}$. The method of maximum likelihood is used to estimate the parameters β_{ij}, with single spells as the unit of observation because of the semi-Markov property of the transition rates. For a completed spell in state i of length t that ends with a transition into state j, the contribution to the sample likelihood is

$$g_{ij}(t) = \tau_{ij}(t) \exp\left\{-\int_0^t \tau_i(s)\, ds\right\}$$

where the hazard from state i is the sum of the transition rates from i into the alternative states $j \neq i$. For right-censored spells, the contribution is the survivor function evaluated at the observed spell length

$$S_i(t) = \exp\left\{-\int_0^t \tau_i(s)\, ds\right\}$$

In Chapter 3, we noted that left censoring poses a more complicated situation when the duration distribution is not exponential because transition rates must be initialized at the start of the observation period. The typical approach is to omit left-censored observations. Weiner includes these spells and treats their starting times as additional parameters.[19]

Weiner works with data for a sample of males, aged 22 or more, taken from the Denver and the Seattle Income Maintenance Experiment (DIME/SIME). As in the studies by Burdett et al. (1985) and Burdett et al. (1984a), the sample is restricted to members of the control groups for each experiment (to avoid treatment effects). Wiener also restricts his sample to those with observed wages, that is, to those with at least one employment spell in the sample period. He recognizes that this may introduce selection bias. On the other hand, Weiner does not note but doubtlessly realized that the wage instruments used in previous studies with the DIME data were not always important in terms of sign and contribution to fit. Overall, there are 1,072 spells for black workers and 1,634 spells for white workers and Weiner fits his model separately for the two groups. The regressors associated with each spell include a quadratic in age, marital status, education, dummy variables for welfare recipiency and Denver as city of residence, younger children, older children, and the log wage in the most recent employment spell. For employment spells, he also includes dummy variables for an unskilled occupation, employment in a goods-producing industry, and government employment.

The number of coefficient estimates precludes a detailed discussion. Since the parameters of particular interest are those pertaining to duration dependence and the wage, we restrict our attention to these. (Remaining results generally accord with expectations.)

The results for the duration dependence parameters are reported in Table 6.3. Note that the sign of α indicates the direction of change in this model. Of course, these results are subject to question because of potential biases from unmeasured heterogeneity. Nevertheless, the similarity between black workers and white workers is quite striking. Qualitatively, the implications are the same across groups. Where significant, the results imply negative duration dependence in transition rates out of employment. On the other hand, variation in the transition rate out of unemployment appears to depend on the destination state. There is some evidence of negative duration dependence in the transition rate between unemployment and employment, but not between unemployment and nonparticipation. Note that both the wage sample selection criteria and unmeasured heterogeneity could produce an understatement of true positive duration dependence that would be consistent with "discouraged worker" theories. The results for movements into the labor force also exhibit dependence on destination. Movements into unemployment appear unaffected by length of time spent out of the labor force, but transition rates into employment decline with duration. This is consistent with a number of hypotheses, such as a declining arrival rate with progressive loss of contacts and human capital depreciation.

The wage has a large impact on some transition rates, but little on others. Transition rates from employment into unemployment are found to be inversely related to wages for workers in both groups, as simple on-the-job search and matching models predict. Higher wages also have a significant negative effect on transitions from employment into nonparticipation for black workers, but the wage level appears irrelevant for transitions in this direction by white workers. The signs for the wage coefficients in the transition rates into employment are also positive, as expected. For the unemployment to employment rate transition, the estimated wage effect for black workers is much larger than the estimated effect for white workers, but the standard errors are relatively large across the board; none of the estimates differs significantly from zero at standard significance levels. Similarly, the wage appears to have little effect on movements between unemployment and nonparticipation in either direction, though it is perhaps worth noting that the wage coefficients are negative for black workers and positive for white workers in the transition from unemployment into nonparticipation.

To summarize his findings, Weiner uses his parameter estimates and sample means

Table 6.3. Weibull Parameter Estimates[a]

| | Baseline: $\lambda_0(t) = t^\alpha$ | | | | | |
	τ_{eu}	τ_{en}	τ_{ue}	τ_{un}	τ_{ne}	τ_{nu}
Black	−0.408	−0.137	−0.132	0.102	−0.120	−0.089
	(0.031)	(0.064)	(0.044)	(0.133)	(0.065)	(0.136)
White	−0.408	−0.133	−0.073	0.058	−0.140	0.192
	(0.026)	(0.051)	(0.037)	(0.107)	(0.051)	(0.140)

[a]From Weiner (1984). Standard errors are in parentheses.

by race to calculate transition rates. These indicate that black and white flows diverge most widely in the unemployment to employment transition, with blacks leaving unemployment at a much slower rate. Moreover, substantial differences across groups remain when Weiner calculates transition rates using the white sample means for skills, education, and wages for both groups. The difference in transition rates appears to arise primarily from differences in intercepts.

Lundberg (1985)[20]

Lundberg uses a three-state model to study the dynamics underlying the "added worker" effect on aggregate labor supply (i.e., additions to the labor force from families whose employed members experience layoffs or restrictions on work hours). In particular, Lundberg focuses on the labor supply response of married women to their husbands' unemployment.

Lundberg extends the three-state model of Burdett et al. (1984a) to the case of a two person household. Specifically, the household is modeled as maximizing the expected present value of a time-separable joint utility function, which depends on total consumption and nonmarket times of the two members in each period. Hours of work when employed and hours devoted to search when unemployed are assumed fixed, so that time allocation within periods is determined by the states occupied by the household members in each period. Job offers can be received only when unemployed and both the distribution of wage offers faced and the arrival rate of offers are known. Employed household members also face uncertainty in that job durations are unknown (i.e., there are random layoffs).

The optimal policy for the household is defined as a set of reservation wages for each member: one that equates the values of employment and unemployment and a second that equates the values of employment and nonparticipation. As in the simpler models of individual behavior, these reservation wages are directly related to levels of nonemployment income and an individual's own mean wage. Also, assuming that the nonmarket times of the two household members are substitutes within periods, each reservation wage is an increasing function of the wage currently received by an individual's spouse. This, in turn, translates into predictions for transition rates that are consistent with the "added worker" hypothesis. In particular, holding nonlabor income and wages constant, the model predicts that transition rates out of nonparticipation and transition rates into employment will be higher for wives with unemployed husbands than for wives with employed husbands. Similarly, transition rates out of employment are predicted to be lower for wives with husbands that are unemployed.

To study the question empirically, Lundberg works with labor market histories for samples of 603 control households from the Denver Income Maintenance Experiment (DIME) and 478 control households from the Seattle Income Maintenance Experiment (SIME).[21] To start, Lundberg fits constant hazard specifications for monthly "household transition rates," defined as individual transition rates between pairs of labor market states, holding spouse's labor market status constant. The explanatory variables include a quadratic in the spouse's actual or predicted wage, a quadratic in the individual's actual or predicted wage, a quadratic in age, other income, number of children less than 6, and dummy variables for race, hispanic origin, and Seattle residence. Actual wages, measured in constant dollars, are used if the initial state is employment. Otherwise, the predicted wages are derived from regressions of average annual wage observations for the full set of controls, stratified by race and sex. Other income includes monthly receipts from earnings of other family members, transfer payments, alimony, and asset income.

Due to sample size limitations, a reasonable fit cannot be obtained for all 72 transition rates (18 for each spouse in each of the two samples locations). In particular, there are too few observations for transitions between nonemployment states. Results for 23 transitions are reported, with substantial variation in the number of observations used to calculate them (34–673).

The results generally suggest that a wife's labor market transitions are affected by her husband's labor market status. In particular, while unemployed and nonparticipant wives' transition rates into employment show some positive response to the mean wage faced in the market, the own-wage response appears to be greater for wives with nonparticipant husbands and much greater for wives with unemployed husbands. A similar set of results appears for the negative own-wage effects on transition rates out of employment; for women with employed husbands, the own-wage effects appear negligible. As for cross-wage effects, there is some evidence that the husband's wage level has a negative effect on transitions from nonparticipation into employment, but wives' transitions out of employment appear unaffected.

The wage effects for husbands are somewhat different. First, the results for transition rates into employment indicate a significant, positive own-wage effect for transitions out of nonparticipation when the wife is a nonparticipant and a weakly significant, positive own-wage effect when the wife is unemployed, but no own-wage effect otherwise. On the other hand, the own-wage effects on transition rates out of employment are small, but significantly negative and almost uniform in size across situations of the wife. The cross-wage effects are also somewhat different. The wife's wage appear to have a positive (though decreasing) effect on the husband's transition rate out of employment when the wife is either employed or out of the labor force, but not otherwise. The cross-wage effects on husbands' transitions into employment are negative when the wife is employed, as expected, but not otherwise.

Higher levels of household nonwage income (including unemployment benefits) have a uniformly significant, negative effect on husbands' transition rates into employment, but only a small, marginally significant, negative effect on wives' transition rates into employment when their husbands are employed and a negligible effect otherwise. The estimated nonwage income effects on transitions out of employment pose a similar contrast. Wives' transition rates into nonemployment seem to be slightly higher when their husbands are either employed or nonparticipants; otherwise, wives' transitions out of employment are unaffected. Husbands' transition rates out of employment appear more responsive to variation in nonwage income. In particular, husbands' transition rates from employment into unemployment decrease significantly with increases in nonemployment income when their wives are employed.

The results for remaining regressors generally seem sensible. In particular, there are significant differences in the coefficients for age, children, race, and ethnic origin between transition rates out of unemployment and out of nonparticipation, as well as into these states, supporting the three-state specification.

To investigate the added worker hypothesis further, Lundberg uses these estimates to calculate transition rates for representative white, black, and hispanic Denver wives with employed and unemployed husbands. (Lundberg notes that characteristics of Seattle women are similar.) Where only few observations are available, group average transition rates are used. These results are mixed. For white wives, the probability of labor market entrance is 25 percent higher when the husband is unemployed, the probability of leaving employment is 28 percent lower, and the probability of labor market exit is reduced by about one-third. These results are consistent with the added worker hypothesis. The estimated probability of an unemployed white wife becoming employed, however, is 35 percent lower when the husband is unemployed; a result of comparable magnitude appears for black wives and the remaining results for black wives are also somewhat puzzling. The probability of labor force exit is 25 percent lower for black wives with unemployed husbands, but the probability of labor force entry is also lower—by a margin of 35 percent. The differences reported for hispanic wives are smaller in magnitude than those reported for black wives, but the sign pattern is the same.

Lundberg offers two potential explanations for these findings, both based on unmeasured heterogeneity. She suggests that the unemployment to employment results may reflect some type of mating pattern. As for the lower labor force entry rates reported for blacks and hispanics, Lundberg notes that unemployment of the husband may represent a lower level of permanent income, as opposed to a transitory drop in income that would give rise to an added-worker effect. An alternative and perhaps simpler explanation would be that the husband's labor market status proxies local labor market demand faced by the wife, since no additional control for local labor market conditions is included in the set of regressors.

Lundberg also reports results form simulations based on the transition rate estimates. Specifically, after calculating the steady-state distribution implied by the full nine-by-nine household transition rate matrix for each race group, Lundberg disturbs the distribution by increasing the proportion of husbands that is unemployed by 5 percent and then traces the adjustment of the system back to its steady-state using monthly transition rates. Results for the wives' labor force participation and employment rates and the husbands' unemployment rates are reported for Denver. (Seattle results are described as similar.) The patterns exhibited for white wives are basically consistent with the added-worker hypothesis. The labor force participation rate increases initially and then declines. The employment rate follows the same path, but with a delay of about 1 month. The responses in both cases are small, however, and take about 6 months to peak. Movements in the rates for black wives are essentially the opposite, that is, both rates drop and then rise. For hispanic wives, the participation rate rises, but the employment rate declines initially and starts to rise only after about 2 months. Caution must be exercised when interpreting these results because many of the estimates used to calculate them are imprecise. Nevertheless, they suggest that the labor market activity of wives is affected by their husbands' experience.

Blau and Robins (1986b)

Blau and Robins use a three-state framework to study potential differences in dynamic labor market behavior between welfare recipients and nonrecipients. Specifically, they attempt to determine whether there are systematic differences in transition rates between those who receive public assistance and those who do not—treating recipiency status as exogenous. Since eligibility and payment levels for public assistance programs typically depend on labor market income and thus on labor market activity, the status exogeneity assumption makes interpretation of their results difficult. Still, their findings are suggestive.

Their data are taken from the baseline household survey of the Employment Opportunity Pilot Project (EOPP) conducted between April and October 1980. These data are well suited to the present analysis because the EOPP intentionally oversampled low income families and, consequently, relatively large numbers of observations are available for welfare recipients. Blau and Robins categorize a person as a welfare recipient in a given spell if the main earner in the person's household reported that the family received Aid to Families with Dependent Children (AFDC) benefits, food stamp benefits, or general assistance during that spell. Durations are measured in months and Blau and Robins restrict their sample to observations on the most recent employment, unemployment, and nonparticipation spells for each individual.

Blau and Robins start their analysis by calculating maximum likelihood estimates for monthly transition rates among unemployment, employment, and nonparticipation separately for recipient and nonrecipient samples of men, married women, single women, and youth.[22] Results for combined samples for each demographic group are also reported. Overall, the signs and magnitudes of the differences in transition rates between recipients and nonrecipients are consistent with findings reported elsewhere based on static analyses of welfare work disincentive effects. Transition rates into the labor force, into employment, and out of unemployment are lower for recipients, while transition rates out of employment, into unemployment, and out of the labor force are lower for nonrecipients. There is some variation in the magnitude of the differences between groups. The largest differences are those reported for transition rates between employment and unemployment. Recipients in all demographic groups except youth appear to move from employment into unemployment about twice as fast as nonrecipients. In the reverse direction, the rate of recipients is roughly half that of nonrecipients in all demographic groups.

Blau and Robins next report estimates for both the steady-state probabilities implied by these transition rate estimates and also for the contributions of the individual transition rates to these probabilities. These results suggest that the primary work disincentive effect of welfare receipt is slowed entry into employment from both unemployment and nonparticipation, although faster movement out of employment also plays an important role for single women.

Blau and Robins also report differences in transition rates based on estimation results for constant hazard models. In addition to a dummy variable for welfare status, the regressors include age, race, ethnic group, education, prior work experience (except for youth), health status, family size, marital status for men, a predicted wage rate, receipt of other transfer payments, nonwage income (including welfare), and local labor market conditions. The results described generally remain intact.[23] In particular, the recipiency results for transitions from both unemployment and nonparticipation into employment change only slightly. The most noticeable change appears in the transition rates out of employment. After controlling for personal characteristics and labor market conditions, it appears that recipient youth, men, and married women move more slowly from employment into nonparticipation than their nonrecipient counterparts, although youth recipients also appear to move more quickly from employment into unemployment.[24]

Flinn and Heckman (1983)

The results for the multistate models discussed thus far suggest that the distinction between nonparticipation and unemployment is more than an artifact of unemployment insurance job search requirements. In this study, Flinn and Heckman formally test the hypothesis that the two states are statistically distinct for a sample of young white males in the United States.

Their specification for the transition rate from state is a Gompertz,

$$\tau_{jk}(t) = \exp[X(s_{jk} + t)'\beta_{jk} + \alpha t + \alpha t^2 + c_{jk}\theta]$$

where s_{jk} denotes the calendar starting date of the spell in state j, the c_{jk} are parameters, and θ is an individual-specific component that is assumed fixed both across and within spells. In estimating the model, Flinn and Heckman specify the distribution of θ as standard normal.

The null hypothesis is that unemployment and nonparticipation are behaviorally the same. This is interpreted to mean that

$$\tau_{ue} = \tau_{ne} = \tau_{Ne}$$

where N denotes nonemployment. This is tested easily using a likelihood ratio test.[25]

Flinn and Heckman carry out this test using data for a sample of 122 workers drawn from the National Longitudinal Survey of Young Men (aged 14–24 in 1966). The sample is restricted to individuals who graduated from high school in spring or summer 1969 and did not return to school by the end of December 1971. These restrictions severely limit both the sample size and the extent to which the results can be generalized. In particular, the number of observed transitions between nonemployment states basically precludes estimation of transition rates between unemployment and nonparticipation. On a positive note, the restrictions serve to lessen the influence of initial conditions; the sample is limited to individuals with little or no labor market experience at the start of the sample period. A time-varying dummy variable for married workers with wife present is the only explanatory variable.

In the unrestricted results for the transition rates out of employment, only the constant term and heterogeneity component are statistically significant at standard levels of significance. In particular, there is no strong evidence of duration dependence in movements from employment into either nonemployment state. In contrast, the unrestricted results for transitions into employment exhibit some sharp differences. The results for duration dependence in the transition rate from nonparticipation into employment imply a significant monotonic increase, but the results for the transition rate from unemployment into employment provide no statistically significant evidence of duration dependence. Flinn and Heckman calculate the paths for both transition rates into employment for nonmarried workers, alone. The results suggest that the transition rate from nonparticipation into employment starts out lower, but overtakes the transition rate from unemployment after about 6 months. Marital status also has a significant positive effect on the former, but no effect on the transition rate from unemployment into employment.

The results for the model with the parameters of τ_{ue} restricted to equal the parameters of τ_{ne} indicate no significant pattern of duration dependence in the transition rate into employment, that is, the unemployment to employment results swamp the nonparticipation to employment effects. According to the likelihood ratio test, the hypothesis of equal parameters can be rejected at the 5 percent level. Thus, Flinn and Heckman provide evidence that the two states are behaviorally distinct, at least for the male high school graduate population sampled here.

Mortensen and Neumann (1984)

This study by Mortensen and Neumann represents a first attempt to distinguish the arrival rate and acceptance probability components of all six transition rates within three-state model. A modified version of the three-state Markov model set out in Chapter 2 serves as the theoretical basis of their analysis. As in the simpler model, information that may alter the values of employment and unemployment for a worker takes the form of independent and identically distributed random vectors that are independent of a worker's actions. Search intensity is also treated as exogenous. The information arrival rates are modeled here as depending on worker characteristics—mean offers in particular. The transition rates in their model are thus defined as

$$\tau_{ij}(z) = \delta_i(z)\pi_j(z)$$

where $\pi_j(z)$ is denotes the acceptance probability for state j. The implications for z from the simpler model are rendered ambiguous by this modification. In particular, the dependence of δ_j on z renders the acceptance probability–mean offer relationship an empirical issue. This, in turn, motivates their interest in identifying the acceptance probability and arrival rate components of the transition rates—which they refer to as "choice" and "chance," respectively.

Since the transition rates are time invariant in their theoretical model, Mortensen and Neumann use the constant proportional hazard specification $\tau_{ij} = \exp(x\beta_{ij})$. They then impose a functional form restriction for the π_j to identify the separate effects of the regressors on δ and π. Specifically, Mortensen and Neumann note that corresponding to their transition rate specification $\tau_{ij}(z) = \delta_i(z)\pi_j(z)$ is a logit specification for the acceptance probabilities π_j. Conversely, if a logit specification is imposed as the functional form for the acceptance probabilities,

$$\pi_j(x) = \frac{\exp\{x\Gamma_j\}}{\sum_k \exp\{x\Gamma_k\}}$$

then the only specification for the δ_j consistent with $\tau_{ij}(z) = \exp(x\beta_{ij})$ is

$$\delta_j(x) = \exp\{x\alpha_j\} \cdot \sum_j \exp\{x\Gamma_j\}$$

It follows that

$$\beta_{ij} = \alpha_i + \Gamma_j, \qquad i \neq j$$

Upon setting one of the Γ_j equal to zero (without loss of generality), the model is overidentified in that there are three α_i, two free Γ_j, and six β_{ij}.[26] Mortensen and Neumann note that the disadvantage of taking their approach to identification is the restriction that the distribution of the information inducing a change in state is in the extreme value form. On the other hand, it has the attractive feature of allowing easy tests of the overidentifying restrictions and the hypothesis that the arrival rates are state independent.

Mortensen and Neumann work with data for the white adult subsample of the

DIME controls analyzed by Burdett et al. (1984b). Specifically, they fit their model separately for males and females, aged 22 or more. A spell represents the contribution to the sample likelihood (because of the Markov property) and they have reasonable sample sizes for each transition for each group.[27] Their specification for the vector of characteristics associated with each spell is the same as that used in Burdett et al.

The results suggest that longer spells of employment observed for high wage workers reflect significantly lower arrival rates of information than those faced by low wage workers. Similarly, the results suggest that the longer spells of nonparticipation observed for low wage workers are a consequence of significantly lower arrival rates than those faced by high wage nonparticipants. No systematic relationship appears between the acceptance probabilities and the level of the wage.

As for other characteristics, there is some evidence that the probability of choosing nonparticipation varies nonlinearly with age among men (negative and then positive), but arrival rates of men do not seem to vary with age in any state. In contrast, arrival rates appear to decrease linearly with age for women who are employed or out of the labor force, but no systematic age and acceptance probability relationships appear. Female arrival rates when out of the labor force are also found to be lower for those with higher levels of educational attainment, higher assets, and more children. Higher education also decreases the probability of choosing nonparticipation among women, but other acceptance probabilities appear unaffected. Higher assets are also associated with a higher probability of choosing employment for women. For men, higher assets are associated with higher probabilities for both alternatives to unemployment and education levels appear irrelevant.

All of these results are sensible, but the results are somewhat disappointing—overall—in that all of the results for the arrival rate when unemployed are imprecise. In particular, there is no evidence of a systematic relationship between the level of the wage and the arrival rate. Thus, the results provide little insight into variation in the rate at which workers move out of unemployment.

van den Berg (1990b)

van den Berg extends the theoretical and econometric models of Narendranathan and Nickell (1985, discussed in Chapter 5) and Ridder and Gorter (1986, discussed in Chapter 4) to fit the three-state model. Precisely, van den Berg models unemployed workers as potentially exiting into either employment or nonparticipation, where transitions into nonparticipation occur according to a Poisson process with parameter τ_{un}, which is independent of the process governing transitions into employment, as in other models discussed in this section. Here, however, expected utility flows in nonparticipation n and unemployment u are modeled as identical. Specifically, the worker's utility in state j is defined as $u(L_j) \log(x_j)$, where L_j and x_j refer to "leisure" and the income flow in state j, respectively; $u(L_e)$ is set equal to unity, $u(L_n)$ and $u(L_j)$ are each set equal to a constant v, and $E(x_n)$ and x_u are set equal to a constant b. The distinction between the two nonemployment states is that nonparticipation is defined as an absorbing state, that is, the arrival rate of information in nonparticipation is restricted to zero (as opposed to assuming that it is lower than the arrival rate in unemployment, as in the three-state models of Burdett et al. (1984a) and others).[28]

The optimal policy for the worker in this model is characterized by a single reservation wage. Using our previous notation, the condition that defines this reservation wage can be written as

$$\log(w^r) = v \log(b) + \frac{\delta}{\tau_{un} + r} \int_{w^r}^{\infty} \{\log(w) - \log(w^r)\} \, dF(w)$$

van den Berg's objective is to estimate a parameterization of this equation. Since he does not have access to special data on the parameters of individual offer distributions $F(w)$, he follows an approach similar to that of Narendranathan and Nickell. Specifically, he specifies lognormal distributions that differ across workers according to age and education and obtains estimates for the parameters of these distributions using wage regressions for a sample of employed workers. van den Berg recognizes that these wage data represent observations on accepted wages, but notes that when corrected for selectivity bias using an inverse Mills ratio, the correction terms are insignificant at standard levels. The offer arrival rate δ and transition rate out of the labor force τ_{ue} are specified as functions of labor market and worker characteristics,

$$\delta = \exp(x'\beta) \quad \text{and} \quad \tau_{un} = \exp(z'\alpha)$$

Thus the parameters of the model are β, α, v, r, and the set of reservation wages w_i^r for all workers. Conditioned on a specific value for r, van den Berg estimates the remaining parameters of the model by applying the method of maximum likelihood to data on x, z, unemployment durations, and destination states, and by imposing the restrictions of the optimality condition. Specifically, the basis of the sample likelihood function is simply a competing risks formulation for the unemployment duration distribution, with destination-specific hazards

$$\tau_{un} = \exp(z'\alpha) \quad \text{and} \quad \tau_{ue} = \exp(x'\beta)\pi(w^r)$$

and the optimality condition is solved numerically for w_i^r for each worker in the sample at each iteration. Using observations on benefit income, he then solves for v.

van den Berg fits the model using data collected in the Netherlands Socio-Economic Panel Survey, a longitudinal survey of a random sample of 12,000 individuals conducted by the Netherlands Central Bureau of Statistics that started in April 1984. In initial interviews, individuals reported their labor market activity over the preceding year. Thereafter, they have reported their activity between interviews held 6 months apart. The sample analyzed here consists of 223 male workers, ages 17 to 65, who were unemployed at the time of their first interviews. The restriction to this group is due to availability of unemployment benefit data; benefit levels are reported only if benefits are being received at the time of an interview. van den Berg works with data collected in the first three interviews (i.e., his sample period is May 1983 to October 1985), but not all workers are followed for the entire period because of attrition.

When specifying his likelihood function, van den Berg incorporates censoring due to attrition and the fixed length of the sample period. Each spell in progress at the first interview is treated as consisting of two parts, with the date of the first interview normalized to zero. The duration of the spell before the first interview thus represents a backward recurrence time and the duration following the interview represents a forward recurrence time. Workers who exit the sample before the second interview, workers who leave after the second interview but before completing their unemployment spells, and workers who remain unemployed at the time of the third interview are all treated as having censored forward recurrence times.

van den Berg also faces another problem with his duration data, which he refers to as a "memory" problem—54 percent of his 112 completed forward recurrence observations "end" on the date of the preceding interview.[29] Since the majority of remaining completed spells in the sample end in the 3 months preceding an interview, van den Berg deals with this measurement problem by entering the probability that the forward recurrence time falls in the first 3 months after the reported spell end. All of the backward recurrence spells are censored at the interview date, but this is easily accommodated. On the other hand, some spells are also censored by the maximum recall period of 1 year and dealing with this is not quite as easy—again because of potential memory problems. van den Berg enters the probability of a spell exceeding 9 months for each spell reported as exactly 1 year long at the first interview.

The explanatory variables included in the specification for the arrival rate are the local unemployment rate, the log of the number employed in a worker's household, categorical variables for age (18–23, 24–29, 30–45) and education level, and dummy variables for new labor market entrant, marital status, household headship, and being Dutch. The specification for the transition rate into nonparticipation includes the new entrant dummy variable and the categorical age variables. All durations are measured in weeks and, for identification, the discount rate is set equal to an annual rate of 10 percent.

Offer arrival rates are found to be significantly higher for married workers than for single workers and higher for workers with more education. They are also significantly higher when additional household members are employed. Remaining variables in the arrival rate specification appear irrelevant. In particular, the coefficients for the age dummy variables are positive, but insignificant at standard levels. The local unemployment rate also appears unimportant, but this variable may be correlated with the variable for employed household members.

The results for the transition rate into nonparticipation are sensible; prime-age workers (24–45) are significantly less likely to leave the labor force than their younger and older counterparts. The estimate for the nonpecuniary utility flow ratio is 0.74 (standard error 0.14). This suggests that a disutility is associated with not working. Note, however, that the estimate is not significantly different from one at the 5 percent level.

van den Berg uses these estimates to calculate offer arrival rate and acceptance probabilities for partitions of his sample by age (18–23, 24–29, 30–45, 46–64) and by education level. Overall, these results suggest that variation in transition rates into employment reflects variation in arrival rates. The average acceptance probability in the sample is 0.97 and there is virtually no variation across age groups. The lowest acceptance probability is 0.94 for workers in the 24–29 group and the highest is 1.00 for workers in the 46–64 group. On the other hand, the arrival rate for the oldest workers is half the size of the arrival rate for workers in the 24–29 group, 0.008 versus 0.016; the sample average is 0.012. (Of course, these estimates must be viewed cautiously because of the imprecise age coefficients for the arrival rate.) The results for the education partition are consistent with the age group results. The acceptance probability ranges from 0.89 for workers in the highest education group to 1.00 for the lowest; the arrival rate estimates for these groups are 0.024 and 0.004, respectively.

The estimate for the transition rate into nonparticipation for the whole sample is 0.004; the estimates for the youngest and oldest workers are the lowest—both are 0.007.

For these workers, it appears that about half of all unemployment spells end with an exit out of the labor force (versus 30 percent for the sample as a whole and less than 20 percent for workers between 24 and 45).

Benefit elasticities are also calculated by age and by education level. These results are quite interesting. The benefit elasticity for the reservation wage is 0.30 for the whole sample, but there is evidence of substantial variation both across age groups and across education groups. The range across age groups is 0.24 for the 24–29 group to 0.46 for the 46–64 group; the range across education groups is 0.16 for the highest education group to 0.44 for the lowest. Though all of these estimates are positive, durations appear insensitive to changes in benefit levels. The elasticity of mean duration with respect to benefits is 0.03 for the sample, with a range of 0–0.05 across age groups and a range of 0–0.1 across education groups. As van den Berg notes, the reasons for this are obvious. As the model is specified, lower benefit levels affect mean durations by lowering the reservation wage and thus by increasing the acceptance probability. Since virtually all offers appear acceptable already, there is no room left for this effect.

van den Berg reports that results for the arrival rate and for the transition rate into nonparticipation are basically unaffected by changes in the value chosen for discount rate. The utility parameter v absorbs the change. Higher discount rates yield higher v values, although they stay below 1 with all discount rate values (even $r = \infty$).[30] A second check on the results allows for variation in worker expectations about exogenously determined wage growth and random layoffs. Again, the results are nearly identical to those described above; the parameter v absorbs the change, but it does not change substantially.

van den Berg does not incorporate unobserved heterogeneity into his specification, but notes that estimating such a model would be a very complicated task. Altering the arrival rate specification to include a multiplicative disturbance term, for example, does not yield an analytical function of the disturbance for the hazard rate. He also presents some formal specification test results for the arrival rate, the transition rate into nonparticipation, and v. Specifically, he uses White's Information Matrix test, an omnibus test that can be interpreted as a test of a null no unobserved heterogeneity. (This application is discussed in Chesher and Spady [1988].) The results for the arrival rate and transition rate do not allow rejection of this null hypothesis at the 5 percent level, but the results for the leisure utility ratio v do. This makes sense, given that v is not parameterized. It is also consistent with the sensitivity of the v estimates to choice of discount rate. Relaxing the assumption of equal utility flows across nonworking states strengthens this line of reasoning.

Summary

The results in this section (summarized in Table 6.4) generally indicate that distinguishing unemployment and nonparticipation is potentially important in the analysis of labor market history data. Failure to do so may lead to biased estimates of the effects of regressors and duration on transition rates. This holds for young workers (particularly young white workers, according to the results presented here) and also for white adult females. For adult males, the distinction between nonemployment states appears to be less clear-cut. This is encouraging, since much of the analysis on nonemployment to employment transitions has focused on this population. Along this line, however, the findings of studies in this section cast additional light on the very different dynamic

Table 6.4. Employment, Unemployment, and Nonparticipation: Hazard Function Studies

Study	Data	Proportional Hazard Model Specification	Findings
Burdett, Kiefer, Mortensen, and Neumann (1984b)	United States, 1971–1974 DIME controls	Constant baseline hazards, by sex and age (18–20, 21 +)	Transition rates into employment increase with wage Transition rates out of employment inversely related to wage Transition rates from unemployment into nonparticipation inversely related to wage for young males, but increase with wage for adult females
Weiner (1984)	United States, 1970–1974 SIME/DIME controls, males	Weibull (t^α) Baseline hazards, by race	Duration dependence: similar results for black and white workers Transitions out of employment: negative both destinations Transitions out of unemployment: negative to employment; none to nonparticipation Transitions into labor force: negative into employment; none to unemployment Wage effects on transitions out of employment: negative in both directions for black workers; negative only into unemployment for white workers Other age effects: negligible
Lundberg (1985) Dynamics of "added worker" effect	United States, 1970–1974 SIME/DIME intact controls, households	Constant baseline hazards, separately for husbands and wives	Wives: positive own-wage effect on transition into employment and negative effect on transitions out of employment if husband is not employed; negligible own-wage effects if husband is employed Husbands: large negative nonwage income effect on transitions into employment No evidence of cross-wage effect
Blau and Robins (1986a,b) Dynamic effects of welfare receipt	United States 1980 EOPP	Constant baseline hazards, separately for men, married women, single women, and youth, by welfare recipiency status	Recipients move more slowly into employment than nonrecipients Recipient men, youth, and married women move more slowly from employment into nonparticipation than nonrecipients Recipient youth move more quickly from employment into unemployment
Flinn and Heckman (1983) Unemployment versus nonemployment	United States, 1969–1971 NLS white young men nonstudent high school graduates	Gompertz hazards, with quadratic in duration and random effects heterogeneity component	Likelihood ratio test rejects hypothesis that hazard rates from unemployment and nonparticipation are the same Duration dependence: positive for nonparticipation into employment; negligible, otherwise
Mortensen and Neumann (1984) Arrival rates versus acceptance probabilities	United States, 1971–1974 DIME controls, adults	Logit, by sex	Arrival rate when employed decreases with mean wage Arrival rate in nonparticipation increases with mean wage Mean wage has negligible effect on acceptance probabilities
van den Berg (1990b)	Netherlands, 1983–1985 NSEPS males	Solution to optimality condition for reservation wage	$\pi(w^r)$: sample 0.97; by age 0.94–1.0; by education 0.89–1.0 δ(week): sample 0.012; by age 0.008–0.016; by education 0.004–0.024 Elasticity of reservation wage with respect to benefits: sample 0.30; by age 0.24–0.46; by education 0.16–0.44 Elasticity of duration with respect to benefits: sample 0.03; by age 0–0.05; by education 0–0.10

behavior of young versus old, male versus female, white versus nonwhite, and low education versus high education workers. In particular, these studies provide additional evidence of substantial differences in the response of workers in different demographic groups to variation in wages faced and to variation in the level of nonwage income. Generalizing the results obtained for adult white males or young white males clearly seems inappropriate. In this respect, the findings of the present section are consistent with those of empirical work based on static labor market analyses. Similarly, the findings from the analyses of the added-worker hypothesis and the distinctive effects of public assistance provide additional insights on these issues, but they are consistent with previous work based on static models. Finally, the findings from the structural analyses discussed here are in line with the findings of previous chapters. They too suggest that variation in transition rates into employment across workers having different characteristics by and large reflects variation in arrival rates of information, as opposed to systematic variation in workers' willingness to accept offers.[31]

Temporary versus Permanent Layoffs

Several of the unemployment duration studies discussed thus far work with samples restricted to workers who are not on "temporary layoff" or at least to those who do not return to their former employers. The reason for this is obvious—it is assumed that search behavior of these workers is distinct from search behavior following a permanent separation. A few of the early empirical search studies actually explored this issue and found evidence that this was the case. Ehrenberg and Oaxaca (1976) and Classen (1977, 1979), for example, both note that the results from duration regressions fit separately for workers on temporary layoff are systematically different from the results for workers on permanent layoff. In particular, Ehrenberg and Oaxaca report a negligible benefit effect for adult males on temporary layoff, while Classen's results imply a benefit elasticity that is roughly half the size of the elasticity for workers not on temporary layoff.[32]

In this section, we review studies that analyze potential behavioral differences between workers on temporary versus permanent layoff more formally within a competing-risks framework. Precisely "new jobs" and "old jobs" are treated as distinct destination states for an unemployed worker. Thus, assuming that recalls and new job offers arrive according to independent Poisson processes, the latent spell duration until an acceptable new job offer is received (T_n) and the latent spell duration until recall (T_r) represent independently distributed random variables, and duration of an unemployment spell is defined as

$$T = \min\{T_r, T_n\}$$

The hazard from unemployment in this case is simply the sum of the two cause-specific hazards,

$$\tau(t) = \tau_r(t) + \tau_n(t)$$

and hazard function methods used in the studies of previous sections in this chapter can be applied directly to estimate the cause-specific hazards.

We start the section with studies by Katz (1986) and Katz and Meyer (1988b) who work with data for workers in the United States. We then turn to studies by Jensen and Westergaard-Nielsen (1989) and Ham and Rea (1987) who analyze data for Danish and Canadian workers, respectively.

Katz (1986)

Katz works with data for a sample of United States workers collected in Waves 14 (1981) and 15 (1982) of the Panel Study of Income Dynamics (PSID). For each household head in the labor force at each interview, the length of the most recent unemployment spell is reported if the spell overlapped at least partially with the calendar year preceding the interview. For example, a spell that began in 1979 and ended in 1980 is reported if the workers was in the labor force at the 1981 Wave interview. A spell that began in 1980 and remained in progress at the 1981 interview is also reproted if the worker was looking for work at the time of the interview. Katz recognizes that this restriction to labor force participants who report unemployment spells is likely to lead to an oversampling of longer spells. A second weakness of the PSID data is the absence of data on unemployment insurance benefit amounts; only benefit receipt is reported. Katz restricts his own sample to spells initiated by either layoffs or dismissals for cause (the two reasons for separation are not reported separately) experienced by workers, ages 20–65, who were household heads at both interviews. Overall, his sample consists of 1,055 spells, with two spells for some workers. Fifty-seven percent are known to end in recall and 20 percent of all spells are censored.

Katz first presents Kaplan–Meier estimates of the total hazard, the new job hazard, and the recall hazard for his full sample. These suggest that the total hazard drops significantly in the first two months of a spell and then declines more gradually thereafter, with the exception of spikes at 25–28, 37–40, and 49–52 weeks. There are sharp differences, however, between the paths of the recall and new job hazards underlying the total hazard path. In particular, the decline in the total hazard appears to reflect the path of the recall hazard, that is, most recalls occur in the first 2 months of a spell; the new job hazard actually appears to increase during the first part of a spell. The spikes appear in both hazards, but they are more pronounced in the new job hazard.

Given that the timing of the spikes coincides roughly with typical exhaustion dates for unemployment insurance benefits (26 and 39 weeks), Katz fits the total, recall, and new job empirical hazards separately for benefit recipients and nonrecipients. The contrast across groups is fairly dramatic. As expected, the spikes in the recipients' hazards are more pronounced than in the full sample hazards, but much smaller for the nonrecipients. A second notable difference regards the new job hazards. For nonrecipients, it starts out higher, but increases at a slower rate than the new job hazard for recipients; the new job spikes are also more pronounced for recipients.

Katz goes on to carry out a parametric analysis of spell durations. Specifically, he uses a Weibull specification for each of the cause specific hazards,

$$\tau_r(t) = at^{a-1} \exp\{x\beta\}, \qquad a > 0$$

and

$$\tau_n(t) = bt^{b-1} \exp\{x\Gamma\}, \qquad b > 0$$

maintaining the assumption that the two are independent. The structure of the sample likelihood function for the model is straightforward. For a spell ending with recall at duration t, the contribution to the likelihood is

$$L_r = \tau_r(t)S(t)$$

where $S(t)$ is the survivor function for unemployment spell duration T,

$$S(t) = \exp\left[-\int_0^t (\tau_r(u) + \tau_n(u))\, du \right]$$

Note that spells ending in recall are treated as censored new job spells. For a spell ending with receipt of an acceptable new job offer at duration t, the contribution is defined analogously as

$$L_n = \tau_r(t)S(t)$$

For right-censored spells, the contribution is the survivor, $S(t)$.

In view of the differences between the empirical hazards for the recipient and non-recipient subsamples, Katz fits the competing risks model separately for each group.[33] The explanatory variables are age, race, sex, marital status, education, the county unemployment rate, industry, and occupation. For comparison, he also reports results for the total hazard $\tau(t)$ for each sample. The total hazard estimates for the Weibull parameter are 0.854 (standard error 0.036) for recipients and 0.722 (standard error 0.050) for non-recipients. These represent fairly strong evidence of negative duration dependence. However, when Katz estimates the competing risks model, he finds substantial differences in the parameters of the new job and recall hazards—particularly for the recipient sample. His Weibull parameter estimates are presented in Table 6.5. Negative duration dependence in the recall hazard cannot be rejected for either recipients or nonrecipients. On the other hand, the results for the new job hazard imply positive duration dependence for recipients and no duration dependence for nonrecipients.

Estimates for remaining parameters in both the single and competing risks models are generally imprecise for the recipient sample. The results for the total hazard results suggest that nonwhite recipients and younger recipients leave unemployment more slowly than their recipient counterparts. In contrast, the competing risks results for recipients imply that the new job hazard declines significantly with age, while the recall hazard increases significantly with age. For the nonrecipient sample, the occupation dummy variables, the local unemployment rate, race, sex, and marital status all have significant coefficients with expected signs in the total hazard results. Again, however, the competing risks results imply a negative age effect on the new job hazard and a positive age effect on the recall hazard. The county unemployment rate also has estimated effects of very different magnitudes for the nonrecipient group; both coefficients are negative, but the effect on the new job hazard is much larger and more precisely determined than the effect on the recall hazard.

Katz presents results for a variety of respecifications. In view of the large jumps in

Table 6.5. Weibull Parameter Estimates[a]

	Baseline: $\lambda_0(t) = \alpha t^{\alpha-1}$	
	b	a
Recipients	1.440	0.732
	(0.091)	(0.044)
Nonrecipients	0.881	0.679
	(0.109)	(0.059)

[a]From Katz (1985, Tables 6 and 7). Standard errors are in parentheses.

the Kaplan—Meier estimates for the cause-specific hazards at 26 and 39 weeks for the recipient sample, he first allows discrete jumps at the 1 week intervals containing these spell lengths using a time-varying dummy variable. The spike estimates at 26 weeks are large and significant at standard levels for both the new job and recall hazards, but no similar results appear at 39 weeks. The results for duration dependence appear robust and results for remaining variables are said to be the same.

Katz next reports results for a model that includes tenure in the job preceding a spell and a dummy variable for unemployment insurance receipt; his sample in this case consists of all recipients and nonrecipients with observed tenures (395 spells). The results suggest that previous tenure has a significant positive effect on the recall hazard and a negative effect on the new job hazard, while age appears irrelevant. Benefit receipt has a significant negative effect on the recall hazard, but a null hypothesis of no effect on the new job hazard cannot be rejected at standard levels. The recall hazard for the pooled sample continues to exhibit negative duration dependence, but the results for the new job hazard do not allow rejection of hypotheses of negative, positive, or no duration dependence at standard levels. However, Weibull parameters for the tenure model fit separately for recipient and nonrecipient samples imply significant positive duration dependence in the new job hazard for recipients and no duration dependence for nonrecipients. The nonrecipients thus appear to dominate in the pooled sample.

Finally, Katz reports Weibull parameter estimates for a single risk model fit separately for recipients and nonrecipients with spells initiated by plant closings. The results imply significant negative duration dependence in the hazard for the nonrecipient sample, but no significant duration dependence for the recipient sample.[34]

Katz and Meyer (1988b)

This study represents an extension of work by Katz (1986) and Meyer (1988b, discussed in Chapter 5). The focus here is the relationship between worker expectations regarding recall and the unemployment experienced by unemployment insurance recipients in the United States. The first objective of the study is to determine the proportions of all unemployment spells and all time spent unemployed accounted for by the layoff–recall process. Katz and Meyer note that previous research reports that temporary layoffs account for a large fraction of unemployment spells, but only a small fraction of total time spent unemployed (e.g., Feldstein, 1975a; Lilien, 1980; Murphy and Topel, 1987). They note, however, that these findings are based on two measures that are likely to be biased downward: (1) the proportion of unemployment spells spent in spells involving no job change (which excludes those who expect to be recalled but then never get recalled or accept new jobs before recall), and (2) the proportion of unemployed workers at a point in time who expect to be recalled (which excludes those with diminished expectations). Katz and Meyer argue that the more appropriate measure is an ex ante measure—a spell should be classified as a temporary layoff spell if the worker expects to be recalled at the time of layoff.

Katz and Meyer investigate the sensitivity of unemployment composition results to the definition used for temporary layoffs using data for unemployment insurance recipients who filed claimed between October 1979 and March 1980 in two states, Missouri (808 workers) and Pennsylvania (691 workers). The data consist of both Continuous Wage and Benefit History (CWBH) records and supplemental survey data. The latter were collected in follow-up telephone interviews in late 1980 and early 1981. The CWBH data were collected when workers filed their claims and provide information on recall expectations, previous income, and demographic characteristics. The supplemental data provide information on whether and when each worker returned to work, whether the worker returned to a previous employer, and the weekly wage on the post-unemployment job. Because these data pertain to just two states and cover a short time span, there is little sample variation in the unemployment insurance program parameters. Obviously, they provide no information about nonrecipients experience. Nevertheless, these data have several attractive features. First, observations on both expectations and outcomes regarding recalls are available. Second, because both self-reported and administrative data are available, alternative duration measures can be constructed. Katz and Meyer work with three duration measures of workers' first spells within their benefit years: FSPELL, based on self-reported spell starting and ending dates; IUSR, based on unemployment insurance claim dates and self-reported ending dates; and PAYSPELL (available for Missouri only), based on the dates of first benefit payments, self-reported numbers of spells, and self-reported spell ending dates.[35]

Seventy-five percent of all workers in the sample expect to be recalled, but only 57 percent have observed recalls (63 percent of all uncensored spells).[36] As Katz and Meyer predict, this difference translates into quite different results for the proportion of time spent unemployed. Using the UISR duration measure, Katz and Meyer find that about 45 percent of all time spent in completed unemployment spells is spent in spells that end in recall, that is, in temporary layoff spells under the ex post definition. However, when censored spells are included and the ex ante definition of temporary layoff is applied, the proportion jumps to 64 percent.[37] Roughly the same results are found for the Missouri sample using the PAYSPELL data. The bottom line is that the majority of workers expecting recall at the time of layoff are recalled, but those who are not recalled experience very long spells.

In view of these findings, Katz and Meyer analyze the distribution of unemployment spell lengths in the Missouri PAYSPELL data using the competing risk framework of Katz (1986). They start by calculating the Kaplan–Meier hazards for the total, recall, and new job hazards. The patterns exhibited here are consistent with those reported by Katz (1986) for the PSID recipient sample. The total hazard trends downward, with a valley between 28 and 36 weeks, but there are distinct differences between the underlying cause-specific hazards. The recall hazard declines rapidly in the first 6 weeks and then tends to decline thereafter, with the exception of spikes at 12, 16, and 25 weeks. The new job hazard, in contrast, tends to rise over time, with an early spike at 22 weeks. Both hazards exhibit the valley just before 35 weeks, but it is more pronounced in the recall hazard. Katz and Meyer also present time-until-exhaustion empirical hazards, calculated using the Kaplan–Meier type estimator with time centered at each individual's exhaustion dates. The total hazard trends downward, with a major spike at the exhaustion date, but the new job and recall hazards again exhibit quite different patterns. The recall hazard starts out high and declines steadily until 5 weeks after exhaustion, with the exception of spikes at 14 weeks and the exhaustion date. Thereafter, it stays close to zero. The new job hazard, on the other hand, starts out low and rises gradually until just a few weeks before exhaustion; it then spikes at exhaustion and remains relatively high thereafter. Overall, these results suggest that workers awaiting recall wait until their benefits run out.[38]

Katz and Meyer also carry out more a formal analysis of the Missouri duration data using a semiparametric approach, as in Meyer (1988b). Specifically, new job and recall hazards for individual i are defined as

$$\tau_{ij}(t) = \lambda_{0j}(t) \exp(x_i(t)'\beta_j)$$

where j denotes the destination state. The $x_i(t)$ are assumed constant over the interval $[t, t + 1)$ and the baseline hazard is parameterized by

$$\alpha_j(t) = \ln \int_t^{t+1} \lambda_{0j}(u) \, du$$

The $\alpha_j(t)$ are estimated along with β_j using the method of maximum likelihood. In the recall hazard, baseline parameters are estimated for the first 30 weeks and longer spells ending in recall are treated as censored. In the new job hazard, baseline parameters are estimated for the first 52 weeks and, again, longer spells are treated as censored. For comparison, results for the total hazard are also presented.

The list of explanatory variables is lengthy. Results are reported for a quadratic in age, sex, race, tenure on the last job, education, the previous net weekly wage, dummy variables to indicate expected recall and definite recall (i.e., a definite date for returning to work), and two unemployment insurance variables. The first is the weekly level of unemployment benefits, entered as a time-varying covariate with potentially different effects before and after exhaustion on both the new job and total (but not recall) hazards. The second is a spline in time-until-exhaustion, with intervals 0 (for the last week before exhaustion), 1 (for the second to last week before), 2–5 weeks, 6–10 weeks, and postexhaustion (i.e., workers with 11 or more weeks of remaining eligibility are the reference group). Number of dependents, marital status, six industry dummies, spell length before filing, and a dummy indicating spells starting before February 1, 1980, are also included, but results are not reported.

The results generally accord with expectations. The estimated effect on the total hazard of "expecting recall" is positive and significant, but its effects on the underlying hazards are quite different. The estimated effect on the recall hazard is positive, large, and significant, while the effect on the new job hazard is negative and significant. The estimated effects of tenure are similar. A small but positive and significant tenure effect on the total hazard represents the combination of a relatively large, positive, and significant recall effect and an insignificant (negative) effect on the new job hazard. The results for all three time–until–exhaustion splines are generally imprecise, except for a large jump of similar magnitude in all hazards in the last week before exhaustion. Education has a positive and significant effect on the new job (but not the recall) hazard, while the previous wage and remaining demographic characteristics appear irrelevant at standard levels for all hazards. Katz and Meyer report that the industry dummies are all insignificant, but that this result is quite sensitive to the inclusion of the expected recall dummy variable. Relative to other industries, construction, durable goods, and nondurable goods are described as having significant higher recall hazards and significantly lower new job hazards. The estimated effects of the benefit level on the total hazard are positive, but small and insignificant. Katz and Meyer note this may be due to limited variation in benefit levels in their sample. However, the estimated benefit effect on the new job hazard is large, negative, and significant before exhaustion, and negligible only after exhaustion. The estimated effect on the recall hazard, constrained to be the same before and after exhaustion, is large, positive, and significant. Katz and

Meyer describe this result as a "puzzle" (p. 29). One explanation would be that higher benefit workers are willing and able to wait for recall, while low benefit workers escape unemployment by entering new jobs. Alternatively, the link between previous wages and benefit levels and the insignificant wage coefficient estimates together suggest that the benefit level coefficients are picking up the effect of relative wage opportunities; that is, workers who had relatively good jobs are willing to wait for recalls. Baseline hazard estimates are not reported, but they are described as consistent with the empirical hazard patterns, that is, an increasing new job hazard and a decreasing recall hazard.[39]

Katz and Meyer also report results with unmeasured heterogeneity entered as a multiplicative disturbance with a unit mean gamma distribution. The estimates for the heterogeneity variance vary across hazards, but all are significantly different from zero (0.836 [standard error 0.257] for the total, 0.88 [standard error 0.368] for the recall, and 1.611 [standard error 0.589] for the new hazard). The coefficient estimates are all smaller in these models, as expected, but there are no qualitative changes in the results.

Jensen and Westergaard-Nielsen (1990)

Jensen and Westergaard-Nielsen investigate the importance of distinguishing temporary and permanent layoffs in the Danish labor market. In particular, their objective is to cast some light on two findings—large numbers of short spells (e.g., Pedersen and Westergaard-Nielsen, 1987) and an ambiguous effect for the benefit replacement rate on the transition rate out of unemployment (e.g., Jensen, 1987a, previously discussed). Their data are drawn from a longitudinal data set for about 240,000 workers in Denmark (about 5 percent of the Danish population) for the 1979–1984 period.[40] Their sample consists of about 11,000 individuals selected randomly from all workers in the full sample who experienced unemployment. Unemployment durations, measured in weeks, are based on administrative records for the unemployment insurance program. Although the data from these records have many desirable features, there are some problems. In particular, returns to former employers and new jobs are not distinguished. Consequently, Jensen and Westergaard-Nielsen rely on alternative administrative data to determine destinations at the end of unemployment spells.[41] By design, their assignment of the label temporary layoff is conservative, but temporary layoffs still appear to represent a large proportion of Danish unemployment spells. For the 6-year sample period, 40 percent of all spells appear to be due to temporary layoffs (ex post). Most of these spells are also relatively short, as anticipated. Their estimate for the proportion of all unemployment represented by temporary layoffs is 16 percent.

Jensen and Westergaard-Nielsen first use these data to estimate a logit model for the probability of temporary versus permanent layoff. Their explanatory variables include a measure of labor market experience,[42] the replacement rate, net taxable wealth, years of schooling, and dummy variables for marital status, sex, nonmetropolitan residence, children age 6 or less, whether a worker had an apprenticeship, industry,[43] occupation, membership in particular unions, part-time enrollment in the unemployment insurance program,[44] and receipt of sickness benefits during the year. Dummy variables for the year of the spell are also included to control for business cycle effects and a dummy variable for spells starting in the last 3 weeks of December is included to control for seasonal effects.

The results indicate that females and residents of Copenhagen have a substantially higher probability of experiencing a temporary layoff. The probability of temporary layoff is also higher for married workers and there is some evidence that it declines with age and education, but rises with experience. Some variation from year to year appears, but there is little evidence of a seasonal effect. The industry and union variables are generally insignificant, although this may reflect colinearity. The replacement rate has a small but nevertheless negative and significant coefficient. Jensen and Westergaard-Nielsen note that if this result is interpreted as evidence that high wage workers are more likely to return to the same employer, it may reflect greater search intensity on the part of those receiving a wage less than the average for workers with similar credentials.

Jensen and Westergaard-Nielsen also fit a competing risks model for unemployment durations separately for sex and age groups (16–24, 25–39, 40–54, 55–77). (Precise sample sizes are not provided.) Their specification for the cause-specific hazards is the Weibull,

$$\tau_j(t) = t^{\alpha_j} \exp\{x\beta_j\}$$

where j = new job and recall. The few spells that end with transitions into nonparticipation are treated as censored when estimating the cause-specific and total hazard rates. The explanatory variables included are those listed for the logit model, except education. For comparison, they also present results for an analogous specification for the total hazard out of unemployment.

Focusing first on total hazard results, there is some variation across groups in the estimates for the Weibull parameter, but all are negative and significantly different from zero. The range is -0.126 to -0.2845, with little variation by age for each sex, but a much larger decline for females. The results for the competing risk model suggest that these estimates reflect a combination of substantial negative duration dependence in the recall hazard and no significant duration dependence in the new job hazard. A second notable difference between the single versus competing risks results appears in the estimates for replacement rate effects. For males in the 25–39 and 55–77 age groups and for females in the 16–24 age group, the total hazard results imply a significant negative effect, but there is no significant effect for the remaining groups. The competing risk results imply that this finding of no replacement rate effect actually represents a large, significant, and negative effect on the recall hazard for the 16–24, 25–39, and 55–77 male age groups and for the 16–24 females age group. For the 25–39 male group, the replacement rate effect on the new job hazard is also negative and significant, but it is insignificant for the remaining groups. The results for the remaining variables indicate additional differences between the two hazards. Overall, a likelihood ratio test allows rejection of the hypotheses that the parameters of the recall and new job hazards are the same.

Ham and Rea (1986)

Ham and Rea work with a discrete time formulation for the unemployment duration distribution, extending the approach taken by Nickell (1979a,b). Their data consist of administrative records for a sample of 282 male recipients in Canada for the 1975–1980 period. A major limitation of these data (like other administrative records) is restricted demographic information; characteristics other than age are not available. More important, accurate inference with respect to the separate effects of benefit levels (or replacement ratios) and wages is essentially impossible. This is in part due to the structure of the benefit system in Canada and in part to the nature of their data for previous earnings. Official replacement rates do not vary across Provinces in Canada; benefits are a constant fraction of previous earnings up to an insurable maximum for all workers. Legislated changes in the official replacement rate over the 1975–1980 period introduce some variation across spells in the data, but not much. Moreover, previous earnings are truncated at the insured maximum for the years 1977 through 1980. Ham and Rea use an instrument for earnings that accounts for the truncation point at the insured maximum, noting that its variance is smaller than the actual earnings variance. Durations are measured as weeks of compensated joblessness, so that very short and very long spells of unemployment are excluded and transitions in and out of the labor force are not distinguished. In contrast to most UI administrative data for the United States, however, individual spells are distinguished here and thus problems of aggregation do not arise. Also, on a more positive note, potential duration of benefits varies within the sample both across individuals and time due to variation in rules across provinces and legislated changes over the sample period. Temporary and permanent layoffs are also distinguished. Since there are relatively few observations on the former, Ham and Rea focus on the new job hazard, treating transitions into former jobs as censored.

Ham and Rea first present Kaplan–Meier estimates of the new job hazard function. Overall, these suggest negative duration dependence through the first 8–9 months and slight positive duration dependence thereafter—with the exception of spikes at 20, 29, 33, and 37 weeks.

Ham and Rea proceed next with a more formal analysis of their data. For a worker i who began his spell at time t_{0i}, their specification for the new job hazard at duration $t_{0i} + t$ is

$$\tau_i(t_{0i}, t) = \{1 + \exp\{-[\theta_i + h(t) + z(s(t_{0i} + t)) + \delta_i t s(t_{0i} + t) + \beta' x_i(t_{0i} + t)]\}\}^{-1}$$

The term $s(t_{0i} + t)$ denotes potential duration of benefits remaining at $t_{0i} + t$ and the function z measures its effect on the hazard; throughout their analysis, they use a quadratic. Ham and Rea start with a sixth-order polynomial for the duration dependence function $h(t)$ and then check the sensitivity of their results with lower order polynomials and a step function. The fourth term in the brackets is an interaction term for entitlement and duration. Initially, θ_i is treated as a constant. Aggregate and local (provincial or regional) unemployment rates, age and seasonal dummy variables, benefit levels, and an instrument for previous wages are included in the vector of regressors.

The results for this basic model suggest that the new job hazard increases as exhaustion of benefits nears, at least when remaining entitlement is 42 weeks or less. Maximum entitlement is about 52 weeks for a claim and the duration of claim cannot exceed a calendar year. The sixth-order polynomial for remaining duration dependence in the hazard also appears to be supported by the data. Interpreting the coefficients for a polynomial of this order is difficult, so Ham and Rea plot the hazard with and without entitlement held constant. With benefit entitlement held constant, the baseline hazard appears to decline to 46 weeks (very few spells last 46 weeks or longer). On the other hand, when entitlement is not controlled, the hazard appears to decline during the first 24 weeks and then rise.

For comparison with previous work, results with a quadratic duration dependence function are presented. The pattern of duration dependence differs in a predictable way from sixth-order model; the hazard declines more smoothly and it begins to rise at an earlier point. When a step function is fit, plots of the hazard are much closer to those for the sixth-order model than those for the quadratic. Variation in the pattern of the entitlement effect is negligible across the alternative specifications for $h(t)$. The same also holds for the coefficients for remaining regressors. The new job hazard decreases with increases in the unemployment rates, as expected. It also declines with age but only through age 49; it appears to rise with age thereafter. The coefficients for the previous wage are negative and differ significantly from zero, while the benefit coefficient are positive, but small relative to their standard errors.

Ham and Rea experiment with alternative models—maintaining their initial specifications for $h(t)$ and $z(s(t_{0i} + t))$. The results for models that include duration in the previous unemployment spell are of particular interest. The motivation here is to capture either true lagged duration dependence or unobserved heterogeneity that remains constant across spells. When entered alone, lagged duration has a significant negative coefficient and remaining parameter estimates are basically unchanged. When the unemployment rate and potential duration of benefits at the start of the previous spell are entered, the lagged duration coefficient is again significantly negative and the coefficients for the unemployment rate and entitlement are positive and significant. Given the close link between benefits and wages in their data, Ham and Rea also investigate the effect of omitting the instrument for previous earnings from the equation. The coefficient for benefits switches sign, but a null hypothesis of no effect cannot be rejected at the standard levels. Similarly, Ham and Rea report that when wages and benefits are interacted with entitlement (to allow for variation in the benefit effect) and with a dummy for age under 25 (roughly following Nickell, 1979a,b), the coefficient estimates for the interaction terms are insignificant.

Ham and Rea next incorporate unobserved heterogeneity into their model. They start by assuming that the intercept θ_i is independently and identically distributed across both spells and individuals, with two mass points. The major effect of this respecification appears in the coefficients for the sixth-order polynomial for the duration dependence function $h(t)$; a null hypothesis that $h(t)$ is a fourth-order polynomial (against the alternative of the sixth-order polynomial previously supported by the data) cannot be rejected on the basis of Wald and likelihood ratio tests. Of course, the specification with heterogeneity involves more parameters, so some power to distinguish hypotheses will have been lost. The results for remaining variables are qualitatively unchanged. In particular, the entitlement effect appears to be strengthened; the coefficients for the quadratic terms are slightly higher, while the coefficient for the duration and entitlement interaction term is negative and significant in this model (versus positive and insignificant at standard levels in the model that ignores unobserved heterogeneity). Ham and Rea note that when a third mass point is added to this model, it is not supported by the data.

Their second specification restricts θ_i to being constant across spells for each individual, that is, a fixed effect. As before, they find that a sixth-order polynomial can be rejected in favor of a fourth-order polynomial for the duration dependence function $h(t)$. A third mass point does appear to be supported in this case, but not a fourth. The results for entitlement and other variables appear similar to the previous results, allowing for both two- and three-point distributions.

As before, detecting the effect of holding potential duration of benefits constant on the duration dependence results is not easily done by viewing the coefficient estimates. Ham and Rea therefore plot the aggregate hazard function with entitlement held constant (following Kennan, 1985). For week t, this can be interpreted as the expected value of the hazard, where the expectation is taken with respect to the distribution of θ_i over those with spells lasting at least t weeks. The hazards for the case in which θ_i is assumed constant across spells appear to be slightly flatter (as expected with the fourth-order polynomial), but they are the same as the results for the nonstochastic model otherwise. On the other hand, the pattern of duration dependence for the model with independence across all spells looks totally different—for no apparent reason. It declines rapidly between 15 and 24 weeks and then rises sharply, with a spike at 39 weeks; Ham and Rea describe the pattern as "somewhat implausible" (p. 349).

Ham and Rea also report results for what they describe as a "parsimonious version of the new job and recall hazards" (p. 333) and the total hazard—accompanied by a warning that the results must be viewed with caution since only 20 percent of all completed spells end with a return to a former employer. Duration is entered as a quadratic and remaining entitlement is entered linearly. Reservations aside, the results do suggest very different behavior between those on temporary versus permanent layoff. While both hazards decline with duration at a decreasing rate, the new job hazard appears much steeper. As in the results reported by Katz, the new job hazard decreases with age, while the recall hazard increases. The new job hazard also decreases with increases in the industrial unemployment rate, while the recall hazard appears unaffected. The benefit effect on the recall hazard is positive, but there is no evidence of a benefit effect on the new job hazard. The total hazard appears to decrease with increases in the wage, but the coefficient in the new job hazards is only marginally significant and the recall hazard appears insensitive. The effect of remaining entitlement is negative and about the same in magnitude across hazards. A likelihood ratio test allows rejection of the hypothesis that the parameters of the two hazards are the same at standard levels.

Summary

The findings reviewed here strongly suggest that distinguishing temporary and permanent layoffs is important (see Table 6.6). Katz (1986), Katz and Meyer (1988b), and Jensen and Westergaard-Nielson (1990) find that negative duration dependence in single risk (or total) hazard models reflects the combination of a decreasing recall hazard and either an increasing or constant new job hazard. The findings of Ham and Rea (1987) for Canada for duration dependence in the new job hazard pose some contrast to these results. Ham and Rea control for the effect of remaining duration of benefits using a quadratic in time-until-exhaustion and find that the new job hazard initially decreases as time-until-exhaustion decreases, but it increases as exhaustion nears when remaining entitlement is 42 weeks or less. After controlling for this effect, Ham and Rea find that the new job hazard increases with duration only after 46 weeks; without this control, it increases after 24 weeks. Using U.S. data, Katz and Meyer fit a linear spline in time until exhaustion and find evidence of a sharp increase in the new job hazard just before the exhaustion date, but only a weak remaining entitlement effect in the preceding period. As noted, Katz and Meyer also report an increasing new job baseline. The difference in benefit entitlement effects across the two studies might be reconciled by noting that the quadratic in time-until-exhaustion could be smoothing out a spike effect (but this is just speculation). As for the remaining duration dependence in the new job hazard, Katz and Meyer do not report their nonparametric baseline estimates. In particular, they do not discuss any spikes remaining after controlling for time-until-exhaustion. The positive slope that Katz and Meyer do report for the new job hazard

Table 6.6. Temporary versus Permanent Layoffs

Study	Data	Hazard Specification	Findings
Katz (1986)	United States, 1980–1982 PSID household heads	1. Proportional hazards, Weibull baseline ($\alpha t^{\alpha-1}$), total, new job and recall, fit separately for UI recipients/nonrecipients	Duration dependence: Total hazard: recipients negative; nonrecipients negative New job: recipients positive; nonrecipients none Recall: recipients negative; nonrecipients negative
		2. As in (1), with dummy for 26 and 39 weeks durations	Large positive effect at 26 (not 39) weeks; other results unaffected
		3. New job and recall as in (1), for full sample with benefit receipt dummy and previous tenure	Duration dependence: New job: none; recall: negative Tenure effect: New job: negative; recall: positive Benefit receipt effect: New job: none; recall: positive
		4. As in (1), with previous tenure, fit separately for UI recipients/nonrecipients	Duration dependence: Recipients: recall: negative; new job: positive Nonrecipients: none
		5. Total hazard for plant closing subsample, fit separately for UI recipients/nonrecipients	Duration dependence: Recipients: none; nonrecipients: negative
Katz and Meyer (1988b) Recall expectations and potential duration of benefits	United States, 1979–1980 CWBH, with follow-up survey, UI recipients, Missouri, Pennsylvania	1. Semiparametric proportional hazards, total, new job, and recall hazards with time-until-exhaustion spline	Duration dependence: Total hazard: negative; new job: positive; recall: negative Recall expectations: Total: positive; new job: negative; recall: positive Benefit level New job: negative before exhaustion, none thereafter; recall: positive Time-until-exhaustion of benefits

Study	Data	Model	Results
		2. As in (1), with gamma heterogeneity distribution	All hazards: jump at one week left Tenure effects Total: positive; new job: none; recall: positive Heterogeneity variance: Total: 0.84 (S.E. 0.26); new job: 1.61 (S.E. 0.59); recall: 0.88 (S.E. 0.36) Above results unaffected
Jensen and Westergaard-Nielsen (1988)	Denmark, 1979–1984	Proportional total, new job and recall hazards, Weibull baseline (t^a), by sex and age	Duration dependence: Total: negative for males 25–39 and 55–77, and females 16–24; none for others New job: negative for males 25–39; none for others Recall: negative for males 16–24, 25–39, and 55–77, and females 16–24; none for others
Ham and Rea (1987) Potential duration of benefits	Canada, 1975–1980 Benefit recipients, administrative records, males	1. Logit, for new job hazard, with sixth-order polynomial in duration and quadratic in time-until-exhaustion	Decreasing hazard through week 46 and then increasing, with control for potential duration of benefits; increases after 24 weeks without control for benefit duration Time-until-exhaustion: hazard increases as exhaustion nears (after initial decrease)
		2. As in (1), quadratic in duration	Similar results
		3. As in (1), except step function in duration	Similar results
		4. As in (1), with 2-point heterogeneity distribution, i.i.d. across all spells	Sixth-order polynomial in duration rejected against fourth order; similar results otherwise
		5. As in (1), with 2- and 3-point heterogeneity distribution, i.i.d. across individuals	Same as above, except third point is supported
		6. Logit for total, new job, and recall hazards, with quadratic duration and linear time-until-exhaustion	Duration dependence: all negative Time-until-exhaustion: all increase as exhaustion nears Benefit level: Total: none; new job: none; recall: positive

S.E. = standard error.

may simply reflect such spikes. Of course, the contrast may simply reflect a difference between populations sampled.

Findings for wages, benefit levels, and replacement rates are somewhat unclear due to limited variation in all samples studied. Benefit level coefficients are generally positive in the recall hazards and negative or negligible in the new job hazards, while wage effects appear negligible. Both variables appear irrelevant in the total hazards. Piecing these results together, it appears that high wage workers (who consequently receive higher benefit amounts) are more likely to await recall if on temporary layoff than workers who received low wages on their previous jobs.

Beyond these findings are some interesting results for age. Katz and Ham and Rea find that the new job hazard decreases with age while the recall hazard increases with age. However, when previous tenure is included by Katz (and by Katz and Meyer), tenure has the contrasting effects on the hazards and age appears irrelevant. A contrast in effects also appears for local labor market conditions. The new job hazard appears more responsive to increases in the unemployment rate. Finally, as in previous chapters, the results from studies of both male and female workers and both white and nonwhite workers suggest some potentially important differences across groups, that is, generalizing results for prime-age white males seems inappropriate.[45]

Alternative Multistate Models of the Labor Market

In previous sections, we consider the consequence of failing to distinguish transitions out of nonparticipation versus unemployment and transitions into new jobs versus old jobs. In this section, we turn to studies based on alternative multistate models. We start with a study by Khandker (1988), who distinguishes transitions into jobs that offer nonwage benefits versus jobs that do not. Narendranathan and Stewart (1990) examine distinctions between transitions into full-time jobs versus alternative destinations from unemployment. Farber (1980) focuses on employment durations and considers the distinction between spells ending with quits and spells ending with layoffs.

Khandker (1988)

Khandker extends the stationary two-state job search model to allow for heterogeneity across jobs in terms of nonwage characteristics. Specifically, an unemployed worker is described as paying a search cost c to receive offers according to a Poisson process with parameter δ. Here, however, an offer is defined as

$$w_k + v_k$$

where $k = 1, 2, \ldots, K$ denotes offer type, v_k is a parameter that represents the imputed dollar value of nonwage characteristics associated with a type k job, and w_k is a money wage drawn from a distribution $F_k(w)$. Job durations also vary across job types; their distributions are assumed to be exponential with parameter a_k. When an offer arrives, the probability that it is a type k offer is P_k, where $\Sigma_k P_k = 1$. These probabilities are treated as exogenous, that is, the worker does not look for jobs of a particular type.

The optimal policy for the worker is a reservation policy. Precisely, when a wage offer for a job of type k arrives, the optimal policy is to accept the offer if it exceeds the reservation wage for a type k job, where the K reservation wages are defined by the conditions

$$w_k^r + v_k = -c + \delta \sum_{k=1}^{K} \left[\frac{P_k}{a_k + r} \int_{w_k^r}^{\infty} (w - w_k^r) \, dF_k(w) \right]$$

simultaneously for $k = 1, 2, \ldots, K$. Each reservation wage thus depends on the entire set of wage offer distributions, the parameters v_k, the offer probabilities P_k, the layoff rates a_k, the arrival rate δ, the discount rate r, and the cost of search c. (Income while unemployed is ignored here, as in the work of Flinn and Heckman [1982b] and Wolpin [1987]). It follows that unemployment durations have an exponential distribution with parameter

$$\tau_u = \sum_k \tau_{uk}$$

where

$$\tau_{uk} = \delta P_k[1 - F_k(w_k^r)]$$
$$= \delta P_k \pi_k(w_k^r)$$

denotes the transition rate from unemployment into a type k job; the second equality uses our previous notation for the acceptance probabilities.

At the empirical stage, Khandker restricts the number of job types to two—type 1 jobs that provide some nonwage benefits as a part of total compensation and type 2 jobs that offer no benefits. His data are for a sample of 1,285 workers collected in the 1980 baseline household survey of the Employment Opportunity Pilot Project (EOPP).[46] His sample consists of workers in their 20s with 12 to 14 years of education, who were paid hourly and who experienced no more than three job changes in the period covered by the retrospective survey period (16–22 months). Khandker restricts his duration observations for each worker to the two most recent completed or right-censored employment and unemployment spells available. Employment spell observations are available for 839 workers, unemployment spell observations are available for 169 workers, and observations on both spell types are available for 277 workers. In the total sample of job spells, 267 (24 percent) provide bonuses, commissions, tips, housing subsidies, or some other kind of nonwage benefit and these are classified as type 1. Others are classified as type 2. All durations are measured in months and accepted hourly wages are observed for all employment spells.

Khandker modifies the approach taken by Flinn and Heckman (1982b, discussed previously), based on treating the sample as randomly selected from a homogeneous population. Specifically, he partitions his sample of employment observations by job type and uses an average of the 10 lowest accepted wages observations for each group. These estimates are $1.873 for a type 1 job and $2.355 for a type 2 job. Normalizing v_2 to zero, the difference between these estimates provide an estimate of the value of the benefits v_1 equal to $0.482. To estimate the remaining parameters of the model, Khandker carries out maximum likelihood estimation conditioned on these estimates. When both completed unemployment and completed employment spells are available, the contribution to the likelihood function is the joint density for the durations and the accepted wage:

$$L(t_{ui}, t_{kei}, w_i | w_1^{r*}, w_2^{r*}) = f_k(w_i)\delta P_k \exp\{-\tau_u(w_1^{r*}, w_2^{r*})t_i\}a_k \exp\{-a_k t_{kei}\}$$

where k denotes the job type accepted and $\tau_u(w_1^{r*}, w_2^{r*})$ represents the unemployment hazard evaluated at the estimated reservation wages. For censored cases, the appropriate survivor functions are used.

Khandker uses two alternative specifications for the offer distributions: normal and lognormal. Under each specification, the mean and variance are restricted to be the same across job types, so that only reservation wages, separation rates, and the probabilities P_k are left to explain differences in the transition rates out of unemployment, τ_{uk}. Khandker notes that when means are allowed to differ across types, their equality cannot be rejected; no comment on the variance restriction is offered.

The cause-specific hazards differ greatly across job types, $\tau_{u1}^* = 0.036$ and $\tau_{u2}^* = 0.11$. Under both offer specifications, this appears to be due to differences in the arrival rates across types. The estimates for the acceptance probabilities are sensitive to the parametric family specified, but they differ only slightly across job types ($\pi_1^* = 0.77$ and $\pi_2^* = 0.73$ under the normal and $\pi_1^* = 1.00$ and $\pi_2^* = 0.97$ under the lognormal). The estimates δ^* are 0.197 for the normal specification and 0.151 for the lognormal. The probability that a job offer is a type 1 offer is only 0.24, however, the arrival rates for type 1 (benefit) offers are effectively 0.046 (normal) and 0.036 (lognormal), versus 0.15 (normal) and 0.11 (lognormal) for type 2 (no benefit) offers. The difference in expected employment spell lengths across job types is also substantial; the estimates for the separation rates are $a_1^* = 0.007$ and $a_2^* = 0.013$, implying jobs that provide benefits last about twice as long. Solutions to the optimality conditions for search costs c under alternative exogenous estimates for the discount rate r are also provided. Letting $r = 0.1$, the estimates are 2.391 under the normal and 2.417 under the lognormal. The negative of these estimates can be interpreted as income net of search costs (b in our notation of Chapter 2).

Narendranathan and Stewart (1990)

Narendranathan and Stewart examine the empirical importance of distinguishing between transitions from unemployment into full-time employment and alternative exits from unemployment. In particular, they consider part-time employment and self-employment. Therewith, they study the sensitivity of their findings to specification of the baseline hazard.

Precisely, Narendranathan and Stewart fit both single risk and competing risk proportional hazards using both Weibull (with $\lambda_0(t) = \alpha t^{\alpha-1}$) and semiparametric specifications. Their data are for a sample of 1,571 men in the United Kingdom who were registered as unemployed in the autumn of 1978. The source of these data is the DHSS Cohort Study, also analyzed by Narendranathan et al. (1985, discussed in Chapter 5). As in that study, unemployment durations are measured in weeks and the sample is restricted to workers with spells of 5 weeks or more (due to uncertain benefit receipt in the first part of workers' spells). The likelihood function is appropriately conditioned on exceeding 4 weeks. The sample used by Narendranathan et al. (1985) is weighted; the present sample is not. The explanatory variables included in all models are log unemployment income (from all sources), log expected income in employment (set equal to the sum of nonlabor income and a fitted value for the mean offered weekly full-time wage, based on regressions by occupational category), the local unemployment rate, redundancy and holding pay, categorical variables for age, education, and housing status, and dummy variables for marital status, ethnic group, disability, union status in the last full-time job, recent labor market experiences (previous tenure less than a year, registered unemployment in the last year, voluntary quit from last job, on-the-job search in last job, and no full-time job in the last year), and no receipt of benefits. Unemployment income, employment income, and the unemployment rate are allowed to take on different values in each quarter. Also, the effect of unemployment income is permitted to vary with age and duration (less than 6 months and more than 6 months, since Earnings Related Supplements cease at 6 months).

This regressor specification is intentionally similar to the basic model of Narendranathan et al. Not surprisingly, the results are quite close across studies for the single risk Weibull model for the hazard out of unemployment. Differences can be interpreted as evidence on the sensitivity to using sampling weights. Overall, they are minor. The Weibull parameter estimate is 1.02 (standard error 0.04) so that a constant hazard cannot be rejected at standard levels of significance. The estimated unemployment income effects on the hazard also exhibit variation with both age and duration of a spell. In the first 6 months, the elasticities of mean duration range from 0.28 for workers ages 45–64 to 0.93 for workers ages 20–24. There is no statistically significant change in the elasticity after 6 months for workers either under age 20 or over age 45, but there is a large change for prime age workers (25–44) and an even greater change for young adults (20–24). For the prime-age group, the initial elasticity is 0.53 (standard error 0.04) and it drops to −0.3. (The estimated change for the hazard elasticity is 0.83 [standard error 0.28]). For young adults, the drop is from 0.93 to 0.10. Findings for remaining regressors are similar to those of Narendranathan et al. Age has a decreasing, negative effect on the hazard. The hazard also decreases with increases in local unemployment and mean employment income (elasticity 0.80). It is also significantly greater for married workers, nonunion workers, workers with more stable work histories, and workers who have completed apprenticeships (though not for those with other educational qualifications).

Results from semiparametric estimation of the single risk model are quite similar. The point estimates for the unemployment elasticities are about 10 percent smaller and standard errors differ only slightly; the pattern described above remains intact. As for duration dependence, the baseline estimates are somewhat different from the Weibull resultsl; for the "standard man" in the sample, there is evidence of weak positive duration dependence initially and then weak negative duration dependence after about 6 months.

The regressor coefficient results for the competing risk model also appear insensitive to the baseline specification, but there are some nonnegligible differences between the single-risk and competing risk results. As might be expected, the variables most closely tied to search-theoretic arguments have a more pronounced effect on the transition rate into full-time jobs. In particular, the coefficient estimates for log employment income are much larger (1.09 [standard error 0.19]) in the Weibull model and 1.04 [standard error 0.19] in the semiparametric model). The log unemployment income coefficients for the first 6 months are also somewhat larger in the full-time job hazard, though the age pattern is the same (−0.38 [standard error 0.08] to −1.11 [standard error 0.09]). The estimated change in the unemployment income effect after 6 months, on the other hand, is reduced somewhat, that is, the single-risk estimates appear to understate responsiveness to unemployment income levels. The Weibull parameter estimate for the full-time job hazard is 0.84 (standard error 0.05), implying negative duration dependence in the hazard. This estimate also implies that elasticities implied by the results are about 20 percent greater than the coefficient estimates in this case (i.e., 1.3 for employment income and 0.45–1.32 for unemployment income in the first 6 months). A comparison of the baseline hazards for the single risk and full-time job in the semiparametric models shows a less marked contrast than in the Weibull models. The full-time job baseline exhibits some negative duration dependence between the fourth and eighth weeks of a spell and a more pronounced decline after 6 months. It also exhibits a much sharper spike at 8 months; the Weibull model most likely picks up the subsequent decline. The full-time job hazard exhibits a sharper decline with age (after 45, in particular). The recent labor market experience coefficients are also larger in absolute magnitude. One very interesting finding is that the full-time job hazard appears insensitive to local labor market conditions, at least when measured by the unemployment rate within a worker's "Travel-to-Work" area. Union membership similarly appears irrelevant. The results for the "other exit" hazard (i.e., non-full-time job) reflect the differences described between the full-time job hazard and the total hazard results.

Results from semiparametric estimation of the transition rate into either a full-time or part-time job (versus other exits) differ only slightly from those for transition rates into a full-time job, although this may simply reflect the small proportion of the sample that makes the part-time transition (3.5 percent). The results are also quite similar when transitions into full-time self-employment jobs are distinguished from wage and salary full-time employment. Putting all of these results together, they suggest that distinguishing exits from unemployment into employment versus nonemployment is potentially important, but making other distinctions such as part-time versus full-time may not be essential, at least for males in the United Kingdom.

Farber (1980)

Farber studies employment duration data and attempts to determine whether quits and firings represent distinct events. Toward this end, he estimates a competing risks model with quits and dismissals defined as alternative exits from employment.

As opposed to specifying a functional form for the hazard, Farber takes the alternative route of specifying the joint duration distribution for log durations. He assumes that log employment durations of each type j, j = q (quit), f (firing), have normal distributions:

$$\ln t_j = x'\beta_j + \epsilon_j$$

where the ϵ_j are standard normal random variables. The joint distribution is bivariate normal with correlation ρ_{qf}. Farber recognizes that the normal specification is restrictive—the hazard rate must rise with duration to a maximum and then decline. Note also that this specification corresponds to an accelerated lifetime model for durations, where the effect of explanatory variables is to rescale time directly (as opposed to rescaling the baseline hazard, as in the proportional hazards model). The coefficients thus measure the proportionate change in duration resulting from a change in an explanatory variable, that is, the role of an explanatory variable is to either accelerate or decelerate the time to exit.[47]

Farber fits the model using data for a sample selected from the random subsample of the Panel Study of Income Dynamics. The sample consists of 513 individuals who were household heads and employed (but not self-employed) at the first round of interviews in 1968 and the data cover the 1968–1977 period. These data have the attractive feature of a long observation period, so that right censoring is minimal (0.19 of the sample). On the other hand, they have one very unattractive feature. Although information on tenure at the start of the sample period is available (and therefore left censoring is not a problem), the durations are reported only in wide interval form. Furthermore, this practice is continued through the first eight waves, that is, 1968–1975, so that subsequent job durations are also measured in interval form. Farber notes that the last two surveys do report job tenures in months, but 84 percent of all jobs held in 1976 are right censored by the 1978 interview. Given the trade-off, he works with the longer panel. In specifying his sample likelihood function, Farber deals with the problem of initial conditions by conditioning all contributions to the likelihood on the lower bounds of the initial tenure intervals—noting that the choice of the lower bound introduces measurement error of an unknown magnitude.[48] To deal with the interval form of data for subsequent durations, he enters the conditional probabilities of job exits in the year intervals observed for uncensored spells and he enters the conditional survivor for censored spells.[49] His specification for the explanatory variables of the model includes dummy variables for sex, race, union membership, less than 12 years of education, more than 12 years, and a constant. Farber notes that observations on industry would be included if available, but these data are not reported until the later waves. He also notes that including age, marital status, and number of children was considered, but he chooses to exclude these variables because of time variation (i.e., both initial levels and all time variation in these variables are included in ϵ_j). Finally, firings are defined as all permanent employer-initiated job separations (i.e., it appears that temporary layoff spells are not included).

For reference, Farber first reports results for an employment duration model. He then reports results for the competing risks specification with and without the coefficients constrained to be equal. Overall, the estimates are imprecise. Females have significantly longer tenures and there is weak evidence that this reflects longer durations until they quit. This variable has the only significant coefficient at the 5 percent level in the entire set of results. In particular, the covariance estimate for the competing risks model is positive, but insignificant. Farber notes that the imprecision is likely the consequence of his poor data. Alternatively, it may reflect the restrictions of the normal specification. The bottom line, however, is the result for the test of the null hypothesis that the marginal distributions for quit durations and the firing durations are the same. On the basis of a likelihood ratio test, the results allow rejection of equality at standard levels of significance. Thus, the study provides at least weak evidence of a difference between the two forms of exit.

Summary

Table 6.7 offers a summary of this section. The findings of Khandker (1988) indicate that transition rates into jobs having different characteristics—nonwage benefits in particular—do differ. As to why they differ, his results suggest that the action is in the arrival rate of offers. Workers appear to move more quickly into jobs that do not offer nonwage benefits because these offers arrive more frequently than benefit job offers. Although his findings for acceptance probabilities appear somewhat sensitive to his specification for the family of the offer distributions (as found in previous structural analyses based on single risk models), the results suggest that workers are not (much) more likely to reject an offer of one type or another. He also finds that jobs offering no

Table 6.7. Alternative Multistate Models

Study	Data	Model	Findings
Khandker (1988) Jobs with versus jobs without benefits	United States, 1978–1980 EOPP	1. Stationary representative agent model, normal offers	Value of benefits: $0.48 $\pi(w')$: benefit job: 0.77; no benefits: 0.73 δ(month): 0.197 Prob (benefit job offer/offer): 0.24 Separation rates: benefit job: 0.007; no benefits: 0.013
		2. As in (1), lognormal offers	$\pi(w')$: benefit job: 1.00; no benefits: 0.97 δ(month): 0.151
Narendranathan and Stewart (1990) Full-time jobs versus alternative exits from unemployment	United Kingdom, 1979 DHSS cohort study, registered unemployed	1. Proportional total and full-time job hazards (versus all other exist), Weibull baseline ($\alpha t^{\alpha-1}$), time and age variation in benefit effect	Duration dependence: Total: none Full-time: negative Unemployment income elasticities: Total: 0.28–0.93 in months 2–6, and drops for workers aged 20–44 after 6 months Full-time job: 0.45–1.32 in months 2–6; drops for workers 20–44 after 6 months
		2. As in (1), with nonparametric baseline	Duration dependence: Total: weak positive and then negative after 6 months Full-time: negative in second month and after 6 months; positive between third and sixth months
		3. "Other" hazard, nonparametric baseline	Duration dependence: Total: weak positive, and then negative after 6 months Full-time: negative in second month and after 6 months but positive between Other results reflect full-time versus total hazard differences listed
		4. Full-time or part-time job, nonparametric baseline	Similar to (2)
Farber (1980) Quits versus firings	United States, 1968–1977 PSID household heads	Accelerated lifetime quit and layoff hazards out of employment	Likelihood ratio test rejects equality of quit and layoff exit rates from employment

benefits end more quickly. Throughout his analysis, Khandker treats arrival rates as exogenous. His results suggest that investigating the appropriateness of this assumption would be worthwhile. Khandker also restricts offer distributions to be the same across job types, so that reservation wages determine the levels of the acceptance probabilities for each type of offer. Investigating the sensitivity of his findings to this restriction also seems in order.

The findings of Narendranathan and Stewart (1990) are both informative and encouraging. The insensitivity of their regressor results to specification of the baseline hazards can be interpreted as favorable evidence for the findings of earlier studies that use parametric methods. The contrast in results for the full-time job versus total hazards is somewhat unsettling. Although the implications of the two models are qualitatively similar, they differ substantially in quantitative terms. The results for the part-time or full-time job hazard are most encouraging. At least for unemployed men in the United Kingdom, it appears that employment versus other exits is the important distinction. Investigating this question for other demographic groups (women, in particular) could produce different findings.

Finally, the results reported by Farber suggest that exits from employment brought about by quits versus firings are distinct. We return to this topic in Chapter 8, where we focus more closely on exits from jobs (versus employment).

The studies reviewed in this chapter address questions relevant for the study of labor market dynamics in the search framework. The studies treating dynamics explicitly have been carried out in a Markovian or semi-Markovian framework. This assumption is typically untested and this needs to be kept in mind in interpreting the results. Failure of this assumption will induce heterogeneity and bias the estimates of duration distributions. Of course, there is no obvious tractable alternative assumption.[50]

One finding that emerges is that the transition rate out of employment declines with the duration of a job. Workers with higher levels of education appear to leave employment more rarely. There is evidence from the multistate models that unemployment and nonparticipation are behaviorally distinct labor market states, especially in the cases of young workers and women. Wage effects on transitions appear to vary substantially across demographic groups. There is indirect evidence that variation in transition rates into employment (from either nonparticipation or unemployment) reflects variation in offer arrivals rather than in acceptance probabilities. There is evidence based on U.S. and Danish data that distinguishing spells initiated by a temporary layoff versus a permanent layoff is important. Transition rates appear sensitive to local labor market conditions. Potential duration of benefit payments appears to be an important determinant of the benefit effect on transitions. Finally, there is evidence that transition rates into jobs depend noticeably on nonwage characteristics as well as the wage (nonwage benefits, in particular). In view of economists' focus on the wage as a summary statistic characterizing a job, at least when the initial acceptance decision is made, this result is disconcerting.

Notes

1. As in previous chapters, we restrict our attention here to analysis of microdata. Toikka (1976) appears to have been the first to study a three state model using gross flow data. Clark and Summers (1979, 1982a,b), Darby et al. (1986, 1987), Ehrenberg (1981), Holt et al. (1977), Jack-

man and Layard (1988), Marston (1975, 1976), and Perry (1972) also present transition rate estimates for a full three-state model calculated using gross flow data. Flaim and Hogue (1985) and
Kiefer et al. (1985) discuss some limitations of the gross flow data for making inferences about
spell lengths and Abowd and Zellner (1985) offer suggestions for making adjustments to gross flow
data to improve estimates.

2. Recall from Chapter 3 that a semi-Markov process is defined as a stochastic process in which
the transition rate out of the state currently occupied may depend on the duration of the current
spell in this state, but not on previous experience in this or alternative states (e.g., previous wages
or unemployment income, previous employment spell lengths, and previous unemployment spell
lengths). This is to be distinguished from the special case of a Markov process in which transition
rates are also independent of duration of the current spell.

3. Lundberg (1981) discusses the construction of individual labor market histories from the
DIME data.

4. Initially, only families were selected for enrollment in the DIME and each had to satisfy
four criteria: (1) the family head had to be white, black, or hispanic; (2) the family had to be single-
or two-headed with one or more dependents; (3) preexperiment earnings had to be below $9,000
for a family of four with a single head and $11,000 for a two-headed family (measured in 1970–
1971 dollars); and (4) the head had to be between the ages of 18 and 58 and capable of gainful
employment. To the extent that low preexperimental earnings reflected transitory income
declines, higher income families may be represented in the sample. Also, individuals who were
once part of a participant family and formed their own household remained eligible for participation in the DIME once the experiment began. Thus, individuals and couples without dependents are included to the sample. Still, the resulting sample should not be regarded as representative of either the U.S. population or the Denver population.

5. The authors report that a specification with the standard correction for censored wage data
was estimated, but the estimated coefficient for the inverse Mills ratio was insignificant.

6. The α estimates decline with the elimination of regressors to 0.659 (standard error 0.0174)
when only the constant is included.

7. Honore and Pederson (1984) present results from an earlier analysis of these data based on
a three-state model. For a more complete description of the data set, see Westergaard-Nielsen
(1984).

8. Labor market experience is based on administrative data collected for worker pensions; the
measure is unusual in that it is related to number of hours worked over the course of a career. For
males, the classification is service, public sector, manufacturing, construction, and other. Note also
that enrollment in the unemployment insurance program is elective for Danish workers.

9. The data analyzed here are taken from the same source as in their study of reservation wage
data, discussed in Chapter 4.

10. The DIME data are discussed in the review of Burdett et al. (1985). The SIME was an
analogous experiment carried out in Seattle between 1970 and 1973. The estimation approach
used in this study is discussed in greater detail by Tuma et al. (1979).

11. Ham and LaLonde present preliminary results from a dynamic analysis of job training
effects on women in the United States. They have even less data on preprogram behavior, making
their task even more complicated than the task faced by Ridder. Using a variety of simpler techniques, Card and Sullivan (1988) find that transition rates into employment of adult males in the
United States are higher following training program participation and that the effect is greater for
classroom training program participants than for on-the-job program participants.

12. Appendix C of this paper consists of a mistaken attack on Kiefer and Neumann (1979b).
Flinn and Heckman describe an estimation procedure different from Kiefer and Neumann's,
attribute it to Kiefer and Neumann, and attack it.

13. An obvious problem with using this reservation wage estimator is its sensitivity to measurement error. If measurement error is present, this and all estimates will be inconsistent. Models

that allow measurement error in wage observations include Kiefer and Neumann (1979a,b), Wolpin (1987), and many others.

14. This normal estimate aligns more closely with lognormal estimates obtained by others using comparable methods (Wolpin, 1987, and Devine, 1988, for example). It seems likely that wages are actually measured in logs here.

15. Note that the estimates for b, using our notation, correspond to estimates for direct costs of search in a model that ignores the receipt of income when unemployed. This is the case in the study by Flinn and Heckman, so that positive direct costs of 0.33 to 2.69 are reported. Chang (1985) uses a variation on this approach to analyze data for a sample of male workers collected in the Employment Opportunity Pilot Project. Specifically, he uses the fifth percentile wage as an estimator for the reservation wage and fits the model separately for subsamples in a partition by age.

16. Our discussion here focuses on this particular paper; earlier versions of this work (Burdett et al., 1980, 1984b) are not discussed separately.

17. This is the same data source used by Burdett et al. (1985, discussed in this chapter). Kiefer and Neumann (1982) present additional analysis of these data.

18. The asset variable is calculated using information on the value of stocks, checking account balances, home and automobile equity, etc.

19. His approach to this is basically to use a modal estimate for the unobserved part of the spell. He discusses his approach in detail.

20. This work is an extension of Lundberg (1981).

21. These data are taken from the same source as the data analyzed by Burdett et al. (1985), discussed in this chapter.

22. The exact numbers of spells are 8,822 male employment (844 recipient), 7,143 married female employment (655 recipient), 5,262 single female employment (1,385 recipient), 4,263 youth employment (886 recipient), 3,155 male unemployment (741 recipient), 1,548 married female employment (321 recipient), 1,907 single female employment (992 recipient), 2,264 youth employment (576 recipient), 7,115 male nonparticipation (1,217 recipient), 10,372 married female nonparticipation (1,681 recipient), 6,024 single female nonparticipation (2,603 recipient), and 6,298 youth nonparticipation (1,737 recipient).

23. Since the model is log linear, the transition rate differences are calculated as

$$r^w - r^{NW} = [\exp(b + cw) - 1]r^{NW}$$

where b is the coefficient for welfare status, c is the coefficient for nonwage income, and w is mean welfare income for welfare recipients. Remaining results are not reported, but Blau and Robins note that the estimated wage and income effects are consistent with predictions of basic search models.

24. Blau and Robins note that further investigation into the higher adult recipient transition rates from employment into unemployment indicates that both quit and layoff rates are higher for recipients, both with and without controls for personal characteristics.

25. Flinn and Heckman note that applying this same test to transition rates out of employment (i.e., testing equality) is correct only when the probability of exiting employment to unemployment equals the probability of exiting employment to out of the labor force. The necessary condition is that the transition rates out of employment into the alternative states be proportional.

26. As in the analysis of Burdett et. al. (1984a), it is assumed that the acceptance set and thus the acceptance probability for a state j do not depend on the state a worker occupies when information arrives. For example, a worker is just as likely to accept a given job offer when unemployed as he or she would be when out of the labor force. This represents a special case of a more general theoretical model considered by Mortensen and Neumann, where the acceptance probability for a state j is defined as π_{ij}. A possible rationale for this might be dependence of the offer distribution on whether one is actively searching. Identification of this more general model requires data on the arrival process, however, since in place of $\beta_{ij} = \alpha_j + \Gamma_j$, we would have $\beta_{ij} = \alpha_j + \Gamma_{ij}$. The

uniformity of the information distribution across states serves as an identifying restriction in the present analysis since arrival rate data are not available. (The theoretical three-state models of Burdett et al. [1984b] and Flinn and Heckman [1982b] represent special cases of the general model presented by Mortensen and Neumann.)

27. Letting e, n, and u denote employment, nonparticipation, and unemployment, respectively, the sample sizes for men are 148 ue, 86 en, 158 eu, 21 un, 99 ne, 26 nu, 211 incomplete e spells, 14 incomplete u spells, and 9 incomplete n spells. For females, the sample sizes are 86 eu, 260 en, 106 eu, 54 un, 296 ne, 67 nu, 197 incomplete e, 15 incomplete u, and 135 incomplete n.

28. Like Narendrananthan and Nickell, van den Berg does not have reservation wage data or any other special wage data, but his theoretical structure is much simpler. In this second respect, he follows Ridder and Gorter. van den Berg suggests that transitions into nonparticipation in his model may be interpreted as a result of rational decision making, but this interpretation is inconsistent with his assumptions about the utilities of nonparticipation and unemployment. He also notes that some transitions can be regarded as forced, e.g., conscription, and this seems a more appropriate way of reconciling the structure of his model with rational choice. Note, however, that the empirical analysis is not restricted to this type of transition.

29. This problem is more generally referred to as recall bias and it is common in longitudinal surveys. It is typically ignored in estimation.

30. Standard errors are not reported, but van den Berg notes that for all reasonable values, a likelihood ratio test allows rejection of the restriction $u = 1$.

31. Gonul (1988) takes a different approach to analyzing the unemployment versus nonparticipation distinction for young male and female high school graduates (14 to 22 in 1979) using data for the New Youth Cohort of the National Longitudinal Survey. She studies transition rates between the two nonemployment states and from each nonemployment state into employment within a stationary framework. Her preliminary findings pose some contrast with those reported here for young workers. The distinction between the two nonemployment states is found to be statistically significant for females (nonwhite females in particular), but generally not for males. The contrast in findings may be due to her assumption of stationarity. Regardless, further investigation into the question appears warranted.

32. Feldstein (1973) was among the first to stress the potential importance of distinguishing temporary and permanent layoff unemployment and the potential effects on employer behavior of the system of imperfect experience rating used in most states to determine employer UI taxes.

33. The recipient sample is the larger of the two with 671 observations. The sample for which results are reported includes the low income subsample in the PSID. Katz notes that omitting the low income subsample leaves a sample about half the size of that analyzed in the paper. Results from estimation using only the random subsample of the PSID are described as consistent with the findings reported here.

34. The plant closing spells are initially excluded because of the impossibility of recall. Obviously, workers dismissed for cause are not likely to be recalled, but this reason for dismissal is not reported separately in the PSID. Katz and Meyer (1988a) present the empirical total, recall, and new job hazards for a PSID sample that consists of both the basic Katz sample and these plant shutdown spells. There are no notable differences.

35. For workers who had single spells that ended before exhaustion, only administrative data are used. For individuals who had single spells that ended after benefit exhaustion or who had multiple spells, self-reported spell completion dates are used. Katz and Meyer report findings from consistency checks on spells of benefit receipt using the information provided across sources for the Missouri sample. Overall, these are not very encouraging. The mean absolute difference is 4.5 weeks.

36. Although the proportions expecting recall are roughly equal across states, only 51 percent were recalled in the Missouri sample, versus 64 percent in Pennsylvania. Mean observed spell lengths also differ substantially. For Missouri, the mean durations are 16.6 IUSR, 19.4 FSPELL,

and 15.3 PAYSPELL. For Pennsylvania, the mean durations are 12.9 IUSR and 16.2 FSPELL (PAYSPELL is not available).

Katz and Meyer note that the Pennsylvania UI program was more generous than the Missouri program in the sample period. The maximum benefit level was $170 and the maximum benefit duration was 30 weeks for all workers in Pennsylvania. In Missouri, the maximum benefit was $105 and the maximum duration was 26 weeks, with variation across workers depending on base period and high quarter earnings. Employer unemployment insurance tax systems also differed. The tax rate increased with a firm's unemployment rate up to 6.3 percent in Missouri, versus 3.6 percent in Pennsylvania, although the marginal changes were greater in Pennsylvania.

37. Of all spells 8.4 percent are censored and these account for 28.5 percent of all unemployment in the combined sample. The results reported by Katz and Meyer should not be translated directly into estimates of the proportion of insured unemployment spent in recall spells (using either definition). The data analyzed here are restricted to lengths of first spells within workers' benefit years, not time spent unemployed in workers' benefit years or any other period of fixed length. This generalization would require assumptions regarding classification (recall versus nonrecall) and the incidence and duration of subsequent spells within benefit years.

38. Katz and Meyer note that when they calculated the hazards for workers who expected recall, there is a marked increase in the new job hazard from 4 weeks before to 4 weeks after exhaustion.

39. Katz and Meyer also note that regressions of the form $\alpha(t) = a + b \ln(t) + \epsilon$ yield positive and negative coefficients for the new job and recall hazards, respectively, that are significant at the 5 percent level.

40. This is an updated version of the data set used by Jensen (1987a, previously discussed). See Westergaard-Nielsen (1984) for a complete description of these data.

41. The Danish unemployment benefit program is quite complex and intertwined with a variety of other programs, including vacation programs. Details are provided in the paper as to how Jensen and Westergaard-Nielsen merge data from pension records in making determinations about temporary and permanent layoffs and the limitations of their approach. Essentially, if the same employer makes a contribution to the supplementary pension program in the 3 months preceding and 3 months following an unemployment spell, the spell is characterized as temporary. They also adjust the original work histories to account for vacations listed as unemployment.

42. This is the same measure used by Jensen (1987a). It is based on administrative data collected for worker pensions and is unusual because it relates to numbers of hours worked over the course of a career.

43. For females, the classification is services, public sector, and other. For males, the classification is service, public sector, manufacturing, construction, and other.

44. Enrollment in the Danish unemployment insurance system is voluntary. Overall, about 82 percent of the labor force is enrolled, while 95 percent of all blue-collar workers are covered. The program includes the option of part-time insurance and, in the sample studied here, 8 percent of the sample elects this coverage.

45. Han and Hausman (1990) also present results from semiparametric estimation of a competing-risk model, but their parameterization for the baseline is inconsistent with a proportional hazards model. Specifically, they set the log integrated (cause-specific) baseline hazard equal to a linear function of regressors and a standard normal random variable. The standard normal specification breaks the link with the proportional hazards model, making their results difficult to compare with other work. (See Proposition 2 in Chapter 3.) Of course, the proportional hazard model is special and not required by economic theory.

46. This is the same source used by Blau and Robins (1986b) that we previously discussed. It appears that both male and female workers are included in the sample.

47. The hazard for this model is
$$\tau_{ij}(t, x) = \lambda_0(t \exp\{-x'\beta\}) \exp\{-x'\beta\}$$

The accelerated lifetime model is discussed in Chapter 3. For additional discussion, see Kiefer (1988b) and Kalbfleisch and Prentice (1980).

48. One way of reducing the coarseness of these data would be to link observations across waves and check for seams in reported tenures, that is, changes in cells occupied between waves. Exact initial tenures, measured in years, would then be known for at least part of the sample. Farber does not note any attempt to explore this possibility, but he does note that the intervals are "wide," particularly for longer tenures. Obviously, very wide intervals would minimize the gain from this procedure.

49. These employment duration data are analogous to the interval unemployment spell data described in Chapter 5 with likelihood (Equation 5.10), except that the exact duration at the first interview is assumed known in that example.

50. Several studies have examined the relationship between incidence and duration of unemployment spells and durations across spells using individual level data. For example, Ellwood (1982), Heckman (1981a), and Borjas and Heckman (1980) study data for youth in the United States, Pedersen and Westergaard-Nielson (1986, 1987) study data for Danish workers, Ebmer and Zweimuller (1990) study data for Austria, and Disney (1979) studies data for the United Kingdom. There is some evidence of a negative correlation between incidence and duration—that is, that workers with more frequent spells experience shorter spells—but this finding appears sensitive to economic conditions, sample composition, and model specification. Using Canadian data, Belzil (1990) finds that receiving UI benefits during a spell of unemployment leads to longer spells of unemployment *and* longer spells of subsequent employment. The evidence on lagged duration independence is fairly weak.

Actual testing of the Markov assumption in economic applications is relatively complicated due to potential effects of unmeasured changes in heterogeneity and other forms of misspecification. See Borjas and Heckman (1980), Corcoran and Hill (1985), and Heckman (1981a) for discussion of tests used outside economics and the difficulties associated with their application to economic data.

7

Search Strategies
and Arrival Rates

In the early job search models of Mortensen (1970a,b) and McCall (1970), variation in the arrival rate of offers played no role in producing variation in unemployment spell lengths. For a fixed cost, the worker received one draw from a known wage distribution each period. Accordingly, this assumption was adopted in early empirical search studies (e.g., Ehrenberg and Oaxaca, 1976; Kiefer and Neumann, 1979a,b, 1981). With the length of a period left undefined, however, this assumption seems arbitrary when turning to the data. A stochastic offer arrival process seems more appropriate—perhaps with the parameters of the process modeled as functions of worker behavior and labor market opportunities. In earlier chapters, we discussed a few studies that attempt to estimate the parameters of the arrival process in the absence of any direct evidence on the frequency of offers or search strategies. Generally, the findings indicate an important role for the arrival rate in producing variation in unemployment spell durations across workers. The findings of these studies open the question of why arrival rates might vary across workers. That is, they do not indicate whether the arrival rate variation reflects variation in search intensity or strategy or variation in demand.

In this chapter, we look at studies of some unusual data on search inputs, search methods, numbers of offers, and (in one case) rejected wage offers, that is, direct evidence on search and the arrival of offers. We start with studies that use regression and discrete choice models to analyze search intensity and choice of search methods. A variety of hypotheses are tested and explored. As in previous chapters, the effects of unemployment benefits receive a fair share of the attention. All of these studies work with U.S. data. In fact, many exploit the same source for their data—a special supplement to the May 1976 Current Population Survey entitled "Jobseeking Activities of the Unemployed." In the second section, we turn to studies that use data on numbers of offers and other unusual data to estimate structural parameters of job search models. Two of these studies examine the empirical relevance of nonsequential search models.

Regression and Discrete Choice Studies

We start this section with two papers by Barron and Mellow (1979, 1981a). The first focuses on the effect of the probability of recall to a former employer on search effort. The second uses a multinomial logit framework to investigate the effects of both search intensity and the reservation wage on changes in labor market status. We next turn to two studies by Barron and Gilley (1979, 1981a,b).[1] In their first study, Barron and Gilley examine the effects of expected future unemployment benefits on search intensity in current spells. In their second, they examine the hypothesis of diminishing returns to random search, defined as direct employer contact without referral. They also study the factors that influence the choice between random and systematic search strategies. Chirinko (1982) also analyzes the returns to random search, but takes an alternative econometric approach. Kahn and Low (1988b) present a simple model allowing random and systematic search and then examine the relative use of the alternative strategies. In their next study (Kahn and Low, 1988a), they focus on the use of intermediaries (i.e., unions or employment agencies) by both unemployed and employed searchers. Holzer (1988) focuses on choice of search methods from a more precisely defined set—family and friends, state employment agencies, newspapers, direct contact, and other—and then analyzes the employment outcomes generated by alternative methods. Keeley and Robins (1985) investigate the manner and extent to which search requirements under employment insurance and other government programs influence the use of different search methods. Finally, St. Louis et al. (1986) present results from a validation study of search activity reported by benefit recipients.

Barron and Mellow (1979)

Barron and Mellow start by setting out a model of search behavior that extends the models of Mortensen (1977), Barron and McCafferty (1977), and Lippman and McCall (1976). Specifically, workers are modeled as allocating both money and time to job search. They also face a nonnegative probability of recall to their former job that is independent of their current labor market activity, that is, workers awaiting recall are allowed to take temporary jobs at wages less than their recall wage. This last assumption represents a response to the claim by Feldstein (1973, 1974, 1975a,b, 1976, 1978) and others that workers on temporary layoff behave differently from those on indefinite or permanent layoff. Let f denote the probability of recall, let s and m denote time search intensity and money search intensity, respectively, let β denote a shift factor reflecting factors that affect the productivity of inputs into the search process, and let w^r refer to the reservation wage for new jobs. Using our previous notation, the transition rate out of unemployment is

$$\tau = \delta\pi(w^r) + f - f\delta\pi(w^r)$$

where the arrival rate is defined as

$$\delta = \delta(s, m, \beta)$$

The model implies that time and money search intensities and the reservation wage are inversely related to the recall wage and positively related to the mean wage and the search productivity shift variable. As in simpler models, an increase in unemployment income is also predicted to have a positive effect on the reservation wage and the benefit effect on search money intensity is predicted to be positive. On the other hand, increases in either unemployment benefit or nonlabor income have a negative effect on search time intensity, which makes sense. All implications for the duration of unemployment are ambiguous—without additional (arbitrary) restrictions—because of opposing direct and indirect effects (i.e., effects due to changes in the reservation wage and the arrival rate).

Barron and Mellow exploit some unusual data to test the implications of their model for search time intensity. In May 1976, unemployed workers in the Current Population Survey (CPS) sample were asked to complete a supplemental survey prepared by the Bureau of Labor Statistics.[2] Among other things, workers were asked the amount of time they had devoted to search in the 4-week period preceding the survey, whether other family members had started looking for work to make up for lost earnings, and whether these individuals had been successful in their search. Barron and Mellow use these data and the standard CPS survey data for a sample of 3,188 workers who had at least 1 week of unemployment and who returned completed questionnaires.

Barron and Mellow start by fitting search intensity regressions, where search intensity is defined as reported time devoted to job search divided by the total number of hours unemployed. This is the number of weeks unemployed (up to 4) times 168 hours. Note that the value of this factor, the same for each individual, does not matter for the results for model fit or significance. The mean number of hours spent searching per week in the sample is reported as approximately 7. The explanatory variables are dummy variables for temporary layoff with recall expected within 30 days, other temporary layoff, and other layoffs (as proxies for the recall probability f),[3] a predicted wage, a dummy variable for individuals seeking part-time work (to account for systematically lower mean wages associated with part-time work), education, dummy variables for central and other city residence as proxies for search productivity, the weekly unemployment insurance benefit received, a dummy variable for receipt of supplemental unemployment benefits, the amount of other nonemployment income for the family, and dummy variables for other family members looking for work and finding work (i.e., added worker effects). The predicted wage is based on a regression of the wage on age, race, sex, education, industry, and occupation.

Overall, the reported results are sensible and appear consistent with the predictions of the model. The estimated coefficients have the correct signs in all cases where the model has unambiguous predictions and all differ significantly from zero at standard levels, except the coefficient for receipt of supplemental unemployment benefits. The dummy variables for type of layoff, used as proxies for the recall probability, all have negative coefficients and the coefficients for temporary layoff types are significant at standard levels—implying that workers on temporary layoff do behave differently.

Barron and Mellow note that workers may engage in systematic search, that is, look into more promising opportunities first, as suggested by Holt (1970) and Salop (1973). They interpret this as meaning that the search productivity parameter β will decline with spell duration. It is not clear that systematic search, as presented by Salop, should be equated with this decline in the productivity shift parameter. However, a number of other factors can produce variation in the productivity of time and money inputs into search (e.g., simple motivation, employers' reactions to time spent searching). Taking all such explanations into account, unambiguous predictions cannot be made. Regardless of interpretation, they report search intensity regressions that include log unemployment spell duration (noting potential simultaneity bias) and it has a significant, negative coefficient, while the results for other variables are essentially unchanged. Results for this regression specification for a subsample that excludes new entrants and reentrants are also reported. The results are essentially unaffected, except that the estimated effect of supplemental benefit receipt becomes significant. Barron and Mellow note that introducing demographic characteristics has no qualitative effect on the results. They report that neither race nor marital status is found to be correlated with search time intensity, but that older workers and females appear to spend less time searching.[4]

Barron and Mellow (1981a)

In this study, Barron and Mellow work with a two-period longitudinal file for a sample of 1,307 workers who were present in both the May and June 1976 CPS samples and who completed the May supplemental questionnaires previously described. These data allow them to estimate a multinomial logit model for the probability of being employed, unemployed, or out of the labor force in June.[5] The explanatory variables include weekly hours of job search, unemployment spell duration reported in May, and dummy variables for permanent layoff, temporary layoff, receipt of unemployment insurance, an application for unemployment insurance benefits not ruled ineligible (i.e., future receipt of benefits), age group, race, sex, and survey month in the CPS sample.[6] The results imply that the probability of being employed in the second period increases significantly with search intensity, while the probability of nonparticipation appears inversely related to search intensity. The probability of moving from unemployment into either alternative state is significantly lower for those who are either receiving benefits currently or expecting receipt; it is also significantly lower for workers with longer spells (i.e., there is some evidence of negative duration dependence).

The May 1976 supplemental survey included a question of the form "What is the lowest wage or salary you would accept ... for this type of work?" Using the 1,090 individuals who provided a response to the question, Barron and Mellow reestimate their model with the ratio of this reservation wage to a predicted wage added to the regressor list. The predicted wage is based on results from a wage regression that includes education, occupation, and regional location fit for CPS workers. The results indicate that higher reservation wages are associated with lower employment probabilities, but there is no evidence of a statistically significant effect on the probability of moving out of the labor force. The results for search intensity and unemployment insurance benefits are essentially the same as before.

Barron and Gilley (1979, 1981a)[7]

Barron and Gilley investigate the effects of unemployment insurance on levels of search intensity. When the basic job search model is modified to allow for endogenous search intensity, higher unemployment benefits and longer periods of benefit eligibility are predicted to reduce unemployed search intensity, raise the reservation wage, and reduce the transition rate out of unemployment, *ceteris paribus*. However, when layoffs are incorporated, the availability of unemployment benefits can have the reverse effects (Burdett, 1979b; Mortensen, 1970a, 1977). The thrust of the argument is that an increased benefit level or longer period of eligibility translates into an increased return to becoming employed—because of an increased value for future unemployment. Thus, for an unemployed worker not receiving benefits in a current spell, higher unemployment benefits and longer periods of benefit eligibility should be associated with greater search intensity, a lower reservation wage, and a shorter current spell length. On the other hand, for a worker currently receiving benefits, the observed benefit effect represents the sum of the standard present benefit effect and the future benefit effect—and the future benefit effect should dominate as exhaustion of benefits nears. Barron and Gilley attempt to determine the relative magnitudes of these effects on the level of search intensity.

Barron and Gilley use data from the special supplement to the CPS in May 1976 to estimate search intensity regressions separately for unemployed workers who were not receiving benefits at the time of the survey because they were ineligible (2,022 workers) and unemployed workers who were either receiving or expecting benefits (1,166 workers).

For each worker in the no (current) benefit group, Barron and Gilley first construct a measure of the expected real value of future benefits using data on maximum allowable periods of benefit receipt, price levels, tax rates, and the results from a regression of benefit levels on age, race, sex, marital status, prior earnings, and geographic region.[8] This variable is then included in a weekly hours of search regression, along with observations on age, sex, race, marital status, a predicted wage, the regional vacancy rate (measured as the new hire rate in manufacturing in the geographic region), real nonwage (nonbenefit) income, educational attainment, and dummy variables for central and noncentral city residence and search for a full-time job. The results provide no evidence of an expected benefit effect on current search behavior; the coefficient is small and insignificant at even the most liberal levels (-0.0003, standard error 0.0009). The results for the other variables are consistent with expectations. Lower levels of nonemployment income, higher predicted wages, and higher educational attainment all have a positive effect on predicted search intensity. Nonwhites, males, older workers, central city residents, and those seeking full-time employment also have higher search intensities.

Barron and Gilley fit an analogous regression for the benefit sample, with the value of remaining benefits included for those already receiving benefits and a predicted value of benefits for those awaiting receipt (comparable to the estimate described above). A dummy variable for those on layoff is also included. Here again, the effect for the value of benefits on search intensity is insignificant.[9] To some extent, this may simply reflect a combination of the requirements of most state UI programs and the self-reported measure of search intensity used. First, Barron and Gilley note that those awaiting benefit receipt have a reported search intensity that is 74 percent higher than those already receiving benefits, but that much of this time is actually devoted to the benefit application process; adding this application time to actual search time should introduce a nonlinearity in the data. They also note that most state UI programs have a search requirement. This might introduce an upward bias in reported time spent searching for those receiving benefits.[10] If the reporting bias is lower for those nearing the end of their period of benefit receipt (i.e., search effort actually does rise, as predicted by Mortensen's model), then the reporting bias might mask the nonlinearity introduced by the initial application time; the estimated effect of the value of remaining benefits would appear negligible. Of course, it is unsatisfactory to argue that a theory is confirmed by an insignificant coefficient, but this is what Barron and Gilley find. As for other variables, workers on layoff are found to have significantly lower search intensities than other workers and the results for remaining variables are consistent with those for nonrecipients, except for the vacancy measure. Increases in regional hiring rates in manufacturing have an estimated effect on intensity that is positive and significant at the 5 percent level.

Barron and Gilley (1981b)

In their second study, Barron and Gilley test the hypothesis of diminishing returns to random search time generated by the model set out by Seater (1979), with random search defined as direct employer contact without referral. The basis of the Seater hypothesis is a spatial argument. Assume that firms are located uniformly across space and are equally likely to make an offer on contact. Then as more firms are contacted, it should take longer to contact another. Hence, the process of generating offers should exhibit diminishing returns to time spent searching.

Barron and Gilley again work with data collected in the special supplement to the May 1976 CPS. In addition to the variables already described, the survey asked workers what search method they used most frequently and the number of firms contacted in the preceding 4-week period. In an attempt to adhere to the assumptions of the Seater model, Barron and Gilley start out by working with a sample of 936 workers who were not on layoff, reported direct application to employers as their most frequently used method (i.e., as opposed to using an employment agency, friends, relatives, a union, answering or placing an ad, or some other intermediary), and reported at least one contact. Barron and Gilley report that the average worker in this sample spent about eight and two-thirds hours on search and contacted just over three employers each week.

Barron and Gilley fit log linear regressions to these data and report the following results:

$$\ln N = -0.06 + 0.45 \ \ln S + 0.13 \ \text{City}, \qquad R^2 = 0.34$$
$$(0.02) (0.05)$$

where N denotes average number of employers contacted per week, S denotes the average number of hours spent searching each week, City is a dummy variable for SMSA residence (intended as a proxy for the density of employers in the worker's area), and standard errors are in parentheses. Barron and Gilley interpret the value for the coefficient for $\ln S$ between zero and one as evidence of diminishing returns to direct random search. This finding is unchanged when demographic and occupation variables are added (though they do find that nonwhite workers make about 25 percent fewer contacts).

Barron and Gilley note that direct employer contact is not the most frequently used method for the majority of workers in the larger sample of 1,923 workers who were not on layoff, had engaged in search activity, and had made at least one contact. The more typical strategy in the sample is one of two methods that Barron and Gilley regard as systematic: self-directed search, where contact is made with the aid of friends or relatives or by placing or answering ads (32 percent of the sample), or indirect search, where contact is made through either a state or private employment agency (14 percent of the sample). To determine the relative effectiveness of these two strategies, they add two dummy variables to their regression, SDS for self-directed search and IS for indirect search, and fit the model for the larger sample. They report the following results:

$$\ln N = 0.03 + \underset{(0.016)}{0.42} \ln S + \underset{(0.039)}{0.07} \text{City} - \underset{(0.042)}{0.39} \text{SDS} - \underset{(0.055)}{0.52} \text{IS}, \qquad R^2 = 0.30$$

In view of these results—that those who engage in systematic search make substantially few contacts—Barron and Gilley investigate the reasons for the majority's choice. In particular, they set out to determine whether workers using these nonrandom methods have a higher probability of getting an offer on contact or have a higher probability of accepting an offer when received. Using a subsample of 727 workers from the longitudinal file constructued by Barron and Mellow (1981a), they estimate a multinomial logit model for the probability of being employed, unemployed, or out of the labor force in June 1976.[12] The explanatory variables in the model include the ratio of the reported reservation wage to a predicted wage,[13] SDS (self-directed search), IS (indirect search), hours of search per week, dummy variables for age group, race, sex, and being on layoff, and a set of dummy variables for the worker's month in the CPS sample to control for "rotation group bias." The results indicate that greater search intensity and a lower value for the reservation wage to offer wage ratio both increase the probability of becoming employed, but there is no indication that the choice of a self-directed or indirect nonrandom search strategy affects this probability. Neither variable has an estimated coefficient that differs significantly from zero at standard levels. As for demographic variation, young workers (20 or less) appear significantly more likely to be employed than prime-age or older workers, and females appear more likely to be out of the labor force, but no significant differences appear between white and nonwhite workers. Barron and Gilley also note that when they substitute number of contacts for search intensity in the employment probability model, the estimated coefficient is insignificant at standard levels and other results are unchanged.

Chirinko (1982)

Chirinko also studies returns to search intensity—measured as the average number of contacts per week—using the May 1976 supplemental survey data. An alternative estimation approach is taken, however, that avoids the sample restriction of at least one contact imposed by the log linear regression specification of Barron and Gilley (1981a). Specifically, Chirinko fits a regression model for the number of contacts per week using an iterated least-squares estimation procedure that yields estimates that are equivalent to maximum likelihood estimates for the expected weekly contact rate.

Following Barron and Gilley, Chirinko first fits his model for a sample of 835 workers who reportedly engaged in "direct" random search. The regressors include a quadratic in search time, interactions of search time with dummy variables for unemployment insurance receipt, temporary layoff, age, race, and sex, and a dummy variable for city residence (used here, as by Barron and Gilley, as a proxy for employer density). On the basis of the results for the quadratic in search time, a null hypothesis of diminishing returns to search time cannot be rejected at standard levels. The coefficients for city residence and the benefit–search time interaction term are both positive and significant, but other regressors appear irrelevant at standard significance levels.

Chirinko also reports results from estimation of this model for a combined sample of 1,647 workers who engaged in either "direct" or "indirect" search (using the same definitions for these strategies as Barron and Gilley), with dummy variables for self-directed and (intermediary) indirect strategies added. The results are essentially the same for the returns to search—a null hypothesis of diminishing returns cannot be rejected. The results for both search strategy variables are also consistent with the results reported by Barron and Gilley; they indicate that self-directed and intermediary strategies result in significantly fewer contacts than a direct employer contact approach.

Kahn and Low (1988b)

Kahn and Low set out a simple model of choice between random search (defined as direct employer contact, as in the studies previously discussed) and systematic search. The model implies that, ceteris paribus, workers with lower stocks of information about individual employers, workers with lower discount rates, and workers with lower unemployment insurance benefits should be more likely to use random search when unemployed. Hence, workers with these characteristics should be more likely to receive an unacceptable offer than workers with the opposite characteristics; the latter should be more likely to engage in systematic search and therefore more likely to apply only for acceptable jobs.

Kahn and Low work with data collected in the May 1976 CPS supplemental survey. In particular, they exploit data on reported numbers of offers received. Their sample consists of 298 unemployed workers who were employed full-time prior to unemployment, who were not enrolled as students, and who had made at least one contact with an employer prior to the survey. Their approach to testing the implications of their model is somewhat indirect. They estimate a Tobit model, with the ratio of the number of offers received to the number of firms contacted as the dependent variable and then equate higher values of this ratio with a higher probability of an unacceptable offer and thus with a higher probability of random search.[14] The explanatory variables include race, sex, years of education, age, marital status, a local unemployment rate for 1976, family income for April 1976 (the job search data pertain to April 18 to May 15), a dummy variable for workers who quit their previous jobs, and the unemployment benefit replacement ratio.

The reported results are generally consistent with the predictions of the model. A higher unemployment benefit ratio is associated with a lower offer to contact ratio. Older workers are also found to be more likely to engage in systematic search as defined here, which may represent the effect of a higher discount rate or a greater stock of firm-specific knowledge accumulated through labor market experience.

Kahn and Low recognize that the unemployment insurance replacement ratio may be correlated with unmeasured ability or search effort. To check the robustness of their unemployment benefit results, Kahn and Low also estimate a Tobit model that includes hours spent searching in the month preceding the survey, dummy variables for indirect search and self-directed search, the number of contacts, current unemployment duration, and a dummy variable for exhaustion of unemployment benefits. Kahn and Low note that these variables are omitted from the initial specification because their values are likely to be affected by the choice of systematic or random search. Current duration has a negative coefficient that differs significantly from zero at the 5 percent level, but other regressors appear irrelevant here. In particular, the coefficient for the unemployment benefit ratio is insignificant.

Kahn and Low (1988a)

In this study, Kahn and Low study the probability of a worker using an intermediary, such as an employment service or union when searching—as opposed to either relying on friends and relatives or searching randomly (i.e., contacting employers directly). Precisely, they estimate probit models for this choice separately for samples of 257 unemployed workers and 538 employed workers. The source of their data is the 1981 interview for the National Longitudinal Survey of the 1979 Youth Cohort and the samples are restricted to nonstudents. The explanatory variables included in both models are current or previous tenure (months), labor market experience (months), current or previous collective bargaining coverage, current or previous log wage, local unemployment rate, number of dependents, education, monthly family income, log mean wage and log wage variance in a worker's one-digit occupation (calculated from the 1979 CPS), and dummy variables for black workers, those living with parents, and intact marital status. The benefit replacement ratio is also included for unemployed workers.

The results for the unemployed worker probit are generally imprecise, but they do provide at least weak evidence that the probability of using an intermediary decreases with previous tenure and that it increases with the replacement rate and the offer variance. These results seem sensible. The tenure result could reflect accumulation of information on the job. The variance result can be interpreted as reflecting the higher value of information when there is more wage variability. As for the benefit effect, this might be interpreted as a subsidy effect—but it might simply be the consequence of job search requirements.

The tenure effect on employed workers' use of intermediaries is also negative, and here it is significant at the 1 percent level. The results for other variables are generally imprecise, except for race and education. The results suggest that black workers and workers with more education are significantly more likely to use a formal search method.

Holzer (1988)

Holzer also considers choice of search strategy, but considers more alternatives than the systematic versus random search categorization used above. Specifically, he extends the endogenous search intensity model presented by Burdett (1979a), so that the arrival rate of offers depends on a worker's choice from a set of five search methods: friends and relatives, newspapers, state employment agencies, direct employer contact without referral, and other. Allowing the different methods to vary in terms of costs and productivity for both an individual worker and across workers, the basic prediction of the model is that optimal choices from the available set reflect the comparison of costs and productivities for different methods.

Holzer uses this model as a guide in examining data on choice of search methods collected for the 1979 Youth Cohort of the National Longitudinal Survey. His sample consists of 608 males, ages 16 to 23, who were neither enrolled in school nor enlisted in the military and who engaged in unemployed search in the month preceding the 1981 interview data. The weighted mean number of methods used by workers in the sample is 3.29, where the weights are those provided with the data set to control for the oversampling of low income white youths, but there is substantial variation in the relative use of alternative methods. The most popular method is asking friends and relatives, which is used by 85 percent of the sample; direct employer contact follows with 80 percent. Reliance on newspapers and state employment agencies rank next in terms of relative use; 58 percent use the former and 54 percent use the latter. The last choice described as "other" includes the use of unions, school placement programs, teacher referrals, etc., and each of these methods is described as having been used by only a few.[15] On average, this pattern of relative reliance on alternative search methods seems consistent with the relative productivities of alternative methods. About one-third of the workers in the sample reports receipt of at least one offer in the month preceding the interview date and 82 percent of these workers report use of either friends and relatives or direct contact. Moreover, 75 percent of workers who accept offers during the month report use of at least one of these two methods.

To examine the hypothesis of his model more closely, Holzer carries out some more formal econometric analysis of these data. Specifically, he works with a two-equation model of the form:

$$S_i = S(Z_i, O_i^*) + e_{si}$$
$$O_i = O(X_i, S_i) + e_{oi}$$

where S_i is a measure of search intensity by individual i, O_i is an ex post employment outcome, O_i^* is the expected value of the employment outcome, Z_i is a set of other variables that may affect search choices, and X_i is a set that may affect offer distributions and arrival rates, and e_{si} and e_{oi} are error terms.

Holzer first estimates the search intensity equation, with S_i defined as the number of methods used by a worker and O_i^* measured first as the probability of getting an offer (based on a first round probit) and then measured as expected unemployment duration (no definition provided). He experiments with different regressor lists but is unable to find a satisfactory fit; the reported R^2 are 0.005 and 0.003 and all coefficient estimates are insignificant at standard levels. Comparable results are reported for probit models for the use of each method.

Holzer next reports estimates for two probit models for the probability of getting an offer, based on the second equation of his model. The first model includes the reported number of methods used, the second model includes the specific search methods reported instead, and age, education, region, urban residence, race, family income, and the local unemployment rate are included as controls in both. These results provide some evidence that choice of search strategy affects the offer probability, given personal characteristics and local labor market conditions. In the first specification, the total number of methods used has an estimated effect that is positive and significant. In the second, relying on relatives and friends and using newspaper ads both appear to have positive and significant effects. Results for the control variables are not reported.

Keeley and Robins (1985)

Transfer programs in the United States and elsewhere often have job search requirements for able-bodied workers. Some programs even require that certain job search methods be used. In this study, Keeley and Robins attempt to determine whether such requirements affect unemployment spell lengths either directly or indirectly, that is, by inducing substitution of required search inputs for more productive search inputs.

Keeley and Robins work separately with samples of 1,974 married men, 1,384 married women, 1,327 single women with children, and 1,641 youths collected in the baseline survey of the Employment Opportunity Pilot Projects (EOPP). The EOPP was an experimental program that provided intensive search assistance to low income workers in 20 geographically dispersed urban and rural areas in the United States and the purpose of the retrospective baseline survey was to provide background data for participants and controls. Low and middle income families were oversampled intentionally for the EOPP; thus, the sample is not representative of the U.S. labor force. Another problem with these data is that behavior may be affected by participation in the program. The attractive feature of these data is the availability of a detailed retrospective work history for each individual for the period between January 1979 and the date of the baseline interview conducted between April and October 1980.

Respondents were asked whether they were required to look for work because of government program participation, the amount of time spent searching per week, and whether specific search methods were used. Keeley and Robins restrict their sample to workers who reported being unemployed following July 1, 1979, and then measure unemployment spell durations as the reported number of weeks of unemployment in the most recent spell after that date. Thus, there are both right-censored and left-censored spells in the sample. The explanation provided for censoring spells in progress on July 1, 1979, is the desire to treat poverty status, program participation, hours worked, and income in the first 6 months of 1979 as exogenous when studying unemployment durations.

Keeley and Robins first fit least-squares regressions for six search "input" measures: the number of methods of job search used, the number of public job search methods used, weekly hours of job search, the weekly rate of employer contact, the weekly rate of employer visits, and the weekly rate of job applications.[16] For each regression, coefficient estimates are reported for the two explanatory variables of primary interest—a dummy variable for UI receipt (and thus UI search requirements) and a dummy variable for search requirements in alternative government programs. (Coefficients for other variables are not reported.) Keeley and Robins note that the UI receipt variable is an imperfect measure for UI search requirements because it measures the effects of benefits levels as well. They note that attempts to identify these separate effects were unsuccessful, but give no futher detail. Note that this income argument could also be rendered against the other search requirement variable.

Setting these reservations aside, the results provide some evidence of modified behavior. For married men, both UI receipt and other search requirements have significant, positive effects on both the total number and number of public search methods used, but the estimated effects of UI receipt on all other search input measures are large and negative. Only weekly hours appear to be affected significantly by imposition of other government search requirements on married men. For both married and single women, the results for numbers of methods used are essentially the same as those for men, that is, requirements increase the numbers of methods used. There is also some evidence that the weekly rate of job applications is lower when unemployment benefits are received by women. For the youth group, receipt of unemployment benefits tend to lower the weekly rates of employer contact, visits, and job applications, but there is no evidence of an effect on numbers of methods used. Other search requirements, however, do appear to increase the number of methods used by youth and their weekly hours devoted to search.

Keeley and Robins also estimate a variety of constant hazard competing risks models for transitions into employment and out of the labor force for each demographic group. Specifically, they estimate four alternative specifications for each hazard rate, where the explanatory variables include the dummy variables for UI receipt and other search requirements, number of methods used, and one of the four remaining input variables (weekly hours of job search, the weekly rate of employer contact, the weekly rate of employer visits, and the weekly rate of job applications). A long list of demographic, income, and labor market variables is also included.

For all groups, the estimated effect of unemployment benefit receipt on transitions into employment is large and negative. The same holds true for transitions out of the labor force for all but the youth group. Other search requirements also have a significant negative effect on the transition rate into employment for married men and youth, but no statistically significant effects for other groups. The most interesting (or perhaps puzzling) results are those reported for each of the search input variables entered separately; for all groups, the results imply that each has a positive and significant effect on both the transition rate into employment and the transition rate out of the labor force. Keeley and Robins interpret the latter result as evidence of a "discouraged worker" effect.

St. Louis, Burgess, and Kingston (1986)

The studies discussed thus far exploit search data (hours, methods, contacts, etc.) generated by survey questions. Consequently, the data are subject to reporting errors. In particular, measured "benefit" effects may reflect systematic overreporting by recipients due to unemployment insurance requirements. St. Louis et al. investigate this possibility using data collected expressly for this purpose in the 1981–1982 Random Audit pilot tests conducted by the U.S. Department of Labor. The sites of the tests were Illinois, Kansas, Louisiana, New Jersey, and Washington, and, in each case, large amounts of time and effort were devoted to verifying job search contacts reported by claimants both on their UI benefit certification forms and in detailed personal interviews. The verification procedures included on-site visits to employers and other forms of follow-up.

Just under half of all reported contracts were found to be legitimate, but only a fifth could be shown to be fictitious or otherwise invalid. The remaining contacts could not be verified. When St. Louis et al. classify claims in the unverified set as valid and invalid using the proportions for the verified claims for each individual, they obtain an estimate of 1.78 for the actual contacts per week, versus the average reported number of 2.67 contacts per week. This difference is striking. Moreover, some clear patterns emerge across groups within the sample. Females, young workers (16–24), long-term unemployed (20+ weeks), nonwhites, hispanics, and workers who were not on layoff all tend to overreport by a larger margin than their counterparts. Obviously, these findings cast doubt on the results for demographic variation reported in the studies discussed above. As an additional check, St. Louis et al. fit regressions using both actual and estimated contact measures as dependent variables. Their explanatory variables are comparable to those included by Barron and Gilley (1979) and others. The list includes the weekly benefit level, the usual weekly wage, spell duration, the state unemployment rate in the month preceding the week of unemployment reviewed, education, sex, race, age variables (less than 25, more than 54), the proportion of the previous year spent working at the normal wage (as a measure of employment stability), a dummy variable for nontemporary layoff due to slack work, and a dummy variable for union members who could fulfill job search requirements by registering with a hiring hall.

Results are reported for the total sample, for union workers (i.e., hiring hall users), for all nonunion workers, for nonunion males, and for nonunion females. For the total sample and for the nonunion subsamples (particularly men), they find that the reported number of contacts increases significantly with duration and it appears significantly higher for white workers, young workers, and nonlayoff workers than their counterparts. However, in the regressions fit for the actual number of contacts, none of these variables has a significant coefficient—even at the 10 percent level. A similar finding appears for the benefit level for the nonunion male sample. On the other hand, actual contacts appear to increase with the weekly wage, but not reported contacts. Only education and the union hiring hall variables have consistent effects across regressions for the total sample; the effects are positive and negative, respectively. For nonunion men, both dependent variables also increase significantly with the wage and education, but these variables appear unimportant for females. The reverse holds true for the employment stability variable, that is, only females' contacts appear to be affected.

Given the method used to classify the unverified cases and the exclusive focus on benefit recipients, these results cannot be pushed too far. Still, they are unsettling.

Summary

Table 7.1 presents a summary of the studies reviewed in this section. Potential biases due to selectivity, simultaneity, and other forms of misspecification make interpretation of reported results less than straightforward. Nevertheless, the findings cast some light on results reported in previous chapters and provide guidance for future research.

Search intensity, defined as time devoted to search, is examined in several studies. Lower local unemployment rates appear to be associated with greater search intensity and there is some evidence that search intensity declines with duration of an unemployment spell. As expected, workers on temporary layoff appear to search less intensively than other unemployed workers. There is also some evidence that females spend less time searching than males, while workers with higher educational attainment, urban residents, workers seeking full-time jobs, and workers facing better wage opportunities all tend to search more intensively than their counterparts. The evidence on differences in search intensity by age, race, and marital status is mixed. Looking across studies, it appears that variation according to these characteristics is tied to reasons for being unemployed and to benefit receipt.

What are the returns to increased search intensity, again defined as more time devoted to search? Barron and Gilley (1981b) and Keeley and Robins (1985) find that the probability of becoming employed increases with search intensity. There is also evidence that the number of employer contacts increases with increased search intensity, though at a decreasing rate, and Keeley and Robins (1985) report that transition rates into employment increase with employer contacts for workers in their EOPP sample. Taken together, these findings suggest that the link between search intensity and employment probabilities may be an employer contact or application effect. However, alternative evidence suggests that more employer contacts do not imply either higher employment probabilities or higher arrival rates for all workers. Barron and Gilley report that substituting the number of contacts for search intensity in their logit model yields a small and insignificant coefficient for contacts for their 1976 CPS sample. Kahn and Low (1988b) also work with data from the 1976 CPS and they find that the number of offers per contact decreases with age and with UI benefit levels, although these results appear quite sensitive to controlling for time devoted to search, use of alternative search

Table 7.1. Regression and Discrete Choice Studies

Study	Data	Model	Findings
Barron and Mellow (1979) Search intensity	United States, 1976 May CPS supplement	Search intensity regression (weekly hours of search)	Intensity decreases as benefits increase and it decreases with duration; Workers on temporary layoff search less intensively
Barron and Mellow (1981a) Search intensity and exits from unemployment	United States, 1976 May and June matched CPS sample	Multinomial logit for labor market status in June (employed, unemployed, or out of LF)	Probability of becoming employed increases with level of search intensity and decreases with spell duration and benefits; Probability of moving from unemployment to nonparticipation decreases as benefits increase
Barron and Gilley (1979, 1981b) Search intensity and expected versus current benefits	United States, 1976 May CPS supplement	Weekly hours of search regression, fit separately for benefit recipients (currently receiving or expecting benefits) and nonrecipients	Neither current nor expected benefits affect search intensity significantly
Barron and Gilley (1981a) Diminishing returns to random search and relative returns to systematic search	United States, 1976 May CPS supplement	Regressions: 1. Log number of employers contacted per week, fit for those using random search (direct employer contact) 2. Log number of employers contacted per week, with alternative methods included as regressors, fit for random and systematic searchers	Number of contacts increases with weekly hours of search, but by proportionately less; Systematic search leads to fewer contacts than random search
	May and June matched CPS sample	3. Multinomial logit for June employment status	Employment probability increases with weekly hours of search and decreases with increases in the reservation wage; Systematic search has no significant effect
Chirinko (1982) Diminishing returns to random search and relative returns to systematic search (versus random)	United States, 1976 May CPS supplement	Regressions: 1. Number of employers contacted per week (estimated using iterated least squares), fit for random searches 2. Same as (1) with self-directed and indirect systematic search variables added, fit for random and systematic searchers	Quadratic in search time supported (i.e., diminishing returns); Benefits and city residence increase search time effects; Quadratic in search time supported; Systematic search leads to fewer contacts than random search
Kahn and Low (1988b) Choice of random versus systematic search	United States, 1976 May CPS supplement	1. Tobit model for number of offers received/number of contacts, interpreted as measure of random search	Offer to contact ratio decreases with increases in benefits and with age

Study	Data	Method	Results
Kahn and Low (1988a) The use of intermediaries	United States, 1980 NLS New Youth Cohort	2. Same as (1), with duration and self-directed and indirect search variables added Probit for use of employment agency or union, by employment status	Offer to contact ratio decreases with duration; benefits and search method irrelevant Use of intermediary: decreases with job tenure among both employed and unemployed; increases with offer variance and benefits among unemployed; higher for black workers; increases with education among employed
Holzer (1988) Search methods and offer probabilities	United States, 1980 NLS New Youth Cohort, males	1. Regression for number of methods (newspaper, relatives/friends, agencies, direct contact, other) 2. Probit for use of each method 3. Probit for probability of an offer	Inconclusive Inconclusive Probability increases with number of methods used and with use of relatives/friends and newspapers
Keeley and Robins (1985) Government program job search requirements, search behavior, and unemployment spell durations	United States, 1979–1980 EOPP	1. Separate regressions for search input levels: number of methods, number of public methods, weekly employer visits, weekly applications, separately for married men, married women, youth, and female household heads 2. Constant hazard competing risks for unemployment durations	Behavior appears altered by program requirements Increased number of methods used for all but youth Application rates lower for youth and female benefit recipients Hours of search increased by non-UI requirements for youth and males Receipt of government transfers (UI or other) decreases transition rates into both employment and nonparticipation; both transition rates increase with the levels of each search input
St. Louis, Burgess, and Kingston (1986) Reported versus actual contacts	United States, 1981–1982 UI claimants, Illinois, Kansas, Louisiana, New Jersey, Washington	1. Regression for reported number of employers contacted per week, separately for union, nonunion, nonunion male, and nonunion female workers 2. Regression for actual number of contacts per week, separately for union, nonunion, nonunion male, and nonunion female workers	Reported number: lower for union (hiring hall) workers; increases with education (males only); increases with employment stability (females only); increases with benefit level (males only); higher for young, white, and nonlayoff workers Actual number: lower for union (hiring hall) workers; increases with education (males only); increases with employment stability (females only), increases with weekly wage

methods, and spell duration. When these variables are included, offers per contact appear to decrease over the course of a spell, and other variables appear insignificant. These findings for the CPS cast some light on the observation that workers in this sample who rely primarily on direct employer contact make more contacts with employers than workers who use alternative methods, but most workers in the sample do not report direct employer contact as their most frequently used method. On average, workers in the sample are more likely to use either an informal intermediary (such as friends or relatives) or a formal intermediary (such as an employment agency or union hiring hall) in their search for employment. Similarly, Holzer (1988) finds that offer probabilities increase with the number of search methods used in his analysis of data for youth in the NLS and Keeley and Robins (1985) find that transition rates into employment increase with the number of methods, but both report variation in the relative use of alternative methods.

Unfortunately, available evidence on how and why search method choices vary with worker characteristics is fragmentary and incomplete. Holzer (1987a) provides descriptive statistics for young workers in the 1979 NLS Youth Cohort and these suggest that nonwhite youth are much more likely to generate an offer when they rely on friends and relatives and that white youth are more likely to generate offers when they use direct employer contact. There is evidence, however, that this observed difference by race may be tied to variation in other characteristics. Kahn and Low (1988a) examine the same NLS data using more formal methods and find little evidence of systematic variation in the use of intermediary search methods with worker characteristics (including race). However, their results also suggest problems with their econometric specification due to simultaneity left unaddressed and this may be the source of their findings; the same comment holds for the results on use of specific search methods presented by Holzer (1988). Not surprisingly, one characteristic that has been analyzed and appears particularly important in sorting out observed search strategy choices is benefit recipiency status. There is some evidence that UI and other income-transfer program search requirements influence the use of alternative search methods (at least in the United States). In particular, it appears that the major effect of program requirements on search activity is to increase use of public employment agencies and, although this effect translates simply into an increase in the number of methods used by some workers, there is evidence of substitution of this method for alternatives by others.

As for results obtained from use of specific search methods, evidence is again scarce. Both direct and indirect evidence suggests that greater reliance on public employment agencies is associated with lower arrival rates or at least lower arrival rates of acceptable offers. (Wiesgosz and Carpenter [1987] and Miller and Volker [1987] provide descriptive evidence for Canada and Australia, respectively, which suggests that the same holds true outside the United States.) Various explanations for these lower arrival rates might be offered. First, there may simply be a lot of noise in the data because of UI requirements. St. Louis et al. (1986) provide reasons to exercise caution when interpreting data on self-reported search activity for samples of unemployment benefit recipients. They find nonnegligible evidence of a positive bias in the numbers of contacts reported and systematic variation in the bias with worker characteristics. On the other hand, there is some evidence that employers are reluctant to list desirable jobs with public employment agencies. (See Barron and Mellow [1982] for descriptive evidence for the United States.) Further investigation into the relationship between the use and productivity of employment services and requirements of transfer programs—in light of both potential supply and potential demand side factors—seems warranted by this array of findings. As for productivity of other search methods, Holzer (1988) finds that reliance on friends and relatives and use of newspaper ads increases the probability of getting an offer for young workers in the NLS. Descriptive evidence for groups other than youth from a variety of sources suggests that workers with less education, blue-collar workers, and males are relatively more likely than their counterparts to find jobs using informal methods such as reliance on friends and relatives (e.g., Bradshaw, 1973; Corcoran et al., 1980; Granovetter, 1974; Rees and Schultz, 1970; Winship, 1982).

If we are willing to assume that workers choose their search methods and search intensities rationally, all of these observations together suggest that the productivity of a unit of search time spent on a particular search method—measured as the change in the probability of getting an acceptable offer—varies across workers, perhaps over a spell, and with local economic conditions. Distinguishing applications, receipt of offers, and acceptance of offers appears important. There is some indication that systematic search—in the sense of Salop (1973)—is the strategy used by some workers in some circumstances. However, it is not yet clear who these workers are or what search methods translate into systematic versus random search. In particular, it is not clear that equating direct employer contact without referral to the theoretical concept of random search is appropriate in all cases. Though not investigated directly, nonsequential search—in the sense of Stigler (1961, 1962)—does not seem entirely irrelevant either.

In summary, it appears that further investigation into the nature of the relationship between search intensity, search methods, and search outcomes is in order.

Structural Studies

In this section, we look at studies that exploit data on search intensity, the offer arrival process, and rejected offers to estimate specific job search models. We start with a study by Blau and Robins (1986a) who modify the Kiefer and Neumann (1979b) approach to exploit data on numbers of offers received by workers. The next two studies estimate nonsequential search models, that is, workers are modeled as choosing the optimal number of offers per period and a reservation wage. Stern (1989) uses rejected wage data to identify the optimal number of offers, while data on numbers of offers are used to estimate the reservation wage in the study by Jensen and Westergard-Nielsen (1989)[17]

Blau and Robins (1986a)

Blau and Robins work with data on both the number of job applications filed and the number of offers received. The data were collected in the baseline survey of the Employment Opportunity Pilot Project (the source used by Keeley and Robins, 1985). The samples of 1,708 men and 1,220 women with which Blau and Robins work separately are restricted to married workers who experienced at least one unemployment spell during the reference period, with unemployment defined as actively engaging in job search throughout the spell. Workers on temporary layoff are thus excluded. In the event of more than one spell, data for the most recent completed or ongoing spell are used and spell durations are measured in days. The total number of offers received by each worker over a spell is observed, although not the timing of receipt. Both the weekly benefit amount received and the duration of benefit receipt are also available. The wage at the time of reemployment is available for all workers employed when interviewed; for workers who began their unemployment spells in January 1979 or later, the previous wage is also reported.

The theoretical basis of the study is the basic job search model set out in Chapter 2, generalized to allow for heterogeneity in the mean of the offer distribution, the arrival rate, net income while unemployed, and the discount rate. Duration dependence in the arrival rate and the reservation wage are also incorporated. The model thus represents a generalization of the model considered in Kiefer and Neumann (1979a,b) and the estimation approach that Blau and Robins take is an extension of their approach (Kiefer and Neumann, 1979a).

Log offers are assumed to be draws from normal distributions that differ across workers in terms of their mean. Letting $\Phi(\cdot)$ denote the standard normal distribution function, and using our previous notation, the hazard for their model can be written as

$$\tau_i(t) = \delta_i(t)\Phi[(x_i'\beta - \ln w_i^r(t))/\sigma]$$

The data on numbers of offers are extremely useful in that these allow Blau and Robins to calculate an instrument for the average weekly arrival rate for each individual in their sample. Specifically, since some workers receive no offers (43 percent of the male sample and 46 percent of the female sample), Blau and Robins first estimate a Tobit specification for the conditional mean arrival rate,

$$\delta_i^c(t) = R_i'\delta + T_i'\theta + \epsilon_1$$

where $\epsilon_1 \sim N(0, \sigma_1^2)$, R_i is a set of regressors, and T_i is a vector of duration dummy variables (10 week intervals up to 50 weeks). They then calculate instruments for the unconditional weekly mean arrival rate for each worker using these results. The next step in their procedure is maximum likelihood estimation of a reduced form specification for individual hazard rates

$$\tau_i(t) = \exp(Z_i'\Gamma + T_i'\alpha)$$

where T_i is as previously defined and the vector Z_i includes x_i, R_i, and other observables that may affect b_i and r_i.

Using these estimates, Blau and Robins next solve for an estimate of the acceptance probability for each worker by taking the ratio of the transition rate to the arrival rate. This estimate is then used to calculate the truncation correction for the means of the accepted wage distributions for each worker. Finally, reservation wage estimates are calculated using the estimated transition rate,

$$\ln w_i^r(t)* = x_i'\beta* - \sigma*\Phi^{-1}[h_i^*(t)/\delta_i^*(t)]$$

where the asterisk denotes an estimate from an earlier stage of estimation.

Blau and Robins report results for the Tobit arrival rate specification, first with θ set equal to zero and then with duration dependence allowed. Their initial specification for R_i includes age, education, race, disability, years of work experience, family size, the local unemployment rate, small or large SMSA residence, state of residence, the UI replacement rate if a worker's previous wage is observed, a dummy that takes on the value of 1 if UI benefits were received but no previous wage observation is available and zero otherwise, and a set of state dummy variables. The results support the search framework and effects of key variables are mostly as expected. Under both specifications and for both men and women, the results indicate that younger workers, white workers,

workers with more education, and workers with no disability have higher average arrival rates than workers with the opposite characteristics. One surprising result is that the coefficient for the local unemployment rate does not differ significantly from zero at standard levels. Results for the benefit replacement rate coefficient are extremely sensitive to the specification for θ. When θ is restricted to zero, the replacement rate effect on the arrival rate is large and negative, which might be interpreted as a search intensity effect. When duration dependence is allowed, the benefit coefficients no longer differ significantly from zero. In particular, the replacement rate coefficient becomes small, both in practical and statistical terms; a null hypothesis of no benefit effect cannot be rejected at standard levels. A similar contrast appears for experience. An alternative specification excludes the UI variables and includes the weekly application rate. The notion here is that the UI effect may be indirect. With and without the duration variables, the application coefficient is positive and significant and the results previously described are not affected by this change. Only the UI model results are used to fit the unconditional arrival rates.

The specification for the regressors Z_i in the hazard model is the same as the R_i specification. Generally, the estimated coefficients have expected signs, but there are some contrasts between the results for men and women. Family size has a significant, negative effect on the male hazard, but no significant effect on the female hazard. The same holds for disability. Evaluated at the sample means, the replacement rate elasticities implied by the parameter estimates are 0.18 for men and 0.26 for women. There is some evidence that the hazard rates for both men and women decline slightly with duration, but the evidence for women is relatively weak and unmeasured heterogeneity may be the source of the observed declines for both groups.

Acceptance probabilities and reservation wages are calculated using group means for different race, sex, benefit recipiency status, and spell length groups. Both vary substantially among groups and there is evidence of a fairly clear negative relation between the two, in accordance with a simple search model. Blau and Robins recognize that all of the acceptance probabilities are low (the maximum among all groups is 11 percent) and all of the reservation wages are high. The minimum (hourly) reservation wage is 4.84 for females who received no benefits and became reemployed within 10 weeks. These results are at odds with all results reported elsewhere—calling the approach taken here or the arrival rate instruments into serious question. Blau and Robins note some inconsistencies in the offer data, such as people entering employment with zero reported job offers. Extreme cases such as this are excluded from estimation of the arrival rate models, but their presence in the sample nevertheless casts some doubt on the validity of the remaining observations.

Stern (1989)

Stern uses data on rejected wages to estimate the parameters of a model that explicitly allows for nonsequential search, that is, workers choose both a reservation wage and an optimal number of job applications to file each period. Exploring the possibility of nonsequential search is important for empirical work in the search framework. If it is the correct specification, then the accepted wage offer distribution differs from the true wage offer distribution by more than truncation at the reservation wage.

Stern starts by specifying

$$G(w) = (1 - \theta) + \theta F(w)$$

as the distribution of nonnegative offer wages, where F is the complete offer distribution, as before, and $1 - \theta$ is the probability of a rejection by an employer once an application has been filed. Treating a rejection as a zero offer, $G(w)$ can be interpreted as the offer distribution faced by the worker. As in the models considered, F and θ are time invariant and assumed known by the worker; uncertainty on the part of workers exists because workers do not know which firms are offering which wages.

When faced with job offers, a worker will accept the highest offer or continue searching. As in the simpler models, a reservation wage policy is optimal, but the worker must also choose the optimal number of job applications for each period, m, given an application cost function $C(m)$. The optimality condition defining the reservation wage in this model is

$$w^r + C(m) - \beta \left[\int_{w^r}^{\infty} (1 - G(w)^m)\, dw + w^r \right] = 0$$

where $\beta = 1/(1 + r)$ and using our earlier notation otherwise.[18] There is also a first-order condition for the choice variable m, conditioned on w^r,

$$\beta \int^{\infty} G_{w^r}(w)^m \ln G(w)\, dw + C'(m) = 0$$

This gives the difference between the marginal benefit cost and marginal benefit of an additional application. A worker's optimal strategy is the pair (w^r, m) that solves these conditions simultaneously. A sufficient condition for a unique optimum is convexity of $C(m)$; Stern uses:

$$C(m) = c_1 m + c_2 m_2$$

The reservation wage in this model can be shown to increase with the mean of the offer distribution μ and the discount factor β and decrease with increases in the rejection probability $1 - \theta$ and the marginal cost of an application $C'(m)$.[19] It can also be shown that the optimal number of applications m is decreasing in r and the marginal cost of an application $C'(m)$, but the implications for θ and μ are ambiguous.

The survivor function in this model is given by

$$S(t) = G(w^r)^{m(t-1)}(1 - G(w^r)^m)$$

and the density for accepted wages is given by

$$F_a(w) = [mg(w)G(w)^{m-1}/(1 - G(w^r))]\, d(w, w^r)$$

where $d(w, w^r)$ is an indicator function that takes on a value of 1 for $w_r \geq w^r$ and zero, otherwise. The contribution to the sample likelihood for an individual observed with a completed spell of length t and accepted wage w^a is thus

$$L(t, w^a) = G(w^r)^{m(t-1)} mg(w^a)G(w^a)^{m-1}\, d(w^a, w^r)$$

while the contribution for an individual with an incomplete spell of length t and rejected offers $w_{rj}, j = 1, 2, \ldots, k$ is[20]

$$L(t, w_{r1}, \ldots, w_{rk}) = G(w^r)^{mt} \prod_{j=1}^{k} (f(w_{rj})/F(w^r))[1 - d(w_{rj}, w^r)]$$

These likelihood functions both contain w^r. If the model is correctly specified, then consistent estimates for the reservation wage are provided by the minimum accepted offer and the maximum rejected offer and maximization of the likelihood conditioned on these estimates will produce consistent estimates of the remaining parameters of the model. On the other hand, if the wage is an incomplete measure of the value of an offer (due to failure to include fringe benefits, for example) or if there is other measurement error in the wage data, that is, if the model is misspecified, then maximum likelihood estimates for the parameters of the model are undefined. Stern addresses this possibility.[21]

Specifically, Stern incorporates the potential measurement error in his offer wage data using a procedure comparable to that of Wolpin (1987) and Kiefer and Neumann (1979a). Letting V denote the log value of a job offer with log wage offer W, W is defined as

$$W = V + Z$$

where Z and V are assumed independently distributed, and Z has density $f_Z(Z)$. The worker's optimization problem is defined in terms of V, with distribution function G previously. In this case, the contribution to the likelihood for an individual with a completed spell of length t and accepted wage w^a is given by

$$L(t, w^a) = G(w^r)^{m(t-1)} \int_{-\infty}^{w^a - w^r} mg(w^a - z)G(w^a - z)^{m-1} \, dF_Z(z)$$

The likelihood contribution for an incomplete spell is given by

$$L(t, w_{r1}, \ldots, w_{rk}) = G(w^r)^{mt} \prod_{j=1}^{k} \int_{w_{rj}^k - w^r}^{\infty} \frac{f(w_{rj} - z) \, dF_Z(z)}{F(w^r)}$$

Upon specifying a functional form for $F_Z(z)$, the unobserved part of W can be integrated out and the distribution parameters for Z can be estimated along with the parameters for the distribution of V. As noted by Stern, this approach is similar to that employed by Kiefer and Neumann (1979a). Stern specifies a Singh–Maddala distribution for log offer values V, a generalization of the Weibull and Sech[2] distributions (Singh and Maddala, 1976). The distribution function for V is thus

$$G(v) = \frac{1 - [1 + (e^v/b)^a]^{-q}}{1 - [1 + (e^s/b)^a]^{-q}}$$

where a, b, q, and s are parameters of the distribution and s is an upper truncation point. The distribution of Z is also specified as a Singh–Maddala distribution, normalized to have unit mean.[22] The final set of parameters to be estimated is thus $\{q, a, b, t, \theta, q_z, a_z, m, w^r\}$.

Stern fits his model using data from the 1981 interviews for the 1979 Youth Cohort of the National Longitudinal Survey. His sample of 1,023 workers consists of unmarried individuals, at least 18 years of age, who were not in school when interviewed in non-summer months, were either actively seeking work or had found a job in the 2 years preceding the interview, were not receiving unemployment insurance benefits, and for whom data on wage offers, accepted wages, spell lengths, and demographic characteristics are available. Stern notes that this cannot be regarded as a representative sample of young workers in the United States. Nevertheless, these data are attractive because they provide observations on rejected offers. Unemployment spell durations are measured in weeks and Stern calculates daily net real wages using state and federal tax rates and regional price indices.[23]

Stern incorporates heterogeneity into his empirical model by grouping his data by sex and education (high school dropouts, high school graduates, and some college attendance). The number of unemployment spells varies substantially across groups—from 104 to 300, with the college groups having the smallest sample sizes. The numbers of rejected offers are much smaller; the range across groups is 7 to 31. Stern notes that not all rejected offers are observed.

For all male groups and female dropouts, the estimated reservation wages and parameters for the job value and mixing distributions are precise in statistical terms.[24] For the female graduate and some college groups, however, Stern reports that convergent estimates could not be obtained under the Singh–Maddala specification for the mixing distribution. Specifically, the parameters estimates tended toward those of an extreme-value distribution.

Overall, both the means and variances for job values calculated using the parameter estimates seem sensible; they are higher for males and for those with higher educational attainment. The daily reservation wage estimates range from $23.19 to $35.60, a relatively high range. Also, although the reservation wage estimates lie below group mean accepted offers, there are observations below the reservation wage in each group sample. The upper truncation points for the distribution of job values range from $145 to $614. These are much higher values than observed in the sample and Stern attributes the discrepancies to the explicit treatment of measurement error in his approach. The results for the mixing distribution parameters suggest that a small, but significant part of variation in observed wages is due to measurement error.

There is some variation in the rejection probability across groups (i.e., the probability of not getting an offer when an application is made), but all estimates are very high; the range is 0.78–0.958. Stern notes that this may be due to the measurement of time. A period is defined as 1 week and the probability of rejection might be lower if a longer period were defined. On the other hand, he also notes that there is no real difference between "frequent rejections" and "infrequent markets"—both imply that the availability of job offers prolongs a spell of unemployment, as opposed to wage offers being too low.

The results for the optimal numbers of applications m are of particular interest. All estimates are significantly greater than 1, implying that individuals search nonsequentially. For those with less than or more than a high school education, the estimates also seem sensible, with values between 1.39 and 2.71. The estimates for high school graduates seem too high, however, the values being 16.6 for male graduates and 19.6 for female graduates.

Informal tests of the offer specification are reported and these results are somewhat discouraging. The Singh–Maddala appears to fit the data rather well for high school graduates and the male college group, but not for the remaining groups. The results for the search cost function obtained by solving the first-order conditions using the m estimates and outside estimates for the discount factor are also somewhat sobering. Setting the annual discount factor equal to 0.8 (i.e., $r = 0.25$), the estimated average cost of an application is about $19.94 for male dropouts, which seems rather high; similar results are reported for female dropouts and females with some college. For the remaining groups, the average cost is negative using reasonable values of the discount factor (i.e., β above 0.70). Stern notes that these negative values may be due to the treatment of job tenure as infinite in his model, since shorter expected job tenures for youth will reduce the present value of a job offer. Estimates for other parameters of the model and some comparative static results are also reported for the male graduate group. These numbers are not very encouraging either. The estimate for the acceptance probability for a random offer is 0.0395, for example, which is extremely low.

Jensen and Westergaard-Nielsen (1987)

Jensen and Westergaard-Nielsen also estimate the parameters of a nonsequential search model. In contrast to Stern (1987), Jensen and Westergaard-Nielsen do not have observations on the value of rejected offers, but they do have data on the numbers of offers received. They exploit these data to estimate individuals' reservation wages using an extension of the empirical approach used by Kiefer and Neumann (1979a,b).

A worker is assumed to apply to m firms per period, where m is a choice variable. The probability that any particular application lead to an offer is θ and the expected number of offers is thus $m\theta$. Offer distributions are specified as lognormal and may vary across individuals, but only in terms of their means, θ_i. Offer probabilities δ are also specified as varying across individuals, but the cost per application c, nonlabor income z, and the discount rate r are assumed to be the same for all workers. Thus, the reservation wage can be written as the function[25]

$$w_i^r = w^r(\mu_i, \theta_i)$$

That is, the only sources of variation in the reservation wage are mean offers and offer probabilities. Following Kiefer and Neumann (1979a) and Lancaster (1985), Jensen and Westergaard-Nielsen approximate this solution with

$$w_i^r = \beta_0 + \beta_2\mu_i + \beta_3\theta_i + \epsilon_i$$

and estimate the parameters using data on unemployment spell lengths, accepted wages, and numbers of offers received.

Jensen and Westergaard-Nielsen work a sample of new law school graduates. The data were collected in Denmark in 1974–1977, between 3 and 29 months after graduation.[26] The particular sample of 306 workers with which they work consists only of workers who sought positions as lawyers assistants; although these jobs are roughly homogeneous, their salaries are unregulated and thus exhibit greater variance than other legal occupations. Data are available on background characteristics for each worker, in addition to the application and offer data. In particular, they have data on work experience during law school, university grade point averages, geographic region of search, whether search was for a part-time position, age, and sex. The mean of the offer distribution is defined as a linear function of these characteristics. Unemployment durations are measured in months and Jensen and Westergaard-Nielsen restrict their period of observation to 1 year.

Estimation of the parameters of the model (i.e., the parameters of the reservation wage equation, the offer variance, and the parameters of the mean offer equation) is carried out using the method of maximum likelihood. In specifying the likelihood function for their sample, Jensen and Westergaard-Nielsen distinguish three types of observations. Letting M_i denote the total number of offers received by individual i and letting n_i denote the number of offers received in the final period of search, the first type of individual is one who searched for only one period and, thus, for whom $M_i = n_i$ (142 observations). The contribution to the sample likelihood in this case is the density for the log accepted wage w_i:

$$n\Phi((w_i - \mu_i)/\sigma)^{n_i-1}\phi((w_i - \mu_i)/\sigma)(1/\sigma)$$

where Φ and ϕ denote the distribution and density function for the standard normal distribution, respectively. The second type of observation pertains to a worker who searched for more than one period, so that $M_i - n_i$ offers were rejected in periods preceding the final period of search. For such cases (156 observations), the contribution to the likelihood function is

$$\Phi((w_i^r - \mu_i)/\sigma)^{M_i-n_i}n_i\Phi((w_i - \mu_i)/\sigma)^{n_i-1}\Phi((w_i - \mu_i)/\sigma)(1/\sigma)$$

with the restriction $w_i \geq w_i^r$ imposed. Finally, there are workers who remain unemployed for the entire period (eight observations) and the probability of this event is entered:

$$\Phi((w_i^r - \mu_i)/\sigma)^{M_i}$$

The results for mean offers are not unusual, that is, higher grade point averages and greater amounts of experience increase the mean. Of greater interest are the reservation wage results. Both higher levels of the mean and higher levels of the offer probability have an estimated effect on the reservation wage that is positive and significantly different from zero. The estimated standard deviation for log offers is also significantly different from zero (0.2655, standard error 0.0342), which can be interpreted as evidence that the potential returns to search are nonnegligible.

Jensen and Westergaard-Nielsen note that a change in Danish law in January 1976 changed the maximum number of assistants per lawyer from one to two and they investigate the effects of this change on the market and the reservation wage. Specifically, they estimate their model for the subperiods before and after the change. Their results indicate that the mean wage did change significantly between periods, but the relationship between the mean wage and the reservation wage remained roughly the same, as predicted by the model.

Summary

Overall, the results reported in this section are somewhat sobering (Table 7.2). As in previous chapters, it seems that fitting precise search models to individual level data may be pushing too far. Still, some interesting issues are raised. In particular, both Stern and Jensen and Westergaard-Nielsen provide evidence that the original nonsequential job search model of Stigler (1961) may have been dismissed too quickly—at least for some groups in the labor force. The results for offer probabilities in this section are consistent with those reported in earlier chapters—variation in unemployment duration again appears to be directly related to variation in the arrival rate. The estimated acceptance probabilities by Blau and Robins and by Stern are much lower than those obtained in Chapter 5 by alternative methods.

There is direct evidence that variation in search intensity (defined as weekly search time) plays a role in producing observed variation in unemployment spell lengths across workers. Details on how this effect operates are unclear. No direct evidence connects search intensity with offer frequencies or with acceptance probabilities for offers

Table 7.2. Structural Studies

Study	Data	Method	Findings
Blau and Robins (1986a) Basic search model	United States, 1979–1980 EOPP	Basic search model with regressors	No evidence of duration dependence in the arrival rate Elasticity of duration with respect to benefits; males 0.68; females 0.26 Maximum $\pi(w^r)$: 0.11; minimum w^r: 4.84
Stern (1989) Nonsequential search	United States 1980 New Youth Cohort	Nonsequential search representative agent model, by sex and education level	Nonsequential search relevant in modeling job search Long durations to low offer probability per application
Jensen and Westergaard-Nielsen (1987) Nonsequential search	Denmark, 1974–1977 Law graduates	Nonsequential search model with regressors	Reservation wage increases with mean offer and offer probability Log offer variance: 0.071

received. Indirect evidence suggests that some search methods are more time-intensive than others in terms of generating employer contacts, but not necessarily in terms of generating acceptable offers—or offers, in general. The characteristics of a worker and surrounding labor market conditions appear potentially important in determining the nature of these relationships.

There is evidence that benefit effects on unemployment durations reported in previous chapters are linked with benefit effects on choice of search strategies. In particular, the effects of UI program search method requirements appear nonnegligible. There is also evidence that demographic variation in unemployment spell lengths may be due to demographic variation in the effects of benefits on search intensity and search method choices, although observed variation in these variables may reflect systematic differences in the reporting of actual efforts made. Search intensity is found to be lower for workers on temporary layoff, but there appears to be no direct evidence on how (or even if) their search strategies differ. The same holds for workers facing less desirable opportunities and for workers who have been unemployed for a long time.

Notes

1. The 1981b paper is a published correction to the 1979 study.

2. Rosenfeld (1977) provides a detailed description of this survey and a summary of the findings. Rosenfeld notes that because of the high nonresponse rate (31 percent), the data should be used with caution.

3. The sample proportions in these groups are 0.02 on 30-day recall, 0.10 on the other temporary layoff, and 0.19 on other layoff. Barron and Mellow note that the CPS standard interview data indicate that the majority in this last group are job-losers.

4. Barron and Mellow (1981b) present additional descriptive evidence on unemployment insurance recipients in this sample.

5. In the June sample, there are 777 unemployed workers, 330 employed workers, and 200 out of the labor force.

6. These survey month dummy variables are entered to control for "rotation group bias," that is, the effect on respondents answers from repeated interviews.

7. A coding error in the data used by Barron and Gilley was detected following the initial publication of their study (Barron and Gilley, 1979). The results discussed here are those reported on reestimation of the model by Barron and Gilley (1981a).

8. The CPS data provide information on residence in one of 27 geographic regions, some of which are states and some of which are sets of states. For individuals in such state sets, Barron and Gilley use averages for program parameters across states.

9. The coding error previously referred to affected the results for this regression; the results described in the text are from their revised report.

10. Just as the UI application process takes time, following the search requirement regulations also takes time that may also increase measured time devoted to job search. Barron and Gilley present results for a logit model for the probability of contacting the state employment agency. The results imply that a worker with an average search intensity is 76 percent is more likely to contact the state employment agency if he or she is awaiting or receiving UI benefits.

11. The average number of contacts for this sample is not reported.

12. In the June sample, 61 percent remain unemployed, 25 percent are employed, and 14 percent are out of the labor force. Barron and Gilley note that their sample includes only those individuals who reported self-directed search, indirect search, or direct employer contact as their most frequent search method. This explains part of the difference in sample sizes between this sample and the sample analyzed by Barron and Mellow (1981); the latter includes persons who reported other methods as their most frequent and those who reported no search activity.

13. This is the same variable used in Barron and Mellow (1981).

14. Kahn and Low note that the fraction of offers rejected would have been used as their dependent variable if it were available, but the data are for workers who are currently unemployed and therefore total numbers of offers are not observed. They also note that their sample is likely to include a disproportionate number of systematic searchers (if systematic search is more time consuming) and a disproportionate number of unlucky random searchers.

15. Holzer notes that although observations on time spent using each method are also available in his data, there are large numbers of missing values, as well as obvious measurement error.

16. Each equation is estimated separately, but Keeley and Robins do note the potential loss in efficiency due to failure to address correlation among the error terms in estimation.

17. Yoon (1981) appears to have been the first to attempt structural estimation of a job search model with variable search intensity. The simultaneity of the choice of reservation wage and optimal search intensity is not treated in his specification, however, making interpretation of his results somewhat difficult. He also notes several problems with his data. Consequently, we do not discuss the study in detail here.

18. Note that the density for accepted wages in this model is simply the density for the mth order statistic for the positive wage distribution,

$$mg(w)G(w)^{m-1}$$

19. As in the studies by Wolpin (1987) and Flinn and Heckman (1982a), income while unemployed is not incorporated explicitly here. Stern excludes individuals who were receiving UI benefits.

20. Stern notes that it is impossible, in principle, to observe rejected offers above the reservation wage in the case of nonsequential search. However, his data do not provide information about when rejected offers were received within 4-week reference periods, so he simply assumes that rejected offers are made prior to acceptance of an offer.

21. An alternative source of misspecification would be failure to incorporate duration dependence. Stern does not incorporate duration dependence, but he does report results from exploratory hazard regressions and these allow duration dependence to be rejected for all but male dropouts.

22. Stern notes that he also experimented with a lognormal specification, but convergence could not be reached.

23. Given the treatment of measurement error in the approach that Stern takes, this adjust-

ment to the wage data is likely to be important. It would be useful to see a comparison of results for adjusted and unadjusted wage data.

24. In carrying out estimation, Stern notes that the values of the parameters of the model were restricted to lie within reasonable ranges (e.g., m is restricted to values greater than 1).

25. Jensen and Westergard-Nielsen define costs as linear in m, that is, $C(m) = cm$, and non-labor income z is included in their model. Otherwise, the model is analogous to that specified by Stern. In particular, the optimality condition that defines the reservation wage is essentially the same and therefore we do not repeat it here.

26. For a complete description of these data, see Westergard-Nielsen (1981a,b, 1984).

8

On-the-Job Search
and Matching

A crucial assumption of the [new microeconomic] theory is that search is significantly more efficient when the searcher is unemployed, but almost no evidence has been advanced on this point. Members of our own profession are adept at seeking and finding new jobs without first leaving their old ones or abandoning not-in-labor-force status.

James Tobin, 1971
Presidential Address to the American Economic Association

Studies reviewed in previous chapters do not distinguish job-to-job transitions when measuring employment spells. Yet, as Tobin observed, a significant share of job changing involves no intervening spell of nonemployment—estimates vary across demographic groups and with economic conditions, but they indicate that roughly half or more of all job changes are direct in the United States and elsewhere.[1] In this chapter, we shift our attention to employed worker behavior in the search framework. Most of the studies we review are based on simple on-the-job search and matching models of labor market mobility, so we will start with a sketch of their basic structures and empirical implications, and then compare these to the implications of on-the-job training models. As in Chapter 2, we consider the case of a risk-neutral worker who discounts future earnings at a positive rate r over an infinite horizon and, for the moment, we also ignore any out-of-pocket costs that might be associated with on-the-job search and job changing.[2]

On-the-Job Search

When a worker accepts a wage offer w, it represents a draw from a known distribution $F(w)$ that will be received throughout tenure on the job. However, in contrast to the model of Chapter 2, the worker in this model can continue to search from the distribution $F(w)$ while "on-the-job"—and he or she will change jobs if an offer above the current wage is received. The arrival rate of alternative job offers when employed δ_e depends on the worker's search intensity s and this will depend on potential gains from search. The quit rate for a worker, currently in a job paying w, is thus

$$q(w) = \delta_e(s(w))[1 - F(w)]$$

228

the product of the arrival rate of new job offers and the new job offer acceptance probability.

Note that there is no wage growth for a worker who stays in one job; workers are paid a wage equal to their productivity on the job and this does not change. Nevertheless, the model implies a positive empirical relationship between wages and both tenure and labor market experience when we look across workers facing $F(w)$—simply because of the sorting process at work in the labor market. Workers in low wage jobs will have higher acceptance probabilities and face greater gains from search. Consequently, they will have higher quit rates and shorter tenures than workers earning high wages. Since workers who have been in the labor market a long time have had more time to search for high wage jobs, wages will also be positively correlated with market experience across workers facing $F(w)$. The model also implies a negative empirical relationship between tenure and quit rates when looking across workers facing $F(w)$—although the quit rate is constant with respect to both tenure in the current job and labor market experience, given the current wage. Workers in high wage jobs simply wait a longer time to get a better offer.

Matching

The central idea of matching models is that both workers and firms are heterogeneous and some matches between workers and firms are more productive than others. Bad matches form, however, because of imperfect information on both sides of the match. Before a match is formed, all workers look alike to a firm and all firms look alike to workers; the true, time-invariant productivity of a worker in a particular match can be learned only over time after employment commences. A job is thus an "experience good." The learning process is such that a noisy observation on true productivity arrives at each date t—where the distribution of the noise is known and the same across all firms in the match distribution faced by a worker. The worker's wage at time t is thus interpreted as the expected value of true productivity in the current job, conditioned on productivity observations prior to t. Now the worker always has the option of restarting the match process at a different firm. Consequently, if the wage on the current job falls below some reservation wage, the current match will be dissolved. Since the value of alternative matches is constant, this reservation wage will be bounded from below by this value. Furthermore, as t increases and more observations are accumulated, the precision of productivity estimates will improve; in particular, the upper tail for the estimates on the current job will be eliminated. Given constant downside risk on all jobs and the increasingly better probability of higher wages on alternative jobs, it follows that—conditional on the current wage—the reservation wage for the current job will increase with tenure. The quit rate for the current job at tenure t, conditioned on the current wage w, may thus be written as

$$q(w, t) = \alpha F_t(w^r(w, t))$$

where $F_t(\cdot)$ denotes the tenure t estimate for the productivity distribution on the current job and α denotes the arrival rate of productivity observations.

Note that productivity is a constant here, but the learning process implies that the wage in a given job will change over time. Specifically, the path of the wage is a martingale with diminishing variance.[3] However, like the on-the-job search model, the matching model implies a positive empirical relationship between wages and tenure when looking across workers facing the same match distribution $F_0(w)$—because only good matches will stand the test of time. Similarly, given the current wage, the model implies that the quit rate will increase with tenure—but a negative correlation between quit rates and tenure may appear when looking across workers facing the same match distribution. A distinguishing empirical implication of this simple matching model is that workers might take a wage cut when changing jobs—because of the relatively higher probability attached to future high wages in alternative jobs.

Both models imply that quit rates decline with the level of the current wage, given tenure. By the same token, they also provide an explanation for an inverse relationship between quit rates and tenure and a positive relationship between wage rates and tenure when we look at data for workers having similar characteristics, that is, among workers facing the same distribution of employment opportunities. These observed relationships are spurious according to both hypotheses—a consequence of job shopping. Out-of-pocket search and moving costs do not alter these basic conclusions; these costs must simply be considered at the margin of the worker's quit decision. Mortensen (1988) demonstrates all of these implications in a general framework that nests the simple on-the-job search and matching hypotheses and a third model from outside the search framework—the on-the-job training hypothesis.[4]

On-the-Job Training

As presented by Becker (1962, 1964), Oi (1962), and Mincer (1958, 1962, 1974, 1986), there is no uncertainty about initial productivity under the on-the-job training hypothesis—but productivity does change over time and the wage changes with it as a worker undergoes job-specific training. Now if the paths of wages in alternative jobs were known prior to employment, no quits would be observed. A worker would start at the best opportunity available and stay there (until dismissed involuntarily). Alternatively, it may be that wage growth follows a stochastic process. Wage increments that are positive and stochastically decreasing in tenure seem a reasonable specification. This implies that the path of the wage is a submartingale with constant variance over time.[5] Suppose that workers can search when employed. This stochastic formulation implies that the reservation wage for alternative job offers will be an increasing function of the current wage, given tenure, and a decreasing function of tenure, given the current wage. The latter follows from increasingly better possibilities for greater wage growth in alternative jobs. Thus, conditioned on the current wage, quit rates in new jobs should increase with tenure and, conditioned on tenure, quit rates should be inversely related to the current wage. Nevertheless, the on-the-job training model implies unconditional job-to-job transition rates will appear to decrease with tenure when looking across workers facing the same offer distribution—again because of self-selection on the part of workers.

In either the matching model or the stochastic on-the-job training models (though not the simplest on-the-job search model), a quit into unemployment may make sense for a worker. Specifically, a quit into unemployment will be optimal if the wage offer in the current job falls below the value of unemployed search. The distribution of current job durations is thus characterized by competing risks in these models—unemployment or a new job. This is where empirical distinctions between the two models come into light.

Both models imply that job-to-job transition rates, conditioned on the current wage, increase with tenure (again, because of greater expected wage growth in the training model and the increasing probability of an alternative match being better in the matching model), but the implications for variation in job-to-unemployment transition rates with tenure, conditioned on the wage, differ. The job-to-unemployment transition rate equals the product of the arrival rate of current job offers and the probability that these offers will fall below the reservation wage for the current job. In both models, the current job reservation wage will increase with tenure (for the same reasons previously given, since alternatives affect the value of unemployed search). In the on-the-job training case, it follows that the quit rate into unemployment, given the wage, will increase with tenure since both direct and indirect effects will work in the same direction. In the matching model, however, the conditional job-to-unemployment transition rate may eventually decrease with tenure if the worker's uncertainty is eliminated. Mortensen (1988) demonstrates this in his general model. See Topel (1986a) and Jovanovic (1984a) also.

No one of these three models can be viewed as a complete description of the realities of labor market mobility. Attempting to determine the relative importance of each hypothesis seems a more reasonable approach to the data. This is the approach we attempt to take in our review of the literature.[6]

We begin with a variety of discrete choice and regression studies, starting with studies of "direct" evidence on the use of on-the-job search. These data are rare—perhaps even more rare than reservation wage data. Since the data are generated by survey questions, their interpretation can also be a problem. Indirect evidence is more readily available, that is, data on quits and job separations. Analyses of these data comprise the rest of the first section. The questions addressed include who chooses to search when employed, who chooses to quit, and why. The findings are interpreted within simple on-the-job search and matching frameworks. Some studies also analyze the returns to on-the-job search versus unemployed search—measured in terms of wage and nonwage changes.

We next turn to the few existing analyses of job duration data and wage data. These studies use techniques discussed in earlier chapters to analyze both single risk and competing risks specifications for the distribution of employment spells.

Finally, we close the chapter with a discussion of some recent analyses of the wage–tenure relationship. These studies use a variety of data and econometric techniques in their attempts to distinguish "true" dependence of the wage on tenure and labor market experience (say, due to on-the-job training and the accumulation of general human capital) and "spurious" dependence resulting from "job shopping." This is no small task. (The jury is still out.)

Regression and Discrete Choice Studies

We start this section with studies of direct evidence on the use of on-the-job search. Black (1981a) sets out to test the implications of simple on-the-job search models by fitting a logit model to data for male workers in the United States. Pissarides and Wadsworth (1988) also use a logit model in their analysis of on-the-job search data for workers in the United Kingdom. (This is the only study of data for non-U.S. workers in this chapter.) Viscusi (1979) sets out a simple job matching model that focuses on the relationship between risk-of-injury on the job and quit behavior. To test its implications, he fits a variety of logit and regression models using both on-the-job search and quit data from several different sources for the United States. Kahn and Low (1982, 1984) also use quit and on-the-job search data in their analysis of the choice between on-the-job search, unemployed search, and (in their second study) no search. Black (1981b) analyzes the wage returns to the use of on-the-job search. Holzer (1987b) analyzes differences in use of search methods and probabilities of receiving and accepting offers between young male unemployed versus employed searchers.

The next studies we review do not have access to "direct" evidence for on-the-job search activity. These studies analyze data on quits—either alone or with wage data. Viscusi (1980) analyzes differences in quit behavior between male and female workers using a logit model based on his risk-of-injury matching model. Blau and Kahn (1981b) focus on young workers and analyze race and sex differences in both the decision to quit and the wage returns to quitting. Mortensen and Neumann (1989) report on wage changes with job changes for men and women in the SIME–DIME data and Bartel and Borjas (1981) look at wage changes with job changes for young and older white men in the NLS, controlling for reasons for job exit. Shaw (1985) focuses on married males and the effects of a wife's labor market activity on her husband's quit decisions. The next papers by Bartel (1982), Datcher (1983), and Gottschalk and Maloney (1985) analyze nonwage returns to on-the-job search and job changing.

In the studies just listed, tenure is treated as exogenous when analyzing current on-the-job search and quit behavior. Since both variables reflect past search and quit decisions, the results are somewhat difficult to interpret. Weiss (1984) deals with the problem of endogeneity by working with a sample of workers at a U.S. firm who have zero tenure at the start of his observation period and then restricting his analysis to the first 6 months of employment. Restricting the sample to workers with zero tenure potentially introduces a problem of selectivity bias, but Weiss argues that this problem is not likely to be substantial because of his very unusual data. We will discuss his reasoning. Flinn (1986) works with a sample of young males in the United States with essentially no labor market experience at the start of his observation period. His objective is to test the empirical relevance of a simple matching model by studying wage and mobility data for his sample.

Black (1981a)

Black studies direct evidence on the use of on-the-job search collected in the 1972 interviews of the Panel Study of Income Dynamics (PSID). His sample consists of 586 black and 1,404 white male household heads who were employed at the time of the 1972 interview, remained household heads from 1971 to 1973, and were neither self-employed nor members of the armed services. Each member of the sample was asked if he had recently engaged in explicit search activity (e.g., made direct employer contacts or used an employment agency) and 5.5 percent of the sample responded yes.

Black uses these data to estimate a logit model for the use of on-the-job search. The key explanatory variable of the model is an imputed measure of the monetary incentive to search—set equal to the negative of the residual from a wage regression divided by the current wage.[7] Additional explanatory variables are age, number of school age children, the PSID index of verbal ability, current tenure (years), the number of previous quits, and categorical variables for education, city size, the county unemployment rate (above 6 percent, below), race, multiple jobs, desire for more hours on the present job, industry (construction, other), and union membership.

Overall, the results are consistent with the predictions of simple on-the-job search models. The coefficient for the wage gap variable is large, positive, and significant. The estimated effects of a college degree and greater verbal ability, included as proxies for search productivity, are also positive and significant. City size has a similar effect. The coefficients for the local unemployment rate variables have the expected signs, but they are insignificant at standard levels; this may simply reflect the use of a categorical variable. Older workers, workers with longer tenure, workers in industries other than construction, and workers with young children are all less likely to search than their counterparts. The results also provide some evidence that union members and black workers are less likely to engage in on-the-job search, but none of the estimated effects for these characteristics are significant at standard levels. The coefficient for previous quit activity is significant at standard levels, but this variable is probably highly correlated with tenure. Finally, the results imply that those working more than one job and those desiring more work hours are both more likely to search. Black notes that this may reflect an hours equilibrating mechanism operating via interfirm mobility.[8]

Pissarides and Wadsworth (1988)

Pissarides and Wadsworth estimate logit models for the use of on-the-job search using direct evidence for both male and female workers collected in the U.K. 1984 Labour Force Survey. Specifically, they work separately with samples of 31,303 employed men aged 15–64 and 22,776 employed women aged 15–59. These data are attractive both in terms of sample size and the availability of on-the-job search information. Each worker was asked whether he or she had looked for a new job to replace a present job during the reference week of the survey. The proportions of males and females in the sample who report on-the-job search activity are 5.1 and 5.5 percent, respectively, which are very close to the percentage reported by Black (1981) for U.S. males. Data on job characteristics and personal characteristics are also available. The major shortcoming of these data is that information on earnings is not available. Pissarides and Wadsworth use regional average hourly earnings in an individual's occupation and regional average hourly earnings in an individual's industry, both measured in logs. Their explanation for including both is based on the observation that workers rarely change occupations, but frequently change industries. The occupation wage is thus used as a proxy for an individual's own wage and the industry wage is used as a measure of the potential wage change faced by a worker (i.e., the higher the wage in the current industry, the less there is to gain from changing jobs). In addition to the earnings variables, the explanatory variables include the vacancy and unemployment rates by region and occupation, a categorical variable for tenure in the current job (less than 6 months, 6 months to 2 years, 2–10 years), a categorical variable indicating whether the worker was employed at the same firm, unemployed, or out of the labor force 1 year before the 1984 interview, age, and dummy variables for marital status, educational qualifications, region, recent migration, council housing tenancy (i.e., public housing), current firm size, current part-time job, and whether the current job is temporary.

The coefficient for the occupation (own) wage is positive, but small and insignificant at standard levels. On the other hand, the level of the industry wage has a significant negative effect on the likelihood of search for both males and females. The age coefficient is large, negative, and significant. On-the-job search decreases significantly with tenure, but only after the first 6 months. The education results indicate that workers with higher qualifications are more likely to search; this may reflect lower search costs for better educated workers or a greater incentive from greater wage dispersion. Workers in permanent and full-time jobs are also significantly less likely to search, but the differences are much greater for men than for women. Finally, the coefficients for the unemployment and vacancy rates have expected negative and positive signs, respectively, but neither is significant at standard levels for either group.

Viscusi (1979)

Viscusi presents a simple matching model for the case of uncertainty about job characteristics. Specifically, he models the worker's choice as a two-armed bandit problem, where the worker must choose between two jobs in each period of his life: a potentially hazardous job with unknown risk of injury properties and a job with known risk of injury properties. The worker starts out with some prior distribution for injury on the uncertain job, but can learn more only through experience on the job. Initially, there exists some compensating wage differential such that the worker will find it optimal to choose the uncertain job. If the worker's experience on the job is sufficiently bad—given the wage being paid—the worker will quit as a result of his or her sharpened assessment of the probability of injury. The implications of this model are consistent with the predictions of the simple matching model of the introduction, that is, lower quit rates will be associated with higher wages and lower mobility costs. Self-selection will also produce an inverse relationship between quit rates and tenure in the data. The key implication of the model is that, given the wage, risk of injury and quit rates should be positively related.

Viscusi tests the injury hypothesis using both cross-sectional and microdata from a variety of sources for the United States. His first results are for log-odds quit rate regressions fit using two- and three-digit manufacturing industry data for 1970 and 1974, respectively. The Bureau of Labor Statistics injury frequency rate, defined as the number of disabling injuries per million hours worked, is used as a measure of risk of injury on the job. The two-digit results are generally imprecise, but the three-digit results for comparable specifications are favorable to his hypothesis; the injury rate and wage coefficients are both significant and have predicted signs. Viscusi notes that similar results are obtained for 1970 three-digit data and 5-year and 15-year average quit rates.

Several sets of results for microdata are presented next, starting with direct evidence on the use of on-the-job search collected in the 1969–1970 University of Michigan Survey of Working Conditions. (The sample size is not reported.) Viscusi estimates logit models using two alternative dependent variables that he interprets as measures of quit intentions. The first indicates a "genuine effort to find a new job with another employer" (p. 46). The second indicates "some" intention. The explanatory variables are race, sex, education, age, health status, union membership, annual earnings, receipt of fringe benefits or pension coverage, answers to a set of job satisfaction questions, and job tenure. The risk of injury measure is a dummy variable indicating whether or not the worker believes that his job exposes him to dangerous or unhealthy conditions. The coefficients for risk of injury and tenure are significantly positive and negative, using both dependent variables. The health variable has a significant positive coefficient, but the results for remaining variables—including earnings—are otherwise imprecise.

Logit results for a sample of 2,071 workers drawn from the 1969–1971 data from the National Longitudinal Survey of Young Men (ages 14–24 in 1966) are reported next. Three quit measures are used as dependent variables: a quit dummy variable for the 2-year sample period, a quit motivated by job satisfaction, and worker dislike of the kind of work or working conditons. Viscusi notes that workers do not report quits and describes the determination of quits as based on "information concerning the individual's work history" (p. 49), without additional detail. The explanatory variables in all three models are age, race, education, union membership, regional economic conditions (no additional definition provided), occupation dummies, hourly wages, tenure, and the BLS injury frequency rate for each worker's industry. In the simple quit model, the coefficient for the hourly wage is negative, as predicted, and significantly different from zero when tenure is excluded. The coefficient for the risk of injury variable is positive, but insignificant at standard levels. When tenure is added to the quit model, all coefficient estimates are imprecise. The results for the alternative dependent variables are also imprecise—with and without tenure.

Viscusi next reports logit results for a sample of 1,932 workers taken from the National Longitudinal Survey of Mature Men (age 45–59 in 1966) for the 1969–1971 period. The dependent variables here are a quit dummy variable and a dummy variable that indicates either a quit or search for a new job. In addition to the variables used for younger men, the explanatory variables include dummy variables for pension coverage, participation in a training program, and overtime work. Viscusi notes that older workers should have sharper assessments of the risk of injury on their jobs and should thus exhibit greater employment stability. This is apparent in his data; only 77 workers quit in the 2-year sample period. The results for the basic quit model indicate that the quit rate declines significantly with age and that union members, nonwhite workers, and workers with pension coverage are less likely to quit. The coefficients for both the wage and injury variables, however, are insignificant at standard levels. The results for the quit or search logit model are qualitatively similar—with the important exception that the injury variable has a significant positive coefficient. In both specifications, the tenure coefficient is negative and significant when included. Moreover, the results for remaining variables do not change when tenure is included.

Viscusi recognizes that coefficients for logit quit models are sensitive to the length of the sample interval. His last results are for tenure regressions fit separately for his younger and older NLS samples. The explanatory variables are those listed for the logit models for each sample, excluding wages; the coefficients for included variables thus incorporate both indirect wage effects and direct effects on quits. The results indicate that significantly shorter tenures are associated with higher injury rates, particularly among older men. The results for young men also indicate that nonwhite workers and workers with less education have longer tenures. The results for older workers provide no significant evidence of important differences in tenure related to race, education, or health, but do indicate that union members have longer job tenures.

Putting all of these findings together, the bottom line is weak support for the hypothesis that uncertainty about risk of injury affects worker quit behavior, that is, workers take jobs under uncertainty, learn about risk characteristics over time, and respond to their findings. This is consistent with the more general matching explanation of worker turnover—since the "wage" in the matching model can be interpreted as a measure of pecuniary and nonpecuniary returns in a given match. Of course, workers typically accumulate information about many job characteristics (not just risk of injury), so exceptionally good fits would be unlikely.

Kahn and Low (1982)

Kahn and Low focus on workers who have already decided to search. Their objective is to determine the extent to which the choice between unemployed search and employed search reflects differences in expected wage offers generated by the alternative methods. Their model consists of three basic equations. The first two pertain to the best wage offer generated by a day's search under each search method,

$$\ln W_u = B'_u X + \epsilon_u$$
$$\ln W_e = B'_e X + \epsilon_e$$

where the subscripts u and e refer to unemployed and employed search, respectively. The third is the condition for unemployed search to be optimal,

$$E(\ln W_u) - E(\ln W_e) > g(C, Z, v)$$

The left-hand side represents the expected gain from unemployed search. The right-hand side represents the marginal cost of becoming unemployed to search C (e.g., current wage loss and fringe benefits), net of the ability to finance unemployed search in the absence of perfect capital markets Z. Direct money costs are assumed the same across search modes. Unmeasured factors influencing the choice are entered in v.[9]

Kahn and Low assume that all offers are draws from the same wage distribution, but they argue that the best unemployed search offer should exceed the best employed search offer for a given worker because of differences in search intensity. However, they also argue that workers who experience successful on-the-job search are likely to have unmeasured characteristics (e.g., good contacts) that increase their returns to on-the-job search relative to the returns faced by those who voluntarily engage in unemployed search. Consequently, the error term v will be correlated with the error terms in the wage equations and consistent estimation of the wage differential requires that this be addressed. Their approach is the three-step procedure used by Lee (1978) in his study of union membership and the union–nonunion wage differential.[10] The first step is a reduced form probit model for the probability of unemployed search; the second step is estimation of the wage equations with selectivity bias correction terms; the third step is estimation of the probit equation for the unemployed search condition again, but using the second-stage mean wage differential estimate $(\hat{B}_u - \hat{B}_e)'X$. The probit coefficient for the differential is then interpreted as an estimate of the true effect of the wage differential on the probability of choosing unemployed search over employed search.

Kahn and Low fit their model using data for a sample of 489 workers collected in the National Longitudinal Survey of Young Men. The data cover the 1969–1971 period and the sample consists of (1) job changers who located new jobs before leaving their 1969 jobs, (2) workers who stayed on their 1969 jobs but reported on-the-job search in the survey, and (3) workers who may or may not have engaged in unsuccessful on-the-job search, but definitely experienced unemployment following a quit in the sample period. Workers in the first two groups are categorized as employed searchers. Workers in the third group are categorized as unemployed job searchers (despite the uncertainty about on-the-job search); by 1971, 118 of the 139 workers in this group were reemployed. Workers who were laid off from their 1969 jobs, part-timer workers, and students are all excluded. Hourly wages for 1971 are used in the offer equations and the explanatory variables in both offer equations are the number of dependents, education, a quadratic in years out of school, the size of the local labor market, the local unemployment rate, the log hourly wage in 1969, and dummy variables for race, marital status, region, and coverage by a collective bargaining agreement in 1969. The additional explanatory variables included in the unemployed search condition are race, marital status, number of dependents, the log 1969 hourly wage, months tenure on the 1969 job as of the survey date, other family income in the year preceding the 1969 survey, and total family assets as of 1969.

Second- and third-stage results are reported. Overall, they are imprecise. In the employed search offer equation, the coefficients for race, education, labor market size, and the log 1969 wage are significant and have expected signs, but only the estimated coefficient for the log 1969 wage is significant at standard levels in the unemployed search offer equation. The coefficients for the selectivity terms are positive, but insignificant at standard levels. Given the imprecision of these offer results, Kahn and Low do not push their implications too hard, but they do calculate the differentials and find evidence of a positive percentage offer advantage for unemployed search relative to employed search for both employed searchers and unemployed searchers. Also, as expected by Kahn and Low, the calculated differential is larger for unemployed searchers than for employed searchers and smallest for employed searchers who do not change jobs.[11] The results for the third-stage probit model are also imprecise. In particular, the coefficient for the wage differential estimate is positive, but null hypotheses of a negative or zero differential cannot be rejected.[12]

Kahn and Low (1984)

Kahn and Low extend the scope of their analysis here to investigate a worker's choice of unemployed search, on-the-job search, or no search. Their approach is based on the assumption that these choices can be equated with successively higher search intensities. Specifically, with search intensity defined as

$$S = B'X + \epsilon$$

they define thresholds μ_1 and μ_2 such that no search corresponds to $S \leq \mu_1$, employed search corresponds to $\mu_1 \leq S \leq \mu_2$, and unemployed search corresponds to $S > \mu_2$. Search intensity S is not observed, but search mode is observed. Kahn and Low use these data to estimate an ordered logit model for the likelihood of each alternative.[13]

Kahn and Low work with data for a sample of 1,377 workers drawn from the National Longitudinal Survey of Young Men for the years 1969–1971. The sample includes all workers in their 1982 study plus workers who remained on their 1969 job through 1971 and indicated no on-the-job search activity (59.9 percent of the present sample). Workers who were laid off from their 1969 jobs, part-time workers, and those who were enrolled in school are excluded, as before. The explanatory variables include all variables listed for the wage regressions and the unemployed search condition in their 1982 study, plus dummy variables for 1969 occupations and industries.

The results suggest evidence that job characteristics have an important influence on workers' choices. Higher current wages have a positive and significant effect on the probability of not searching and a negative and significant effect on the probability of employed search. The same pattern also appears for coverage by a collective bargaining agreement and government employment. Both employed and unemployed search decline significantly with tenure. Signs of remaining coefficients are consistent with predictions, but none differs significantly from zero at standard levels.

Black (1981b)

In this study, Black focuses on the returns to on-the-job search activity—measured by wage changes. As in his other study, he works with data collected in the Panel Study of Income Dynamics; the sample analyzed here consists of 425 black and 1,084 white male workers who were employed at the 1972 interview, household heads from 1971 through the 1974 interview date, and who worked at least 500 hours in 1973. The analysis focuses on the percentage change in the average wage rate between 1971 and 1973; the first two restrictions thus serve data requirements. The hours restriction serves to restrict attention to workers who planned on staying in the labor force when quitting. Also excluded are those who were either self-employed or in the armed services over the 1971–1972 period.

Results for four log 1973 wage regressions are reported. The basic specification includes the log 1971 average wage,[14] experience, education, an index of verbal ability, city size in 1971, and dummy variables for race, recent disability, a decrease in the local unemployment rate over the 1971–1973 period, an increase in the local unemployment rate over the 1971–1973 period, one or more quits in the 1968–1971 period, a quit following the 1972 interview, and a quit following the 1972 interview to become self-employed. The education and verbal ability variables are included as controls for on-the-job human capital investment over the period. City size is added to control for differential growth rates across localities; an alternative interpretation would be differences in employment density that affect the arrival rate of offers.

The results for this basic model indicate a significantly smaller wage change for all quitters relative to stayers and an even smaller change for those who quit to become self-employed. Significantly larger wage changes for white workers, workers in larger cities, and workers with more education are also implied. The coefficient estimates for remaining variables are imprecise, including changes in local unemployment. Black notes that the national economy deteriorated throughout the sample period, and the results for local labor market conditions might thus be swamped.

In his second specification, Black adds a dummy variable for on-the-job search, both additively and interactively with the quit dummy.[15] Thus, each individual is classified as either searching but not quitting, quitting without searching, both searching and quitting, or neither. The results suggest that those who engage in search but do not quit within the sample period fare somewhat better than those who quit without prior search, but both experience wage decreases relative to those who do neither. Meanwhile, those who search on-the-job and then quit neither gain nor lose relative to those who do neither. Note, however, that no control for intervening unemployment spells is included.[16] It may be the case that those who quit following successful on-the-job search fare better, while those who search on-the-job and then quit to engage in unemployed search do not. As Black notes, it is not clear which quits are voluntary and which quits are not. The results for remaining variables are essentially unaffected by the addition of the on-the-job search variables.

A third specification includes the wage gap variable used in Black's 1981 on-the-job search choice study, both alone and interacted with the quit dummy, the on-the-job search dummy, and the quit and search interaction terms. The coefficient for the wage gap is large, positive, and significant, indicating that those who had been paid less than their observational equivalents in 1971 tended to experience larger wage increases. The coefficient on the unrestricted log 1971 wage is also significantly less than 1, indicating that those earning relatively high 1971 wages obtained smaller percentage wage increases. The coefficient for the on-the-job search variable is negative, as before, but its interaction with the wage gap has a large, positive, and significant coefficient—which works to offset the predicted wage decline for searchers who are underpaid. The coefficient for the quit variable is slightly more negative than in the second specification and the coefficient for its interaction with the wage gap is insignificant at standard levels.[17] Finally, the coefficient for the search and quit dummy variable is significantly negative here, as before, but its interaction with the wage gap has a large negative coefficient. Together the results imply that workers who are initially underpaid improve their situation through job changes, while those who are initially above the average stand to lose—at least in the short run. Among the results for remaining variables, the only noticeable change is a sharp decrease in the magnitude of the education coefficient.

Black's final specification includes interaction terms of the local unemployment rate with all of the search, quit, and wage gap variables. These results indicate that higher local unemployment tends to offset the wage gains for the initially underpaid—both from search without quitting and from search followed by a quit.

Holzer (1987b)

Holzer presents direct evidence on unemployed versus employed search choices and outcomes for a sample of young men. His data were collected in the 1981 interviews of New Youth Cohort of the National Longitudinal Survey and his sample consists of males, ages 16–23, who were not enrolled in school, not in the military, and who reported that they had searched for work in the month preceding the interview. Both those who were unemployed at the time of the interview and those who searched for and accepted jobs in the preceding month are classified as unemployed searchers. This classification is somewhat arbitrary and complicates interpretation of his findings. In particular, it is not clear that observations on key variables—rejected and accepted offers, reservation wages, and time spent using alternative search methods (friends and relatives, direct employer contact, state agency, newspapers, and other methods [private agencies, school placement offices, unions, and community organizations])—pertain to the previous spell of unemployment. Nevertheless, his sample using this classification consists of 609 unemployed and 438 employed searchers and he uses weights to correct for the NLS oversampling of the low income population throughout his analysis.

The descriptive statistics for the two groups of searchers pose some interesting contrasts. They suggest that unemployed searchers use more methods than employed searchers and that they spend more time on all methods except newspapers. On average, unemployed searchers also have relatively lower reservation wages, face offer distributions with just slightly lower means, but also face greater wage dispersion. (The mean ratios of the reservation wages to offered wages are 1.32 for the employed and 0.99 for the unemployed.) As for the arrival of offers, the proportions of the samples receiving at least one offer in the 4-week period are surprisingly close—0.34 for the unemployed and 0.294 for the employed. (Note, however, that numbers of offers may still differ across methods.) In contrast, the difference in the proportions reporting an offer rejection over the recall month is substantial—0.19 among the unemployed who reported receipt of one or more offers and 0.583 among the employed with offers.

Holzer uses these data to fit probit models for the probability of receiving an offer and for the acceptance probability. The results suggest that employment status has a negligible effect on the probability of receiving an offer after controlling for personal and labor market characteristics (age, education, marital status, race, religion, urban residence, family income, the local unemployment rate), the number of search methods used, and time spent on each method. The number of methods and the use of "other" methods appear to play key roles. (Coefficients for demographic and labor market variables are not reported.) The acceptance probability probit model includes the log ratio of the reservation wage to the previous wage, in place of the search choice variables. In this case, the coefficient for being unemployed is large and significant. The log reservation wage ratio also has an expected negative coefficient, but it is significant only at the 10 percent level. (Again, coefficients for control variables are not reported.) Probits for the probability of entering a new job are also fit. The explanatory variables include the search variables, the log reservation wage, the controls listed above, and a dummy variable for job leavers. Again, being unemployed has a significant, positive effect. The number of methods used and time spent on "other" methods also have significant, positive effects. Remaining variables (including the reservation wage) have only negligible effects.

Offered wage and accepted wage regressions are also fit using the same variables. The log reservation wage is included only in the accepted wage regression and it has the only significant coefficient in either regression; that is, neither choice of search method intensities nor employment status appear important in determining either variable, given their indirect effects through the reservation wage.

Viscusi (1980)

In this study, Viscusi analyzes differences in quit activity between male and female workers using data for samples of 2,609 females and 3,178 males taken from the Panel Study of Income Dynamics for the years 1975–1976. Specifically, Viscusi fits logit models for the probability of quitting jobs held in 1975 separately for each sex using two specifications—a first that includes the 1975 wage rate and a second that includes the worker's predicted wage gap for 1975 (i.e., defined as the difference between the worker's observed wage and a predicted wage).[18] In both models, the additional explanatory variables are education, number of children, tenure, the BLS industry injury rate (previously defined), the percentage of female workers in the worker's industry, and dummy variables for age, race, health impairment, union membership, and job tenure under a year.

Looking at the sample means, the female quit rate is about twice that for males (0.167 for females and 0.084 for males), and the logit results shed some light on this difference. For both the wage and wage gap specifications, chi-square tests allow rejection of the hypothesis that all coefficients are the same across sexes. Moreover, the results for individual variables for each sex are essentially the same across specifications—both imply some very sharp differences across sexes, in terms of direction and magnitude. Education and higher injury rates, for example, have significantly positive effects on the female quit rate, but negligible negative effects on male quits. For both groups, the coefficient for tenure is insignificant at standard levels, but the coefficient for tenure of less than 1 year is positive and significant—and the estimate for females is more than twice the size of the estimate for males. Similarly, the wage and wage gap variables have significantly negative coefficients for both groups, but the estimate for females is substantially larger than the estimate for males. On the other hand, the results indicate that black workers of either sex are less likely to quit—but the difference is much larger for males. The coefficients for age and health impairment are similar for males and females, both in direction and magnitude (negative and positive, respectively). Being married is associated with a lower quit probability for both groups, but other variables appear irrelevant.[19]

As a summary measure, Viscusi calculates predicted quit rates with average personal and job characteristics exchanged between males and females. The difference in average quit rates is not only diminished—it is reversed. The same holds true when only job characteristics are exchanged (i.e., wage, union membership, injury rates, and industry percent female).

Blau and Kahn (1981b)

Blau and Kahn study quit behavior of young workers—with a focus on differences by both race and sex. They also analyze returns to quitting, measured in terms of short-run and long-run changes in earnings. Their data are for samples of 2,031 white males, 775 black males, 1,604 white females, and 602 black females collected in the National Longitudinal Surveys of Young Men and Young Women (age 14–24 in 1966). The male data are for quits between 1969 and 1970 and between 1970 and 1971. The female data are for quits between 1970 and 1971 and between 1971 and 1972. All samples are restricted to nonagricultural, wage and salary workers who were employed at the time of either first year interview and who were not enrolled in school.[20]

For each of the four race and sex groups, Blau and Kahn estimate a probit model for 1-year quit probabilities. The explanatory variables include education, a quadratic in experience (age − [age upon leaving school]), number of dependents (excluding spouse), net family assets, other family income, months tenure on initial job, the average annual SMSA unemployment rate, months of military experience (for males), local labor market size, and dummy variables for marital status, coverage by a collective bargaining agreement, white-collar occupation, industry group, initial year of observation, and draft status (males only). Two earnings measures are also included—the log average hourly wage (deflated to November 1970) and the log median income of workers of the same sex in a worker's three-digit occupation (calculated from 1970 Census data); the latter is their measure of long-run earnings potential.

For all groups, job characteristics appear to play an important role in quit decisions. In particular, the estimated effects of both earnings variables are large, negative, and significant for all groups. Coverage by a collective bargaining agreement also has a negative effect for all groups except black females. White males in white-collar jobs and black males in basic industry appear more likely to quit than their counterparts, but the occupation and industry variables appear irrelevant otherwise. More education and being married are associated with higher quit probabilities for white females, but there is no additional evidence that personal characteristics have a significant effect on quitting—either within or across groups. For all groups, the quit probability declines significantly with tenure.

Blau and Kahn use these results to calculate quit probabilities for 1970–1971—with and without subsample characteristics exchanged. For both black workers and white workers, the results indicate that the substantially higher predicted quit probabilities for females reflect differences in job characteristics. The same holds for the slightly higher predicted quit probabilities for black workers relative to white workers, both male and female.

Blau and Kahn analyze race and sex differences in the returns to quitting by fitting log earnings change regressions to both the own-wage and occupation earnings data. Their samples here are restricted to workers who were employed at two consecutive survey dates and who did not report an involuntary separation in the year between. Recognizing the endogeneity of quits, they use instruments calculated from first-stage probits for the subsamples using the specifications described above. All of the explanatory variables listed are included in the log earnings change regressions, except assets and other income.

Only the quit coefficients are reported for the alternative wage and industry earnings specifications. In the wage change results, all of the estimates are positive, but only the coefficient for the black female group differs significantly from zero at standard levels. On the other hand, the coefficients in the occupation earnings regressions are all positive and only the coefficient for black males is insignificant at the 5 percent level. Blau and Kahn recognize the possibility of selectivity bias due to their sample employment restriction. To investigate both the endogeneity of quits and sample selection, they estimate log wage and log occupation earnings change regressions that include a simple dummy variable for quits, with and without an inverse Mill's ratio correction variable for sample selection (following Heckman, 1979). The quit coefficients are not sensitive to the addition of the selectivity term, but they do pose some contrast to the instrumental variables results. For white males and females, the quit coefficients are negative, although significant only for white females. For black males, the estimates from the wage change equation are also negative, though insignificant.

Mortensen and Neumann (1989)

Mortensen and Neumann examine data from the SIME–DIME experiments which provide detailed information on the timing of the job changes over a 4-year period. They find that turnover is nonnegligible even for workers over age 40, though it is much higher for younger workers. About 60 percent of job changes by men in the sample do not involve a spell of nonemployment; the figure for women is 50 percent. On average, job changers receive higher wages, though about 34 percent receive wage cuts. Indeed, about 29 percent of those who move without a spell of unemployment receive wage cuts. This is inconsistent with the simple on-the-job search model.

Log wage regressions are estimated by sex and by age group. Controlling for previous earnings, personal characteristics are unimportant, as is tenure on the previous job. This suggests that the duration dependence implied by matching and specific-capital models is not quantitatively relevant.

Bartel and Borjas (1981)

Bartel and Borjas examine returns to job-changing, measured as 2-year wage changes of movers relative to nonmovers, using data for white workers from the NLS Surveys of

Younger Men and Older Men. In contrast to other studies we discuss, they distinguish reasons for quits. This produces some suggestive results.

Their samples are restricted to workers who were not in school and who remained in the labor force over the sample period of their data, 1967–1973. Partitioning this period into 2-year intervals, they treat each observation for each individual as independent; this yields samples of 3,665 observations for younger men and 4,475 for older men. Linear and log linear wage change regressions are fit for each group. The regressors include alternative sets of reason for job-exit dummy variables and controls for education, potential postschool experience, tenure, military experience, union membership, health limitation, marital status, wife's wage (older men only), wife's earnings (younger men), local labor market size, the local unemployment rate, weeks of unemployment in the intervening 2 years, and calendar period of observation. Only results for the job-exit variables are reported and, given the pooling of samples and potential endogeneity and selectivity biases, one must proceed cautiously in drawing conclusions. Nevertheless, the results are interesting. When quits are simply distinguished from layoffs, there is weak evidence of a greater wage change for young men who quit, relative to both stayers and laid-off workers; for older men, all job changers appear to lose substantially. When more detailed reasons for non-layoff job exits are included, substantial differences appear for both groups. The results suggest that (1) workers who leave jobs for health-related and other personal reasons (e.g., family related) experience large negative wage changes relative to stayers—even larger than laid-off workers, (2) workers who quit because of job dissatisfaction experience about the same wage changes as stayers, and (3) workers who report that they quit because they found a better job experience significantly greater wage changes than stayers. The finding for the dissatisfied workers is perhaps the most interesting. Bartel and Borjas note that about 85 percent of all quits in the young sample and 73 percent of all quits in the older sample are job related and that about half of these are reportedly due to job dissatisfaction. Moreover, although wages are on the list of possible reasons for job dissatisfaction, most workers report nonwage reasons (e.g., disliked co-workers, hours, or other working conditions). Overall, these findings suggest that nonpecuniary returns provide nonnegligible motivation for job-changing.

Additional OLS results are reported for wage-change regressions for movers prior to and following their moves, again relative to stayers and treating job exits as exogenous. There is little evidence of a difference in either case.

Shaw (1985)

Shaw investigates the relationship between marital status and male quit rates using a household human capital allocation model that draws heavily on portfolio models of the finance literature. The household's problem is to maximize expected utility through allocation of its human capital wealth across jobs, where each job has a stochastic rate of return (i.e., jobs are analogous to assets in the finance framework), subject to the constraints that individuals' allocations be nonnegative and sum to current wealth. Shaw follows the approach of the empirical finance literature and assumes that the household's preferences can be represented by a function of the mean and variance of returns. To focus on the husband's quit decision, Shaw also assumes that the husband's human capital can be allocated to one of two options—quitting (and whatever follows) or staying on the current job; that the allocation of the wife's human capital is fixed;

and that the husband's quit option is the only option with any risk. She also assumes that there are transactions costs associated with exercising the quit option. The household's problem is thus reduced to choice between a risky quit and riskless stay on the current job for the husband, conditional on the wife's allocation of human capital. This represents the choice of one corner solution or the other and the household's decision rule follows directly: the husband should quit if

$$(r_q - r_s - c)/p\sigma^2 - (\tfrac{1}{2})(1 - \alpha_w) > 0$$

and stay otherwise, where r_j denotes the return to choice j, $j = $ q (quit) or s (stay), c denotes transactions costs, p denotes the parameter of constant relative risk aversion, σ^2 denotes the variance of the net return to quitting, and α_w denotes the wife's share of the household's human capital wealth allocated to the market. The model thus implies that increases in the wife's share of household wealth will increase the husband's propensity to quit.

Shaw tests this hypothesis by fitting a probit model to data from the Panel Study of Income Dynamics for the years 1971–1977 and 1981. The gap is due to missing tenure data. For each year, she restricts her sample to males from the random subsample of the PSID, ages 16–59, who were married, had working wives, and reported either no job separation in the previous year or a quit from their last job. (Only last separation data are available for each year.) After deleting observations due to missing data, there are up to eight observations for each individual and the total sample consists of 1,455 quit observations, which Shaw treats as independently and identically distributed both across time and individuals. Shaw works separately with age group subsamples, 16–19, 20–29, 30–39, and 40–49, based on age at the start of sample period, 1971. However, because of the longitudinal nature of her data, the actual age grouping is 16–29 (350 observations), 20–39 (388 observations), 30–49 (339 observations), and 40–59 (368 observations).[21]

Results for a standard quit model are reported first. The explanatory variables include education, tenure with the current employer, years of labor market experience, the ratio of other income to total household income, the ratio of transfer payments to total family income, the log hourly wage on the current job, a dummy variable for race, the local unemployment rate, and a constant. All variables are described as measured prior to the quit decision, but no detail is provided as to when. There may be substantial measurement error if, for example, the data were collected in the preceding interview. The treatment of wages and tenure as exogenous variables also makes interpretation of the results somewhat difficult. Nevertheless, the results are generally consistent with those reported elsewhere. The tenure coefficients are significantly negative at standard levels for all groups. Higher wages are associated with lower quit rates for workers over 40, but the results for the younger groups provide weak evidence of a positive effect. The quit probability also declines significantly with education and experience for the 20–39 group, but there is no evidence of significant effects for other age groups. Remaining variables appear irrelevant.

When Shaw adds the wife's income share variable, the results are consistent with her hypothesis. The coefficient is positive for all groups, significant at the 5 percent level for both the 20–39 and 30–49 groups, and significant at the 10 percent level for the 16–29 and 40–59 groups. Number of children is also added in this specification, but it has only a negligible effect. The results for the first specification remain fairly stable; the only notable change is that the education effect for the youngest group becomes significantly negative.

Shaw investigates her finding for the wife's income share in a number of ways. She first makes an effort to distinguish the relative contributions of risk aversion, transaction costs, and the variance in transaction costs that together determine the wife's share coefficient. This involves a variety of specifications that include interaction terms of education, unemployment rate, age, and race with the wife's income share variable and with each other. Interpreting the results as intended is difficult, but they are still quite interesting. They imply that the response of white males' quit behavior to wife's income share declines with education at a decreasing rate, while exactly the opposite effect appears for black males. Assuming that quit transactions costs decrease with education, this result would imply that better educated black males are either more risk averse or face a much higher wage variance. The coefficients for the age interactions are negative and the coefficients for the local unemployment rate are positive, but all are imprecise. Experimentation with alternative unemployment measures yields similar results. Shaw also explores the roles of savings and financial obligations, but neither signficantly influences the effect of the wife's income share.

Shaw checks for bias due to endogenous labor supply of the wife by estimating a dummy endogenous-censoring model with cross equation correlation of errors, that is, the probit model described and a Tobit model for the wife's share variable. The explanatory variables in the Tobit model are the husband's quit decision, number of children, husband's education, wife's education, age, and race. Results reported for the 20–49 group imply that the cross equation errors are correlated and also that husband's quits have a large, positive effect on the wife's share of income. The results for the quit equation are incredibly close to the single equation results, however, and thus provide little evidence of simultaneity bias.

Shaw notes that when labor force participation is substituted for the share variable, the results are much weaker, that is, it is not just being in the market that matters. Experimentation with the error structure of the basic probit model (i.e., dropping the assumptions of independence across time and individuals) is said to yield qualitatively similar and quantitatively stronger results. Also, Shaw notes that a likelihood ratio test allows rejection of selectivity bias due to the wife working restriction when the inverse Mill's ratio is included as a correction.

The bottom line of the study is a decomposition of the total contribution of marital status to male quit propensities. Shaw estimates her basic probit model using both married male and single male quit decision observations with a marital status dummy variable added, with and without the wife's income share variable. The results indicate that married men are less likely to quit than their single counterparts—but the estimated effect is not significant at standard levels and the wife's share in household income significantly offsets it. To illustrate the magnitude of the wife's income effect, Shaw reports the following quit probabilities for males age 30–49 calculated at the married workers' mean characteristics: 0.064 for married males with wife's income share equal to 0.40, 0.044 for married males with wife not working, and 0.064 for unmarried males. Furthermore, the unmarried male predicted quit probability rises to 0.071 when calculated using the unmarried sample means—indicating that marital status may be correlated with other variables.

Bartel (1982)

Bartel studies the relationship between job exits and nonwage job characteristics using data from the NLS for Young Men and Mature Men merged with data from alternative sources. Specifically, Bartel works with NLS data for the 2-year periods 1967–1969 and 1969–1971 and, for each period, she restricts her samples to full-time white workers who were employed at the start and finish of the interval and who were neither retired nor enrolled in school. Treating observations across 2-year periods as independent for individuals, this yields samples of 2,116 observations for young men (1,292 blue collar) and 3,393 observations for mature men (1,878 blue collar). She then merges these data with industry fringe benefit–wage ratios calculated from 2-digit BLS and 3-digit Census of Manufacturers data on compensation components and 3-digit occupation character- istic data from the Dictionary of Occupational Titles (DOT). The characteristics included are bad working conditions (hazards, extreme climate conditions, etc.), phys- ical strength requirements, stressful conditions, repetitive tasks, and limited responsi- bility, and all are measured within a range zero to one. The sample means for these nonwage job characteristics, calculated for each age group for all occupations and sep- arately for blue-collar workers, suggest that young workers face significantly lower wages and fringe benefits and that they are significantly more likely to hold jobs with negative characteristics, with the exception of job stress. Within age groups, jobs held by blue- collar workers offer higher fringe benefit–wage ratios, but lower wages and more nega- tive nonwage job characteristics.

Results from 2-year quit probits are reported for those nonwage variables and the wage. These suggest that older men give fringe benefits and the wage substantial consid- eration when making quit decisions, but other characteristics appear unimportant. For young men, the wage is again important, but fringes are not. On the other hand, all young workers appear more likely to quit jobs with repetitive work conditions and blue- collar workers tend to quit jobs with high risks of injury. Controls for education, a qua- dratic in potential postschool experience, a quadratic in tenure, health limitation, mar- ital status, wife's labor force status, local labor market size, local unemployment rate, industry, and calendar period of observation are also included in these probits, but results are not reported.

To examine returns to quitting, Bartel fits regressions in which the dependent vari- able is the change in a given job characteristic between the start and finish of a 2-year interval (they thus range from negative one to positive one, except for the log wage). The regressors include a quit dummy variable, a layoff dummy variable, and controls for education, experience, marital status, health limitation, and calendar period. Results are reported for the quit dummy variable coefficients in the log wage, fringe benefit– wage ratio, and DOT characteristics change regressions and also for a reported change in job satisfaction regression. Given that other returns to quitting are free to vary in each of these regressions and given the potential endogeneity of the quit decision, these results cannot be pushed too far. Nevertheless, they present some interesting contrasts. The results for young workers in blue-collar jobs suggest that quits produce wage gains and reductions in repetitiveness. On the other hand, the results for all young workers suggest an increase in overall job satisfaction, but other gains appear negligible, that is, there appear to be some distinct differences in the gains and losses associated with quit- ting blue-collar versus white-collar jobs. Among older blue-collar men, stress actually appears to increase for quitters, relative to stayers and those laid off, but other relative changes seem negligible. The results for all older workers suggest that white-collar quitters are also more likely to wind up in more stressful jobs, more likely to increase the level of repetitiveness of their jobs, and more likely to reduce the extent of bad working conditions. There is no evidence of a relative wage or fringe benefit gain or loss for older quitters, but this may simply reflect the averaging over changes in other characteristics.

As a check on her results, Bartel fits quit probits using data on job characteristics collected directly from workers in the Quality of Employment Survey for 1973–1977. The differences by age are of particular interest, so she fits a probit model comparable to that described which includes interactions of age with alternative job characteristic variables. Her key NLS finding holds up. Quits are higher for jobs with repetitive tasks, but the effect decreases significantly with age. Other nonwage variables appear unimportant.

Datcher (1983)

Datcher examines a somewhat different question from those examined above—the extent to which use of informal search methods (i.e., friends and relatives) improves an applicant's knowledge about a job before employment commences. Her approach is indirect. Specifically, she considers the effect of knowing someone at the place of employment prior to accepting an offer on the probability of quitting, holding constant the wage, tenure, personal characteristics (age, education, and race), and whether the relative or friend had any "clout" (i.e., helped the worker obtain an offer).

Datcher works with data for a sample of 1,472 male household heads, ages 25–44, collected in the Panel Study of Income Dynamics. The connection data are available from the 1978 interviews and quit observations are based on 1979 and 1980 interview responses. Close to half of all workers in the sample reported that they knew someone and about two-thirds of these workers reported that this associate had at least some say in getting the worker an offer.

Datcher examines her question using a probit model for a quit in either 1979 or 1980. As in other studies, longer tenure and higher current wages are found to decrease the probability of a quit. Black workers also have significantly lower quit rates than white workers. Neither years of education nor age appears important, but her results do imply that knowing someone before entering employment does reduce the probability of a quit. Moreover, her findings are consistent with the hypothesis that it is the improvement in information gathering that counts; help with getting the job offer appears unimportant. The magnitude of the informal contact effect also appears to be greater for black workers and for workers with more than a high school education.

Datcher uses her estimation results to predict quit probabilities separately for black workers and white workers, distinguishing those with some college education from those with no college education. These are quite interesting. Among workers who knew someone before getting their jobs, the quit rates are essentially the same across education groups for each race, but much higher for whites than blacks given education level. Overall, this is consistent with the summary statistics for this sample as a whole (and those reported by others). On the other hand, among those who knew no one, college educated black workers appear to have a slightly higher quit rate than their white counterparts and there is little difference between white worker and black worker quit rates among those with no college. Together these results suggest that the relatively low quit rate observed for black workers in the sample reflects the very low quit rate for black workers who knew someone. In particular, it more than offsets the fact that the typical black worker in the sample was less likely to know someone than was the typical white worker.

Gottschalk and Maloney (1985)

Gottschalk and Maloney address a question slightly different from those discussed thus far. They ask whether type of termination or unemployment experience affects the probability that a worker will find a new job that is preferable to an old job. Their analysis is based on a simple extension of the matching model that allows permanent layoffs—with and without some finite period of notification. The implication of the model is that type of termination should matter simply because an involuntary termination restricts a worker's choice set. Given the type of termination of the old job, however, the fact that a worker experiences unemployment should not affect the likelihood of being better off on the new job. In the event of a positive but finite notification period, for example, a worker initially faces the choice between on-the-job or unemployed search and will choose the method with the lowest cost. For the worker who chooses on-the-job search, it follows that search costs jump at the end of the notification period and the reservation wage must therefore decline as the layoff date approaches (as in the case of benefit exhaustion). The probability that a new job will represent an improvement over an old job thus increases with the length of notification. If voluntary separations in the absence of layoff notification are equated with infinite notification periods, the basic implication of the model follows directly.

Gottschalk and Maloney test this implication using data for a sample of 2,657 male household heads collected in the 1978–1979 interviews of the Panel Study of Income Dynamics.[22] The sample consists of workers, ages 23–61 in 1979, who were employed at the 1978 interview, but neither self-employed nor farmers. Their measure of relative well-being in the new job is based on responses to the question: "On the whole, would you say your present job is better or worse than the one you had before?" (p. 115). Gottschalk and Maloney recognize the potential interpretation problems with this measure: how often will an individual admit to either a mistaken move or failure to live up to a better opportunity in the past? Their rationale for using this measure is to capture workers' own valuation of nonwage aspects of employment.[23] A second problem with the question is that only reemployed individuals were asked (413 of 484 workers who were not on the same job at the 1979 interview). Also, the precise timing of events and the incidence of multiple job separations over the course of the year are not reported.

Gottschalk and Maloney report results for a bivariate probit model for the probability of being reemployed at the second interview, conditioned on a job separation, and the probability of feeling better off, given a job separation and reemployment by the 1979 interview. The correlation across the two equations is negative and significant, as expected. The results for the selection question indicate that the probability of being reemployed is significantly lower for workers who experience involuntary unemployment and significantly higher for married workers and white workers. The tenure coefficient is positive, but only marginally significant; this may be due to measurement error.[24] The results for the probability of being better off are consistent with the predictions of the model. Involuntary termination is associated with a significantly lower probability of a worker feeling better off. The coefficient for unemployment is also negative, but insignificant.

Gottschalk and Maloney also present results with the involuntary termination dummy variable omitted from both equations. The results for the sample selection equation are qualitatively unchanged, but the correlation between equations is insignificant and the unemployment coefficient in the well-being equation is significantly negative—indicating that it picks up the termination effect.

Weiss (1984)

Weiss analyzes quit behavior over the first 6 months of employment using a very unusual data set. His sample consists of 2,431 workers hired by a U.S. firm in either 1977 or 1979 to perform semiskilled production work at two of its plants (one in the South and one in the Midwest). The available data include observations on sex, age, race, years of education, marital status, whether a worker was employed at the time of application, scores on each part of the Crawford Physical Dexterity Test, whether a worker quit, whether the worker was laid off due to demand conditions, whether the worker was hired for a fixed term, separation dates, and a measure of job complexity at the time of entry.[25] What makes these data exceptional are the firm's personnel policies and the close monitoring of a union. At each location, all entry-level workers face the same pay schedule, promotion opportunities, and fringe benefits—regardless of age, experience, race, sex, etc. Only complexity of job assignments differs across entry-level workers—but initial assignment is random and subsequent transfers are according to seniority. Hiring procedures are almost as random. Interviews are granted on the basis of time of application (except for some influence of EEOC guidelines with respect to race and sex) and performance on the Crawford Physical Dexterity Test is about the only criterion used in the actual hire decision (but it has no other influence thereafter).[26]

Weiss bases his analysis on a very precise formulation of the on-the-job search model. First, the possibility of future job changes is incorporated into the calculation of lifetime utilities on current and alternative jobs, with the probability of a change assumed independent of whether the worker changes jobs in the observation period. Second, the discounted values of future opportunities in the present job $V(PJ_{it})$ and alternative jobs $V(AO_{it})$ both change exponentially at a rate δ, assumed constant across individuals. High expected wage growth corresponds to a large positive value for δ, while a negative δ corresponds to a high discount rate. Letting age be denoted by a_i, assuming that all work ends for all workers at age 65, and also that costs of changing jobs C are constant, the quit condition for a worker is

$$\frac{[\exp\{\delta(65 - a_i)\} - 1]}{\delta}[V(\overline{AO}_{i0}) - V(\overline{PJ}_{i0})] > C_i$$

where the overbar denotes an expectation. The specifications for the job values and costs of quitting are

$$V(\overline{AO}_{i0}) = X_{1i}\beta_1$$
$$V(\overline{PJ}_{i0}) = X_{2i}\beta_2$$

and
$$C_i = X_{3i}\beta_3 + \theta_i + \epsilon_i$$

where θ_i and ϵ_i denote unobserved nonpecuniary costs of moving. The ϵ is defined as normally distributed random noise with a zero mean. The θ is defined as institutional loyalty and general "stick-to-itiveness," which Weiss predicts will have a positive effect on costs. Assuming these variables are highly correlated with education S_i, the quit condition becomes

$$f(a_i|\delta)[X_{1i}\beta_1 - X_{2i}\beta_2] - X_{3i}\beta_3 - \beta_4 S_i > \epsilon_i$$

which leads naturally to a probit specification. The role of the constant growth rate δ is obvious; it allows the separate influences of explanatory variables on gains and costs associated with quitting to be distinguished.

Weiss restricts his sample to 1,532 workers with no missing data who were neither laid off in their first 6 months nor initially hired for a fixed term. Overall, 12 percent of his sample quits in the first 6 months. The explanatory variables are marital status and education, entered as measures of costs of quitting, and interactions of the age function with education, employment status at the time of application, job complexity, sex, age, the separate parts of the Crawford test, plant location, an interaction of race and location, and a measure of the match of education level and complexity of initial assignment (the product of the deviations of education and job complexity from their means).

A special feature of the data is that all workers have zero tenure at the start of the observation period. In the studies discussed above, tenure is typically included as an explanatory variable in modeling current quit and job search behavior. Current tenure reflects past quit and search activity, however. Therefore, the error terms in propensity to quit and probability of search equations are likely to be correlated with the explanatory variables—making the results difficult to interpret. Here, variation in tenure in the current job cannot explain variation in quit behavior. On the other hand, workers do have varied labor market experience when applying to the firm and the zero tenure restriction potentially introduces another problem—selectivity bias. For example, older workers in this sample may have unmeasured characteristics that increase their quit probabilities relative to their counterparts who stay on their former jobs. Weiss recognizes the problem, but argues that it is not likely to be serious here because of relatively high wages offered by the firm and its (almost) random hiring procedures.

Results based on three values for δ and two alternative education specifications for C_i are reported. Using years of education, the results show some sensitivity to δ. Specifically, when δ is set equal to 0.05 or 0, the effect of education on the quit propensity (due to changes in costs of moving) is negative and significant, as expected.[27] When δ is set equal to -0.05, the estimated coefficient for education remains negative and it is about the same magnitude, but the standard error is large and the effect appears insignificant at standard levels. The second education specification consists of the natural log of years of education and a dummy variable for high school graduates. Results for δ set equal to 0 and -0.05 are reported and both indicate that high school graduates have significantly lower quit propensities. The coefficients for log years of education are also negative, but insignificant; this may simply reflect the selectivity bias noted. On that note, the coefficients for age interaction terms are also insignificant. The results for all specifications imply that white workers in the South, workers given more complex job assignments, and workers who were not employed at the time of application have greater propensities to quit. Remaining coefficients are imprecise across all specifications. Weiss also notes that when number of job changes or number of unemployment spells in the previous 3 years are included, each is insignificant but the employment at application time effect remains negative and significant.

Qualitatively, the results are essentially the same for a simple probit model, that is, without the $f(a_i)$ term. The only notable difference is a significant, negative coefficient for age—as expected.

Flinn (1986)

Flinn carries out a structural analysis of wages and mobility of young men based on a parameterization of the matching model developed by Jovanovic (1979a,b, 1984b). Formally, the productivity of worker i with tenure t at firm j is defined as

$$w_{ijt} = z'_{it}\beta + \mu_i + \theta_{ij} + \epsilon_{it}$$

where z_{it} denotes observable characteristics (both fixed and time varying) that affect productivity uniformly across all firms; μ_i represents unobservable individual-specific, time-invariant characteristics that also affect productivity uniformly across firms; θ_{ij} is an unobservable time-invariant, match-specific parameter for worker i when employed at firm j; and ϵ_{it} is pure noise. All three observables are specified as independently distributed normal random variables with zero means and precision $\pi_k (= 1/\sigma_k)$ for $k = \mu_i, \epsilon_{it},$ and θ_{ij}.

When a match is formed, the worker knows both individual-specific terms that affect his productivity ($Z'_{it}\beta$ and μ_i), but information on the match-specific and noise components is restricted to knowledge of their distributions. Thereafter, the worker observes their sum in each period $r_{ijt} = \theta_{ij} + \epsilon_{it}$. In deciding whether to stay with firm j or to quit at the start of period t, the worker's approach is to update his prior estimate of the quality of the match q using information obtained in the previous period, that is, the r observation, and compare this estimate to the cost of quitting. Letting h denote the precision of the worker's match quality estimate and letting q' and h' denote one period updates, it follows from the assumption of normality that these are defined as

$$q' = \frac{hq + \pi_\epsilon r}{h + \pi_\epsilon}$$

and
$$h' = h + \epsilon_\epsilon$$

where the initial estimates are $q = 0$ and $h = \pi_\theta$. The optimal policy for the worker is a reservation policy: to quit in the current period if and only if the current estimate of the match component q falls below a critical value, $q^*(h)$. It is shown that q^* is monotonically increasing in the precision of the estimate h. Since the precision improves with successive observations on the sum r, it follows that the reservation value increases with tenure. The model thus predicts that mean wages should be systematically lower for movers than for stayers and, given the wage, quits should increase with tenure.

Flinn works with data for a sample of 248 workers collected in the National Longitudinal Survey of Young Men (ages 14–24 in 1966). To be included in his sample, an individual had to be (1) enrolled in school full-time and not in the labor force full-time at the time of the 1966 interview and (2) employed full-time and not in school full-time at each of the 1967, 1968, and 1969 interview dates. In addition, data had to be available on hourly wages at each of the 1967–1969 interview dates, job changes between interviews, years of schooling in 1967, age, and race. Although stringent, these selection criteria serve to avoid concern over initial conditions. In the simple matching model, a worker's current quit decision depends on estimates for the match component of productivity and the precision of this estimate. These, in turn, depend on all previous wages on the job. In the absence of complete wage histories with the beginning-of-sample-employer for a worker, it follows that the likelihood of moving during the sample period must be conditioned on presample wages and then integrated with respect to the correct wage density—a less than straightforward procedure. (Of course, matters are even more complicated if initial tenure is unobserved.) In the sample selected by Flinn, workers essentially have no labor market history at the start of the sample period and their subsequent experiences over a 3-year period are observed. In particular, their wage histories are observed for this period.[28]

Flinn works with a partition of his sample by mobility patterns between 1967 and 1969: MM includes those who move in both the 1967–1968 and 1968–1969 periods (42 workers), MS includes those who move only in the 1967–1968 period (55 workers), SM includes those who move only in 1968–1969 (36 workers), and SS includes those who never move (115 workers).

Although group sample mean wages and sample mean wage changes provide only rough evidence, they are consistent with the pattern predicted under the simple matching story, that is, movers have lower mean wages. The model also implies several restrictions on the covariance structure of the wages, both within and across mobility groups and Flinn tests these restrictions using a minimum distance test. He reports a χ^2 (11 *d.f.*) statistic of 9.81 and, given that the probability of a greater value exceeds 0.5, the restrictions cannot reasonably be rejected. Thus, the data appear consistent with the matching model.[29]

Flinn next calculates maximum likelihood estimates for the parameters of the model [β, σ_μ^2, σ_ϵ^2, σ_θ^2]. Given the precise structure of the model and the completeness of the data, this is straightforward in principle, but computationally demanding. Consequently, only data for the first 2 years of the sample period are used. Age, sex, and education are included as determinants of the match-invariant wage component and these results are consistent with most wage regression results; younger workers and nonwhite workers have relatively low mean wages. The only unusual result is a small and insignificant education coefficient.[30] Of particular interest are the variance estimates, which are all precise. The estimate for the total variance of log wages is 0.178, with 38 percent due to match variation (θ) and 44 percent due to unobserved variation across individuals (μ).

Summary

Interpretation of the findings of studies in this section is complicated by several issues. There are potential biases due to simultaneity and self-selection. Intervals of different length are used in the probit and logit models in different studies. Still, looking at the results for key variables that are summarized in Table 8.1, some consistent patterns emerge.

As predicted by the simple on-the-job search model, the studies of "direct evidence" find that search is less likely for those with current wages above the mean, given tenure. They also find that search decreases with tenure, given the current wage, and that it is less prevalent among older workers. The findings of quit studies are similar.

The results for *returns* to on-the-job search and quits are less straightforward. Black (1981a), Gottschalk and Maloney (1985), and Mortensen and Neumann (1989) report that nonnegligible proportions of the job changers in their samples experience wage decreases. These observations confirm those of Reynolds (1951) and other early studies of local labor market data reviewed by Parnes (1954). Overall, this consistency might be taken as evidence against the pure on-the-job search model. At the same time, these and other findings point to some fundamental questions regarding specification and measurement that must be addressed before drawing conclusions.

The first issue is the appropriate definition of a *wage*. Bartel and Borjas (1981) and Bartel (1982) find that *nonpecuniary* concerns motivate a significant share of observed quits in their samples of male workers from the NLS. (See Akerlof et al. [1988] for additional tabulations and discussion of these findings in the NLS data.) Similarly, non-pecuniary returns to job-changing—such as reductions in job stress or repetitiveness, hours adjustments, or just reported increases in job satisfaction—appear significant for at least some workers. These findings are also consistent with those of earlier studies (Parnes, 1954) and this consistency, in turn, suggests that a broader interpretation of the wage may be appropriate when testing hypotheses generated by search and matching models. The studies reviewed here also focus on *current* wage changes with job changes, but the findings of Pissarides and Wadsworth (1988), Blau and Kahn (1981b), and Weiss (1984) suggest that long-run earnings potential in a job may be important. Of course, distinguishing current and future wages conflicts with the simplest formulations of matching and on-the-job search models. In the next section of this chapter, we review studies that examine the empirical relevance of this distinction.

The findings of Blau and Kahn (1981b) suggest that negative wage change predictions may simply be a consequence of failing to address the endogeneity of quits in estimation. The findings of Bartel and Borjas (1981) suggest that controlling for alternative reasons for quits can also affect predicted wage changes substantially. A related issue is the sensitivity of wage change results to the particular calendar period sampled. Black (1981b) notes that his finding of negative wage returns to quitting may reflect slack conditions in the economy during his sample period. All of these findings point to a second serious measurement issue—the distinction between a *quit* and a *layoff*. If a layoff is imminent, say due to an anticipated plant shutdown, slackness in the product market, or even "cause" that will lead to dismissal, it may be averted by a worker—in which case a quit will be observed. Similarly, an employer may dissolve a match if a quit is anticipated.[31] In practice, we observe both voluntary and involuntary separations between workers and firms and most evidence suggests that workers who experience permanent layoffs fare worse than quitters in terms of wage and nonwage returns to job-changing, not to mention the costs associated with time spent unemployed. Negative wage changes for quitters may in part reflect rational responses to anticipated layoffs.

Contract provisions and/or legal obligations may be important in determining observed separation behavior. Deere and Wiggins (1989) offer a simple theoretical analysis of contract provisions for advance notice to workers in the event of an anticipated plant closing. They show, not surprisingly, that some notice is an efficient contract provision under reasonable assumptions, but notice is not likely to be given in practice unless there is a future that constrains self-interested rent-seeking at the end of contractual arrangements. A few recent studies empirically examine the effects of advance notice using data for workers in the United States from the Displaced Worker Surveys in the 1984, 1986, and 1988 January CPS. There is some ambiguity in the notice question used in these surveys and there are problems with the methods used to measure unemployment spells. On the upside, all workers who reported being displaced were surveyed, even those who experienced no unemployment between jobs. In a comprehensive study of the 1984 data, Ehrenberg and Jakubson (1989) find evidence that

Table 8.1. Regression and Discrete Choice Studies

Study	Data	Model	Findings
Black (1981a) On-the-job search	United States, 1972 PSID male household heads	Logit for on-the-job search	Likelihood of on-the-job search inversely related to deviations of the current wage from the mean, age, and tenure
Pissarides and Wadsworth (1988) On-the-job search	United Kingdom, 1984 Labour Force Survey: males (15–64), females (15–59)	Logit for on-the-job search, by sex	Likelihood of on-the-job search inversely related to the mean industry wage, age, and tenure (after 6 months)
Viscusi (1979) On-the-job search, quits, and risk of injury	United States, 1969–1971: 1. 1969–1970 Survey of Working Conditions 2. 1969–1971 NLS young men 3. 1969–1971 NLS mature men	Logit for on-the-job search Logit for quits Logit for quit or on-the-job search Tenure regressions, separately for young and mature men (wage excluded)	Likelihood of on-the-job search increases with level of risk of injury and decreases with tenure Quits decrease with wage and increase with risk of injury (sensitive to including tenure) Both search and quits decrease with age and tenure; neither is sensitive to wage level; search increases with risk of injury Tenure decreases with risk of injury
Kahn and Low (1982) Differences in mean offers and the choice of on-the-job versus unemployed search	United States, 1969–1971 NLS young men	1. Probit for unemployed search 2. Log wage offer regressions, separately for unemployed and employed searchers 3. Probit, with offer differential estimate	Weak evidence that unemployed search yields higher offers than employed search for typical worker
Kahn and Low (1984) Unemployed search, on-the-job search, and no search	United States, 1967–1971 NLS young men	Ordered logit for no search, on-the-job search, and unemployed search	Likelihood of search inversely related to current wage and tenure
Black (1981b) Returns to on-the-job search	United States, 1971–1973 PSID male household heads	Log 1973 wage regressions	Returns to on-the-job search and quitting depend directly on current relative wage opportunities
Unemployed versus employed search	United States, 1981 NLS New Youth Cohort	Probits for 1. month before interviews, 2. acceptance probability, and 3. accepting new employment	Offer probability: increases with number of search methods used and time spent using less popular methods; not affected by employment status; acceptance probability: higher for unemployed; probability of new job represents combination of above
Viscusi (1980) Quit behavior of young males versus females	United States, 1975–1976 PSID	Logit for quits, by sex	Quits most likely in first year (especially females); tenure appears irrelevant after 1 year Quits decrease with current wage and increase with wage gap (especially females) Higher female quit rate reflects differences in job characteristics
Blau and Kahn (1981b) Race and sex	United States, 1969–1972 NLS young women	1. Probit for one-year quits, by race and sex	Quits inversely related to current wage, wage within occupation, and tenure; higher predicted quit

Study	Data	Method	Results
differences in quit probabilities and returns to quitting	(1970–1972), young men (1969–1971)	2. Log earnings change regressions by sex and race, using instrument for quits	rates for female (vs. male) and black (vs. white) workers reflect differences in job characteristics; Evidence of potential long-run wage gain with change of occupation
Mortensen and Neumann (1989)	SIME/DIME	OLS log wage regressions, by sex and age	60 percent (male) and 50 percent (female) of job changes occur without nonemployment; 34 percent take wage cuts; Previous tenure unimportant with previous wages included
Bartel and Borjas (1981) Wage changes and reasons for job exit	United States, 1967–1973 NLS young men, NLS mature men, white workers	Linear and log wage regressions	Wage change for quitters depends on reason for exit: large negative if for health and family reasons; negligible negative if due to job dissatisfaction; large positive if found better job
Shaw (1985) Husbands' quits and wives' income	United States, 1971–1977, 1981 PSID	Probit for quits (one year)	Husband's quit probability directly related to wife's share of household income and inversely related to tenure; decreases with the current wage for workers over 40
Bartel (1982) Quits and nonwage job characteristics	1. United States, 1967–1971 NLS young men, NLS mature men, white workers	1. Probits for 2-year quits, by age group and separately for blue-collar workers	Quit probability increases with wage for all groups; higher for all young in repetitive jobs; higher for blue-collar young if working conditions bad; decreases with fringe benefit–wage ratio only for older men; other nonwage characteristics irrelevant for older men
	2. United States, 1973–1977 Quality of Employment Survey males	2. Nonwage and wage change regressions Probit for quits	Young quitters reduce and older quitters increase job repetitiveness; Similar results
Datcher (1983) Preemployment connections	United States, 1978–1980 PSID male household heads	Probit for quits (one year)	Quit probability inversely related to wage and tenure; Preemployment connection
Gottschalk and Maloney (1985) Nonwage returns to search	United States, 1978–1979 PSID male household heads	Bivariate probit for probabilities of reemployment and (subjective) job improvement	Perceived job improvements more likely after quitting than after layoffs
Weiss (1984) Quit behavior of new hires	United States, 1977–1979 new hires at a U.S. firm	Probit for quits in first 6 months	Quit probability is lower for workers employed at application time; decreases with age and increases with job complexity
Flinn (1986) Test of simple matching model	United States, 1967–1969 NLS young men, new entrants in 1967	1. Log wage and log wage change regressions	Covariance restrictions of matching model cannot be rejected (χ^2 test)
		2. MLE of log wage model	Log wage variance 0.178, with 38 percent due to match variation and 44 percent due to individual fixed effects

advance notice increases the probability of a direct job-to-job transition. (For additional discussion of these data, see our discussion of the study by Podgursky and Swaim [1987] in Chapter 5.)

Though somewhat limited in scope, available evidence on systematic variation in search and job-exit behavior with worker characteristics suggests that it is substantial. The likelihood of on-the-job search appears to be inversely related to education and skill level, and perhaps is lower for married workers and females.[32] In his sample of male household heads from the PSID, Black (1981b) also finds that black workers are relatively less responsive to relative wage opportunities. The studies reviewed here and alternative sources of relevant evidence suggest that demographic differences in job-exit behavior may be tied to demographic differences in the relative importance attached to nonwage job characteristics. Zax (1990), for example, examines personnel records for a single Detroit firm and finds that commuting distances may be particularly important for both nonwhite workers and females when considering job exits. Similarly, Bartel (1981) finds significant variation with age in the importance attached to both fringe benefits and particular job characteristics in her samples of white males. She also finds evidence of differences between blue-collar and white-collar workers. The findings of Viscusi (1980) suggest that young females are more responsive to risk of injury than are young males. Gender differences in union membership also appear important in producing observed gender differences in quit rates, at least among young workers. Reasons for this are not really clear.

Differences in unemployment benefit eligibility and payment levels across workers may play an important role in determining observed quits versus layoffs. The potential effects of UI financing arrangements on the incidence of temporary versus permanent layoffs have received a substantial amount of attention (e.g., Adams, 1987; Baily, 1977; Brechling, 1977,1981; Feldstein, 1973, 1974, 1975a,b, 1976, 1978; Osberg, 1986; Topel, 1980, 1984b; Topel and Welch, 1983; Wolcowitz, 1984). Available evidence suggests that imperfect experience-rated financing arrangements (i.e., arrangements in which the value of benefits received by unemployed workers exceeds their incremental cost to employers) have a nonnegligible effect on the incidence of temporary layoffs. These findings are often regarded as evidence of effects on demand-side decisions, but this interpretation is not clear. Employer decisions should be conditioned on the anticipated quit behavior of their workers. On the flip side, employer behavior should be influenced by voluntary leaver provisions available in some states, but analysis of these provisions has focused solely on employee quit behavior. An interesting course for future research would be to attempt to sort out employer and employee separation responses to variation in UI program structures.[33]

Job Duration Data

The studies in this section examine job exits using duration data techniques. Meitzen (1986) fits hazard functions for job durations of men and women. Berkovec and Stern (1988) estimate a model of the decision to retire (or quit) using data for a sample of mature men. Gronberg and Reed (1989) address the question of workers' marginal-willingness-to-pay for job attributes within the search framework.

Meitzen (1986)

Meitzen takes a hazard function approach to study differences in job-quitting behavior between males and females in the United States. His data are for samples of 1,256 males and 1,503 females collected in the Employment Opportunity Pilot Project Employers' Survey (EOPPE). These data are not perfect. The sample is not representative for the U.S. labor force (low-wage firms were intentionally oversampled in the EOPPE). The period for which information is collected, January 1978 to either March or May 1980, is somewhat short (particularly in terms of job durations).[34] Nevertheless, these data have some very attractive features. Meitzen restricts his sample to workers who were hired during the reference period and, for each worker, a precise work history with the firm is observed up to either a separation date or the date of the interview.[35] Completed and right-censored job durations, measured in days, are thus available. Data are also available for several firm characteristics and basic demographic characteristics. Also, workers' occupations and labor market locations are both known, which allows auxiliary data on occupation and local labor market characteristics to be merged with the EOPP data.

Meitzen uses a Gompertz proportional hazards model,

$$\tau(t; x) = \exp(x'\beta + \alpha t)$$

This specification allows only monotonic change in the hazard with duration, as in a Weibull specification, but it allows the change to occur at a faster rate. The parameter α measures the proportionate change in the hazard with duration. Meitzen fits the model separately for his male and female samples, noting that a likelihood ratio test allows rejection of equal parameters across the two hazards. The explanatory variables are age, a categorical education variable (less than high school, more than high school, college graduate), a dummy variable indicating hazardous work conditions in the worker's occupation, log employment at the firm in December 1979, industry dummy variables, categorical variables for the percentage of the firm's nonsupervisory employees covered by a collective bargaining agreement (1–25, 26–50, 51–75, 76–100 percent), the percentage of the firm's workforce in a craft, the number of hours spent by the firm in hiring (recruiting, screening, and interviewing), the starting wage, the top wage for a worker's initial job slot, a dummy variable to indicate a difference between the top and bottom wage in a worker's job slot, the expected amount of time required to reach average performance in an initial job slot, the average manufacturing wage in the worker's local labor market, and the percentage change in local labor market employment between 1977 and 1979.

The annual exit rates are 0.242 for males and 0.248 for females in the sample, but the results from estimation indicate some major differences in the determinants of the hazard. In particular, the estimates for the duration dependence parameter α are both significant, but have opposite signs. The estimate for males is -0.00109 (standard error 0.00047), implying an elasticity of -0.294 when evaluated at the sample mean tenure. On the other hand, the estimate for females is 0.000812 (standard error 0.00036), implying an elasticity of 0.233 at the mean. For males, higher top wages and higher percentages of the firm's workforce in craft occupations significantly lower the exit rate. For females, the estimated effect of the top wage level is insignificant, but the dummy variable indicating a difference between top and bottom wages has a significant negative coefficient. At least weak evidence that higher local market wages increase the female exit rate also appears.[36] The exit rate is also significantly lower for older females and for females in occupations that do not involve substantial exposure to hazardous conditions, but neither of these variables appears significant at the 5 percent level for males. The same contrast appears for time invested by the firm in the hiring process. Both males and females at larger firms have significantly lower exit rates. The coefficients for remaining variables are insignificant at the 5 percent level.

Meitzen examines the contrast in tenure results using a variety of respecifications. Most interesting are the results for an interaction of tenure with a dummy variable for age greater than 30. The results reported for the simpler model remain stable. In particular, although the age–tenure interaction terms are positive and negative for males and females, respectively (indicating an offsetting tenure effect with age), both coefficients are small in absolute value and insignificant at standard levels. Results are also reported for a model that includes only a constant and tenure. For both groups, the estimates for α are smaller, as expected, and it is insignificant for females.

Berkovec and Stern (1988)

Berkovec and Stern present and estimate a discrete-time dynamic programming model of the job exit behavior of older men. In each period, an employed worker is modeled as choosing either to continue in his current job, to retire, or to change jobs to an alternative full- or part-time job. Two specifications are estimated, one in which the discount factor is equal to zero, so that a static maximization is made each period, and one in which the discount factor is nonzero (but prespecified, not estimated). In the latter case, the possibility of returning to employment after retirement is considered. The problem is set up in a finite horizon dynamic programming framework, similar to that of Wolpin (1987, discussed in Chapter 5), and the optimal policy is obtained numerically. However, the model is fit (unlike Wolpin) using a full set of explanatory variables and the method of simulated moments (e.g., Lerman and Manski, 1981; McFadden, 1989) is used to estimate the parameters. This is a method of moments estimator, equating theoretical moments predicted by the model (which are functions of parameters) to sample moments. However, the theoretical moments from the model are approximated here by simulating data from the model, conditional on parameter values, and taking averages. Berkovec and Stern also allow random effects particular to the individual, to the job, and to the match of the individual to the job. These are integrated out by averaging the conditional transition probabilities over a Monte Carlo sample of the random effects. The computational effort involved in estimating this model is thus substantial.

Berkovec and Stern fit their model using work histories for a sample of 500 workers in the National Longitudinal Survey of Mature Men who were aged 55 to 59 at the start of the survey in 1966 and remained in the NLS sample through 1983. Although roughly 40 percent of these workers holds a single full-time job and then retires permanently during the sample period and another 15 percent remains retired throughout, a nonnegligible amount of movement among labor market states is observed for the remaining workers in the sample. About 5 percent of the sample makes at least one transition out of retirement, more than 10 percent holds more than one full-time job, and more than 20 percent makes a transition into a part-time job (either from a full-time job or from retirement).

As might be expected, Berkovec and Stern find that bad health and aging increase retirement probabilities, while education tends to decrease them. The results on random effects are interesting: 60–70 percent of wage variation is estimated to be due to individual effects and another 25 percent to match effects. Point estimates are not sensitive to assumptions on the discount factor, but the dynamic implications of the model are sensitive. This is disturbing, since the authors report that their attempts to identify this parameter using the available data are unsuccessful.

Gronberg and Reed (1989)

The objective of this study is to estimate workers' marginal willingness to pay for job attributes (MWP) within a job search framework. The basic idea is that workers will remain longer at jobs having desirable characteristics, given the wage. Thus, differences in job durations should yield information on relative values of job attributes.

More precisely, the simple on-the-job search model of Burdett (1978), which we sketch in the introduction to this chapter, is extended to allow for multidimensional jobs. Letting the utility of a job with characteristics X_i, $i = 1, \ldots, n$, be denoted by $u(X)$, and also assuming that the new job arrival rate is proportional to search intensity, the quit rate is written as

$$q(u(X)) = \delta_e S(u(X))[1 - F(u(X))]$$

The parameter δ_e in this case is defined as the market determined search efficiency parameter and, assuming that search costs are convex in intensity S, the optimal intensity is well defined. Now the marginal willingness of a worker to pay for the ith job attribute (X_i) must equal the ratio of the marginal utility of the attribute to the marginal utility of the wage. It follows (from differentiation of the quit rate) that

$$MWP_i = \frac{\partial q(X)}{\partial X_i} \bigg/ \frac{\partial q(X)}{\partial w}$$

for attributes $i = 1, \ldots, n$. Thus, the ratio of the estimated marginal effects of an attribute and the wage on the quit rate can be used as an estimate of MWP_i (i.e., the ratio of the coefficients).

The basic on-the-job search model, as extended here, implies that completed job durations have an exponential distribution. However, to allow flexibility in the effects of unobserved heterogeneity on the duration distribution, Gronberg and Reed use an accelerated failure time specification, $\ln t = X'\beta + \epsilon$, with a generalized gamma distribution specified for the error term. Thus, their model admits Weibull, exponential, and lognormal distributions as special cases. Moreover, estimation is fairly straightforward; the method of maximum likelihood is applied. (See Propostion 3 in Chapter 3.)

The model is fit using data for a sample of 662 white males from the New Youth Cohort of the National Longitudinal Survey. Specifically, their sample is restricted to workers who were employed at the 1979 interview, but not enrolled in school, self-employed, in the military, or working without pay at that time. Job tenure as of 1979 is available and workers are followed through 1985 interviews. Job attributes are not directly available in the NLS, but occupations are observed. Gronberg and Reed use these occupation data together with the Dictionary of Occupational Titles to determine whether each worker's job had any or all of four characteristics: bad working conditions (extremes of heat, cold, wetness, vibrations, or hazards), involved repetitious work, required heavy lifting, or required frequent stooping, kneeling, crouching, or crawling. The regressors in the hazard model include dummy variables for these negative job characteristics, the log wage, the local unemployment rate, a quadratic in experience, educational attainment, a dummy variable for more than 30 days of job-specific training, and dummy variables for job requirements in language, math, and reading.

As in other job duration studies, the coefficients for the unemployment rate, education, and the log wage are negative and significant at the 5 percent level. Experience (measured as age − education − 6) appears unimportant, but this could reflect the use of the proxy or the age range of the sample. Among the general human capital variables, a reading requirement appears to be marginally important, though tenure is shorter in such jobs. On the other hand, the coefficient for the specific training variable is negative and significant, as expected. The parameters for the heterogeneity distribution also allow rejection of both exponential and Weibull durations (and thus the proportional hazards model). Remaining coefficients are insignificant at the 5 percent level. In particular, the estimated job characteristic coefficients are positive, as expected, but imprecise. Only the coefficient for bad working conditions is significant at the 10 percent level.[37]

Gronberg and Reed use the job characteristic coefficient estimates to calculate the MWP for each characteristic at the mean wage for the sample ($4.43) (acknowledging the imprecision of potential conclusions). The point estimates range from $0.02 for no heavy lifting to $1.24 for no bad working conditions. For comparison, Gronberg and Reed fit an OLS ("hedonic") log wage regression—the conventional method for obtaining estimates of MWP_i. All four of the job characteristics have significant regression coefficients, with expected negative signs except for required stooping, kneeling, etc. Given the imprecise hazard function results, a comparison of point estimates for the MWP_i across methods is of limited value. Still, a comparison of results does suggest that the conventional approach understates the values of job attributes. This finding is consistent with theoretical predictions of the equilibrium wage distribution model of Mortensen (1988), which suggests that additional work on this question with alternative data could be useful.

Summary

The findings of these job durations studies are consistent with some of the findings reported in the preceding section but pose contrasts to others (see Table 8.2). Meitzen (1986) finds significant differences in the effects of age and other explanatory variables on the hazard rates of males versus females in his sample of new hires, which is not surprising. However, he also finds a decreasing hazard for males and an increasing hazard for females, while studies discussed previously found that quit rates were generally higher for females in their first 6 months to a year on a job and then decreased. One explanation for Meitzen's finding might be the combination of a monotonic baseline hazard and maximum-2-years-at-risk duration data. Gronberg and Reed (1989) produce a second surprising result. In contrast to the findings of Bartel (1982), they find that nonwage job characteristics, including job repetitiveness, are irrelevant to young white males' quit decisions. Gronberg and Reed include a control for specific training and this may pick up the repetitiveness effect, but this is just speculation. Another notable aspect of the Gronberg and Reed study is the rejection of the proportional hazards model. The findings of Berkovec and Stern (1989) for older men are consistent with the

Table 8.2. Job Duration Data

Study	Data	Model	Findings

Meitzen (1986)
  Male vs. female job
  exits
	United States, 1978–1980
	  EOPPE new hires
		Proportional hazards,
		  Gompertz baseline,
		  by sex
			Duration dependence: negative
			  for males; positive for females
			Hazard decreases with firm size
			  and with potential wage growth
			Hazard for females: decreases with
			  age; higher in risky jobs;
			  increases with local market
			  wage rate
			Hazard for males: no similar
			  effects
			Equal hazards rejected

Berkovic and Stern (1989)
  Job exits to retirement
  and other jobs
	United States, 1966–1983
	  NLS mature men
		Dynamic programming
		  model, with
		  individual and job
		  match random
		  components
			Education decreases and health
			  limitations and age increase
			  probabilities of retirement and
			  reduced hours
			Wage variation components: 60–
			  70 percent individual, about 25
			  percent match

Gronberg and Reed
  (1989)
  Nonwage job
  characteristics
	United States, 1979–1985
	  NLS New Youth
	  Cohort, white males
		Accelerated failure
		  time, generalized
		  gamma distribution
			Hazard inversely related to local
			  · unemployment, wage,
			  education, and specific training
			Proportional hazard model
			  rejected
			Nonwage job characteristics
			  irrelevant

findings of others. They find that most wage variation is due to person-specific effects; variation in match effects is next in importance. They also find that retirement at a given age is less likely for workers with more education and better health.

Wage–Tenure Relationship

Some of the studies in the first section look at wage changes with job changes. Here, we turn our attention to studies of wage growth in a single job that address issues raised by search theory. Few empirical results have attained the level of acceptance occupied by the positive coefficient for tenure in an OLS log wage regression. Indeed several theories have been advanced to explain this empirical truth. As discussed in the introduction to this chapter, specific human-capital theories explain the relationship in terms of worker investments in job-specific skills (e.g., Becker, 1962, 1964; Jovanovic, 1979a [in a matching model]; Oi, 1962; Mincer, 1958, 1962, 1974, 1986; Mortensen, 1978 [in an on-the-job search model]; Parsons, 1972; Hashimoto, 1979, 1981; Rosen, 1972, 1974). Monitoring or agency theories describe the relationship as a method designed to reduce shirking (e.g., Becker and Stigler, 1974; Lazear, 1979, 1981; Lazear and Rosen, 1981; Viscusi, 1980; Rosen, 1986, 1988). A third explanation is based on an insurance motive. Workers are guaranteed a wage equal to their expected productivity, minus an insurance premium. As productivity is revealed, relatively more productive workers leave if not compensated adequately, while less productive workers stay. Assuming all productivity information becomes common knowledge, the positive wage–tenure profile is implied (e.g., Harris and Holmstrom, 1982). Adverse-selection models describe the positive wage–tenure relationship as a device used by employers to discourage workers from applying if they are highly mobile or not likely to be productive (e.g., Salop and Salop, 1976; Nickell, 1976; Guasch and Weiss, 1981).[38]

Unfortunately, cross-sectional evidence of a positive correlation between wages and tenure need not reflect the "true" positive relationship implied by any of these models, that is, actual wage growth. As discussed in the introduction to this chapter, a positive correlation between observed wages and tenure may simply reflect job-shopping activity. Similarly, a positive correlation between wages and labor market experience may reflect search activity—as opposed to life-cycle plans for human capital investment.

In this section, we discuss recent attempts to distinguish "true" versus "spurious" dependence of the wage on tenure. Toward this end, a variety of methods and data are used to estimate log wage regressions of the form

$$\ln w_{ijt} = b_0 Z_{it} + b_1 X_{it} + b_2 T_{ijt} + e_{ijt}$$

for a worker i in job j at time t, where $t = 0$ corresponds to labor market entrance, X_{it} is labor market experience as of t, T_{ijt} denotes tenure on the job j as of t, and Z_{it} denotes observable characteristics that control for variation in the offer or match distributions faced by different workers.[39] The thrust of the arguments presented is that the error term is not orthogonal to T or X if on-the-job search and matching are important, that is, if the error term contains a match-specific component. Thus, it is argued that applying OLS to this equation produces an estimate for b_2 that is biased upward, while b_1 estimates are biased downward. Complicating matters, not all individual characteristics that influence the offer distribution faced by a worker are observable. If job mobility is systematically related to such person-specific effects (i.e., more "able" workers are either more or less mobile, on average), an additional source of bias must be considered. All of this suggests a specification for the error of the form

$$e_{ijt} = \theta_{ij} + \mu_i + \epsilon_{ijt}$$

where the components on the right refer to unobservable match-specific characteristics, person-specific characteristics, and pure noise, respectively. Ascertaining the true wage–tenure relationship requires that this structure be addressed in estimation.

We start our discussion with a review of the OLS results presented by Mincer and Jovanovic (1981). Many studies present similar results, but this study is often used as a "reference case." Thereafter, we turn to a study by Marshall and Zarkin (1987), who estimate a switching regression system for log wages of movers and stayers, with the mobility decision treated as endogenous. In the next set of studies we discuss, Topel (1986a), Abraham and Farber (1987), and Altonji and Shakotko (1987) take different approaches to fit error component models like the one previously described. Across the board, their findings suggest that earlier OLS results for the wage–tenure profile are seriously off target. That is, when these studies control for unobserved match and person-specific determinants of the wage, pure tenure effects on the wage appear negligible and general labor market experience effects appear substantial—evidence consistent with the job-shopping theories.

We close with two still more recent studies that reverse what seemed to be the new consensus. Hersch and Reagan (1990) and Topel (1988) use different methods and data—but both studies produce evidence consistent with the positive wage–tenure relationship implied by the earlier OLS studies.

Mincer and Jovanovic (1981)

Mincer and Jovanovic analyze the relationship between wages and tenure using data for males in the United States. Specifically, they work with 1971 NLS interview data for a sample of 1,442 young men (ages 19–20), 1973 NLS interview data for a sample of 982 older men (ages 52–66), and 1976 PSID interview data for a sample of 1,560 males of all ages. The regressor specifications are simple. They start with education and a quadratic in experience, then add a quadratic in tenure, (T), and then a mobility variable (either the number of prior job changes in the survey period [PSID, NLSYM] or the number of years in which job changes took place [NLSOM]), or its interaction with experience. Some interesting patterns across groups emerge. For younger men, the results for the last specification imply that each year of tenure increases wages by about $7.8–1.1T$ percent, which is certainly a nonnegligible amount. The results for the alternative model are similar. The experience effect on wages is essentially linear and about 4 percent per year. Prior mobility appears irrelevant for the young males using either measure. A very different picture appears for older men. First, additional experience has a negligible effect at this stage in a career. Second, the quadratic in tenure appears to be supported by the data when prior mobility variables are excluded, but this tenure effect is completely offset when either prior mobility term is included; the mobility coefficients are only weakly significant, though negative. Since quits and layoffs are not distinguished here, this result might reflect worker heterogeneity (in terms of a propensity to invest in specific-human capital)—or simply bad luck. The PSID sample results can be interpreted as representing experience at mid-career. These imply that an additional year of tenure increases the wage by about $2.49–0.12T$ percent, while the experience effect is about $4.04–0.14T$ percent. Here, however, both mobility variables have non-negligible negative coefficients—suggesting that workers who are highly mobile at mid-career have lower wages and face flatter earnings profiles. As expected, the tenure coefficients are reduced when the mobility terms are included.[40]

Marshall and Zarkin (1987)

Marshall and Zarkin criticize OLS log wage regressions from a simple matching point of view. They model the employer as making an offer to the worker in each period for the next period wage. If the offer exceeds the worker's reservation wage, then the offer is the observed wage in the next period. Otherwise, the worker is observed in a new match and the offer from the previous employer is never observed, that is, the wage offer data are censored.

On this basis, Marshall and Zarkin specify a model for the joint determination of wages offered by firms and the mobility decision. The log wage offer for period t is specified as a function of worker characteristics in period $t − 1$ (education, a quadratic in experience at $t − 1$, and the number of interfirm moves between school and $t − 1$) and a quadratic in tenure at time t, where the lag accounts for the timing between offers and receipt of wages. The log reservation wage is specified as a function of these variables and search and mobility costs in $t − 1$ (the local unemployment rate, number of dependents, marital status, and spouse's income). The errors in these equations are assumed jointly normally distributed and this leads directly to a first-stage probit specification for the mobility decision. These results are then used to calculate selectivity correction terms that are included in second-stage offer equations for stayers and new hires. The latter are estimated using the method of maximum likelihood.

The model is fit using data for a sample of 1,522 young males collected in the National Longitudinal Survey of Young Men (aged 14–24 in 1966) for the years 1970 and 1971. The sample is restricted to workers who were employed in both years, not enrolled in school full-time, and had no missing data. Observations for 1971 are used for the wage and tenure variables and 1970 data are used for the remaining variables.

Marshall and Zarkin find that the probability of a separation decreases with tenure at a decreasing rate, decreases with education, and increases with prior mobility. The quit probability is also significantly lower for married workers, but (in contrast to the results presented by Shaw, for example) the level of a wife's income has a negligible effect after controlling for marital status.

The second-stage wage results attribute all wage growth to experience. The coefficient for tenure is actually negative, though very imprecise, while the experience effect is just about linear and implies an increase in wages of about 3.7–3.8 percent per year for both new job and current job offers. The results for prior mobility are a bit surprising. New job offers are not affected, but offers on the current job are increased significantly. The coefficients for the selectivity terms are large and positive—suggesting that behavior is consistent with income-maximizing search. The results also imply that reservation wages and offer wages are highly correlated and that the variance of log reservation wages (1.74) significantly exceeds the variance of offers (0.16) (as found by Kiefer and Neumann [1979a,b] in their study of unemployed search).[41]

Marshall and Zarkin calculate mean log wage offers on the current job and mean accepted wages; the period zero estimates here refer to new jobs. These estimates imply that the mean offer to workers with 1 year of tenure is about 31 percent higher than the mean wage they accept in period zero, which is about 25 percent higher than the initial mean offers. After 1 year on the job, however, job offers do not grow in any systematic way; they are just about constant.[42]

Topel (1986a)

Topel takes an approach to studying the wage–tenure relationship that extends the work of Marshall and Zarkin. Topel studies the observed wages of both movers and stayers, with the effects of the mobility decision incorporated into the specifications for both—but he departs from the Marshall and Zarkin model in that he incorporates individual-specific terms into his specification for the offer distribution. Specifically, his model consists of three equations. The first is a new job offer equation,

$$\ln w_t^* = A(X_t) + \theta + \mu$$

where X refers to experience and θ and μ are match-specific and person-specific components, respectively. The second equation is for the wage on the current job,

$$\ln w_t = \ln w_{t-1} + B(X_t, T_t) + \epsilon_t$$

where T refers to tenure and ϵ_t is white noise. The third is a reservation wage for new jobs,

$$\ln w_t^r = \ln w_t + C(X_t, T_t)$$

where the C function denotes costs of moving, given current labor market experience and tenure. (Any lags between offers and observed wages are ignored here and at the empirical stage.) Assuming that ϵ_t and θ have a bivariate normal distribution, a probit model for the mobility decision based on the offer and reservation wage models follows directly. However, it is complicated in this case by the presence of the individual effect μ. A move is optimal if

$$\theta - \epsilon > \ln w_{t-1} + B(X, T) - A(X) + C(X, T) - \mu$$

Topel treats these μ terms as fixed effects and estimates them directly—assuming that the length of his panel is long enough. Using the results from this first stage probit, corrections for the mobility decision are calculated directly for both movers and stayers. The parameters of the current wage equation—the experience and tenure effects, in particular—are obtained simply from change-in-log-wage regressions for stayers. The offer wage parameters are also identified under the assumption that the arrival rate of new job offers is exactly one per period (set equal to a quarter here).

Topel fits his model using data taken from the Longitudinal Employee–Employer Data (LEED) file for the period 1957–1972. These data have several attractive features. In particular, the data provide quarterly observations on social security earnings and job-changing activities of new entrants to the labor force. Therefore, neither jobs spells nor careers are left censored. Topel restricts his sample to white males, aged 18 or less in 1957, who were observed for at least 52 quarters after entering the panel, worked full time at least 75 percent of that time, and had no spell of joblessness of 8 quarters or more. Labor market experience is measured as starting at one's eighteenth birthday or the start of the first job thereafter. The major constraint of these data is the limited demographic data; only age, race, and sex are observed. On the other hand, firm size, industry, and location data for the firm are available. The current employer for each worker is defined as the major contributor to the worker's social security fund. Overall, the sample consists of 600 match observations.

Focusing first on the exit probability, Topel fits the probit model separately for job-to-job changers and all exits—with and without the quarterly wage. The additional explanatory variables are a quadratic in experience, an interaction of experience with tenure after 1 year, and dummy variables for tenure less than a year, first job, a gap in employment, and firm size. Conditioning on the wage reduces the estimated effect experience. Without conditioning on the wage, a small negative experience effect appears when quit destinations are treated alike, but this disappears on conditioning. On the other hand, the estimated effect of experience on the probability of a job-to-job transition is positive and significant, with and without conditioning on the wage, and the magnitude increases substantially with conditioning. All results suggest that exit rates decline significantly over the first year on the job, but there is no evidence of a significant tenure effect thereafter. Both the conditional and unconditional exit rates appear higher on first jobs in a career and in smaller firms; conditioning on the wage reduces the magnitude of these effects, but only slightly. Finally, given tenure and experience, the exit probability decreases sharply with increases in the current wage.

Turning to the second-stage wage results, Topel finds that the combined effect of experience and tenure on wages in the current job is about 5.1 percent per quarter—but the net effect of tenure alone is essentially zero. On the other hand, the estimated effect of experience on (new job) offers is about 6.2 percent. Overall, the results imply that substantial sorting among workers occurs, that is, the movers receive better outside offers.

Abraham and Farber (1987)

Abraham and Farber use two simple approaches to examine the extent of true versus spurious wage growth with tenure. Both approaches are based on the argument that if "good matches last" because of job-specific or person-specific factors, then controlling for the completed length of a match should eliminate the bias in the estimated tenure effect. Their first approach is simply to use the deviation of actual tenure from completed tenure as an instrument for tenure. The second approach is to directly include completed tenure on a job.

Their data are for male household heads, aged 18–60, collected in the Panel Study of Income Dynamics (PSID) for the years 1968–1981. They restrict their sample to members of the random subsample of the PSID who were living in the Continental United States and were neither retired nor self-employed. Their unit of observation is a job match and they exclude all union, government, clerical, and sales jobs. Overall, they have observations on 985 white-collar matches (professional, managerial, and technical) for 706 workers and 1,417 blue-collar matches for 831 workers. Throughout their analysis, they work with these samples separately. Although the length of the observation period makes these data attractive for the purpose at hand, there is one serious problem—tenure is not well measured. For the early years of the sample period, tenures are reported only in broad interval form and Abraham and Farber therefore use a substantial amount of smoothing. Also, completed match durations are observed for only 40 percent of the blue-collar matches and 55 percent of the white-collar matches. Estimation of the wage equations thus requires that an instrument be used for completed tenure in all remaining cases.

Abraham and Farber calculate tenure instruments using results for a Weibull proportional hazards model fit separately for the white-collar and blue-collar samples. With the baseline defined as $\lambda_0(t) = \alpha t^{\alpha-1}$ the estimates for α are quite close across samples and imply strong, negative duration dependence in the job exit rate (0.38 [standard error 0.028] for white-collar matches and 0.394 [standard error 0.017] for blue-collar matches). The results from this stage also suggest that more educated workers and married workers have longer matches and that differences between white and nonwhite workers are negligible. One interesting result is that additional prejob labor market experience has only a negligible effect on lengths of white-collar matches, but a large, positive and significant effect on the length of blue-collar matches. Wages are not included. When using these results to calculate predicted tenures, Abraham and Farber condition on observed job duration and an assumption that all workers retire at age 65. Results are not reported, but all regressions include controls for education, race, marital status, disability, occupation, industry, region, and year of observation.

The second-stage log wage results have essentially the same implications across the alternative approaches. For white-collar workers, the estimated return to tenure is about 0.5 percent per year; for blue-collar workers, there is no statistically significant effect at standard levels. On the other hand, Abraham and Farber do find that earnings increase by about 2 to 3 percent in white-collar matches with each additional year of labor market experience, and by about 1 to 2 percent in blue-collar matches. They also find that longer matches are substantially better paying matches from the start—as implied by simple quit and matching models. Abraham and Farber use a variety of methods to check the sensitivity of their results to the use of predicted values for completed duration and to the potential measurement error in the tenure data. In all cases, they find essentially the same results.

Altonji and Shakotko (1987)

Altonji and Shakotko also take an instrumental variables approach to control for the endogeneity of tenure in the log wage regression, but they use a different instrument. Specifically, they use the deviations of tenure and tenure squared from their respective sample means for each match. By construction, these variables are uncorrelated with fixed person- and match-specific components of the error term, but there are potential problems with these instruments, which Altonji and Shakotko describe. First experience may be correlated with the match-specific term, in which case the coefficient for experience will be biased upward and the tenure effects will be biased downward. Second, if the transitory term is serially correlated (say due to a firm-specific change in technology or demand), then the tenure deviations will be correlated with this term.

An additional problem with using the deviations as instruments arises from measurement error in the tenure data. Like Abraham and Farber, Altonji and Shakotko work with data collected in the PSID for 1968–1981. Their sample differs, however, in that it is not restricted to the random subsample of the PSID, nor to nonunion jobs, but it is restricted to white workers. Overall, there are 15,138 wage observations for 2,163 individuals in 4,334 job matches. Altonji and Shakotko also take a different approach to dealing with the interval tenure data for the early years of the sample period. Specifically, they use interval midpoints for changes within intervals. The problem with using the deviations as instruments is that they serve to magnify the measurement error associated with these interval observations. Altonji and Shakotko also note that there is ambiguity in the question about job changes; in some years, the question refers to an employer change (which is what they want), while in others it refers to a change in position (which might not involve an employer change).

An additional issue associated with using the deviations as instruments is that the person-specific and match-specific components left in the error term are definitely serially correlated; GLS applied to the instrumental variable model is thus relatively efficient and they use it. In addition to the tenure deviations variables, Altonji and Shakotko report results for a quadratic in education, a cubic in experience, a dummy variable for jobs in progress more than a year, and an interaction of experience with education; marital status, union membership, health status, city size, SMSA residence, and region are also included, but results are not reported.

A lot of results are reported—OLS, GLS, IV, IV-GLS, and others (as checks on the potential biases discussed). The bottom line is that all of the instrumental variables results suggest a negligible tenure effect and a large experience effect. Specifically, using the model described, they find that the first 10 years of tenure result in a wage increase of about 2.7 percent, while the 10 years of general labor market experience accumulated during this period raises the wage by 53.7 percent. Upon investigation, they find empirical evidence that this estimate is most likely biased downward. Their "preferred" estimate of the 10 year tenure effect is 6.6 percent, with 5 percent being in the first year alone—after allowing for biases due to job shopping over the course of a career (i.e., correlation between the match component and experience).

Topel (1988)

In this study, Topel presents evidence of a nonnegligible tenure effect on earnings—in contrast with the recent work previously discussed (including his own). Specifically, he presents estimates of an upper bound for the experience effect on wages of 6.2–6.6 percent per year initially (that declines eventually) and lower bounds for the tenure effects on wages of 10.7–13.3 percent in the first year and an additional 16.5–19 percent increase over the next 10 years.

His route to obtaining these estimates is a straightforward two-step procedure. The first step is simply estimation of a first-difference wage equation. This yields an estimate of the combined effect of a 1 year increment to both tenure and experience with an additional year on a given job, which is consistent under an assumption that unobserved job quality follows a random walk (i.e., $E(\theta_{ijt}) = \theta_{ijt-1}$). Topel also considers the case of fixed match components ($\theta_{ijt} = \theta_{ij}$). In this case, deviations from the match sample means provide a more efficient first-stage estimator, although if the true process is a random walk, the deviations estimator is inconsistent. His data suggest that wages follow a random walk with drift, but for completeness he reports both sets of results. The second step of his procedure is simply a regression of the form

$$\ln w_t - Z\Gamma = X_0\beta_x + \epsilon_t$$

where $Z\Gamma$ denotes the first-stage estimate of the combined experience and tenure effect on wage growth within the match, including higher order terms, and X_0 denotes experience on entering the match. Topel recognizes that OLS estimates of the experience coefficient in this equation may be subject to selectivity bias due to search and matching activity over the course of one's career. As opposed to correcting for this by modeling the mobility decision explicitly, Topel notes the bias here and focuses on its sign. Basically, unless the effects of job-changing decisions on wage growth and match durations are negligible, the estimate must be biased upward and thus it can be interpreted as an upper bound for the effect of experience on wage growth. Letting B denote the first round estimate of the combined experience and tenure effect on wages and letting β_x^* denote the second step experience estimates, it follows that

$$\beta_t^* = B - \beta_x^*$$

can be interpreted as an estimate of the lower bound for the tenure effect.

Topel fits the model using the data for white males, aged 18–60, collected in the first 14 interviews (1968–1981) of the Panel Study of Income Dynamics (PSID). His sample is restricted to members of the random subsample of the PSID in the Continental United States, who were neither self-employed nor employed in agriculture or government. Overall, there are 3,082 match observations for 1,502 individuals. Average hourly earnings are deflated by a white male wage index calculated from CPS files that net out real aggregate wage growth and price level changes. Wages are thus measured in uniform units. Topel deals with the tenure data problems in the PSID in a fairly straightforward manner. For spells in progress at the first interview, initial tenure is determined from the maximum reported for the job and it is incremented by 1 year in each year between. Topel notes that this leaves many ambiguities, such as negative changes in reported tenure with no reported employer change. Topel deletes these inconsistent observations (3,931 out of 16,000) and reports that this has minor effects on his results. All regressions include controls for education, race, marital status, disability, occupation, industry, region, and year of observation. Additional explanatory variables included in the second-stage regressions are SMSA residence, and a dummy variable for union membership. For both tenure and experience, a cubic is used, with a separate first year tenure effect allowed. These appear to be supported by the data.

The estimates obtained for the first difference and deviations specifications differ only slightly. (The first difference tenure estimates are the larger of the two reported.) Moreover, they are quite close to the "naive" OLS estimates for the effects of experience (linear term 4.8 percent) and tenure (17 percent in the first year and 22 percent over the next 10 years).

Given that his findings are at odds with other recent findings for the same data source, Topel explores the sources of the contrast.

Focusing first on the work by Altonji and Shakotko, he notes that part of the difference may be due to their use of deviations as an instrument for tenure. As noted, the coefficient estimate for tenure (experience) will be biased downward (upward) if the match component of wages follows a random walk, as opposed to being a fixed effect. This bias is identified empirically, however, and (at least in the sample analyzed here) it is small. Instead, the major source of the difference in the findings seems to be the different methods used to deal with measurement error in the tenure data. Topel notes that when he carries out estimation using midpoints of reported intervals (following Altonji and Shakotko), he also finds a negligible tenure effect.

Topel next considers the Abraham and Farber results. Here, the difference is attributed to method. Recall that Abraham and Farber use an estimate of completed duration of a match as an instrument for unobservable match and person-specific terms in a log wage regression. The problem with this approach is not the use of the completed tenure variable as a proxy. Instead, Topel argues that their estimate for wage growth within a match is biased downward because their approach requires a much longer panel, that is, complete labor market histories. As it stands, their approach does not account for the potential correlation between mean tenure for observed jobs and error terms, as implied by job shopping. More precisely, the coefficient for mean observed years in a job and deviations from the mean are effectively restricted to be the same. (They are not measured separately.) If the coefficient for mean tenure is inconsistent, as job shopping implies, the estimator for wage growth is inconsistent. Topel presents results for the Abraham and Farber model that support his claim.

Topel also examines variation in wage–tenure profiles across occupations. Specifically, he fits his model separately for workers in three broad categories: professional and service, union blue-collar, and nonunion blue-collar. As in the full sample, wage growth appears to follow a random walk in each category. (A notable feature of the covariance estimates is a much smaller wage variance for union workers.) The findings for experience are about the same across groups, but the findings for the wage–tenure profile are quite different. The path followed by white-collar wages is essentially the same as the full sample path. The nonunion blue-collar wage path differs somewhat; it is slightly steeper and there is no major first year effect. The union profile is most striking. The first year tenure effect is a 19.7 percent increase in wages, while the annual tenure effect is not significantly different from zero thereafter.

Hersch and Reagan (1990)

Hersch and Reagan take a very different approach to studying the wage–tenure relationship. Specifically, they exploit a matched sample of workers and firms to estimate a two-equation model for wages and tenure. Their results are consistent with those of Topel (1988). They find that wages increase by about 50 percent in the first 10 years on a job—suggesting that Topel's lower bound is a very conservative lower bound for the population sampled here.

The data were collected by Hersch and Reagan in the Eugene, Oregon SMSA. The employer sample consists of 12 manufacturing firms, 5 warehouses, and a large commercial laundry firm in the Eugene area, each with 40 or more employees, that were willing to participate in the study (50 percent of those invited). The employee sample consists of all workers at these firms who were willing to complete anonymous questionnaires during lunch hour or a coffee break (for $5). In the present study, the employee sample is restricted to 307 full-time, blue-collar, male workers (mean age 39.94).

Hersch and Reagan use these data to fit a model of the form:

$$\ln W_{ijt} = a_1 T_{ijt} + a_2 X_{it} + a_3 Y_{ijt} + a_4 M_{ij} + U_{ijt}$$
$$T_{ijt} = \quad\ b_1 W_{ijt} + b_2 Age_{it} + b_3 Z_{ijt} + b_4 M_{ij} + V_{ijt}$$

where T, W, and X are tenure, the current wage, and experience (as above). Age, tenure, and experience are all entered as quadratics. M_{ij} denotes observable match quality variables—a dummy variable that indicates whether a worker is likely to make a serious effort to find a job in the next year and a job satisfaction variable (on a scale of 0 to 10). Y_{ijt} and Z_{ijt} denote firm, job, and worker characteristics that affect wages and tenure, respectively. Both Y and Z include education, race, marital status, union membership (for an individual), years of (company-provided) on-the-job training, number of employees at the firm, and percentage of the work force laid off in the previous year. The wage equation also includes a dummy variable for disability, an occupation dummy variable ("craftsman, foreman, operative or kindred worker" versus other), and a dummy variable that indicates previous work experience that was useful for getting or doing the current job. The tenure equation includes capacity utilization of the firm over the current year, the percentage of the work force that is part-time, and the percentage of the work force that is seasonal. The bases of these restrictions are assumptions that firms respond to shocks by adjusting employment but not wages, and that individual characteristics, human capital, and job characteristics affect wages but not tenure. Given that the error terms are likely to be correlated, Hersh and Reagan use three-stage least squares to estimate the model. For reference, they also report the OLS results.

The linear tenure equations have no straightforward interpretation and the identifying restrictions might be viewed as ad hoc. Nevertheless, the results are quite interesting. As noted, the wage equation results imply a concave and relatively steep tenure profile; the estimated effect is $5.9 - 0.26T$ percent per year. This linear term is relatively large, which may reflect a smoothing of the first year effect found in other studies. The more striking results are for the experience coefficients in the wage equation. Although having "useful" previous experience increases the wage level by about 5.5 percent, years of labor market experience have a negligible effect. Moreover, this general experience result is insensitive to controlling for useful experience but it is sensitive to allowing for correlation in equation errors. The OLS results imply a large, significant annual experience effect on wages. This is the only variable for which the implications actually differ qualitatively across methods. The education coefficient in the wage equation is large and significant, but on-the-job training appears irrelevant here and both appear irrelevant in the tenure equation. The union and occupation coefficients in the wage equation are positive and large, while the effect of union membership on tenure is negative but imprecise. Age has a significant effect on tenure; tenure appears to decrease through age 29 and then increase. There are no significant differences in either wages or tenure between white and nonwhite workers in this sample. Similarly, married workers and single workers have similar tenures in this sample, although the former do earn significantly higher wages. Consistent with theory, tenure increases significantly with the wage. Of course, the variables of key interest here are the match and firm characteristics. The capacity utilization variable has its expected positive sign and it is significant at standard levels. Surprisingly, tenure appears to be longer at smaller firms in this sample, while the other work force composition and layoff variables appear to have no significant effect on tenure. The coefficients for the likelihood of search variable suggest that wages are significantly lower among searchers, but tenure is neither longer nor shorter. In both equations, job satisfaction (given search intentions) appears irrelevant. As far as the role of these variables as proxies for match quality is concerned, their omission produces a slight increase in the tenure coefficient. Hersch and Reagan recognize that unobserved firm effects may induce a spurious correlation between wages and tenure and reestimate their model with firm fixed effects in both equations. Though 13 of the 17 firm dummy variables in the wage equation and 7 in the tenure equation have coefficients that are significant at the 5 percent level, none of the results described is affected qualitatively. In particular, although the tenure coefficients are reduced in magnitude, they remain large.

Summary

Do wages rise with job tenure? The results from recent studies—summarized in Table 8.3—suggest that some part of wage growth in a match can be attributed to a pure tenure effect, but there is no consensus on what proportion this represents. The findings have gone full circle and beyond—the *most* recent results suggest that early OLS results attributed too small a share of wage growth to tenure and too much to labor market experience.

One thing that is clear from this section is that future work on this question will require better data. The problems with the tenure data in the PSID make any results from its analysis suspect. As discussed, Topel (1988) attributes most of the difference between his results and those of Altonji and Shakotko (1987) to the use of alternative methods to clean up the tenure data. Of course, representative matched samples of employers and employees in the United States and elsewhere would be very desirable. The analysis by Hersch and Reagan (1990) just hints at what might be found.

All of the studies reviewed here attempt to control for match and individual fixed effects in the error terms and then attribute remaining within-job wage growth to on-the-job human capital accumulation or alternative explanations. A few recent studies take what can be described as the opposite approach to explaining wage–tenure profiles; that is, they attempt to test the on-the-job training hypothesis against all alternatives. Brown (1989), for example, studies the relationship between "direct evidence" on training available for household heads interviewed in the 1976 interviews of the PSID and subsequent within-job wage growth for these workers. After fitting a wide variety of wage growth regressions, Brown concludes that observed wage growth can be attributed to training, as opposed to alternative explanations. Given the problems in the PSID tenure data and the fact that he does not control for the potential endogeneity of job exits, this

Table 8.3. The Wage–Tenure Relationship

Study	Data	Method	Findings
Mincer and Jovanovic (1981)	United States, 1970s NLS young men, 1971	OLS log wage regressions	Wage growth effects: tenure $(7.8 - 1.1T)$ percent/year; experience $(4 - 0.27T)$ percent/year
	NLS mature men, 1973 PSID (all ages), 1976		No growth Tenure $(2.49 - 0.12T)$ percent/year; experience $(4 - 0.14T)$/year
Marshal and Zarkin (1987)	United States, 1971 NLS young men	Regression model for log wage offer of movers and stayers, with endogenous mobility decision probit	Wage growth effects: tenure negligible Experience: 3.7–3.8 percent/year increase in current wage and new job offers Calculated wage offer growth: 31 percent first year, negligible increases thereafter Movers receive high new job offers
Topel (1986a)	United States, 1957–1972 LEED young white men	Regression model for log wages of movers and stayers, with endogenous mobility decision probit with person-specific fixed effects	Probit results: given the wage, quit probability decreases over first year of tenure, but no further decline with tenure; given tenure, quit probability decreases with wage Wage results: tenure negligible Experience: current job 5.1 percent/quarter; new job 6.2 percent/quarter Movers get better new job offers
Abraham and Farber (1987)	United States, 1968–1981 PSID nonunion male household heads	Nonunion log wage regression, with completed tenure estimate used as instrument for unobserved match/person effect, by white-collar/blue-collar workers Weibull $(\alpha t^{\alpha-1})$ hazard function for employment durations, by white-collar/blue-collar workers	Wage growth results: white-collar: tenure 0.5 percent/year; experience 2–3 percent/year; blue-collar: tenure negligible; experience 1–2 percent/year Negative duration dependence: white-collar: $\alpha = 0.38$ (S.E. 0.03); blue-collar: $\alpha = 0.39$ (S.E. 0.02)
Altonji and Shakotko (1987)	United States, 1968–1981 PSID white male household heads	Log wage regression, with deviations of tenure variables as instruments	Wage growth results: tenure 2.7 percent/10 years; experience 53.7 percent/10 years; after allowing for shopping effects: tenure 5 percent/first year, 6.6 percent first 10 years
Topel (1988)	United States, 1967–1971 PSID white male household heads	Two-step procedure to obtain "bounds": (1) log wage difference regression; (2) log wage regression Same model, fit separately for white-collar, nonunion blue-collar, union blue-collar workers	Wage growth results: tenure ("Lower bound") 10.7–13.3 percent/first year; experience ("Upper bound") 6.2–6.6 percent/year Experience bound approximately the same "Tenure bounds": white-collar approximately the same; nonunion blue-collar 5.1 percent/first year, 24.9 percent/next 10 years; union 19.7 percent/first year, 7.6 percent/next 10 years
Hersh and Reagan (1990)	United States, 1986 matched employer-employee data set, Eugene, Oregon, blue-collar males	Two-equation model for wages and tenure	Wage growth results: tenure $(5.9 - 0.26T)$ percent/year Experience negligible Tenure increases with wage, convex in age (minimum at 29)

S.E. = standard error.

conclusion is perhaps best interpreted as tentative. The quality of the training data in the PSID and elsewhere is also subject to debate. After analyzing direct observations on training for young males in the 1979 NLS New Youth Cohort, Parsons (1989) concludes that we are basically in the dark insofar as the training effect on wages is concerned—and we will remain there until better data are collected. Brown's approach and findings are nevertheless suggestive. If better direct evidence does become available, attempting to test the shopping and training hypotheses jointly might be a useful objective.

Finally, the work reviewed here focuses on males in the United States (and white males exclusively in some cases). Corcoran and Duncan (1979) examine the effects of life-cycle labor force attachment on observed cross-section wage differences by race and gender using observations on time spent in and out of the labor force and the PSID training data studied by Brown (1989). They find that variation in patterns of withdrawal from the labor market explains little of observed wage variation, but differences in time devoted to on-the-job training explain a substantial amount. These results are obviously subject to the measurement error problems previously discussed. Still, along with the findings reviewed in previous sections of this chapter, they suggest that expanding the scope of future analysis to consider demographic variation in the wage–tenure relationship might yield some interesting findings.

What have we learned about the process that produces employer–employee separations? Direct evidence shows that search by employed workers is less likely when wages are above average, given tenure, and for older workers. Essentially the same effects are found for quits (as expected). There is a nonnegligible amount of job-changing to lower wages, but potential problems with selectivity and with the definitions of wages and quits must be addressed before search or matching models can be rejected on the basis of this observation.

Some surprising results emerge from the studies of job duration data. In particular, although Meitzen (1986) finds a decreasing hazard for males, he finds an increasing hazard for females. This finding for females is not consistent with the quit rate studies of the first section, nor is it consistent with the results from employment duration studies discussed in Chapter 6. It may reflect the restriction to short job spells imposed by the length of the sample period, combined with the specification of a monotonic baseline hazard. Future analyses might investigate nonmonotonicity. A second, related result in this section is the rejection of the proportional hazards model by Gronberg and Reed (1989).

The basic statistical relationship between wages and tenure holds up in a variety of data sets. The economic interpretation of the partial correlation and the economic role of tenure are completely open. This is currently an active area of research—although a breakthrough is likely to come from looking at new or different data.

More complex search and matching models of labor market mobility within careers are available. These models may prove fruitful in analysis of occupational change over the life-cycle, which available evidence suggests is substantial (e.g, Shaw, 1987). For example, Miller (1984) extends the simple matching framework by incorporating distinct categories of jobs. Specifically, workers are modeled as facing different job types, where two jobs are categorized as the same if the worker's prior beliefs about them are identical. Using the theory of multiarmed bandit processes, Miller investigates both the optimal order to sample jobs within and across categories and the optimal duration for each job. To support his theory, Miller presents data on occupational change which suggest that career paths are (at least roughly) consistent with the rational planning implied by his model. McCall (1990) offers an extension of Miller's model. In McCall's model, initial wages in all jobs are known and identical within each occupation, but wages in a match change over time and the information that arrives has additive occupation-specific and job-specific components. The key implication of the model is that the quit rate for a current job will decrease with previous tenure for those who do not switch occupations between jobs—if occupational matching is important. Using data for the NLS New Youth Cohort and both parametric and nonparametric hazard function specifications, McCall finds evidence that supports this hypothesis. Ingram (1990) takes a route to explaining career paths that cover more than one job type which is somewhat less conventional. In the simplest version of her model, job attributes are known at the time of match formation, but preferences over job attributes are not. That is, a worker does not know his or her suitability for each job. Through experience on a job of a particular type, preferences over attributes are learned and preferences over all job types are updated accordingly.

Search activity associated with sectoral transitions represents another mobility topic that is essentially open. Sectoral shift theories of unemployment are based on the straightforward idea that, following shocks to one or more sectors of the economy, workers will reallocate themselves until cross-sectoral wage differentials are eliminated. On this basis, it is argued that a significant part of measured unemployment represents time-consuming movement between sectors in response to shocks. Lucas and Prescott (1974), for example, assume independent and identically distributed shocks across time and sectors of the economy and this leads to a "natural rate" of unemployment. Lilien (1982) and others argue that cyclical fluctuations in the unemployment rate are due to variation in the variance of sectoral shocks over time, which in turn implies movement in the natural rate. The latter formulation is generally referred to as "the sectoral shift hypothesis." (See Hall [1970] and Hall and Lilien [1986], for example, for additional discussion of the basic ideas, and Davis [1985, 1987] for an extension. These theories can also be linked with the basic on-the-job search and matching models. For this, see Bull and Jovanovic [1987, 1988] and Jovanovic [1987].)

There have been numerous attempts to determine the potential of the sectoral shift hypothesis for explaining the secular rise in the unemployment rate in the United States in the 1970s and early 1980s. The most common approach has been to study movements in pairs of industry level aggregates such as wage levels, employment levels, and vacancy rates, but there appears to be no consensus on the appropriate pair of aggregates or whether this approach will yield any insights at all (e.g., Davis, 1985, 1987; Riordan and Staiger, 1987; Smith, 1990). Recent studies of unemployment incidence and sectoral shifts arrive at opposite conclusions on the relevance of sectoral shocks. Murphy and Topel (1987), for example, study data from the March CPS for 1968 through 1985 and find little evidence of cyclical fluctuations in the incidence of unemployment among industry changers. They instead find that unemployment incidence among stayers fluctuates, which might be interpreted as evidence against the sectoral shift hypotheses. On the other hand, Loungani et al. (1989) present incidence tabulations from the PSID which suggest that the Murphy and Topel results follow from the CPS restriction to observation periods of at most 15 months for individual workers and perhaps from their industry definitions. Their results support the hypothesis. Given the motivation and search-theoretic basis for the sectoral shift hypothesis, one surprising aspect of this literature is the tendency to neglect the search activity of workers who move between sectors in response to shocks.[43] Loungani et al. (1989) present some tabulations and regression results for unemployment duration data from the PSID and these suggest that differences in spell lengths between industry changers and stayers were important in determining relative group contributions to aggregate unemployment during the period in question. This, however, appears to be the only analysis of microlevel duration data in light of the hypothesis. Additional analysis could prove fruitful.

Notes

1. Mattila (1974), for example, provides estimates in the range 50–60 percent for the United States. For the complete text of Tobin's speech, see Tobin (1972).

2. Our discussion here is based on the on-the-job search model of Burdett (1978), generalized to allow choice of search intensity by Burdett and Mortensen (1978), and the matching model of Jovanovic (1979a,b). Johnson (1978) presents a simpler job-shopping model that yields similar implications. Additional results on matching are given in Crawford and Knoer (1981), Dagsvik et al. (1985), Deere (1987), Harris and Weiss (1984), Lippman and McCall (1981), McCall (1988, 1990), Pitts (1986), and Wilson (1980).

3. A martingale is a stochastic process $\{X_t\}$ with the property
$$E_t[X_{t+1} | X_t, X_{t-1}, \ldots, X_0] = X_t.$$

4. Frameworks that nest the hypotheses are also presented by Jovanovic (1984a), Topel (1986a), and Mortensen and Neumann (1988). Stationary on-the-job search models that incorporate moving costs are presented by Hey and McKenna (1979), Holmlund (1984), Holmlund and Lang (1985), Burgess (1988), and van den Berg (1989). The implications of the models sketched here generally hold up, unless the moving costs are a nonconstant function of the current wage; in this case, an optimal policy may not be well-defined (see van den Berg, 1989). Hughes and McCormick (1985), for example, examine evidence for workers in the United Kingdom and their findings suggest that moving costs may be quite important in determining who searches on the job. Moving costs become crucial in the search approach to migration. This is a well-established empirical area including Bartel (1979), Farber (1983), Fields and Hosek (1977), Fields (1990), Goss and Schoening (1984), Harris and Todaro (1970), Herzog et al. (1985), Herzog and Schlottman (1983), McCall and McCall (1987), and Todaro (1969).

5. A submartingale is a stochastic process $\{X_t\}$ such that
$$E_t[X_{t+1} | X_t, X_{t-1}, \ldots, X_0] \geq X_t.$$

6. We restrict our attention to studies of microdata. These microlevel studies were preceded by a fairly large number of analyses of aggregative turnover data (i.e., cross-sectional and time-series data at the state and industry level), for example, Pencavel (1972), Hall (1972), Parsons (1973), Mattila (1974), and Barron and McCafferty (1977). In short, these studies found that a large share of job changing does not involve intervening unemployment, higher wages are associated with lower quit probabilities, high mobility costs (e.g., pension losses) are associated with lower quit probabilities, and quit rates tend to decline with tenure. Parsons (1977) presents a survey of this early economics literature. A recent (and somewhat unusual) survey of the management literature on turnover is provided by Cotton and Tuttle (1986). The findings are essentially the same as those reported in the economics literature.

7. This incentive variable is calculated using 1971 wage data (to avoid the effects of successful search). The regression results used to calculate the predicted wage are not reported but are described as consistent with results reported by others, with $R^2 = 0.36$. The explanatory variables are a quadratic in age, education, an index of verbal ability, farm background, veteran status, father's education and occupation, city size, local labor market conditions, and interactions of all variables with race.

The current wage in the denominator is entered as a proxy for the marginal cost of search, and the numerator is used as a proxy for the deviation of the mean of the acceptable wage distribution from the worker's acceptance (i.e., current reservation) wage. Black notes that a referee pointed out that the predicted wage is not computed from a distribution truncated at the worker's acceptance wage and that it should be interpreted as the mean of the entire wage offer distribution. Although the former point may be correct, note that the latter interpretation is clearly incorrect. All observed wages are observations on accepted wage distributions.

8. Altonji and Paxon (1988) examine data from the PSID and find that annual hours changes for job changers are 2 to 4 times larger than hours changes for those who do not change jobs. This is consistent with Black's speculation.

9. Note that the parts of the wage equation errors that influence a worker's choice of search mode must be known to the worker (although not the econometrician) and therefore enter the worker's expectation of the wage.

10. This approach is described in Maddala (1983), chapter 8.

11. Differentials calculated using unreported OLS results with and without the selectivity correction terms are also reported. The OLS selectivity corrected estimates are slightly larger than the GLS estimates, but the pattern is the same. In contrast, the simple OLS differentials are large and negative.

12. Blau and Kahn (1983) study the relationship between job search and union–nonunion status. Their hypothesis is the following: If the distribution of union wages is centered above the distribution of nonunion wages, then workers with high income net of search costs and therefore higher reservation wages should be the workers who end up in union jobs (controlling for relative costs of generating an offer from the alternative distributions and maintaining the structure of the basic search model otherwise). To test this hypothesis, they use the NLS job-changer data analyzed here and again fit a Lee (1978) model. The choice rule in this case is based on the relative net benefits of taking a union job, which they specify as depending on supply-side determinants of the reservation wage. Observed weeks of unemployment is included in the third-stage probit but not the first probit and its estimated coefficient is negative and significant. Despite concerns about endogeneity and potential model misspecificiation, this result suggests that the probability of obtaining a union job tends to decrease as a spell continues.

13. See Maddala (1983) for a discussion of the ordered logit model.

14. A wage incentive variable constructed using $\ln W_{71}$ is introduced in the third specification, so Black fits all regressions with $\ln W_{71}$ on the right-hand side of the equation for ease of comparison.

15. Black reports that 14 percent of all white workers and 10.4 percent of all black workers in this sample engaged in on-the-job search—much higher percentages than reported in Black (1981). Black also reports that 41 percent of all white quitters and 20 percent of all black quitters reported on-the-job search, while 20 percent of all white searchers and 14 percent of all black searchers quit.

16. The exclusion of those with less than 500 hours employment may be interpreted as an unemployment control. However, this restriction allows unemployment spells of up to three-fourths of 1973.

17. Black notes that unreported results for regressions fit separately for white and black workers indicate significant racial difference for the quit and quit/wage gap interaction variables. For black workers, neither variable has a significant coefficient. For whites, the quit variable has a large negative coefficient, but the wage gap interaction term has a significant positive coefficient, that is, underpaid white workers may gain. However, the wage gap must be on the order of 150 percent, that is, more than substantial.

18. The predicted wage is based on results from a regression for each sex that includes age, industry injury rates, marital status, health impairment, union membership, tenure, education and a quadratic in age.

19. Results are also reported for the wage specification for subsamples of full-time workers under 65 (3,075 males and 2,233 females, respectively). On average, these subsamples are not very different for either sex and the logit results are essentially the same as those described in the text.

20. Note that the male sample is drawn from the same source as the sample analyzed by Viscusi.

21. Shaw notes that the upper tails of these age group distributions are fairly thin because of the 3 year gap in the data. Given that observations are treated as independent over time and across individuals, it is not clear why the initial age partition is not maintained (i.e., why workers cannot move from one group to the next over time). Alternatively, given that the initial age partition is maintained, it is not obvious why the 1981 data are used at all—given the relatively large sample size available for 1971–1978 and the age group distributions created by the 1981 data. As the data stand, it is not clear how to interpret variation in results across age groups (e.g., 16–29 versus 20–39), even if the upper tails are thin.

22. Gottschalk and Maloney choose data for 1978–1979 because they represent the most recent period (relative to 1984) in which there was no major recession.

23. Gottschalk and Maloney note that finding negative wage returns to job changes are not unusual. In the present sample, 41 percent of those reporting themselves better off have lower wages in their new jobs. The proportion of those worse off with higher wages is not reported, but it would certainly be an interesting thing to know.

24. Tenure is observed only for workers under 45 in 1978 and Gottschalk and Maloney use data collected in the 1977 interviews for workers age 45 or more.

25. The measure of job complexity is the natural log of the necessary number of weeks for an average worker to learn the task, as determined by industrial engineers.

26. Weiss notes that the wages offered by the firm are relatively high. Specifically, the average wage gain for workers employed at the time of application is 103 percent. Consequently, workers start lining up to apply about 36 hours before the distribution of applications. Time of application actually pertains to the time stamped on the workers application at the time of distribution. He also notes that 78 percent of all interviewees were hired and, among those rejected, 85 percent had test scores that were too low.

27. Note that there appears to be no sample restriction based on school enrollment. This education effect may simply be students going back to school.

28. Note that for job changers, it may be the case that multiple job and wage changes may occur between the interview dates, with and without intervening spells of unemployment. Also, workers who experience long spells of unemployment are likely to be excluded.

29. The residuals used in carrying out this test are based on log wage regressions that include age, race, and sex as explanatory variables.

30. Flinn also reports first round OLS log wage results fit using 1967 wage observations for the entire sample. These results are close to the maximum likelihood estimates, except for the education coefficient. The OLS estimate is large and significant.

31. For additional discussion of theoretical distinctions between quits and layoffs, see McLaughlin (1989).

32. Reid (1972) provides additional descriptive evidence on demographic and skill variation for a sample of British workers who expected to be laid off from their firms. First, 46.5 percent of all men versus 24 percent of all women engaged in job search prior to being laid off. Less than 20 percent of all unskilled workers versus more than half of all skilled workers in the sample began their job search prior to being laid off. Among males, prime-age men were most likely and teen-aged males were least likely to engage in on-the-job search. Among females, the youngest were the most likely to search before layoff. Of course, sample proportions such as these are averaged over alternative wage and nonwage opportunities and other characteristics, but they are suggestive. The source of these data is the same as that used by MacKay and Reid (1972), discussed in Chapter 5.

33. In an early study, Marston (1979) analyzed pooled data from the March CPS for 1973–

1975 and state-level data for 1972–1974 and found little evidence of a significant expected benefit level effect on quit behavior. Ragan (1984) and Solon (1985) present more recent analyses of the effects of alternative UI benefit program provisions on quit behavior based on state-level data and also fail to find evidence of significant effects. Further analysis based on less aggregate data may present a different picture.

34. To support his use of these data, Meitzen reports that the BLS estimates for average tenure are 2.4 years for females and 3.3 years for males in the occupations covered in his sample. However, these estimates are likely to be based on incomplete durations and thus likely to be biased downward.

35. Meitzen describes his work as an analysis of quits, but he does not indicate what he does with workers who were laid off during the sample period.

36. Meitzen notes that the sample mean top wage for females is \$4.71 compared to \$5.80 for males. He interprets this as potential evidence of discrimination. Note, however, that distinguishing the effects of shorter tenures and discrimination is not possible in the reported results.

37. These results are also obtained when the distribution of ϵ is restricted to extreme value, that is, to an exponential distribution for durations.

38. See Parsons (1986) for a discussion of this literature.

39. These variables would be expected to have the same effect on productivity in all job opportunities faced by worker i. Entering higher order terms in X and T in these equations does not affect the basic argument and, in the studies to be reviewed, these terms are included.

40. Mincer and Jovanovic also fit linear job exit probability models. The variables are those included in the wage equation and, thus, they can be interpreted as unconditional exit rates (i.e., averaged over the current wages). The results suggest that the exit probability is convex in tenure at all ages and marginally concave in experience from the middle to the end of a career.

41. To check the effects of incorporating the lag between offers and wage payments, alone, Marshall and Zarkin fit an OLS log wage regression for their full sample. As expected, the tenure coefficients are slightly smaller than those reported by Mincer and Jovanovic (1981), and the coefficients for remaining variables are slightly larger—but there are no substantive differences. They also fit OLS log offer equations for stayers and movers with no correction for censoring. The tenure coefficient for stayers is smaller than the full sample OLS estimate, but is still significant. All other coefficients are similar in both magnitude and significance across groups, with the exception of the prior mobility variable. These OLS results imply that prior mobility has a significant negative effect on the offers faced by movers, but no effect on the offers received by stayers.

42. Garen (1988) offers an overview of the empirical matching literature that appeared through 1987, including results from his own analysis of the PSID data using a two-step procedure comparable to that of Marshall and Zarkin (1987). His findings are similar, though less pronounced. Controlling for selectivity bias reduces estimates for within-job wage growth attributable to tenure to about half the size of simple OLS estimates.

43. Sectoral shift studies of microdata based on models in which it is assumed that transitions between sectors are either instantaneous or exactly one period long have also appeared (Keane, 1990; Shaw, 1989).

9

Experimental Studies

To many economists, "empirical research" means the application of econometric techniques to data that are generated passively and typically collected in surveys or compiled by government agencies. In some rare cases, the data are generated by a social experiment, where subjects participate in a special program (e.g., negative income tax, job training, or search assistance). This description of empirical research applies to the studies discussed in previous chapters—but not to the research reviewed here. The data analyzed here are generated by *controlled laboratory experiments*—a relatively new endeavor in economic research.

As described by Vernon Smith (1982), leading proponent of experimental economics,

> The fundamental objective behind a laboratory experiment in economics is to create
> a manageable "microeconomics environment in the laboratory where adequate con-
> trol can be maintained and accurate measurement of relevant variables guaranteed."
> (p. 930)

The single most important element of an experiment is control over individual preferences. A reward structure and system of property rights must be designed to induce *prescribed* monetary valuation on experimental outcomes. Measurements are taken on the set of messages that experimental subjects send in the trials of an experiment, which have a form and potential content that are well defined in the experimental design. Statistical analysis then follows. This is an ambitious agenda—even when testing the most basic hypotheses of economics. This has served as the basic objective of experimental research thus far. Experimentalists view the primary value of their approach as resting in its ability to allow rejection of fundamental theoretical results that would otherwise remain untested.[1]

Here we review three attempts to test job search theory in the laboratory setting. The studies differ in terms of their experimental designs and precise objectives, but all focus on fundamental aspects of the search paradigm. Moreover, the bottom lines are the same. When put to the test in a laboratory setting, the basic results of job search theory appear robust.

Schotter and Braunstein (1981, 1982)[2]

Schotter and Braunstein present findings from their laboratory tests of several job search hypotheses, conducted using 56 undergraduate students recruited from principles level economics courses at New York University as subjects. Their experimental design was straightforward. Each subject was scheduled for an individual, hour long session that took place in an enclosed room—the "laboratory." In addition to a researcher, the only other items in the room were a computer terminal on which the experiment was carried out, a table, and two chairs. At the start of the session, the subject was given 10 pages of written instructions to read, which were then reviewed by the researcher. The instructions stated explicitly that the purpose of the experiment was to investigate how people go about searching when wages and prices represent draws from some probability distribution—which may or may not be known by the economic agent. They also provided details on the number of trials in the experiment (8 to 12) and the nature of each individual trial, that is, a description of the distribution from which wages would be drawn, the search cost per draw, the availability of offer recall, and the potential number of searches (unlimited in all but a few cases). The search process itself was quite simple in each trial. To start, the subject typed "search," and a wage offer would appear. If satisfied, the subject type "stop" and then proceeded to the next trial. If not satisfied, he or she typed "search," etc. The experimental payoff from a trial consisted of the accepted wage minus any costs incurred, both measured in "points," and the instructions clearly stated the method that would be used to translate experimental payoffs into U.S. dollars for each trial. Also, before starting the actual experiment, several practice trials were conducted—to familiarize the subject with the search procedure and the various wage distributions he or she would face during actual trials. In all cases only simple continuous distributions were used—rectangular, symmetric triangular, left triangular, right triangular, or truncated triangular.

The subjects were separated into three groups that participated in three different experiments. Differences between the first two experiments were designed to induce alternative preferences. In the first, the conversion of experimental payoffs was a penny for a point—to induce risk-neutral behavior. In the second experiment, subjects faced a concave function of the experimental payoffs—to induce risk-averse behavior. There was some variation in the use and ordering of particular trial designs across the first two experiments, but all differences across trials involved changes in the offer distribution, changes in search costs, the introduction of discounting, limits on the number of searches, the possibility of recall, or some other well-defined and simple change designed to test a basic search hypothesis. Wages ranged between 0 and 200 points (except when the distributions were truncated or contracted) and the basic search cost was 5 points; the potential earnings for the subjects were thus considerable, given the time commitment. The third experiment used the same risk-neutral conversion schedule for payoffs as the first experiment, but the structure of the trials differed. Specifically, several of the trials in the third experiment were designed to test the effects of various forms of uncertainty about the offer distribution (e.g., subjects were told that they faced one of four distributions, but not which one).

In addition to engaging in the actual search trials, all subjects responded to a set of questions. Before each trial, a subject was asked the minimum payoff he or she would accept not to search in that trial. In the last trial (where all subjects unknowingly faced the same wage offers on the first six searches), a subject was also asked the minimum payoff question before each successive search. At the end of the experiment, subjects were asked to write a paragraph on their views about the optimal way to search and the method they had actually used in the experiment.

Schotter and Braunstein use their experimental results to investigate a variety of hypotheses from the search literature, starting with the most basic: (1) Do searchers actually have the ability to calculate the optimal reservation wage? and (2) Do searchers act as if they set reservation wages? As a test of the ability hypothesis they compare the average pretrial responses to the minimum offer question and the actual optimal reservation wages for each trial. For the risk-neutral group, they find no significant difference. In fact, the responses are remarkably close. Furthermore, the lowest accepted wages and highest rejected wages from the actual search trials in the risk-neutral experiment are consistent with the reported reservation wages, that is, workers appear to behave as if they use a reservation wage policy. On the other hand, the reservation wages reported by the risk-averse group are generally below their optimal level—indicating that subjects exaggerate the designated degree of their risk aversion. Still, the average deviation from the optimal reservation wage is not statistically significant at standard levels and the actual acceptance and rejection behavior of the subjects in the risk-averse group is consistent with their reported reservation wages.

Schotter and Braunstein go on to examine the effects of search subsidies for both limited and unlimited numbers of searches, mean-preserving spreads, a finite horizon, and the possibility of offer recall. In each case, the results are consistent with the predictions of the simple search model. The results for the effects of uncertainty about the wage distribution and the minimum wage are mixed, but they note that these may be due to problems in trial designs.

The most striking finding of the study is a failure of the constant reservation wage hypothesis for participants in the risk-neutral experiment. Although there is no significant change in the reservation wages for subjects in the risk-averse group, a regression of the responses given in the last trials for the risk-neutral group on numbers of searches (i.e., duration) suggests a 4 percent decline between successive searches.

Cox and Oaxaca (1988)

Cox and Oaxaca take issue with several aspects of the Braunstein–Schotter experimental design and design their own experiment with these issues in mind.

They start by noting that if job search models are to serve as "reasonably accurate predictors of job search behavior," then labor market behavior must be consistent with two hypotheses:

> (a) normally-intelligent human beings are capable of making choices in a dynamic, uncertain decision environment as if they were finding the optimal solutions to stochastic dynamic decision problems; and
>
> (b) the income stream that results from search dominates other possible determinants of job search behavior. (p. 2)

These are the basic hypotheses tested by Braunstein and Schotter, (1) and (2). However, Cox and Oaxaca point out that when hypotheses (a) and (b) are tested jointly, by using terms such as *job* and *income from working* in experimental instructions and by explicitly asking subjects to "engage in job market role-playing" (as in the Braunstein and Schotter experiment), it must be assumed that laboratory role-playing and actual labor market participation are equivalent when interpreting the results. Specifically, if behavior apears consistent with the hypothesis, it cannot be determined whether hypothesis (b) is really tested, that is, whether the role-playing is taken seriously. It may be the case that only hypothesis (a) holds. On the other hand, if behavior appears inconsistent with the hypothesis, it cannot be determined which hypothesis fails to hold. Therefore, Cox and Oaxaca set out to test the more primitive hypothesis (a) alone, which they view as a first step. This is done simply by avoiding emotive terms related to the labor market when instructing their subjects. The subjects are told that they are participating in "an experiment in the economics of decision-making," and nothing more.

Their second major point of contention relates to the Braunstein–Schotter finding of declining reservation wage for risk-neutral searchers. Cox and Oaxaca question the appropriateness of interpreting an unlimited number of searches per experimental trial as corresponding to an infinite horizon search. They argue that an infinite number of searches is impossible in an experiment and that the finding of a declining reservation wage by Braunstein and Schotter may thus reflect the experimental subjects' perception of the experiment as a finite search horizon problem. Furthermore, they note that an infinite number of searches is impossible in the real world. On the basis of both arguments, they maintain a finite search horizon framework throughout their experiment in their test of hypothesis (a). Precisely, Cox and Oaxaca set out a simple, finite search model with a nonzero probability of no offer per search, and solve for the optimal path of the reservation wage for the cases of risk-neutral searchers.

In translating this into an experiment, Cox and Oaxaca use a design that is even simpler than the Braunstein and Schotter design. (Among their minor points of contention is a practical concern about subjects' ability to understand computer-generated draws from continuous probability distributions.) Their search procedure consists of two steps in each round (i.e., search). First, a subject drew from a container of prespecified numbers of white and black balls (two and two in the baseline) to determine whether an offer would be drawn at all. If a white ball was drawn, then an offer was generated by a bingo cage. In the basic case, the bingo cage contained 10 balls numbered 1 to 10, so that the probability of any potential offer was 0.1. After drawing from the bingo cage, the subject then chose between repeating this two-step procedure (up to 20 times) or accepting the offer and moving on the next trial. A number of trials involved deviations from the basic case—to test specific hypotheses. In particular, the effects of differences in discount rates, and search costs or subsidies were examined. Variation in arrival rates and offer distributions were explored by altering the numbers of balls in the container and bingo cage. For example, leaving only the balls numbered 4 to 7 in the bingo cage corresponded to mean-preserving contractions. One major difference between the Cox and Oaxaca and Braunstein and Schotter designs was the approach used to examine differences in behavior arising from risk aversion on the part of the searchers. Cox and Oaxaca did not incorporate risk aversion into their design directly (i.e., by altering the payoff structure). Instead they tested the consistency of the observed search distribution and payoffs with those theoretically implied under an assumption of risk-neutral behavior.

As in the Braunstein and Schotter experiment, the subjects of the experiment that generated the results in the present paper were undergraduate students, namely, 60 students at the University of Arizona. The subjects were split randomly into two groups that were administered separate experiments. The logistics also appear to have been roughly the same (i.e., individual meetings in enclosed rooms, the reading and reviewing of instructions, etc.). Each experiment lasted 30–45 minutes.

Overall, the behavior of the experimental subjects is reasonably close to the behavior predicted for risk-neutral agents. About 77 percent of all terminations are consistent with optimal risk-neutral stopping times and results from various statistical tests are favorable. In particular, the results from a Kolmogorov–Smirnov test of the observed and theoretically implied duration distributions, conditioned on draws, are favorable. Deviations from risk-neutral behavior suggest risk-averse behavior; 94.2 percent of all observed terminations are consistent with either optimal risk-neutral or optimal risk-averse stopping times.

When considered alone, the results of the baseline case might not be viewed as substantial evidence of behavior consistent with the ability hypothesis (a); observed behavior might reflect the use of some "naive decision rules" such as a fixed maximum number of searches or a fixed target earnings level. Cox and Oaxaca note, however, that the overall consistency of behavior described takes both the baseline trial results and the treatment results together. With the exception of a treatment that shortened the length of the search horizon for one group, subjects generally responded to treatments in predicted ways; that is, they appeared to use the optimal stopping rules.[3]

Harrison and Morgan (1987)

Results are presented here from an experimental comparison and evaluation of three search strategies: (1) the fixed-sample size (FSS) studied by Stigler (1961, 1962), which restricts an agent to exactly one sample of offers, but allows choice of sample size; (2) the pure-sequential (SEQ) discussed in Chapter 2, which allows an unlimited or finite number of samples of size one; and (3) the variable-sample size (VSS) studied by Benhabib and Bull (1983) and others, which combines the FSS and SEQ strategies so that both numbers of samples and sample sizes are defined as choice variables. Clearly, the VSS is the optimal strategy, since it yields a payoff at least as large as the alternatives. Harrison and Morgan seek to discover which, if any, of the three strategies are consistent with the observed behavior of experimental subjects. Like Braunstein and Schotter and Cox and Oaxaca, Harrison and Morgan recognize the possibility that subjects may not be able to calculate the optimal strategies accurately. They thus treat testing the ability hypothesis as a primary concern. Precisely, they calculate the theoretical opportunity costs for deviations from optimal behavior under the alternative strategies and ask whether these deviations are "too expensive" to be attributed to limited computational ability.

The experimental design used by Harrison and Morgan shares features with the designs of each of the studies previously discussed. Following Cox and Oaxaca, they avoid issues associated with interpreting the unlimited search case as an infinite horizon problem by maintaining a finite search horizon. On the other hand, the instructions given to subjects stated explicitly that the purpose of the experiment was to "find out how people go about searching for prices and wages" (p. 12) and the wage represented the only job characteristic of concern to searchers. The experiment was carried out on a computer, with offers generated from one of four alternative beta distributions in each trial. As in both of the experiments previously discussed, undergraduate students were used as subjects; 30 students at the University of Western Ontario served in this case.

Table 9.1. Experimental Studies

Study	Subjects	Model	Findings
Braunstien and Schotter (1981, 1982)	New York University students	Stationary infinite horizon sequential search model	Reservation wage declines with duration for risk-neutral agents
Cox and Oaxaca (1988)	University of Arizona students	Finite horizon sequential search model	Observed behavior consistent with optimizing behavior; some evidence of risk-averse behavior
Harrison and Morgan (1988)	University of Western Ontario students	Finite horizon fixed-sample-size, sequential and variable-sample-size models	Observed behavior consistent with most flexible optimal strategy available

All subjects participated in the same 23 trials, with differences across trials geared toward isolating choice of strategy when faced with different search costs, offer distributions, and horizons. The main logistical departure of the Harrison and Morgan design from the other designs discussed was the use of a "training session" several days before the paid experimental sessions. Beyond a lesson on the search procedure using 14 practice trials, students were given a printout that listed both their actions and outcomes in each trail.

Harrison and Morgan find that subjects generally employ the least restrictive and thus potentially most remunerative strategy available. When permitted samples of size greater than 1, subjects choose larger samples and when permitted to sample more than once, they do. These results hold up under a variety of statistical tests. On the other hand, the realized earnings of the experimental subjects are not significantly higher when the more flexible strategies are used, that is, potential gains are not realized. Harrison and Morgan note that this may be a consequence of the ordering in trials in their design, VVS–SEQ and VVS–FSS within pairs of trials that were otherwise the same; their intention was to avoid interpretation problems due to learning. The use of the training session might be viewed as weakening this line of argument, but this is just speculation. As Harrison and Morgan note, the presence of the side effects in their design cannot be dismissed without additional experimentation.

Summary

The results of laboratory economic experiments are most useful when they allow rejection of a theoretical result or hypothesis. This is noted by Smith and the researchers engaged in the experiments we have discussed (Table 9.1). So far, the basic finding is that search theory has not done too badly in the laboratory setting.

Notes

1. Smith (1982) presents a discussion of the methodology and function of experimental economics.

2. Both of these papers present results from the same experiment and therefore we do not discuss them separately.

3. Additional statistical analysis of these experimental results is presented in Cox and Oaxaca (1989a,b).

10

How the Other Half Searches: Evidence from the Demand Side of the Labor Market

Employers play a passive role in the studies previously reviewed. Workers are modeled as facing a distribution of employment opportunities and it is their optimizing behavior that is the focus of attention. Even in the studies based on matching models, only minor attention is paid to attempts by employers to learn about the productivity of prospective employees before hiring. This emphasis in the empirical search literature has not reflected ignorance about the presence of uncertainty on the demand side of the labor market. Nor has it been a matter of favoritism on the part of the researchers. It simply reflects the relative scarcity of demand-side data. Microdata sets for firms are rare. Moreover, when firm level data have been collected, the data have typically been taken from records kept by firms—and firms rarely keep records on search activity.

The studies discussed in this chapter exploit available microdata on demand-side search—using approaches that are by and large mirror images of those in the supply-side studies. Employers with vacancies are modeled as facing a distribution of workers with different productivities, but they do not know which workers have which productivities. Workers are relegated to a passive role.

The first studies we discuss by Barron et al. (1985), Barron and Bishop (1985), and Bishop and Barron (1984) focus directly on employer search activity. Specifically, they analyze screening, recruitment, and interviewing practices using data for large samples of U.S. firms. Their objective is to determine the factors that influence both the level of resources an employer devotes to information gathering and the allocation of these resources across alternative methods of information gathering. Barron et al. (1985) set out a simple optimal control model of the employer's problem when seeking to fill a position. This serves as a guide in the empirical work in both studies. Barron and Bishop (1985) note that some firms accept applications even when there are no open positions. They look into the causes and effects of this "stockpiling" practice. The next study, Rynes and Boudreau (1986), examines the college recruiting activities of large firms using data from a mail survey of college recruitment directors. Rynes (1990) discusses an empirical literature on recruiting that appears primarily in personnel and applied psychology journals. We review some of her conclusions briefly.

We turn next to analyses of vacancy duration data. Beaumont (1978) analyzes vacancy data constructed from the records of two Scottish Employment Registers. Roper (1988) analyzes vacancy data collected in a nationwide employer survey in the United Kingdom. van Ours (1988) and Renes (1989) study data from a nationwide employer survey in the Netherlands. Different econometric approaches are taken in these studies, but all are primarily descriptive, as opposed to behavioral or structural. As Beaumont (1980) puts it,

> As yet no specific model has been developed to analyze vacancy duration so that the variables entered in our estimating equations were chosen on the basis of certain rather *ad hoc* hypotheses about the likely factors involved in differential vacancy duration. (p. 80)

As in the early studies of data on unemployment durations, the work presented here is guided by a variety of search theoretic arguments—but it is primarily exploratory.[1]

Search Strategies

Barron, Bishop, and Dunkelberg (1985)

Barron et al. analyze search activity data for a sample of employers in 28 local labor markets in the United States. The data were collected in April–June 1980 in the first of two surveys designed to evaluate the Employment Opportunity Pilot Project (EOPP), an experiment conducted in 10 of these sites by the Department of Labor. These data have some unattractive features. There are potential experimental effects on behavior. Gulf Coast cities are overrepresented in the sample design and the Northeast is under-represented. Low-wage and large firms are intentionally oversampled in each market. Nevertheless, these data provide some rare information. All 5,300 employers in the sample were asked if they had hired since January 1, 1978, and 69 percent responded yes. The sample analyzed here consists of 2,094 employers in this group who provided complete answers to questions about the process involved in their most recent hiring. In particular, employers were asked to report the total number of hours the firm spent recruiting, screening, and interviewing applicants for the position, the number of applicants interviewed for the position, and the number of offers rejected. Data on the current starting wage, education requirements, occupation, and the amount and type of training associated with the position were also collected. Characteristics of the firm were recorded as a part of the general survey. These include industry, size of the work force, percentage of the work force covered by a collective bargaining agreement, the annual quit rate, and the annual number of applicants.

Barron et al. characterize employer search as proceeding along both extensive and intensive margins—as suggested by Rees (1966) and Rees and Schultz (1970). The extensive margin pertains to the number of applicants considered; the intensive margin pertains to the amount of information gathered per applicant. The number of interviews per offer serves as their measure of extensive search. The total number of applicants for the position in question is not known here; they note that extensive search would be measured as in the number of applicants per offer, otherwise. The hours spent per applicant interviewed serves as their measure of intensive search. Total hiring costs are defined as the product of these two variables and the number of offers extended. (Ninety percent of the firms reported just one offer.)

Results are reported for regressions of the natural log of each of these three variables on all of the employer and position characteristics listed, except the starting wage. None of the results indicates substantial explanatory power for the specification (the adjusted R^2 ranges from 0.04 to 0.13). Nevertheless, some interesting patterns emerge. First, orientation training by personnel and supervisory staff is the only variable that has a significant coefficient with the same sign in both the intensive search and extensive search regressions—the effects are large and positive. Additional training in the first month, education requirements of a high school diploma or more, larger firm size, and higher annual flow rates of applicants (defined as the annual number of applicants per position) are all associated with greater search on the extensive margin. Except for the annual flow rate of applicants, which has a negative effect, none of these variables has a significant effect on intensive search. Neither the annual quit rate nor the level of unionism has a statistically significant effect on search activity along either margin, even at the most liberal levels. This is somewhat surprising. Not surprisingly, intensive search is significantly higher for positions in professional and technical occupations, relative to blue-collar positions, while extensive search is greater for clerical positions. Industry appears irrelevant. The results for the total cost regression basically follow the extensive search results. The only new piece of information is that significantly fewer resources are devoted to hiring for service positions than to hiring for positions in other occupations.

Results are also reported for a regression of the log starting wage on all of the firm and position characteristics, the hours spent per interview (intensive search), and the number of interviews per offer (extensive search). Both of the search measures have large, positive, and significant effects. Somewhat surprisingly, the training variables have negligible, negative effects after controlling for resources devoted to screening.

Barron and Bishop (1985)

Barron and Bishop work with data collected in the second round of interviews in the survey used by Barron et al. Specifically, second interviews were conducted by Gallop, Inc., in January and February 1982, with 3,400 of the 5,300 employers in the original sample. In this round, employers were asked about their last hire prior to September 1981 and the sample analyzed here consists of 2,264 employers who indicated hiring activity and provided complete information. In addition to information collected in the first interviews, the second round of interviews inquired about the proportion of skills learned in the position that would be useful outside the firm, the number of firms in the local labor market having jobs that required these skills, the current cost of the most expensive machine used in the position, whether the employers had advance notice of a vacancy (a more precise definition was not used), whether the position was part-time, temporary, or seasonal, whether there was more than one vacancy for the position, and whether there was a great deal of paperwork required to fire an employee at the firm. Longer term training information and the numbers of employment inquiries by phone and in person in the 10 days preceding the second interview were also recorded.

The approach taken to analyze these data is broadly similar to the approach of Barron et al. Intensive search is measured as hours per applicant and extensive search is defined as number of applicants per offer extended. These were their preferred measures in the study previously discussed, but the required data on the number of applicants per position are available only from the second round of interviews. Separate regressions are fit using the log number of applicants per interview and the log number of interviews per offer as dependent variables—to sort out effects on the two components of extensive search. Regression models for log total hours per applicant, log total hours per position, and log number of offers per position are also fit. The explanatory variables in all five regressions include all of the variables available from the second (but not first) interviews listed, the percentage of the labor force covered by a collective bargaining agreement, the size of the work force, and training associated with the position; education requirements for the position are not included.

The explanatory power of these regression models is low (the adjusted R^2 ranges from 0.01 to 0.14), as in the results reported by Barron et al. However, some interesting patterns emerge. First, the difficulty involved in firing a worker has a large positive effect on the amount of resources devoted to search—on both intensive and extensive margins. Moreover, both the numbers of applicants screened and the number of interviews are significantly higher when the employer perceives the amount of firing difficulty as substantial. As found by Barron et al., search activity on both margins also increases with the amount of training associated with the position to be filled. The new finding here is that there is little variation in the training effect with the transferability of the skills or the existence of competing employers nearby. Also, the training results reported here suggest that the increase in extensive search reflects an increase in the number of interviews per offer extended, as opposed to recruiting larger numbers of applicants. Both larger employers and firms with other divisions or subsidiaries engage in more extensive search than small and single plant employers—but the level of intensive search is about the same. The results for the multiple-opening variable provide some evidence of economies of scale in search; hours of search per applicant are significantly lower, while the number of offers for each position is slightly higher. These findings might reflect unmeasured characteristics of the jobs involved when there are multiple vacancies. Extensive search is significantly higher when an employer knows about a vacancy ahead of time, but there is no significant difference in intensive search. Search activity is generally lower for part-time and seasonal jobs. Not surprising, intensive search is directly related to the cost of capital associated with a position. Finally, in contrast to the results reported by Barron et al., the results reported here indicate that the total cost of filling a vacancy is inversely related to the extent of unionism in the firm; the number of applicants per interview increases with unionism, but the number of hours per applicants, the number of interviews per offer, and the number of offers per position are all significantly lower. Additional results are not reported, but Barron and Bishop note that including the starting wage, occupation, industry, quit rates, and the existence of a probationary period for new hires has little effect on these results. The findings for these additional variables are consistent with those of Barron et al. Intensive search is higher for positions in managerial and professional occupations and extensive search is higher for positions in clerical and sales occupations. The starting wage also has a significant effect on intensive search and, when it is included, capital cost seems irrelevant.

Bishop and Barron (1984)

This paper considers the recruitment strategy of "stockpiling" job applications, as opposed to recruiting only for existing openings. Firms increase the pool of applicants by accepting applications without having openings, thus increasing the extent of search.

There is also a potential "supply" effect. Workers may be more likely to apply for a position with a firm that reviews stockpiled applications when openings arise. The data set is that used by Barron et al. (1985). A dummy variable for stockpiling, set equal to 1 if the firm had called a stockpiled applicant for an interview in the past year, is used as an independent variable along with many others in a set of regression models. The coefficient is 0.34 when the dependent variable is the log of applications per offer. This can be broken down into a coefficient on log applications per interview of 0.18 and log interviews per offer of 0.16. Thus, firms that stockpike applications have more applications to review and do more interviewing per offer than other firms. The coefficient on the stockpiling dummy when the dependent variable is log hours per applicant is -0.21, indicating that the intensity of employer search declines with stockpiling. All of these coefficients have t ratios greater than 3.7. No statistics on the fit of the equations are reported. A regression of the log of the number of applications received during the 2-week period preceding the survey on the stockpiling dummy, firm size, and other variables is fit in an effort to get at the supply effect. The coefficient for the stockpiling dummy is 0.367 in this case.

The authors next turn to the determinants of stockpiling. What firms collect and keep applications? Thirty-five percent of all firms in the sample called in a prior applicant for an interview when they were filling a new position. However, 58 percent of the largest firms (more than 250 employees) did so. Stockpiling appears most common for service jobs. Logit results for stockpiling suggest that employer size, on-the-job training, quit rates, unionism, and multiple openings all have positive effects. The starting wage has a negative effect, implying that stockpiling is more prevalent for low wage jobs.

Rynes and Boudreau (1986)

This study reports results from a survey of college recruiting directors in the 1985 *Fortune* 1000 companies. Unfortunately there were only 207 responses. Of these, 40 reported no recruiting and 22 reported data that were not useful, leaving a sample of 145 organizations, disproportionately representing large firms. Nevertheless the data are interesting in view of the scarcity of information on this side of the market. The survey shows that job requirements are set primarily by line managers rather than personnel staff. Thus, job requirements are not set on the basis of availability of candidates (or, at least, adjustment to availability is slow). Starting salaries are also set primarily by line managers and not by the recruiting staff. Salary ranges, measured as average low to average high by BA field, are business 19,200–22,700, engineering 24,800–28,800, and computer science 22,400–26,000. Offers were left outstanding for 1 to 12 weeks, with an average of about 3 weeks (there was substantial nonresponse on this question).

Rynes (1990)

Apparently, many firms do not collect information allowing evaluation of recruitment strategies and policies. In particular, data relating employee performance to the method of recruitment are rarely collected. In this paper, Rynes reviews empirical research based on available data.

There are findings in this literature of differences in performances of employees hired by different methods. Unfortunately these findings are not very consistent. There is evidence that performance is highest for employees hired by referrals from existing employees and for employees rehired after layoffs. Newspaper advertisements appear to be effective in generating applications and filling vacancies, but there is some weak evidence that employees hired through newspaper ads do not perform as well as others. There is some evidence that "realistic" recruitment versus "selling" the job to applicants leads to lower turnover. Requirements for formal screening, such as pencil and paper tests, reduce the flow of applicants. (This is consistent with a rational response to an increase in the cost of search.) There is a literature on "job attribute ranking" that attempts to find the characteristics of a job that are most important to recruits. Examples of characteristics studied are opportunity for promotion, type of work, pay, job security, and location. There seems to be no clear consensus on what is most important to recruits—an alarming situation considering our focus on the wage.

Rynes notes the lack of information and consensus, as well as the selectivity problem in almost all of the studies she reviews. These studies examine only those recruits hired—recruitment, selection, and self-selection effects are thus confounded.

Vacancy Durations

Beaumont (1978)

This study represents a response to employer complaints of labor shortages in high unemployment areas of Scotland. The duration data are constructed from the records of two employment exchanges and consist of observations on 1,731 vacancies that were either filled through the exchange (1,173 observations) or cancelled (558 observations) during the October 1973 and December 1975 period. (Only "standing" and permanent listings are excluded from the sample.) The duration of a filled vacancy is defined as the number of days between registration of the vacancy and the date of referral of the applicant who got the job. For cancelled vacancies (i.e., vacancies not filled by the registry), only an interval for the ending date is observed (the date of the last referral by the exchange and the date that the employer informed the exchange that the vacancy was no longer open). Beaumont uses the mean of these dates in measuring durations. Almost half of all vacancies were registered in multiple listings by firms, but Beaumont treats each as an independent observation.

Not all vacancies in the local labor markets appear in these data; in particular, very short spells are likely to be excluded (as in the case of unemployment insurance records). Nevertheless, these data provide some useful (and, in some ways, surprising) information. First, the summary statistics indicate that roughly two-thirds of all filled vacancies last 5 days or less, but the distribution of spell lengths is highly skewed; 10 percent of filled vacancies last more than 30 days. On the other hand, less than one-third of all cancelled vacancies have lengths of 5 days or less and about one-third have lengths exceeding 30 days. On average, the filled vacancies that were registered individually lasted 10.7 days and the multiple listing vacancies lasted 14.6 days. Cancelled vacancies, on the other hand, lasted an average of 40 to 50 days.

Beaumont reports results for a log duration regression fit separately for cancelled and filled vacancies. His specification includes the weekly wage rate and dummy variables for "antisocial" hours of work, unskilled occupation, industry, a 1975 starting date (to capture the general deterioration in labor market conditions), and location of the exchange. The explanatory of the model seems reasonable for both duration types (R^2 = 0.28 for filled and R^2 = 0.43 for cancelled vacancies). The results for the year and location variables suggest that both general and local labor market conditions have a significant direct effect on vacancy durations. The coefficients for the wage are negative in both regressions, but small and insignificant at all standard levels. The lengths of filled vacancies are also shorter in the service, food, construction, and engineering industries, but (surprisingly) antisocial hours have no significant effect. On the other hand, the durations of cancelled vacancies are significantly longer for positions having undesirable hours and for positions in the engineering, metal, and textile industries. Finally, both sets of results indicate that vacancies in unskilled occupations have shorter durations than vacancies for skilled positions.

Beaumont also looks at data on the number of submissions (i.e., applicant referrals) per vacancy—to gain some further insight to the numbers and lengths of cancelled vacancies. For about half the vacancies in the sample, just one or two referrals were made, but more than five referrals does not appear unusual—in the case of either filled or cancelled vacancies.

Beaumont's bottom line is that a firm level panel survey would be useful, given his findings. This seems an appropriate conclusion—and it was followed up with the survey that generated the data studied by Roper (1988).

Roper (1988)

Roper focuses on the effects of choice of recruitment method on the durations of vacancies. The idea here is that choice of recruitment methods can affect both the numbers of applicants and the distribution of applicant characteristics, that is, the arrival rate and acceptance probability of a firm. His data were collected in the Survey of Employers' Recruitment Practices, conducted between November 1976 and February 1977 in the United Kingdom (i.e., in the middle of the 1970s downturn). The survey sample consisted of 1,294 firms with 10 or more employees, located in 100 local labor markets. Each firm was asked about their one or two most recent manual and nonmanual hires and the sample analyzed here consists of 1,539 manual and 1,481 nonmanual vacancies. For each, Roper observes whether the vacancy was for a temporary position, the required skill level, the starting wage, the starting date of the vacancy, and the employer's use of both formal and informal recruitment methods for each vacancy. In about a quarter of all cases, the method that proved successful is also reported. Observations on these variables make this data source attractive, but there are some major shortcomings. The local labor market is not identified, making it impossible to measure local labor market conditions in any accurate manner; the only measure is the employer's response when asked if recruitment for the positions was easy. Firm size is reported, but industry data are limited; only manufacturing and nonmanufacturing firms are distinguished. Most important, the duration data are available only in interval form (0–7, 8–14, 15–21, 22–28, 29–56, and 56+ days). Unfortunately, Roper responds to this grouped duration data situation by using an ordered probit model for log durations.[2]

Results are reported for a variety of specifications, fit separately for manual and nonmanual vacancies. The explanatory variables include different subsets of the variables listed above, measured in categorical form. Overall, the manual vacancy results are more precise than the nonmanual results. The percentage of outcomes correctly predicted is also higher for the manual vacancies, although both are fairly low (63–65 percent for manual, versus 51–52 percent for nonmanual). The manual results suggest that vacancies at relatively small and relatively large firms, vacancies in manufacturing firms, and vacancies for skilled positions all last significantly longer than vacancies having the opposite characteristics. The results for the wage variables also indicate that the duration of manual vacancies increases significantly with the wage level. This might be interpreted as evidence of endogeneity of the starting wage, that is, the response to difficulty in filling a vacancy over time. The results for the nonmanual sample suggest that skill level has a positive effect on duration, but the effect is only marginally significant. Industry appears irrelevant, but firm size seems important. The results again imply that vacancies at the smallest and largest firms last longer. The nonmanual vacancy results also indicate seasonal variation; vacancies starting in the spring and in the fall are filled more quickly. (This does not appear in the manual results.) As for wages, no systematic relationship appears for the nonmanual sample.

Choice of recruitment method seems to have an important effect on the duration of a vacancy. Among formal methods (employment agencies, advertising in newspapers, etc.), listing with a public Jobcentre seems to produce the fastest results for both manual and nonmanual vacancies. However, informal methods (personal contacts, direct application) are significantly faster than all formal methods.

van Ours (1988)

van Ours takes a hazard function approach to study vacancy data from a two-stage survey of Dutch employers by the Organization for Strategic Labor Market Research (OSLMR). The original sample design consisted of a stratified random sample of 1,288 medium sized and 625 large employers from the private sector (excluding employment agencies). Between November 1986 and January 1987, each employer in the sample was asked if they had vacancies that they wished to fill immediately. In the total sample, 648 employers reported that they had one or more vacancies and 580 cooperated when asked about the characteristics of these vacancies. The second round of interviews took place 3 to 4 months later. Here, 581 employers cooperated when questioned about the status of earlier reported vacancies and the characteristics of the employees hired to fill them. After deleting observations due to missing data and observations on vacancies that either ceased to exist or came into being between interviews, van Ours has a sample of 1,850 vacancies, 524 of which remained unfilled at the second interview. Although the scarcity of vacancy duration data makes these data valuable, they have several limitations. First, the maximum recorded duration at the first interview was 12 months; although censoring at some fixed length is common in cross-section samples of spell durations, observations with durations of more than 12 months at the initial survey date were actually deleted from the original sample in this case. The maximum potential duration for a vacancy in the sample is thus 15 or 16 months (depending on the data of the second interview). Second, precise data on vacancy durations were not collected in either interview. For some vacancies, starting dates and ending dates are reported only as falling at the beginning, middle, or end of a particular month; van Ours uses these data to calculate durations, measured in days, with the beginning, middle, and end of the month defined as the 5th, 15th and 25th. For other vacancies, the date within either the starting or ending month is not reported. In these cases, the 15th of the month is assigned as the relevant date. Together, there are 1,100 vacancies of these types and van Ours accounts for both sources of measurement error when specifying his likelihood function. For the remaining 226 vacancies, starting month data are available, but all that is known about the ending date is that it falls between the first and second interviews. van Ours also accounts for this in his likelihood specification. The average filled vacancy duration is about 26 weeks and the average unfilled vacancy is censored at about 31 weeks.

van Ours specifies a Weibull model for the distribution of vacancy durations, with unobserved heterogeneity incorporated using a gamma mixing distribution. The hazard is thus $\tau_v(t, x) = \alpha t^{\alpha-1} \exp\{x'\beta\}v$. The explanatory variables are the local unemployment rate, the size of the firm, whether the vacancy was part of a multiple listing, whether the position involved unpleasant working conditions, categorical occupations variables, categorical variables for education and labor market experience requirements, and dummy variables for alternative recruitment methods.

The Weibull parameter estimate is 1.43 (standard error 0.09), implying positive duration dependence.[3] Various interpretations of this result are possible. Firms may vary search intensity with vacancy duration, and thus increase the arrival rate of applicants. Alternatively, they might alter their offer wage and thereby increase the probability of offer acceptance. They might also adjust their reservation level of productivity downward. The rest of the results also seem sensible. Vacancies for positions with higher vocational or academic education requirements and vacancies at larger firms take longer to fill, while vacancies for service positions have significantly shorter durations than vacancies in other occupations. Labor market experience requirements and undesirable working conditions have no significant effect on durations, nor does the existence of multiple vacancies. Relative to internal recruiting channels, the use of any external recruiting channel (including informal methods) is associated with significantly longer durations. Finally, the estimated variance for the heterogeneity component is only marginally significant (0.10 [standard error 0.06]) and the rest of the results are essentially unaffected when unmeasured heterogeneity is ignored. In particular, the finding of positive duration dependence remains.

As a check on the stability of the coefficients in the model, van Ours also analyzes his duration data in terms of backward and forward recurrence times, relative to the first interview. The coefficients are quite stable across periods—except for the response to regional unemployment. The hazard decreases significantly with increases in the unemployment rate in the period before the first interview, but moves with the unemployment rate afterward. There is no obvious explanation for this finding.

Renes (1989)

Renes studies vacancy duration data from the same OSLMR panel survey as van Ours, but fits a more flexible hazard model. Specifically, Renes fits a step function of the form

$$\lambda(t) = \lambda_j, \qquad t_{j-1} \leq t < t_j,$$
$$= \exp(\beta_j x)$$

Variation in the effects of explanatory variables with duration is thus allowed, while the constant picks up remaining duration dependence and residual heterogeneity. The intervals used are 0–2 months, 2–3 months, 3–4 months, 4–5 months, 5–6 months, and more than 6 months. Renes also works with a slightly different sample from that of van Ours. In particular, she excludes all observations for which the exact ending date is not observed at the second interview, in addition to new and cancelled vacancy observations and observations with missing data; this produces a sample of size 1,391. A third difference between this study and that of van Ours is the set of regressors included. The variables specified as having potentially time-varying coefficients include a dummy variable for part-time job vacancies, dummy variables for required levels of experience, dummy variables for required education levels, dummy variables for vocational training requirement levels, and dummy variables for broad occupation categories; all of these are included by van Ours, except for the part-time dummy. Firm size, industry dummy variables, and a dummy variable indicating whether a firm used a newspaper ad are also included, but with constant coefficients. Relative to van Ours's specification, the variables excluded by Renes are the local unemployment rate, controls for multiple listings and undesirable working conditions, and additional recruitment strategy variables. Even with these omissions, however, there are 85 parameters estimated in Renes's model.

The results reported by Renes pose some nonnegligible contrasts to the results reported by van Ours. Most important, there appears to be significant variation in the effects of different characteristics as duration increases; that is, the hazards for vacancies having alternative sets of characteristics do not follow the same time path. The "reference case" is a vacancy for a full-time job in the mining industry which requires a primary education and at most 2 months experience; the hazard in this case is U-shaped. Taken alone, the effect of part-time status is to increase the hazard initially, then decrease it sharply in the fourth through sixth months, and increase it sharply thereafer; that is, its U-shape is more pronounced than the reference case. Overall, mean durations for part-time job vacancies are predicted to be shorter. A similar contrast appears between jobs requiring different education and vocational training levels. Looking across categories, the magnitude of changes in the hazard across intervals essentially follows the ordering of required credentials; in particular, hazards for vacancies for jobs that require a university degree or a high vocational credential start out relatively low and change most. The net predicted effect, however, is consistent with that found by van Ours—mean durations are predicted to increase with required credentials. In contrast to van Ours, Renes finds that experience requirements reduce the hazard significantly, although the effects are smaller in absolute magnitude than the effects of skill requirements and part-time status. Relative to the reference case, the hazards for vacancies with greater experience requirements start out lower, increase through the fifth month (versus fourth), and then decline sharply; that is, the effect of experience requirements is to offset and, to some extent, invert the U. The occupation coefficient estimates are generally imprecise, although there is some evidence that clerical and business jobs are relatively more likely to fill in the first few months. Among the controls, the advertisement variable has a positive coefficient, which might be viewed as conflicting with van Ours's findings for formal versus informal methods. There is also some evidence of industrial variation; in particular, nonfinancial services are included in "other" and the hazard appears to be significantly higher for vacancies in this category, manufacturing, and transportation (all relative to mining—the reference case). One surprising result is that firm size has a negligible effect on the hazard.

As a check on her specification, Renes fits a proportional hazards model with constant coefficients and a step function for the baseline. The regressor coefficients are all significant and have signs consistent with the general patterns for the more flexible model. The key difference is in the baseline—it increases through the fifth month and then declines slightly. As for the relative fits of the two models, results from a likelihood ratio test allow rejection of the coefficient restrictions and thus rejection of a proportional hazards specification.

Summary

The findings reviewed in this chapter are consistent with several conclusions of the earlier supply-side chapters (Tables 10.1 and 10.2). It appears that firms do not make a lot of offers for each position they wish to fill, particularly when measured against the numbers of applications received. This finding is consistent with Stern's finding of a very high rejection probability on application (Stern, 1989, discussed in Chapter 7). It is also consistent with the more general finding that workers' acceptance probabilities are in the range of 0.8 to 1 and unemployment durations are largely determined by the arrival rate of offers. The employer search strategy studies find that more resources are devoted to filling positions with higher skill and education requirements, while the vacancy duration studies suggest that it generally takes longer to fill these positions. These findings are consistent with the supply-side finding that offer arrival rates increase with education.[4] The tentative finding that informal search methods are associated with better employee performance is interesting. This seems consistent with direct evidence that offer probabilities are higher for workers who rely on informal methods (Chapter 7), and also with Datcher's finding that workers are less likely to quit when they find their jobs using contacts within firms (Datcher, 1983, discussed in Chapter 8). The finding that use of informal search methods by employers reduces the time it takes to fill a vacancy also seems consistent with this pattern of results.[5]

The work discussed in this chapter also raises some basic questions of definition and measurement that future research must address. Exactly what constitutes a "vacancy"? This is not a new question—an NBER conference dealt with this subject as early as the mid-1960s (Holt and David, 1966)—but it remains unsettled. Is passive willingness to hire, should the right worker come along, the same (in principle) as actively seeking employees? This behavior might be modeled as distinct from active search, just as we distinguish "nonparticipation" and "unemployment" when analyzing search on the supply side of the market. However, if we do make this distinction, then we must figure out what to do with the practice of "stockpiling" applications. Similarly, it is not clear that we should omit vacancies that cease to exit between interviews in a panel survey—but how they should be interpreted is not straightforward either. They may be evidence of cancelled jobs. They may reflect "discouraged employers" responding to conditions in the market. Along this line, Renes (1989) suggests that her finding of U-shaped hazards may reflect a temporary reduction in recruitment efforts, but this is just speculation. Direct observations on changes in employers' strategies with duration of a vacancy are not available in her data set. We might want to distinguish search to fill new job vacancies from search to fill employee replacement vacancies—just as we distinguish new entrants and re-entrants from workers who are separated from previous jobs. Similarly, search to fill vacancies for known future job openings (say due to the advance notice of a separation from an employee to an employer or vice versa, or perhaps due to anticipated expanded production) might be very different from search for a job that is unfilled (i.e., after an employee leaves a position or the new production date arrives). For a particular employer, the costs of continued search are likely to differ between the two situations (in much the same way that an employed worker who anticipates a layoff or who winds up in an otherwise bad match faces search costs that differ from the costs faced after a layoff or quit). An employer might respond to such a change in the status of a vacancy by adjusting search intensity, the requirements for the job, or the offered wage. Since changes in costs between the two situations are likely to vary with the char-

Table 10.1. Search Strategies

Study	Data	Methods	Findings
Barron, Bishop, and Dunkelberg (1985)	United States, 1978–1980 EOPP first round interviews, 28 local labor markets	Regressions: 1. Extensive search: log number of interviews per offer	Mean number: 5.67 Increases with firm size, education requirements, and on-the-job training staff
		2. Intensive search: log total hours per interview	Mean number: 1.76 Increases with on-the-job training (personnel staff only): higher for professional/technical positions
		3. Total cost: log total hours per offer	Mean number: 8.04 Increases with firm size, education requirements, and training; lower for service positions
		4. Log wage	Directly related to level of extensive and intensive search; no training effect
Barron and Bishop (1985)	United States, 1980–1981 EOPP second round interviews, 28 local labor markets	Regressions: 1. Extensive search: log number of applicants per interview	Mean number: 2.93 Higher if very difficult to fire, if there is advance notice, and at large firms; increases with unionism
		2. Extensive search: log number of interviews per offer	Mean number: 4.48 Higher if very difficult, if trained, if there is advance notice, and at large firms; decreases with unionism
		3. Intensive search: log total hours per applicant	Mean number: 2.09 Higher if very difficult to fire and if trained; increases with cost of capital and decreases with unionism
		4. Log number of offers per hire	Mean number: 1.08 Slightly higher if difficult to fire and if hiring for more than one position; decreases with unionism
		5. Total cost: log total hours per hire	Mean number: 9.87 Increases with difficulty of firing, training, and advance notice; decreases with unionism
Rynes and Boudreau (1988)	United States, 1985 Survey of *Fortune* 1000 companies	Tabulations of author-collected data	Job requirements and starting salaries set by line managers, not personnel staff
Rynes (1988)	Review of many empirical papers	Various: focus on performance by method of hire	Referrals by current employees are relatively reliable
Bishop and Barron (1984)	United States, 1978–1980 EOPP	Regressions: 1. Log number of applicants per offer	Applications per interview/offer higher and interviews per offer lower when employers stockpile applications
		2. Log number of applicants per interview	
		3. Log number of interviews per offer	
		Logit: stockpiling applications	Large firms stockpile more often

Table 10.2. Vacancy Duration Data

Study	Data	Method	Findings
Beaumont (1978)	United Kingdom, 1973–1975 Registered vacancies at two Scotland employment exchanges	Log duration regression, separately for filled and cancelled vacancies	General and local labor market conditions important; skilled position vacancies last longer
Roper (1988)	United Kingdom, 1976–1977 SERP, 100 local labor markets	Ordered probit for long duration, separately for manual and nonmanual vacancies	Manual: durations are longer at very small and very large firms, in manufacturing, and for skilled positions and high wage jobs
			Nonmanual: durations are longer at very small and very large firms; vacancies starting in spring and summer are filled faster
			Both: informal search methods are quickest
van Ours (1988a)	Netherlands, 1986–1987 Nationwide private sector	Proportional hazards model, Weibull baseline ($\alpha t^{\alpha-1}$) and gamma heterogeity distribution	$\alpha = 1.43$ (S.E. 0.09)
			Duration increases with required skill and education requirements and with firm size
			Vacancies in service occupations are shorter
			Internal channels are most effective recruiting method
Renes (1989)	Netherlands, 1986–1987	Step function for hazard, with time-varying coefficients	U-shaped hazard
			Part-time, low skill, and low experience requirement jobs fill faster
			Proportional hazards model rejected

S.E. = standard error.

acteristics of jobs to be filled and with firm characteristics, it seems reasonable to expect that the nature, time, and overall magnitude of employers' responses will vary. Variation of this sort may be responsible in part for the systematically different time paths found by Renes (1989) for vacancies for jobs with different characteristics—but again this is just a guess.

On balance, the supply side of the labor market is well studied if not perfectly understood. The demand side is wide open. The results discussed in this chapter are intriguing, but they must be supplemented by additional studies before the findings can be considered solid. The major effort required in this area is data collection.

Notes

1. We restrict our attention here to studies of microlevel data. Pissarides (1986), for example, offers an analysis of vacancies and unemployment based on aggregate data for the United Kingdom and Schager (1987) analyzes aggregate vacancies and unemployment data for Sweden. Dunne and Roberts (1987) analyze employer data for U.S. employment flows aggregated to the industry level. Holzer (1989) studies vacancy data from the EOPP aggregated to the local labor market level.

2. See Maddala (1983) for a description of the ordered probit model.

3. Kooreman and Ridder (1983) also find evidence of positive duration dependence when they fit a proportional hazards model for vacancy durations using aggregate data.

4. Jackman et al. (1984) present additional evidence for the United Kingdom from the National Survey of Engagements and Vacancies. Here, as in the data analyzed by Roper, vacancies durations are found to be directly related to skill levels. Holzer (1989) presents summary statistics for vacancy duration data collected in the EOPP surveys studied by Barron et al. Specifically,

questions about the most recent hire included a question about the number of days between the recruitment starting date and the new hire's starting date. These data suggest that vacancies for managerial and clerical jobs remain open the longest and that laborer positions fill most quickly. Durations for jobs requiring less than a high school diploma also tend to be shorter than those requiring more education. These findings are consistent with those reported for the United Kingdom and the Netherlands. One surprising finding is that vacancy durations for positions requiring a high school diploma are about the same length, on average, as those requiring some college education.

5. These findings on informal search methods are also consistent with early descriptive evidence on the Chicago labor market presented by Rees and Schultz (1970) and with findings for the market for economists (Carson and Navarro, 1987).

11

Conclusions

We have examined—at length—an impressive collection of empirical studies. Data range from answers to hypothetical questions ("What wage would you accept?") to large and complex panel data sets. Statistical approaches range from simple interpretation of partial and multiple correlations to maximum likelihood estimation of tightly specified theoretical models. Objectives include program evaluation, investigating the determinants of the natural rate of unemployment, and tests of specific models. The feature common to all studies in our review is a relevance to some aspect of search in the labor market. Clearly, an enormous amount of energy and talent has been devoted to this area since Kasper's 1967 study of "asking wages." What have these efforts accomplished?

The first search studies used regression analysis to examine reservation wage data collected for local labor markets. Their results suggested that reservation wages are not constant over the course of a spell of unemployment; a very slight decline seemed to be present in all samples. Early results also suggested that reservation wages vary systematically with observed worker-specific variables (unemployment benefit receipt and benefit amounts, in particular) and with unobserved characteristics. Interrelationships between these two sources of variation in reservation wages—pure duration effects and effects of covariates—have since been examined. In particular, the link between variation in benefit receipt and duration dependence in the reservation wage has been studied and appears important. Continued research has uncovered some potentially serious measurement errors in available reservation wage data; for example, workers frequently accept wages below their reported reservation wages. This disconcerting behavior may reflect a combination of duration dependence in the reservation wage and the timing of interviews. Alternatively, job characteristics other than the wage may be given more consideration by the worker than the studies generally allow.

The next major advance following the direct study of reservation wages was the realization that analysis within the search framework does not require observations on reservation wages. This has been recognized since the early 1970s. Analysis can be carried out using data on spell durations and accepted wages. The 1979 studies by Kiefer and

Neumann demonstrated that it is possible to fit tightly specified nonlinear models within the search framework, and thus identify the effects of variables on the reservation wage (unemployment benefits, in particular), without having observations on reservation wages—but with strong assumptions. Indeed, search models (albeit very simple models) have been among the first stochastic dynamic programming models to be fit to data (both with and without reservation wage observations). The 1979 study by Lancaster and Nickell marked another major advance: the beginning of a large literature that studies economic duration data by modeling the hazard function directly. Current structural modeling efforts involve state-of-the-art econometric and numerical techniques and countless computing cycles.

Subsequent sections of this chapter review results on offers, acceptances, and systematic search; the importance of the type of spell of unemployment; unions and search; effects of unemployment benefits; duration dependence; causes of job separations; demographic and other characteristics; and demand-side search. Before turning to these results we consider the data sets available—not exhaustively, but to illustrate some of the problems involved in making inferences. Of course, no data set is perfect. Despite the problems with currently available data, some common themes do appear. As necessary in assessing an empirical literature, we have looked for results that hold up across data sets and specifications—maintaining the hope that inadequacies of the data cancel out as findings reappear. Following the discussion of substantive results we note some of the econometric advances developed in the course of fitting search models. We then turn to theoretical developments and indicate briefly where more theory would be useful. Throughout, we speculate about potentially productive areas for future research.

Data

The content and quality of available data have clearly influenced the course taken by empirical research in the search framework. The studies we review use data sets from a variety of sources for several countries. The variety reflects ingenuity and enterprise on the part of researchers—no sample was collected for the purpose of assessing the search approach to labor market analysis. Of course, this situation has a downside.

The most common type of data set consists of individual worker interview data, either in a cross section or a panel format. Almost all major sources of supply-side data have certain limitations—an absence of reservation wage data, an absence of information on search methods and intensity, an absence of information on offers declined, a failure to distinguish job spells and employment spells (i.e., job-to-job transitions are not observed), an absence of information on nonwage job characteristics (including nonwage compensation), and limited information on nonemployment income other than unemployment benefits. Special supplements to standard surveys provide some information on reservation wages, job search methods, and receipt of offers, but such instances are rare and there are typically other problems with these data.

First, most samples in use are not representative. Data from social experiments, such as the SIME/DIME and the EOPP, oversample low income individuals or households and are confined to specific labor markets. Treatment effects for noncontrol portions of the samples are also present. Other large surveys, such as the PSID and the NLS, also oversample low income groups. A random sample can be identified in the PSID, but at the cost of a serious reduction in sample size. The NLS also has a cohort structure and survey instruments vary substantially; some research questions can be addressed for some groups, but not others. Similarly, although the PSID is a household survey, questions related to labor market experience have varied over the years and some potentially important questions are addressed only to household heads. Administrative records have been exploited extensively (UI records in the CWBH for the United States, in particular). Here, there are basic problems of take-up and eligibility. For example, about 90 percent of all jobs in the United States are currently covered under the UI system, but less than one-third of unemployed workers actually receive UI benefits at a time. (See Blank and Card [1988], Fields [1977], Gritz and MaCurdy [1988], and Marston [1975]. Glenday and Alam [1982] present similar evidence for Canada.) In terms of substantive conclusions, the consequence of working with nonrepresentative samples is obvious. We may know a lot about benefit recipients and low income workers (low income, white, male high school graduates, in particular), but can the findings be generalized for these narrowly defined groups?

A second basic problem with available worker data concerns the measurement of spell durations. Surveys do not always collect spell duration data in a useful form. For example, total weeks of unemployment in the year between interviews might be collected, but not broken down by spell; the number of spells may not be known. When data on individual spells are reported, long retrospective periods can provide reason for concern. Brief spells may be forgotten. (See, for example, Akerlof and Yellen [1985], Duncan and Hill [1985], Mellow and Sider [1983], Poterba and Summers [1986], and Summers [1986] for discussion of measurement error in labor market data.) The monthly CPS data are useful for analysis of many labor market phenomenon because of large sample sizes, the representativeness of the samples, and detailed labor market data. Using the CPS for longitudinal analysis is complicated, however, by the rotation group structure of the sampling plan and the use of residences as the basic sampling units. Gross flow data constructed by the BLS from the CPS are too aggregated for many purposes. The duration data in UI administrative records are typically limited to observations on weeks of benefit receipt within a benefit year, possibly aggregated over multiple spells. (Earnings data in UI records are also generally censored at program levels of maximum insured earnings, and information on demographic and other characteristics is limited.)

Data from the SIPP, a longitudinal household survey conducted by the U.S. Bureau of the Census since October 1983, are only now becoming available. These may prove to be a useful source for future analysis of labor market dynamics. First, each SIPP Panel (i.e., sample) is large and representative for the United States. Moreover, since a new Panel is started each February, even larger samples can be constructed. Labor market activity is collected for each week in the survey period (about 2.5 years for each Panel) and the detail of the survey questions is sufficient to allow temporary layoffs and spells of nonparticipation to be distinguished. Information on rejected offers and reasons for rejection are also available for the 1985 and 1986 Panels (although numbers of offers and their timing and nonwage characteristics of rejected offers are not reported). Work history data are available for the 1984 and 1986 Panels (though tenure and ongoing unemployment spells are measured perhaps too roughly for the 1984 Panel to be very useful for search analysis). Reservation wage data are also available for a subsample of the 1984 Panel. Outside the United States, new data sets are also being developed. For the United Kingdom, the DHHS has served as a major source of information on the unemployed, although benefit receipt in the first 4 weeks in a spell is uncertain. The group studying the Danish labor market at the Aarhus Business School has a representative panel from the Danish work force; this is likely to be an important source of information as well.

Demand-side data are extremely thin. In the United States, the EOPP represents the major source of data on employer search activity; like the supply-side EOPP, however, there are problems of representativeness. Vacancy duration data are available for the Netherlands and the United Kingdom, and these have proved useful. Microlevel vacancy duration data for the United States have yet to be analyzed. The SIPP data have the potential for being matched with employer data from the Census of Manufacturers. This would be an important advance.

Findings

Offers, Acceptance, and Systematic Search

Perhaps the most important conclusion is that the reservation wage may be less important than was first thought. Variation in the arrival rate of offers appears at least as important in producing variation in transition rates into employment—across workers, over the course of a spell, and across states of the economy. Direct evidence on offers is extremely limited, but available data (for the United States and United Kingdom) suggest that offer rejections are rare. Most of the evidence is indirect, that is, based on wage and duration data and assumptions. The studies that sort out acceptance probabilities and arrival rates typically find little variation in acceptance probabilities. Indeed, the typical acceptance probability is high—in the range of 0.8–1.0. Workers appear to search in markets in which almost all jobs are acceptable. Thus, variation in unemployment durations appears to arise primarily from variation in the likelihood of receiving offers.

Arrival rates of offers are often modeled as exogenous and fixed, but there is evidence that arrivals are endogenous. Studies that look at direct evidence on search intensity and search strategies find systematic variation across individuals. There is evidence that this leads to variation in job "contacts," but less evidence that this leads to variation in numbers of actual offers received. This lack of evidence is due not to insignificant coefficients, but to an absence of data instead. Studies of reservations wages suggest that these are affected by offer arrival probabilities (more frequent arrivals implies a higher reservation wage). There is also some evidence that search intensity and offer arrival rates decline with durations of spells of unemployment.

One finding that emerges, indirectly but consistently across several studies, is the relevance of both systematic search and nonsequential search. The model in which workers are indifferent about the order in which firms are sampled, and in which offers are sampled and decided on one at a time, may be too restrictive. A delay between the time of application for a job and the time that an offer is made may imply that a worker can have more than one outstanding offer. Further, workers may prefer one firm to another. Such considerations have not been considered widely, but they have appeared relevant when entertained.

Types of Unemployment Spells

Studies that consider search behavior and unemployment spell durations by reasons for unemployment find significant differences. First, distinguishing new entrants from the experienced labor force appears important. Distinguishing reasons for unemployment among experienced workers also seems important, although here there are complex problems of definition and measurement.

One case that has received a great deal of attention is the distinction between temporary layoffs and permanent layoffs. In some data sets, this question is essentially moot; the two are not distinguished in any way. In other data sets, it is known whether a worker returns to a former employer. It is not clear, however, that the distinction between permanent and temporary layoffs is this sharp. What appears to matter is a worker's subjective probability of recall. Indeed, not all temporary layoffs are the same—layoffs with definite, fixed-in-advance return dates and layoffs with indefinite durations are undoubtedly different. Of course, there is the basic question of whether a worker on layoff with a recall date should be classified as unemployed, that is, if such workers search, perhaps this should be categorized as "on-the-job" search? Regardless of definition, all of the studies that distinguish temporary and permanent layoffs do find evidence that unemployment duration and search behavior differ along this line of classification. Workers on temporary layoff—either expecting recall or those who are known to return to former employers—have lower search intensities. Workers who expect to be recalled to a job, but who are not recalled, tend to experience longer spells than workers who never expect to be recalled. In sum, the distinction between permanent and temporary layoffs appears to be a potentially important source of heterogeneity in unemployment duration data. Additional attention to issues of definition and measurement along this line seems warranted in future research.

Permanent layoffs can arise involuntarily or voluntarily, as with quits. Involuntary permanent layoffs can be due to dismissal for cause, or due simply to elimination of a job. Distinctions at this fine a level are not well established empirically, but available results suggest that they may be important.

Unions and Search

The effect of unions on search was recognized early in the theoretical search literature (e.g., Holt, 1970; Eaton and Neher, 1975), but empirical examinations have been rare—perhaps due to difficulties with data. Unemployed union workers appear to have higher reservation wages than comparable nonunion workers. There is also some evidence that union members experience longer spells of unemployment, but this is much less clear. Union members may have a higher offer arrival rate, offsetting the effect of the higher reservation wage. We suspect that the union-duration effect is sometimes confounded with temporary layoff effects. We found no studies that examined union effects and permanent–temporary layoff effects simultaneously, but a general finding is that unemployment durations are shorter for construction and other goods-producing workers than for service workers. This may be due to the higher incidence of temporary layoffs in construction, which in turn may be linked to a higher incidence of union membership. Unionism may have an effect on the productivity of time spent searching—on both sides of the market. Job search requirements for receipt of unemployment insurance benefits may be satisfied by registration with a union hiring hall, at least in some states in the United States. This registration seems to be associated with a higher number of employer contacts per week. On the demand side, firms attempting to staff a "union" job see a higher applicant flow than the flow when staffing comparable nonunion jobs. This is perhaps due to hiring hall referrals. By the same token, firms with higher levels of unionism expend a smaller amount of resources (time, in particular) per offer made. Once employed, union workers have smaller wage variance after controlling for observable characteristics. Available data also suggest that they engage in less on-the-job search, and have lower quit rates and longer tenures than nonunion workers. Apparently, the male–female quit rate differential (women quit more, at least in the first year or two on a job) can be explained in part by male–female differences in union membership. Unemployment insurance is linked closely to union membership in Denmark and coverage is thus largely voluntary. Jensen and Pedersen (1987) use aggregate data to examine the decision to be insured via union membership. Not surprisingly, they find that increases in unemployment are accompanied by surges in union membership. Similar relationships could hold elsewhere.

Overall, the presence of unions in the labor market appears to have some real effects on its dynamics. Additional attention to union effects may prove useful.

Unemployment Benefits

The difficult issue of the effect of unemployment benefits on unemployment durations is still unsettled. The "benefit effect," defined (for example) as the elasticity of expected duration with respect to the level of benefits or with respect to the replacement ratio (benefit amount divided by the previous wage), appears to be positive, but with uncertain magnitude. Estimates vary across samples and there is evidence that the benefit effect varies with labor market conditions (responsiveness declines with increases in local unemployment rates), elapsed duration, and age. Benefits also appear to have different effects on the behavior of workers on temporary layoff, relative to the effects on behavior of workers on permanent layoff. There is some empirical evidence that benefits affect search intensity and the choice of search method on the supply side of the market. Estimates also vary with estimation techniques and this sensitivity suggests specification error in modeling the effect of benefits. In particular, potential duration of benefits may be as important as the benefit level. Demand-side analysis of benefit effects within the search framework has been rare, but limited evidence suggests that effects on firm behavior are potentially more important.

To sum up, benefits appear to affect unemployment durations in a complicated way. There is probably no single number—a "benefit effect"—that applies to all workers and to each worker in all circumstances. Sharper modeling of the effects of benefit program parameters on the generation of offers (including layoffs and recalls of workers by firms) would be a useful course for future research, especially in view of the finding that reservation wages are less important empirically than the arrival rate of offers.

Duration Dependence

Results on duration dependence in the transition rate into employment are quite sensitive to specification. Findings of strong negative duration dependence in the hazard appear to result from uncontrolled heterogeneity. As expected, the estimates of the extent of duration dependence decline as heterogeneity is controlled. There is some evidence of positive duration dependence in the hazard. As noted, reservation wage studies tend to find a slight decline in the reservation wage with duration, which is consistent with this finding of an increasing hazard in duration data studies. Additional evidence suggests that increases in the hazard with duration are due in part to the effect of potential duration of benefits—ignoring this effect leads to overestimation of the extent of positive duration dependence. Fixed assets in a world of imperfect capital markets could potentially produce the same results. A number of studies find that duration dependence is insignificant after controlling for heterogeneity with a suitable list of explanatory variables (time-varying variables, in particular) or with a mixing distribution for unobserved heterogeneity. The bottom line here seems to be that additional attention to modeling time-varying processes (comparable to time variation in the level of benefits) could yield interesting results.

Duration dependence in the employment hazard is perhaps more firmly established. The rate of leaving employment appears to decline with duration. However, most studies have used specifications that impose monotonicity. There is some weak evidence that this hazard may not be monotonic—it may increase and then decline.

Separations

The process of leaving jobs is still not well understood. On-the-job search seems to be less common among workers who experience an intervening spell of unemployment, but questions regarding the direction of causation remain open. The wage–tenure relationship represents an active area of current research. The significant positive correlation (and regression coefficient) in the cross section is well established, but the underlying economic interpretation remains unclear. A surprising number of job changes (with and without on-the-job search) involve wage cuts. This can be interpreted as evidence consistent with a variety of search and matching theories—but this observation also calls into question the importance of nonwage considerations on the part of workers moving about in the labor market. The wage may not be a "sufficient statistic" characterizing job attributes. It may make sense for a worker to concentrate on the wage in making the decision to accept a job with many unknown attributes. As these attributes are learned, however, the relative importance of the wage may decline. Nonwage compensation also appears important when measured, particularly for older workers. (It is somewhat disconcerting that studies in the personnel area regard the wage as one of many job attributes—not necessarily the most important.)

We know that unemployment spells differ by the reasons for their origins. However, the type of origin of a spell may well be endogenous. There is a strong possibility that modeling type of separation and unemployment duration as jointly endogenous will be useful.

Demographic and Other Characteristics

Throughout our review, we find evidence of distinct differences in the experience of workers having different characteristics. This holds for the cases previously noted—benefit recipients versus nonrecipients, workers on temporary layoff versus workers on permanent layoff, and union members versus nonmembers. It also holds for demographic differences—older workers versus younger workers, males versus females, and (perhaps most clearly) white workers versus nonwhite workers. When examined, results that vary across workers in different demographic groups include those for the effect of benefits on unemployment durations. A negligible effect is found for nonwhites in almost every sample, for example, and results for females generally contrast with those for males within age–race cohorts. Results from tests of the distinction between unemployment and nonparticipation also suggest nonnegligible differences across groups. The difference may not be important for adult males. Studies of job-exit behavior find evidence of systematic age and gender differences (although currently available evidence on the latter is restricted to youth)—both in terms of motivation and returns. In many cases, findings on demographic differences are only secondary, that is, not the direct objective of researchers. The strength and breadth of such findings, however, suggest that a more direct focus would be useful.

Variation with level of educational attainment comes across clearly in almost every case considered. Differences also appear according to occupation, industry, geographic location, and marital status. Unlike age, race, and sex, these characteristics reflect choice on the part of workers, given opportunities faced. They are not part of one's initial endowment. Some work has been done on the links between some of these choices and search considerations. Additional work on these questions—both theoretical and empirical—could be productive.

Demand

The results of the few existing demand-side studies are consistent with the supply-side findings and complement them in several ways. Firms apparently do not make a lot of offers per position, indicating a belief that acceptance probabilities are high. The length of time and resources it takes to fill a vacancy appear to vary substantially with job characteristics and requirements. There is evidence of nonlinearity in the hazard function for vacancies, but the behavior giving rise to this nonlinearity is unclear.

Search Experiments

Laboratory experiments involving student subjects in search situations have found behavior consistent with the implications of search theory. A reservation wage policy can be induced and the reservation wage apparently declines with duration. There are not yet many studies in this framework. There is one study of choice of search strategy. It would be interesting to design an experiment to study search intensity, and perhaps a comparison of on-the-job versus unemployed job search behavior.

Econometrics

Econometric techniques have improved markedly as this literature has accumulated, which has allowed more information to be extracted from available data. Matters of selectivity and censoring are now given careful attention. Application of nonlinear methods and models are now routine. The study of duration data, in particular, has become substantially more sophisticated in the last decade. Indeed, the development of sophisticated techniques for modeling heterogeneity was a direct response to an empirical puzzle. Namely, simple calculations of hazard functions for unemployment durations implied that the probability of leaving unemployment decreased as spell length increased. Of course, search models implied that this probability is either constant or increasing, as the reservation wage falls (ignoring potential effects of learning). It was quickly recognized that heterogeneity led to a spurious impression that the hazard was decreasing—as those individuals most likely to be reemployed become reemployed, the remaining pool of individuals in the sample become dominated by those least likely to be reemployed. Thus, even if each individual has a constant hazard, the aggregate would appear to decline.

A number of areas still need improvement. Left censoring in models with duration dependence still poses a difficult problem. Most of the duration studies (by a large margin) are carried out in the proportional hazards framework; there is no economic justification for this restriction and alternatives need more attention. In many cases the proportional hazard assumption is rejected when tested. Similarly, most of the dynamic models of turnover have restricted attention to Markov (or semi-Markov) processes. Again, there is no solid justification for this and alternatives should be explored. Complicated, nonlinear models can be extraordinarily sensitive to seemingly innocuous assumptions. Consequently, methods for specification analysis, often involving generalized notions of residuals, should be applied routinely. Tests and diagnostics have been developed for a number of models. Guidelines for their use and interpretation, as well as evaluation of their performance, should be developed. The literature on estimation of general dynamic programming models is beginning to advance. Estimation of job search models was an early application and will certainly continue to be a proving ground for these techniques.

Theory

Theoretical analysis of job search has advanced along with applications. Models cover risk-averse search, finite-horizon search, search with benefits that run out, multistate search, and many other topics. Most of the effort has concentrated on worker behavior—characterizing the reservation wage or sequence of reservation wages, in particular. There is work on time allocated to search by workers, but more work on the determination of offer arrivals would be worthwhile. Attention should be paid to the demand side—the generation of vacancies and the mechanisms by which they are filled.

Equilibrium models offer potential empirical payoff. Theoretical analyses of search equilibrium include Albrecht and Axell (1984), Axell (1977), Albrecht, Axell, and Lang (1986), Allen and Azariadis (1988), Barron et al. (1988), Burdett (1988), Burdett and Judd (1983), Burdett and Mortensen (1989), Burdett and Vishwanath (1988a), Butters (1977), Diamond (1971, 1981, 1982, 1984), Greenwald and Stiglitz (1988), Lang (1990), MacDonald (1982, 1983, 1988), MacMinn (1980), McKenna (1987), Montgomery (1989), Mortensen (1982, 1986a, 1990a), Pissarides (1984a,b, 1985a,b, 1988), Ramaswami (1983), Reinganum (1979), Rothschild (1974), Saloner (1985), Stiglitz (1985), Wernerfelt (1988), Wilde (1977), Wilde and Schwartz (1979), and Wilson (1980). Burdett (1990) presents a detailed survey of the results obtained in this research to date. Eckstein and Wolpin (1989) attempt to fit a version of the Albrecht–Axell equilibrium model. Their results are mixed but not disastrous; the theoretical model is quite simple and they work with data for a demographic group whose experience is typically difficult to explain—a sample of young nonstudent high school graduates from the New Youth Cohort of the NLS. Equilibrium modeling is the beginning of a potentially important line of work in the search framework. We expect rapid theoretical and empirical advances.

The search approach has led to a focus on dynamics in understanding the labor market. We now know quite a bit about these flows and their variation with regressors and across demographic groups. "Structural" interpretation of these flows is more problematic. In the Markovian framework we are accustomed to, it is these flow rates that determine the equilibrium or natural unemployment rate. Policies affecting the flow rates are likely to have long-term effects; those focused on the stock at a particular period in time will have only short-term effects. This notion has been crucial in the discussion of unemployment insurance policy and its effect on the natural rate of unemployment. Of course, the intuition leading to this generalization is based on Markovian (or semi-Markovian) models, and this specification is rarely checked.

Looking across studies, we have found evidence that the empirical (and theoretical) work on search would benefit from changes of emphasis. First, the evidence shows that we have perhaps overemphasized the setting of reservation wages as a research area. There are definite advances to be made in studying the process by which workers get offers (on the job or otherwise). Second, more attention to systematic search, rather than random sequential search may be productive. Finally, much more attention needs to be paid to nonwage characteristics of a job. It is natural (for economists) to focus on the wage as the most important job characteristic a worker considers when taking or rejecting a job, especially when we consider that the worker is searching in a particular industry or occupation. However, nonwage characteristics are also important in acceptances and may be crucial in determining separations.

The search framework will doubtless continue to be a useful way to model the labor market. We look forward to the next round of empirical advances. Some of these will undoubtedly be a result of availability of new data.

References

Abowd, J. and A. Zellner (1985): "Estimating Gross Labor–Force Flows." *Journal of Business and Economic Statistics* 3, 254–283.

Abraham, K. G. and H. S. Farber (1987): "Job Duration, Seniority, and Earnings." *American Economic Review* 77(3), 278–297.

Adams, J. D. (1985): "Permanent Differences in Unemployment and Permanent Wage Differentials." *Quarterly Journal of Economics* 100, 29–56.

Adams, J. D. (1986): "Equilibrium Taxation and Experience Rating in a Federal System of Umployment Insurance." *Journal of Public Economics* 29, 51–77.

Akerlof, G. and B. Main (1980): "Unemployment Spells and Unemployment Experience." *American Economic Review* 70, December, 885–893.

Akerlof, G. and B. Main (1980): "Unemployment Spells and Unemployment Experience." *American Economic Review* 70, December, 885–893.

Akerlof, G. and B. Main (1981): "An Experience-Weighted Measure of Employment and Unemployment Durations." *American Economic Review* 71, December, 1003–1011.

Akerlof, G. A., A. K. Rose, and J. L. Yellen (1988): "Job Switching and Job Satisfaction in the U.S. Labor Market." *Brookings Papers on Economic Activity* 2, 495–582.

Alaouze, C. M. (1987): "Empirical Evidence on the Sign of the Slope of the Hazard Rate from Unemployment from a Fixed Effects Model." *Journal of Applied Econometrics* 2, 159–168.

Albrecht, J. W. and B. Axell (1984): "An Equilibrium Model of Search Unemployment." *Journal of Political Economy* 92(4), 824–840.

Albrecht, J. W., B. Axell, and H. Lang (1986): "General Equilibrium Wage and Price Distributions." *Quarterly Journal of Economics* 101(407), 687–706.

Albrecht, J. W., B. Holmlund, and H. Lang (1986): "Job Search and the Transition to Employment: Theory." Mimeo, University of Stockholm.

Allen, B. and C. Azariadis (1988): "Informational Theories of Employment." *American Economic Review Proceedings* 78(2), May, 104–109.

Alpern, S. and D. J. Snower (1988): "'High-Low Search' in Product and Labor Markets." *Amercian Economic Review Proceedings* 72(2), May, 356–362.

Altonji, J. G. and C. H. Paxson (1988): "Labor Supply Preferences, Hours Constraints, and Hours-Wage Trade-Offs." *Journal of Labor Economics* 6(2), 254–276.

Altonji, J. and R. Shakatko (1987): "Do Wages Rise with Job Seniority?" *Review of Economic Studies* 54, 437–459.

Ashenfelter, O. and J. Blum (eds.) (1976): *Evaluating the Labor Market Effects of Social Programs.* Princeton University Press, Princeton.

Ashenfelter, O. and W. Oates (eds.) (1977): *Essays in Labor Market Analysis.* Halstead Press, New York.

Atkinson, A. B. and J. Micklewright (1985): *Unemployment Benefits and Unemployment Duration.* Imediaprint Limited, London.

Atkinson, A. B., J. Gomulka, J. Micklewright, and N. Rau (1984): "Unemployment Benefit, Duration and Incentives in Britain." *Journal of Public Economics* 23, 3–26.

Axell, B. (1977): "Search Market Equilibrium." *Scandinavian Journal of Economics* 79(1), 20–40.

Baily, M. N. (1977): "On the Theory of Layoffs and Unemployment." *Econometrica* 45, July, 1043–1063.

Baily, M. N. (ed.) (1982): *Workers, Jobs, and Inflation.* The Brookings Institution, Washington, D.C.

Baker, J. M. and P. K. Trivedi (1985): "Estimation of Unemployment Duration from Grouped Data: A Comparative Study." *Journal of Labor Economics* 3(2), 153–174.

Barnes, W. F. (1975): "Job Search Models, the Duration of Unemployment, and the Asking Wage: Some Empirical Evidence." *Journal of Human Resources* 10, Spring, 230–240.

Barron, J. M. (1975): "Search in the Labor Market and the Duration of Unemployment." *American Economic Review* 65, 934–942.

Barron, J. M. and J. Bishop (1985): "Extensive Search, Intensive Search and Hiring Costs: New Evidence on Employer Hiring Activity." *Economic Inquiry* 23, July, 363–382.

Barron, J. M. and O. Gilley (1979): "The Effect of Unemployment Insurance on the Search Process." *Industrial and Labor Relations Review* 32, 363–366.

Barron, J. M. and O. Gilley (1981a): "Erratum." *Industrial and Labor Relations Review* 34, 533.

Barron, J. M. and O. Gilley (1981b): "Job Search and Vacancy Contacts: Note." *American Economic Review* 71, September, 747–752.

Barron, J. M. and S. McCafferty (1977): "Job Search, Labor Supply and the Quit Decision." *American Economic Review* 67(4), September, 683–691.

Barron, J. M. and W. Mellow (1979): "Search Effort in the Labor Market." *Journal of Human Resources* 14, Summer, 389–404.

Barron, J. M. and W. Mellow (1981a): "Changes in Labor Force Status among the Unemployed." *Journal of Human Resources* 16, Summer, 427–441.

Barron, J. M. and W. Mellow (1981b): "Unemployment Insurance: The Recipients and Its Impact." *Southern Economic Journal* 47(3), 606–616.

Barron, J. M. and W. Mellow (1982): "Labor Contract Formation, Search Requirements, and Use of a Public Employment Service." *Economic Inquiry* 20, July, 381–387.

Barron, J. M., J. Bishop, and W. C. Dunkelberg (1985): "Employer Search: The Interviewing and Hiring of New Employees." *Review of Economics and Statistics* 67, 43–52.

Barron, J., D. Black, and M. Lowenstein (1987): "Employer Size: The Implications for Search, Training, Capital Investment, Starting Wages, and Wage Growth." *Journal of Labor Economics* 5(1), 76–89.

Barron, J. M., D. A. Black, and M. A. Lowenstein (1988): "A Simple Equilibrium Job Matching Model." Working Paper E-128-88. University of Kentucky.

Barron, J., D. Black, and M. Lowenstein (1989): "Job Matching and On-the-Job Training." *Journal of Labor Economics* 7(1), 1–19.

Bartel, A. P. (1979): "The Migration Decision: What Role Does Job Mobility Play?" *American Economic Review* 69, 775–786.

Bartel, A. P. (1980): "Earnings Growth on the Job and between Jobs." *Economic Inquiry* 18, 123–137.

Bartel, A. P. (1982): "Wages, Nonwage Job Characteristics, and Labor Mobility." *Industrial and Labor Relations Review* 35, 578–589.

Bartel, A. P. and G. Borjas (1981): "Wage Growth and Job Turnover: An Empirical Analysis." In S. Rosen (ed.), *Studies in Labor Markets*. University of Chicago Press, Chicago, pp. 65–90.

Bean, C., R. Layard, and S. Nickell (1987): *The Rise of Unemployment*. Basil Blackwell, New York.

Beaumont, P. B. (1978): "The Duration of Registered Vacancies: An Exploratory Exercise." *Scottish Journal of Political Economy* 25, 75–87.

Becker, G. S. (1962): "Investments in Human Capital: A Theoretical Analysis." *Journal of Political Economy* 70, October, 9–49.

Becker, G. S. (1964): *Human Capital*. NBER, University Microfilms, Ann Arbor.

Becker, G. S. and G. Stigler (1974): "Law Enforcement, Malfeasance, and Compensation of Enforcers." *Journal of Legal Studies* 3, 1–18.

Belzil, C. (1990): "Unemployment Insurance, Unemployment and Labor Market Transitions: An Empirical Analysis with Canadian Data." Ph.D. Thesis, Cornell University, Ithaca, N.Y.

Benhabib, J. and C. Bull (1983): "Job Search: The Choice of Intensity." *Journal of Political Economy* 91, 747–764.

Ben-Horim, M. and D. Zuckerman (1987): "The Effect of Unemployment Insurance on Unemployment Duration." *Journal of Labor Economics* 5(3), 386–390.

Berkovec, J. and S. Stern (1988): "Job Exit Behavior of Older Men." Working Paper, University of Virginia.

Berkovitch, E. (1990): "A Stigma Theory of Unemployment Duration." In Y. Weiss and G. Fishelson (eds.), *Advances in the Theory and Measurement of Unemployment*. Macmillan, London, in press.

Bishop, J. and J. Barron (1984): "Stockpiling Job Applicants." *Proceedings of the Thirty–Seventh Annual Meeting of the Industrial and Labor Relations Association* 107–114.

Black, M. (1981a): "An Empirical Test of the Theory of On-the-Job Search." *Journal of Human Resources* 16, Winter, 129–140.

Black, M. (1981b): "Pecuniary Implications of On-the-Job Search and Quit Activity." *Review of Economics and Statistics* 62, May, 222–229.

Blackwell, D. (1965): "Discounted Dynamic Programming." *Annals of Mathematical Statistics* 36, 226–235.

Blank, R. and D. Card (1988): "Recent Trends in Insured and Uninsured Unemployment." Working Paper 243, Princeton University.

Blau, D. M. (1988): "Search for Nonwage Job Characteristics: A Test of the Reservation Wage Hypothesis." Working Paper 88-6, University of North Carolina.

Blau, D. M. and P. K. Robins (1986a): "Job Search, Wage Offers, and Unemployment Insurance." *Journal of Public Economics* 29, 173–197.

Blau, D. M. and P. K. Robins (1986b): "Labor Supply Response to Welfare Programs: A Dynamic Analysis." *Journal of Labor Economics* 4(1), 82–104.

Blau, F. and L. M. Kahn (1981a): "Causes and Consequences of Layoffs." *Economic Inquiry* 19, April, 270–296.

Blau, F, and L. M. Kahn (1981b): "Race and Sex Differences in Quits by Young Workers." *Industrial and Labor Relations Review* 34, July, 563–577.

Blau, F. and L. M. Kahn (1983): "Job Search and Unionized Employment." *Economic Inquiry* July, 412–430.

Blundell, R. and I. Walker (1986): *Unemployment, Search and Labour Supply*. Cambridge University Press, Cambridge.

Borjas, G. and M. S. Goldberg (1978): "The Economics of Job Search." *Economic Inquiry* 16, 119–125.

Borjas, G. and J. Heckman (1980): "Does Unemployment Cause Future Unemployment? Definitions, Questions, and Answers from a Continuous Time Model of Heterogeneity and State Dependence." *Economica* 47, May, 247–283.

Bowers, J. K. and D. Harkess (1979): "Duration of Unemployment by Age and Sex." *Economica* 46, 239–260.

Bradshaw, T. (1973): "Job Seeking Methods Used by Unemployed Workers." *Monthly Labor Review* 96, 35–40.

Brechling, F. (1977): "The Incentive Effects of the U.S. Unemployment Insurance Tax." In R. Ehrenberg (ed.), *Research in Labor Economics,* Vol. 1. JAI Press, Greenwich, Conn., pp. 41–102.

Brechling, F. (1981): "Layoffs and Unemployment Insurance." In S. Rosen (ed.), *Studies in Labor Markets.* University of Chicago Press, Chicago, pp. 187–208.

Brown, J. (1989): "Why Do Wages Increase with Tenure?" *American Economic Review* 79(5), 971–991.

Bull, C. and B. Jovanovic (1987): "The Role of Matching and Relative Demand Shocks in Generating Turnover." *Review of Economic Studies* 54.

Bull, C. and B. Jovanovic (1988): "Mismatch versus Derived-Demand Shift as Causes of Labour Mobility." *Review of Economic Studies* 55, 169–175.

Burdett, K. (1973): "Theories of Search in the Labor Market." Technical Analysis Paper No. 37. U.S. Department of Labor, Washington, D.C.

Burdett, K. (1975): "Systematic Search, Search Order, and Risk in a Labor Market." World Congress, Toronto.

Burdett, K. (1978): "A Theory of Employee Job Search and Quit Rates." *American Economic Review* 68, 212–220.

Burdett, K. (1979a): "Search, Leisure, and Individual Labor Supply." In S. Lippman and J. McCall (eds.), *The Economics of Job Search.* North Holland, New York, pp. 157–170.

Burdett, K. (1979b): "Unemployment Insurance Payments as a Search Subsidy: A Theoretical Analysis." *Economic Inquiry* 17(3), 333–342.

Burdett, K. (1988): "Micro Equilibrium Wage Distributions." Mimeo, Cornell University, July.

Burdett, K. (1990): "Search Market Models: A Survey." Working Paper, University of Essex.

Burdett, K. and K. Judd (1983): "Equilibrium Price Dispersion." *Econometrica* 51(4), July, 955–970.

Burdett, K. and D. T. Mortensen (1978): "Labor Supply Under Uncertainty." In R. Ehrenberg (ed.), *Research in Labor Economics,* Vol. 2. JAI Press, Greenwich, Conn., pp. 109–157.

Burdett, K. and D. T. Mortensen (1980): "Search, Layoffs, and Labor Market Equilibrium." *Journal of Political Economy* 88, August, 652–672.

Burdett, K. and D. T. Mortensen (1989): "Equilibrium Wage Differentials: Compensating and Otherwise." Mimeo, Cornell University.

Burdett, K. and L. Muus (1989): "Logconcavity and the Economics of Information." Mimeo, Cornell University.

Burdett, K. and J. Ondrich (1985): "How Changes in Labor Demand Affect Unemployed Workers." *Journal of Labor Economics* 3(1), 1–10.

Burdett, K. and S. Sharma (1988): "On Labor Market Histories." Mimeo, Cornell University, August.

Burdett, K. and T. Vishwanath (1988a): "Balanced Matching and Labor Market Equilibrium." *Journal of Political Economy* 96, 1048–1065.

Burdett, K. and T. Vishwanath (1988b): "Declining Reservation Wages and Learning." *Review of Economic Studies* 55(184), 655–665.

Burdett, K. and R. Wright (1986): "The Effects of Unemployment Insurance on Layoffs, Hours per Worker, and Wages." Working Paper, Cornell University, March.

Burdett, K., N. Kiefer, D. Mortensen, and G. Neumann (1980): "A Dynamic Model of Employment, Unemployment and Labor Force Participation: Estimates from the DIME Data." Manuscript, Cornell University.

Burdett, K., N. Kiefer, D. Mortensen, and G. Neumann (1984a): "Earnings, Unemployment, and the Allocation of Time over Time." *Review of Economic Studies* 51, 559–578.

Burdett, K., N. Kiefer, D. Mortensen, and G. Neumann (1984b): "Steady States as Natural Rates in a Dynamic Discrete Choice Model of Labor Supply." In G. Neumann and N. Westergaard-Nielsen (eds.), *Studies in Labor Market Dynamics.* Springer-Verlag, Heidelberg, pp. 74–97.

Burdett, K., N. Kiefer, and S. Sharma (1985): "Layoffs and Duration Dependence in a Model of Turnover." *Journal of Econometrics* 28, 51–69.

Burgess, S. M. (1988): "Search, Job Changing Costs and Unemployment." Mimeo, University of Bristol.

Burgess, P. L. and J. L. Kingston (1971): "Unemployment Insurance, Job Search, and the Demand for Leisure: Comment." *Western Economic Journal* 9(4), 447–450.

Burgess, P. L. and J. L. Kingston (1974): "Worksearch Knowledge, Schooling, and Earnings." *Industrial and Labor Relations Review* 8(3), October, 308–312.

Burgess, P. L. and J. L. Kingston (1975): "Unemployment Insurance and Unemployment Duration." *Quarterly Review of Economics and Business* 15(4), 65–79.

Burgess, P. L. and J. L. Kingston (1977): "Impact of Unemployment Insurance Benefits on Reemployment Success." *Industrial and Labor Relations Review* 30(3), July, 25–31.

Butler, J. S., K. H. Anderson, and R. Burkhauser (1989): "Work and Health after Retirement: A Competing Risk Model with Semiparametric Unobserved Heterogeneity." *Review of Economics and Statistics* 71, 48–53.

Butters, G. R. (1977): "Equilibrium Distributions of Sales and Advertising Prices." *Review of Economic Studies* 44, 465–491.

Cain, G. and H. Watts (eds.) (1973): *Income Maintenance and Labor Supply.* Academic Press, New York.

Card, D. and D. Sullivan (1988): "Measuring the Effects of Subsidized Training Programs on Movements in and out of Employment." *Econometrica* 56(3), May, 497–530.

Carson, R. T. and P. Navarro (1988): "A Seller's (& Buyer's) Guide to the Job Market for Beginning Academic Economists." *Journal of Economic Perspectives* 2(2), 137–148.

Chamberlain, G. (1985): "Heterogeneity, Omitted Variable Bias, and Duration Dependence." In J. Heckman and B. Singer (eds.), *Longitudinal Analysis of Labor Market Data.* Cambridge University Press, New York, pp. 3–38.

Chang, H. (1985): "Age and the Length of Unemployment Spells: A Structural Hazard Analysis." Ph.D. Thesis, Cornell University, Ithaca, N.Y.

Chapin, G. (1971): "Unemployment Insurance, Job Search, and the Demand for Leisure." *Western Economic Journal* 9(1), 102–107.

Chesher, A. (1984): "Testing for Neglected Heterogeneity," *Econometrica* 52, 865–872.

Chesher, A. and T. Lancaster (1981): "Stock and Flow Sampling." *Economic Letters* 8, 63–65.

Chesher, A. and T. Lancaster (1983): "The Estimation of Models of Labour Market Behavior." *Review of Economic Studies* L, 609–624.

Chesher, A. and T. Lancaster (1985): "Residuals, Tests, and Plots with a Job Matching Illustration." Mimeo, University of Bristol.

Chesher, A. and R. Spady (1988): "Asymptotic Expansions of the Information Matrix Test Statistic." Discussion Paper, University of Bristol.

Chirinko, R. (1982): "An Empirical Investigation of the Returns to Job Search." *American Economic Review* 72, 498–501.

Christensen, B. J. and N. M. Kiefer (1990): "The Exact Likelihood Function for an Empirical Job Search Model." Center for Analytic Economics Working Paper, Cornell University.

Clark, K. B. and L. H. Summers (1979): "Labor Market Dynamics and Unemployment: A Reconsideration." *Brooking Papers on Economic Activity* 1, 13–72.

Clark, K. B. and L. H. Summers (1982a): "The Dynamics of Youth Unemployment." In R. Freeman and D. Wise (eds.), *The Youth Labor Market Problem.* University of Chicago Press, Chicago, pp. 199–234.

Clark, K. B. and L. H. Summers (1982b): "Unemployment Insurance and Labor Market Transitions." In M. N. Baily (ed.), *Workers, Jobs, and Inflation*. The Brookings Institution, Washington, D.C., pp. 279–324.

Classen, K. P. (1977): "The Effect of Unemployment Insurance on the Duration of Unemployment and Subsequent Earnings." *Industrial and Labor Relations Review* 30(8), 438–444.

Classen, K. P. (1979): "Unemployment Insurance and Job Search." In S. Lippman and J. McCall (eds.), *Studies in the Economics of Search*. North-Holland, New York, pp. 191–219.

Corcoran, M. and G. Duncan (1979): "Work History, Labor Force Attachment, and Earnings Differences between the Races and Sexes." *Journal of Human Resources* 14, Winter, 3–20.

Corcoran, M. and M. S. Hill (1985): "Reoccurrence of Unemployment among Adult Men." *Journal of Human Resources* 20(2), Spring, 165–183.

Corcoran, M., L. Datcher, and G. J. Duncan (1980): "Most Workers Find Jobs through Word of Mouth." *Monthly Labor Review* 103, 33–35.

Cotton, J. and J. Tuttle (1986): "Employee Turnover: A Meta-Analysis and Review with Implications for Research." *Academy of Management Review* 11, 55–70.

Cousineau, J. M. (1985): "Unemployment Insurance and Labour Market Adjustment." In F. Vaillancourt (ed.), *Income Distribution & Economic Security in Canada*, Vol. 1. Royal Commission on the Economic Union and Development Prospects for Canada, Toronto.

Cox, D. R. (1962): *Renewal Theory*. Methuen, London.

Cox, D. R. (1972): "Regression Models and Life Tables." *Journal of the Royal Statistical Society B* 34, 187–220.

Cox, D. R. (1975): "Partial Likelihood." *Biometrica* 62, 269–276.

Cox, D. R. and D. Oakes (1984): *Analysis of Survival Data*. Chapman & Hall, London.

Cox, J. C. and R. L. Oaxaca (1988): "When Enough Is Enough: Direct Tests of the Reservation Wage Property of Sequential Search Models." Working Paper, University of Arizona.

Cox, J. C. and R. Oaxaca (1989a): "Direct Tests of the Reservation Property." Working Paper, University of Arizona.

Cox, J. C. and R. L. Oaxaca (1989b): "Laboratory Experiments with a Finite Horizon Job Search Model." *Journal of Risk and Uncertainty* 2, 301–330.

Crawford, V. P. and E. M. Knoer (1981): "Job Matching with Heterogeneous Firms and Workers." *Econometrica* 49, 437–450.

Cripps, T. F. and R. J. Darling (1974): "An Analysis of the Duration of Male Unemployment in Great Britain." *Economic Journal* 84, 289–316.

Crosslin, R. and D. Stevens (1973): "The Asking Wage-Actual Wage Relation." *Proceedings of the Business and Economics Section, American Statistical Association,* December.

Crosslin, R. and D. Stevens (1977): "The Asking Wage-Duration of Unemployment Relation Revisited." *Southern Economic Journal* 43, 1298–1302.

Dagsvik, J., B. Jovanovic, and A. Shepard (1985): "A Foundation for Three Popular Assumptions in Job-Matching Models." *Journal of Labor Economics* 3(4), 403–420.

Danforth, J. (1979): "On the Role of Consumption and Decreasing Absolute Risk Aversion in the Theory of Job Search." In S. Lippman and J. McCall (eds.), *Studies in the Economics of Search*. North Holland, New York, pp. 109–131.

Danziger, S., R. Haveman, and R. Plotnick (1981): "How Income Transfer Programs Affect Work, Savings, and the Income Distribution: A Critical Review." *Journal of Economic Literature* 19, September, 978–1028.

Darby, M. (1976): "Three-and-a-Half Million U.S. Employees Have Been Mislaid: Or, an Explanation of Unemployment, 1934–41." *Journal of Political Economy* 84, 1–16.

Darby, M. R., J. C. Haltiwager, and M. W. Plant (1985): "Unemployment Rate Dynamics and Persistent Unemployment under Rational Expectations." *American Economic Review* 75, September, 614–637.

Darby, M. R., J. C. Haltiwager, and M. W. Plant (1986): "The Ins and Outs of Unemployment: The Ins Wins." UCLA Discussion Paper No. 411.

Datcher, L (1983): "The Impact of Formal Networks on Quit Behavior." *Review of Economics and Statistics* 56, 491–495.

Davis, S. J. (1985): "Allocative Disturbances and Temporal Asymmetry in Labor Market Fluctuations." Brown University, January.

Davis, S. J. (1987): "Fluctuations in the Pace of Labor Reallocations." *Carnegie-Rochester Conference Series on Public Policy* 27, Autumn, 335–402.

Deere, D. R. (1987): "Labor Turnover, Job-Specific Skills, and Efficiency in a Search Model. *Quarterly Journal of Economics* 102(4), November, 815–833.

Deere, D. R. (1988): "Unemployment Insurance and Employment." Working Paper, Texas A&M University, January.

Deere, D. R. and S. N. Wiggins (1989): "Plant Closings, Advance Notice, and Private Contractual Failure." Mimeo, Texas A&M University.

DeGroot, M. H. (1970): *Optimal Statistical Decisions.* McGraw-Hill, New York.

Devine, T. J. (1988a): "Arrivals versus Acceptance: The Source of Variation in Reemployment Rates across Demographic Groups." Working Paper, The Pennsylvania State University, April.

Devine, T. J. (1988b): "Interpreting Reemployment Patterns in the Search Framework." Ph.D. Dissertation, Cornell University.

Diamond, P. (1971): "A Model of Price Adjustment." *Journal of Economic Theory* 3, 156–168.

Diamond, P. (1981): "Mobility Costs, Frictional Unemployment, and Efficiency." *Journal of Political Economy* 89, 798–812.

Diamond, P. (1982): "Wage Determination and Efficiency in Search Equilibrium." *Review of Economic Studies* 49, 217–227.

Diamond, P. (1984): *A Search-Equilibrium Approach to the Micro Foundations of Macroeconomics.* MIT Press, Cambridge.

Diamond, P. and M. Rothschild (1978): *Uncertainty in Economics.* Academic Press, New York.

Disney, R. (1979): "Recurrent Spells and the Concentration of Unemployment in Great Britain." *Economic Journal* March, 109–119.

Duncan, G. J. and D. H. Hill (1985): "An Investigation of the Extent and Consequences of Measurement Error in Labor-Economic Survey Data." *Journal of Labor Economics* 3(4), 508–532.

Dunne, T. and M. Roberts (1987): "The Duration of Employment Opportunities in U.S. Manufacturing." Working Paper, The Pennsylvania State University.

Dunne, T., M. J. Roberts, and L. Samuelson (1989): "Plant Turnover and Gross Employment Flows in the U.S. Manufacturing Sector." *Journal of Labor Economics* 7(1), 48–71.

Dynarski, M. and S. Sheffrin (1987): "New Evidence on the Cyclical Behavior of Unemployment Durations." In K. Lang and J. Leonard (eds.), *Unemployment and the Structure of Labor Markets.* Basil-Blackwell, New York, pp. 164–185.

Eaton, B. C. and P. A. Neher (1975): "Unemployment, Underemployment, and Optimal Job Search." *Journal of Political Economy* 83, 355–375.

Ebmer, R. and J. Zweimuller (1990): "Do They Come Back Again? Job Search, Labour Market Segmentation and State Dependence as Explanations of Repeat Unemployment." University of Linz, Austria.

Eckstein, Z. and K. I. Wolpin (1990): "Estimating a Market Equilibrium Search Model from Panel Data on Individuals." *Econometrica,* in press.

Ehrenberg, R. G. (1981): "The Demographic Structure of Unemployment Rates and Labor Market Transition Probabilities." In R. G. Ehrenberg (ed.), *Research in Labor Economics,* Vol 3. JAI Press, Greenwich, Conn., pp. 241–291.

Ehrenberg, R. G. and G. Jakubson (1989): *"Advanced Notice Provisions in Plant Closing Legislation: Do They Matter?"* W.E. Upjohn Insititue, Kalamazoo.

Ehrenberg, R. G. and R. L. Oaxaca (1976): "Unemployment Insurance, Duration of Unemployment, and Subsequent Wage Gain." *American Economic Review* 66, 754–766.

Ehrenberg, R. G. and R. Smith (1988): *Modern Labor Economics,* 3rd ed. Scott Foresman, Glenview, Ill.

Elbers, C. and G. Ridder (1982): "True and Spurious Duration Dependence: The Identifiability of the Proportional Hazard Model." *Review of Economic Studies* XLIX, 403–409.

Ellwood D. (1982): "Teenage Unemployment: Temporary Blemish or Permanent Scar?" In R. Freeman and D. Wise (eds.), *The Youth Labor Market Problem.* University of Chicago Press, Chicago, pp. 349–390.

Farber, H. (1980): "Are Quits and Firings Actually Different Events? A Competing Risk Model of Job Duration." Working Paper, MIT.

Farber, S. C. (1983): "Post Migration Earnings Profiles: An Application of Human Capital and Job Search Models." *Southern Economic Journal* 49(3), 693–705.

Feinberg, R. M. (1977): "Risk Aversion, Risk, and the Duration of Unemployment." *Review of Economics and Statistics* 59, 264–271.

Feinberg, R. M. (1978a): "The Forerunners of Job Search Theory." *Economic Inquiry* 16, 126–132.

Feinberg, R. M. (1978b): "On the Empirical Importance of Job Search Theory." *Southern Economic Journal* 45, 508–521.

Feldstein, M. (1973): "The Economics of the New Unemployment." *Public Interest* 33, 3–42.

Feldstein, M. (1974): "Unemployment Compensation: Adverse Incentives and Distributional Anomalies." *National Tax Journal* June, 231–244.

Feldstein, M. (1975a): "The Importance of Temporary Layoffs: An Empirical Analysis." *Brookings Papers on Economic Activity* 3, 725–745.

Feldstein, M. (1975b): "Unemployment Insurance: A Time for Reform." *Harvard Business Review* 53, 51–61.

Feldstein, M. (1976): "Temporary Layoffs in the Theory of Unemployment." *Journal of Political Economy* 84, October, 937–957.

Feldstein, M. (1978): "The Effect of Unemployment Insurance on Temporary Layoff Unemployment." *American Economic Review* 62, December, 834–846.

Feldstein M. and J. Poterba (1984): "Unemployment Insurance and Reservation Wages." *Journal of Public Economics* 23, 141–167.

Fields, G. S. (1976): "Labor Force Migration, Unemployment and Job Turnover." *Review of Economics and Statistics* 58, 407–415.

Fields, G. S. (1977): "Direct Labor Market Effects of Unemployment Insurance." *Industrial Relations* 16, 1–14.

Fields, G. S. (1990): "On-the-Job Search in a Labor Market Model: Ex-Ante Choices and Expost Outcomes." *Journal of Development Economics,* in press.

Fields, G. S. and J. R. Hosek (1977): "Labor Market Choice and Unemployment." Discussion Paper, October.

Fields, G. S. and G. H. Jakubson (1985): "Labor Market Analysis Using SIPP." *Journal of Economic and Social Measurement* 13(3–4), 281–286.

Fishe, R. (1982): "Unemployment Insurance and the Reservation Wage of the Unemployed." *Review of Economics and Statistics* 64, 12–17.

Flaim, P. O. and C. R. Hogue (1985): "Measuring Labor Market Flows: A Special Conference." *Monthly Labor Review* 108, July, 7–17.

Flinn, C. J. (1986): "Wages and Job Mobility of Young Workers." *Journal of Political Economy* 94(3), pt. 2, S88–S110.

Flinn, C. and J. Heckman (1982a): "Models for the Analysis of Labor Force Dynamics." In R. Basmenn and G. Rhodes (eds.), *Advances in Econometrics,* Vol. 1. JAI Press, Greenwich, Conn., pp. 35–95.

Flinn, C. and J. Heckman (1982b): "New Methods for Analyzing Structural Models of Labor Force Dynamics." *Journal of Econometrics* 18, 115–168.

Flinn, C. and J. Heckman (1983): "Are Unemployment and Out of the Labor Force Behaviorally Distinct Labor Force States?" *Journal of Labor Economics* 1(1), 28–42.

Frank, R. H. (1978): "How Long Is a Spell of Unemployment?" *Econometrica* 46, 285–302.

Freeman, R. and D. Wise (eds.) (1982): *The Youth Labor Market Problem.* University of Chicago Press, Chicago.

Garen, J. E. (1988): "Empirical Studies of the Job Matching Hypothesis." In R. G. Ehrenberg (ed.), Research in Labor Economics, Vol. 9. JAI Press, Greenwich, Conn., pp. 187–224.

Glenday, G. and J. Alam (1982): *The Effects of Unemployment Insurance Benefits on Employment in Seasonally and Cyclically Sensitive Sectors.* Employment and Immigration Commission, Ottawa.

Gonul, F. (1988): "New Evidence on Whether Unemployment and Out-of-the-Labor Force Are Distinct States." Working Paper, Carnegie Mellon University, September.

Goss, E. P. and N. C. Schoening (1984): "Search Time, Unemployment, and the Migration Decision." *Journal of Human Resources* 19, 570–579.

Gottschalk, P. (1988): "The Impact of Taxes and Transfers on Job Search." *Journal of Labor Economics* 6(3), 362–375.

Gottschalk, P. and T. Maloney (1985): "Involuntary Terminations, Unemployment, and Job Matching: A Test of Job Search Theory." *Journal of Labor Economics* 3(2), 109–123.

Granovetter, M. (1974): *Getting a Job: A Study of Contacts and Careers.* Harvard University Press, Cambridge.

Greenwald, B. and J. E. Stiglitz (1988): "Pareto Inefficiency of Market Economies: Search and Efficiency Wage Models." *American Economic Review Proceedings* 72(2), May, 351–355.

Gritz, M. G. and T. MaCurdy (1988): "Unemployment Experiences and Use of Unemployment Insurance among Young Workers." Mimeo, Stanford University.

Gronau, R. (1971): "Information and Frictional Unemployment." *American Economic Review* 61(3), 290–301.

Gronberg, T. J. and W. R. Reed (1989): "Estimating Workers' Marginal Willingness to Pay for Job Attributes Using Duration Data." Mimeo, Texas A&M University.

Guasch, J. L. and A. Weiss (1981): "Self-Selection in the Labor Market." *American Economic Review* 71, June, 275–284.

Hall, R. (1972): "Turnover in the Labor Force." *Brooking Papers on Economic Activity* 3, 709–756.

Hall. R. (1979): "A Theory of the Natural Unemployment Rate and the Duration of Employment." *Journal of Monetary Economics* 5, April, 153–169.

Hall. R. (1982): "The Importance of Lifetime Jobs in the U.S. Economy." *American Economic Review* 72, 716–724.

Hall, R. and D. Lilien (1986): "Cyclical Fluctuations in the Labor Market." In O. C. Ashenfelter and R. Layard (eds.), *Handbook of Labor Economics,* Vol. 2. North-Holland Amsterdam, pp. 1001–1035.

Hall, R., S. A. Lippman, and J. J. McCall (1979): "Expected Utility Maximizing Job Search." In S. A. Lippman and J. J. McCall (eds.), *Studies in the Economics of Search.* North-Holland, New York, pp. 133–155.

Ham, J. C. and R. J. LaLonde (1990): "Using Social Experiments to Estimate the Effect of Training on Transition Rates." In J. Hartog, G. Ridder, and J. Theewes (eds.), *Panel Data and Labor Market Studies,* in press.

Ham, J. C. and S. Rea (1987): "Unemployment Insurance and Male Unemployment Duration in Canada." *Journal of Labor Economics* 5(3), 325–353.

Hamermesh, D. (1977): *Jobless Pay and the Economy.* Johns Hopkins University Press, Baltimore.

Hamermesh, D. (1979): "Entitlement Effects, Unemployment Insurance, and Employment Decisions." *Economic Inquiry* 17, July, 317–332.

Hamermesh, D. and A. Rees (1988): *The Economics of Work and Pay.* Harper & Row, New York.

Han, A. and J. Hausman (1990): "Flexible Parametric Estimation of Duration and Competing Risk Models." *Journal of Applied Econometrics,* in press.

Harris, M. and B. Holmstrom (1982): "Theory of Wage Dynamics." *Review of Economic Studies* 49, 315–333.

Harris, M. and Y. Weiss (1984): "Job Matching with Finite Horizon and Risk Aversion." *Journal of Political Economy* 92(4), 758–779.

Harrison, G. W. and P. Morgan (1987): "Search Intensity in Experiments." Mimeo, University of Western Ontario, December.

Hartog, J. (1984): "On the Efficiency of Labor Markets." *De Economist* 132(3), 279–299.

Hashimoto, M. (1979): "Bonus Payments, On-the-Job Training, and Lifetime Employment in Japan." *Journal of Political Economy* 87, October, 1086–1104.

Hashimoto, M. (1981): "Firm-Specific Human Capital as a Shared Investment." *American Economic Review* 71, June, 475–482.

Hayes, J. and P. Nutman (1981): *Understanding the Unemployed: The Psychological Effects of Unemployment.* London, Tavistock Publication.

Heckman, J. J. (1979): "Sample Selection Bias as a Specification Error." *Econometrica* 47, 153–161.

Heckman, J. J. (1981a): "Heterogeneity and State Dependence." In S. Rosen (ed.), *Studies in Labor Markets.* University of Chicago Press, Chicago, pp. 91–140.

Harris, J. R. and M. P. Todaro (1970): "Migration, Unemployment, and Development: A Two Sector Analysis." *American Economic Review* 60, 126–142.

Heckman, J. J. (1981b): "The Incidental Parameters Problem and the Problem of Initial Conditions." In C. Manski and D. McFadden (eds.), *Analysis of Discrete Data.* MIT Press, Cambridge.

Heckman, J. J. and B. Singer (1984a): "Econometric Duration Analysis." *Journal of Econometrics* 24(1), January/February, 63–132.

Heckman, J. J. and B. Singer (1984b): "The Identifiability of the Proportional Hazard Model." *Review of Economic Studies* 51, April, 231–241.

Heckman, J. J. and B. Singer (1984c): "A Method for Minimizing the Impact of Distributional Assumptions in Econometric Models for Duration Data." *Econometrica* 52, March, 271–320.

Heckman, J. J. and B. Singer (1985): *Longitudinal Analysis of Labor Market Data.* Cambridge University Press, New York.

Hersch, J. and P. Regan (1990): "Job Match, Tenure, and Wages Paid by Firms." *Economic Inquiry,* in press.

Herzog, H. W., Jr. and A. M. Schlottmann (1983): "Migrant Information, Job Search, and the Remigration Decision." *Southern Economic Journal* 50, 43–56.

Herzog, H. W., Jr., R. A. Hofler, and A. M. Scholottmann (1985): "Life on the Frontier: Migrant Information, Earnings, and Past Mobility." *Review of Economics and Statistics* 67, 373–382.

Hey, J. D. and K. G. Mavromaras (1981): "The Effect of Unemployment Insurance on the Riskiness of Occupational Choice." *Journal of Public Economics* 16, December, 317–341.

Hey, J. D. and C. J. McKenna (1979): "To Move or Not to Move?" *Economica* 46, 175–185.

Heyman, M. and J. Sobel (1982): *Stochastic Models in Operations Research.* McGraw-Hill, New York.

Hicks, J. R. (1964): *The Theory of Wages.* 2nd ed. Macmillian, London.

Holen, A. (1977): "Effects of Unemployment Insurance Entitlement on Duration and Job Search Outcomes." *Industrial and Labor Relations Review* 30(3), July, 445–450.

Holen, A. and S. A. Horwitz (1974): "The Effect of Unemployment Insurance and Eligibility Enforcement on Unemployment." *Journal of Law and Economics* 17, 403–431.

Holmlund, B. (1984): "Labor Mobility." Mimeo, University of Stockholm.

Holmlund, B. and H. Lang (1985): "Quit Behavior under Imperfect Information: Search, Moving, Learning." *Economic Inquiry* 13, 383–393.

Holt, C. C. (1970): "Job Search, Phillips' Wage Relation, and Union Influence: Theory and Evidence." In E. S. Phelps (ed.), *Microeconomic Foundations of Employment and Inflation Theory.* W. W. Norton, New York, pp. 53–123.

Holt, C. C. and M. H. David (1966): "The Concept of Job Vacancies in a Dynamic Theory of the Labor Market." In Holt, C. C. and M. H. David (eds.), *The Measurement and Interpretation of Job Vacancies.* National Bureau of Economic Research, New York, pp. 73–110.

Holt, C. C., W. J. Scanlon, and R. S. Toikka (1977): "Extensions of a Structural Model of the Demographic Labor Market." In R. Ehrenberg (ed.), *Research in Labor Economics,* Vol. 1. JAI Press, Greenwich, Conn., pp. 305–332.

Holzer, H. J. (1986a): "Are Unemployed Young Blacks Income Maximizers?" *Southern Economic Journal* 52, 777–784.

Holzer, H. J. (1986b): "Reservation Wages and Their Labor Market Effects for Black and White Male Youth." *Journal of Human Resources* 21, 157–177.

Holzer H. J. (1987a): "Informal Job Search and Black Youth Unemployment." *American Economic Review* 77, 446–452.

Holzer, H. J. (1987b): "Job Search by Employed and Unemployed Youth." *Industrial and Labor Relations Review* 40, 601–611.

Holzer, H. J. (1988): "Search Method Use by Unemployed Youth." *Journal of Labor Economics* 6(1), 1–20.

Holzer, H. J. (1989): *Unemployment, Vacancies and Local Labor Markets.* W. E. Upjohn Institute, Kalamazoo.

Honore, B. E (1990): "Simple Estimation of a Duration Model with Unobserved Heterogeneity." *Econometrica,* in press.

Honore, B. E. and P. J. Pedersen (1984): "Estimation of a Three State Model—A Pilot Example." Working Paper 84-6, Aarhus School of Economics and Business Administration, Institute of Economics, University of Aarhus, July.

Horowitz, J. L. and G. Neumann (1987): "Semiparametric Estimation of Employment Duration Models." *Econometric Reviews* 6(1), 5–40.

Horrigan, M. W. (1987): "Time Spent Unemployed: A New Look at Data from the CPS." *Monthly Labor Review* 110(7), July, 3–15.

Hosek, J. (1975): "Unemployment Patterns among Individuals." The Rand Corporation.

Hosios, A. J. (1985): "Unemployment and Recruitment with Heterogeneous Labor." *Journal of Labor Economics* 3(2), 175–187.

Hughes, G. and B. McCormick (1985): "An Empirical Analysis of On-The-Job Search and Job Mobility." *The Manchester School,* March, 76–95.

Hutt, W. H. (1939): *The Theory of Idle Resources: A Study in Definition.* Jonathan Cape, London.

Ingram, D. (1990): "Learning about Yourself: Occupation Choice with Unknown Own-Preference." Mimeo, University of Kentucky.

Ioannides, Y. M. (1981): "Job Search, Unemployment and Savings." *Journal of Monetary Economics* 7, May, 355–370.

Jackman, R. and R. Layard (1988): "Does Long-Term Unemployment Reduce a Person's Chance of a Job? A Time-Series Test." Working Paper No. 883R, Centre for Labour Economics, London School of Economics, March.

Jackman, R., R. Layard, and C. Pissarides (1984): "On Vacancies." Discussion Paper No. 165, Centre for Labour Economics, London School of Economics.

Jackman, R., R. Layard, and S. Savouri (1987): "Labour Market Mismatch and the 'Equilibrium' Level of Unemployment." Working Paper No. 1009, Centre for Labour Economics, London School of Economics.

Jensen, P. (1987a): "Testing for Unobserved Heterogeneity and Duration Dependence in Econometric Models of Duration." Mimeo, University of Aarhus, Denmark.

Jensen, P. (1987b): "Transitions between Labour Market States—An Empirical Analysis with Danish Data." In P. Pedersen and R. Lund (eds.), *Unemployment: Theory, Policy, and Structure.* Walter de Gruyter, Berlin and New York, pp. 67–80.

Jensen, P. and P. J. Pedersen (1987): "The Unemployment Insurance Propensity among Danish Workers—An Econometric Analysis." Mimeo, University of Aarhus, Denmark, February.

Jensen, P. and N. C. Westergard-Nielsen (1987): "A Search Model Applied to the Transition from Education to Work." *Review of Economic Studies* LIV, 461–472.

Jensen, P. and N. C. Westergard-Nielsen (1990): "Temporary Layoffs." In J. Hartog, G. Ridder, and J. Theeuwes (eds.), *Panel Data and Labor Market Studies.* North-Holland, Amsterdam, in press.

Johansen, S. (1978): "The Product Limit Estimator as a Maximum Likelihood Estimator." *Scandinavian Journal of Statistics* 5, 195–199.

Johnson, W. R. (1978): "A Theory of Job Shopping." *Quarterly Journal of Economics* 92(2), 261–277.

Jones, R. (1988): "The Relationship between Unemployment Spells and Reservation Wages as a Test of Search Theory." *Quarterly Journal of Economics* 103(415), 741–765.

Jovanovic, B (1979a): "Firm-Specific Capital and Turnover." *Journal of Political Economy* 87(6), 1246–1260.

Jovanovic, B. (1979b): "Job Matching and the Theory of Turnover." *Journal of Political Economy* 87(5), pt. 1, 972–990.

Jovanovic, B. (1984a): "Matching, Turnover, and Unemployment." *Journal of Political Economy* 92, 108–122.

Jovanovic, B. (1984b): "Wages and Turnover: A Parameterization of the Job-Matching Model." In G. R. Neumann and N. C. Westergaard-Nielsen (eds.), *Studies in Labor Market Dynamics. Springer-Verlag, Heidelberg, pp. 158–167.*

Jovanovic, B. (1987): "Work, Rest, and Search: Unemployment, Turnover, and the Cycle." *Journal of Labor Economics* 5(2), 131–148.

Kahn, L. M. (1978): "The Returns to Job Search: A Test of Two Models." *The Review of Economics and Statistics* 60, November, 496–503.

Kahn, L. M. (1987): "Unemployment Insurance, Job Queues, and Systematic Job Search: An Equilibrium Approach." *Sourthern Economic Journal* 54, October, 397–411.

Kahn, L. M. and S. A. Low (1982): "The Relative Effects of Employed and Unemployed Job Search." *Review of Economics and Statistics* 64, May, 234–241.

Kahn, L. M. and S. A. Low (1984): "An Empirical Model of Employed Search, Unemployed Search, and Nonsearch." *Journal of Human Resources* 19(1), Winter, 104–117.

Kahn, L. M. and S. A. Low (1988a): "The Demand for Labor Market Information." Working Paper, University of Illinois.

Kahn, L. M. and S. A. Low (1988b): "Systematic and Random Search: A Synthesis." *Journal of Human Resources* 23, 1–20.

Kaitz, H. (1970): "Analyzing the Length of Spells of Unemployment." *Monthly Labor Review* 93, November, 11–20.

Kaitz, H. (1979): "Potential Use of Markov Process Models to Determine Program Impacts." In F. Bloch (ed.), *Research in Labor Economics,* Supplment 1. JAI Press, Greenwich, Conn.

Kalachek, E. D. and F. Q. Raines (1976): "The Structure of Wage Differences among Mature Male Workers." *Journal of Human Resources* 11, 484–506.

Kalbfleish, J. and R. Prentice (1980): *The Statistical Analysis of Failure Time Data.* Wiley, New York.

Kaplan, E. and P. Meier (1958): "Nonparametric Estimation from Incomplete Observations." *Journal of the American Statistical Association* 53, 457–481.

Kapteyn, A., A. van Soest, and I. Woittiez (1989): "Labour Supply, Income Taxes, and Hours Restrictions in the Netherlands." Center Working Paper, Tilburg University.

Karlin, S. and H. Taylor (1975): *A First Course in Stochastic Processes,* 2nd ed. Academic Press, New York.

Kasper, H. (1967): "The Asking Price of Labor and the Duration of Unemployment." *Review of Economics and Statistics* 49(2), 165–172.

Katz, A. and J. E. Hight (eds.) (1977): "The Economics of Unemployment Insurance: A Symposium." *Industrial and Labor Relations Review* 30(3), July, 431–437.

Katz, L. (1986): "Layoffs, Recall, and the Duration of Unemployment." Working Paper No. 1825, National Bureau of Economic Research.

Katz, L. and B. D. Meyer (1988a): "The Impact of the Potential Duration of Unemployment Benefits on the Duration of Unemployment." Discussion Paper No. 1406, Harvard Institute of Economic Research, October.

Katz, L and B. D. Meyer (1988b): "Unemployment Insurance, Recall Expectations and Unemployment Outcomes." National Bureau of Economic Research Working Paper No. 2594, May.

Keane, M. (1990): "Sectoral Shift Theories of Unemployment." Mimeo, University of Minnesota.

Keeley, M. and P. Robins (1985): "Government Programs, Job Search Requirements, and the Duration of Unemployment." *Journal of Labor Economics* 3, 337–362.

Kennan, J. (1985): "The Duration of Contract Strikes in U.S. Manufacturing," *Journal of Econometrics, Annals* 28, April, 5–28.

Khandker, R. (1988): "Offer Heterogeneity in a Two State Model of Sequential Search." *Review of Economics and Statistics* 70, 259–265

Kiefer, N. M. (1984a): "An Integral Occurring in Duration Models with Heterogeneity." *Economic Letters* 11, 251–256.

Kiefer, N. M. (1984b): "A Simple Test for Heterogeneity in Exponential Models of Duration." *Journal of Labor Economics* 2(4), 539–549.

Kiefer, N. M. (1985a): "Evidence on the Role of Education in Labor Turnover." *Journal of Human Resources* 20(3), 445–452.

Kiefer, N. M. (1985b): "Specification Diagnostics Based on Laguerre Alternatives for Econometric Models of Duration." *Journal of Econometrics, Annals* 28, 135–154.

Kiefer, N. M. (1987): "A Proposition and Example in the Theory of Search." *Journal of Labor Economics* 5, 211–220.

Kiefer, N. M. (1988a): "Analysis of Grouped Duration Data." In *Statistical Inference for Stochastic Processes* 80, 107–137. AMS Series in Contemporary Mathematics, Providence.

Kiefer, N. M. (1988b): "Economic Duration Data and Hazard Functions." *Journal of Economic Literature* 26, 649–679.

Kiefer, N. M., and G. R. Neumann (1979a): "An Empirical Job Search Model with a Test of the Constant Reservation Wage Hypothesis." *Journal of Political Economy* 87, 89–107.

Kiefer, N. M. and G. R. Neumann (1979b): "Estimation of Wage Offer Distributions and Reservation Wages." In S. A. Lippman and J. J. McCall (eds.), *Studies in the Economics of Search,* pp. 171–190. North-Holland, New York.

Kiefer, N. M. and G. R. Neumann (1981): "Individual Effects in a Nonlinear Model: Explicit Treatment of Heterogeneity in the Empirical Job Search Model." *Econometrica* 49, July 965–979.

Kiefer, N. M. and G. R. Neumann (1982): "Wages and the Structure of Unemployment Rates." In M. N. Baily (ed.), *Workers, Jobs, and Inflation.* pp. 325–357. The Brookings Institution, Washington, D.C.

Kiefer, N. M. and G. R. Neumann (1989): *Search Models and Applied Labor Economics.* Cambridge University Press, Cambridge.

Kiefer, N. M., S. Lundberg, and G. R. Neumann (1985): "How Long Is a Spell of Unemployment?" *Journal of Economic Statistics* 3, 118–128.

Killingsworth, M. (1983): *Labor Supply.* Cambridge University Press, Cambridge.

Kohn, M. G. and S. Shavell (1974): "The Theory of Search." *Journal of Economic Theory* 9, 93–123.

Kooreman, P. and G. Ridder (1983): "The Effects of Age and Unemployment Percentage on the Duration of Unemployment." *European Economic Review* 20, 41–57.

Laird, N. (1978): "Nonparametric Maximum Likelihood Estimation of a Mixing Distribution." *Journal of the American Statistical Association* 73, 805–811.

Lancaster, T. (1979): "Econometric Methods for the Duration of Unemployment." *Econometrica* 47(4), July, 939–956.

Lancaster, T. (1985a): "Generalized Residuals and Heterogeneous Duration Models: With Applications to the Weilbull Model." *Journal of Econometrics, Annals* 28(1), 155–169.

Lancaster, T. (1985b): "Simultaneous Equations Models in Applied Search Theory." *Journal of Econometrics, Annals* 28(1), 113–126.

Lancaster, T. (1990): *The Econometric Analysis of Transition Data.* Cambridge University Press, New York.

Lancaster, T. and A. Chesher (1983): "An Econometric Analysis of Reservation Wages." *Econometrica* 51(6), 1661–1776.

Lancaster, T. and A. Chesher (1984): "Simultaneous Equations with Endogenous Hazards." In G. Neumann and N. Westergaard-Nielsen (eds.), *Studies in Labor Market Dynamics.* Springer-Verlag, Heidelberg, pp. 16–44.

Lancaster, T. and S. Nickell (1980): "The Analysis of Reemployment Probabilities for the Unemployed." *Journal of the Royal Statistical Society Series A* 135, 257–271 and 143, pt. 2, 141–165.

Landsberger, M. and D. Peled (1977): "Duration of Offers, Price Structure, and the Gain from Search." *Journal of Economic Theory* 14, 17–37.

Lang, H. (1985): "On Measuring the Impact of Unemployment Benefits on the Duration of Unemployment Spell." *Economic Letters* 18, 277–281.

Lang, H. (1986): "Comparative Statistics in Dynamic Programming Models of Economics." Mimeo, University of Stockholm.

Lang, K. (1990): "Persistent Wage Dispersion and Involuntary Unemployment." Mimeo, Boston University.

Lang, K. and J. Leonard (1987): *Unemployment and the Structure of Labor Markets.* Basil-Blackwell, New York.

Lawless, J. (1982): *Statistical Models and Methods for Lifetime Data.* Wiley, New York.

Layard, R. and S. Nickell (1986): "Unemployment in Britain." *Economica* 53, S121–S169.

Lazear, E. P. (1979): "Why Is There Mandatory Retirement?" *Journal of Political Economy* 87, 1261–1284.

Lazear, E. P. (1981): "Agency, Earnings Profiles, and Hours Restrictions." *American Economic Review* 71, 606–620.

Lazear, E. P. and S. Rosen (1981): "Rank-Order Tournaments as Optimum Labor Contracts." *Journal of Political Economy* 89, 841–864.

Lee, L. (1978): "Unionism and Wage Rates: A Simultaneous Equations Model with Qualitative and Limited Dependent Variables." *International Economic Review* 19, June 415–433.

Lerman, S. R. and C. F. Manski (1981): "On the Use of Simulated Frequencies to Approximate Choice Probabilities." In C. F. Manski and D. McFadden (eds.), *Structural Analysis of Discrete Data with Econometric Applications.* MIT Press, Cambridge.

Levine, P. B. (1989): "Testing Search Theory with Reemployment Bonus Experiments: Cross-Validation of Results from New Jersey and Illinois." Working Paper No. 257, Industrial Relations Section, Princeton University.

Lichtenberg, F. R. (1983): "Employment Duration among Public Sector Employees." Mimeo, Columbia University.

Lilien, D. (1980): "The Cyclical Patterns of Temporary Layoffs in United States Manufacturing." *Review of Economics and Statistics* 62, February, 24–31.

Lilien, D. (1982): "Sectoral Shifts and Cyclical Unemployment." *Journal of Political Economy* 90, August, 777–793.

Lininger, C. A. (1963): "Unemployment Benefits and Duration." Institute for Social Research, University of Michigan.

Lippman, S. A. and J. J. McCall (1976): "The Economics of Job Search: A Survey," Parts I and II. *Economic Inquiry 14,* 155–189 and 347–368.

Lippman, S. A. and J. J. McCall (eds.) (1979): *Studies in the Economics of Search.* North-Holland, New York.

Lippman, S. A. and J. J. McCall (1980): "Search Unemployment: Mismatches, Layoffs, and Unemployment Insurance." *Scandinavian Journal of Economics* 82, 253–272.

Lippman, S. A. and J. J. McCall (1981): "The Economics of Belated Information." *International Economic Review* 22, 135–146.

Lippman, S. A. and J. J. McCall (1990). *The Economics of Search.* Blackwell, Oxford, in press.

Loungani, P., R. Rogerson, and Y-H. Sonn (1989): "Labor Mobility, Unemployment and Sectoral Shifts: Evidence from the TSID." Mimeo, University of Florida.

Lucas, R. and E. Prescott (1974): "Equilibrium Search and Unemployment." *Journal of Economic Theory* 7, February, 188–209.

Lundberg, S. J. (1981): "Unemployment and Household Labor Supply," Ph.D. Dissertation, Northwestern University, Evanston, Ill.

Lundberg, S. J. (1985): "The Added Worker Effect." *Journal of Labor Economics* 3(1), pt. 1, 11–37.

Lynch, L. M. (1983): "Job Search and Youth Unemployment." *Oxford Economic Papers* 35, 271–282.

Lynch, L. M. (1985): "State Dependency in Youth Unemployment: A Lost Generation?" *Journal of Econometrics, Annals* 28, 71–85.

MacDonald, G. M. (1982): "A Market Equilibrium Theory of Job Assignment and Sequential Accumulation of Information." *American Economic Review* 72, 1038–1055.

MacDonald, G. M. (1980): "Person-Specific Information in the Labor Market." *Journal of Political Economy* 88, June, 578–597.

MacDonald, G. M. (1983): "Job Mobility and the Information Content of Equilibrium Wages: Part I. A Finite State Space Economy." Working Paper, Economics Research Center/NORC.

MacDonald, G. M. (1988): "Job Mobility in Market Equilibrium." *Review of Economic Studies* 55, 153–168.

MacKay, D. I. and L. Reid (1972): "Redundancy, Unemployment, and Manpower Policy." *Economic Journal* 82(328), December, 1256–1272.

MacMinn, R. D. (1980): "Search and Market Equilibrium." *Journal of Political Economy* 88, April, 308–327.

Maddala, G. S. (1983): *Limited-Dependent and Qualitative Variables in Econometrics.* Cambridge University Press, Cambridge.

Maki, D. R. (1975): "Regional Differences in Insurance-Induced Unemployment in Canada." *Economic Inquiry* 13, 389–400.

Malinvaud, E. (1970): *Statistical Methods of Econometrics.* American Elsevier, New York.

Malinvaud, E. (1985): *The Theory of Unemployment Reconsidered,* 2nd ed. Basil-Blackwell, New York.

Marshall, R. C. and G. Zarkin (1987): "The Effect of Job Tenure on Wage Offers." *Journal of Labor Economics* 5, July, 301–324.

Marston, S. T. (1975): "The Impact of Unemployment Insurance on Job Search." *Brooking Papers on Economic Activity* no. 1, 13–60.

Marston, S. T. (1976): "Employment Instability and High Unemployment Rates." *Brookings Papers on Economic Activity, Vol. 1.* The Brookings Institution, Washington, D.C., pp. 169–210.

Mattila, P. (1974): "Job Quitting and Frictional Unemployment." *American Economic Review* 64, 235–239.

McAuley, A. (1975): "An Analysis of the Structure and Duration of Male Unemployment in Great Britain, 1962–1973." Discussion Paper No. 66, University of Essex.

McCafferty, S. (1978): "A Theory of Semi-Permanent Wage Search." *Southern Economic Journal* 45(1), 45–62.

McCall, B. P. (1988): "Job Search, Matching Information, and the Behavior of Reservation Wages over an Unemployment Spell." Working Paper No. 235, Industrial Relations Section, Princeton University, July.

McCall, B. P. (1989): "A Theory of Job Search and Learning Behavior." Working Paper, University of Minnesota.

McCall, B. P. (1990): "Occupational Matching: A Test of Sorts." *Journal of Political Economy* 98(1), February, 45–69.

McCall, B. P. and J. J. McCall (1981): "Systematic Search, Belated Information, and the Gittins' Index." *Economic Letters* 8, 327–333.

McCall, B. P. and J. J. McCall (1987): "A Sequential Study of Migration and Job Search." *Journal of Labor Economics* 5(4), pt. 1, 452–476.

McCall, J. J. (1965): "The Economics of Information and Optimal Stopping Rules." *Journal of Business* 38, 300–317.

McCall, J. J. (1970): "The Economics of Information and Job Search." *Quarterly Journal of Economics* 84(1), 113–126.

McCall, J. J. (ed.) (1980): *The Economics of Information and Uncertainty.* University of Chicago Press, Chicago.

McFadden, D. (1989): "A Method of Simulated Moments for Estimation of Discrete Response Models without Numerical Integration." *Econometrica,* 57, 995–1026.

McKenna, C. J. (1987): "Labour Market Participation in Matching Equilibrium." *Economica* 54(215), August, 325–333.

McLaughlin, K. J. (1989): "The Quit-Layoff Distinction in a Joint Wealth Maximizing Approach to Labor Turnover." Working Paper No. 103, Rochester Center for Economic Research.

Meitzen, M. E. (1986): "Differences in Male and Female Job-Quitting Behavior." *Journal of Labor Economics* 4(2), 151–167.

Mellow, W (1978): "Search Costs and the Duration of Unemployment." *Economic Inquiry* 14, 155–189.

Mellow, W. and H. Sider (1983): "Accuracy of Response in Labor Market Surveys: Evidence and Implications." *Journal of Labor Economics* 1(4), October, 331–344.

Melnik, A. and D. H. Saks (1977): "Information and Adaptive Job-Search Behavior: An Empirical Analysis." In O. Ashenfelter and Oates (eds.), *Essays in Labor Market Analysis.* Halstead Press, New York.

Meyer, B. (1986): "Semiparametric Hazard Estimation." Mimeo, MIT.

Meyer, B. (1988a): "Implications of the Illinois Reemployment Bonus Experiments for Theories of Unemployment and Policy Design." Working Paper No. 242, Industrial Relations Section, Princeton University.

Meyer, B. (1988b): "Unemployment Insurance and Unemployment Spells." National Bureau of Economic Research Working Paper No. 2546, March.

Miller, P. and P. Volker (1987): "The Youth Labor Market in Australia: A Survey of Issues and Evidence." Discussion Paper No. 171, Australian National University, May. Condensed version in *The Economic Record* 63, 203–219.

Miller, R. (1984): "Job Matching and Occupational Choice." *Journal of Political Economy* 92, April, 1086–1120.

Miller, R. G. (1981): *Survival Analysis.* Wiley, New York.

Mincer, J. (1958): "Investment in Human Capital and the Personal Income Distribution." *Journal of Political Economy* 66(4), 281–302.

Mincer, J. (1962): "On-the Job Training: Costs, Returns, and Some Implications." *Journal of Political Economy* 70(5), pt. 2, 50–79.

Mincer, J. (1974): *Schooling, Experience and Earnings.* Columbia University Press, New York.

Mincer, J. (1986): "Wage Changes in Job Changes." In R. G. Ehrenberg (ed.), *Reserach in Labor Economics.* Vol. 8, Part A. JAI Press, Greenwich, Conn., pp. 171–197.

Mincer, J. and B. Jovanovic (1982): "Labor Mobility and Wages." In S. Rosen (ed.), *Studies in Labor Markets.* University of Chicago Press, Chicago, pp. 21–64.

Moffitt, R. (1985): "Unemployment Insurance and the Distribution of Unemployment Spells." *Journal of Econometrics* 28, 85–101.

Moffitt, R. and W. Nicholson (1982): "The Effect of Unemployment Insurance on Unemployment: The Case of Federal Supplemental Benefits." *Review of Economics and Statistics* 64, 1–11.

Morgan, P. B. (1983): "Search and Optimal Sample Sizes." *Review of Economic Studies* 50, October, 659–675.

Morgan, P. B. and R. Manning (1985): "Optimal Search." *Econometrica* 53, July, 923–944.

Mortensen, D. T. (1970a): "Job Search, the Duration of Unemployment, and the Phillips Curve." *American Economic Review* 60(5), 505–517.

Mortensen, D. T. (1970b): "A Theory of Wage and Employment Dynamics." In E. S. Phelps (ed.), *Microeconomic Foundations of Employment and Inflation Theory.* Norton, New York, pp. 167–211.

Mortensen, D. T. (1976): "Job Matching under Imperfect Information." In O. Ashenfelter and J. Blum (eds.), *Evaluating the Labor Market Effects of Social Programs.* Princeton University Press, Princeton, pp. 194–238.

Mortensen, D. T. (1977): "Unemployment and Job Search Decisions." *Industrial and Labor Relations Review* 30(3), 505–517.

Mortensen, D. T. (1978): "Specific Capital and Labor Turnover." *The Bell Journal of Economics* 9(2), 572–586.

Mortensen, D. T. (1982): "The Matching Process as a Noncooperative Game." In J. J. McCall (ed.), *The Economics of Information and Uncertainty.* University of Chicago Press, Chicago, pp. 233–258.

Mortensen, D. T. (1986a): "Closed Form Equilibrium Price Distributions." Mimeo, Northwestern University.

Mortensen, D. T. (1986b): "Job Search and Labor Market Analysis." In O. C. Ashenfelter and R. Layard (eds.), *Handbook of Labor Economics,* Vol. II. North-Holland, Amsterdam, pp. 849–919.

Mortensen, D. T. (1988): "Wages, Separations, and Job Tenure: On the Job Specific Training or Matching?" *Journal of Labor Economics* 6(4), 445–471.

Mortensen, D. T. (1990a): "Equilibrium Wage Distributions: A Synthesis." In J. Hartog, G. Ridder, and J. Theewes (eds.), *Panel Data and Labor Market Studies,* in press.

Mortensen, D. T. (1990b): "A Structural Model of UI Benefit Effects on the Incidence and Duration of Unemployment." In Y. Weiss and G. Fishelson (eds.), Advances in the Theory and Measurement of Unemployment. Macmillan, London, in press.

Mortensen, D. T., and G. R. Neumann (1984): "Choice or Chance? A Structural Interpretation of Individual Labor Market Histories." In G. R. Neumann and N. Westergaard-Nielsen (eds.), *Studies in Labor Market Dynamics.* Springer-Verlag, Heidelberg, pp. 98–131.

Mortensen, D. T. and G. R. Neumann (1988): "Estimating Structural Models of Unemployment and Job Duration." In W. A. Barnett, E. R. Berndt, and H. White (eds.), *Dynamic Econometric Modeling, Proceedings of the Third International Symposium in Economic Theory and Econometrics.* Cambridge University Press, Cambridge, pp. 335–355.

Mortensen, D. T. and G. R. Neumann (1989): "Interfirm Mobility and Earnings." In N. M. Kiefer and G. R. Neumann (eds.), *Search Models and Applied Labor Economics.* Cambridge University Press, Cambridge, pp. 247–283.

Montgomery, J. (1988): "Equilibrium Wage Dispersion and Inter-Industry Wage Differentials." Mimeo, MIT.

Munts, R. and I. Garfinkel (1974): *The Work Disincentive Effects of Unemployment Insurance.* Upjohn Institute for Employment Research, Kalamazoo, Mich.

Murphy, K. and R. Topel (1987): "The Evolution of Unemployment in the United States: 1968–1985." NBER Macroeconomics Annual, Vol. 2.

Narendranathan, W. and S. Nickell (1985): "Modelling the Process of Job Search." *Journal of Econometrics* 28, 29–49.

Narendranathan, S. W. and M. B. Stewart (1990): "An Examination of the Robustness of Models of the Probability of Finding a Job for the Unemployed." In J. Hartog, G. Ridder, and J. Theewes (eds.), *Panel Data and Labor Market Studies,* in press.

Narendranathan, W., S. Nickell, and J. Stern (1985): "Unemployment Benefits Revisited." *Economic Journal* 95, 307–329.

Neumann, G. R. and N. C. Westergaard-Nielsen (eds.) (1984): *Studies in Labor Market Dynamics.* Springer-Verlag, Heidelberg.

Newton, F. and H. Rosen (1979): "Umemployment Insurance, Income Taxation, and the Duration of Unemployment: Evidence from Georgia." *Southern Economic Journal* 45, 773–784.

Nickell, S. J. (1976): "Wage Structure and Quit Rates." *International Economic Review* 17, February, 191–203.

Nickell, S. (1979a): "The Effect of Unemployment and Related Benefits on the Duration of Unemployment." *Economic Journal* 89, March, 34–49.

Nickell, S. (1979b): "Estimating the Probability of Leaving Unemployment." *Econometrica* 47(5), September, 1249–1266.

OECD (1988): *National Accounts, vol. 1 (Main Aggregates) 1960–1986.* Organization for Economic Cooperation and Development, Department of Economics and Statistics.

Oi, W. (1962): "Labor as a Quasi-Fixed Factor." *Journal of Political Economy.* 70, 538–555.

Oi, W. (1983): "Heterogeneous Firms and the Organization of Production." *Economic Inquiry* 21(2), 147–171.

Ondrich, J. (1985): "The Initial Conditions Problem in Work History Data." *Review of Economics and Statistics* 67, 411–421.

Osberg, L., R. Apostle, and D. Clairmont (1986): "The Incidence and Duration of Individual Unemployment: Supply Side or Demand Side?" *Cambridge Journal of Economics* 10(1), March, 13–34.

Parnes, H. (1954): *Research on Labor Mobility.* Social Science Research Council, New York.

Parsons, D. O. (1972): "Specific Human Capital: An Application to Quit Rates and Layoff Rates." *Journal of Political Economy* 80, November/December, 1120–1143.

Parsons, D. O. (1973): "Quit Rates over Time: A Search and Information Approach." *American Economic Review* 63, June, 390–401.

Parsons, D. O. (1977): "Models of Labor Market Turnover: A Theoretical and Empirical Survey." In R. Ehrenberg (ed.), *Research in Labor Economics,* Vol. 1. JAI Press, Greenwich, Conn., pp. 185–225.

Parsons, D. (1986): "The Employment Relation: Job Attachment, Work Effort, and the Nature of Contracts." In O. Ashenfelter and R. Layard (eds.), *Handbook of Labor Economics.* North-Holland, Amsterdam, pp. 789–848.

Parsons, D. (1989): "On-the-Job Training and Wage Growth." Mimeo, The Ohio State University.

Pedersen, P. J. (1983): "Unemployment Spells and Duration: A Note." Institute of Economics, University of Aarhus, Denmark, March.

Pedersen, P. J. and N. Smith (1983): "Duration of Unemployment in the Case of Mixed Censored and Noncensored Spells." Institute of Economics, University of Aarhus, Denmark, March.

Pedersen, P. and N. C. Westergaard-Nielson, (1986): "A Longitudinal Study of Unemployment: History Dependence and Insurance Effects." In R. Blundell and I. Walker (eds.), *Unemployment Search and Labor Supply.* Cambridge University Press, Cambridge, pp. 44–59.

Pedersen, P. and N. C. Westergaard-Nielson, (1987): "Multiple Spells of Unemployment—The Danish Experience." In P. Pedersen and R. Lund (eds.), *Unemployment: Theory, Policy, and Structure,* Walter de Gruyter, New York, pp. 105–128.

Pencavel, J. H. (1972): "Wages, Specific Training, and Labor Turnover in U.S. Manufacturing Industries." *International Economic Review* 13(1), 53–64.

Perry, G. L. (1972): "Unemployment Flows in the U.S. Labor Market." *Brooking Papers on Economic Activity* no. 2, 245–292.

Phelps, E. S. (ed.) (1970): *Microeconomic Foundations of Employment and Inflation Theory.* Norton, New York.

Phelps, E. S. (ed.) (1972): *Inflation Policy and Unemployment Theory.* Norton, New York.

Pissarides, C. A. (1976): "Job Search and Participation." *Economica* 43, 33–49.

Pissarides, C. A. (1979): "Job Matchings with State Employment Agencies and Random Search." *Economic Journal* 89, 818–833.

Pissarides, C. A. (1982): "Job Search and the Duration of Layoff Unemployment." *Quarterly Journal of Economics* 97, November, 595–612.

Pissarides, C. A. (1984a): "Efficient Unemployment with Endogenous Jobs and Job Rejection." *Economic Journal Conference Series* 94, 97–108.

Pissarides, C. A. (1984b): "Search Intensity, Job Advertising, and Efficiency." *Journal of Labor Economics* 2(1), 128–143.

Pissarides, C. A. (1985a): "Taxes, Subsidies, and Equilibrium Unemployment." *Review of Economic Studies* 52, 121–134.

Pissarides, C. A. (1985b): "Short-Run Equilibrium Dynamics of Unemployment, Vacancies, and Real Wages." *American Economic Review* 75, 676–690.

Pissarides, C. A. (1986): "Unemployment." *Economic Policy* 3, 499–559.

Pissarides, C. A. (1987): "Search, Wage Bargains, and Cycles." *Review of Economic Studies* LIV, 473–483.

Pissarides, C. A. (1988): "The Search Equilibrium Approach to Fluctuations in Employment." *American Economic Review Proceedings* 78(2), May, 363–368.

Pissarides, C. A. and J. Haskel (1987): "Long-Term Unemployment." Discussion Paper No. 983, London School of Economics.

Pissarides, C. and J. Wadsworth (1988): "On-the-Job Search: Some Empirical Evidence." Discussion Paper No. 317, London School of Economics.

Pitts, A. (1986): "A Queuing Approach to Labor Turnover." Working Paper, UCLA.

Podgursky, M. and P. Swaim (1987): "Duration of Joblessness following Displacement." *Industrial Relations* 26(3), 213–226.

Poterba, J. M. and L. H. Summers (1986): "Reporting Errors and Labour Market Dynamics." *Econometrica* 54(6), November, 1319–1338.

Prentice, R. and L. Gloeckler (1978): "Regression Analysis of Grouped Survival Data with Application to Breast Cancer Data." *Biometrics* 34, 57–67.

Ragan, J. F., Jr. (1984): "The Voluntary Leaver Provisions of Unemployment Insurance and Their Effect on Quit and Unemployment Rates." *Southern Economic Journal* 51(1), 135–146.

Ramaswami, C. (1983): "Equilibrium Unemployment and the Efficient Job-Finding Rate." *Journal of Labor Economics* 1(2), 171–196.

Reder, M. W. (1978): "An Analysis of a Small, Closely Observed Labor Market: Starting Salaries for University of Chicago M.B.A.s." *Journal of Business* 51(2), 263–297.

Reed, W. R. and T. Gronberg (1989): "Estimating Workers' Marginal Willingness to Pay for Job Attributes Using Duration Data." Texas A&M University.

Rees, A. (1966): "Information Networks in Labor Markets." *American Economic Review* 56, 559–566.

Rees, A. and G. Schultz (1970): *Workers and Wages in an Urban Labor Market.* University of Chicago Press, Chicago.

Reid, G. L. (1972): "Job Search and the Effectiveness of Job Finding Methods." *Industrial and Labor Relations Review* 25, 479–495.

Reinganum, J. F. (1979): "A Simple Model of Equilibrium Price Dispersion." *Journal of Political Economy* 87, August, 851–858.

Renes, G. (1989): "Vacancy Durations: Shortages and Surpluses in the Labour Market." Working Paper, University of Leiden, the Netherlands.

Reynolds, L. (1951): *The Structure of Labor Markets.* Harper & Row, New York.

Ridder, G. (1984): "The Distribution of Single-Spell Duration Data." In N. C. Westergard-Nielsen and G. R. Neumann (eds.), *Studies in Labor Market Dynamics.* Springer-Verlag, Berlin.

Ridder, G. (1986a): "An Event History Approach to the Evaluation of Training, Recruitment and Employment Programmes." *Journal of Applied Econometrics* 1(2), 109–126.

Ridder, G. (1986b): "Life Cycle Patterns in Labor Market Experience." Ph.D. Dissertation, University of Amsterdam, Amsterdam, The Netherlands.

Ridder, G. (1986c): "The Sensitivity of Duration Models to Misspecified Unobserved Heterogeneity and Duration Dependence." Manuscript, University of Amsterdam.

Ridder, G. (1988): "On Generalized Accelerated Failure Time Models." Mimeo, Rijksuniversiteit, Gronongen, July.

Ridder, G. and K. Gorter (1986): "Unemployment Benefits and Search Behavior: An Empirical Investigation." Manuscript, Cornell University, May.

Ridder, G. and W. Verbakel (1986): "On the Estimation of the Proportional Hazards Model in the Presence of Unobserved Heterogeneity." Mimeo, University of Groningen.

Riordan, M. and R. W. Staiger (1987): "Sectoral Shocks and Structural Unemployment." Working Paper, Stanford University, July.

Roberts, K. S. and M. L. Weitzman (1980): "On a General Approach to Search and Information Gathering." Working Paper, MIT.

Roper, S. (1988): "Recruitment Methods and Vacancy Duration." *Scottish Journal of Political Economy* 35, 51–64.

Rosen, H. (1976): "Taxes in a Labor Supply Model with Joint Wage-Hours Determination." *Econometrica* 44, 485–507.

Rosen, S. (1972): "Learning by Experience as Joint Production." *Quarterly Journal of Economics* 86, August, 366–382.

Rosen, S. (1974): "Learning and Experience in the Labor Market." *Journal of Human Resources* 7, 326–342.

Rosen, S. (1977): "Comment: Unemployment Insurance and Job Search Decisions." *Industrial and Labor Relations Review* 30(4), 518–520.

Rosen, S. (1981): *Studies in Labor Markets.* University of Chicago Press, Chicago.

Rosen, S. (1985): "Implicit Contracts." *Journal of Economic Literature* 23, September, 1144–1175.

Rosen, S. (1986): "Prizes and Incentives in Elimination Tournaments." *American Economic Review* 76, 701–715.

Rosen, S. (1988): "Transactions Costs and Internal Labor Markets." *Journal of Law, Economics, and Organization* 4(1), 49–64.

Rosenfeld, C. (1977): "Job Search of the Unemployed." *Monthly Labor Review* 100, 39–43.

Rothschild, M. (1973): "Models of Market Organization with Imperfect Information: A Survey." *Journal of Political Economy* 81, 1283–1308.

Rothschild, M. (1974): "Searching for the Lowest Price When the Distribution of Prices Is Unknown." *Journal of Political Economy* 82, July/August, 689–711.

Rynes, S. L. (1990): "Recruitment, Job Choice, and the Post-Hire Consequences." In M. D. Dunnette (ed.), *Handbook of Industrial and Organizational Psychology,* 2nd ed. Consulting Psychologists Incorporated, in press.

Rynes, S. L. and J. W. Boudreau (1986): "College Recruiting in Large Organizations: Practice, Evaluation and Research Implications." *Personnel Psychology* 39, 729–757.

Salant, S. W. (1977): "Search Theory and Duration Data: A Theory of Sorts." *Quarterly Journal of Economics* 91, February, 39–57.

St. Louis, R. D., P. L. Burgess, and J. L. Kingston (1986): "Reported vs. Actual Job Search by Unemployment Insurance Claimants." *Journal of Human Resources* 21(1), Winter, 92–117.

Saloner, G. (1985): "The Old Boys' Network as a Screening Mechanism." *Journal of Labor Markets* 3, 255–267.

Salop, J. and S. C. Salop (1976): "Self-Selection and Turnover in the Labor Market." *Quarterly Journal of Economics* 90, 619–627.

Salop, S. C. (1973): "Systematic Job Search and Unemployment." *Review of Economic Studies* 41(2), 191–201.

Sandell, S. (1980a): "Is the Unemployment Rate of Women Too Low: A Direct Test of the Economic Theory of Job Search." *Review of Economics and Statistics* 62, 634–638.

Sandell, S. (1980b): "Job Search of Unemployed Women: Determinants of the Asking Wage." *Industrial and Labor Relations Review* 33, April 368–378.

Sant, D. T. (1977): "Reservation Wage Rules and Learning Behavior." *Review of Economics and Statistics* 59, 43–49.

Sargent, T. J. (1987): *Dynamic Macroeconomic Theory.* Harvard University Press, Cambridge.

Schager, N. H. (1987): "Unemployment, Vacancy Durations, and Wage Increases." Research Report No. 29, The Industrial Institute for Economic and Social Research, Stockholm, Sweden.

Schmidt, R. M. (1974): "Determinants of Search Behavior and the Value of Additional Unemployment." Graduate School of Management, University of Rochester.

Schotter, A. and Y. M. Braunstein (1981): "Economic Search: An Experimental Study." *Economic Inquiry* 19, January, 1–25.

Schotter, A. and Y. M. Braunstein (1982): "Labor Market Search: An Experimental Study." *Economic Inquiry,* 20, January, 133–144.

Seater, J. (1977): "A Unified Model of Consumption, Labor Supply, and Job Search." *Journal of Economic Theory* 14(2), 349–372.

Seater, J. (1979): "Job Search and Vacancy Contacts." *American Economic Review* 69, 411–419.

Sharma, S. (1988): "On the Existence and Uniqueness of Value Functions in Models of Labor Market Dynamics." *Economic Letters* 24, 349–352.

Sharma, S. (1989): "Specification Diagnostics for Econometric Models of Durations." Working Paper, University of California, Los Angeles, March.

Shavell S. (1979): "The Optimal Payment of Unemployment Insurance Benefits over Time." *Journal of Political Economy* 87, 1347–1362.

Shaw, K. L. (1985): "The Quit Decision of Married Men." *Journal of Labor Economics* 5(4), pt. 1, 533–560.

Shaw, K. L. (1987): "Occupational Change, Employer Change, and the Transferability of Skills." *Southern Economic Journal* 54, 702–719.

Shaw, K. (1989): "Wage Variability in the 1970s: Sectoral Shifts or Cyclical Sensitivity?" *Review of Economics and Statistics* 71, 26–35.

Sider, H. (1985): "Unemployment Duration and Incidence: 1968–82." *American Economic Review* 75, June, 461–472.

Silcock, H. (1954): "The Phenomenon of Labour Turnover." *Journal of the Royal Statistical Society, Series A* 107, 429–440.

Singh, S. K. and G. S. Maddala (1976): "A Function for the Size Distribution of Incomes." *Econometrica* 44, 963–970.

Siven, C-H.(1974): "Consumption, Supply of Labor and Search Activity in an Intertemporal Perspective." *Swedish Journal of Economics* 76(1), 44–61.

Smith, B. D. (1990): "Unemployment, the Variability of Hours, and the Persistence of 'Disturbances': A Private Information Approach." *International Economic Review* 30, in press.

Smith, V. L. (1982): "Microeconomic Systems as an Experimental Science." *American Economic Review* 72, December, 923–955.

Solon, G. (1984): "The Effects of Unemployed Insurance Eligibility Rules on Job Quitting Behavior." *Journal of Human Resources* Winter, 118–126.

Solon, G. (1985): "Work Incentive Effects of Taxing Unemployment Benefits." *Econometrica* 53(2), 295–306.

Spencer, M. K. (1987): "Reservation Wages of Mexican Americans: The Pessimists Are Pleasantly Surpised." *Review of Social Economy* 45(2), 163–177.

Steinberg, D. and F. A. Montforte (1987): "Estimating the Effects of Job Search Assistance and Training Programs on the Unemployment Durations of Displaced Workers." In K. Lang and J. Leonard (eds.), *Unemployment and the Structure of Labor Markets.* Basil-Blackwell, New York, 186–206.

Stephenson, S. P. (1976): "The Economics of Youth Job Search Behavior." *Review of Economics and Statistics* 58, February, 104–111.

Stephenson, S. P. (1981): "A Turnover Analysis of Joblessness for Young Women." Working Paper, Pennsylvania State University.

Stern, S. (1989): "Search, Applications, and Vacancies." In Y. Weiss and G. Fishelson (eds.), Advances in the Theory and Measurement of Unemployment. Macmillan, London.

Stern, S. (1989): "Estimating a Simultaneous Search Model." *Journal of Labor Economics* 7(3), 348–369.

Stigler, G. J. (1961): "The Economics of Information." *Journal of Political Economy* 69, June, 213–225.

Stigler, G. J. (1962): "Information in the Labor Market." *Journal of Political Economy* 70, October, 94–105.

Stiglitz, J. E. (1985): "Equilibrium Wage Distributions." *Economic Journal* 95(3), September, 595–618.

Stone, J. A. (1982): "The Impact of Unemployment and Compensation on the Occupation Decisions of Unemployed Workers." *Journal of Human Resources* 17(2), 299–306.

Stone, L. D. (1975): *Theory of Optimal Search* Academic Press, New York.

Summers, L. H. (1986): "Why Is the Unemployment Rate So Very High Near Full Employment?" *Brookings Papers on Economic Activity* 339–383.

Summers, L. H. (1988): *Understanding Unemployment.* MIT Press, Cambridge.

Tobin, J. (1972): "Inflation and Unemployment." *American Economic Review* 62, 1–18.

Todaro, M. P. (1969): "A Model of Migration and Urban Unemployment in Less Developed Countries." *American Economic Review* 59, March, 138–148.

Toikka, R. S. (1976): "A Markovian Model of Labor Market Decisions by Workers." *American Economic Review* 66, 821–834.

Topel, R. (1983): "On Layoffs and Unemployment Insurance." *American Economic Review* 73, September, 541–559.

Topel, R. (1984a): "Equilibrium Earnings, Turnover, and Unemployment: New Evidence." *Journal of Labor Economics* 2, October, 500–522.

Topel, R. (1984b): "Experience Rating of Unemployment Insurance and the Incidence of Unemployment." *Journal of Law and Economics* 27, April, 61–90.

Topel, R. (1986a): "Job Mobility, Search and Earnings Growth: A Reinterpretation of Human Capital Earnings Functions." In R. G. Ehrenberg (ed.), *Reserach in Labor Economics,* Vol. 8. JAI Press, Greenwich, Conn., pp. 199–223.

Topel, R. (1986b): "Unemployment and Unemployment Insurance." In R. G. Ehrenberg (ed.), *Research in Labor Economics,* Vol 7. JAI Press, Greenwich, Conn., pp. 199–233.

Topel, R. (1988): "Wages Do Rise wtih Seniority." Working Paper, Graduate School of Business, University of Chicago.

Topel, R. and M. P. Ward (1983): "Early Career Mobility and the Duration of Jobs." Working Paper, Graduate School of Business, University of Chicago.

Topel, R. and F. Welch (1980): "Unemployment Insurance." *Economica* 47, 351–379.

Trussell, J. and T. Richards (1985): "Correcting for Unmeasured Heterogeneity in Hazard Models Using the Heckman–Singer Procedure." In N. B. Tuma (ed.), *Sociological Methodology.* Jossey-Bass, San Francisco, pp. 242–276.

Tuma, N. B. and P. K. Robins (1980): "A Dynamic Model of Employment Behavior: An Application to the Seattle and Denver Income Maintenance Experiments." *Econometrica* 48(4), 1031–1052.

Tuma, N. B., M. T. Hannan, and L. P. Groeneveld (1979): "Dynamic Analysis of Event Histories." *American Journal of Sociology* 84, January, 820–854.

Tunali, I. (1986): "A General Structure for Models of Double-Selection and an Application to a Joint Migration/Earnings Process with Remigration." *Research in Labor Economics* 8B, 235–282.

van den Berg, G. J. (1989): "A Structural Dynamic Analysis of Job Turnover and the Costs Associated with Moving to Another Job." Mimeo, Groningen University.

van den Berg, G. J. (1990a): "Nonstationarity in Job Search Theory." *Review of Economic Studies,* in press.

van den Berg, G. J. (1990b): "Search Behavior, Transitions to Nonparticipation and the Duration of Unemployment." *Economic Journal,* in press.

van Ours, J. C. (1988): "Durations of Dutch Job Vacancies." Working Paper 1988-6, Free University, Amsterdam.

Viscusi, W. K. (1979): "Job Hazards and Worker Quit Rates: An Analysis of Adaptive Worker Behavior." *International Economic Review* 20, February, 29–58.

Viscusi, W. K. (1980): "Sex Differences in Worker Quitting." *Review of Economics and Statistics* 62, 388–397.

Vishwanath, T. (1986): "Job Search, Scar Effect, and the Escape from Unemployment." Discussion Paper, Northwestern University.

Vishwanath, T. (1988): "Parallel Search and Information Gathering." *American Economic Review Proceedings* 72(2), May, 110–116.

Vishwanath, T. (1989): "Job Search , Stigma Effect, and Escape Rate from Unemployment." *Journal of Labor Economics* 7(4), 487–502.

Vroman, S. B. (1985): "No Help-Wanted Signs and Duration of Job Search." *Economic Journal* 95, September, 767–773.

Waldman, D. M. (1985): "Computation in Duration Models with Heterogeneity." *Journal of Econometrics, Annals* 28, 127–134.

Warner, J. T., J. Poindexter, and R. Fearn (1980): "Employer-Employee Interaction and the Duration of Unemployment." *Quarterly Journal of Economics* XCIV(2), 211–233.

Weiner, S. E. (1984): "A Survival Analysis of the Adult Male Black/White Unemployment Differential." In G. R. Neumann and N. Westergaard-Nielsen (eds.), *Studies in Labor Market Dynamics.* Springer-Verlag, Heidelberg, pp. 132–157.

Weiss, A. M. (1980): "Job Queues and Layoffs in Labor Markets with Flexible Wages." *Journal of Political Economy.* 88(3), 526–538.

Weiss, Y. (1984): "Determinants of Quit Behavior." *Journal of Labor Economics* 2(3), 371–387.

Weiss, Y. and G. Fishelson (1990): *Advances in the Theory and Measurement of Unemployment.* Macmillan, London, in press.

Weitzman, M. L (1979): "Optimal Search for the Best Alternative." *Econometrica* 47, May, 641–654.

Welch, F. (1977): "What Have We Learned from Empirical Studies of Unemployment Insurance?" *Industrial and Labor Relations Review* 30(3), July, 451–461.

Wernerfelt, B. (1988): "General Equilibrium with Real Time Search in Labor and Product Markets." *Journal of Political Economy* 96(4), 821–831.

Westergaard-Nielsen, N. C. (1981a): "Pre- and Post-Graduation Search." Mimeo, Institute of Economics, University of Aarhus, Denmark.

Westergaard-Nielsen, N. C. (1981b): " A Study of a Professional Labor Market—Introduction and Data." *Studies in Labor Market Dynamics,* No. 81-2, Institute of Economics, University of Aarhus, Denmark.

Westergaard-Nielson, N. C. (1984): "Description of Danish Longitudinal Data Base." *Studies in Labor Market Dynamics,* No. 81-2, Institute of Economics, University of Aarhus, Denmark.

Whipple, D. (1973): " A Generalized Theory of Job Search." *Journal of Political Economy* 81, September, 1170–1183.

Wielgosz, J. B. and S. Carpenter (1987): "The Effectiveness of Alternative Methods of Searching for Jobs and Finding Them." *American Journal of Economics and Sociology* 46(2), 151–164.

Wilde, L. (1977): "Labor Market Equilibrium under Nonsequential Search." *Journal of Economic Theory* 16, 373–393.

Wilde, L. (1979): "An Information-Theoretic Approach to Job Quits." In S. H. Lippman and J. J. McCall (eds.), *Studies in the Economics of Search.* North-Holland, New York, pp. 35–52.

Wilde, L. L. and A. Schwartz (1979): "Equilibrium Comparison Shopping." *Review of Economic Studies* 46, July, 543–553.

Wilson, C. (1980): "A Model of Job-Search and Matching." Working Paper, University of Wisconsin.

Winship, C. (1982): "Comment." In R. Freeman and D. Wise (eds.), *The Youth Labor Market Problem.* University of Chicago Press, Chicago, pp. 465–468.

Wolcowitz, J. (1984): "Dynamic Effects of the Unemployment Insurance Tax on Temporary Layoffs." *Journal of Public Economics* 25, 35–51.

Wolpin, K. (1987): "Estimating a Structural Search Model: The Transition from School to Work." *Econometrica* 55(4), 801–818.

Woodbury, S. and S. Speigelman (1987): "Bonuses to Workers and Employers to Reduce Unemployment: Randomzied Trials in Illinois." *American Economic Review* 77, September, 513–530.

Woytinsky, W. S. (1942): *Three Aspects of Labor Dynamics.* Social Science Research Council, Committee on Social Security, Washington, D.C.

Wright, R. (1986a): "Job Search and Cyclical Unemployment." *Journal of Political Economy* 94, February, 38–55.

Wright, R. (1986b): "The Redistributive Roles of Unemployment Insurance and the Dynamics of Voting." *Journal of Public Economics* 31, 1–23.

Wright, R. (1987): "Search, Layoffs, and Reservation Wages." *Journal of Labor Economics* 5(3), 354–365.

Wright, R. and J. Hotchkiss (1988): "A General Model of Unemployment Insurance with and without Short-Time Compensation." In R. G. Ehrenberg (ed.), *Research in Labor Economics,* Vol. 9. JAI Press, Greenwich, Conn., pp. 91–131.

Wright, R. and J. Loberg (1987): "Unemployment Insurance, Taxes, and Unemployment." *Canadian Journal of Economics* 20, February, 36–54.

Wurzel, E. (1990): "Staggered Entry and Unemployment Durations: An Application to German Data." In J. Hartog, G. Ridder, and J. Theewes (eds.), *Panel Data and Labor Market Studies,* in press.

Yoon, B. J. (1981): "A Model of Unemployment Duration with Variable Search Intensity." *Review of Economics and Statistics* 63, November, 589–609.

Zax, J. S. (1990): "Quits and Race." *Journal of Human Resources* 24(3), 469–493.

Zuckerman, D. (1985): "Optimal Unemployment Insurance." *Operations Research* 33, 263–276.

Author Index

Abowd, J., 196
Abraham, K. G., 262, 266, 267, 269, 272
Adams, J. D., 256
Akerlof, G., 45, 253, 301
Alam, J., 301
Alaouze, C. M., 99
Albrecht, J. W., 307
Allen, B., 307
Altonji, J., 262, 267, 269, 271, 272, 276
Anderson, K. H., 99
Apostle, R., 256
Ashenfelter, O., 325
Atkinson, A. B., 100, 103, 104, 120, 121
Axell, B., 307
Azariadis, C., 307

Baily, M. N., 256
Baker, J. M., 45
Barnes, W. F., 47–49, 64
Barnett, W., 326
Barron, J. M., 76, 202–8, 212–14, 216, 225,
    226, 285–89, 296, 297, 307
Bartel, A. P., 232, 242, 243, 246, 247, 253, 255,
    256, 260, 275
Beaumont, P. B., 286, 290, 291, 297
Becker, G. S., 230, 261
Belzeil, C., 200
Benhabib, J., 283
Ben-Horim, B., 27
Berg, G. J. van den, 27, 63, 71–76, 159, 170–
    74, 198, 275
Berkovec, J., 256, 258–61
Berkovitch, E., 27
Berndt, E., 326
Beveridge, W., 10
Bishop, J., 285–89, 296
Black, D., 307
Black, M., 231–33, 238, 239, 252–54, 276

Blackwell, D., 28
Blank, R., 301
Blau, D. M., 28, 159, 166, 167, 174, 197, 199,
    217–19, 225, 232, 241, 242, 253, 255, 276
Blum J., 325
Blundell, R., 311
Borjas, G., 27, 28, 200, 232, 242, 243, 253, 255
Boudreau, J. W., 285, 289, 296
Bowers, J. K., 45
Bradshaw, T., 217
Braunstein, Y. M., 280–84
Brechling, F., 256
Brown, J., 271, 273
Bull, C., 274, 283
Burdett, K., 7, 27, 28, 76, 143–47, 156–62,
    164, 170, 174, 196, 197, 204, 209, 259,
    275, 307
Burgess, P. L., 78, 80, 81, 87, 94, 140, 212, 215
Burgess, S. M., 275
Burkhauser, R., 99
Butler, J. S., 99
Butters, G. R., 307

Cain, G., 10
Card, D., 196, 301
Carpenter, S., 216
Carson, R. T., 298
Chamberlain, G., 99
Chang, H., 197
Chapin, G., 140
Chesher, A., 47, 61–63, 65, 66, 68, 71, 74, 75,
    97, 99, 124, 132, 141, 142, 173
Chirinko, R., 202, 207, 214
Christensen, B. J., 36, 38
Clairmont, D., 256
Clark, K. B., 195
Classen, K. P., 78, 84–86, 88, 92, 94, 95, 140,
    175

335

Subject Index

accelerated lifetime model, 43, 192
acceptance sets, 24
acceptance probability, 17, 71, 72, 73, 131, 134, 137, 156, 169, 172, 190, 219, 229, 240
accepted wages, distribution of, 30, 32
added worker effect, 164
advance notice of layoffs, 248, 253
aggregate data, 140
Aid to Families with Dependent Children (AFDC), 167
arrivals, offer, 7, 69, 72, 131–34, 139, 156, 169, 172, 175, 190, 201, 202, 229, 238, 239
Australian Longitudinal Survey (ALS), 52, 148

business cycles, 20, 120

censoring, 29, 31, 32, 79, 92, 96, 162
Census of Employment 1970, 53
Census of Manufactures, 246
Census of Population 1970, 89, 241
collective bargaining. See unions
competing risks, 29, 43, 179, 192
Continuous Wage and Benefit History (CWBH), 84, 85, 104, 109, 112, 114, 178
controlled laboratory experiments, 279
covariates. See explanatory variables
Crawford Physical Dexterity Test, 249
Current Population Survey, Displaced Worker Survey (DWS), 106–7, 253
Current Population Survey, May 1976 Supplement (CPS), 54, 146, 203, 204, 205, 206, 208, 274

Danish administrative data, 147
demographic variables, 33, 52, 93, 104, 107, 154, 204, 212, 257, 305

Denver Income Maintenance Experiment (DIME), 146, 149, 151, 160, 162, 164, 170
Department of Health and Social Cohort Study of the Unemployed (DHSS), 108, 131, 190
Dictionary of Occupational Titles (DOT), 246, 259
discouraged worker effect, 163, 212
discrete choice models, 9
discrete time models, 97
distribution
  discrete, 97
  duration, 6
  exponential, 6, 7, 40, 66, 74, 116, 145, 146, 149, 150, 155–56
  extreme value, 42, 169
  gamma, 99, 134, 181, 259
  geometric, 6
  Gompertz, 168
  log logistic, 117, 118
  lognormal, 117, 118, 135, 171, 190, 223
  mixing, 98–99, 106
  normal, 124, 130, 135, 155, 156, 190, 218, 224
  Pareto, 33, 59, 61, 63, 66, 71
  Singh-Maddala, 221
  truncated, 36, 77, 133
  unknown offer, 49, 76
  Weibull, 41, 93, 100, 104, 106, 108, 114, 116, 117, 118, 146, 148, 149, 162, 163, 176, 177, 182, 190, 257, 266
Downriver Community Conference Economic Readjustment Activity (DCC), 117
duration data models, 38
duration dependence, 39, 61, 67, 70, 93–94, 98, 101, 102, 106, 108, 116, 126, 129, 146, 148, 149, 161, 162, 177, 183, 204, 219, 242, 257
  lagged, 106
dynamic programming, 27

341